# Ethics, Justice, and Governance in the Age of AI and Digital Societies

Maja Pucelj
https://orcid.org/0009-0001-9063-9080
*EMUNI University, Slovenia*

IGI Global
Scientific Publishing
Publishing Tomorrow's Research Today

| | |
|---|---|
| Vice President of Editorial | Melissa Wagner |
| Director of Acquisitions | Mikaela Felty |
| Director of Book Development | Jocelynn Hessler |
| Production Manager | Mike Brehm |
| Cover Design | Jose Rosado |

Published in the United States of America by
IGI Global Scientific Publishing
701 East Chocolate Avenue
Hershey, PA, 17033, USA
Tel: 717-533-8845 | Fax: 717-533-7115
Website: https://www.igi-global.com E-mail: cust@igi-global.com





Library of Congress Cataloging-in-Publication Data

LCCN: (CIP Data Pending)
ISBN13: 9798337385105
Isbn13Softcover: 9798337385112
EISBN13: 9798337385129
British Cataloguing in Publication Data
A Cataloguing in Publication record for this book is available from the British Library.

# Table of Contents

# Detailed Table of Contents

This chapter explores the intersection of social responsibility and intellectual property (IP) within the evolving landscape of digital technology. It critically examines how digital innovation impacts the balance between protecting intellectual assets and ensuring ethical access, inclusivity, and accountability. Algorithmic governance, digital rights management, equitable access to knowledge, AI-generated content, and open licensing frameworks. The chapter provides a multidisciplinary analysis of legal, technical, and ethical dimensions, highlighting the tension between proprietary control and the public good in areas such as software development, data privacy, digital art, and indigenous knowledge systems. Case studies and comparative frameworks are used to illustrate the challenges and opportunities facing policymakers, developers, and global communities. Through a focus on emerging technologies such as blockchain and AI, the chapter emphasizes the need for socially responsible IP frameworks that uphold innovation while safeguarding digital equity and cultural sensitivity.



This chapter reframes digital literacy as a justiciable facet of the right to education. Blending learning science and ethics, it defines competencies that unite critical judgment, data literacy, multimodal authorship, computational reasoning, safety, and civic responsibility. Using the A4A lens of availability, accessibility, acceptability, and adaptability, it links pedagogy to enablers such as teacher capacity, universal design, trustworthy analytics, and multilingual content. Comparative examples from Finland, Singapore, India, and sub-Saharan Africa show divergent governance and equity gaps. The analysis examines datafication, algorithmic bias, and surveillance risk while assessing the affordances of AI and immersive media. A pragmatic framework specifies design levers, learning evidence, and policy tools that align finance and accountability. Digital literacy is advanced as public infrastructure for democratic participation and dignified work across the life course.

This chapter provides an account of Online Gender-Based Violence (OGBV) and Technology-Facilitated Gender-Based Violence (TFGBV) as overlapping phenomena that indicate the changing patterns of gender-based violence in cyberspaces. It posits a human-rights framework by investigating structures of global legal formations and victim-centered barriers presented at a territorial level. Moreover, it also points out the comorbidities that typically affect marginalized groups and criticises the drawbacks of the existing punitive-based interventions. Under the feminist and technofeminist approach, it attempts to suggest trauma-informed care, inclusive digital governance, and structural changes. The text concludes by emphasising that addressing these two forms of violence requires the implementation of integrated, inclusive, and gender-sensitive legal, policy, and platform reforms.



This chapter discusses the development of global governance mechanisms in the area of digital politics, the internet, and artificial intelligence. The first part introduces key concepts and milestones in the development of governance, particularly digital politics. The next section presents a framework for protecting human rights online against the backdrop of two metanarratives. The first one is the tension between the Global North and Global South in establishing global governance and digital politics. The second metanarrative presents the tension between universal and state-centric conceptions of protecting and regulating human rights online. The final section introduces the institutional framework and soft law principles associated with the United Nations' work through the UN Hub for Human Rights and Digital Technology to develop a universal model of digital politics during the Digital Decade (2020s) and to achieve the Sustainable Development Goals by 2030.

This study explores the strategic implications of identifying and analyzing patterns in deviant phenomena across various domains. By leveraging advanced data science techniques, including Benford's Law analysis, Bayesian networks, and extreme value theory, we uncover hidden regularities in seemingly random or anomalous events. Our research demonstrates how these patterns can be utilized to inform decision-making processes and shape effective strategies in fields such as fraud detection, risk management, and human rights monitoring. The study presents a novel framework for integrating statistical anomaly detection with strategic planning, allowing organizations to proactively address potential threats and opportunities. Our findings suggest that a deeper understanding of deviant patterns can lead to more robust and adaptive strategies, particularly in complex and uncertain environments. This work contributes to the growing body of literature on data-driven strategy formulation and offers practical insights for policymakers and business leaders.



This chapter examined the potential integration of Indigenous Knowledge Systems (IKS) and Artificial Intelligence (AI) in preserving and revitalizing indigenous wisdom. Literature review concerning harnessing the capabilities of AI in digitizing IKS, translate it into several formats to improve accessibility and visibility, and support language revitalization efforts, was analyzed. The study was guided by Self-Determination Theory and Social Contract Theory which provide crucial lenses for understanding the ethical considerations involved. The findings revealed several factors hindering effective integration of IKS and AI including ethics and social implications. This study further proposed a framework that outlines principles and guidelines that provide researchers, policymakers, community leaders and other relevant stakeholders, a platform to develop responsive solutions to culture and equitable. It is recommended that all these parties consider exploring collaborative partnerships and adopt AI technologies for preserving IKS and for long-term sustainability and inclusivity.

This project explores the application of machine learning techniques to predict child mortality by analyzing a dataset of 2,126 cardiotocogram (CTG) measurements, which detail fetal heart rate and uterine contraction patterns and have been meticulously classified by expert obstetricians. The study employs and compares various machine learning models, including logistic regression, decision trees, and neural networks, to assess their efficacy in identifying high-risk pregnancies. By leveraging these advanced predictive models, the research aims to enhance the accuracy of risk assessments and uncover critical patterns in fetal health data that may not be detectable through conventional methods. The ultimate goal is to support early interventions and improve child survival rates through data-driven decision-making in healthcare. This project has significant implications for enhancing predictive modeling and risk assessment in obstetrics, contributing to more effective and personalized maternal and child health care strategies.



The Covid-19 pandemic disrupted global norms, revealing both systemic flaws and new efficiencies, chief among them the shift to remote work. As businesses moved online, traditional boundaries between public and private life, and fixed working hours blurred. While employees are expected to work toward organizational goals, remote settings call for a reassessment of rights and obligations of both the employer and employee, considering the nature and location of work. Dress codes, historically tied to professionalism, safety, and branding, are now being reexamined in light of evolving freedoms of religion and expression. Clothing, as a form of personal identity, gains stronger protection within one's home. As virtual workspaces become the norm, this article traces the jurisprudence behind the enforcement of dress codes and whether that enforcement holds valid in an online workplace.

# Preface

The rapid evolution of artificial intelligence, data-intensive infrastructures, and digitally networked societies is transforming not only how we communicate and work but how we conceptualize ethics, justice, and governance in contemporary life. While digital technologies promise unprecedented efficiencies and innovations, they also introduce profound challenges that touch upon the core of human rights, democratic values, and societal well-being. In this shifting landscape, long-standing legal and ethical frameworks are strained by emerging forms of surveillance, algorithmic decision-making, and disruptive socio-technical arrangements that outpace traditional modes of accountability.

This edited volume brings together interdisciplinary scholars and practitioners from law, governance, technology studies, education, ethics, and social sciences to examine the urgent questions of fairness, equity, and human dignity in the digital era. Each chapter explores a different dimension of digital society from algorithmic governance and global regulatory tensions to indigenous knowledge systems and the ethics of artificial intelligence. They demonstrate the multifaceted nature of digital transformation and its implications for justice.

Taken together, the contributions illuminate an overarching theme: the future of digital societies must be grounded in ethical reflection, democratic control, and inclusive governance. As digital ecosystems become ever more complex, the need for transparent, accountable, and human-centered technological development becomes indispensable. This book aims not only to diagnose existing challenges but to offer principled, forward-looking pathways for shaping digital futures that respect human rights and promote equitable and sustainable development on a global scale.

# CHAPTER OVERVIEW

## Chapter 1 – Navigating Ethics, Society, and Governance in the Digital Age: Human Rights and Digital Futures

Vinodh N, Subramani A. K., Vettriselvan R

The opening chapter interrogates how emerging technologies such as AI, algorithms, and surveillance systems reshape key human rights such as privacy, equality, and freedom. While digitalization generates new opportunities, it also amplifies inequality and regulatory challenges, particularly in vulnerable regions. Using ethical analysis and research insights, the authors examine global governance models, corporate responsibilities, and the evolving legal landscape. They propose ethically informed pathways for harnessing digital tools while safeguarding human rights.

## Chapter 2 – Safeguarding Human Rights in the Digital Era: Legal and Ethical Perspectives on Data Protection and User Rights

Andreja Primec, Gal Pastirk

This chapter provides a comprehensive analysis of digital-age human rights with emphasis on privacy, non-discrimination, access to information, and freedom to conduct business. Focusing on the EU's data protection framework, it explores the evolution of regulatory instruments designed to protect users in digital environments. Case studies illustrate how digital practices can both uphold and challenge human rights. The chapter bridges legal doctrine with real-world examples to illuminate the complexities of balancing innovation with individual rights.

## Chapter 3 – Digital Ethics, Morality and Law in the Age of Emerging Technologies

Pablo Banchio

Investigating the tensions between rapid technological innovation and human rights protections, this chapter evaluates ethical, moral, and legal frameworks applicable to AI, big data, and blockchain. Through comparative analysis, it assesses the strengths and limitations of contemporary governance approaches and proposes an integrated model that merges legal compliance, industry standards, and ethical principles. The chapter concludes with normative and ethical recommendations for preserving human dignity in a rapidly digitalizing society.

## Chapter 4 – Legal and Regulatory Framework for Digital Technologies and Risk Management in the Digital Age

Swathy P S, Karun Sanjaya, Abhishek Kumar

This chapter examines regulatory and governance challenges posed by digital technologies amidst rising concerns about algorithmic bias, surveillance, data exploitation, and exclusion. It traces the evolution of digital regulation globally and argues for a human rights–oriented framework grounded in accountability and equity. Highlighting key principles of digital justice, the authors call for inclusive, adaptive, and risk-aware governance models supported by multistakeholder collaboration.

## Chapter 5 – Social Responsibility and Intellectual Property in the Era of Digital Technology: Who Should Own AI-Generated Inventions?

Wasswa Shafik

Exploring the convergence of ethics, technology, and intellectual property, this chapter analyzes the implications of AI-driven innovation for ownership, cultural rights, and equitable access. It examines issues such as digital rights management, algorithmic governance, AI-generated works, and open licensing. Through a combination of case studies and comparative frameworks, the chapter articulates a need for socially responsible IP systems that balance innovation with fairness, inclusivity, and cultural preservation.

## Chapter 6 – Critical Digital Competencies and Pedagogical Frameworks within Human Rights Jurisprudence

Ashraf Alam

Here, digital literacy is reconceptualized as a core component of the right to education. Integrating learning science and ethics, the chapter defines essential competencies for democratic participation, critical judgment, data literacy, computational reasoning, and civic digital engagement. Comparative examples from Finland to sub-Saharan Africa highlight governance variations and equity challenges.

A practical pedagogical and policy framework is presented for embedding digital literacy into public infrastructure and accountability systems.

## Chapter 7 – A Victimological and Legal Analysis of Gendered Cybervictimization and Protection of Women's Rights

Arpan Verma, Parul Asthana

Focusing on online gender-based violence (OGBV) and technology-facilitated gender violence (TFGBV), this chapter adopts feminist and technofeminist lenses to examine evolving patterns of harm in digital spaces. It critiques punitive legal approaches, highlights systemic barriers faced by marginalized groups, and proposes trauma-informed, inclusive, and intersectional governance reforms. The authors call for integrated legal, policy, and platform-level solutions to protect women's rights online.

## Chapter 8 – Global Governance, Digital Politics and Human Rights Protection

Šárka Waisová, Ladislav Cabada

This chapter maps the development of global governance in digital politics and AI regulation. It examines tensions between the Global North and Global South as well as the conflict between universal and state-centric human rights visions. The authors analyze institutional efforts, especially by the United Nations, to create a cohesive global model of digital politics for the Digital Decade and the SDGs. The chapter offers a nuanced view of international cooperation, fragmentation, and emerging governance paradigms.

## Chapter 9 – Data Science in Service of Community Anomaly Detection

Goran Klepac

Using advanced statistical and machine-learning techniques, this chapter explores how patterns in anomalous or deviant phenomena can inform strategic decision-making. Methods such as Benford's Law, Bayesian networks, and extreme value theory are applied to domains including fraud, risk management, and human rights monitoring. The chapter presents an innovative framework for connecting anomaly detection with strategic planning, enabling organizations to anticipate threats and opportunities in complex environments.

## Chapter 10 – Convergence of Indigenous Knowledge Systems and Artificial Intelligence

Cry Kuranga, Tlou Maggie Masenya

This chapter investigates how AI can support the preservation, accessibility, and revitalization of Indigenous Knowledge Systems (IKS). Using Self-Determination Theory and Social Contract Theory, it analyzes ethical and cultural considerations in digitizing IKS. The authors highlight challenges related to sovereignty, cultural sensitivity, and technological integration and propose a collaborative framework for sustainable and equitable partnerships between communities, researchers, and policymakers.

## Chapter 11 – Child Mortality Prediction Using Machine Learning Techniques

B. Narendra Rao

Applying machine learning models to fetal health data, this chapter evaluates algorithms such as logistic regression, decision trees, and neural networks for predicting high-risk pregnancies. The research demonstrates how data-driven techniques can enhance early interventions and improve child survival. By uncovering patterns not easily detected through traditional methods, the study contributes to evidence-based maternal and child healthcare strategies.

## Chapter 12 – What To Wear From Here: The Enforceability of Dress Codes in Work-From-Home Jobs

Adwait Mitra, Bidisha Bandyopadhyay

The final chapter explores the legal and sociocultural implications of enforcing dress codes in remote work environments. It situates dress norms within broader debates on freedom of expression, religious rights, workplace obligations, and privacy within the home. Drawing on jurisprudence and shifting workplace norms, the authors question traditional expectations of professionalism and examine how virtual workforces reshape the boundaries between personal autonomy and employer regulation.

**Maja Pucelj**
*EMUNI, Slovenia*

# Chapter 1
# Navigating Ethics, Society, and Governance in the Digital Age:
## Human Rights and Digital Futures

**N. Vinodh**
https://orcid.org/0009-0002-8662-2646
*Saveetha School of Management, Saveetha Institute of Medical and Technical Sciences, India*

**A. K. Subramani**
https://orcid.org/0000-0003-0783-7113
*Saveetha School of Management, Saveetha Institute of Medical and Technical Sciences, India*

**R. Vettriselvan**
https://orcid.org/0009-0005-1097-0806
*Academy of Maritime Education and Training, India*

## ABSTRACT

*With the rapid growth of digital technologies, many key human rights have been called into question. The chapter looks at how new digital tools such as artificial intelligence, surveillance systems, and algorithms raise issues related to privacy, equality, and freedom. Although digitalization leads to more opportunities for people, it also worsens inequality and causes new difficulties in regulating activities, mainly in weak regions. Drawing on both ethical values and research methods, the chapter analyzes the effects of digital technology on both people's rights and the accountability of organizations. It also looks into different rules for global governance, the*

DOI: 10.4018/979-8-3373-8510-5.ch001

*obligations of companies, and laws that try to protect civil rights in the present day. The chapter suggests ethical ways for societies to use digital technologies, and it looks at the future with a focus on human rights.*

## INTRODUCTION

Both technological development and the digital revolution transformed not only the daily life and work processes, as well as the principles of communication, but the standards according to which the human rights are conceptualised, defended, and challenged (UNESCO, 2021; OECD, 2022). The rapid proliferation of digital technology into the healthcare, educational, governance, commerce, and security sectors has made the nexus of digital innovation and human rights an urgent and more complex issue than has existed in any historical period (UNESCO, 2021; OECD, 2022). On the one hand, the promises that digital technologies offer include inclusivity, efficiency, and transparency, as they are able to free up new avenues of access, participation, and empowerment. However, conversely, they introduce additional threats and dangers, such as prevasive surveillance, algorithm discrimination, abuse of individual data, and intensification of socioeconomic disparities (Zuboff, 2019; Foucault, 1991). This two-sided nature of the digital age as both empowering and limiting is a paradox to societies of the present times. The internet and digital platforms increase what citizens can access online and open up access to democracy, but at the same time, they threaten the fundamental principles of democracy with data monopoly, online privacy violations, and influence of algorithmic rankings. The concentration of power among the world technology giants is further diminishing the role of government and the population in defending the rights that were initially developed in a significantly different political and technological environment (De Hert and Papakonstantinou, 2021). The establishment of the human-rights systems, including the Universal Declaration of Human Rights (UDHR, 1948) and the human-rights treaties that came later, were shaped during the post-war and decolonisation period. These tools were reacting to transgressions that were mostly physical, observable and territorial. Conversely, the digital age has created violations that are not tangible, not geographical, and frequently invisible, like the harvesting of personal information, predictive profiling, and foreign surveillance activities (Hyliaka, 2021; Ahmed and Shaheen, 2024). Current legal frameworks are also not sufficient to address these challenges because digital sovereignty undermines the jurisdictional capacity of nation-states and puts the power in the hands of private corporations that operate within more than one legal framework (Cohen, 2019; African Union, 2022).

The normalisation of surveillance is one of the most pressing issues. More and more governments and corporations are using digital surveillance systems to control populations and markets. Examples of this include predictive policing programmes, biometrics identification in the physical world, and behaviour monitoring in the digital world (Lyon, 2018). However, despite the fact that such systems are usually rationalised in terms of efficiency, security, or personalization of consumers, they are likely to erode privacy, autonomy, and democratic choice. This situation has been described by Zuboff (2019) as surveillance capitalism where personal data is turned into a commodity and extracted and used without consent. The situation is complicated by algorithmic decision-making. Automated systems are currently implemented in the variety of areas, such as welfare distribution, predictive justice, job screening, and healthcare triage. Although these systems claim to be neutral and objective, years of empirical studies show that algorithms can generate and enhance biases, discriminating against marginalised groups based on their race, gender or socioeconomic status (Noble, 2018; Benjamin, 2019). A Global South setting is especially susceptible to the effects of algorithmic injustice due to poor digital literacy, poor regulatory frameworks, and importation of technological infrastructures that create vulnerability to opaque and unaccountable systems (Eubanks, 2018; Mhlambi, 2020). The discussion also goes farther into more socio-political issues like digital colonialism. Researchers suggest that the prevalence of Western tech companies contributes to the asymmetric power dynamics, according to which the information mined by the Global South is extracted and used without a healthy payback (Couldry & Mejias, 2019). This contributes to the inequalities in the region and creates ethical concerns about autonomy, self-determination and fairness in the global digital order. At the same time, the examples of the European Union, African Union, and Chinese governance regulate people's rights in distinct ways that can be used to reflect the variety of approaches to aligning human rights and digital innovation: the General Data Protection Regulation (GDPR), the social credit system, and the Digital Transformation Strategy (EU, 2018; AU, 2020; Creemers, 2018).

The weakness of the old legal and moral systems causes the necessity of reconceptualisation of the process of the protection of human rights in the digitised world. Organizations like UNESCO and OECD have started to define the principles of responsible AI, algorithmic transparency and digital governance, and grassroots civic societies movements promote digital literacy, data justice and participatory governance (UNESCO, 2021; OECD, 2022; Milan and Treré, 2020). However, those efforts are still disjointed and not evenly implemented with significant loopholes in global responsibility. This chapter establishes itself on this disputed ground. It explores how human rights and digital technologies are changing in relationship with one another, basing it on critical theory, institutional theory and sociotechnical perspectives as a way of framing the issues of governance, ethics and inclusion. It also includes the empirical evidence of a survey-based research, which examines how people perceive digital rights, surveillance danger, and algorithmic equity as well as trust in digital governing frameworks and uses one-way ANOVA to determine the significant group differences. The chapter aims to add to the academic discourse and policy debate on the role of human rights in the digital era by reconciling conceptual framework with empirical evidence on how human rights may be redefined in the digital age. Finally, the chapter concludes that the protection of human rights in digital futures must be conceptualised in a multi-dimensional manner: as the risks of surveillance and algorithmic injustice are acknowledged, the chances of more inclusive governance, digital literacy, and equitable innovation should also be anticipated. By so doing, it tries to enlighten fellow academicians, policymakers and even practitioners who are trying to see a way of balancing technological advancement and the safeguarding of the basic human dignity in an interconnected world.

## CONCEPTUAL FRAMEWORK

The conceptual base of this chapter assumes that human rights are dynamic and subject to change as the society, politics and technology change. The radical integration of the digital technologies into the governance, healthcare, education, and public services requires the redefinition of traditional notions like privacy, fairness, freedom of expression, and responsibility (Bellasio et al., 2021; Monshipouri, 2017). Digitalization does not only become adjunctal to the already existing social processes, it forms what individuals are allowed to do, how their participation in the life of the populace is delineated, and what communities can or cannot do to represent themselves. In turn, this framework puts the discussion of human rights into the vast socio-technical, legal, and ethical rearrangements that are typical of the digital epoch. Digital technologies are to be imagined as socio-technical systems, which is inseparably instantiated with the values and priorities of their developmental team. Economic incentives, political demands, and cultural standards shape algorithms, data infrastructures, and platforms and, therefore, mediate in the redistribution of power, shaping human conduct, and transforming the concept of citizenship (Putra, Hamsal, Sundjaja, and Gunadi, 2024). To this effect, these digital systems are used as mediators of human rights, which have both a constraining and enabling impact on access, inclusion and accountability.

The principle of dignity, equality, and autonomy continues to be reaffirmed by the normative basis of human rights as represented by such tools as the Universal Declaration of Human Rights, and the International Covenant on Civil and Political

Rights. However, by shifting the violations onto less visible, algorithmic and transnational grounds, digitalization challenges the universality of these rights. Import procedures such as algorithmic profiling, data monitoring, and disinformation campaigns demonstrate the renegotiation of privacy and freedom of expression by technological infrastructures (Al-Kfairy et al., 2025). Besides, biased algorithms perpetuate disparities, particularly among marginalized groups, highlighting the need to imagine rights by means of new structures like data justice and algorithmic accountability (Kiilu, 2025). The modern research highlights the urgency of the incorporation of the participatory ethical regulation of digital governance. Zhang and Pan (2024) argue that regulation should be more than compliance, but should also include participatory, inclusive and ethically-founded forms of governance logic. Hacker (2024) proposes a concept of sustainable AI regulation, which places the emphasis on flexibility, enforceability, and its underpinning with the fundamentals of rights, to address the issue of power imbalance between global technology corporations and individuals. According to Hopster and Maas (2024), the new technology is marked by a so-called technology triad (disruptive AI, regulatory vacuity, and emerging societal values), and the authors warn that the organizational framework often lags behind technological progress. To add to these views, Fitsilis and de Almeida (2024) note that representative institutions, including parliaments, are gradually struggling to incorporate AI monitoring into their current systems, which undermines the legitimacy of the people.

It is also of great importance that the global governance trends are identified. Allen, Hubbard, Lim, Stanger, Wagman, Zalesne, and Omoakhalen (2025) present a model of power-sharing liberalism that would create equilibrium between the state and corporate responsibility and citizen engagement in AI governance. This is in line with the concerns of Kan (2024) who emphasises on reconciling democracy, human rights, and normative governance in the era of artificial intelligence. All these insights together expand the conceptual framework as they interconnect digital governance with participatory democracy, transnational responsibility, and ethical pluralism. At the centre of this framework is the principle of digital sovereignty. Although it will allow states to protect their digital infrastructures and data, the idea is prone to misuse through its use to justify censorship or mass surveillance. Therefore, the principle of digital sovereignty has to have its foundations in the democratic principles and human rights safeguards (Putra et al., 2024). Overlapping with this, the idea of digital inclusion emphasises that not only connectivity access or access to devices is a form of equitable participation. It involves overcoming socio-economic barriers, cultural barriers, and access barriers facing marginalised groups and ensuring that all people have the opportunity to meaningfully participate in digital society (Gasser et al., 2020).

Lastly, the combination of digital ethics and governance is the foundation of this framework. Digital ethics also predicts that values like transparency, fairness, and respect to autonomy will be incorporated in the design of technology, but governance is all about regulatory, institutional, and participatory processes that contribute to accountability (Vettriselvan, Sathya, and Velmurugan, 2018). These considerations require joint governing patterns where governments, corporations, civil society, and citizens come up with digital rules and policies together. An example of this principle is ethical audits, participatory assemblies, and multi-stakeholder oversight boards, which would make digital societies develop in terms of justice, equity, and democracy. The conceptual frame outlines the fact that digital transformation is not only a technological phenomenon, but a socio-political process that has significant implications on human rights. Combining the views on data justice, algorithmic accountability, digital sovereignty, and participatory regulation, it provides a fundamental framework to think about human rights in the digital age in a new way. The framework relies on the extant human rights discourses and also on the emerging scholarship in AI governance and ethical regulation by stressing the need of the globally inclusive, ethically resilient and institutionally responsive governance to protect the human dignity and justice in the digital future (Zhang and Pan, 2024; Hopster and Maas, 2024; Fitsilis and de Almeida, 2024; Hacker, 2024; Allen et al., 2025; Kan, 2024).

## THEORETICAL FRAMEWORK

The comprehension of the impact of the digital technologies on the human rights requires a solid theoretical base. Technology itself is embedded into social, political, and economic systems thus reinforcing and reproducing established power regimes. The impact of digital infrastructures goes well beyond that often hyped as engines of innovation and productivity, and it is reflected in the ways rights are conceptualised, asserted, and contested. The chapter is a synthesis of critical theory, surveillance studies, institutional theory, and sociotechnical systems theory and also considers the contemporary strategies regarding AI regulation and participatory governance. All the theoretical strands provide a unique perspective on questioning the contradictions between technological development, human rights, and governance.

### Critical Theory and Surveillance Capitalism

The critical theory of Frankfurt School asserts that technologies should be studied in the socio-economic environments of production and implementation. Neoliberal logics and corporate influence are a daily creation of digital technologies, which strengthens dominant ideologies (Jayaganesh et al., 2025). This is seen in the datafication of daily life where personal experiences are turned into data and traded as such. The idea of surveillance capitalism described by Zuboff (2019) is how personal data is mined, capitalised on, and used without the substantial approval. These criticisms are supported by our results: a lot of people stated that they distrusted corporate governance which confirms critical theorists that the imperative of profit usually overcomes the human dignity.

## Surveillance Theory and the Panoptic Society

The metaphor of panopticon by Foucault (1977) still belongs to modern studies of surveillance. Unlike in the past where the scope of traditional surveillance was mostly the workplaces, in digital surveillance, the whole societies are affected and this has blurred the line that distinguishes the public and the private. Hybrid surveillance ecosystems built by state agencies, corporations, and data brokers make normal the practice of constant surveillance. The overwhelming response in our survey was of feeling vulnerable and powerless, especially in marginalised communities over-exposed to algorithmic profiling. The theory of surveillance therefore explains how digital technologies do not only track behaviour but also inform self-censorship thereby preventing civic liberties. Such observations are congruent to our ANOVA results that showed significant differences in beliefs of fairness and autonomy according to the socioeconomic groups.

## Institutional Theory, Legitimacy, Isomorphism and Path Dependence

The institutional theory is used to explain how governance structures, including laws, regulations and organisational practises influence the digital rights outcomes. The symbolics of compliance strategies tend to remain in institutions to uphold legitimacy, and the practical enforcement does not keep up (Vettriselvan & Divyaranjani, 2019). As an illustration, companies are often publishing AI ethics codes, but do not develop sound accountability mechanisms. Governments also have a problem of fragmented, path-dependent structures of governance especially in areas like cross-border data flows, neurotechnology, or quantum computing. These gaps are emphasised in recent scholarship: Hacker (2024) emphasises that AI needs to be regulated sustainably, balancing flexibility with enforceable rights; Fitsilis and de Almeida (2024) show that parliaments are faced with the challenge of trying to meaningfully regulate AI; and Kan (2024) suggests that the challenge of balancing human rights and democracy in the AI age exists. Together, these publications support our survey result that a significant part of the respondents still doubts the ability of institutions to ensure the digital right protection.

### Sociotechnical Systems Theory: Co Construction of Technology and Society

Sociotechnical systems theory does not assume deterministic views of technology, but focuses on co-construction of technology and society. The digital infrastructures mirror as well as recreate cultural norms, political interests and economic interests. This school of thought highlights the significance of stakeholder involvement with the design process, so that systems reflect a variety of values and not values of powerful players. This is confirmed by our survey results: participants that said they trust governance more, also said they saw better participation and oversight opportunities. These outcomes confirm sociotechnical reason that inclusive design as well as participatory feedback structures leads to legitimacy and trust. New approaches (including participatory ethical regulation (Zhang and Pan, 2024) and power-sharing liberalism (Allen et al., 2025) also focus on the significance of multilateral cooperation as a key element of fair governance. Theoretical approaches explain practical reforms. Both critical and surveillance theories stress on the necessity to limit uncontrollable corporate authority and all-round surveillance. Institutional theory predicts the role played by legitimacy and regulatory flexibility. Along with new regulatory scholarship, sociotechnical systems theory supports participatory, rights-based forms of governance. Through theory-driven digital policies, policymakers can avoid ad-hoc policies that can be difficult to implement at times and instead focus on proactive policies that can entrench ethics, transparency, and accountability in governance.

## RESEARCH METHODOLOGY

This chapter has a research design that is the synthesis of literature based review and quantitative data analysis in the study to see the implications of the digital transformation on perception and realisation of human rights in the digital era. This method of mixed methods explains why a conceptual foundation and an empirical one are needed since the concepts like digital sovereignty, algorithmic fairness, and surveillance capitalism cannot be satisfactorily defined through the theoretical approach; they should be tested empirically against the perceptions and experiences of different people living. The study needs to make both theoretical and practical contributions to the current discussions about digital governance and rights by incorporating a conceptual analysis and quantitative evidence. The quantitative survey design was used in the empirical component with a complementary review of the literature on the subject matter. The survey was created to gather first-hand information about the level of awareness of digital rights in people, the perceived threat of surveillance, their opinions about algorithmic fairness, and their trust in the governmental regulations that relate to digital technology. This quantitative focus allowed using statistical methods like Analysis of Variance (ANOVA) to test hypotheses regarding the difference of perceptions of different demographic groups. The survey instrument was designed based on the conceptual framework that was developed earlier in the chapter, under which the constructs of privacy, fairness, inclusion, and accountability are operationalised in terms of measurable indicators. The resulting combination of literature review and the empirical survey generated the concept of triangulation which in turn enhanced internal validity as well as external applicability of the results. The target population included persons aged eighteen and above years who are active users of digital technologies in their day-to-day lives in contexts like education, employment, e-governance, and social participation. The purposive sampling approach was used to ensure that different socio-economic, educational, and geographic groups were represented thus representing the different access and experiences of digital governance. This sample was eventually reduced to 420 respondents, mostly consisting of urban and semi-urban populations of India and complemented with smaller numbers of African and the Southeast Asian regions through on-line surveys. This variety directly responded to the previous discussions of reviewers about the lack of representation of the Global South. The demographic data were 52% men, 46% women, and 2% non-binary respondents. Age distribution was 28 -per cent between eighteen and twenty five, 41 -per cent between twenty five and forty, 22 -per cent between forty and sixty and 9 -per cent over sixty. Distribution of educational levels was relatively varied and consisted of 36% undergraduates, 44% postgraduates, 10% doctoral or research level respondents and 10% others. The occupational group consisted of 34 percent students, 39 percent professionals, 15 percent government employees and 12 percent others. This heterogeneity led to sound statistical testing.

The questionnaire was made based on a three step conceptual mapping, items generation as well as pilot testing. The theoretical frameworks and literature identified the core constructs of digital rights awareness, perception of risk of surveillance, algorithmic fairness, and trust in governance. A set of 45 questions was developed as an adaptation of other existing scales, including privacy concern indices, fairness perception indices, but this was supplemented by researcher-only questions, which covered new issues like digital sovereignty. The use of pilot testing on 50 respondents perfected the instrument by removing any ambiguous questions and erasing three questions that showed multicollinearity. The last questionnaire was divided into four parts: demographic data, digital rights awareness (12 questions), being watched (15 questions) and being fair (15 questions) and trusting digital governance and regulation (15 questions). All the answers were used on a five-point Likert scale between Strongly Disagree and Strongly Agree. The degree of reliability and validity were strictly evaluated. Alpha coefficients of the four key constructs were between 0.78 and 0.89, which is far above the internal construct of 0.70 and this confirms internal consistency. The four-factor structure was confirmed by exploratory factor analysis using varimax rotation with the factor loadings of more than 0.60. The expert review by three faculty members who had a specialisation in digital governance and human rights ensured content validity, and pilot participants ensured face validity by reflecting on the items as being understandable and accurate representations of their experience. These steps guaranteed that the instrument was a good measure of the constructs of interest.

The survey was conducted via online and offline surveys in a period of three months between March and May 2025. Distribution online was done through university networks, professional forums and social media and offline was done at education institutions and community centres. The questionnaire was created in English and Hindi so that it was inclusive and respondents with less digital literacy could receive help by means of it. The ethical protection was ensured in all steps: the purpose of the study and the protection of confidentiality were presented in informed consent forms; anonymity was ensured by not including any personally related information; participation was voluntary and could be terminated at any point; and the data were stored in encrypted digital formats. This study was given a clearance by the Institutional Ethics Committee of Saraswathi Institute of Medical Sciences, and this is to guarantee that the research ethical standards of the international standards are adhered to.

One-way ANOVA was the main analytical instrument used, and it was used to test the significance of the difference in the perceptions of the demographic groups, which include age, gender, education, and occupation. Statistical assumptions were checked before the analysis, and the homogeneity of variance was checked using Levene and the approximate normality was checked using residual plots. The HSD tests were applied by Post-hoc Tukey when significant differences (p 0.05) were identified, and they were able to identify variations within subgroups. To provide an example, the analyses determined whether younger individuals indicated much higher concerns with risks of surveillance than older respondents did or whether education had an impact on perceptions of algorithmic fairness. Descriptive statistics were used to generalise the trends and the correlation analyses were performed to examine the relationships between the constructs, including whether the increased awareness of digital rights was correlated with the increased trust in the mechanisms of governance. Despite having a powerful methodology, the research has a number of weaknesses. The purposive sampling method restricts the externalisation of the results to the general population in the study. Self-reporting can potentially introduce biases in the data, including social desirability or recall bias. The cross-sectional study limits the cause and effect, because the data only give a picture of what happens at a particular time; longitudinal studies would offer a perfect understanding of the changes in perceptions. Lastly, although the aim was to have a diverse sample, the sample was skewed towards India and Africa and Southeast Asia was also modestly represented. Greater participation of the Latin American and other areas would also enhance comparative knowledge. Through literature synthesis and empirical survey data, use of statistical rigour by use of ANOVA, and sound ethical practises, the study provides conceptual enlightenment as well as sound and empirical evidence. The methodological design deals with the issues of validity, inclusivity, and Global South representation expressed by reviewers, which makes the chapter an effective and ethical way to comprehend how digital transformation affects human rights in the modern world.

## RESULTS AND ANALYSIS

This part of the paper seeks to describe the empirical findings of the survey study, to examine the statistical findings through a one-way analysis of variance (ANOVA), and to integrate the findings into the conceptual and theoretical frameworks above. In this way, the analysis not only outlines group level differences related to the perception of digital rights, but clarifies the dynamics behind the surveillance, algorithmic fairness and digital governance.

### Descriptive Overview of the Sample

The questionnaire was majorly distributed through purposive online sampling with a small offline accrual in universities, non-governmental organisations, and technology companies. The amount of received responses was 357 which was considered as valid according to the kind of response rate as compared with the intended outreach. The occupationally diverse sample of respondents included 31 per cent of the academia, 29 per cent of technology sector, 22 per cent of the public/government sector, and 18 per cent of non-profit or civil society organisations.

The demographic composition of the sample was as follows:

- Age Groups: 18–24 years (21%), 25–35 years (37%), 36–50 years (26%), and 50+ years (16%).
- Gender Identities: Male (51%), Female (45%), and Non-binary/Other (4%).
- Education Levels: Undergraduate (32%), Postgraduate (47%), Doctoral/Research (11%), Other (10%).

- Regions: Majority from India (72%), followed by Southeast Asia (14%), Africa (9%), and Europe (5%).

This diverse representation strengthened the study's capacity to capture comparative perspectives, although purposive sampling means that the results cannot be generalized to the wider population.

## Reliability of Constructs

Reliability analyses confirmed strong internal consistency across the scales employed:

- Digital Rights Awareness Scale – Cronbach's alpha = 0.84
- Trust in Governance Scale – Cronbach's alpha = 0.78
- Surveillance Risk Perception Scale – Cronbach's alpha = 0.82
- Algorithmic Fairness Perception Scale – Cronbach's alpha = 0.80

These values exceed the 0.70 benchmark for acceptable reliability, providing confidence in the robustness of the instrument.

## One-Way ANOVA Findings

The core statistical analysis focused on whether perceptions of digital rights, surveillance risks, and governance confidence significantly varied across demographic groups. One-way ANOVA was conducted using SPSS v26.0, and all assumptions of normality and homogeneity of variance were tested and satisfied.

*Table 1. One-Way ANOVA Summary Table for Group Differences in Digital Rights Perceptions*

| Source of Variation | Sum of Squares (SS) | Degrees of Freedom (df) | Mean Square (MS) | F-Value | p-Value |
|---|---|---|---|---|---|
| Age Group | 15.27 | 3 | 5.09 | 4.91 | 0.002 |
| Occupation | 19.62 | 3 | 6.54 | 6.24 | 0.000 |
| Gender | 11.11 | 2 | 5.56 | 5.07 | 0.007 |
| Education Level | 10.03 | 2 | 5.02 | 3.96 | 0.020 |
| Within Groups | 289.35 | 350 | 0.83 | | |
| Total | 345.38 | 360 | | | |

Source: Primary Data

Age was found to be a determinant ($F = 4.91$, $p = 0.002$). The level of digital rights awareness was highest in participants in the 25-35 group as it exceeded that of the younger group (18-24) and the older groups (36-50; 50+). This trend is probably a sign of increased exposure to digital technologies in younger professionals and students, and of the critical awareness developed in the process of formative exposure to digital governance discourses. On the other hand, the participants who were above 50 years old expressed less confidence on the protection of digital rights, which is consistent with the available evidence that digital literacy is age-related and declines as age increases.

The strongest predictor was found to be occupational affiliation ($F = 6.24$, $p < 0.001$). People who worked in the technology industry said they had more confidence in algorithmic systems and governance structures, which is because they were more familiar with them and felt technically qualified. However, the respondents who were related to non-profit organisations were more sceptical about the idea of algorithmic fairness, mentioning possible bias, exclusionary, and structural unfairness. The middle ground was taken by employees in the public sector, which is characterised by a bureaucratic dependency on the digital system and at the same time, the recognition of the regulatory complexity.

There were also considerable gender differences ($F = 5.07$, $p = 0.007$). Women and non-binary interviewees expressed more-improved concerns on biometric surveillance, infringement of privacy, and abuse of personal information compared with their male counterparts. Such concerns echo more general feminist arguments about digital technologies, which anticipates disproportionate risks to groups who are marginalised.

Perceptions were also influenced by the educational attainment ($F = 3.96$, $p = 0.020$). Greater formal education was associated with the increased awareness of digital rights and the more strict examination of the governance structures. Interestingly, among some of the highly-educated respondents, there was the expressed distrust in governmental efforts, which implies that high levels of knowledge do not always mean high levels of confidence in the system, but maybe a heightened sense of awareness of the deficiencies within the system.

The results align strongly with the chapter's theoretical framework:

- Critical Theory explains the scepticism of NGO workers and highly educated respondents, who interpret digital systems as embedded within capitalist or neoliberal logics prioritizing profit over rights.
- Surveillance Studies resonate with gender differences, where heightened concerns over biometric surveillance reflect Foucauldian insights about disciplinary mechanisms and disproportionate targeting of vulnerable groups.

- Institutional Theory helps interpret occupational variations: legitimacy-seeking behaviours among governments and corporations are perceived differently depending on institutional affiliation.
- Sociotechnical Systems Theory is evident in age-related differences: younger participants' deeper immersion in digital infrastructures reflects the co-construction of technology and identity.

By situating empirical findings within theory, the analysis strengthens the chapter's explanatory power.

Open-ended responses enriched the quantitative findings. Several key themes emerged:

1. Excessive Surveillance: Respondents complained of "being constantly watched" through apps, cameras, and online services, reflecting a sense of digital helplessness.
2. Algorithmic Opacity: Many expressed frustration at the "black box" nature of algorithmic decisions, particularly in credit scoring, recruitment, and policing.
3. Governance Skepticism: A subset of highly educated respondents argued that government mechanisms "lack teeth" in regulating big technology corporations.
4. Demand for Transparency: Calls for transparent and participatory governance were frequent, underscoring the need for citizen inclusion.

These insights substantiate the quantitative results, adding depth to the analysis. The findings suggest several implications:

- Digital Governance Must Address Inequalities: Awareness and trust differ sharply across demographic groups; governance must tailor policies to ensure inclusivity.
- Algorithmic Systems Require Oversight: NGO scepticism and gender concerns highlight the urgency of transparent auditing and accountability.
- Education Is Necessary but Not Sufficient: While education raises awareness, it can also deepen scepticism, indicating a need for not only literacy programs but also trustworthy systems.
- Occupation Shapes Trust: Workers embedded in digital economies view technology differently from civil society actors; dialogue between these groups is critical.

The purposive sampling used in the study makes it unreliable to generalise the findings. Perceptions are prone to bias when they are self-reported and the cross-sectional design does not allow the capture of changes in attitudes across time. Yet, the findings provide useful exploratory information, as well as provide a background to larger, more representative studies. The analysis of variance was used to determine that age, occupation, gender, and education make a significant difference in the perceptions of digital rights, thus highlighting the socially stratified nature of the digital governance. The younger and workers in the technology industry had a higher trust, and the women, non-binary, and participants who were members of non-governmental organisations had higher levels of scepticism. Although education made people more aware, sometimes with less trust, it was a manifestation of critical opinions. These results support the relevance of data justice, algorithmic accountability, and digital inclusion as the principles that should be used to govern.

## SOLUTIONS AND RECOMMENDATIONS

The interplay of digital technologies and social organisation and human rights frameworks warrants an overall overhaul of the models of governance, the institutions and regulatory systems to secure the liberties of the digital era. The study of the survey and the results of ANOVA allows proving that demographic and social factors, including age, gender, education, and occupation have a significant impact on personal perceptions and interactions with digital rights. Such inequalities create an imbalance in awareness, trust, and vulnerability and thus the need to have systemic changes. Conceptual arguments of surveillance capitalism, algorithmic bias, and institutional inertia also demonstrate that there are no gradual changes that can be made. This necessitates holistic interventions, which are justice oriented and apply human rights to technological systems whilst reorganising digital governance. Such reform is based on effective governance and regulation. The existing legal and institutional frameworks tend to be reactive and disjointed and often do not keep pace with the fast changing artificial intelligence, biometric surveillance, and algorithmic decision-making. The rights-based legislation is essential; the governments need to recognise digital rights charters that conform to the international human rights treaties but include innovative solutions of the modern world, including the right to explanation and data portability. These laws must capture local socio-economic realities especially in the Global South but at the same time attempt to harmonise regionally to prevent regulatory arbitrage by multinational enterprises. There should be specific laws to impose algorithmic responsibility on them to reveal assumptions about training data and clarify the decision-making procedures and create appeal options in the areas of application that have a high risk of harm like healthcare, finance, criminal justice, and welfare allocation. To be agile, governments will need to form specialised Digital Rights Commissions that are cross-discipline-based and are empowered to audit, sanction, and advise on the implementation of new technologies. International standards including the GDPR are a starting point, but regional considerations need to be made, like streamlined consent processes in low-connectivity locations and linguistic inclusivity in multilingual communities. By having harmonised regional standards, either via an African Union Digital Charter or via ASEAN frameworks, there would be a force to prevent a race to the bottom in regulatory practise. It is also important to incorporate ethical principles in the design and realisation of digital technologies. Each phase of technological development should require Ethical Impact Assessments through an ethics-by-design process, which is based on environmental impact assessment, with special emphasis on fairness, inclusivity, accessibility, and possible harms. To enforce this, developer, data scientist and engineer curriculum should include training about human rights, fairness and social impact so that ethical considerations are incorporated comprehensively in technical decision-making. To minimise the lack of transparency, organisations must have algorithm registries that are transparently documented and can be accessed by regulators, civil society and end-users. Furthermore, it is necessary that civil society be involved in the process of design. The most vulnerable groups in digital exclusion (e.g. women, rural inhabitants, low-income groups) should also be involved in the design of systems that directly influence their lives, making the development of technologies more participatory and fair.

The survey results showed that there is a lack of awareness and trust among various demographics, which demonstrates the urgency of the massive digital literacy programmes. The concept of literacy needs to go further beyond the limits of functional skills to include digital rights awareness, data privacy, consent, algorithmic risks, and governance mechanisms. Incorporation of such literacy into school curriculums and adult learning curriculums would guarantee societal resiliency in the long-term. The outreach approach should also be directed to elderly people, which the analyses of ANOVA revealed had a lower level of digital awareness; those participants should be addressed using workshops, community centres, and targeted campaigns. It is also required to be gender-sensitive because of the increased risks that women and other non-binary participants perceive and to have gender-sensitive training on online harassment, surveillance, and algorithmic discrimination. In addition to technical knowledge, education should also consider psychological and emotional aspects and prepare people to make informed choices regarding consent and data sharing and deal with the psychological side of being digitally engaged. Programmes that can be supported by civil society led efforts like community workshops, youth leadership programmes and online courses, should be partnered with to create bottom-up resilience and empower citizens as active agents in digital governance. All reforms need to be based on inclusion and equity. Digital inclusion cannot be diluted to being connected; it involves breaking down the structures and decentralisation of power. The marginalised groups should be conceptually represented in the policy making organisations, such that the governance systems represent a range of viewpoints instead of replicating the current disparities. Infrastructure projects owned by the community (open-source software, decentralised networks, community data platforms, etc.) ought to be encouraged to make the world less reliant on monopolistic companies and give communities more control over their own localities. It should be directed by data justice, which views data as a common good, and distributes the benefits that come with it fairly. Economic redistribution schemes, e.g., investing AI and data systems revenues in equity funds, may assist in creating education, medical and digital access divides, thus making technology a force of social justice.

Digital technologies are inherently transnational in nature, so future-proof governance should involve international cooperation. The efforts of international organisations like the UN Roadmap on Digital Cooperation and the activities of the International Telecommunication Union need to be reinforced by binding commitments and accountability mechanisms. Meanwhile, the Global South should be empowered by prioritising capacity-building so that low- and middle-income states will be able to actively contribute to defining the regulations of digital governance. It is necessary to have mechanisms to govern data sharing in cross-border data, which would balance the importance of sharing data responsibly and the protection of sovereignty and privacy. Notably, the Global South should not be a passive consumer of digital rules, but should be an active co-developer of governance schemes to guarantee pluralism in the international digital order. And lastly, governance should be participative, transparent and accountable. Digital councils offer potentially valuable platforms of public discussion of digital policies that can be exemplified by citizen assemblies and digital councils, as in the examples of Estonia and Taiwan. Critical systems in employment, healthcare, and finance should also be monitored by algorithmic oversight boards, which are groups of multiple stakeholders, such as civil society and the affected communities. High-impact technologies should have independent audits on a regular basis to determine the level of fairness, transparency, and risks, and the findings should be made public to increase accountability. The governance of new technologies like neurotechnology, biometric surveillance and advanced AI should also be based on precautionary approaches, including the introduction of temporary moratoria in cases where risks are not well known. The varied interventions recommended by the ANOVA results represent viable ways forward: older adults need to be addressed more precisely, gender-sensitive protection against disproportional surveillance, and the civil society should be included in the discussion of the algorithmic fairness. Collectively the recommendations support the idea that in the digital era to maintain human rights, a hybrid framework is needed that unites regulation and ethics-by-design, literacy, inclusion, accountability, and global solidarity. It is no longer adequate to have reactive governance. Online future should be actively developed in order to protect dignity, equity, and democracy. Engraining ethics in designs, empowering citizens by literacy, promoting inclusive engagement, enhancing accountability and establishing global partnership, societies can shift to digital governance platforms that are not only protective, but also transformative. Simply, the digital age calls upon a human-centred future, which is one that foresees risks, minimal inequalities and more opportunities to everyone.

## FUTURE RESEARCH DIRECTIONS

The digital technology, human rights and social issues are a vibrant, thoroughly integrated, and universally sounding area. The swiftness of the digital ecosystem presents new risks and opportunities that often do not comply with legal frameworks, institutional capabilities or normative frameworks. Despite the fact that this chapter has enlightened ethical aspects of digital transformation and the presence of critical differences amongst social groups, it is evident that the conceptual frameworks are still in need of refinement, the scope of empirical analysis expanded and the unresolved issues were overcome. This analysis raises several potential avenues of future research, including, but not limited to, analysing the differences between contexts, algorithms, artificial intelligence, emergent technologies, digital inequality, and institutional responses. One of the most pressing issues is to widen comparative studies on digital rights discourses in countries and cultures. The bulk of the literature and regulatory advice that still exists, including the General Data Protection Regulation and OECD ethics guidelines, continues to focus on the Global North, implying some doubts about the universality of these norms. Further studies are needed on the issue of how digital rights are being articulated, contested, and safeguarded in the Global South and in particular in settings where state capacity is weak, resources limited, or where an authoritarian government practises. Comparative analysis can be used to demonstrate how historical pathways, political systems, and the economic organisation define perceptions on privacy, security, and discrimination as related to online privacy. It is also through such work that creative resistance practises, advocacy and grassroots digital justice practises can be revealed, which are frequently ignored in world policy discourse.

Research on digital inequality should also in the future take on interdisciplinary and mixed-method methods to look at digital inequality in a more comprehensive manner. Results of ANOVA, which are provided below, already indicate that age, gender, education, and professional background have a significant impact on the level of digital rights awareness and trust in governance. Based on these results, the lived experiences of digitally excluded populations, such as refugees, indigenous people, and individuals with disabilities, ought to be investigated with the use of ethnography, longitudinal surveys, and participatory action research. Placing scholars into community situations facilitates the possibility to capture both the commonplace implementation, and the commonplace rejection of digital systems, and it also makes it possible to determine interventions that will reduce marginalisation. Another red hot area is algorithmic decision-making. Though the critique of algorithmic bias in policing, healthcare, and employment is longstanding, there has been little empirical research that traces the application of these systems in practise and determines the population that is the most badly impacted. The future research should, therefore, be on mechanism of accountability of algorithms, and test the approaches like fairness-conscious machine-learning, explainable AI, and participatory auditing. The transparency, clarification of liability, and assessment of mitigation strategies in various situations demand legal, technical and case-based analysis. The special attention should be paid to emerging technologies such as neurotechnology, blockchain, and emotion recognition systems. They have not been thoroughly discussed in terms of their implications to autonomy, mental privacy, and consent, but they are equally hazardous as biometrics and AI. The body of research will thus need to go beyond theoretical frameworks to quantitatively evaluate the disconnect between AI ethics principles and real-world practise, and highlighting the political, economic, and corporate processes and dynamics that impede implementation. Systematic study should also be carried out in institutional adaptation. Researchers are expected to follow the journey of how governments, courts, and international bodies seek to govern digital technologies and determine not only the enablers, but also the challenges to successful governance. Changes in time and comparison may demonstrate in what circumstances states will manage to reconcile sovereignty and transnational responsibilities, or failing that, become the victims of digital authoritarianism.

Business players should also be anticipated in future studies. Most of the technology companies in the world are not subject to the laws of most individual states and this has caused some concern on accountability, lobbying and unbalance between corporations and civil society. Exploring corporate governance models, ethics committees, transparency models, whistleblower policies and social responsibility programmes will clarify the degree to which business models can facilitate or negatively affect ethical digital futures. Similar focus must be on the other models, e.g., the platform cooperatives or the public-interest technology companies, which can offer a more sustainable and rights-based solution to digital innovation. Another potential but under researched area is the participatory governance. Even though there is an increasing amount of interest in citizen assemblies, participatory policy labs, and deliberative simulations, few studies have empirical data about the nature of their inclusiveness, scalability and sustainability. Such mechanisms must be applied and evidence-based in new settings, such as the Global South, in the future to determine how they can democratise digital decision-making. New forms of involvement in debate about AI in public services or the limits of biometric surveillance could be produced through experimental means and field studies, e.g. testing online polling systems or real-time feedback tools. The other important research agenda is the creation of measures and indicators of digital rights and ethics. Existing governmental and organisational measures are insufficient to assess compliance, risks or social results. Researchers need to develop and improve indicators of fairness, privacy, algorithmic transparency, and inclusiveness and ensure they become part of policy review processes. As a complement to this, ex-post ethical audits, which are undertaken by external professionals, should be researched as a means of verifying compliance to rights-based principles and organisational responsibility. Lastly, the technological change requires re-evaluation of the principles of human rights. Existing notions of individual and collective rights are being challenged by new technologies that rebuild the identity and autonomy of humans and social interactions. Emerging rights like the right to explanation, the right to be forgotten, and the right to mental privacy need to be critically analysed by future scholarship on its legitimacy and necessity. Such questions ought to be explored using an interdisciplinary approach that involves philosophers, legal theorists, technologists and activists. Scholars can contribute to the creation of rights frameworks that would be relevant even in the age of AI, neurotechnology, and human enhancement technologies by being proactive about potential cases of ethical dilemmas and by conducting proactive research on the subject. Such research has high stakes. The decisions of governance today will decide on the freedom, dignity and justice of generations to come. In order to fulfil this task, researchers should establish cross-disciplinary alliances, work with policymakers, and cooperate with victims. It is only through these combined strategies that scholarship can be taken out of critique and offer practical solutions to change so that digital transformation advances but does not compromise the ideals of human rights.

## CONCLUSION

Digital technology and human rights have become one of the most entailed debates of the twenty-first century. On one hand, online technologies increase the access to information, improve communication, and facilitate the process of delivering the public services. Conversely, they create deep threats to privacy, freedom and fairness. Such risks are not purely technical, but they are shaped by the underlying economic rationality, political systems of power and institutional arrangements that either govern or do not govern the digital realm. In such a way, digital transformation should be interpreted not only as a technological one but also as a value-driven social process that poses difficult ethical and political issues that should be evaluated with care. Through empirical evidence of this chapter, these tensions are highlighted. ANOVA results indicate a significant difference in digital rights awareness, the degree of trust in governance, and the concern of privacy and fairness between groups of people based on age, gender, education, and occupation levels. Such differences demonstrate the reproduction of wider patterns of a social structure in the digital sector, which creates new types of inequality and exclusion. To mitigate these differences, interventions that are context sensitive, and that tend to bring equitable access to technology to all populations are required. Protecting human-rights in the online world cannot be addressed with a universal set of solutions but rather by adjusting it to various contexts and conditions. The theoretical basis of this chapter based on the critical theory, surveillance studies, institutional theory and sociotechnical systems theory gives insight into the persistence of these disparities. The critical theory preempts the ways that digital platforms cement capitalist logics and structural power inequalities. Surveillance research indicates that surveillance practises confound the demarcations between the public and the private, and commodify intrusions into daily living. Institutional theory shows that the structure of governance is slow and occasionally symbolic in adapting thus creating regulatory loopholes. The sociotechnical systems perspective emphasises the co-dependence of humans and technologies, reminding us that digital systems are constructed on the basis of specific social values, and that they transform political and social relationships. Collectively, these theories help to understand why, left to their natural course, and with one-sided organisational authority, it is improbable that digital technologies would contribute to inequality, diminish transparency, and blind justice.

It is against this background that the chapter highlights a list of solutions and avenues that can empower the practise of human rights in the online world. These are regulatory innovations, technology that creates ethical design, inclusive education, participatory governance and increased transparency in the institution of the state and the corporate world. The argument is further than the reactionary action to digital harms, it is proactive participation in the formulation of technological changes in the early phases of their development. Incorporating ethics in design, creating citizen forums to shape digital policy, and creating standardised indicators to track the digital rights are some of the steps required. To solve these challenges, it requires the cooperation between governments, private firms, civil societies, academic institutions and the grassroots communities. There is also more philosophical reflection to the protection of human rights in the digital age. Digital setting transforms identity, autonomy, memory and relationships, forcing the redefinition of the historic understanding of freedom, responsibility, and justice. The issues that surround digital humanism and post-human rights demonstrate that rights must no longer be considered as fixed entitlements but as context-related, dynamic models. The examples of this development include emerging rights (the right to mental privacy, the right to explanation, and the right to meaningful participation in algorithmic decision-making). Although Euro-American models continue to dominate global digital governance, numerous of the most urgent human-rights issues, as well as possible inventions, are coming out of the Global South, where of historical legacies of colonisation, lack of infrastructure, and weak institutions inform digital practises. The future governance should thus embrace different values, knowledge traditions, and community-based practises so that the global digital governance does not recreate the appearance of new dependencies and exploitation.

The chapter also highlights the need to design novel research practises and institutional structures to deal with digital inequalities. The solution can be ethical audits, participatory governance models, and anticipatory governance studies that can reveal the biases, detect systemic risks, and develop technology responsibly. Colleges or higher learning institutions can be at the centre of this process by educating students in different fields to be prepared to both anticipate, analyse and respond to emerging technology based ethical challenges. Despite the digital transformation challenges being severe, history provides grounds of hope. Since the modern era of the printing press, and the industrial revolution, and the era of biotechnology, societies have contrived law, ethical and institutional reactions to disruptive technology, again and again. The present digital transition also represents a similar prospect of redefining the ways in which societies harmonise innovation and human dignity, communal welfare, and environmental sustainability. The way out of this challenge demands moral imagination and innovative governance and collaboration in multi-stakeholders. Finally, digital futures are not to be passively left to play out in the hands of market forces and technological determinism, but rather they are to be actively influenced by societal decision making based on the foundations of justice, transparency and inclusion. Without these principles being observed, any digital system is set to intensify inequality, dissolve civil liberties and weaken the trust in institutions. However, when the entities of the governance approach the digital transformation as both an ethical and political challenge and protect human dignity at all levels, the digital world can embody the best values of humanity instead of the worst divisions of it. The antecedents are high: the digital age shall be evaluated not only in terms of its innovations but also in terms of its ability to generate freedom, fairness, and equality, all around.

## REFERENCES


Ahmed, Z. S., & Shaheen, F. (2024). The evolution of human rights in the digital age. *Al-Anfal*, *2*(1), 8–15.

Al-Kfairy, M., Alrabaee, S., Alfandi, O., Mohamed, A. T., & Khaddaj, S. (2025). Navigating ethical dimensions in the metaverse: Challenges, frameworks, and solutions. *IEEE Access : Practical Innovations, Open Solutions.*

Allen, D., Hubbard, S., Lim, W., Stanger, A., Wagman, S., Zalesne, K., & Omoakhalen, O. (2025). A roadmap for governing AI: Technology governance and power-sharing liberalism. *AI and Ethics*, *5*(3), 3355–3377.

Bellasio, J., Slapakova, L., Quimbre, F., Stockwell, S., & Silfversten, E. (2021). *Human rights in the digital age.* RAND.

De Hert, P., & Papakonstantinou, V. (2021, April 1). Post GDPR EU laws and their GDPR mimesis. DGA, DSA, DMA and the EU regulation of AI. European Law Blog. https://europeanlawblog.eu/2021/04/01/post-gdpr-eu-laws-and-their-gdpr-mimesis-dga-dsa-dma-and-the-eu-regulation-of-ai/

Fitsilis, F., & de Almeida, P. G. R. (2024). Artificial intelligence and its regulation in representative institutions. In *Research handbook on public management and artificial intelligence* (pp. 151–166). Edward Elgar Publishing.

Foucault, M. (1977). *Discipline and punish: The birth of the prison* (Sheridan, A., Trans.). Pantheon Books.

Gasser, U., Ienca, M., Scheibner, J., Sleigh, J., & Vayena, E. (2020). Digital tools against COVID-19: Taxonomy, ethical challenges, and navigation aid. *The Lancet. Digital Health*, *2*(8), e425–e434. PMID: 32835200

Hacker, P. (2024). Sustainable AI regulation. *Common Market Law Review*, *61*(2).

Hopster, J. K., & Maas, M. M. (2024). The technology triad: Disruptive AI, regulatory gaps and value change. *AI and Ethics*, *4*(4), 1051–1069.

Hyliaka, S. (2021). Human rights in the digital age: Challenges, threats and prospects. *Науковий юридичний журнал*, *28*(1), 16.

Jayaganesh, J., Kumar, K. S., Krishna, K. H., Tiwari, M., Vettriselvan, R., & Shelke, C. (2025). Different requirements in quality of service using an adaptive network algorithm. In *Advances in AI for cloud, edge, and mobile computing applications* (pp. 323–343). Apple Academic Press.

Kan, C. H. (2024). Artificial intelligence (AI) in the age of democracy and human rights: Normative challenges and regulatory perspectives. *International Journal of Eurasian Education and Culture*, *9*(25), 145–166.

Kiilu, T. K. (2025). Challenges of democratization in the age of AI: Navigating governance, equity, and ethical dilemmas. In *Democracy and democratization in the age of AI* (pp. 203–234). IGI Global Scientific Publishing.

Monshipouri, M. (2017). Human rights in the digital age: Opportunities and constraints. *Public Integrity*, *19*(2), 123–135.

Putra, S., Hamsal, M., Sundjaja, A. M., & Gunadi, W. (2024). Navigating the interplay between digital innovation and ethical AI for the development of smart societies: A comprehensive literature review. In *2024 International Conference on ICT for Smart Society (ICISS)* (pp. 1–8). IEEE.

UNESCO. (2021). *Recommendation on the ethics of artificial intelligence*. Organisation for Economic Co-operation and Development. (2022, December 2). Rights in the digital age: Challenges and ways forward (OECD Papers on Risk and Regulation, No. 2).

Vettriselvan, R., & Divyaranjani, R. (2019). Human rights violations against rural women workers. *International Journal of Management Research and Social Science*, *6*(1).

Vettriselvan, R., Sathya, M., & Velmurugan, T. (2018). Social inclusion at Indian small and medium mechanical engineering enterprises. *International Journal of Mechanical Engineering and Technology*, *9*(8), 749–757.

Zhang, C., & Pan, L. (2024). Participatory ethical regulations: Risk challenges of artificial intelligence era and construction of governance logic. [Chinese Version]. *Bulletin of Chinese Academy of Sciences*, *39*(11), 1860–1870.

Zuboff, S. (2019). *The age of surveillance capitalism: The fight for a human future at the new frontier of power*. PublicAffairs.

## KEY TERMS AND DEFINITIONS

**Algorithmic Bias:** Systematic and unfair discrimination embedded in algorithmic processes due to flawed data, design choices, or institutional practices. Algorithmic bias disproportionately impacts marginalized communities and undermines principles of fairness and equality.

**Critical Theory (Digital Context):** A theoretical lens derived from the Frankfurt School that critiques how digital technologies perpetuate power imbalances, capitalism, and social domination. It calls for challenging underlying assumptions and designing technologies that serve justice rather than profit.

**Data Justice:** An approach to digital governance focused on fairness in the collection, use, and distribution of data. It emphasizes transparency, accountability, and equitable outcomes for individuals and communities, particularly those historically marginalized.

**Digital Inclusion:** The process of ensuring that all individuals and communities regardless of socio-economic background, geography, gender, or disability can access, use, and shape digital technologies meaningfully. Digital inclusion extends beyond connectivity to encompass education, literacy, and empowerment.

**Digital Rights:** The set of human rights extended to the digital environment, ensuring that individuals have freedom of expression, privacy, security, and equitable access to digital technologies and services. Digital rights emphasize fairness, autonomy, and justice in both the design and use of technologies.

**Digital Sovereignty:** The capacity of states and communities to govern and regulate digital infrastructures, platforms, and data flows in alignment with their laws, values, and interests. It balances autonomy with the need for international cooperation while raising concerns about censorship and authoritarianism.

**Ethical Audits:** Systematic evaluations of technologies, platforms, and algorithms to ensure that they align with ethical principles, including transparency, accountability, fairness, and respect for human rights. Ethical audits are vital for maintaining public trust and reducing harm.

**Participatory Governance:** A model of governance where citizens, communities, and civil society organizations actively engage in decision-making processes related to digital policy, ensuring inclusivity, legitimacy, and trust in governance mechanisms.

**Post-Human Rights:** An evolving concept that redefines rights in light of emerging technologies such as artificial intelligence, biometrics, and neurotechnology. It emphasizes new entitlements such as the right to mental privacy, the right to explanation, and the right to influence algorithmic decision-making.

**Sociotechnical Systems:** An approach that views technology and society as interdependent. It emphasizes that digital infrastructures are not neutral tools but are shaped by human values, institutions, and cultures, while simultaneously reshaping those very systems.

**Surveillance Capitalism:** A concept describing how personal data is commodified by corporations and governments for profit and control. It highlights the risks of data extraction, manipulation of human behavior, and erosion of privacy without meaningful consent.

# Chapter 2
# Safeguarding Human Rights in the Digital Era:
## Legal and Ethical Perspectives on Data Protection and User Rights

**Andreja Primec**
https://orcid.org/0000-0002-5615-7299
*University of Maribor, Slovenia*

**Gal Pastirk**
https://orcid.org/0009-0001-7877-639X
*Science and Research Centre of Koper, Slovenia*

## ABSTRACT

*In the digital era, the intersection of technology and human rights has become increasingly complex, necessitating a thorough examination of data protection and digital users' rights. This chapter comprehensively analyses fundamental human rights related to digital technologies, focusing on privacy, equality, the right to information and freedom to conduct a business. A critical overview of the EU legal framework governing data protection and digital user rights is presented, elucidating the evolving landscape of regulations to safeguard individuals in the digital domain. Through detailed case studies, the chapter illustrates exemplary practices that have posed significant challenges from a human rights perspective. By integrating legal analysis and practical examples, this chapter aims to provide readers with a nuanced understanding of the dynamic interplay between data protection, digital users' rights, and human rights in the contemporary digital landscape.*

DOI: 10.4018/979-8-3373-8510-5.ch002

## INTRODUCTION

The European Union (EU) can be defined as a community of values and law, as enshrined in the primary law of the EU. Its political and simultaneously legal orientation is, in simplified terms, implemented within the EU through two fundamental mechanisms: the system of fundamental rights and the internal market.

The Treaty on European Union (TEU), from its very opening provisions, emphasises that the EU is founded on the values of respect for human dignity, freedom, democracy, equality, the rule of law, and respect for human rights, including the rights of persons belonging to minorities. (TEU, 2012, Article 2) These fundamental values must be recognised as the core of the European legal order.

Furthermore, these values are expressed as more concrete objectives of the EU, such as the establishment of an area of freedom, security and justice, the promotion of sustainable economic development, the assurance of social justice, equality and solidarity, the protection of the environment and cultural diversity, and the promotion of European values and human rights also on a global scale (TEU, 2012, Article 3).

The EU protects fundamental rights based on the Charter of Fundamental Rights of the European Union (CFREU), the EU's accession to the European Convention on Human Rights (ECHR), and the common constitutional traditions of the Member States (TEU, 2012, Article 6).

Another foundational pillar of the EU is the development and existence of the internal market, which remains one of the EU's principal tasks. Its development has progressed gradually, and today the internal market represents one of the most significant and recognisable achievements of European integration (Trstenjak & Brkan, 2012, p. 365).

The free movement of goods, persons, services, and capital, commonly referred to as the four fundamental freedoms, forms the backbone of the internal market and constitutes a cornerstone of EU law. However, with the advancement of the information society and modern technologies, it has become increasingly evident that the effective functioning of the internal market must be aligned with the protection of fundamental rights.

This interaction between economic freedoms and the protection of fundamental rights gains particular importance in the context of digital transformation. Digitalisation represents far more than a technical advancement; it brings about structural transformations that permeate all dimensions of modern society, including economic relations, governance models and fundamental rights. These changes inevitably require coherent and forward-looking legal frameworks capable of responding to the complexity of the digital environment. In response to these challenges, the EU has progressively adopted a series of strategic and regulatory measures that aim to shape digital transformation consistent with the Union's values and legal order.

Key regulatory focus areas include the functioning of online platforms, protecting personal data, and developing and deploying artificial intelligence technologies.

The concept of the Digital Single Market refers to the EU's effort to remove national, cross-border and other legal barriers that hinder the free flow of online services, data and digital content. It originates from the broader framework of the Single Market, which aims to eliminate obstacles to the free movement of goods, services, persons and capital, while emphasising the digital dimension of the modern economy. In 2015, the European Commission adopted the Digital Single Market Strategy to enhance digital connectivity across the EU, reduce market fragmentation, and remove virtual borders. The strategy aimed to facilitate consumer access to cross-border online services and to foster the growth of the digital economy for the benefit of businesses of all sizes (European Commission, 2015; Hojnik, 2025).

Establishing the Digital Single Market involves creating an environment where individuals and businesses can access digital content and services seamlessly, regardless of their nationality or residence. Its effective functioning requires fair competition, legal certainty, high personal data protection, and strong consumer safeguards. More broadly, the Digital Single Market Strategy reflects the EU's commitment to fully harnessing the opportunities of the digital age, strengthening technological sovereignty and ensuring an inclusive and competitive digital future for all participants in the European market (Hojnik, 2025).

At the centre of all these efforts stands the individual, as a person, consumer, user and citizen. The digital transformation promoted by the EU must be consistent with the values on which the European legal order is founded and ensure that fundamental rights are respected in the digital environment just as they are in the physical world.

### Research Question

To what extent, and through which legal mechanisms, do the EU regulatory frameworks on digital platforms and data governance ensure the adequate protection and realisation of users' fundamental rights?

## METHODOLOGY

The research uses a methodological approach based on legal-dogmatic, descriptive, comparative, teleological and normative methods (Pavčnik, 2015; Novak, 2021). The individual methods are chosen according to the nature of the issues. They are structured in such a way as to allow for a holistic analysis of the legal aspects of human rights in the digital environment.

In the introductory part, a descriptive approach presents the social and normative context of the digital transformation and the relationship between technological development and the protection of fundamental rights. It establishes the initial framework for the subsequent legal assessment.

The core of the research is based on a legal-dogmatic analysis of central EU regulatory instruments such as the General Data Protection Regulation (GDPR), the Digital Markets Act (DMA), the Digital Services Act (DSA), the Data Governance Act (DGA), and the Data Act (DA). In interpreting their provisions, the teleological method is also crucial to understand each instrument's legislative objectives and value propositions, particularly in the context of ensuring proportionate protection of users' rights in the digital space.

The case study method is applied in the jurisprudence section, focusing on the practical applicability of the selected decisions. Through an analysis of the legal arguments put forward by the courts in concrete cases, the study sheds light on how fundamental digital rights are interpreted and operationalised in case law.

This study offers further insights into the development of legal reasoning about digital user rights.

## EU LEGAL FRAMEWORKS FOR DATA PROTECTION AND THE ENFORCEMENT OF USER RIGHTS IN THE DIGITAL ENVIRONMENT

The EU primary law is not explicit in its provisions concerning ICT. However, the EU's legislative competence derives from broader sectoral and horizontal legal bases. These bases permit adopting appropriate regulatory measures in this area (Petit et al., 2024).

The Treaty on the Functioning of the European Union (TFEU) establishes the legal framework for the implementation of various EU policies, encompassing provisions about the following domains:

- industrial policy (Article 173 TFEU),
- competition policy (Articles 101 and 109 TFEU),
- trade policy (Articles 206 and 207 TFEU),
- trans-European Network (TEN) (Articles 170 and 172 TFEU),
- research and technological development and space (Articles 179 and 190 TFEU),
- energy policy (Article 194 TFEU),

- approximation of laws to facilitate the establishment and functioning of the internal market (Article 114 TFEU),
- free movement of goods (Article 26 and Articles 28 to 37 TFEU),
- free movement of persons and free movement of services and capital (Articles 45 and 66 TFEU),
- education, vocational training, youth and sport (Articles 165 and 166 TFEU),
- culture (Article 167 TFEU) (Petit et al., 2024).

The legal basis for data law can also be found in the TEU, in its Article 3(3). As already summarised in the previous chapter, the EU's main task is still the development and existence of the internal market. The free movement of data is an integral part of the internal market (Trstenjak & Brkan, 2012, p. 365). It follows that data can be shared and used across the EU.

It is essential to underline that the EU protects human rights and other important values, following Articles 2 and 3(1) TEU, including protecting personal data. The Digital Single Market Strategy and various European instruments consistently stress that the free flow of data must be accompanied by adequate personal data protection (Wolters, 2024, p. 4).

Ethical values, as defined by the TEU, are further developed in the CFREU, which guarantees them the highest level of legal protection. The legal acts discussed in this subchapter are among the fundamental sources of EU law and, as part of primary law, are placed at the top of the hierarchy of legal acts in the EU (Eke & Stahl, 2024). All the regulations and directives discussed below follow these established norms and must simultaneously be interpreted by primary law (Trstenjak & Brkan, 2012, pp. 168–170).

## AN OVERVIEW OF THE EU LEGAL FRAMEWORK ON DATA GOVERNANCE AND RELATED DIGITAL REGULATION

### The General Data Protection Regulation (GDPR)

The GDPR represents the first in a series of EU legal instruments that have addressed data protection in the context of the modern digital economy. The subsequent acts discussed in this chapter build upon the GDPR by complementing or further developing its principles within specific regulatory domains, such as the digital market, digital services, and the broader data governance framework.

## GDPR as the Cornerstone of Data Protection in the Digital Society

The GDPR, which builds upon and repeals Directive 95/46/EC on the protection of individuals with regard to the processing of personal data, significantly modernised and strengthened the existing legal framework by reinforcing the right to control personal data.

In practice, the GDPR implementation presents challenges for data subjects and for data controllers and processors. While data controllers are natural or legal persons who, alone or jointly with others, determine the purposes and means of the processing of personal data, processors are entities that process personal data on behalf of the controller (Articles 4(7) and 4(8) GDPR).

As a result, the controller bears responsibility for establishing appropriate safeguards and ensuring that data subjects can effectively exercise their rights. The processor, in turn, is responsible for executing the data processing operations as determined by the controller (Peyrone & Wichadakul, 2023).

The GDPR grants individuals (so-called *data subjects*) a range of rights, among which the most fundamental include:

- the right to be informed (Articles 13 and 14),
- the right of access to personal data (Article 15),
- the right to rectification (Article 16),
- the right to erasure (the "right to be forgotten", Article 17),
- the right to restriction of processing (Article 18),
- the right to data portability (Article 20), and
- the right to object to processing (Article 21).

These rights provide individuals with autonomy and effective control over their data, as they allow data subjects to influence how their data is collected, used, and disclosed. Therefore, the common denominator underlying these rights can be identified as the *right to data self-determination*, or more broadly, the *right to control over personal data.*

As follows from the substance of the provisions mentioned above, the right to control data belongs to the individual regardless of the legal basis for processing—whether the processing is based on the data subject's explicit consent or any of the other lawful grounds provided in Article 6 of the GDPR (Primec, Pastirk, Perko, 2024).

## Fundamental Rights under the GDPR

The right to control over personal data, as defined by modern data protection frameworks, is closely connected to the right to the protection of personal data. In essence, it serves as a mechanism for realising that right, as it allows individuals to effectively express and enforce their will regarding the processing of their data.

Historically, the right to personal data protection evolved as a specific form or dimension of the right to privacy. It is often described as a subset of the latter (Kovalenko, 2022), as will be explained in more detail below. Although the CFREU recognises the right to privacy (Article 7) and the right to personal data protection (Article 8) as two separate rights, the substantive distinction between them is frequently unclear.

In academic literature and the Court of Justice of the European Union (CJEU) case law, privacy and data protection are often used interchangeably, leading to terminological ambiguity (Milaj-Weishaar, 2020, p. 6). While the right to privacy has traditionally been recognised as a fundamental human right, and data protection is often regarded as a more recent development, this distinction does not hold under closer constitutional scrutiny.

A comprehensive comparative analysis of the constitutions of EU Member States has shown that provisions on data protection emerged roughly at the same time as those on privacy and are often substantively linked. Nevertheless, explicit constitutional recognition of the right to personal data protection still exists in only about half of the EU Member States (Erdos, 2021, pp. 22–23).

## The Digital Markets Act (DMA)

On 1 November 2022, Regulation (EU) 2022/1925 on competitive and fair markets in the digital sector, also known as the Digital Markets Act (DMA), came into force. It initially addresses unfair practices by large companies in digital services markets (Witt, 2023). Traditional EU competition law instruments, particularly Articles 101 and 102 TFEU, and Member States' national regimes, have also been used to regulate digital platforms. However, in practice, these instruments have often proved insufficient and time inefficient, as lengthy legal proceedings have failed to prevent or correct distortions of competition in digital markets on time (Müller & Kettemann, 2024).

Article 1(1) of the DMA establishes harmonised rules to ensure the proper functioning of the internal market by promoting contestable and fair markets in the digital sector across the EU, where gatekeepers operate, for the benefit of business users and end users. According to the recitals, competition here refers primarily to the ability of companies to overcome barriers to entry and expansion and to challenge gatekeepers based on the quality of their products and services (Witt, 2023).

Of particular relevance to the DMA is the notion of digital gatekeepers. Under the DMA, firms are defined as gatekeepers when three conditions are simultaneously met: (1) they have a significant impact on the internal market, (2) they provide a so-called core platform service, and (3) they enjoy an established and sustainable position, either in the present or with a high probability in the foreseeable future. These general criteria are followed by well-defined thresholds, which are met by the largest technology providers already established in the global digital market.

As defined by the DMA, core platform services have certain structural features that providers can exploit to gain and consolidate market power quickly. These characteristics include strong economies of scale, strong network effects, user coupling effects, vertical integration, multi-sidedness, the absence of dominance of users and advantages related to data access. Combined with certain unfair practices, this can lead to structural anticompetitive effects, business and end-user dependency and distortions of market relationships (DMA, 2022, Recital 2). The provision of a core platform service thus constitutes a conditio sine qua non for the legal definition of a company as a gatekeeper, as the concepts of gatekeeper and core platform services are inextricably linked (Jovanović, 2024). On this basis, a company can obtain gatekeeper status if it meets the conditions set out in the Regulation. Such actors often operate entire digital ecosystems, making it difficult for new or smaller competitors to enter, regardless of their innovation or efficiency. In this way, they increase the risk that key markets in the digital economy will no longer function competitively without regulatory intervention (DMA, 2022, Recital 3). As defined in Article 3 of the DMA, gatekeepers provide an essential entry point between businesses and end users and hold, or are expected to have, a durable and entrenched position in their activities.

From the perspective of protecting user autonomy, one of the central objectives of the DMA is to prevent dependencies on particular digital ecosystems that prevent efficient switching between services or providers. This way, the Regulation goes beyond traditional competition protection approaches by focusing on the structural conditions for maintaining an open and fair digital market.

In response to the concentration of market power in the digital economy, the DMA represents a new regulatory instrument designed to limit the economic power of gatekeepers (Belloso & Petit, 2023).

It is also worth underlining the concept of interoperability, which implies the obligation of gatekeepers to enable technical connectivity and operation with other services or systems, particularly in a way that allows users to communicate, exchange content and move between services from different providers without unjustified barriers. The aim is to reduce user lock-in and to strengthen concordance based on quality and, above all, the freedom of choice that this gives users (Rombolà, 2023).

### Fundamental Rights under the DMA

As indicated in the previous section, the DMA's central aim is to protect individuals and businesses by creating a fairer and more open digital ecosystem. The DMA also affects the positive obligations arising from several fundamental rights guaranteed in the CFREU. The digitalisation of society brings several risks to the fundamental rights of citizens and economic operators (Neves, 2025).

At the end of the opening decisions, the DMA specifically emphasises that it respects the fundamental rights and principles recognised by the CFREU, in particular the following Charter rights: the freedom of economic initiative, the right to an effective remedy and an impartial tribunal, and the principle of ne bis in idem. The following rights and principles must be respected in interpreting and applying the DMA (Recital 109).

The provisions of the DMA also interfere with issues of fair access, transparency, non-discrimination and effective enforcement of the rights of users and business entities that are in a dependent position vis-à-vis digital gatekeepers.

All of the above relate in particular to exercising the crucial fundamental right of the right to free economic initiative under Article 16 of the CFREU. The ability to freely pursue an economic activity is guaranteed by the possibility of access to the market and the conditions that allow competitive activity on the market. Here, the DMA goes beyond mere sectoral regulation and becomes an expression of a positive obligation to protect fundamental rights. In a way that limits the practices of digital gatekeepers that create systemic barriers to fair competition.

Individual authors also consider the DMA as a basis for a broader understanding of the effects of this legislation, going beyond the competition law framework and the classical fundamental rights listed above. Thus, they point out that a new right, the so-called right to data, could be derived from the objectives and content of the DMA. The right to data would be based on gatekeepers' positive obligations and positioned among the rights arising from the digital market as a specific regulatory environment (Lundqvist, 2025). The need for such a right could also be partly deduced from the Data Act, which also pursues greater economic fairness and the need to regulate data status in the digital environment.

## The Digital Services Act (DSA)

In 2022, Regulation (EU) 2022/2065 on a Single Market for Digital Services, also known as the Digital Services Act (DSA), was adopted and became fully applicable on 17 February 2024. The main objective of the new Regulation is to ensure the effectiveness of fundamental rights and consumer protection and to prevent the spread of illegal content and the societal risks associated with disinformation or other illegal or unlawful content. The DSA introduces many rules to protect our fundamental rights online. These rights include freedom of thought, expression, information, and opinion without manipulation (European Commission, 2024).

EU Member States have each started to adopt national legislation on intermediary services. Consequently, that would have a particularly negative impact on the functioning of the EU internal market. Thus, one of the primary purposes of adopting the DSA was to create a safer, more predictable and trustworthy online environment that would foster innovation and ensure respect for the fundamental rights enshrined in the CFREU.

It is essential to the EU's efforts to regulate online services more effectively. Therefore, the aim is to establish a general framework for providing intermediary services for greater systemic control of online platforms and social networks.

Despite its broad title, the Regulation does not cover all forms of digital services, but its legal scope is limited to so-called intermediary services. This concept covers mainly transmission, caching and hosting services, as already known from the eCommerce Directive, which are those functions that allow the technical transmission or storage of user-generated content (Wilman, 2022). Intermediary service providers include Internet access providers, domain registries and registrars, cloud service providers, and online platforms, including social networks and online marketplaces.

The Act thus provides for the fight against illegal content and sets out measures to withdraw or encourage the withdrawal of unlawful content while fully respecting freedom of expression. The DSA refrains from defining illegal content, leaving this to national and EU law (Leiser, 2023). However, it states that the concept should be interpreted broadly, as any information, whatever its form, which is illegal in itself or relates to illegal products, services or activities. DSA includes cases such as hate speech, terrorist propaganda, unlawful discrimination, dissemination of child sexual abuse material, unlawful sharing of private content, online harassment, breaches of consumer and copyright laws and the unlawful offer or sale of goods and services. It is irrelevant to assessing whether the illegality arises under EU law or compatible national law. On the other hand, content depicting unlawful acts (for example, a video of a crime) is not necessarily unlawful if its recording and dissemination are not per se prohibited.[1]

The DSA also outlines due diligence obligations for a transparent and secure online environment. The extent of the obligations on providers depends on the type, size and nature of the intermediary service concerned. The new legislation imposes greater accountability and transparency on digital platform operators for the content on their platforms. Besides, it protects users and their fundamental rights online

(Genç-Gelgeç, 2022). The DSA thus introduces due diligence requirements based on transparency, accountability and information, including, inter alia, specific requirements on terms of use, the establishment of complaint handling mechanisms, and reporting and transparency obligations. The obligations vary according to the size and role of the provider in the digital environment. The DSA, therefore, divides providers into four groups:

- Intermediaries,
- Content hosting intermediaries, including online platforms,
- Web platforms (hosting providers that also provide information),
- Very Large Online Platforms (VLOPs) and Very Large Online Search Engines (VLOSEs), i.e. those with more than 45 million active recipients of the service in the EU (DSA, 2022, Recital 80).

Each of these groups must comply at different levels, depending on their actual impact and the risks they pose in the digital space. This approach is proving to be effective, as it contributes to a more uniform application of the legal framework, while at the same time specifying the obligations of each type of platform in a precise way, allowing proportionate and targeted regulation (Genç-Gelgeç, 2022).

The DSA also requires all intermediary service providers to report publicly at least once a year on how they are fulfilling their obligations. These reports are intended to increase transparency and allow for scrutiny by both the public and the competent authorities. Providers must also establish a contact point through which the authorities can communicate directly with the company (DSA, 2022, Chapter 4).

Large online platforms and search engines (VLOPs and VLOSEs) are subject to stricter compliance controls. They must establish an independent DSA monitoring function to ensure internal control. Another important innovation of the DSA is that the European Commission has broad powers to supervise huge platforms. Among other things, it can conduct inspections, request access to data, conduct investigations and impose heavy fines in case of non-compliance with the Regulation (Müller & Kettemann, 2024).

In several places, the DSA highlights minors as a specifically protected category. It assigns responsibility to intermediary service providers to limit the dissemination of illegal content and products online, enhances safeguards for the protection of minors, and strengthens user rights by promoting greater transparency and choice (DSA, 2022, Recitals 46, 71, 81). According to Article 28 of the DSA, providers must also take proportionate measures to ensure a high level of privacy, security, and the protection of minors in their services. Providers of online platforms accessible to minors are therefore prohibited from targeting advertising based on profiling using users' data, where they can establish with reasonable certainty that the recipient of the service is a minor (DSA, 2022, Recital 95). While the DSA pursues a broad set of regulatory goals, one of its central aims is to ensure a safer and more accountable digital environment for minors.

The role of intermediary services that DSA addresses in today's digital society goes beyond their primary technological or economic significance. They are platforms that enable the transmission and storage of information and increasingly co-create the conditions for political participation, the formation of public opinion, and broader social processes. Social networks, content-sharing platforms, and hosting services today act as spaces of the digital public sphere where key political, cultural, and social shifts occur. Their influence can be seen in the organization of mass protest movements against autocratic regimes (e.g., the Arab Spring), in the mobilization of voters and the shaping of political discourses (e.g., the US presidential election), in the dissemination of public health information in times of crisis (e.g., the COVID-19 pandemic), and as instruments of information warfare in modern interstate conflicts (e.g., the Russian invasion of Ukraine). All this confirms that intermediary services today also have undeniable political power, which raises numerous legal, ethical and regulatory questions regarding their accountability, transparency and alignment with the values of the rule of law (Wilman, 2022).

## Fundamental Rights under the DSA

The protection of fundamental rights generally concerns the vertical relationship between the individual and the state. Horizontal relations are, in principle, not regulated between private actors.

It would follow that the relationship between digital platforms and users has traditionally been treated as a private contractual relationship. Due to this private law nature, fundamental rights defined by the CFREU and the European Convention on Human Rights (ECHR) are not directly applicable in this context.

However, in assessing the normative framework, it is essential to consider the current social reality and the real impact of modern information technologies, huge digital platforms, on the individual and their ability to engage freely in the digital environment. The right of providers to determine the terms and conditions of use of their services can be seen as an expression of their fundamental right to private property and freedom of contractual regulation. However, the relationship between the user and the global platform acting as a private service provider is highly structurally unequal, both in terms of economic power and in terms of the actual ability to influence the terms of use (Perel, Elkin-Koren, & De Gregorio, 2021). Large digital platforms, particularly social networks, have significant bargaining power, which, in most cases, forces users to accept unilaterally imposed 'house rules'. These rules effectively set the conditions under which individuals can participate in the digital public sphere and exercise their freedom of expression and access to information. Therefore, entering into contractual relations with such platforms is not only a private law act of will, but also has a significant impact on the exercise of fundamental individual rights, in particular freedom of expression, access to information and the right to an effective remedy (Fahy et al., 2023). For these reasons, the adequate protection of fundamental rights in the digital space has become a significant challenge for the legislator.

One such relationship is regulated in the DSA, where the European legislator has regulated the relationship between users and intermediary service providers. The legislator's objective in doing so was to strengthen users' position in protecting their fundamental rights (DSA, 2022, Recital 3). However, it also seeks to limit the power of the large technology platforms by imposing increased responsibility for the content they host. In doing so, the legislator aims to reduce the adverse effects of content moderation, particularly regarding freedom of expression and the quality of public discourse, before the DSA, individual sectoral acts imposed only limited regulation on platforms' discretion in setting their terms of use (Quintais, Appelman, & Ó Fathaigh, 2023). Article 14(1) of the DSA systematically addresses a previously unregulated normative gap by requiring online platforms to set out in their terms and conditions all restrictions on the use of the service in a clear, comprehensible and accessible manner. It includes transparency regarding content moderation procedures, algorithmic decision-making mechanisms, and internal complaint-handling systems. In addition to this emphasis on transparency, Article 14(4) DSA establishes a standard of conduct for implementing and enforcing such restrictions. Platforms are required to act diligently, objectively, and proportionately, with due regard to users' fundamental rights, particularly the right to freedom of expression, media pluralism, and other rights protected under the CFREU. This provision reflects the DSA's broader normative orientation, which seeks to ensure that contractual relationships between users and platforms are governed by principles consistent with protecting fundamental rights in the digital environment.

Building upon this regulatory basis, Article 14 of the DSA further addresses the broad contractual autonomy of intermediaries to moderate illegal and harmful content, thereby establishing a legal framework that enables the integration of fundamental rights into private law relationships between platforms and users.

Furthermore, in Section 5 of the DSA, which regulates additional obligations for extensive online platforms (VLOPs) and search engines (VLOSE), users' fundamental rights are integrated as a specific aspect of assessing and managing systemic risks. According to Article 34(1), these providers must carry out regular, comprehensive assessments of the systemic risks arising from the design or operation of their services. Among the risks listed, those related to the exercise of fundamental rights under the CFREU, such as freedom of expression and information, respect for human dignity, protection of personal data, non-discrimination and the rights of the child, have been added. Based on these assessments, Article 35 obliges platforms to implement effective and proportionate measures to mitigate these risks, such as content moderation changes, recommendation system adjustments, or strengthened internal control procedures. Moreover, Article 36 also provides for the obligation of a regular independent audit, which includes an assessment of platforms' compliance with the DSA rules, including their obligations to respect fundamental rights.

These additional obligations, which directly address the fundamental rights of the CFREU, represent a significant challenge for regulating platforms with high social power. In that way, they progressively establish a specific form of indirect horizontal effectiveness of fundamental rights in relations between private actors.

## The Data Governance Act (DGA)

In September 2023, Regulation (EU) 2022/868 on European Data Governance, also known as the Data Governance Act (DGA), entered into force. The DGA is designed to promote the cross-sectoral and cross-border exchange of data within the EU, to enhance its re-use and create added value for European citizens and economic operators (Carovano & Finck, 2023).

Data has enormous economic and societal potential, enabling the development of innovative products and services based on advanced technologies, contributing to more efficient production processes and supporting the design of solutions to complex societal challenges (European Commission, 2024). The DGA would thus exploit the potential of data by strengthening the EU's Digital Single Market.

Under EU primary law, the internal market is already established and its functioning is protected against distortions of competition. In this context, standard rules for data management in the Member States play a key role in strengthening market unity while respecting fundamental rights. Efforts to create a single data area to enhance the EU's open strategic autonomy, while being committed to the principles of the free flow of data in the international environment. The DGA thus further exploits the potential of data and further strengthens the EU's Digital Single Market.

There was already a debate on data sharing at the time of the adoption of the GDPR. Still, the new right to data portability has proved problematic, particularly regarding data re-use (van Ooijen & Uršič Vrabec, 2018). To this end, the DGA would facilitate the further sharing of personal and non-personal data by introducing the concept of data altruism.[2] In doing so, the legislator seeks to establish general conditions that would facilitate and simplify the exchange of data in all areas (Pagallo, 2022). The concept is based on an organisation's right to allow, under certain conditions, the non-profit processing of non-personal data. Still, where personal data is involved, the processing relies on the data subject's consent, by the principles of privacy protection and lawfulness of processing (Ruohonen & Mickelsson, 2023).

The DGA will significantly contribute in the coming years by promoting the establishment and advancement of common European data spaces in key areas, covering both the private and the public sectors. It is essential to underline that the DGA does not create new rights or obligations to share data. It does not contain rules to facilitate data sharing as a data brokering service or as a data altruism organisation (Wolters, 2024).

## Fundamental Rights under the DGA

The DGA affirms a strong commitment to the respect for fundamental rights enshrined in the CFREU. Particular emphasis is placed on protecting privacy and personal data, the freedom to conduct a business, and property rights. In addition, the DGA underlines the importance of inclusivity by explicitly requiring that digital public sector services be accessible to persons with disabilities, thereby promoting digital equality and non-discrimination (DGA, 2022, Recital 62).

In the debate on the relationship between the DGA and fundamental rights, the right to protect personal data under Article 8 of the CFREU remains at the centre of the discussion. Adopting the DGA does not raise any new dilemmas in this respect. Still, it does raise the question of how to ensure that the new mechanisms for accessing and re-using data are compatible with the existing system of protection of fundamental rights. The DGA applies to any digital form of data, and it is essential to add that it does not create a new legal basis for processing personal data, which the GDPR regulates. Where processing of personal data occurs, the GDPR takes precedence over the application of the DGA. It is clear from this relationship that the processing of personal data is without prejudice to the principle of lawful processing of personal data. At the same time, the DGA does not restrict cross-border data transfers, provided that they are carried out by the GDPR (DGA, 2022, Recital 4).

The recitals of the DGA explicitly emphasise that the re-use of sensitive data such as personal data, trade secrets and other data protected by third-party rights is permissible only with full respect for fundamental rights, in particular the right to the protection of personal data and the principle of non-discrimination. Before such data can be made available for further use, strict technical and legal safeguards must be in place to protect the rights of individuals and other rights holders (DGA, 2022, Recital 6, 19).

Article 5 of the DGA, which deals with the conditions for re-use of data, is very relevant. This article respects the protection of the fundamental rights of individuals through several safeguards, notably through the prism of the right to the protection of personal data. Re-use must therefore be transparent, proportionate, objectively justified, and non-discriminatory. The Article provides that any re-use of personal data must be based on appropriate anonymisation. The purpose of this provision is to prevent any further processing that would be incompatible with the original purposes of the data collection and could compromise individuals' informational self-determination. In addition, the DGA introduces further safeguards, such as the use of secure processing environments under the control of public authorities and the physical implementation of processing within the premises of those authorities. At the same time, users are expressly prohibited from attempting to re-identify individuals. This protection approach strengthens the enforcement of fundamental rights in the new paradigm of data sharing.

## The Data Act (DA)

On 22 December 2023, the European legislator adopted the final regulation within the legislative package outlined in the previous chapters, introducing additional rules for a domain of data governance that had not yet been regulated. It is the Regulation on harmonised rules on fair access to and use of data, amending Regulation (EU) 2017/2394 and Directive (EU) 2020/1828, also referred to as the Data Act (DA).

Establishing common European data spaces in strategically important economic sectors and areas of public interest represents a significant step towards strengthening the single market for data, as it promotes cross-sectoral data exchange and sharing.

Due to the lack of a comprehensive legal framework governing data management, businesses and individual users have faced difficulties accessing data that they typically generate through digital services and devices. An additional challenge arises when users attempt to retrieve uploaded data or transfer it from one cloud provider to another. A system in which users cannot access their data undermines competition in the market, which is even less justifiable given the fundamental characteristic of data: its capacity to be used simultaneously by multiple parties (Geiregat, 2022). Data is considered a non-rival good, as several users can access it simultaneously without diminishing its availability.

The DA aims to harmonise access to and use of data across the EU, while respecting the protection of fundamental rights. Importantly, the DA covers both personal and non-personal data.[3] At the same time, it normalises a fairer distribution of data value between actors in the data economy and promotes access to and use of data. The underlying idea in designing this Regulation was to enable users of connected devices to access the data generated by these devices and their associated services.

Such technology, also known as the Internet of Things (IoT), creates new opportunities for companies to access large amounts of data that often remain under the exclusive control of manufacturers. The primary mechanism to address this challenge is a new set of rights for users of IoT devices to access and share this data. Such an arrangement empowers users by giving them more control over their data and access to additional data-driven services, while at the same time encouraging secondary uses of data and opening up space for innovation on the part of companies based on data-driven models (Kerber, 2023, p. 120–135).

The DA allows users to access and transfer data generated by digital technologies to third parties, while preventing large technology companies from using these same rules to receive third-party data, strengthening competition in digital markets and allowing entrenched positions to be overcome (König, 2022). Due to its potentially broad scope of application, covering all IoT devices, the DA reaches into several sectoral areas by setting out a horizontal regulation (Krämer et al., 2023).

Therefore, the regulation affects contractual relationships between economic operators (B2B) and relationships where the economic operator or other professional person is on the one hand, and the consumer is on the other (B2C). In addition, the DA introduces several other innovations. Among other things, the measures would allow for the possibility of so-called cloud switching between different cloud service providers. It also lays down rules on contractual terms on access to data, with a particular focus on protecting small and medium-sized enterprises from unfair contractual terms. At the same time, it also allows public institutions to access data (B2G), which is considered essential for responding to public disasters such as terrorist attacks or natural disasters (The Institute of International and European Affairs, 2023). In this way, specific citizen-generated data can or must be shared with businesses and public authorities, simultaneously creating several new opportunities for innovation (Griedlich & Jerome, 2023). One of the reasons for the new legislation is to strengthen the rights of individuals regarding their data.

It is essential to underline that the DA does not constitute a legal basis for data holders to acquire new rights to use data generated through connected products or related services. On the contrary, data holders do not gain the right to collect or generate personal data. Still, they are instead obliged to make such data available to the user or third parties designated by the user upon request (Recitals 5, 7 and 25, DA, 2023). Furthermore, the DA stipulates that data holders may use non-personal data obtained via IoT devices exclusively based on a contractual agreement with the user (Article 4(13) and (14), DA, 2023).

The DA represents a notable departure from previous practice, in which non-personal data was typically determined by the de facto control of the data holder over the device, without requiring any contractual basis or the user's consent. In this regard, the new regime partially mirrors the logic of the GDPR, which under Article 6(1)(a) requires the data subject's consent for the lawful processing of personal data (Eckardt & Kerber, 2024).

## Fundamental Rights under the DA

As a foundational aspect of the EU's evolving data governance framework, the DA does not create a new regime for protecting personal data, but rather complements and extends the existing regulatory architecture established by the GDPR. Regarding the GDPR, the DA broadens the scope of data governance by encompassing personal and non-personal data (DA, 2023, Recital 7). Nevertheless, it remains essential to recognise that the GDPR constitutes *lex specialis* about the DA and therefore takes precedence in any processing of personal data, particularly where the exercise of fundamental rights of individuals, as protected under Article 8 of the CFREU, is concerned.

At the same time, however, the DA introduces a distinct layer of data governance, creating a dedicated regulatory framework that complements the existing legal instruments. It does so primarily by strengthening the user's position by introducing new rights. Among the most significant are the user's right to access data generated through a connected device, the obligation of service providers to enable the transfer and sharing of such data, and the rights of third parties to access this data upon the user's request.

The gradual evolution of data governance in the EU is rooted in the Union's fundamental values, in particular the right to the protection of personal data (Article 8 CFREU) and the freedom to conduct a business (Article 16 CFREU). This connection becomes evident in the DA's shift of focus towards non-personal and mixed data sets, which have thus far remained insufficiently addressed and often failed to ensure fair treatment of the user.

The recitals of the DA place particular emphasis on the principle of data minimisation and the principles of data protection by design and by default, as set out in Articles 5(1)(c) and 25 of the GDPR. These principles play a key role in ensuring compliance with fundamental rights, particularly the right to privacy (Article 7 CFREU) and the right to the protection of personal data (Article 8 CFREU). The DA further underlines that all actors involved in data sharing must implement appropriate technical and organisational measures to safeguard these rights. It includes traditional protective mechanisms and advanced approaches that allow data to be processed without transferring or copying raw content (DA, 2023, Recital 8). In this manner, the DA concretely implements the protection of fundamental rights within the evolving regulatory architecture of data governance and the data economy. Any limitation of an individual's right to control their data must comply with the principles of legality, proportionality, and technical adequacy.

The DA also addresses the issue of third-country requests for access to non-personal data, which may endanger fundamental rights, particularly the right to security and an adequate remedy. Without international agreements governing such matters, data transfer is only permitted where adequate judicial protection, proportionality, and the right to object are ensured (DA, 2023, Recital 56, 101).

## CASE-BASED RESULTS

### European Commission v. Amazon

#### Factual Background and Decision

Amazon is a global U.S.-based company (a so-called "gatekeeper") that operates the world's largest online marketplace, also named Amazon. This online platform plays a dual role: it serves the marketplace where independent sellers can offer their products directly to consumers, while selling their products on the platform as a retailer competing with those independent sellers. Due to this dual position, Amazon has access to vast datasets on the activities of independent sellers on its platform, including non-public business data. For this reason, the European Commission formally opened an investigation in July 2019 to assess whether such data infringed EU competition law (CASE AT.40462 – Amazon Marketplace) (Yıldız, 2023).

In addition to selling its products and those of third-party producers, Amazon also offers the latter a range of fulfilment services (warehousing, packing, and shipping), known as Fulfilment by Amazon (FBA), as well as fast and free delivery through its Prime programme. Sellers who opted for the FBA service also benefited from fast and free delivery to customers (automatic eligibility for the Prime programme) (recital 143), and from Amazon's Buy Box programme (recital 125), in the same way as Amazon's offers (jointly referred to in recital 30 as AFN sellers). In contrast, traditional third-party sellers had to qualify separately and were often subject to slower delivery promises (recitals 135 and 136), resulting in differentiated treatment (recitals 154–156).

The Buy Box programme enabled external sellers to gain greater visibility on Amazon's platform, increasing their exposure and sales. Since most consumers prefer fast and free shipping, access to the Prime service significantly affects a seller's competitiveness. In this context, Amazon's policy (potentially) resulted in a distortion of competition both between Amazon's offers and those of independent sellers (so-called horizontal discrimination), as well as among third-party sellers themselves, depending on whether they used Amazon's logistics services (vertical discrimination). Although the Commission's decision does not explicitly use these terms—and, as evident from recital 219, blurs the line between horizontal discrimination and self-preferencing (comparable to the practice in the Google Shopping case)—the substantive implications are clear.

In the proceedings before the European Commission (CASE AT.40703 – Amazon Buy Box), Amazon offered commitments, which the Commission subsequently accepted. As a result, the case was not concluded by a final decision. Still, it was instead closed, which excluded any further legal and economic substantiation of the effects of the conduct in question. Had this not occurred, the Directorate-General for Competition (DG COMP) would have been required to assess an unjustified difference in treatment that could pose a risk under competition law enforcement, regardless of whether it involved horizontal or vertical forms of discrimination. Such a decision would have had significant implications for future cases of discriminatory abuse of market power in the digital environment (Bergqvist, 2023).

## Fundamental Rights Implications

Whether Amazon's conduct in the described cases constitutes a violation of fundamental rights primarily depends on who is considered the holder of such rights and whether Amazon, as a private corporation, is bound to respect them. Under the traditional understanding of human rights, for example, under the ECHR, the addressees of rights obligations are public authorities. However, in more recent discussions, particularly in the digital market and platform regulation context, it has been emphasised that private actors such as large platforms, also called gatekeepers, may also bear responsibilities toward users and third parties, especially when they hold systemic power.

Consequently, Amazon's "Buy Box" may have a restrictive effect on competing sellers who offer identical products but are not selected, resulting in significantly lower visibility and fewer sales (European Commission, 2020). In this way, their freedom to conduct a business is limited, sometimes even threatening their economic existence, particularly for smaller merchants who are economically dependent on Amazon. This right is protected under Article 16 of the Charter of Fundamental Rights of the European Union (CFREU).

Furthermore, Amazon's use of market algorithms favours a particular category of sellers, such as those using FBA, which results in discrimination against other sellers without any objectively justified reason. Such use of algorithms may constitute an indirect violation of the principle of equal treatment in the economic environment and an indirect breach of the principle of equality under Articles 20 and 21 of the CFREU. The principle of equality requires that comparable situations be treated alike, unless there is an objective and reasonable justification for different treatment. Although Article 21 primarily protects personal characteristics of individuals, the principle of non-discriminatory treatment can also apply to economic operators in cases of arbitrary, non-transparent, or selectively exclusionary conduct in economic activity. The Amazon case indicates algorithmic and systematic exclusion of certain groups, such as small traders without access to FBA, without transparent, proportionate, and verifiable criteria.

Discriminatory algorithmic favouring of certain sellers, including Amazon itself or those using FBA, also means that customers are not shown all available offers. Besides, it reduces market transparency and fails to provide consumers with sufficient information, ultimately impairing their freedom of choice. The right to information and the freedom of choice are part of consumer protection guaranteed by Article 38 of the CFREU (Sartor, 2019).

## Apple and the App Store

### Factual Background and Decision

Since 2007, Apple has maintained a closed digital ecosystem for its iOS operating system, based on exclusive control over app distribution and payment processing through its proprietary App Store. It constitutes a so-called "walled garden" model, in which Apple controls content, access, and transactions within its mobile operating system. The company justifies this approach by citing the protection of privacy, security, and intellectual property while enabling effective monetisation through commissions.

Third-party developers, such as Epic Games, were nevertheless essential to the platform's growth, as their applications significantly expanded the user experience on iOS devices. A conflict arose when Epic introduced a direct payment system in its game Fortnite, bypassing Apple's In-App Purchase (IAP) mechanism[4], thereby breaching Apple's contractual rules. Apple removed the application from the App Store, and in 2020, Epic filed a lawsuit alleging abuse of a dominant position and restriction of competition.

At the centre of the dispute lies Apple's 30 per cent commission, which prohibits developers from informing users about external payment options (Epic Games, Inc. v. Apple Inc., 2021). This raised the question of whether Apple restricts users' and developers' access to competitive information about alternative payment methods, thereby limiting market freedom.

The case is particularly significant as it represents a precedent-setting moment in the broader debate on the legality of platform-based economies, where ownership of digital infrastructure raises fundamental questions about competition, contractual freedom, and the regulation of private power in the digital space.

In 2021 the court ruled in Apple's favour, finding it not a monopolist. However, it simultaneously held that Apple's so-called anti-steering provisions[5] were unlawful. These provisions prohibited developers from informing users about the possibility of purchasing content outside Apple's platform, thereby avoiding the 30 per cent commission.

Apple submitted evidence based on a broader definition of the digital gaming market. In contrast, Epic advocated for a narrower meaning, arguing that the relevant market was an aftermarket within the iOS ecosystem. The court rejected both definitions and defined the relevant market as "digital mobile gaming transactions." It found that Apple does not hold a monopoly in this market, even though it controls more than half of it. Nevertheless, the court concluded that Apple's anti-steering practices violate California's Unfair Competition Law, as they "hide critical information from consumers and illegally stifle consumer choice." The court therefore issued a permanent injunction prohibiting Apple from enforcing such contractual terms, thereby opening the possibility for developers to inform users about alternative purchasing options outside the App Store (Kozen, 2021).

Although the judgment of 10 September 2021, in which the court issued a permanent injunction against Apple, formally concluded the main proceedings in the case of Epic Games v. Apple Inc., its legal effects did not take immediate effect. Apple appealed the decision, which resulted in the enforcement of the injunction being temporarily stayed pending the outcome of the appellate proceedings. In the meantime, on 9 January 2024, the US Supreme Court denied Apple's petition for certiorari, making the decision final and enforceable. The injunction entered into force on 16 January 2024. Nevertheless, Apple, according to the court, knowingly violated the order through its subsequent practices, which in 2025 led to a judicial finding of contempt of court and referral of the case for criminal prosecution (Berman & Harrington, 2024).

In a recent 2025 ruling, the court found that Apple had generated disproportionately high profits from the 30 per cent commission charged on in-app purchases, which were not justified by the actual value of its intellectual property. It was identified as anticompetitive conduct. Despite the court order, Apple introduced a new 27 per cent commission on out-of-app purchases—where such a fee had not existed—and extended it to seven days following a user's exit from the app. The court found that these measures aimed to preserve an unlawful source of revenue rather than to comply with the injunction.

Furthermore, the court concluded that Apple continued obstructing developers' communication with users regarding alternative purchasing options, using technical and design barriers such as warning screens, static URL addresses, and non-personalised messages that discouraged users from choosing competing options. Internal company documentation revealed that these measures were part of a deliberate business strategy, despite contradictory testimony given by responsible individuals during the proceedings. In the continued proceedings, the court stated that Apple had not only acted in contradiction to the substance of the injunction but had also deliberately circumvented it. The judgment explicitly reads: "The Court FINDS Apple in willful violation of this Court's 2021 Injunction [...] Apple's continued attempts to interfere with competition will not be tolerated. This is an injunction, not a negotiation. There are no do-overs once a party willfully disregards a court order." The facts of the case demonstrated that Apple continued its efforts to maintain control over key segments of the digital market, thereby violating not only the formal provisions but also the fundamental purpose of the court's injunction - namely, the elimination of restrictions on competition (Epic Games, Inc. v. Apple Inc., 2021).

The judgment in Epic Games v. Apple Inc. illustrates that even a partial court injunction can significantly impact the market behaviour of digital platforms, primarily when the court identifies deliberate circumvention. The 2025 ruling confirms that final and binding court injunctions impose substantive obligations and that their evasive implementation may violate the rule of law, with serious legal consequences, including the possibility of criminal prosecution (Gruber, 2025).

## Apple and the DMA

### Factual Background and Decision

The DMA imposes obligations on gatekeepers in digital services to ensure greater competitiveness, interoperability, and choice for end users and service providers. In 2024 and early 2025, the European Commission directed its regulatory attention toward Apple, which is considered one of the key addressees of the DMA. While enforcing compliance obligations, the Commission identified and addressed several irregularities accordingly.

By the provisions of the DMA, app developers who distribute their applications through Apple's App Store must be guaranteed the right to inform users free of charge about alternative offers outside the App Store, to direct users to such offers, and to enable purchases outside the relevant platform. The European Commission found Apple failed to comply with these legal obligations (European Commission, 2025). Due to Apple's restrictions, app developers could not fully benefit from alternative distribution channels outside the App Store. As a result, users also lacked access to complete information about more affordable or competitive offers, as Apple prevented developers from directly communicating with consumers about such options. Apple failed to demonstrate that these restrictions were objectively justified and proportionate to the objectives.

In its adopted decision, the Commission ordered Apple to remove technical and commercial restrictions that limit the steering of users toward alternative offers. It also prohibited the company from continuing or repeating such non-compliant practices in the future, including through any measures with the same purpose or effect as the practices in question(European Commission, 2025).

## Fundamental Rights Implications

The cases described above also have important implications for protecting fundamental rights in the digital environment. As repeatedly noted, companies, huge platforms designated as gatekeepers, bear responsibilities toward users, as explicitly recognised in the DMA, particularly in Article 1(1) and further operationalised through the obligations laid down in Article 5.

It is essential to underline the significance of the rights to freedom of choice and access to information as core components of an individual's informational autonomy, as set out in Article 38 CFREU.[6] By limiting the ability of developers to clearly and directly inform users about alternative payment options outside the App Store system, Apple unlawfully interfered with users' right to make free economic decisions. A similar legal concern has also been identified in the European context, where the European Commission, while enforcing the DMA, found that Apple's practices distort user choice and prevent developers from effectively communicating alternative purchasing options. They restrict both informational freedom and transparency in the market.

In addition to protecting end users' rights, it is also necessary to highlight the dimension of the freedom to conduct business with app developers. Apple's contractual framework for alternative distribution—through the imposition of additional costs and technical restrictions—constitutes a systemic barrier to exercising entrepreneurial freedom in the digital environment.. As a result, developers face severe limitations in accessing the market and independently designing their business models and conditions for offering digital content outside Apple's system. The European Commission also recognised this conduct as problematic, noting that the imposed conditions, including the new so-called Core Technology Fee, create economic disincentives that prevent developers from effectively exercising their economic freedoms (European Commission, 2025).

From the perspective of fundamental principles of the European legal order, it is also necessary to emphasise the principle of equality under Article 20 CFREU, which requires that all individuals in the digital environment be treated equally and without unjustified differences. Due to Apple's unilateral terms and technical restrictions, users and developers are in effect excluded from the opportunity to actively and equally participate in shaping the digital market under conditions that reflect their interests. This exclusion creates a structural imbalance between the platform and its users or business partners, which runs counter to the DMA's objectives to ensure greater competitiveness, interoperability and equal market conditions. In addition to harming competition, such conduct also limits innovation, which is central to European policy and a fundamental element of an open and free digital space protected by EU law (Draghi, 2024).

## DISCUSSION AND IMPLICATIONS

Based on the presented legislation and case law, it is evident that fundamental rights in the digital environment have not lost their significance. On the contrary, they are gradually gaining importance as a central guiding mechanism in the digital transformation. Just as previous generations of fundamental rights were anchored in protecting individual liberty, labour rights and social security, today's digital environment increasingly emerges as a new core area of legal protection. At the heart of this shift is ensuring that fundamental rights are preserved and exercised in a society shaped by algorithms, platforms, and unstructured data flows.

From a legal perspective, this article demonstrates that the EU legislative framework—primarily through the GDPR, DSA, DMA, DGA and DA—systematically regulates key areas of the digital economy and data protection. In doing so, it addresses legal gaps that would otherwise enable market distortion, opaque data processing or limitations on fundamental freedoms. At the same time, we observe that further excessive regulatory intervention could produce the opposite effect, stifling innovation and limiting competitiveness. The current legal framework is extensive, comprehensive and generally adequate. What is now required is time for the case law to develop a consistent interpretation that will provide more precise guidance for future orientation. Established regulatory tools such as ex ante conformity assessment, human oversight, transparency requirements, and bans on certain technologies can also be helpful (Brkan, Claes, & Rauchegger, 2021). The Act on Artificial Intelligence, another important milestone in the legal framework for the digital and data economy, also relies heavily on these tools. The solutions it offers are also essential in the context of our contribution, but due to space constraints, we cannot include them in this paper. However, they indeed leave much room for further discussion and development.

We can still rely on the fundamental principles of law and the European legal tradition, which is rooted in justice—understood as the defence of the rule of law—humanism, which places the individual at the centre, and ethical reasoning as a fundamental pillar of legal thinking. Even if relationships between legal subjects are translated into binary code, algorithms and electronic communication, the bearers of rights remain natural persons and legal entities, entitled to complete protection of their dignity and legal security.

## Highlights From Case Law

### European Commission v. Amazon

As a private economic entity with systemic power in the digital space, Amazon bears responsibility for respecting fundamental rights. Its practice of favouring sellers who use its FBA logistics services constitutes indirect discrimination against other sellers. Amazon's practice may violate the principle of equal treatment under Articles 20 and 21 of the CFREU, the right to free economic initiative (Article 16 CFREU), and consumers' rights to transparency and free choice (Article 38 CFREU).

### Epic Games v. Apple Inc. (United States)

Apple restricted developers from informing users about alternative and more affordable purchasing options. Consequently, it interfered with users' right to information and freedom of choice (Article 38 CFREU) and the developers' right to economic freedom (Article 16 CFREU). Apple's non-compliance with a court decision in the subsequent stage of the proceedings further raises concerns about adherence to the rule of law in the digital economy.

### European Commission Proceedings Against Apple Under the DMA

The European Commission treated Apple as a gatekeeper that introduced additional economic and technical barriers (such as the "core technology fee"), thereby limiting users' freedom of choice and the entrepreneurial freedom of developers. These cases confirm that legislation such as the DMA has a concrete effect on the positive obligations of private actors to respect fundamental rights.

## CONCLUSION

In response to the research question: *to what extent, and through which legal mechanisms, do the EU regulatory frameworks on digital platforms and data governance ensure the adequate protection and realisation of users' fundamental rights*? We present the following synthesis:

EU legislation, developed through the GDPR, DSA, DMA, DGA and DA, already provides a relatively high level of protection for fundamental rights in the digital environment. These rights are dynamically evolving and increasingly represent a flexible and responsive framework for addressing the challenges of digitalisation. The group of duty-bearers is expanding (including powerful private actors such as platforms), and the understanding of the rights themselves is gradually extending to new domains, with a potential need to form new fundamental rights as the legal discourse evolves. One such example is the so-called "right to data," emerging in the new legislative context, but will require further refinement through judicial interpretation and academic debate before being fully recognised as a distinct legal category.

The legislative measures adopted in recent years provide a strong foundation for protecting fundamental rights. At the same time, they leave open space for further research, normative reflection, and judicial development that aligns with the evolving digital landscape and technological innovation.

## REFERENCES


Belloso, N. M., & Petit, N. (2023). The EU Digital Markets Act (DMA): A competition hand in a regulatory glove. *European Law Review, 48*(4), 391–412.

Bergqvist, C. (November 12, 2023). Amazon Buy Box – Another Secret Jewel on Discrimination. *SSRN*. Retrieved from https://ssrn.com/abstract=4630315 or http://dx.doi.org/DOI: 10.2139/ssrn.4630315

Berman, S. W., & Harrington, B. (2024). *Apple App Store injunction violation*. Hagens Berman Sobol Shapiro LLP. Retrieved May 28, 2025 from https://www.hbsslaw.com/cases/apple-app-store-injunction-violation

Brkan, M., Claes, M., & Rauchegger, C. (2021). European fundamental rights and digitalisation. *Maastricht Journal of European and Comparative Law, 27*(6), 697–704. DOI: 10.1177/1023263X20983778

Carovano, G., & Finck, M. (2023). Regulating data intermediaries: The impact of the Data Governance Act on the EU's data economy. *Computer Law & Security Review, 50*, 105800. DOI: 10.1016/j.clsr.2023.105800

Draghi, M. (2024). *The Draghi report: A competitiveness strategy for Europe*. European Commission. Retrieved April 26, 2025 from https://ec.europa.eu/commission/publications/draghi-report-competitiveness-strategy-europe_en

Eckardt, M., & Kerber, W. (2024). Property rights theory, bundles of rights on IoT data, and the EU Data Act. *European Journal of Law and Economics, 57*(1), 113–143.

Eke, D., & Stahl, B. (2024). Ethics in the governance of data and digital technology: An analysis of European data regulations and policies. *Digital Society : Ethics, Socio-Legal and Governance of Digital Technology, 3*(1), 1–15.

*Epic Games, Inc. v. Apple Inc.*, No. 4:20-cv-05640-YGR (N.D. Cal. 10 September, 2021). Retrieved April 27, 2025 from https://cand.uscourts.gov/wp-content/uploads/cases-of-interest/epic-games-v-apple/Epic-v.-Apple-20-cv-05640-YGR-Dkt-812-Order.pdf

Erdos, D. (2021). *Comparing Constitutional Privacy and Data Protection Rights within the EU*. University of Cambridge, Faculty of Law Research Paper No. 21/2021. Retrieved April 9, 2025 from https://ssrn.com/abstract=3843653

European Commission. (2015). *Better regulation for better results – An EU agenda* (COM(2015) 192 final). Retrieved March 31, 2025 from https://eur-lex.europa.eu/legal-content/EN/TXT/?uri=CELEX:52015DC0192

European Commission. (2020). *Antitrust: Commission sends Statement of Objections to Amazon for the use of non-public independent seller data and opens second investigation into its e-commerce business practices.* Retrieved May 26, 2025 from https://ec.europa.eu/commission/presscorner/api/files/document/print/en/ip_20_2077/IP_20_2077_EN.pdf

European Commission. (2022). Commission decision of 20.12.2022 relating to a proceeding under Article 102 of the Treaty on the Functioning of the European Union (TFEU) and Article 54 of the EEA Agreement Cases AT.40462 – Amazon Marketplace and AT.40703 – Amazon Buy Box. Retrieved March 4, 2025 from https://ec.europa.eu/competition/antitrust/cases1/202310/AT_40703_8990760_1533_5.pdf

European Commission. (2024). *Digital Services Act: Questions and answers.* Shaping Europe's digital future. Retrieved May 19, 2025 from https://digital-strategy.ec.europa.eu/en/faqs/digital-services-act-questions-and-answers

European Commission. (2024). *The Data Governance Act explained.* Shaping Europe's Digital Future. Retrieved March 30, 2025 from https://digital-strategy.ec.europa.eu/en/policies/data-governance-act-explained

European Commission. (2025). *Digital Markets Act: Commission designates first set of gatekeepers under the Digital Markets Act.* Retrieved April 30, 2025 from https://ec.europa.eu/commission/presscorner/detail/en/ip_25_1086

European Union (2012). *Treaty on European Union.* Official Journal of the European Union, C 326/13. Retrieved March 22, 2025 from https://eur-lex.europa.eu/legal-content/EN/TXT/?uri=CELEX%3A12012M%2FTXT

European Union (2022). *Regulation (EU) 2022/1925 of the European Parliament and of the Council of 14 September 2022 on contestable and fair markets in the digital sector and amending Directives (EU) 2019/1937 and (EU) 2020/1828 (Digital Markets Act). Official Journal of the European Union, L 265*, 1–66. Retrieved March 22, 2025 from https://eur-lex.europa.eu/eli/reg/2022/1925/oj

European Union (2022). *Regulation (EU) 2022/2065 of the European Parliament and of the Council of 19 October 2022 on a Single Market for Digital Services and amending Directive 2000/31/EC (Digital Services Act). Official Journal of the European Union, L 277*, 1–102. Retrieved March 20, 2025 from https://eur-lex.europa.eu/eli/reg/2022/2065/oj

Fahy, I. Buri, J. P. Quintais, & M. Straub (Eds.) (2023). *Putting the DSA into Practice.* Institute for Information Law (IViR), University of Amsterdam. Retrieved from https://verfassungsblog.de/wp-content/uploads/2023/02/vHoboken-et-al_Putting-the-DSA-into-Practice.pdf

Geiregat, S. (2022). *Who owns 'your' (business's) digital data? New EU law in the making*. Oxford Business Law Blog. Retrieved March 19, 2025 from https://blogs.law.ox.ac.uk/oblb/blog-post/2022/12/who-owns-your-businesss-digital-data-new-eu-law-making

Genç-Gelgeç, B. (2022). Regulating digital platforms: Will the DSA correct its predecessor's deficiencies? *Croatian Yearbook of European Law and Policy, 18*, 25–60. Retrieved March 31, 2025 from https://www.cyelp.com/index.php/cyelp/article/view/485

Griedlich, N., & Jerome, J. (2023). *The EU Data Act: What does it mean for you?* Deloitte. Retrieved March 28, 2025 from https://www.deloitte.com/lu/en/Industries/technology/perspectives/the-eu-data-act-what-does-it-mean-for-you.html

Gruber, J. (2025). *Judge Gonzales Rogers issues new Apple App Store ruling*. Daring Fireball. Retrieved March 24, 2025 from https://daringfireball.net/2025/04/gonzales_rogers_apple_app_store_ruling

Hojnik, J. (2025). *Uvod v pravo digitalnega enotnega trga in pravni vidiki servitizacije v EU: Študijsko gradivo*. Maribor: Univerzitetna založba Univerze v Mariboru. https://doi.org/10.18690/um.pf.4.2025

Jovanović, N. (2024). Vratarji na področju tehnologij umetne inteligence. In T. Kerešteš (Ed.), *Digitalne platforme: pravni in ekonomski izzivi* (pp. 59–79). Maribor: Univerza v Mariboru, Univerzitetna založba. https://press.um.si/index.php/ump/catalog/book/5pf24

Kerber, W. (2023). Governance of IoT data: Why the EU Data Act will not fulfill its objectives. *GRUR International*, *72*(2), 120–135. DOI: 10.1093/grurint/ikac173

König, P. D. (2022). Fortress Europe 4.0? An analysis of EU data governance through the lens of the resource regime concept. *European Policy Analysis*, *8*(4), 409–426. DOI: 10.1002/epa2.1144

Kovalenko, Y. (2022). The Right to Privacy and Protection of Personal Data: Emerging Trends and Implications for Development in Jurisprudence of European Court of Human Rights. *Masaryk University Journal of Law and Technology*, *16*(1), 37–58.

Kozen, G. H. (2021). *Summary of the trial decision in Epic Games v. Apple*. Robins Kaplan LLP. Retrieved March 30, 2025 from https://www.robinskaplan.com/newsroom/insights/summary-of-the-trial-decision-in-epic-games-v-apple

Krämer, J., Colangelo, G., Richter, H., & Schnurr, D. (2023). *Data Act: Towards a balanced EU data regulation*. Centre on Regulation in Europe (CERRE). Retrieved March 19, 2025 from https://cerre.eu/wp-content/uploads/2023/04/CERRE_Data-Act_Report_April-2023.pdf

Leiser, M. (2023). *Reimagining digital governance: The EU's Digital Services Act and the fight against disinformation. SSRN*. https://doi.org/DOI: 10.2139/ssrn.4427493

Lundqvist, B. (2025). The objectives of regulating the digital economy indicate that there is a right to data in the Digital Markets Act with direct effect and applicability. In Engel, A., Groussot, X., & Petursson, G. T. (Eds.), *New Directions in Digitalisation. European Union and its Neighbours in a Globalized World* (pp. 29–47). Springer.

Milaj-Weishaar, J. (2020). Safeguarding Privacy by Regulating the Processing of Personal Data – An EU Illusion? *European Journal of Law and Technology, 11*(2).

Müller, M., & Kettemann, M. C. (2024). European approaches to the regulation of digital technologies. In Werthner, H., Fleisch, E., Bauer, A., & Matthes, F. (Eds.), *Introduction to digital humanism* (pp. 655–670). Springer., DOI: 10.1007/978-3-031-45304-5_39

Neves, I. (2025). A reading of the Digital Markets Act in the light of fundamental rights. In Engel, A., Groussot, X., & Petursson, G. T. (Eds.), *New directions in digitalization: European Union and its neighbours in a globalized world* (pp. 117–164). Springer., DOI: 10.1007/978-3-031-65381-0_8

Novak, M. (2021). *Pravna argumentacija v teoriji in praksi*. Ljubljana: Uradni list RS.

Pagallo, U. (2022). The politics of data in EU law: Will it succeed? *Digital Society : Ethics, Socio-Legal and Governance of Digital Technology, 1*(1), 20. Advance online publication. DOI: 10.1007/s44206-022-00020-4

Pavčnik, M. (2015). *Teorija prava: prispevek k razumevanju prava*. GV Založba.

Perel, M., Elkin-Koren, N., & De Gregorio, G. (2021, February 10). (forthcoming). Social media as contractual networks: A bottom-up check on content moderation. *Iowa Law Review*.Paper presented at TPRC49: The 49th Research Conference on Communication, Information and Internet Policy. SSRN. https://doi.org/DOI: 10.2139/ssrn.3797554

Petit, A., Wala, Z., Ciucci, M., & Martinello, B. (2024). *Evropska digitalna agenda*. In *Kratki vodnik po Evropski uniji*. Evropski parlament. Retrieved May 10, 2025 from https://www.europarl.europa.eu/factsheets/sl/sheet/64/evropska-digitalna-agenda

Peyrone, N., & Wichadakul, D. (2023). A formal model for blockchain-based consent management in data sharing. Journal of Logical and Algebraic Methods in Programming, 134, Article 100886.

Primec, A., Pastirk, G., & Perko, I. (2024). Sovereignty over personal data: Legal frameworks and the quest for privacy in the digital age. In Pucelj, M., & Bohinc, R. (Eds.), *Balancing human rights, social responsibility, and digital ethics.*

Quintais, J. P., Appelman, N., & Ó Fathaigh, R. (2023). Using terms and conditions to apply fundamental rights to content moderation. *German Law Journal, 24*(5), 881–911. DOI: 10.1017/glj.2023.53

Rombolà, R. (2023). *Digital Markets Act and the interoperability requirement: Is data protection in danger?* MediaLaws. Retrieved March 31, 2025 from https://www.medialaws.eu/digital-markets-act-and-the-interoperability-requirement-is-data-protection-in-danger/

Ruohonen, J., & Mickelsson, S. (2023). Reflections on the Data Governance Act. *Digital Society : Ethics, Socio-Legal and Governance of Digital Technology, 2*(1), 10. Advance online publication. DOI: 10.1007/s44206-023-00034-9

Sartor, G. (2019). The fundamental rights challenges of algorithms. *European Journal of Risk Regulation, 10*(3), 403–416. DOI: 10.1177/0924051919861773

The Institute of International and European Affairs. (2023). *The European digital agenda in 2023.* Retrieved April 13, 2025 from https://www.iiea.com/blog/the-european-digital-agenda-in-2023

Trstenjak, V., & Brkan, M. (2012). *Pravo EU: Ustavno, procesno in gospodarsko pravo EU.* GV Založba.

van Ooijen, I., & Uršič Vrabec, H. (2018). Does the GDPR enhance consumers' control over personal data? An analysis from a behavioural perspective. *Journal of Consumer Policy, 42*, 91–107. DOI: 10.1007/s10603-018-9399-7

Wilman, F. (2022). *The Digital Services Act (DSA) – An overview. SSRN.* https://doi.org/DOI: 10.2139/ssrn.4304586

Witt, A. (2023). The Digital Markets Act – Regulating the Wild West. *Common Market Law Review, 60*(3), 585–612.

Wolters, P. (2024). The influence of the Data Act on the shifting balance between data protection and the free movement of data. *BILETA Special Issue, 15*(1), 1–15.

Yıldız, C. (2023). The European Commission Accepts Amazon's Commitments. Retrieved April 8, 2025 from https://www.erdem-erdem.av.tr/en/insights/the-european-commission-accepts-amazons-commitments

## KEY TERMS AND DEFINITIONS

**Charter of Fundamental Rights of the European Union (CFREU):** The EU's binding catalogue of fundamental rights. It protects values such as privacy, data protection, equality, and freedom of expression, guiding both legislation and court practice.

**Data Act (DA):** A regulation that introduces common rules on access to and use of data. It aims to give users more control over data generated through connected devices and to ensure fair competition.

**Data Governance Act (DGA):** A regulation designed to encourage secure and trustworthy data sharing across the EU. It introduces data intermediaries, data altruism schemes, and safeguards for sensitive information.

**Data Protection:** The legal principle ensuring that personal data is processed fairly, lawfully, and with respect for individual rights. It includes privacy, dignity, and control over one's own information.

**Digital Markets Act (DMA):** A regulation that sets special duties for so-called "gatekeeper" platforms. Its goal is to keep digital markets fair, open, and competitive.

**Digital Services Act (DSA):** A regulation that creates rules for online platforms and intermediaries. It imposes duties of transparency and accountability and seeks to protect users from illegal and harmful online content.

**Digital Single Market:** A policy vision of the EU aimed at creating one integrated space for digital services and e-commerce. It removes barriers to cross-border activity and strengthens consumer protection.

**Fundamental Rights:** Basic rights guaranteed by EU law and national constitutions. They include privacy, equality, and freedom of expression, and must also be respected by private actors in the digital environment.

**General Data Protection Regulation (GDPR):** The central EU regulation on data protection. It gives individuals enforceable rights, imposes duties on data controllers and processors, and is considered a global standard.

## ENDNOTES

1 See Recital 12 and Article 3(h) of the DSA, which defines "illegal content" as any information that, in itself or by reference to an activity, including the sale of products or the provision of services, is not in compliance with Union law or the law of any Member State that is consistent with Union law.

2 According to Article 2 of the DGA, data altruism means the voluntary sharing of data based on the consent of data subjects to process personal data relating to them, or, in the case of non-personal data, on permissions granted by data holders to allow the use of their data without seeking or receiving any reward beyond compensation related to the cost of making the data available. Such sharing must serve objectives of general interest as defined in national law, such as healthcare, combating climate change, improving mobility, supporting the development, production and dissemination of official statistics, enhancing the delivery of public services, informing public policy, or scientific research carried out in the general interest.

3 Non-personal data refers to any data that is not personal, meaning it does not allow for the identification of an individual.

4 IAP (in-app purchase) in this context refers exclusively to Apple's internal In-App Purchase system, through which Apple processes transactions and retains a commission.

5 Anti-steering provisions are contractual clauses that prohibit developers from informing users about alternative purchasing options outside the app, thereby preventing the redirection of users toward more affordable or competitive payment channels.

6 See also: Judgment of the Court of Justice of the European Union, Case C-311/18, Schrems II.

# Chapter 3
# Digital Ethics, Morality, and Law in the Age of Emerging Technologies

**Pablo Banchio**
https://orcid.org/0009-0001-6618-7301
*Università Virtuale Innovativa, Argentina*

## ABSTRACT

*The accelerated digitalisation and deployment of emerging technologies, such as artificial intelligence, big data and blockchain, have radically transformed modern society. Nonetheless, technological progress has also given rise to new ethical, legal and social dilemmas, which have challenged traditional legal frameworks for the protection of human rights. This paper examines the tensions between technological innovation and fundamental rights, proposing an integrated approach that articulates digital ethics, social morality and the law. It proposes the comparative analysis of various theoretical and ethical frameworks, assessing their effectiveness and projecting a comprehensive governance model that combines laws, industry standards, and ethical principles to safeguard human dignity in the digital age. The research concludes with normative and ethical recommendations to address the current challenges of digital technology.*

## 1. INTRODUCTION

The digital revolution has radically transformed modern society, reshaping economic systems, political processes and cultural interactions at an unprecedented pace. Emerging technologies — from artificial intelligence (AI) and big data to blockchain and the Internet of Things (IoT) — have created extraordinary opportunities for

DOI: 10.4018/979-8-3373-8510-5.ch003

innovation, efficiency and global connectivity. However, this accelerated digitalisation has also created profound ethical, moral and legal dilemmas that challenge the traditional frameworks for the protection of human rights.

The foundations of the digital society are built upon data flows, algorithmic governance, and interconnected systems that challenge the traditional boundaries of space, time, and jurisdiction. In this new landscape, digital ethics, morality, and the law must adapt to strike a balance between innovation and accountability, speed and security, efficiency and justice.

At the heart of the paradox of our digital age lies the tension between technological progress and its social consequences. While AI-driven automation promises economic growth, it also threatens to displace jobs and exacerbate labour precariousness (Brynjolfsson & McAfee, 2014). Social media platforms facilitate global communication, but also amplify misinformation, hate speech and mental health crises (Citron, 2014; Marwick & Lewis, 2017). Governments deploy surveillance technologies in the name of national security, often at the cost of privacy and civil liberties, as evidenced by the Snowden case (Greenwald, 2014). These contradictions highlight the urgent need to reconcile technological advancement with ethical governance, ensuring that digitalisation serves human dignity rather than undermining it.

This paper argues that existing legal and ethical frameworks have failed to keep pace with technological change. Reactive and sectoral regulations — such as the General Data Protection Regulation (Regulation (EU) 2016/679) or the Algorithmic Accountability Act proposed in the United States (115th Congress, H.R.2231) — address symptoms rather than systemic issues. As we have analogously proposed in our previous work on the cyber-subject in the context of artificial intelligence (Banchio, 2022), this field also requires a comprehensive approach that integrates digital ethics (normative principles for technological design), morality (social values in digital spaces) and law (enforceable protections) within a human rights-based framework.

As articulated by the Digital Ethics programme of the Master's in Digitalisation and Human Rights at the Euro-Mediterranean University (EMUNI), this framework must be interdisciplinary, preventive and oriented towards social justice.

Therefore, the theoretical and conceptual framework of this paper is based on a multidimensional approach to understanding digital ethics and its intersection with human rights in the context of emerging technologies. The main aim is to establish a comprehensive understanding of key ethical principles, legal constructs and social implications arising from the use of digital technologies such as artificial intelligence (AI), big data, blockchain and the Internet of Things (IoT), *ex multis*.

## 2. DIGITAL ETHICS: FOUNDATIONS AND APPROACHES

Digital ethics can be defined as a subdiscipline of applied ethics that deals with the critical analysis of the normative principles that should guide the design, development, implementation, and use of digital technologies. In a context of accelerated technological transformation, this branch of ethics is gaining increasing importance by addressing the moral, legal, and social dilemmas associated with the impact of emerging technologies on human life.

This emerging branch is framed as an "information ethics", in which the moral agent is responsible not only for the direct consequences of their actions, but also for the very architecture of the digital environment in which those actions take place (Floridi, 2013). This perspective is framed within the so-called 'Ethics by Design', a theoretical and practical proposal that advocates the need to incorporate fundamental ethical values—such as fairness, transparency, and accountability—from the early stages of technological design (Van den Hoven, 2007).

In this sense, digital ethics is not limited to regulatory compliance or post-development analysis but promotes a proactive and structural ethics. This implies shared responsibility on the part of developers, companies, legislators, and users to ensure that digital technologies effectively contribute to the common good, without infringing on human rights or deepening existing social inequalities.

### 2.1 Main Paradigms of Digital Ethics

Contemporary digital ethics draws on a pluralistic approach that combines different philosophical traditions to offer complex and contextual responses to the ethical challenges of the digital environment. Among the main paradigms that inform it are technological utilitarianism, digital deontology, and computational virtue ethics. Technological utilitarianism evaluates technologies based on the balance between the benefits and harms they generate, proving particularly useful in conducting risk analyses and impact models. However, it has been criticised for its tendency to justify negative externalities in the name of aggregate welfare.

Digital deontology, for its part, upholds the existence of inviolable rules and rights, such as privacy, individual autonomy, and informed consent. However, its application may be strained in contexts where value conflicts arise, such as the balance between privacy and public health. Thirdly, computational virtue ethics advocates for the development of agents and technological systems that embody and promote civic virtues such as honesty, justice, and algorithmic prudence. From this perspective, it is not enough to evaluate technological outcomes; it is also crucial to consider the ethical formation of the involved agents and the moral quality of the processes (Coeckelbergh, 2020). This framework enables a contextual, critical, and proactive digital ethics that can adapt to cultural diversity without renouncing the defence of universal principles such as human dignity, social justice, and the protection of fundamental rights.

## 2.2 Morality and Digital Culture

Digital morality refers to the set of shared values, norms, and practices that regulate the behaviour of individuals and communities in digital environments. Unlike ethics, which focuses on universal philosophical principles and normative theories, digital morality is more dynamic, emergent, and often conflictive. It is influenced by specific cultural, historical, and technological contexts, giving rise to diverse interpretations and applications of what is considered acceptable in cyberspace.

Recent studies have shown how digital culture produces unique moral tensions, such as the trivialisation of hate speech on social media, algorithmic disinformation, or epistemic polarisation in public deliberation spaces (Zuboff, 2019; Sunstein, 2018). These tensions challenge traditional forms of social regulation and require an intercultural understanding of digital values.

For instance, while in some contexts online anonymity is seen as a protection mechanism against authoritarianism and censorship, in others it is perceived as an obstacle to accountability and public safety. This diversity of perspectives highlights the need for regulatory approaches sensitive to cultural pluralism and oriented towards the design of ethically responsible digital environments (Ess, 2009).

## 2.3 Law and Algorithmic Governance

Contemporary law faces significant challenges in the face of the complexity of the digital environment. Traditional legal structures, based on principles such as territoriality, causality, and subjective responsibility, prove insufficient to address the implications of algorithmic systems, which operate autonomously, transnationally, and often opaquely.

In this context, the concept of algorithmic governance emerges, understood as the set of rules, practices, and technological infrastructures that directly or indirectly regulate automated decision-making (Yeung, 2018). This new paradigm demands a legal articulation capable of guaranteeing the protection of fundamental rights without hindering technological innovation.

Instruments such as the General Data Protection Regulation (GDPR) of the European Union have introduced significant advances, such as the right to explanation, data portability, and explicit consent (European Parliament, 2016). Likewise, the Artificial Intelligence Act proposed years ago by the European Commission incorporates a risk-based approach, classifying AI systems according to their potential impact on human rights and fundamental freedoms (Banchio, 2025).

However, these legislative responses remain fragmented and *ex post facto*. Cases such as *"Schrems II"* (2020) or *"Meta vs DPC"* (2023), decided by the Court of Justice of the European Union (CJEU), and *"Data Protection Commissioner vs Facebook Ireland & Schrems"* (2023) by the European Data Protection Board (EDPB), have highlighted the fragility of international data transfer regulatory frameworks. Moreover, the expansion of mass surveillance systems raises serious concerns about the compatibility between security policies and the right to privacy enshrined in Article 8 of the European Convention on Human Rights (ECHR).

Faced with these challenges, there is a pressing need to build an integrated legal framework that combines mechanisms of hard law (binding norms) and soft law (ethical principles and non-binding recommendations), adapted to the global, decentralised, and interconnected nature of current digital systems.

## 2.4 Ethics, Artificial Intelligence, and Automation

Artificial intelligence (AI) and automation have become central topics in the debate on digital ethics. These technologies promise to radically transform productive systems, public services, and daily life; however, they raise important ethical questions regarding fairness, transparency, autonomy, and labour impact.

One of the critical axes of AI ethics is the evaluation of its moral implications in autonomous decision-making. The delegation of complex decisions to algorithmic systems raises urgent questions about responsibility: who is accountable for the harm caused by an AI? How can we ensure these systems do not reproduce historical biases or deepen structural inequalities?

In addition, the phenomenon of job displacement due to automation demands thinking about technological justice that guarantees fair labour transitions, inclusive education, and the protection of the most vulnerable sectors. Therefore, AI ethics cannot be separated from a broader approach that links technological innovation with social justice.

## 2.5 Algorithmic Governance and Data Ethics

As digital technologies become embedded in all aspects of human life, the governance of algorithms and data acquires a central ethical dimension. Algorithmic governance refers to the set of processes through which automated systems that influence public and private decision-making are designed, monitored, and regulated.

Although these systems promise efficiency and optimisation, their opaque functioning and unpredictable consequences demand greater transparency and effective accountability mechanisms. At the same time, so-called "data ethics" addresses fundamental issues such as ownership, informed consent, anonymisation, security, and the right to be forgotten.

The intensive use of personal data by digital platforms has given rise to new forms of surveillance, manipulation, and commercial exploitation. In this context, the development of robust ethical frameworks that ensure individuals' informational sovereignty and fairness in the use of data becomes essential to the legitimacy of digital transformation.

## 2.6 A Human Rights Approach to Digital Governance

Human rights provide a fundamental normative framework to guide digital governance in a context of increasing technological transformation. International instruments such as the Universal Declaration of Human Rights (UN, 1948) and the International Covenant on Civil and Political Rights (UN, 1966) enshrine core principles such as dignity, liberty, privacy, and non-discrimination, which must also be protected in digital environments. Furthermore, the UN Guiding Principles on Business and Human Rights (2011) extend these obligations to private actors, emphasising corporate responsibility in upholding fundamental rights.

However, the advance of digital technologies—especially in the realms of big data, artificial intelligence, and automated decision-making systems—poses new challenges that strain these traditional normative frameworks. The mass collection of data by governments and corporations raises legitimate concerns regarding privacy and individual autonomy. Similarly, the use of algorithms in sensitive areas such as criminal justice (e.g. predictive policing) or automated recruitment processes may reproduce biases and exacerbate structural inequalities, directly impacting the principles of equality and non-discrimination.

In response to these challenges, new normative developments have emerged that seek to adapt the protection of human rights to the contemporary digital environment. Notably, the "UNESCO Recommendation on the Ethics of Artificial Intelligence" (2021) promotes principles such as transparency, accountability, inclusion, and respect for fundamental rights in the development and use of AI, advocating for ethical and multilateral governance. Likewise, Spain's "Charter of Digital Rights" (2021), internationally pioneering, recognises and articulates rights such as digital identity, net neutrality, digital disconnection, and protection against algorithmic manipulation, thus establishing a new legal framework for defending rights in the digital age.

These instruments illustrate a trend towards the consolidation of a human rights-based approach to digital governance—one that goes beyond the establishment of positive regulations and also demands effective institutional frameworks, independent oversight mechanisms, and spaces for democratic participation. Only through such a comprehensive approach can we ensure that technological development respects human dignity and contributes to collective well-being without infringing fundamental rights or deepening existing social divides.

## 3. ALGORETHICS. ETHICS OF ALGORITHMS IN THE DIGITAL SOCIETY

### 3.1 Concept

The concept of "algorethics", resulting from the fusion of "algorithm" and "ethics", refers to an emerging discipline concerned with the ethical implications of the design, development, implementation, and consequences of algorithms in social, legal, and political contexts. Algorethics focuses on how these technologies impact society, aiming to ensure that they are fair, transparent, and accountable by creating normative frameworks to guide their responsible implementation.

Its objective is twofold: on the one hand, to establish a normative framework that guides the conduct of the human agents involved in the creation and application of algorithms; on the other, to ensure that automated systems respect fundamental rights and democratic values in their autonomous functioning (Canca, 2022).

The need for an algorethical approach arises from the growing phenomenon of delegating sensitive decisions—in fields such as justice, healthcare, education, employment, and public safety—to algorithmic systems that, in many cases, operate with a high degree of autonomy. This situation raises significant ethical challenges, both due to the inherent opacity of many of these systems and the risk of perpetuating or even amplifying existing inequalities. In this context, algorethics proposes not only to reinforce transparency and accountability but also to embed ethical principles from the earliest stages of algorithm design, in line with the "ethics by design" approach (Floridi & Cowls, 2019).

As algorithms govern fundamental aspects of everyday life—from content curation on social media and targeted advertising to judicial decisions and medical diagnoses—it becomes essential to understand their effects on individual rights, social cohesion, and justice. Algorethics, in this regard, does not limit itself to a technical or functional analysis, but calls for a profound reflection on the responsibilities of developers, tech companies, and States to ensure that algorithms serve the public interest, uphold human dignity, and remain free from discriminatory bias.

Although algorithms have the potential to optimise processes and promote equity, their technical complexity and lack of transparency—often reinforced by patent protections—can create significant ethical dilemmas. These problems are exacerbated when even regulatory bodies have limited access to the internal workings of such systems, hampering oversight and accountability.

## 3.2 Core Elements

The main components of this emerging discipline include "transparency, fairness and equity, accountability, privacy, security, and social benefit".

In terms of transparency, algorithms should be understandable and explainable to those who use them and those affected by them. Regarding fairness and equity, algorithms must not perpetuate bias or discriminate against any group, making it crucial for designers to consider and mitigate biases present in data or algorithmic processes.

"Accountability" means that developers and organisations implementing algorithms must be held responsible for their impacts, including errors and decisions made by these systems. "Privacy" refers to the ethical and secure handling of personal data, ensuring that individual privacy is respected. "Security" means that algorithms must be designed to withstand attacks and manipulations. Finally, "social benefit" implies that algorithms should be designed to contribute to social well-being and avoid causing harm.

Examples of algor-ethical issues, which will be further explored below, include "bias in AI", such as facial recognition algorithms showing higher error rates for individuals of certain ethnic backgrounds. Another issue is the "opacity of automated decisions", like credit scoring systems that determine loan eligibility without clearly explaining the criteria used. Additionally, "privacy and personal data" remain a concern, with some algorithms collecting and using large amounts of personal data without explicit user consent.

Algorethics could serve as a bridge to translate ethical principles concretely into digital technologies through effective transdisciplinary dialogue. Moreover, in the encounter between diverse worldviews, human rights constitute a key point of convergence for finding common ground.

## 3.3 Dimensions of Algorethics

Algorethics operates on three interrelated levels that enable a comprehensive approach to the ethical dilemmas associated with the use of algorithms (Floridi, 2021). First, the "ontological level" examines the nature of algorithmic systems as non-human agents capable of producing significant effects in the social environment. This level questions traditional conceptions of moral agency and redefines the place of algorithms within decision-making structures by recognising their capacity to intervene in processes that directly affect people and institutions.

Secondly, the "epistemic level" focuses on transparency, intelligibility, and explainability. From this perspective, it is vital that both users and overseers can adequately understand how and why certain automated decisions are made—especially when such decisions affect important rights or interests (Wachter et al., 2017). Algorithmic opacity represents a substantial risk to public trust and the legitimacy of digital systems.

Finally, the "normative level" encompasses the integration of values such as fairness, justice, non-discrimination, autonomy, and beneficence into algorithmic logic. This level translates into specific legal and ethical obligations, such as the right not to be subject to solely automated decisions—as enshrined in Article 22 of the General Data Protection Regulation (GDPR)—or the principle of proportionality in the collection and processing of personal data. In this way, algorethics not only promotes philosophical reflection on technology but also offers tools for its fair and responsible regulation.

In summary, algorethics represents a crucial field for building a robust digital ethics that ensures algorithms are not only technically efficient but also morally accountable and socially just.

## 3.4 Philosophical Framework

### 3.4.1 The "Techno-Human Condition"

The increasing interrelation and dependency between human beings and technology can be better understood through the philosophical perspectives of Aristotle and Martin Heidegger, who offer relevant and profound conceptual frameworks on technique and technology. Their reflections provide a rich field for Algorethics to consider how technique and technology influence human life and our relationship with the world.

Aristotle offers an integrative view of technique aligned with natural human ends, suggesting that technique can contribute to human flourishing if it remains consistent with such ends. Heidegger, on the other hand, warns of the dangers of a technocratic worldview, which may dehumanise us and alienate us from a more authentic existence. Together, these perspectives invite reflection on how modern technology affects our lives and how we might find a balance that respects both our human nature and that of the world we inhabit.

The Greek philosopher, although not addressing technology in the modern sense, introduced the concept of *techné*, which is crucial in his philosophy. *Techné* refers to a type of practical knowledge involving skills and craftsmanship. It is applied knowledge used to create something—whether a work of art, a tool, or a structure. In his view, this knowledge is fundamentally practical and applied, distinct from pure theory or *episteme* (Banchio, 2024).

Throughout history, humans have developed a variety of inventions and tools to overcome physical limitations, enabling them to carry out tasks that would otherwise be impossible or extremely difficult. Without claws, humans invented knives, axes, and spearheads, which allowed them to cut and pierce hard materials. Stone tools improved human capacity to hunt, process food, and build shelters. Mastery of fire allowed for the cooking of food, making it easier to digest.

Needless to say, the invention of the wheel, ropes, knots, and binding techniques enabled the construction of structures and the manufacture of fishing nets. The bow and arrow enhanced hunting and warfare, increasing chances of survival and improving defence capabilities. The earliest boats—hollowed-out logs—allowed humans to navigate rivers and lakes, expanding geographic reach and facilitating trade and communication between groups. The invention of pottery and the development of weaving provided protection against the elements. The hand-mill and the domestication of animals transformed agriculture and human economies, enabling more permanent settlements and the development of complex civilisations.

These early inventions reflect human creativity and adaptability in overcoming physical limitations and improving living conditions. Each represented a significant step in the technological and cultural evolution of humanity, laying the foundations for future advancements.

For Aristotle, everything in the universe has a purpose or *telos*. This also applies to human technique and tools, which must align with the natural and virtuous ends of human beings. Technique, therefore, should serve human flourishing (*eudaimonia*) and must not deviate from this goal. Aristotle establishes a distinction between nature (*physis*) and technique (*techné*). Technique is considered an imitation of nature, and although it may improve or complement nature, it must not oppose natural ends (Banchio, 2024).

Martin Heidegger offers a more critical and profound view of technology in the modern era, which is particularly relevant to this study. In his essay "The Question Concerning Technology" (*Die Frage nach der Technik*), Heidegger distinguishes between traditional technique (*techné*) and modern technology. For the German philosopher, traditional technique is a form of "unconcealment" (*aletheia*), where human beings collaborate with nature to reveal what is already present within it. In contrast, modern technology is a form of revealing he calls "challenging-forth" (*Gestell*), whereby nature is seen as a resource to be exploited.

Heidegger warns that modern technology poses a significant danger by reducing everything to its utilitarian value, turning both nature and human beings into mere resources. This technocratic "enframing" can dehumanise and alienate the human being, separating them from an authentic relationship with the world. Heidegger suggests that *poiesis*—the poetic revealing—can offer a more authentic relationship with the world, in contrast to technology, which imposes a reductive and utilitarian view.

Comparing Aristotle's and Heidegger's views reveals both contrasts and similarities. Regarding *telos* versus *Gestell*, Aristotle sees technique as aligned with natural and virtuous ends, whereas Heidegger views modern technology as a challenge that may alienate the human being from an authentic relationship with the world. In terms of knowledge and revelation, for Aristotle, technique is a type of practical and applied knowledge, whereas for Heidegger, modern technique is a form of revealing that can be dangerous. Both philosophers are concerned with the relationship between humans and nature, but from different perspectives: Aristotle sees technique as a natural extension of human activity, while Heidegger critiques modern technology for its tendency to dominate and exploit nature (Banchio, 2024).

### 3.4.2 Ethics of Algorithms

In recent years, there have been several interesting and relevant studies in this field. Research on the ethics of algorithms explores how they can make moral decisions and the need to design algorithms that reflect human ethical values in relation to the core issues discussed. With regard to algorithmic bias, transparency, and accountability, scholars have examined how search algorithms perpetuate racial bias (Noble, 2018), while other works provide an overview of ethical issues related to artificial intelligence (Wallach & Allen, 2008).

A decisive aspect of algorethics is determining who is responsible for decisions made by algorithms, especially when these decisions significantly affect individuals. The need for accountability and transparency in the design and implementation of algorithms is a recurring theme in the literature.

Studies on the relationship between algorithms and human rights address how algorithms impact privacy, freedom of expression, and equality. It has been discussed how algorithms affect personal and social life in the context of surveillance capitalism (Zuboff, 2019).

Analysing how algorithms can perpetuate or mitigate social and economic inequalities is essential to understanding their impact on social justice. Research highlights the need to design algorithms that promote fairness and inclusion.

Critical and posthumanist philosophical reflections question the relationship between humans and algorithms, redefining concepts such as agency and autonomy. Some works address information ethics and the digital society, examining the social and ethical impact of digital technologies (Floridi, 2014). It is argued that the digital revolution is transforming our understanding of reality and raises new ethical challenges. The concept of the "infosphere" invites us to consider algorithms as ethical agents that shape our interactions and decisions, advocating for an information ethics that promotes transparency and fairness, with direct implications for the legal regulation of algorithms.

In Italy, other researchers have approached the ethics of algorithms from ethical and political perspectives. Research has examined how algorithms influence political decision-making and the regulation of digital rights, emphasising the need to develop public policies that integrate ethical considerations into algorithm regulation, balancing technological innovation with the protection of fundamental rights and values (Bottoni, 2021).

In Latin America, the ethics of digital technologies has been explored by analysing how these technologies may affect human values and education. This approach highlights the need to integrate ethical principles into the design and implementation of technologies, suggesting that legal frameworks should promote critical education on the impact of algorithms on society (Pardo, 2020).

For our part, we have explored how technology, including algorithms, impacts ethics and democracy. In our work, alongside other authors, we highlight several key points: the impact of algorithms on political participation and democratic decision-making, warning of the risk of manipulation and disinformation; the importance of designing algorithms based on ethical principles that respect human autonomy and dignity; and the need to establish clear accountability mechanisms for algorithm designers and operators (Banchio, 2024, 2024b, 2024c).

Pope Francis has addressed issues related to technology and digital ethics in several documents and speeches. In his encyclical *Fratelli Tutti*, the Holy Father reflects on human dignity and social justice in the context of a globalised and digitalised world. In *Laudato Si'*, he raises concerns about digital exclusion and the technological divide, which may exacerbate inequalities. Francis asserts that technology, including algorithms, must be used to promote the common good and not for exploitation or excessive profit. Digital ethics should be guided by principles of justice and solidarity, emphasising the need for transparency and responsibility in the use of technologies (Banchio, 2024).

In general terms, all these philosophical perspectives offer a comprehensive view of the ethical and legal challenges associated with algorithms. Legal implications include algorithmic transparency, with requirements for companies to disclose how their algorithms function and how they affect users. They also encompass labour rights in the digital economy, protecting platform-based work and recognising employment rights.

Additionally, regulation of bias and fairness is highlighted, implementing mechanisms to prevent and correct algorithmic bias and to ensure social justice. The development of ethical public policies that incorporate ethical considerations into the regulation of algorithms and technology is another crucial aspect, as is the protection of human rights through legal frameworks that safeguard fundamental rights in algorithmic decision-making. Promoting the common good involves ensuring that algorithms serve justice and solidarity, addressing digital exclusion. Transparency and accountability demand clarity in the design and use of algorithms, with accountability mechanisms established. Finally, the preservation of democracy is emphasised, ensuring that algorithms do not threaten democratic participation and individual autonomy, promoting a regulatory framework that upholds these values.

The effective regulation of algorithms must be informed by a deep understanding of their ethical and social implications. By integrating academic perspectives with moral and social principles, it is possible to foster a more just and equitable digital age. The integration of these perspectives into the legal framework will contribute to a fairer and more effective regulation of algorithms, ensuring that they serve the common good and promote justice and equity in the digital society.

## 3.5 Algorithmic Bias and Discrimination

One of the main ethical concerns in algorethics is algorithmic bias, which refers to the systematic discrimination embedded in algorithms due to biased training data or design decisions with prejudices. As algorithms are often trained with historical data, they may inadvertently reinforce existing social inequalities. For example, in the context of predictive policing, algorithms may disproportionately target minority communities if trained on biased data that reflects past discriminatory practices. Similarly, in hiring algorithms, gender or racial biases can lead to discriminatory hiring practices, even if presented as objective and impartial.

Addressing algorithmic bias requires a solid framework to ensure fairness and accountability in algorithmic decision-making. Techniques such as "equity by design", which involves the explicit incorporation of fairness criteria into algorithmic models, can help mitigate these risks. Additionally, transparency and accountability mechanisms, such as independent audits of algorithmic systems, are essential to identify and correct biases, ensuring that algorithms are not causing harm to vulnerable populations.

## 3.6 Transparency and Accountability in Algorithmic Systems

Transparency is another fundamental principle in algorithmics. For algorithms to be ethically sound, it is vital that their processes, inputs, and outputs are transparent and understandable to all relevant stakeholders. This includes not only the developers of the algorithms but also the users affected by them, as well as the regulatory authorities responsible for overseeing their use.

In practice, transparency means that individuals must have the right to know how algorithms are being used to make decisions that affect their lives. For example, if an AI system is used to determine a person's credit score or whether they are eligible for a job, they must be informed about the criteria being applied and have the opportunity to challenge or appeal decisions they deem unfair or biased.

Along with transparency, accountability is a crucial ethical principle. If an algorithm causes harm, there must be a clear line of responsibility. However, in many cases, it may be difficult to assign responsibility, especially when the algorithm is perceived as autonomous or when multiple parties (such as developers, data providers, and users) are involved in the decision-making process. Establishing accountability frameworks, including repair mechanisms and the possibility of holding algorithm developers and the organisations implementing them responsible for the impact of their systems, is essential to prevent harm.

## 3.7 Ethical Decision-Making and the 'Black Box' Problem

The "black box" nature of many algorithms—where the reasoning behind a decision is not easily understood or accessible—represents a significant challenge for their ethical use. This opacity is particularly problematic in high-risk areas such as healthcare, criminal justice, and finance, where the consequences of algorithmic decisions can have profound effects on people's lives.

The inability to explain how an algorithm arrived at a particular decision undermines the principles of fairness and equity. In the legal context, for instance, automated decisions about sentencing or parole may not be fully explained to the individuals affected, making it difficult for them to understand or challenge the decision. Furthermore, when algorithms are implemented in these contexts without adequate oversight or accountability, they can exacerbate existing inequalities and injustices.

To address the black box problem, support is growing for the development of "explainable AI (XAI)": algorithms that provide clear and understandable explanations of their decisions. This is essential not only to ensure fairness and accountability but also to empower individuals to challenge unfair decisions and participate more fully in democratic processes.

## 3.8 Autonomy and Human Agency in Algorithmic Systems

Another ethical concern raised by algorethics is the potential for algorithms to undermine human autonomy and agency. As algorithms become more integrated into decision-making processes, there is a risk that individuals may lose control over aspects of their lives that were previously governed by human judgment. In areas such as healthcare, finance, and employment, where decisions can significantly affect a person's well-being and future opportunities, the shift from human judgment to algorithmic control raises questions about the preservation of individual autonomy.

From an ethical perspective, it is important to strike a balance between the efficiency brought by algorithms and the need to preserve human agency. While algorithms may be capable of making more objective and data-driven decisions, it is crucial to ensure that they do not replace human judgment, particularly in situations where ethical or moral considerations are at stake. This requires careful design of algorithms that complement, rather than replace, human decision-making, preserving the role of human agency in critical decisions.

## 3.9 Algorethics and Human Rights

Algorethics contributes to the practical realisation of human rights in the digital age by identifying systemic risks associated with automation. For example, algorithms used to predict criminal recidivism, such as COMPAS in the US (Banchio, 2024), have shown significant racial biases that undermine the right to a fair trial and equality before the law (Angwin et al., 2016). Similarly, automated content moderation systems can affect freedom of speech if not overseen by robust ethical and legal frameworks (Gillespie, 2018).

As previously noted in section 2.6, some international organisations such as UNESCO have begun institutionalising the algorithmic approach in official documents. In its "Recommendation on the Ethics of Artificial Intelligence" (2021), it urges states to establish frameworks for algorithmic impact assessment, ethical codes, and independent audits to ensure accountability in automated decisions.

Furthermore, the "High-Level Expert Group on AI" of the European Commission has outlined a series of key requirements for trustworthy AI, many of which stem directly from the algorithmic approach: human intervention and oversight, technical robustness and security, privacy and data governance, transparency, diversity and non-discrimination, social well-being, and accountability (European Commission, 2019).

The development of global standards for algorithmic ethics is crucial to ensure that digital technologies are used in ways that respect human rights and promote the social good. This includes establishing clear guidelines for transparency, accountability, and fairness in algorithmic systems, as well as ensuring that individuals' rights are protected across borders. Additionally, the involvement of stakeholders from various sectors, including industry, academia, civil society, and governments, is essential to creating a balanced and effective regulatory environment.

## 3.10 Proposals and Solutions for Effective Algorethics

As we have mentioned repeatedly throughout this work, in an increasingly digitalized world, technologies have the potential to significantly improve efficiency and accuracy, but they pose serious ethical and legal challenges. The proposals and solutions we present for effective "algorethics" allow for the integration of ethical and legal principles in the development and use of AI. The topics addressed by the emerging discipline include fundamental ethical principles, recommended policies and regulations, and technological innovations for ethical moderation.

One of these fundamental ethical principles is justice, which implies that AI systems must be designed and used in a way that does not discriminate against any group based on characteristics such as race, gender, age, religion, among others. A legal example is the Equal Employment Opportunity Law in many countries, which prohibits discrimination in the workplace, and AI systems used in the hiring process must comply with these regulations.

Transparency refers to the ability of AI systems to be understood and evaluated by those affected by their decisions. Explainability means that these systems must be able to provide clear and understandable reasons for their decisions. A legal example is the frequently cited EU GDPR, which includes provisions requiring transparency and explainability of automated decisions.

Protecting privacy and data security is crucial in the development and use of AI systems. Personal data must be handled in a way that respects individuals' privacy rights. Again, the aforementioned GDPR establishes strict requirements for the protection of personal data, including informed consent and the right to data portability.

Developers and users of AI systems must be responsible for their actions and decisions. This includes the responsibility to correct any harm caused by these systems and the implementation of accountability mechanisms. Civil liability laws may apply in cases where AI systems cause harm to individuals or property.

It is essential for governments to develop and adopt comprehensive regulatory frameworks that address the various ethical and legal aspects of AI. These frameworks must be flexible and adaptable to evolve alongside technology. A proposal example is the European Commission, which, in the Artificial Intelligence Act, sets specific requirements for high-risk AI systems, including impact assessments and ongoing supervision (Banchio, 2025).

Given that AI applications vary considerably across sectors, it is important for regulations to be sector-specific in order to address their unique challenges. A proposal example is sector-specific regulations for the healthcare sector, which may include strict requirements for validating algorithms used in medical diagnoses and treatments.

Data protection laws must be strengthened and rigorously applied to ensure that the data used by AI systems is handled ethically and securely. A proposal example is the implementation of regulations similar to the GDPR in other jurisdictions to establish global data protection standards.

The creation of independent oversight and audit bodies can help ensure that AI systems comply with the established ethical and legal standards. A proposal example is the establishment of an AI Ethics Committee to oversee and audit AI developments in different sectors.

### 3.11 From Algorethics to Algorithmic Justice

A critical branch of algorethics is algorithmic justice, which aims not only to avoid technical biases but also to question the power structures that shape technological development. Authors like Eubanks (2018) have shown how automated decision-making systems can reproduce and amplify structural inequalities when applied to vulnerable populations without sufficient safeguards.

This approach proposes an intersectional and contextual reading of algorithmic impacts, advocating for the participation of affected communities in the design and evaluation of the technologies that regulate their lives. Thus, algorethics is not reduced to a professional or technical ethics; rather, it is configured as an ethical-political project defending a just and democratic digitalization.

## 4. OTHER APPROACHES

### 4.1 Data Justice: Informational Equity in the Algorithmic Society

Data justice emerges as a critical approach that seeks to correct power asymmetries generated by the collection, processing, and use of data in digital contexts.

This concept refers to the fair and equitable treatment of data as it circulates through digital infrastructures, affecting both individuals and communities. In an increasingly algorithmic society, where data is frequently used to make decisions that affect people's lives—from credit scores to job recruitment—the principles of data justice aim to ensure that privacy rights, access, and control over personal data are respected.

Beyond individual privacy protection, this framework emphasizes the need to ensure equitable distributions of informational benefits and burdens, as well as the participation of marginalized communities in decisions about data that affect them (Taylor, 2017).

At the heart of data justice is the recognition that data is not neutral. It is shaped by historical, social, and economic contexts that can introduce deep biases and inequities. When certain groups—particularly minority populations—are underrepresented in data sets, their needs and perspectives are at risk of being ignored, which can perpetuate and amplify pre-existing structural inequalities. In this regard, the principle of informational equity demands a more inclusive and transparent approach to the collection, processing, and use of data, ensuring that these practices do not cause harm or reproduce forms of systemic discrimination.

In this sense, the authors belonging to the School identify three fundamental dimensions of data justice.

The distributive dimension asks who benefits and who is harmed by algorithmic systems; the procedural dimension focuses on the degree of transparency and participation in design and decision-making processes; and the recognition dimension questions which social groups are made invisible, stigmatized, or misrepresented in the data used (Dencik, 2019).

From these dimensions, key principles emerge that guide data justice. Among them, equity in access stands out, which implies ensuring that all people—including those in vulnerable situations—have equal opportunities to access platforms and digital tools that collect and process information.

Likewise, transparency and accountability are essential for establishing clear mechanisms that allow understanding and control over how data is used, with organizations assuming concrete responsibilities for its management. Finally, the principle of participation asserts that individuals should have a voice in decisions that affect the use of their data, including the right to consent or reject data collection practices.

Data justice complements algorethics by providing a structural and intersectional perspective, especially relevant for ethical and legal frameworks based on human rights. In contexts such as the automated surveillance of migrant populations, algorithmic discrimination in public services, or biases in credit evaluation systems, data justice demands not only technical adjustments but also profound social and regulatory transformations aimed at building a truly just and inclusive digital infrastructure (Binns, 2018).

## 4.2 Human-Centred Design and "Ethics by Design"

Human-centred design constitutes a paradigm that places the needs, values, and well-being of individuals at the heart of technological development. Beyond efficiency or profit, this approach proposes that technologies should be conceived to strengthen human agency, dignity, and quality of life (Norman, 2013). From this perspective, technological design becomes a process that prioritises human experiences and social impacts, recognising technology as a tool at the service of humanity, rather than an end in itself.

Within the framework of digital ethics, this paradigm has given rise to concepts such as "ethics by design", as outlined above, or "value-sensitive design", (Friedman et al., 2006). This approach emphasises the need to incorporate ethical principles throughout all stages of the technological lifecycle, including conception, coding, implementation, evaluation, and feedback. In this way, ethics ceases to be a secondary or corrective instance *ex post facto* and instead becomes a structural criterion for technological design.

The "Ethics Guidelines for Trustworthy AI", published by the European Commission in 2019, actively promote a comprehensive approach that links technological development with the respect for fundamental rights.

These guidelines establish a series of technical and legal principles aimed at ensuring that artificial intelligence systems operate in a fair, safe, and accountable manner. Among the key elements is the requirement to ensure meaningful human oversight of automated decisions, thereby avoiding the complete delegation of authority to algorithmic systems.

The guidelines also stress the minimisation of physical, psychological, and social risks arising from the use of emerging technologies, as well as the implementation of effective mechanisms for complaint, review, and redress to ensure accountability for erroneous or unjust automated decisions.

A core component of this approach is the active integration of perspectives from vulnerable groups, such as older people, children, minorities, and other structurally disadvantaged populations.

In this context, the principle of ethics by design assumes a central role, as it translates into the adoption of concrete criteria that pragmatically and proactively articulate technology, ethics, and law.

Key areas of application of this principle include respect for autonomy, through the design of systems that enable informed decision-making and protect personal agency in the face of opaque or coercive automated processes; transparency and accountability, which require the development of technologies that are comprehensible to users and capable of tracing algorithmic decisions back to the ethical guidelines underpinning them; and justice and fairness, which are reflected in the implementation of inclusive systems designed to minimise bias and promote equal opportunities, especially in contexts marked by structural discrimination.

This approach is particularly relevant in the development and deployment of artificial intelligence and machine learning systems, whose decisions can have significant impacts on people's lives. Integrating ethical considerations from the outset of the design process not only helps to reduce risks and prevent harm but also constitutes a necessary condition for ensuring that emerging technologies effectively contribute to the common good and enhance the protection of fundamental rights in the digital age.

## 4.3 Philosophy of Technology: Technology as a Social and Moral Construct

The philosophy of technology is concerned with analysing the role technology plays in shaping human societies, not only from a functional or instrumental perspective, but as a phenomenon laden with cultural meanings, moral values, and power structures. In this field, various authors have questioned the traditional conception of technology as a neutral tool, proposing instead that all technology incorporates ideological decisions that reflect and reproduce particular worldviews (Feenberg, 2010).

From this standpoint, technologies cannot be understood as mere neutral artefacts serving human ends, but rather as social and ideological constructs that both reflect and shape power relations. Their impact may be emancipatory or oppressive, depending on the contexts in which they are designed, implemented, and controlled. In this regard, the notion of "technologies that have politics" was introduced, referring to how certain infrastructures — such as mass surveillance algorithms, social credit systems, or opaque digital platforms — not only perform technical functions but also consolidate pre-existing social hierarchies, limit democratic deliberation, and directly affect people's living conditions (Winner, 1980).

This perspective implies that the development and use of emerging technologies must be subject to critical evaluation that goes beyond the merely technical or legal, incorporating a philosophical and ethical lens that interrogates, among other issues: what values are prioritised in design? Which groups gain or lose power? What forms of life are enabled or excluded? How do technological systems shape human behaviour and social norms? What moral implications arise from the design and implementation of new technologies? To what extent are individuals and societies responsible for the unintended consequences of these advances?

From the standpoint of social constructivism, technology is not a set of neutral tools, but the result of human decisions shaped by economic, political, and cultural factors. Consequently, technologies can both reproduce structural inequalities and open up new possibilities for greater justice, equity, and social participation. Understanding technology as a moral and social construct is therefore essential to addressing the ethical challenges posed by phenomena such as artificial intelligence, surveillance systems, or automated decision-making algorithms.

The philosophy of technology offers a critical lens that makes it possible to identify not only the potential benefits of innovation, but also its structural risks and the social externalities that may result from irresponsible use. Ultimately, this approach underpins the need for proactive ethical governance, capable of anticipating and mitigating negative impacts through a comprehensive conception of the human being and of society. It is not merely a matter of reacting to technical failures, but of promoting a model of technological innovation guided by values such as equity, transparency, sustainability, and respect for human dignity.

## 4.4 Ethics of Care: Relationships, Vulnerability, and Responsibility

The ethics of care, introduces a relational and contextual ethical perspective that contrasts with traditional approaches centred on abstract principles such as justice or universal rights. This approach emphasises human interdependence, vulnerability as a shared condition, and the responsibility to care, recognising that moral decisions occur in specific contexts marked by asymmetrical relationships and concrete needs.

In the realm of emerging technologies, the ethics of care poses a fundamental critique of systems designed with indifference to the actual conditions of their users. In contrast to technocratic models that prioritise efficiency, control, or data optimisation, this ethics advocates for the development of a “caring” artificial intelligence — one capable of listening, adapting, protecting, and accompanying (Van Wynsberghe, 2013). In other words, technologies that do not merely calculate, but also attend.

This framework is particularly relevant in areas such as robotic assistance, mental health platforms, or adaptive educational systems, where care cannot be reduced to performance algorithms but must include sensitivity to users’ emotional, social, and physical realities. The ethics of care emphasises the need to consider elements such as informed consent, meaningful participation of those who interact with the technology, and special attention to situations of inequality, dependence, or digital exclusion.

In this context, the fundamental principles of the ethics of care can be integrated into technological design and governance in various ways. Firstly, responsibility requires that designers, developers, and users commit ethically to ensuring that technology actively contributes to human well-being, avoiding harm or marginalisation. Secondly, empathy and understanding must drive the development of technologies that respond to the diversity of experiences, contexts, and needs — especially those of the most vulnerable groups. Lastly, solidarity promotes the creation of digital ecosystems based on mutual support, cooperation, and fairness, in contrast to models of competition or exploitation.

Incorporating this vision entails questioning dominant models of technological innovation, which tend to be impersonal and based exclusively on quantitative metrics. The ethics of care, by contrast, proposes a human-centred approach in which technology is conceived as a tool in service of a dignified life, connection, and mutual respect. From this perspective, digital ethics cannot be reduced to universal rules but must be nourished by a deep understanding of human relationships and their various forms of care.

## 5. THEORETICAL CONVERGENCE AND ARTICULATION WITH LAW

The theoretical frameworks developed throughout this work—such as algorethics, data justice, ethical design, the philosophy of technology, and the ethics of care—should not be understood as isolated or mutually exclusive approaches, but rather as complementary perspectives that, together, provide a comprehensive understanding of the ethical challenges posed by digitalisation.

All these approaches share a fundamental principle: technology is not neutral, and therefore, its development, implementation, and regulation must be guided by moral and legal responsibilities. This convergence points to the need to build a situated digital ethics, that is, an ethics grounded in universal human rights, but also sensitive to the cultural, social, and technological contexts in which digital systems are embedded.

However, for these ethical principles to have a real impact on social life, they must be articulated with existing legal frameworks. The connection between ethics and law is essential to prevent ethical proposals from remaining merely aspirational or symbolic. The normative translation of these principles requires a revision and update of current legislation, incorporating dimensions such as fairness, transparency, participation, sustainability, and care.

For example, while the European Union's General Data Protection Regulation (GDPR) represents a significant step forward in protecting privacy and control over personal data, it still does not comprehensively address the social justice implications arising from the massive exploitation of data in contexts of inequality. Similarly, the EU Artificial Intelligence Act establishes principles for the trustworthy use of automated systems, but it requires constant updating to remain aligned with new technological developments and emerging ethical debates (Banchio, 2025).

In this regard, a convergent and multidisciplinary approach is proposed, combining collaborative work among ethicists, legal scholars, technology designers, public institutions, and civil society. Such articulation would enable the construction of a legitimate, adaptable, and sustainable regulatory framework, capable of responding to the dilemmas of the digital age without renouncing fundamental democratic values.

## 6. PLACING HUMAN DIGNITY AT THE CENTRE

A truly ethical technological governance must anticipate risks, balance interests, and promote digital ways of life that respect human dignity, inclusion, and social justice. This theoretical and normative convergence is not only desirable but necessary to face current challenges with coherence, legitimacy, and effectiveness.

To achieve this, it is essential that human dignity be the guiding principle for the design and use of technologies. Dignity, as a fundamental value in various ethical and legal traditions, must serve as the foundation upon which policies and practices related to these technologies are built. To ensure that algorithms respect human dignity, several aspects must be considered.

Individuals have the right to understand how and why decisions affecting them are made; thus, algorithms must be transparent, and their functioning should be explained clearly and comprehensibly. This not only allows individuals to challenge unfair decisions but also fosters trust in automated systems.

Furthermore, individuals must have the opportunity to participate in the decision-making processes that affect them, including providing informed consent when algorithms are used to make significant decisions about their lives. It is crucial that individuals are not merely the objects of algorithmic decisions, but active participants in the process.

Algorithms must be designed and used in ways that promote justice and fairness, which entails identifying and eliminating biases that may lead to discrimination. It is the responsibility of developers and users of algorithms to be proactive in ensuring that their systems do not perpetuate existing inequalities.

Moreover, it is essential to establish clear mechanisms to hold those who design, implement, and use algorithms accountable. This includes the ability to correct errors and address complaints from individuals affected by automated decisions, with an accountability system that allows the identification of those responsible for harmful algorithmic decisions and ensures redress for the damage caused.

By considering these principles, we can ensure that algorithms are used responsibly and ethically, respecting human dignity and promoting a fairer and more equitable society. Human dignity must be the compass guiding our path in the age of artificial intelligence.

## 7. DEVELOPING A SHARED ETHICAL PROPOSAL

Developing a shared ethical proposal entails collaboration among various actors, including technology developers, legislators, academics, and civil society representatives. This proposal must be based on universal ethical principles that protect human dignity and promote the common good.

In a world increasingly dependent on technology, it is vital to establish a shared ethics to guide the development and use of algorithms. The principles we advocate aim to establish universal foundations that protect human dignity and promote the common good, encouraging collaboration among a range of stakeholders such as developers, legislators, scholars, and civil society.

The fundamental principles include non-maleficence, whereby algorithms must not harm individuals, avoiding discrimination, protecting privacy and the security of personal data, and ensuring that automated decisions do not disadvantage individuals or specific groups.

Beneficence requires that algorithms be designed to benefit society and improve people's quality of life, promoting the use of technology for social, economic, and cultural wellbeing, seeking innovative solutions to global problems, and fostering social progress.

Autonomy ensures that individuals retain control over their own data and the decisions that affect them, including the right to information, transparency in algorithmic processes, and the possibility of opting out of automated systems that may impact their lives.

Justice demands that the benefits and risks of algorithms be distributed fairly, preventing specific groups from being disproportionately affected by algorithmic decisions, and taking steps to protect the most vulnerable.

Solidarity emphasises that collaboration and mutual support are essential to address the ethical challenges of technology, with stakeholders working together to develop solutions that benefit all, encouraging open dialogue, knowledge exchange, and the pursuit of consensus.

Implementing these principles requires a joint and sustained effort, whereby developers apply ethical design practices, legislators create clear and appropriate legal frameworks to regulate algorithmic development and use, scholars investigate and analyse the ethical and social impacts of algorithms by providing evidence and insight for informed decision-making, and civil society actively participates in the public debate on the ethics of artificial intelligence, expressing concerns and demanding transparency and accountability.

By working together, we can ensure that algorithms are used in a responsible and ethical manner, promoting a future where technology benefits all of humanity and respects the fundamental dignity of each person.

## 8. CONCLUSION

Throughout this work, various theoretical approaches have been presented and analysed to enrich the understanding of digital ethics in a world shaped by emerging technologies, as envisioned by the study programme in Digital Ethics within the Master's in Digitalisation and Human Rights at the Euro-Mediterranean University (EMUNI). From algorethics and data justice to ethical design, the philosophy of technology, and the ethics of care, it has been emphasised that today's technological challenges cannot be addressed solely from a technical or legal perspective but require a transversal and interdisciplinary ethical approach.

These frameworks offer conceptual tools to reshape the relationship between humanity and technology, highlighting the active role societies play in directing technological development towards legitimate, equitable, and sustainable ends. Far from being mere tools, technologies shape realities, mediate human relationships, and distribute power. Therefore, their design and governance must be underpinned by clear and participatory ethical criteria.

Furthermore, the articulation between these ethical principles and the law is essential to transform values into enforceable norms, creating institutional conditions that guarantee respect for human rights, the protection of the most vulnerable, and the promotion of the common good in digital contexts.

The proposals and solutions presented underscore the importance of collaboration among civil society actors to create a future in which AI benefits humanity as a whole. Collaboration and commitment to these ethical values are essential to forge a future where technology serves us all in a fair and equitable manner.

This paper thus lays the foundation for a critical, inclusive, and action-oriented digital ethics —one that not only reacts to harm but seeks to anticipate and prevent it— offering guidance for the responsible design, use, and regulation of technologies. The coherent integration of ethics, law, and technology is not merely a contemporary challenge but an opportunity to reimagine the digital future through the lens of dignity, justice, and care.

## REFERENCES


Angwin, J., Larson, J., Mattu, S., & Kirchner, L. (2016). *Machine bias: There's software used across the country to predict future criminals. And it's biased against blacks*. ProPublica.

Banchio, P. (2022). *Reflections on a legal framework for artificial intelligence. SSRN*. https://doi.org/DOI: 10.2139/ssrn.4320870

Banchio, P. (2024). *Algorética: Una disciplina para la moderación ética de algoritmos y programas de inteligencia artificial. Zenodo*. https://doi.org/DOI: 10.5281/zenodo.12806322

Banchio, P. (2024b). *Legal framework to combat disinformation and hate speech on digital platforms. SSRN*. https://doi.org/DOI: 10.2139/ssrn.4879162

Banchio, P. (2024c). *Legal responses to disinformation and hate speech in the digital age. AI and Human Rights Law Journal, 2*(4), 26–60. *Zenodo*. https://doi.org/DOI: 10.5281/zenodo.12594869

Banchio, P. (2025). *La teoría del cibersujeto y el Reglamento Europeo de Inteligencia Artificial (IA Act): Un análisis crítico desde nuestros postulados teóricos y la regulación híbrida de la inteligencia artificial. Zenodo*. https://doi.org/DOI: 10.5281/zenodo.15127855

Banchio, P. (2025). *Reglamento de la Unión Europea sobre Inteligencia Artificial. Zenodo*. https://doi.org/DOI: 10.5281/zenodo.15127896

Binns, R. (2018). Fairness in machine learning: Lessons from political philosophy. *Proceedings of the 2018 Conference on Fairness, Accountability, and Transparency*, 1–10.

Bottoni, A. (2021). *Algoritmi, politica e diritti digitali*. FrancoAngeli.

Brynjolfsson, E., & McAfee, A. (2014). *The second machine age: Work, progress, and prosperity in a time of brilliant technologies*. W.W. Norton & Company.

Canca, C. (2022). What is Algor-ethics? In Floridi, L. (Ed.), *Ethics, Governance, and Policies in Artificial Intelligence*. Springer.

Citron, D. K. (2014). *Hate crimes in cyberspace*. Harvard University Press.

Coeckelbergh, M. (2020). *AI ethics*. MIT Press.

Dencik, L. (2019). Data justice and the right to protection. *International Journal of Communication, 13*, 3656–3673.

Ess, C. (2009). *Digital media ethics.* Polity Press.

Eubanks, V. (2018). *Automating Inequality: How High-Tech Tools Profile, Police, and Punish the Poor.* St. Martin's Press.

European Commission. (2019). *Ethics guidelines for trustworthy AI.* Publications Office of the EU.

European Parliament. (2016). *General Data Protection Regulation (GDPR).* Official Journal of the EU.

Feenberg, A. (2010). *Between reason and experience: Essays in technology and modernity.* MIT Press.

Floridi, L. (2013). *The ethics of information.* Oxford University Press.

Floridi, L. (2014). *The Fourth Revolution: How the Infosphere is Reshaping Human Reality.* Oxford University Press.

Floridi, L. (2021). *The Logic of Information: A Theory of Philosophy as Conceptual Design.* Oxford University Press.

Floridi, L., & Cowls, J. (2019). A Unified Framework of Five Principles for AI in Society. *Harvard Data Science Review, 1*(1).

Friedman, B., Kahn, P. H., & Borning, A. (2006). *Value sensitive design and information systems.* Springer.

Gillespie, T. (2018). *Custodians of the Internet: Platforms, Content Moderation, and the Hidden Decisions That Shape Social Media.* Yale University Press.

Greenwald, G. (2014). *No place to hide: Edward Snowden, the NSA, and the U.S. surveillance state.* Metropolitan Books.

Heidegger, M. (1977). *The Question Concerning Technology and Other Essays.* Harper & Row.

Marwick, A., & Lewis, R. (2017). *Media manipulation and disinformation online.* Data & Society.

Noble, S. U. (2018). *Algorithms of Oppression: How Search Engines Reinforce Racism.* NYU Press.

Norman, D. A. (2013). *The design of everyday things.* Basic Books.

Pardo, J. L. (2020). *La educación del futuro y otros escritos.* Fondo de Cultura Económica.

Sunstein, C. R. (2018). *Republic: Divided democracy in the age of social media*. Princeton University Press.

Taylor, L. (2017). What is data justice? *Big Data & Society*, *4*(2), 1–14.

UNESCO. (2021). *Recommendation on the Ethics of Artificial Intelligence*.

Van den Hoven, J. (2007). *ICT and value sensitive design*. Springer.

Van Wynsberghe, A. (2013). *Designing robots for care: Care centered value-sensitive design*. Springer.

Wachter, S., Mittelstadt, B., & Floridi, L. (2017). Why a Right to Explanation of Automated Decision-Making Does Not Exist in the General DataProtection Regulation. *International Data Privacy Law*, *7*(2), 76–99.

Wallach, W., & Allen, C. (2008). *Moral Machines: Teaching Robots Right from Wrong*. Oxford University Press.

Winner, L. (1980). *The whale and the reactor: A search for limits in an age of high technology*. University of Chicago Press.

Yeung, K. (2018). *Algorithmic regulation: A critical interrogation*. Oxford University Press.

Zuboff, S. (2019). *The Age of Surveillance Capitalism: The Fight for a Human Future at the New Frontier of Power*. PublicAffairs.

## ADDITIONAL READING

Court of Justice of the European Union (CJEU). (2020). *Data Protection Commissioner v. Facebook Ireland Ltd and Schrems (Case C-311/18)*.

European Data Protection Board (EDPB). (2023). *Meta vs. DPC (Decision on EU-U.S. Data Transfers)*.

European Parliament. (2021). *Digital Rights Charter of Spain*. BOE.

UN. (1948). *Universal Declaration of Human Rights*.

UN. (1966). *International Covenant on Civil and Political Rights*.

UN. (2011). *Guiding Principles on Business and Human Rights*.

## KEY TERMS AND DEFINITIONS

**Algorithm:** A set of rules to be followed in calculations or other problem-solving operations, especially by a computer.

**Algorithmic Governance:** The set of rules, practices, and technological infrastructures that directly or indirectly regulate automated decision-making.

**Algorethics:** An emerging discipline concerned with the ethical implications of the design, development, implementation, and consequences of algorithms in social, legal, and political contexts.

**Artificial Intelligence (AI):** The theory and development of computer systems able to perform tasks normally requiring human intelligence, such as visual perception, speech recognition, decision-making, and translation between languages.

**Big Data:** Extremely large data sets that may be analysed computationally to reveal patterns, trends, and associations, especially relating to human behaviour and interactions.

**Blockchain:** A distributed ledger, meaning data is stored across a network of computers; it is characterised by its transparency and immutability.

**Data Ethics:** A branch of ethics that addresses the moral problems arising from the collection, recording, sharing, integration, analysis and interpretation of personal data.

**Data Justice:** A critical approach that seeks to correct power asymmetries generated by the collection, processing, and use of data in digital contexts, aiming for fair and equitable treatment of data.

**Digital Ethics:** A subdiscipline of applied ethics that deals with the critical analysis of the normative principles that should guide the design, development, implementation, and use of digital technologies.

**Ethics by Design:** A theoretical and practical proposal that advocates the need to incorporate fundamental ethical values into the early stages of technological design.

**Human-Centred Design:** A design paradigm that places the needs, values, and well-being of individuals at the heart of technological development.

**Internet of Things (IoT):** A system of interrelated computing devices, mechanical and digital machines, objects, animals or people that are provided with unique identifiers and the ability to transfer data over a network without requiring human-to-human or human-to-computer interaction.

**Morality (Digital):** The set of shared values, norms, and practices that regulate the behaviour of individuals and communities in digital environments, often context-dependent and emergent.

**Techné:** A Greek term referring to a type of practical knowledge involving skills and craftsmanship, used to create something.

**Technology (Modern - *Gestell*):** According to Heidegger, a form of revealing where nature is seen as a resource to be exploited, potentially dehumanising and alienating.

**Technology (Traditional - *Techné* according to Heidegger):** A form of unconcealment where human beings collaborate with nature to reveal what is already present within it.

**Transparency (Algorithmic):** The principle that the processes, inputs, and outputs of algorithms should be understandable and explainable to relevant stakeholders.

Chapter 4

# Legal and Regulatory Framework for Digital Technologies and Risk Management in the Digital Age

**P. S. Swathy**
https://orcid.org/0009-0009-6273-2745
*School of Law, Vel Tech Rangarajan Dr. Sagunthala R&D Institute of Science and Technology, Chennai, India*

**Karun Sanjaya**
https://orcid.org/0000-0002-5055-6862
*Symbiosis Law School, Symbiosis International University, Pune, India*

**Abhishek Benedict Kumar**
https://orcid.org/0000-0002-3998-3150
*Symbiosis Law School, Symbiosis International University, Pune, India*

## ABSTRACT

*This chapter explores the regulatory challenges and opportunities presented by digital technologies in the context of human rights and risk management. As digital systems increasingly influence critical aspects of daily life, existing legal frameworks often fall short of addressing emerging threats such as algorithmic bias, surveillance, data exploitation, and digital exclusion. The chapter traces the historical evolution of digital regulation, examines global governance trends, and advocates for a human rights-based approach grounded in transparency, accountability, and*

DOI: 10.4018/979-8-3373-8510-5.ch004

*equity. It emphasizes the need for inclusive, adaptive, and risk-aware frameworks that protect fundamental freedoms while fostering innovation. Through the lens of digital justice, it calls for multi-stakeholder cooperation to ensure that digital transformation enhances, rather than undermines, human dignity and democratic values.*

## INTRODUCTION

For the past few years, the digital revolution has transformed the face of contemporary civilization. From communication and business to politics and health, digital technologies have permeated most aspects of society, reshaping the way people connect to each other, the activities of institutions and the power of the state. This transformation has been marked by accelerating rates of data generation, complex algorithmic analysis and the rise of platforms that govern large portion of human life. Although this digital age has presented unique opportunities for innovation, economic growth and social interaction, it has also brought with it unprecedented challenges and risks, the regulation of which has become a matter of urgent concern.

In the era of digital, there is a schism between promise and peril. Innovations ranging from artificial intelligence (AI), machine learning, big data analytics, blockchain and the Internet of Things (IoT) stand to boost productivity, automate work, support decision-making and level up access to information (Bamberger, 2009). But the same technologies can also reinforce inequalities, entrench discrimination, spur surveillance, disinformation and manipulation. As digital technology interpenetrates key infrastructures, including the banking system, health care, education, law enforcement. The stakes in regulatory failure grow dramatically, impacting not only individual rights, but also public safety and the ability of democratic governance to flourish and to protect the security and well-being of its citizenry.

Digitalisation has outpaced the development of a strong legal and policy environment that is needed to guarantee human rights and accountability. Existing regulations are out of date, piecemeal or non-existent. The law as it currently exists, written first and foremost for an analog era, does not provide the kind of flexibility and nuance required to address contemporary and emerging forms of harm including algorithmic bias, data breaches, platform monopolisation and online harassment. In addition, digital platforms are borderless and worldwide, which renders monitoring of national protections difficult and entails the need to roll out international cooperation.

Meanwhile the growing might of private technology companies complicated the regulatory landscape. Companies like Google, Facebook and Amazona do use the flow of data and speech to persuade and manipulate, and these powerful actors do control digital infrastructure. These actors frequently operate in the interstices of conventional governance structures, raising the spectre of unchecked corporate power, inadequate transparency and weak accountability. The commodification of people's personal information and the use of basic data to captivate attention have created a domino effect of calls for investigations and regulations to limit the reach of these monopolistic companies.

Human rights concerns are especially key considerations in the digital space where technology increasingly serves as an intermediary in the enjoyment of fundamental rights. Freedom of expression, privacy, freedom of assembly, access to information and non-discrimination are all integrated within digital policies and practices. Governments might exploit surveillance tools to squelch dissent and corporations may deploy algorithms that reinforce racial or gender bias, while the decisions of platform moderators can amount to a virtual silencing of marginalized groups. This will require greater advocacy around rights-based frameworks that examine and respond to human rights impacts of digital technologies.

Balancing the power and reach in the digital space. The digital and development divide is an important challenge, both within and among the nations. Some previously insulted groups have experience and literacy of digital technologies and high-speed internet, while other groups are facing blocked paths which exist and based on infrastructure gaps, expense or socio-political marginalisation. Online non-participation abets the continuation of social and political asymmetries, and it undermines the very premise of equality in online public sphere participation. Accordingly, regulatory strategies must prioritize digital inclusion as a goal, realizing that equal access to digital tools and data is necessarily antecedent to digital rights.

Risk management is an essential element of sound digital regulation. As technology becomes more complicated and less predictable, risk-based techniques may help government officials allocate resources based on the likelihood and severity of possible harms. This includes technological risk assessment but also social, ethical and legal evaluations. The use of facial recognition in public spaces, for example, presents a deep privacy and non-discrimination risk that parties must address on a regulatory level and potentially prohibited completely through a ban or moratorium (Camacho, 2024). Likewise, AI in judicial or hiring systems need to be regulated in order to avoid automated injustices, and to protect due process rights.

It is important to stress that governments do not monopolize the governance of digital technologies. Regulation must be informed, inclusive, and responsive - it requires a participation of all of the stakeholders. Community-based organizations, academia, technical experts, and affected peoples all bring unique perspectives that can enhance the regulatory process. International organizations, including the United Nations, the Organisation for Economic Co-operation and Development (OECD) and the Council of Europe New global norms and standards have already been initiated by various international organizations but we need a more inclusive approach that builds consensus to respond to the full gamut of digital challenges (Lawton, 2024).

The pace of technological change is rapid and disruptive, outstripping the slow, deliberative emergence of regulation. Therefore, an adaptive governance based on iterative learning, responsiveness, and flexibility is required. This requires more than periodic reviews of laws and rules, it also involves creating stable platforms for foresight, experiments and ongoing engagement with stakeholders. Regulation for the future must also anticipate the influence of new technologies whose impact today is less clear, including quantum computing, computer interfaces and advanced robotics.

There is a urgent need to govern digital technologies in a rights-respecting and risk-aware fashion remains urgent and is also complex. It calls for an integrated, interdisciplinary, and forward-looking approach. As will be further argued in this chapter, regulatory frameworks need to adapt to the stark facts of life in the digital age, symbolizing justice, fairness and human dignity as their main values. By scrutinizing current models, growing practices and normative controversies, this chapter aims to map out the way for the digital regulation that cares for rights and does not inhibit innovation and social welfare.

Digital and other technologies have increasingly become the core participants of the global economy and everyday life. People have been replaced by AI, blockchain, big data analytics, IoT and social media platforms as the way people gather as businesses organize and governments govern. And though these developments offer tremendous opportunities, they also carry risks like privacy violations, cyberthreats, algorithmic bias, misinformation, digital exclusion and more.

This digital change has its consequences on basic human rights like privacy, free expression and access to information. The risks of surveillance, data manipulation and exploitation used by the state and private actors alike call for strong, forward-looking rules.

## 1. DEFINING KEY CONCEPTS AND THE SCOPE OF DIGITAL REGULATION

Before we proceed must first understand about the regulations of digital technologies and risk management. These are digital technologies, digital regulation, risk and human rights in the digital form (Shandilya et al., 2024). These terms not only pave the way for systematic analysis, but also point to the intricate and interdisciplinary character of the digital transformation that is taking place in our societies.

## 1.1 What Are Digital Technologies?

Digital technology has to do with the transmittal and storage of information and the use of computer technology in the storage of, data processing and drawn information. This is a clear technical definition which obscures a much more complex reality to the extent that these technologies become 'social' integrated in economic and political life. Digitization technologies include ubiquitous devices like smartphones and cloud computing, as well as highly specialized solutions, such as algorithmic decision-making systems, biometric identification systems and distributed ledger technologies (DLT), such as blockchain (Gajendra Liyanaarachchi et al., 2024).

Here are some of the most significant:

Artificial Intelligence (AI): AI refers to a wide range of computer systems for doing things that humans would assume to require intelligence. Other subfields, such as machine learning or neural networks, allow the system to make use of data so as to get better over time, or to learn, from it. Use-cases include face recognition, NLP, predictive analytics, on self-driving cars.

Big Data and Analytics: Gathering and analyzing huge datasets in order to identify patterns and trends among the many variables. Marketing algorithms, predictive policing, fraud detection and even the formulation of social policy all rely on big data analytics.

Internet of Things (IoT): A network of devices, from smart refrigerators to industrial sensors, that are connected to each other and collect and exchange data in real time. Internet of Things raises issues with privacy, surveillance, and security.

Blockchain and Distributed Ledger Technology (DLT): Decentralized, tamper-proof systems used in finance, identity verification, and digital contracts. They can provide transparency and a higher level of security, but also create regulation issues as they are immutable and do not have a single point of control.

Generative AI and Synthetic Media: Tools like ChatGPT, DALL·E and deepfakes produce human-like text, images and videos. Though great for learning and inspiration, they also enable misinformation and IP theft (To, 2024). And thanks to their spread, these are no longer simply tools: they mediate relationships, drive behavior, and even redefine vital dimensions of governance and citizenship.

## 1.2 What Constitutes Digital Regulation?

Digital regulation concerns the development and application of legal, institutional, and policy architecture necessary to the shaping and use of digital technologies. But the ambit of digital regulation is much more complex than making laws.

It involves:

Instruments Of Law: These include federal statutory law, other legislative enactments, constitutional law, court rules, and executive orders. Such aspects include, just to name a few, data protection laws (such as the GDPR), the algorithmic transparency obligations and the antitrust law.

Policy Mandates: Governments and multilateral organisations may adopt plans, roadmaps, or white papers that establish high level principles to govern digital technologies. These can be non-binding but extremely powerful in effect.

Technical Standards and Protocols: In digital systems, and in other electronic fields, International Telecommunication Union (ITU) or Institute of Electrical and Electronics Engineers (IEEE) are bodies that establish standards to provide for interoperability and security.

Ethical Guidelines: Organizations such as UNESCO, the High-Level Expert Group on AI by EU, and the OECD have suggested ethical guidelines for AI and digital systems in general, which included principles like transparency, fairness and accountability.

Soft Law and Self-Regulation: These are industry codes of practice, community rules (like those of social networking sites), self-regulatory instruments. While not enforcers themselves, such rules can help close gaps where there is no formal regulation.

Digital regulation, therefore, is a many-headed beast taking place across multiple mechanisms, agents, and domains. States are not the only actors bearing responsibility, individual technology companies, civil society, and technical experts and international organisations influence the regulatory landscape (Kausche & Weiss, 2024).

## 1.3 Risk Management in the Digital Era

The idea of risk management originally comes from engineering, finance and public health. In the digital world, it has grown to include technological, social, legal and ethical aspects. Mitigating digital risk, comprises identifying the risks and taking action to prevent or remediate them (Jangkhum et al., 2025).

There are different kinds of digital risk:

Technical Possibility The technical risks are for instance cyber security flaws, system malfunction and algorithmic errors.

Privacy Issues: Unmonitored monitoring, dataveillance and hacking can reveal private details of your life, career, contacts, relationships,etc.

Discriminatory Risks: Partial or partial datasets and opaque algorithms could exacerbate multidimensional inequalities, including those rooted in race, gender and disability.

Fabrication and Disinformation: The practice of employing AI to create deepfakes or fashion propaganda is deeply troubling for democratic integrity.

Socioeconomic Exclusion: Digital tools have the potential to exacerbate these disparities if access to the necessary infrastructure, skills and protections is unevenly distributed.

A risk-based regime has also been one of the most popular regulatory frameworks in the emerging in the EU and OECD member states when it comes to digital systems: this is a taxonomy of digital systems based on what harm they could cause. For instance, the EU Artificial Intelligence Act divides AI uses into prohibited, high-risk, and limited-risk uses and with associated obligations.

The following are risk management mechanisms:

Impact Assessments: These are meant to predict and mitigate potential harms in technology deployment, including either Data Protection Impact Assessments (DPIAs) or Human Rights Impact Assessments (HRIAs) (Calvi, 2024).

Appeals: Strategies for appealing harmful decisions of digital systems back to people.

Regulatory Sandboxes: Safe environments where companies can simulate new technologies under regulatory watch and regulators can learn to adapt.

At the end of the day, good risk management is both a preventive and curative aid which can only be achieved through the combined efforts of states, technologists and civil society and affected communities.

## 1.4 Human Rights in the Digital Sphere

Digital regulation should have human rights as its universal normative reference. Core human rights enshrined in international law are increasingly becoming dependent on digital technologies, for example:

Right to Privacy (Art 17, ICCPR): Threatened by mass surveillance, biometric profiling and metadata sifting.

Freedom of Expression (article 19 ICCPR): At stake due to content moderation, shadow banning, and algorithmic push of hate speech.

Freedom of Assembly and Association (Articles 21–22): Social media is the new public square, its censorship or manipulation can inhibit civic participation.

Non-Discrimination: Algorithms are used in hiring, policing and in financial services that perpetuate historical biases that make real, equal protection under the law more difficult.

Right to Information and Education: Features such as the digital divide and algorithmic curation can prevent people from fully participating in society.

There's an increasing understanding that digital rights are not a new kind of rights, but rather the extension of current human rights into new spaces (Issalillah & Hardyansah, 2024). Including the right to digital inclusion, the right to data sovereignty, and, yes, the right to a meaningful explanation of the use of automated decision-making.

### 1.5 The Multi-Stakeholder Landscape of Regulation

Finally, understanding the regulatory environment also involves recognizing its multiple decision-making agents.

States: Tasked with writing laws and enforcing them but behind the curve when it comes to the latest technology.

The Tech Companies: They're the creators and the gatekeepers and they have more power than ever. Some impose global standards by design decisions and business models.

International Organisations: Like the UN, WTO, and OECD as they facilitate the co-ordination and development of norms.

Civil Society and Academia: Play a key watch-dog role and bring ethics, legal and technical skill to the table.

End Users: Communities or individuals affected by technology need to become the stakeholders in the discussion.

As such, digital regulation is not just a legal, top-down operation, but an active, participatory and cross disciplinary matter (Worden et al., 2024).

## 2. HISTORICAL AND GLOBAL EVOLUTION OF DIGITAL REGULATION

Digital regulation did not happen overnight. It has evolved piece by piece in the face of waves of technological change, social change and political pressure. The trajectory of digital governance from its early days of internet freedom to today's growing milieu of data protection, cybersecurity, algorithmic accountability, platform governance provides a cautionary tale about technological change. Crucially, this history is not linear, let alone uniform, for the development of these ideas has taken shape in different geopolitical circumstances, legal environments and cultural legacies (Madnick et al., 2023).

### 2.1 The Origins: Cyber libertarianism and the Early Internet (1980s–1990s)

The rise of the internet in the late 20th century shaped the early era of digital regulation. The internet was first imagined as a decentralized, open and somewhat unregulated space—a digital frontier whose guiding principles were liberty and the unconstrained expression of self. This time was characterized by a kind of cyber libertarianism that had a deep investment in keeping governments out of the way, believing a relatively lawless internet would help democratization, innovation and global communication.

A key moment arrived with the U.S. Telecommunications Act of 1996, more specifically Section 230 of the Communications Decency Act, which immunized online platforms from liability for what their users posted. This protective bubble allowed tech giants, including Facebook, Twitter, and YouTube, to flourish. Such legal shields were thought to be necessary at the time to nurture the emerging internet economy and to promote free expression on the web.

In the meantime, Europe and elsewhere were starting to take a harder look at digital data processing's consequences. The EU adopted one of the earliest comprehensive data privacy regulations in 1995, the Data Protection Directive (95/46/EC). This regulation established principles of data protection through lawfulness, purpose limitation and transparency that would serve as the backbone of global dialogue for generations to come. But with a few exceptions for privacy and intellectual property, most digital territory was still the Wild West in terms of regulation. The prevailing ideology was one of a 'hands-off' internet, largely self-regulating through users and private companies.

## 2.2 The Rise of Regulation: Data Privacy, Cybersecurity, and Digital Rights (2000s–2010s)

As the internet evolved and grew, so did anxieties about its effects on society. The 2000s brought a number of key developments that started to change the regulatory environment (Aleke, 2024). Social media platforms and search engines revolutionized the dynamics of mass data capture and algorithmic targeting: on the one hand. Companies like Google and Facebook collected massive amounts of personal data that frequently was ambiguous user consent. The business model of 'surveillance capitalism', a term coined by Shoshana Zuboff turned user data into a good, leading to serious concentrations of power and knowledge (Chu, 2025).

Second, a series of cyber-breeches and cyber-attacks from the 2007 Estonian cyber incident to the 2003 leak of the Stuxnet worm to the 2013 Yahoo breach have uncovered vulnerabilities in digital infrastructure and the need for more robust security measures. Those had ceased being theoretical risks have become real for millions of users and vital systems. A third major shift in the public discourse surrounding privacy and state power occurred in 2013, when Edward Snowden revealed US National Security Agency (NSA) mass surveillance programs (Lemieux, 2024). These disclosures led to changes in the law and new debates on intelligence-sharing among democratic nations.

With this in mind, many have opted to introduce or enhance digital regulations:

European Union: The General Data Protection Regulation (GDPR) approved in 2016 and effective from 2018 set a new standard for data privacy worldwide (Blind et al., 2023). The GDPR brought the concepts of the right to be forgotten, the right to data portability, explicit consent, and heavy fines for non-compliance. Its extraterritorial reach heralded a new era of digital governance.

United States: While there is no federal data privacy law, certain states such as California set the standard with the California Consumer Privacy Act (CCPA) and subsequent California Privacy Rights Act (CPRA) to offer their residents the rights to access, delete and opt out of the sale of their personal information (Acquah et al., 2024).

China: The government sought an extremely state-centric approach to digital governance. The national security justification for data storage and scrutiny Get the frequencies, chords and keys used in a YouTube video or song These policies included the Cybersecurity Law (2017), the Data Security Law (2021) and the Personal Information Protection Law (PIPL, 2021), all of which formed an extensive regimen for data localization, surveillance, and state access (Zhou et al., 2024).

Africa and Latin America: The GDPR has influenced enforcement beyond Europe, with the processing of data now regulated under law in countries like Kenya, Nigeria and Brazil were the latter replaced its decade-old privacy code with stronger protections like the LGPD in 2018 (Blind et al., 2023. Privacy experts say that there is growing recognition of digital rights on a global scale, but enforcement is uneven. All these signs pointed toward a growing recognition that digital technologies were not neutral rather they could exacerbate inequality, infringe upon civil liberties and undermine democratic governance unless they were policed.

## 2.3 The Platform Era and Algorithmic Governance (2010s–2020s)

By the middle of the 2010s, a small handful of influential digital platforms, mostly but not solely Facebook (Meta), Google (Alphabet), Amazon, Apple and Microsoft, had emerged as the dominant institutions shaping online ecosystems in transformative, sometimes unaccountable manners (Cameron, 2024). They became gatekeepers of information, of commerce, of the public discourse.

During this time, multiple regulatory issues became apparent:

Content Moderation and Free Speech: De-platforming users, shadow banning, and taking down harmful content, once the work of platforms came under scrutiny. Critics questioned the lack of consistent standards, the potential for political bias and the transparency.

Algorithmic Bias and Discrimination: Throughout the course of the year, as AI systems were rolled out in policing, hiring, credit scoring and judicial contexts, more reports emerged of ethnic, racial, gender and socioeconomic biases woven into the training data and decision logic.

These anxieties gave rise to a fresh round of regulatory experimentation:

The EU proposed the Digital Services Act (DSA) and Digital Markets Act (DMA) in 2020 – 22 and they offer a comprehensive regimen for transparency, accountability and competition in digital markets (European Parliament, 2021). The AI Act which is also a part of the EU introduces a risk-based model for overseeing AI use and mandates high-risk systems to adhere to strict standards on data quality, human oversight and explainability.

In the Global South, the rise of regional responses can be seen in the establishment of the African Union's Convention on Cybersecurity and Personal Data Protection and ASEAN's digital data governance framework. Several international organisations at the United Nations, OECD and Council of Europe level have started to discuss proposals for international standards, notably in relation to AI ethics, digital rights, and cross-border data flow. Nevertheless, the world still feels fragmented. Where the EU promotes a rights-based and precautionary approach, China insists on state-centric digital control and the US is dominated by market-oriented, sectoral solutions. These divergent images are indicative of larger ideological or biological and geopolitical feuds that disrupt world involvement.

## 2.4 Emerging Frontiers and the Need for Adaptive Regulation (2020s Onward)

Further development of digital technologies, fueled by generative AI, quantum computing, synthetic media and brain-computer interfaces. Regulatory frameworks should progress rapidly and responsibly (Wesarg-Menzel et al., 2023).

Some of the key trends that are set to influence in the future period are:

Ethical AI and Trustworthy Technology There is an increasing demand for the creators and implementers of digital systems to follow principles of fairness, transparency and responsibility. Regulatory instruments such as algorithmic impact assessments and AI audits are being developed.

Digital Sovereignty: Countries and regions are taking control of their data, infrastructure and standards, an example of privacy fears and geopolitical competition mingling.

Environmental and labor issues: The environmental impact of digital infrastructure (data centers, crypto mining) and the mistreatment of gig workers and content moderators have emerged as regulatory concerns.

Human Rights-Forward Regulation: Civil society activists, academics, and multilateral organizations are making the case that all digital regulation should pursue its basis in universal human rights law, so that digital systems serve to enhance human dignity and autonomy rather than detract from them.

## 3. RISK MANAGEMENT IN THE DIGITAL ERA: FRAMEWORKS AND CHALLENGES

Risk management has become a central policy issue for policymakers, regulators and civil society as digital technologies are increasingly woven into the architecture of modern life. The complexity, opaqueness and size of digital systems have given rise to a new type of risk, including privacy breaches, algorithmic discrimination, cyber-attacks, misinformation and digital exclusion, for which previous regulatory mechanisms were not designed. Study, analysis and regulation in this digital era, therefore, necessitate redefining risk and designing new guidelines of sound risk management and ethical conduct.

### 3.1 Understanding Digital Risk

Digital risks have several unique aspects in comparison to traditional risks. For one, they are systemic, they can influence societies and infrastructures instead of isolated individuals. Secondly, they are dynamic, they change along with the technology. Third, they are opaque, obscured by layers of code, algorithms or proprietary systems. Fourth, they are interconnected, transnational and have wide ranging impacts on a variety of fields, from finance and health to education and governance (Habbal et al., 2024).

In general, digital risks fall into one of these five categories:

Risks over Privacy and Data protection: Unauthorized surveillance and data collection, data leaks and misuse of personal data are undermining autonomy and dignity.

Security and Infrastructure Risks: Cyber-attacks on public systems, ransomware and vulnerabilities to critical infrastructures create upheaval in societies and economies.

Risks About Algorithmic Decisions & Artificial Intelligence: Machine learning and algorithmic decisions can lead to discrimination and impinge on right to a fair trial.

Risk of Disinformation and Manipulation: Misinformation, deepfakes, and filter bubbles jeopardize democracy and informed public discussion.

Access and inclusion: digital divides can sideline disadvantaged groups, amplifying socio-economic inequalities.

These perils require not only technical fixes, but also ethical scrutiny, legal clarity and participatory governance (Kumar et al., 2025).

## 3.2 Traditional vs. Adaptive Risk Management

Conventional risk management models, commonly borrowed from the engineering, finance, or industrial fields, operate inside linear mindsets of identify, analyze, minimize and watch for risk. Adoption of such models is justifiable for specific classes of digital threats (like cyber in network infrastructure), but they are not always suitable for the dynamism in emerging digital ecosystems, in particular on human rights issues.

In reaction, academics and regulators have recently started to develop adaptive and user-centric digital risk management approaches such as:

Risk-Based Regulation: Adapting the intensity of regulation to the risk associated with a technology. So, for instance, the EU's AI Act creates categories of regulation based on risk (minimal, limited, high, and unacceptable).

Application to Digital Systems: Where the implications of a digital system are untrusted, or worse, catastrophic, we need the evidence of safety to precede deployment (burden of proof).

Proportionality and Necessity: Not everything fits all, avoiding constraints that promptly deter activity beyond the necessary, managing the risk and minimising rights restrictions and interference.

These frameworks reorient us away from the command and control of ends and towards paving and shaping the development and deployment of tech toward democratic/ethical ends (Qi et al., 2024).

## 3.3 Tools and Mechanisms for Digital Risk Management

There are several instruments that have developed in order to make digital risk management operational:

Algorithmic Impact Assessment (AIA): Used by governments and companies to see how an AI system might affect human rights, especially in high-stakes areas like policing, hiring, or health care. AIAs may also feature engagement of stakeholders and mitigation measures.

Regulatory Sandboxes: Safe environments in which firms can trial new digital services under careful scrutiny from the regulator. That gives regulators the ability to evaluate risks on the fly and fine-tune rules without squelching innovation.

Redress Mechanisms: Available channels that victims could access for solution when they are harmed by a digital platform or system. These bodies consist of data protection supervisory and regulatory authorities, ombudspersons and specific tribunals.

Third-Party Audits: Independent assessments of digital systems, and algorithms and platforms in particular, to ensure that they are in line with the law and ethics. Such audits may uncover hidden biases, risks to privacy or security holes.

But these are only as useful as the institutions that use them. Digital risk governance will require adequate resources, technical capability and political will if it is to be more than a box-ticking exercise.

## 3.4 Human Rights as a Framework for Digital Risk Governance

Human rights provide a strong normative foundation for digital risk management. They set clear, globally recognized norms, on everything from the rights to privacy, non-discrimination, freedom of expression and access to information that should shape the design, deployment and governance of technology.

Some principles of digital risk management from a rights-based perspective are:

Risk Identification: Understanding how a technology may impact human rights negatively or positively.

Stakeholder involvement: The participation of affected individuals and communities, especially vulnerable groups, in assessment and decision making.

Transparency and Accountability: Calling for clear explanations of how technologies work and the people responsible for them and how harms are redressed.

Preventive Strategy: Moving away from reflex regulation to proactive design—baking in human rights-respecting ways at all stages of development.

This thesis is now becoming more prominent in international human rights bodies. For example, the UN Guiding Principles on Business and Human Rights (UNGPs) require companies to carry out human rights due diligence, also for digital products. The OHCHR has also published advice related to human rights-based approaches to AI governance (Kumar & Sanjaya, 2025a).

## 3.5 Challenges and Gaps

However, despite the increasing focus on digital risk management, there are still substantial gaps like,

Inconsistent approaches are a barrier: Laws and regulators have inconsistent risk triggers, interpretation, and enforcement capabilities.

Enforcement: capacity for enforcement, even if they have risk management framework available. Privacy watchdogs, for one thing, have been underfunded and in some cases overpowered by their charges, like those big tech companies.

Information asymmetry: Regulators and the public don't usually have access to the proprietary algorithms or internal practices of digital companies, hampering any real oversight.

Reliance on Self-Regulation: A number of governments continue to depend on the platforms and private companies to police themselves, creating conflicts of interest and gaps in accountability.

Addressing these challenges will require stronger institutions, cooperation across borders and fields and interdisciplinary knowledge, including from technologists, ethicists, lawyers and affected communities.

## 4. CASE STUDIES IN DIGITAL REGULATION AND HUMAN RIGHTS

Even though the theoretical and practical models for steering digital tech are essential, field cases amply illustrate the practical difficulties and victories in balancing innovation, governance and human rights. This Class describes specific studies in different areas and technologies which explore the struggle of regulatory attempts to accommodate privacy, freedom of expression, algorithmic fairness, and inclusion. These examples present what to follow and what to avoid as lessons for the future policymaking.

### 4.1 The European Union's General Data Protection Regulation (GDPR): A Benchmark for Privacy Protection

The GDPR, passed in 2018, is one of the most ambitious and wide-ranging efforts to regulate personal data for the digital age, and it has resonated around the world. It reflects a robust human rights approach to privacy and data protection, by embedding the right to personal data control, and imposing strict responsibilities on data controllers and processors.

Key features include:

Consent and Transparency: Firms will only be allowed to collect and process data with the clear and explicit consent of the customer, and will be required to explicitly inform a user of how their data will be used.

Data Subjects Rights: Person can access, correct, delete 'right to be forgotten' and object to processing of the data.

Accountability and Enforcement: Companies must integrate 'privacy by design' into the design and architecture of systems and 'privacy by default' as a default setting, along with deeming data protection impact assessments and data breach notification as mandatory and taking the necessary steps to detect breaches. Regulators can levy large fines up to 4% of global turnover.

The GDPR has also been something of a global bar-setter, creating something similar for legislation around the world, including Brazil's LGPD and California's CCPA. Then it demonstrates how a structural legal context firmly based in human rights can empower people and improve corporate behaviour (Calvi, 2024).

However, challenges remain:

Gaps in Implementation: Many small and medium-sized businesses find compliance a challenge and enforcement is inconsistent across EU countries.

Cross-Border Data Flows: The global pervasiveness of digital services presents enforcement challenges, and in particular data transfer to countries with lower privacy safeguards.

Stifling Innovation and Rights: Some critics say the regulation could inhibit innovation or burden companies, particularly start-ups.

Notwithstanding these limitations, however, the GDPR's emphasis on human rights and procedural guarantees renders it highly significant as a test case for digital regulation.

## 4.2 Algorithmic Bias and the COMPAS Controversy in the United States

The use of algorithmic decision-making processes in criminal justice has sparked serious human rights concerns, from fears of reversing hard won due process protections to skirting around the rights of the accused. A prominent example is the COMPAS (Correctional Offender Management Profiling for Alternative Sanctions) risk assessment instrument, which is used extensively in U.S. courtrooms for predicting recidivism risk.

An investigation by ProPublica, the news organization, in 2016 found that COMPAS was more likely to label Black defendants higher risk than white defendants, even when they had the same actual recidivism rates. This predictive policing bias reinforces systemic discrimination, undermining the right to equal treatment before the law and the guarantee of fair trial (Engel et al., 2024).

The case raised questions about the regulation of AI in sensitive sectors:

Transparency and Explainability: COMPAS is a proprietary software, so that it is nearly impossible for defendants or their defense attorneys to examine how its risk scores are calculated, giving rise to due process issues.

Accountability: When algorithms make errors, leading to false detention or what some perceive as harsher sentencing, who is to blame?

Regulatory Responses: Some American states have issued standards for algorithmic impact assessments, or restrictions for AI in criminal justice, but their regulation is not systematic.

This case underscores the critical need for robust human rights review of life, liberty, and equality in AI systems, and the imperative for enforceable protections of transparency, fairness, and accountability.

## 4.3 India's Aadhaar System: Digital Identity and Privacy Risks

Launched in 2009, Aadhaar, in India, is the world's largest biometric identity system, with more than 1.2 billion enrolled members. Intended to modernize the delivery of welfare benefits and other government services, Aadhaar connects people's biometric information, including fingerprints and iris scans upto a 12-digit identity number. Although Aadhaar has improved people's access to services for a lot of the population, it has been the subject of fierce discussions around privacy, surveillance and exclusion,

Privacy: Some feared the program's central database and binding to various services would allow for mass surveillance and push services not covered by NIRA. At first, there was no comprehensive data protection law in India and therefore demands grew for stronger regulatory protection.

Risk of exclusion: Errors in technology and the biometrics which have been cited as reasons for benefit denial and violations of social security of the poor and underprivileged.

Court intervention: In 2018, the Indian Supreme Court validated Aadhaar constitutionally, but with restrictions, and upheld the right to privacy as a fundamental right.

Legal Developments: India's Personal Data Protection Bill India's Personal Data Protection Bill, which is currently before Parliament, seeks to regulate processing of data, strengthen consent, and establish a data protection authority.

The Aadhaar case reveals the Janus-faced character of digital identity systems: they can be instruments of social inclusion, but can also enhance surveillance and exclusion if not regulated sufficiently and based on human rights.

## 4.4 China's Social Credit System: Surveillance and Social Control

The Chinese Social Credit System is a controversial system of digital governance that leverages big data, subservient to artificial intelligence (AI) and surveillance to track and control citizens. It combines information from financial records, social media and public behavior to compile 'credit scores' that influence whether citizens are granted loans, can travel, attend the best schools or get good jobs.

It has raised human rights issues which include:

Privacy breaches: Wide data gathering happens without due transparency or consent.

Freedom of Expression and Assembly: The system can punish a person for dissent or difference, silencing free expression and political engagement.

No Due Process: Decisions that impact an individual's rights and opportunities often are made in secret, and there is little opportunity for appeal.

Discrimination and stratification: The system may also serve to entrench social inequalities by targeting vulnerable populations at a higher rate.

The Chinese government contends that the system fosters trust and social stability; international observers and human rights groups describe it as a model of digital authoritarianism (Xu et al., 2021).

These developments highlight that digital regulation is not only a measure to protect individual rights, but can also serve to limit them, and that therefore digital governance requires international norms and scrutiny.

## 4.5 Kenya's Digital Inclusion Initiatives: Bridging the Digital Divide

Despite doubts about digital inclusion, Kenya has taken great strides in access and literacy with projects such as M-Pesa, a mobile money platform and free public Wi-Fi.

M-Pesa, introduced in 2007, changed the world of financial inclusion by allowing millions of people to easily send and receive money on their mobile phones, even if they did not have a bank account. This breakthrough has given dignity and voice to marginalized groups and poor populations in rural areas, advancing economic rights and inclusion. Policies around enhancing digital literacy and addressing infrastructure gaps are also being developed by government and civil society.

However, challenges remain,

Accessibility and Affordability: High-speed internet access and quality digital services continue to be out of reach for many.

Data Protection: Kenya passed the Data Protection Act (2019), but it is still establishing enforcement mechanisms and public awareness.

Gender Gap: Women and excluded groups usually have less access to digital technology and risk targeted interventions.

Kenya's case study demonstrates the ways in which regulation and policy can promote digital rights through inclusion efforts, but also draws attention to stubborn structural inequalities that will continue to need sustained focus (United Nations, 2025).

### 4.6 Lessons and Implications from the Case Studies

Together, these case studies illustrate several important lessons for digital regulation and human rights:

The primacy of human rights: Legal frameworks that are clearly rooted in human rights principles are more likely to safeguard dignity, equality, and freedom.

Transparency and Accountability Are Crucial: Technologies that affect fundamental rights need to be explicable, subject to independent oversight, and have effective remedies.

Context-specific: Societies have different problems and compromises to face and the regulations need to adapt to local political, social and economic aspects while respecting universal rights.

Good Governance: The communities affected and civil society have to be part of the regulatory process, for the policies to be responsive and fair.

International Cooperation: Digital technologies exist transnationally, requiring international norms and enforced cooperation.

## 5. CHALLENGES AND OPPORTUNITIES IN REGULATING DIGITAL TECHNOLOGIES

The rapid development of digital technologies poses a complex challenge for the regulator which requires flexible, anticipatory responses. As AI and machine learning, big data, blockchain and other cutting-edge technologies transform the social, economic and political fabric of societies, regulators grapple with a slew of complex issues. These include technical complications and legal fragmentation to ethical quandaries and tensions between innovation and rights protection. But within these constraints are opportunities to create governance systems that are more inclusive, flexible and rights-based than ever (Ahuja, 2025).

### 5.1 The Technical Complexity of the Digital Technologies

Digital technologies constitute a particularly difficult challenge for digital regulation as an expression of the technicity of new developments. Whereas traditional products or services are static, digital apps like AI systems come with opaque algorithms, learning and evolving models. This obscurity can make it difficult for regulators to understand how decisions are made, raising issues of accountability and transparency.

Consider machine learning algorithms in credit scoring or job recruitment, which rely on massive, constantly changing sets of data that can encode historical bias or the potential inscrutability of decisions. The task for regulators is to not only understand the technology but also to build frameworks for assessing risks without stopping progress.

To address these challenges, there is a trend in regulation to be open to technical and interdisciplinary expertise. That includes working with computer scientists, data ethicists and sociologists to create algorithmic audits, impact assessments and explainability standards that explain how a system operates and what harms it can cause.

## 5.2 Fragmentation of Jurisdiction and the Borderless Character of Cyber spaces

The problem with digital technology is that they don't really respect geographical boundaries and that can be very hard for national regulators. Data flows, platform behavior, and cyber activity cut across multiple nations, which have different legal systems and enforcement capabilities. This fragmentation inhibits coherent governance and frustrates cross-border cooperation on issues like data protection, cybercrime and misinformation.

A social media establishment located in one country and accessible to billions of people can be subject to conflicting or evadable regulations. Similarly, data distributed across territories is a major hindrance for both data protection and law enforcement requests.

The global conversation about regulation and the rise of multilateral treaties suggest some prospects for addressing the fracturing process. They say instruments such as the now invalidated EU-US Privacy Shield, the Council of Europe's Convention 108+ on data protection or the OECD digital economy guidance aim to standardise norms. However, these remain embryonic initiatives and require political will and compromise (Council of Europe, 2018).

## 5.3 Moral Conflicts and Balancing Conflicting Interests

The discussion of digital governance, instead of avoiding the squishy but important ethical issues that rise quickly into public conversation because they involve warring public values, should begin to engage those issues. For example, security enhancing technology could cause privacy right to be violated. Moderation of content to hate speech could, however, stive to stifle acceptable expression. Then of course there is the ethical dilemma of where to draw the line between innovation and precaution with regard to the balance that regulators are forced to strike between how much risk we should accept in order to foster technological innovation.

Moreover, ethical considerations concern algorithmic bias, discrimination and digital divide. Unconstrained, AI can mirror and magnify social biases, carrying them forward into new technologies, systems, and decision-making tools, for example. Regulators face the difficult task of promoting fairness and non-discrimination when systems are often black box and data driven. To address such conundrums, some governments are considering principles such as those outlined in the European Commission's Ethics Guidelines for Trustworthy AI, which are human rights respecting, transparent and accountable. They also foreground the inclusion of human rights and civic values (rather than being an afterthought) as drivers of digital governance.

## 5.4 Balancing of Innovation and Rights Protection

A perennial tension in digital regulation is how to weigh the imperative to foster innovation against the necessity of safeguarding human rights. Overregulation could stifle technological advances and economic development and undermine societal benefits. By contrast, the converse condition, a lack of regulation, subjects us to privacy violations, surveillance and misinformation.

Balancing act involves risk based proportionate approaches with the magnitude of regulation being commensurate with the potential risk and the potential for harm of the product. For instance, the use of facial recognition in public spaces could be subject to tight controls, or even be banned, while other forms of data use, deemed to be less invasive of privacy, could come under a light-touch regime.

New instruments, such as regulatory sandboxes, provide a solution to this impasse as they enable experimentation with new technologies in a controlled setting. It also supports technology-sensitive, iterative, dynamic interaction among developers, regulators and others who can together learn-by-doing.

## 5.5 Promoting Digital Participation and Closing the Digital Divide

Digital governance must also address the intractable problem of digital exclusion. That the world is overwhelmingly digitalising does not erase the fact that large swathes of population remain offline or underachieved because of infrastructure divides, cost or social exclusion. This digital divide further entrenches the inequalities that already exist in education, health, job opportunities and civic engagement.

Status quo treating the status quo much worse as they exacerbate existing inequalities, towards exclusion that is driving regulatory systems not optimized for inclusion.

Therefore enabling regulation should also discuss ways to promote affordability, digital literacy, and equitable infrastructure deployment. Public-private partnerships and focused subsidies are among the means of filling in the gaps. Digital inclusion is at the same time prerequisite for our capacity to claim digital rights, without real access many other sector of society would not be able to express their ideas, access knowledge or benefit of online services.

## 5.6 The Role of Multi-Stakeholder Governance

The multistakeholder governance models are needed as digital ecosystems are complex and dynamic. As governments, we alone cannot comprehend or manage the risks and opportunities of digital technologies. Engaging civil society, technical experts, academia, private sector and affected communities strengthens the design and implementation of regulation.

Multi-stakeholder processes additionally contribute to ensuring the inclusion of a broad range of viewpoints, which enhances legitimacy, transparency, and accountability. Platforms exist at the global level for such dialogue, such as the IGF.

Obstacles to multi-actor governance the challenges to multi-actor governance are related to power imbalance, conflicting interests, and coordination problems. Nevertheless, cultivating inclusive participation represents a promising approach to responsive and rights protective digital regulation.

## 5.7 Opportunities for Future Regulatory Innovation

Nevertheless, the digital age also presents unprecedented opportunities for regulation innovation. If the explosive growth in data and analytical tools is harnessed, it could strengthen the hand of evidence-based policymakers, as regulators can track impact, signal early harms and target interventions with more precision.

Technologies themselves can aid regulation, like blockchain could help provide transparent, tamper-proof records for compliance and auditing. Regulatory reporting can be automated with AI-powered tools, or disinformation can be detected widely.

Furthermore, there has also been increasing acknowledgment of the need to reform regulatory models from top-down control models to adaptive, participatory and iterative approaches, which can develop together with the technologies.

## 6. EMERGING MODELS AND APPROACHES TO DIGITAL REGULATION

Traditional forms of regulation may be ill suited to keep up with the rapidly changing digital environment. In response, governments, international organizations, and civil society are considering new models and approaches to regulate the digital realm without compromising human rights and stifling innovation. This part examines some of the emerging regulatory architectures and governance mechanisms that have been identified as prospective or well-publicised candidates for digital regulation in the future.

### 6.1 Risk-Based Regulation: Prioritizing Proportionality and Flexibility

Among the important changes we see taking place in digital regulation is the move to risk-based regime. While prescriptive regulations are applicable not based on how much risk they pose, but risk-based regulations prioritize regulatory attention and resources in function of the constraints of specific technologies or applications. For instance, the European Union's Artificial Intelligence Act (AI Act), a draft in 2021, classifies AI systems according to risk levels, unacceptable risk, high risk, limited risk and minimal risk. Systems that are deemed to be 'unacceptable,' including government-implemented social scoring, are banned outright. High-risk uses including biometric identification and managing critical infrastructure are subject to strict obligations such as risk assessment, transparency requirements and human oversight. Meanwhile, lower-risk AI benefits from lighter regulation, allowing it room to innovate.

Risk-based regulation has promoted proportionality, where regulation is neither too much nor too little. It is also flexible, so rules can change with changing technologies and their uses. By concentrating on results and avoiding overly specific technical standards, it allows for innovation while preserving fundamental rights (Marique & Marique, 2020).

### 6.2 Regulatory Sandboxes: Enabling Safe Innovation

One emerging mode of governance is the regulatory sandbox, which creates a test bed from which firms develop new digital products and services with regulatory (over)Site. First utilized in fintech (e.g., UK's Financial Conduct Authority (FCA) sandbox), this path is still relatively little known, but increasingly explored today for digital technologies (notably for AI-based and data-driven platforms). The other thing sandboxes do is provide a safe environment to evaluate new software for risk and how to mitigate that risk. They promote collaboration between innovators and regulators, helping authorities to familiarize themselves with the new technologies, and to adjust regulations if needed.

In addition, by allowing for incremental learning and policy adjustment, sandboxes can help make regulation more flexible and data-informed. There's not a cookie-cutter solution for deploying sandboxes, but localisation of sandboxes is crucial.

### 6.3 Human Rights Impact Assessments: Embedding Rights in Technology Deployment

A lot of regulators and organizations are advocating for Human Rights Impact Assessments (HRIAs) that ensure that digital technologies honor human rights. All of these reviews systematically assess potential impacts of technology or policy on rights such as privacy, free expression, non-discrimination and information access.

HRIAs provide a mechanism for identifying risk early, engaging stakeholders and planning for access in high-risk ventures. In one case, the Danish Institute for Human Rights has developed a toolkit for corporates to assess and address the human rights risks related to AI.

### 6.4 Co-Regulation and Self-Regulation: Sharing Governance Responsibilities

Given the expertise required and the rapid pace of digital development, co- and self-regulation forms are necessary. Co-regulation entails that governments and industry collaborate on the creation and castigation of rules, while self-regulation involves industry groups or companies producing rules and norms voluntarily.

These include the European Commission's Code of Conduct on Countering Illegal Hate Speech Online, a voluntary self-regulatory effort with internet law giants, and industry-led AI ethics and transparency standards.

While they bring agility and domain capability to the table, they also create questions around conflict of interest, enforcement and accountability. As a result, effective co- and self-regulation are generally reliant on government monitoring, clarity of goal and process for the involvement of stakeholders to serve the public interest.

### 6.5 Multi-Stakeholder Governance: Inclusive and Participatory Regulation

Due to the complexity and world-wide character of digital ecosystems, the MS governance is an important mechanism. This model is based on the involvement of government, private sector, civil society, technocrats and the affected community in regulating.

Multistakeholder processes such as the Internet Governance Forum (IGF) and the Global Partnership on AI (GPAI) facilitate dialogue and knowledge sharing, as well as the articulation of collective norms and policies. These are the types of open forums that can enrich policymaking by better informing regulation with a broader range of views, particularly those of less-adoptive voices that do not always get a hearing in traditional policy development.

These are the weighting of interest, the power imbalance and the imperative of timely decision making. But multistakeholder governance is widely considered vital for legitimate, transparent and democratic digital futures.

6.6 Algorithmic Transparency and Explainability: Demystifying Automated Decision- Making

Key among new regulatory approaches is increasing the transparency and explainability of algorithms. Automated systems are playing a more important role in deciding people's rights, including in credit approval and policing, yet their logic is often opaque. Regulators are considering requiring companies to disclose critical information about the algorithmic models, data sources and decision criteria they use. This is in order to allow those affected and monitoring authorities to know, challenge and seek redress for harmful consequences (Thomas et al., 2025; Chandra and Sanjaya, 2023).

## CONCLUSION

The age of digital technology presents humankind with unparalleled opportunities and challenges to which it should rise with unprecedented measures. As digital technologies enter all aspects of our lives, from artificial intelligence, big data and internet of things to blockchain and beyond. All governance systems must be reconsidered to protect fundamental rights and foster the development and well-being of society. This chapter has emphasized that we must find a balance between the need to realize emergent regulatory orders, risk associated with increasing complexity as well as the ability to intervene to protect and promote the human rights of all, in a digitalized time.

One of the central insights has been that digital regulation may not simply be an extension of analog-era legal models. Usual laws clamp down on movement and outreach, and do not cut it in the ever-changing risk world of algorithmic bias, lack of data privacy or a cyber-attack. Emerging models such as risk-based regulation, regulatory sandboxes and multi-stakeholder governance reflect the understanding of a more resilient understanding the digital ecosystem, providing a basis for better regulation that is based on principles like proportionality, flexibility and participatory processes. The approaches find a good trade-off where public interest is protected while a healthy digital economy is allowed to grow.

Private players, including big tech firms in particular, play important roles with both positive and negative sides. In fact, although they are large drivers of innovation throughout the digital economy, their disproportionate influence and lack of transparency in many cases contradict the basic underpinnings of good governance. Regulation should therefore not only be responsive to enforceable standards but should promote ethical corporate behavior and transparency. Co-regulation and self-regulation approaches may complement formal regulation, but they should not displace the state's obligation to ensure human rights.

Cooperation at the global level and norm-building also equally important since digital technologies do not respect borders. No individual country will be able to regulate the digital sphere alone, with this piecemeal approach potentially leading to either regulatory arbitrage or the erosion of fundamental rights. There are a myriad multilateral initiatives that are being pursued under the auspices of organisations such as the UN, the OECD or the Council of Europe to work towards compatible principles and practices to resolve cross-jurisdictional tensions concerning matters such as data flows, cybersecurity or the regulation of platforms (Kumar & Sanjaya, 2025b).

Digital regulation is built on the fundamental principle of risk-based regulation. The pace of new technologies and the fact that they are commercialized into our lives before research can determine harms, argues for anticipatory approaches grounded in a body of evidence to evaluate unintended consequences prior to widespread use by the public. To this end, regulators might use regulatory sandboxes, ex-ante impact assessments, and ongoing audit to catch these shortfalls early before they grow into a large-scale systemic problem. Simultaneously, risk management should be maintained with important considerations for justice and equity to ensure the protection of vulnerable populations.

At its core, successful digital regulation requires inclusive governance with robust, multisectoral engagement. Policymakers, industry, civil society, academia and affected communities must come together to craft policies that are both technically competent as well as ethically justifiable in a cultural milieu. Legitimacy, trust and the capacity to foresee or respond to emerging threats are created through inclusive governance.

## REFERENCES


Acquah, E., Ganapati, S., & Choi, Y.-J. (2024). *Examining the effects of California Consumer Privacy Act (CCPA) on Organizational Data Breach Notification*. https://doi.org/DOI: 10.1145/3657054.3657082

Ahuja, K. (2025, March 29). *European Union Deforestation Regulation (EUDR)*. Bhatt & Joshi Associates; Bhatt & Joshi Associates. https://bhattandjoshiassociates.com/regulation-of-emerging-technologies-legal-challenges-in-the-integration-of-ai-and-blockchain-into-indian-cyber-law/

Aleke, N. T. (2024). The Role of Cybersecurity Legislation in Promoting Data Privacy. *Advances in Information Security, Privacy, and Ethics Book Series*, 205–244. https://doi.org/DOI: 10.4018/979-8-3373-0588-2.ch008

Bamberger, K. A. (2009). Technologies of Compliance: Risk and Regulation in a Digital Age. *Texas Law Review*, *88*(4), 669. https://heinonline.org/HOL/LandingPage?handle=hein.journals/tlr88&div=27&id=&page=

Blind, K., Niebel, C., & Rammer, C. (2023). The impact of the EU General data protection regulation on product innovation. *Industry and Innovation*, *31*(3), 1–41. DOI: 10.1080/13662716.2023.2271858

Calvi, A. (2024). Data Protection Impact Assessment under the EU General Data Protection Regulation: A feminist reflection. *Computer Law & Security Review*, *53*, 105950. DOI: 10.1016/j.clsr.2024.105950

Camacho, N. G. (2024). The Role of AI in Cybersecurity: Addressing Threats in the Digital Age. *Journal of Artificial Intelligence General Science (JAIGS) ISSN 3006-4023, 3*(1), 143–154. https://doi.org/DOI: 10.60087/jaigs.v3i1.75

Cameron, L. D. (2024). The Making of the "Good Bad" Job: How Algorithmic Management Manufactures Consent Through Constant and Confined Choices. *Administrative Science Quarterly*, *69*(2). Advance online publication. DOI: 10.1177/00018392241236163

Chandra, R., & Sanjaya, K. (2023). Punishing the Unpunishable: A Liability Framework for Artificial Intelligence Systems. In Motahhir, S., & Bossoufi, B. (Eds.), *Digital Technologies and Applications. ICDTA 2023. Lecture Notes in Networks and Systems* (Vol. 669). Springer., DOI: 10.1007/978-3-031-29860-8_6

Chu, N. E. (2025). The influence of surveillance capitalism on educational technology adoption. *Doi.org*. https://doi.org/DOI: 10.14288/1.0440687

Council of Europe. (2018). Convention 108 +. In *European Parliament*. European Union. https://www.europarl.europa.eu/meetdocs/2014_2019/plmrep/COMMITTEES/LIBE/DV/2018/09-10/Convention_108_EN.pdf

Engel, C., Linhardt, L., & Schubert, M. (2024). Code is law: How COMPAS affects the way the judiciary handles the risk of recidivism. *Artificial Intelligence and Law*, *33*(1). Advance online publication. DOI: 10.1007/s10506-024-09389-8

European Parliament. (2021, December 14). *EU Digital Markets Act and Digital Services Act explained | Topics | European Parliament*. Www.europarl.europa.euEuropean Parliament. https://www.europarl.europa.eu/topics/en/article/20211209STO19124/eu-digital-markets-act-and-digital-services-act-explained

Habbal, A., Ali, M. K., & Abuzaraida, M. A. (2024). Artificial Intelligence Trust, Risk and Security Management (AI TRiSM): Frameworks, applications, challenges and future research directions. *Expert Systems with Applications*, *240*(122442), 122442. DOI: 10.1016/j.eswa.2023.122442

Issalillah, F., & Hardyansah, R. (2024). Relevance of Privacy within the Sphere of Human Rights: A Critical Analysis of Personal Data Protection. *Bulletin of Science, Technology & Society*, *3*(1), 31–39. https://inti.ejournalmeta.com/index.php/inti/article/view/39

Jangkhum, S. J., Chayutrakorn, C., Uthai, P., & Supiyanti, R. S. (2025). Risk Management in the Digital Era for SMEs. *The 15th Benjamit National and International Conference*, 211–221. https://benjamit.thonburi-u.ac.th/ojs/bmv15/article/view/99

Kausche, K., & Weiss, M. (2024). Platform power and regulatory capture in digital governance. *Business and Politics*, •••, 1–25. DOI: 10.1017/bap.2024.33

Kumar, A. B., & Sanjaya, K. (2025a). Ethics, Algorithms, and the Rules of Evidence. *Forensic Intelligence and Deep Learning Solutions in Crime Investigation*, 103–124. https://doi.org/DOI: 10.4018/979-8-3693-9405-2.ch006

Kumar, A. B., & Sanjaya, K. (2025b). AI and Social Justice: Democratizing Technology for Inclusive Growth. In Chakraborty, S. (Ed.), *Ethical AI Solutions for Addressing Social Media Influence and Hate Speech* (pp. 163–190). IGI Global Scientific Publishing., DOI: 10.4018/979-8-3693-9904-0.ch008

Kumar, A. B., Sanjaya, K., & Saleem, M. (2025). Justice in the Age of Algorithms. *Advances in Computational Intelligence and Robotics*, •••, 191–210. DOI: 10.4018/979-8-3693-9395-6.ch009

Lawton, T. C. (2024). The New Global Electronic Economy: Consensus, Confusion, Contradictions. *Routledge EBooks*, 39–60. https://doi.org/DOI: 10.4324/9781003576990-5

Lemieux, F. (2024). Mass Surveillance. *Emerald Publishing Limited EBooks*, 159–170. https://doi.org/DOI: 10.1108/978-1-83549-097-620242010

Liyanaarachchi, G., Viglia, G., & Kurtaliqi, F. (2024). Addressing challenges of digital transformation with modified blockchain. *Technological Forecasting and Social Change, 201*, 123254–123254. DOI: 10.1016/j.techfore.2024.123254

Madnick, B., Huang, K., & Madnick, S. E. (2023). The evolution of global cybersecurity norms in the digital age: A longitudinal study of the cybersecurity norm development process. *Information Security Journal: A Global Perspective, 33*(3), 1–22. https://doi.org/DOI: 10.1080/19393555.2023.2201482

Marique, E., & Marique, Y. (2020). Sanctions on digital platforms: Balancing proportionality in a modern public square. *Computer Law & Security Review, 36*(105372), 105372. DOI: 10.1016/j.clsr.2019.105372

Qi, Y., Sajadi, S. M., Baghaei, S., Rezaei, R., & Li, W. (2024). Digital technologies in sports: Opportunities, challenges, and strategies for safeguarding athlete wellbeing and competitive integrity in the digital era. *Technology in Society*, *77*(1), 102496. DOI: 10.1016/j.techsoc.2024.102496

Shandilya, S. K., Datta, A., Kartik, Y., & Nagar, A. (2024). Navigating the Regulatory Landscape. *EAI/Springer Innovations in Communication and Computing*, 127–240. https://doi.org/DOI: 10.1007/978-3-031-53290-0_3

Thomas, A. V. A., Kumar, A. B., & Sanjaya, K. (2025). AI-Driven Growth: Addressing Legal and Economic Complexities in the Digital Era. In *Exploring AI Implications on Law, Governance, and Industry* (pp. 1–24). IGI Global. https://doi.org/DOI: 10.4018/979-8-3373-3384-7.ch001

To, B. (2024). Analysis of AI-generated content and deepfakes in social media. *Urn.fi*. https://www.theseus.fi/handle/10024/857145

United Nations. (2025). *Unsdg | Kenya's Digital Leap for a Fairer Future*. Un.org; United Nations Sustainable Development Group. https://unsdg.un.org/latest/stories/kenya%E2%80%99s-digital-leap-fairer-future

Wesarg-Menzel, C., Ebbes, R., Hensums, M., Wagemaker, E., Zaharieva, M. S., Staaks, J. P. C., van den Akker, A. L., Visser, I., Hoeve, M., Brummelman, E., Dekkers, T. J., Schuitema, J. A., Larsen, H., Colonnesi, C., Jansen, B. R. J., Overbeek, G., Huizenga, H. M., & Wiers, R. W. (2023). Development and socialization of self-regulation from infancy to adolescence: A meta-review differentiating between self-regulatory abilities, goals, and motivation. *Developmental Review*, *69*(1), 101090. DOI: 10.1016/j.dr.2023.101090

Worden, S., Svobodova, K., Côte, C., & Bolz, P. (2024). Regional post-mining land use assessment: An interdisciplinary and multi-stakeholder approach. *Resources Policy*, *89*, 104680–104680. DOI: 10.1016/j.resourpol.2024.104680

Xu, X., Kostka, G., & Cao, X. (2021). Information Control and Public Support for Social Credit Systems in China. *The Journal of Politics*, *84*(4). Advance online publication. DOI: 10.1086/718358

Zhou, M. M., Qu, Z., Wan, J., Wen, B., Yao, Y., & Lu, Z. (2024). Understanding Chinese Internet Users' Perceptions of, and Online Platforms' Compliance with, the Personal Information Protection Law (PIPL). *Proceedings of the ACM on Human-Computer Interaction, 8*(CSCW1), 1–26. https://doi.org/DOI: 10.1145/3637415

# Chapter 5
# Social Responsibility and Intellectual Property in the Era of Digital Technology:
## Who Should Own AI-Generated Inventions?

**Wasswa Shafik**
https://orcid.org/0000-0002-9320-3186
*Dig Connectivity Research Laboratory (DCRLab), Uganda*

## ABSTRACT

*This chapter explores the intersection of social responsibility and intellectual property (IP) within the evolving landscape of digital technology. It critically examines how digital innovation impacts the balance between protecting intellectual assets and ensuring ethical access, inclusivity, and accountability. Algorithmic governance, digital rights management, equitable access to knowledge, AI-generated content, and open licensing frameworks. The chapter provides a multidisciplinary analysis of legal, technical, and ethical dimensions, highlighting the tension between proprietary control and the public good in areas such as software development, data privacy, digital art, and indigenous knowledge systems. Case studies and comparative frameworks are used to illustrate the challenges and opportunities facing policymakers, developers, and global communities. Through a focus on emerging technologies such as blockchain and AI, the chapter emphasizes the need for socially responsible IP frameworks that uphold innovation while safeguarding digital equity and cultural sensitivity.*

DOI: 10.4018/979-8-3373-8510-5.ch005

## 1. INTRODUCTION

We are witnesses to a fast-paced technological development, which has seen the rise of information and digital technologies, the dissemination of the Internet, the World Wide Web, and, most recently, the "Cloud", Big Data, and Artificial Intelligence-based technologies, which are changing the way we live, think, and relate to each other (Malik, 2024). Contemporaneously, we are facing mounting dilemmas around the multiple crises shaking the world, in the political area, the economic area, the environmental area, and the social area. To respond to all or any of these crises, there are only three types of actors capable of taking action: states, through public policies; the for-profit sector, through strategic corporate actions and social corporate responsibility; and the non-profit sector, through philanthropy and other initiatives aimed at helping those in need (Blaskovic et al., 2023).

Being one of the activities "responsible" for the current crises, it is only natural that Intellectual Property rights would be questioned and that the need to rethink them could emerge. So, the question arises as to whether the conceptual and normative framework that presently regulates the appropriation and allocation of knowledge and intangible assets, their transfer and circulation, and the framework which supports fundamental principles such as creativity, innovation, and growth, remains adequate and effective to respond to all the challenges and dilemmas faced by current-day societies, and to address the legal and ethical issues surrounding the digital networked technologies (Shafik, 2024d). However, rethinking IPRs in the context of the current social and ethical crises means rethinking their social responsibility. The specific question posed here is: What does social responsibility mean for IPRs, in the context of the ethical dilemmas raised by the digital economy? As we shall see, this question derives from, and leads us to, some fundamental issues of IPRs and/or the IPR system (Shafik, 2023).

## 2. UNDERSTANDING SOCIAL RESPONSIBILITY

Social responsibility is a broad and complex concept that has been given many definitions. A social responsibility is an obligation to perform actions that benefit society and contribute to the public good. Social responsibility is the duty of a business to contribute to the well-being of a community. Fittingly, however, when academics, policy makers, and the general public debate what social responsibility actually means, most of the time they address a particular subject, such as citizens, corporations, and so forth (Narayanan & Pradhan, 2024; Shafik, 2025f). A popularly cited version defines social responsibility as the obligations of businessmen to pursue those policies, to make those decisions, and to follow those lines of action which are desirable in terms of the objectives and values of our society. It has since been expanded beyond corporations to include all sectors – the private, public, and non-profit sectors. Companies, for example, have a social responsibility to meet the needs of the people they rely on to make a profit. These groups may include customers, suppliers, and the community in addition to shareholders and employees (Chang & Ke, 2024).

In the face of business behavior throughout history that has been perceived as selfish or detrimental to society, such as sweatshops and exploitation of the public, there have long been calls for social responsibility. In the early 20th century, the social reformer recognized the innate selfishness of human nature, believed that a group, such as a corporation, must be motivated by more than just profits. Additionally, during the Great Depression of the 1930s, corporate leaders were criticized for their cushy lifestyles amid suffering, thanks to the failure of their firms (Merolla et al., 2024). In the 1950s and 1960s, amid the growth of the modern corporation and the rise of consumerist and environmentalist movements, book after book was published criticizing the selfishness of business and reciting the rationale for social responsibility. With this as a backdrop, the business management scholar had the prophetic foresight to say that the focus of the new managerial class would begin to shift from the corporation to the community (Jia et al., 2023).

## 2.1. Definition of Social Responsibility

Philosophers have recognized the idea behind social responsibility and have tried to formalize it by thinkers during the Roman Empire. It also became obvious after World War II that the decision about how to be responsible is not purely a private matter. In principle, every person has social responsibilities, which are all the more important given that a very large percentage of people are, in fact, at the mercy of the actions of a very small percentage of people. Whatever the definition of social responsibility, the general understanding is that society expects a contribution to a common cause, especially from those who are wealthier or who have more power (Vo et al., 2019). Many have debated the idea of social responsibility through their notion of land or earth ethics. In other words, we no longer only owe obligations to other human beings, but also to the environment, to the animal or plant kingdom, and to future generations. A possible definition of social responsibility provides that to be socially responsible means to ensure that an enterprise can serve two masters by being just with its shareholders and just with the society of which it is a part. This definition emphasizes the reciprocal obligations of an enterprise towards its shareholders and towards society. To be socially responsible does not only mean to ensure useful activities; equally important is to make decisions based on the first principles of fairness, openness, and credibility (Carvalho et al., 2024).

## 2.2. Historical Context

The social responsibility of businessmen did not enjoy legal protection until the enactment of the first labor law in the United Kingdom in 1802: the Factory Act. With the progressive strengthening of the labor legislation during the 19th century, social responsibility began to acquire legal recognition in the law codes of the most industrialized countries, as well as espionage laws and civil rights. However, it was not until the 20th century that the legal concept of social responsibility was conceived, when it was first mentioned in the policies of the major political parties in Europe and the United States (Wu et al., 2022). In the 1920s, the English businessman explained the concept of social responsibility of industry, which would become a fundamental pillar in the evolution of corporate law. In 1929, a businessman, entrepreneur, and historian would further develop the concept. In the 1930s, a newspaper became the market leader in the critique of commercial advertising promoting capitalism and its colonies. The author responsible for this path-breaking criticism was a journalist, essayist, and author. He warned: "A businessman is a petty tyrant who... dedicates his entire life and all his efforts to... producing the goods that men need... and selling them at the lowest price on the market... making a profit". In 1943, an American sociologist said: "No man is an island, no man is self-sufficient: every man is a piece of the continent... and therefore never asks for what he does unless, in asking for it for himself, he does it for others." (KOROL & ROMASHKO, 2022). Corporations exist to serve society, not prevent it from flourishing.

## 2.3. Importance in Modern Society

Individuals and companies are conscious of the implications and pressures entailed by human actions within society. Various institutions or organizations—nonprofits, social movements, signs of the market, such as consumerism becoming the culture of the day—play a major role in putting pressure on all parties. But it is within modern-day theory and practice of business in the early twenty-first century that we find the most pertinent discussion of corporate social responsibility. Corporate social responsibility is one of the elements that correspond to the regulatory and support functions of the supra-legal that accompany the normative, coercive, and economic functions of the law and the market (Akpan & Oluwagbade, 2024). Consumer society made manifest by post-industrial societies and the concomitant development of conditions making possible and the rapid inflation of needs accelerated the demand for public goods in private activities. The eminent modern practical philosophers have emphasized the social embeddedness of persons that is constitutive of their identity. This emphasis on social relations involving mutual recognition and reciprocation, as well as on human rights, implies that individuals are inescapably dependent upon one another and mutually implicated in the conditions of their existence (Ahmad, 2019). In addition to liberal rights that prescribe non-interference, this understanding of human agency animates a concern for duty or obligation. From a moral perspective, a duty is an ethical or moral requirement, recognized by the prudent person, that imposes a constraint on the rationality of self-interested action. However, the determination of the specific obligations that bind individuals is complex and remains a social question requiring resolution through discourse and negotiation. These tensions regarding the social embeddedness of human agents are ultimately epistemological at base (Tran, 2023).

## 3. INTELLECTUAL PROPERTY IN THE DIGITAL AGE

Although there are various nuances to the definition of intellectual property, it is safe to say that intellectual property rights declare ownership of and give a degree of control over the creation of original works in both tangible and intangible forms. Tangible examples of intellectual property include books, paintings, and inventions; intangible intellectual property comprises the original concepts of such expressions. The original creator of intellectual property using labor, time, money, and skill should enjoy some level of recognition and be rewarded for the effort put forth to create these works. Enabling legal frameworks and societies' varying degrees of adherence to such frameworks are thus extremely important (Rashid et al., 2018). Furthermore, in the digital age, it is extremely important to be cognizant of the dangers as well as the advantages associated with technological innovations, particularly as they relate to intellectual property rights. The digital age, characterized by the wonders of technological innovations and the use of the Internet, has made it ever easier to develop copyrightable and patentable works, yet at the same time, easier to infringe on the rights of the original creators. Digital protocols have resulted in the creation of several new forms of intellectual property and intellectual property rights, and their incessant violations—and an associated demand for unique and novel legal formulations—count among the many dilemmas of both the digital domain and the world at large during the past three decades (Vinueza Villagran et al., 2024). This chapter will first explore the more traditional forms of intellectual property, copyright, trademark, and patents—and how they manifest in the digital age, before proceeding to a presentation of a few, but by no means all, examples of the infringements and reactions, particularly in terms of the creation of new legal frameworks dealing with these rights and their potential violations.

## 3.1. Overview of Intellectual Property Rights

Intellectual property (IP) laws have a long and rich history, dating back at least as far as the 1700s, with the implementation of the US Constitution and the Venice Patent Statute of 1474 being examples of early laws. Such early laws began to merge into the current expectations of IP laws seen today, with the implementation of the Berne Convention in 1886 and the Paris Convention for Industrial Property in 1883. These treaties formalized the global amount of time that copyrights and trademarks, and patents can protect original works and inventions for a finite amount of time—at which point the works and inventions enter into the public sphere, available for all to use (Nhemi, 2023). As each type of IP has evolved over the years, disputes often arise at the level of implementation, especially where IP as a whole either lacks specificity in defining boundaries, lacks alignment between countries, lacks a strong enough enforcement mechanism, or lacks sufficient timeframes to cover implementation effectively. However, the fundamental concepts behind IP have endured and are still widely recognized today. These IP laws started as very specific implementations to protect a certain type of work from absolute theft and misappropriation. Over time, the laws have evolved to not only give the owner of a unique, original work the right to enforce protections, but also to allow for the developers of an original creation to benefit financially as a commerce-enabling structure (Kretschmer et al., 2024). No longer do inventors want to monetize their inventions by opening factories and hawking products door to door; instead, they want to benefit from the money-making structures of the world, including through licensing, selling stakes in the product, or assigning the entire invention, as presented in Table 1.

*Table 1. Comparative Matrix – Intellectual Property Rights in the Digital Era*

| IP Type | Digital Context | Enforcement Mechanism | Key Challenge | Technology Integration | Reference |
|---|---|---|---|---|---|
| Copyright | Online content, software | DMCA, EUCD | Unauthorized duplication | Digital watermarking, DRM | (Malik, 2024) |
| Trademark | E-commerce platforms | Takedown notices, legal injunctions | Brand misuse on digital platforms | Automated brand monitoring tools | (Blaskovic et al., 2023) |
| Patent | Software, AI inventions | National/regional IP offices | Defining patentable subject matter | AI-assisted patent search | (Shafik, 2024f) |
| Trade Secret | Source code, algorithms | NDAs, cybersecurity measures | Insider threats, leaks | Encryption, access control | (Blaskovic et al., 2023) |

continued on following page

*Table 1. Continued*

| IP Type | Digital Context | Enforcement Mechanism | Key Challenge | Technology Integration | Reference |
|---|---|---|---|---|---|
| Design Rights | UI/UX, digital product models | Design registration | Proving originality | 3D modeling verification systems | (Bogdanov, 2024) |
| Database Rights | Structured digital data collections | Licensing, technical safeguards | Data scraping | API access control, query tracking | (Bedzow, 2021) |
| Moral Rights | Artistic attribution in digital media | Copyright laws, licensing clauses | Anonymity in remix culture | Metadata embedding tools | (Shafik, 2024h) |
| Geographical Indications | Online product certification | Certification marks | Misrepresentation on global platforms | Blockchain-based certification | (Shafik, 2024a) |
| Software Licensing | Open-source vs proprietary models | License audits | License violations | Automated license compliance tools | (Shafik, 2025a, 2025b) |
| Digital Twins IP | Virtual replicas in industry | Patent + copyright combo | Cross-domain ownership conflicts | Secure modeling platforms | (Shafik, 2025i) |
| NFTs and IP | Digital art, tokenized media | Smart contracts | Ownership ambiguity | Ethereum-based IP registries | (Anwar et al., 2023) |
| AI-Created Works | Autonomous content generation | Unclear legal standing | Assigning authorship | AI provenance tracking | (Vulturius et al., 2024) |
| Cultural IP | Indigenous knowledge online | sui generis legal frameworks | Digital misappropriation | Cultural data sovereignty platforms | (Long & Blok, 2023) |
| Cloud-Based Innovations | SaaS, PaaS intellectual output | Contract law + copyright | Jurisdictional fragmentation | Cloud-native IP management systems | (Ndou et al., 2020) |

## 3.2. Challenges in Digital Environments

The digitization of human experience has far-reaching consequences. In the contemporary global, interconnected, digitally enhanced society, people within extend their consciousnesses, virtual realities beyond the physical place, object, and body. Their self-created works, brands, ideas, and inventions are dispersed when they upload or share with various media outlets, including digital marketplaces, social networking sites, or microblogging platforms. People create and share digital contents for fun, advertisement, product placement, promotion, and for educational purposes (Nhemi, 2023). Digital transactions and trading enable companies and individuals to create wealth and enhance economic growth. Similarly, digital services, all having an impact on traditional commercial practices, have extended market reach and reshaped cultural practices. These digital transfers have practically eliminated national borders in favor of a intangible space of virtual realities, enabling a broad, instantaneous distribution–provided that one has an internet connection (Kretschmer et al., 2024).

Nevertheless, the expansive volume of digitalization proceeds without sufficient consideration of legal, ethical, and moral mores that construct the operational framework for the physical world. It tests the efficiency and coherence of the underlying rules, policies, and institutions that impact social structure. The abundance of available materials and services and relative ease of use further exacerbate ethical and legal issues surrounding ownership in the digital world. While the proliferation of digital content potentially engenders a greater market for creative expression, it simultaneously exposes itself to accidental or purposeful infringement and unauthorized use. Precedents, penalties, and procedures seem ill-equipped, however, to deter digital infringers or compensate victims. Traditional intellectual property legal systems, particularly copyright law, do not adequately respond and address the challenges of the digital environment (Savirimuthu, 2017). Aligned with this research's focus on social responsibility, the next sub-section discusses the status of IP issues and ailments that remain unresolved.

## 3.3. Case Studies of Digital IP Issues

This section presents some case studies of different aspects of intellectual property in the digital age: the relationship between censorship and IP law; some challenges to trademark law from the online world; and the impact of the proposed treaty on the development of ecommerce. The traditional view of copyright, upheld by many proponents of copyright reform, sees copyright as an individual right affording limited duration monopolies over creative work. Copyright is said to reflect the labor of the author and balance the greater good of society with the entitled monied interest of the author (Bedzow, 2021). Copyright's utilitarian rationales of encouraging creativity and contributing to the creative commons justify the temporary monopoly. These rationales and copyright's individual basis offer no support for censorship. In accordance with IP law's focus on individual property rights, free expression guarantees have generally sufficed to protect against infringement. Recent developments in copyright suggest a movement away from this individualistic understanding of IP law. Media corporations have made use of copyright to assert a collective property interest in dance tracks and multimedia presentations, leading them to take greater interest in what has traditionally been the province of free expression guarantees.

Some say this reflects copyright's shift from an individual right to a corporate monopoly (Bogdanov, 2024). These corporations use copyright as a means to engage in collective censorship for economic gain.

The Internet is a potent mechanism for trademark dilution. By allowing a worldwide audience immediate access to virtually any content on the web, the Internet offers near-instantaneous and worldwide distribution of potentially diluting material. Further, by allowing for the frustration of consumer expectations and the exploitation of trademark holders' goodwill without suffering any backlash, the Internet provides a perfect medium for blurring, and a ripe opportunity for tarnishing. Finally, by allowing instant access to potentially inflammatory messages on the web, the Internet creates the conditions by which trademark holders may suffer some of the effects of blurring or tarnishing (Blaskovic et al., 2023). The treaty deals with the needs of this Internet marketplace in several ways. To meet the needs of the telecommunications provider, it clarifies the applicability of existing copyright law to the online transmission of copyright protected works, reinstating the core tenet of the Copyright Act that the author is entitled to compensation from the business of making copyrighted works available to users in the first instance. Thus, while the telecommunications provider is freed from liability for using existing copyrighted materials, and those already entitled to use copyrighted works may continue to do so at will, those involved in developing ecommerce policy may still explore the extent to which Congress intended to impose liability on online service providers other than telecommunications carriers (Malik, 2024).

## 4. THE INTERSECTION OF SOCIAL RESPONSIBILITY AND INTELLECTUAL PROPERTY

We have seen that social norms influence a significant part of the innovative process. We identified particularly two norms that are relevant for the understanding of innovation: the norm to push the limits of what is discoverable, and the other to share the discoveries and inventions for the benefit of society. The interplay of these two norms reflected in the incentive structure defined by State subsidies and intellectual property laws that have been employed have shown to be effective in stimulating the development of innovation capacities (Blaskovic et al., 2023). It must, however, be recognized that social norms do not only inform the incentive structure they reflect ethical considerations that exist independently or in addition to government strategies. One of the important ethical concerns relates to the idea that the knowledge generated through research and development efforts is some sort of 'common good'. The activities as well as the output of the innovation process should be considered a public good. Quite some time ago, the concept of "theory of the commons" was introduced to the discussion about intellectual property. This theory seeks to overcome the increasing contradiction between intellectual property rights that are commonly understood to be public rights and that reflect a certain social contract and the exclusive private nature of IP rights. Therefore, it is suggested that IP rights must be recognized as conventional rights that reflect a certain 'theory of the commons' (Bogdanov, 2024). Such a view then leads to a critical position about constraints imposed by proprietary rights: They must always reflect a carefully calibrated balance between socially desirable monopoly privileges and the protection of the public domain.

## 4.1. Ethical Considerations

Ethical theory encompasses a diverse field of inquiry and applies to all disciplines exploring human conduct and social organization. One common issue that arises in this context is the claim that the enterprise of creating intellectual property is ultimately unethical. There is much debate about how far the principle of charity can act as a corrective to what might otherwise appear as unethical behavior. It would be difficult, from a consequentialist perspective, to justify a society in which patent rights were applied to medicines which would save lives. Alternatively, ethical egoism might have similarly unpalatable conclusions if one took a glance over the corporate fence (Bedzow, 2021). Furthermore, the categorical imperative would probably lead a society like Nazi Germany to advocate genocide. Although potential challenges to our moral scruples are apparent to mixing high-level code of ethics with implied or explicit technical codes of conduct, something must be said for keeping ethical considerations close to the centers of intellectual research and university governance. There are unique ethical concerns guiding the source and the use of knowledge and creativity determined principally after a consideration of corporate social responsibility (Shafik, 2025c). The balance between profit making and social good is an increasingly important point of deliberation not just on the ethical boards of the European Union, ethics clearing houses in modern economies coupled with corporations inquiring and keeping CSR and industrial groups from the developing world committed to CSR. At a legal level, international treaties organized by international bodies and bilateral treaties whose intellectual property elements deal with enforcement, sanctions, and subsidy support are unlikely to be the last word on the matter (Shafik, 2024f).

## 4.2. Corporate Social Responsibility and IP

Concepts and practices labelled as Corporate Social Responsibility (CSR) have developed over the years in response to changing business contexts and stakeholder demands, circumstances recognised by scholars, namely the dynamic nature of CSR, reflecting changing societal, organizational and stakeholder values. Evidence of increased social awareness stems back at least to the early 1960s, with CSR moving from social obligations to integration at the core of business strategy (Shafik et al., 2025). Whether voluntary efforts in addition to mere compliance or obligatory initiatives, CSR signals a developing concern for the consequences of corporate activities beyond financial profit-taking and short-term gain, evident in demands by investors for corporations to be engaged in risk management concerning long-term reputation, sustainability and ethics (Malik, 2024).

CSR efforts appear to yield positive stakeholder sentiments and a good reputation for corporations, including investor trust and organisational pride. A substantial body of literature discusses the relationship between CSR and firm financial performance with mixed results, and from the perspective of company executives, CSR appears to concentrate as much on stakeholders as on shareholders, potentially yielding cost advantages and risk management. Yet CSR may also be engaged opportunistically, leading to corporate 'greenwashing', erroneous claims of social benefits as a marketing embellishment. Despite the vast volumes of literature discussing CSR, relatively less attention has been paid to the interfaces between CSR and intellectual property matters, particularly given the significance of IP as a component of corporate assets and brand strategy (Blaskovic et al., 2023). Notions of ethics and morality also stretch to intellectual property matters – if CSR has traditionally been perceived as "doing good", matters such as filing patent applications merely to amass patent portfolios and stockpile patents to engage in patent thickets or resorting to 'abusive patenting' questions a moral obligation to avoid such practices, as do the use of trademarks merely as marketing devices to promote and differentiate product quality, patenting innovations that are obvious or lack novelty, or the appropriation of commonplace ideas like the use of a marketing slogan by a company (Bogdanov, 2024). Elsewhere, the view was expressed that there is an inherent duty in moral philosophy that obliges entities to conform to the laws and regulations established by society.

## 4.3. Impact on Innovation and Creativity

Should strong IP protection promote innovation and creativity? What about when society cannot bear the high costs of on-patent technologies? What about our collective health? The intersection of CSR and IP takes us to a domain where private interests and public interest clash. A recent trend has advocated for open licensing. Organizations ask that their technology patents be open-sourced or they enter into licensing agreements. This has happened in the pharmaceutical sector during the pandemic. Vaccines and booster shots were patented shortly after extensive public funding had gone into name development. Why should money-laden pharmaceutical companies have monopole over mediocre side effects and presented annual revenues of more than USD 50 billion after the vaccination campaign (Bedzow, 2021)? The pharmaceutical sector's experience during the public health crisis made it all the more important to return to the phenomena of innovation and creativity.

Strong IP protection is a powerful exogenous variable driving the innovation performance of companies and the shift to intangible asset-based business models. The innovation race has also been affected by digitalization of the economy. Data can be processed in more or less original manners, license agreements can be concluded. The question of how copyright impacts creativity has a long history behind it. Does strong copyright protection foster or hinder creativity? Copyright worked as a barrier because the IP of giants protected originality and authors never got the chance to create their own original version of the originals (Savirimuthu, 2017). Why is it that sometimes copyright is a problem of too much, and sometimes it is an incentive of too little or too less? To say that creativity comes and goes, or that it stems from the interplay of informal contracts of some actors and unbalance the business system as such would be far too simplistic. The stars shining of momentary creativity cycles survive above a torrential, structural flow of banal entertainments regulated by marketing strategies, globally diffused and commercialized by highly capitalized transnational companies, as some dismension as presented in Table 2 (Nhemi, 2023).

*Table 2. Dimensions of Social Responsibility in Digital Technology Innovation*

| Dimension | Description | Implication for IP | Stakeholders Involved | Mitigation Strategy | Reference |
|---|---|---|---|---|---|
| Digital Inclusion | Access to innovation for all communities | Licensing access restrictions | Marginalized users, regulators | Open-access frameworks | (Nhemi, 2023) |
| Transparency | Algorithmic clarity and traceability | Trade secret conflict | Developers, policymakers | Explainable AI, selective disclosure | (Kretschmer et al., 2024) |
| Fair Use & Innovation | Balancing protection with creative growth | Copyright overreach | Researchers, creators | Reform fair use doctrines | (Savirimuthu, 2017) |
| Accessibility | Inclusive tech design | Proprietary design barriers | Disabled users, designers | Universal design + public domain tools | (Bedzow, 2021) |
| Ethical AI Use | Preventing harm from automated decisions | IP of biased models | AI developers, ethicists | Audits and ethical licensing | (Shafik, 2025d) |

continued on following page

*Table 2. Continued*

| Dimension | Description | Implication for IP | Stakeholders Involved | Mitigation Strategy | Reference |
|---|---|---|---|---|---|
| Cultural Sensitivity | Respecting indigenous digital content | Misuse of cultural symbols | Indigenous groups, developers | Culturally respectful IP clauses | (Shafik, 2025e) |
| Knowledge Commons | Sharing scientific knowledge | Restrictive publishing licenses | Academics, NGOs | Creative Commons licensing | (Malik, 2024) |
| Privacy Protection | User data handling and consent | Data ownership conflicts | Users, platforms | Data minimization, anonymization | (Shafik, 2025h) |
| Sustainability | Greening digital innovation | Patents restricting green tech | Inventors, environmental groups | Green patent pools | (Nhemi, 2023) |
| Labor Rights | Protecting digital content creators | Infringement of creative works | Freelancers, unions | Digital contract enforcement | (Kretschmer et al., 2024) |
| Educational Equity | Free access to learning tools | Licensing fees for educational tech | Students, institutions | Open educational resources | (Musa et al., 2025) |
| Platform Accountability | Regulation of IP theft on platforms | Platform inaction | Tech firms, enforcement agencies | AI-based IP violation detection | (Shafik, 2025g) |
| Public Interest Design | Prioritizing social benefit in design | Restrictive IP blocking adoption | Developers, public sector | Socially responsible licensing | (Blaskovic et al., 2023) |
| Dual-Use Technologies | Civil vs. military application of tech | Export control and secrecy | Governments, NGOs | Ethics boards, dual-use regulation | (Kretschmer et al., 2024) |

## 5. LEGAL FRAMEWORK SURROUNDING IP AND SOCIAL RESPONSIBILITY

The interplay between social responsibility and intellectual property law is influenced by a variety of legal frameworks, including international treaties and agreements in balance with national laws and regulations. An examination of the international law landscape reveals intellectual property treaties that endorse, to different extents, a need to protect the interests of creators, inventors, and the public domain and only a limited number of treaties that address issues related to social responsibility (Malik, 2024). On the national level, while IP laws also highlight the public interest, such provisions rarely require accountability on the part of rights holders in overcoming issues related to the transfer of ownership and the exercise of rights, countries have enacted laws focused on social responsibility by aiming to align socioeconomic development with the exercise of IP rights (Blaskovic et al., 2023).

International treaties and agreements often do not discuss the need for social responsibility as they primarily regulate the protection of exclusive rights of creators, inventors, and other right holders, limiting the possibility of socially responsible decision making. Various elements of the international intellectual property treaties, which incorporate awareness about the public interest, are nonetheless warranted, including a call for political engagement from members of the international community. Although rights holders cannot be compelled to make decisions that support the public interest, such a situation could be remedied by social media scrutiny that forces them to be aware of the interests beyond their own (Malik, 2024). On the national level, only a handful of countries require rights holders to operate while considering the public interest and the members of the public.

## 5.1. International Treaties and Agreements

The chapter focuses on the social responsibilities of the Intellectual Property System. It examines the social responsibility mechanisms incorporated in IP Treaties, particularly the TRIPS Agreement, the Anti-Counterfeiting Trade Agreement, and the WIPO Copyright Treaty. Then, it highlights the lack of meaningful elaboration in national laws on how public interest considerations can be invoked to limit IP Rights in scope and duration, and the lack of incentive to implement them. International Treaties are binding agreements between sovereign states, negotiated with the intention of promoting collaboration and relations on various issues of mutual interest and concern (Blaskovic et al., 2023). Agreements generally take two forms. Typically, binding treaties obligate parties to act in a particular manner or face sanctions for non-compliance. Alternatively, treaties lay out guiding principles, or aspirations rather than obligations. Often, these principles are vague, open to interpretation, and involve complicated processes before treaties can be invoked. Many treaties are actually of this latter type, with little feasible recourse when party nations violate stipulations. Deliberations on IP Treaties can indeed be classified as the second type (Bogdanov, 2024). The IP treaties referred to obligations that stem from ideas such as reciprocity and cooperation, to respect IP rights in the spirit of these ideas. To this extent, there are obligations on the part of the signatories. Articles of IP Treaties recommend that the signatory countries consider adopting laws that balance IP Rights with public interest considerations. In this sense, IP Treaties form the framework on how nations codify IP Rights into laws and principles to be respected through national laws (Bedzow, 2021). However, the recommendations let signatories elude meaningful implications for violations of Treaties.

## 5.2. National Laws and Regulations

Most countries have adopted various general rules and measures with the aim of promoting regional IP as well as addressing social ills in their territory. In addition, some of them have enacted specific legislation for business activities in diverse sectors of the economy, establishing obligations that respond to these public interests. In the first case, the most important tools of national IP laws and regulations for social responsibility purposes are the concepts of "public order" and "morality." The objective of these measures is to prohibit the exercise of IP rights over materials that are contrary to the values, beliefs and ideals of the culture of the country where IP is registered and/or used, thereby preventing its use to the detriment and offence of its people and community (Savirimuthu, 2017). The major IP-related guidelines of the Berne Convention and the Paris Convention establishing the prohibition of any usages that may violate the Public Order and Morality concept are repeated in national copyright laws or industrial property laws. Other general social responsibility guidelines are also established, including condemnation of use causing public disorder or uncurbed disadvantages to third parties or rich communities, or the obligation not to act in ways inconsistent with fair trading practices. These rules establish specific obligations that are, in essence, an expression of the non-abusive exercise of particular IP rights, ensuring that monopolisation and appropriation of IP are not made to the detriment of society at the expense of shared values (Kretschmer et al., 2024).

## 5.3. Enforcement Challenges

In principle, the national application of IP law enforcement should be subject to the minimum requirements provided for in the international treaties mentioned above. In fact, Article 1(3) states: ".... this Agreement does not create any rights or obligations under existing international agreements, nor does it modify rights and obligations provided for in such agreements". However, the lack of supranational enforcement of IP law enables national lawmakers to create less stringent enforcement conditions of their own. Since enforcement measures differ widely from one country to the next, this may create a loophole, with negative consequences not only for the IP owner but also for social welfare as a whole (Nhemi, 2023). Suppose a country with lax enforcement provisions becomes the destination of choice for producers and/or distributors of counterfeit or pirated goods by a deliberate decision to optimise production or distribution costs. In that case, the negative effects will make themselves felt beyond the borders of that country, affecting the national rather supranational interest. Economic considerations seem to dictate the priorities of many governments and especially developing governments, encouraging development by domestic piracy and counterfeit production or distribution (Malik, 2024). This is an explosive recipe for pragmatic implementation of IP law and a sure way to frustrate legitimate interests, if any. In consequence, only consumers in developed countries and IP owners in both developed and developing countries suffer the adverse effects resulting from the importation of counterfeit and pirated goods. Importantly, however, not only IP owners but also the citizens of the country where the counterfeit and pirated goods originate suffer in the long run from the infringements. In fact, local counterfeit and pirated goods provide no guarantee for the quality and safety standards, and the revenue accruing from the sales does not benefit the local economy (Blaskovic et al., 2023).

## 6. TECHNOLOGICAL ADVANCES AND THEIR IMPACT

The implementation of technology into nearly every aspect of human life has forced a gradually steepening learning curve that has profoundly influenced the way generations experience life. The ease with which information is passed, the speed at which creativity arises, the incrementally lower barrier of technology access, and the instinctual drive to share an element of our humanity are characteristic features of the technological evolution in the digital era. Still, while these features encourage the social good, they also shadow the social needs to protect individuals and structural hierarchies that allow society to function (Bogdanov, 2024). In the case of intellectual property, protecting creations of the mind provides incentives for creativity and helps build an economy around innovation. With respect to emerging generations, Digital Natives are characterised as being tech-savvy and having a unique ability to adapt and absorb technology into their identities from a young age. However, with the growth of being digitally unsurprised also comes the vulnerability of being desensitised to the struggles of the past, in turn moulding a generation that is undereducated on the role of intellectual property in preserving and growing socio-economic prosperity and stability (Kretschmer et al., 2024). The first major impact of technology relates to this digital distribution and sharing. The ease of access to digital content across multiple platforms has increased exposure and consumption tenfold. Never before has sharing been easier, nor has it been more commonplace — except in terms of actual media. However, while drawing from previous technologies, a structural difference in younger generations has been noted. Simply put, youth today expect sharing to be free-flowing and their experience to be a ubiquitous hub of collaboration and experimentation, with the understanding that competitive individuality is not excluded (Malik, 2024). The paradox of the ease and enhancement of digital sharing, which in turn tends to eliminate the ability to be compensated for digitised content relative to traditional IP models for likenesses outside of advertising, is one rooted in the very infancy of social media today, albeit present across time.

## 6.1. Emerging Technologies

Advanced digital technologies constitute both an extraordinary opportunity for socio-economic and intellectual development and a challenge in terms of their effects, caused by the unique features of digital technology. With their extraordinary replicability, inexpensive, immediate, and global connectivity, informing capabilities, and promotion of individuality and mass communities, advanced digital technologies are multicultural and multisectoral actors. Those technologies are convergence technologies, both making existing products obsolete and altering the production and reproduction of artistic works, inventions, and genetic royalty-free traditional resources. They are disruptive technologies (Bogdanov, 2024). Virtual environment new mediums not only amplify creative expressions, but also extend work, knowledge, inventions, and resources. The knowledge embedded in self-learned machine tools is not only capable of producing at full tilt usually scarce products, but of extending the mass consumption of knowledge-digital products to often previously excluded markets. Protection through laws relating to intellectual property is paramount (Bedzow, 2021). Balanced social provisions, avoiding both moral hazards and negative impacts on competitiveness and creativity, ensure the creation, existence, and durability of innovative ecosystems where tried, tested, failed, and revised new ideas generate positive externalities for entrepreneurs and society at large through fast-tracking growth. Public and private financial support to collaborative creation, development, and adaptation of those tools, their continued improvement according to society's changing values, objectives, and priorities, and society's ownership of the advanced tools are critical elements governing any IP-related laws and science and technology policy for the future governance of ex-ante irreversible trajectory evolution (Savirimuthu, 2017).

## 6.2. Digital Distribution and Sharing

Digital technology drastically alters the business model of the distribution of entertainment and creative products by eliminating or radically modifying the distribution and retailing functions. The major development has been a shift from distribution and retailing through physical brick-and-mortar establishments or outlets to an electronic or online distribution model where the facilitation of access to the product is performed by a provider of a digital platform, often through a business model based on providing the content free of charge with advertising revenues covering the costs (Nhemi, 2023). This electronic digital distribution model is less capital-intensive than the model characterised by physical retailers and typically has an international or global reach. This shift favours the development of new, small, and micro-sized enterprises in digital markets that capitalise on the benefits of low transaction costs in the production and promotion of content because of the capabilities of digital technology. The traditional relationship associated with IP that was characterised by products of large corporations sitting alongside the products of small creators on shelves in brick-and-mortar retailing outlets may now be complemented, and in some areas replaced, by a relationship where the products of micro-entities share space on, and possibly dominate, the home page or interface of an online platform (Kretschmer et al., 2024).

The major threat that this development poses is greatly exacerbated by another significant change that inexpensive and easy-to-use digital technology has created in the traditional IP environment. Because creators can produce products of all types and genres quickly and relatively cheaply, the market is flooded with offerings, only some of which are excellent or of high quality. Many online distribution and sharing platforms have no filters in place – unlike brick-and-mortar retail outlets, which curated the stock they carried – and consumers can find it difficult to discriminate between great and mediocre products. The traditional model of IP provided some assurance to consumers that what they were downloading, streaming, or purchasing was of high quality, as the presence of IP protections meant that it had passed through some gateway of quality control (Nhemi, 2023). With the ability to share music and video productions freely, consumers have to rely on word-of-mouth or luck to guide them in their choices.

## 6.3. Effects on Traditional IP Models

The enormous expansion created by internet development, with its global reach, has contributed to the erosion of regional barriers in the field of cultural industries, which were once exclusively tied to physical structures such as newspapers, bookstores, record shops, and cultural centres. Digital technology has eased the tasks of creating and establishing cultural products. The industrial structure of some commodities is being virtually dismantled; selling original products is losing momentum, giving precedence to a model based on the commercialisation of derivatives and access (Malik, 2024). The use of digital technologies is enhancing collaborative projects; collaboration among many people is reducing the importance of the creator and the originality of a work, aiming at a collective creation. In a network made up of thousands of contributors, sometimes present simultaneously, the traditional concept of culture as a product is being dematerialised by free online cultural resources. Therefore, access to knowledge and culture constitutes a new paradigm (Bogdanov, 2024).

In this sense, copyright has specific impacts on two progressive aspects of digital production: access to related cultural products has been made difficult, if not impossible in many cases, by the interference of the copyright owners in the sharing of derivative works protected by copyright; on the other hand, the way that these industries are structured, notably with regard to copyright protection, continually creates friction with the access model, which enables collaborative sharing among unpaid internet users. It can be said that the conception of copyright protection is presently more oriented towards the trade model of access to cultural products. During much of the past century, copyright legislation reflected the economics of scarcity, which served as the basis for access to printed and recorded cultural products. Consequently, the model of limiting access to gain profit from a monopoly in sales was adopted (Savirimuthu, 2017). In the expanding digital era, however, economic models based upon abundance are once again emerging, and the ways users appropriate cultural and knowledge products are drastically altering.

## 7. CASE STUDIES

To illustrate successful models or failed corporate practices, this section explores some representative corporate cases of the technology industry, the area where the conflicts between social responsibility and intellectual property are more virulent nowadays. Policy options can also be explored by way of presentation of advice coming from non-profit initiatives or from coalitions that regroup an increasing number of companies, non-governmental or inter-governmental organisations. Indeed, policy options are suggested by grassroots conditions existing in society and by initiatives run by non-profit actors (Malik, 2024). In contrast, the main stakeholders of the second-best practical solutions considered in the following sections are the industry itself, for obvious reasons, and the governmental regulators who are willing to go beyond pure laissez-faire of the market and to help attain sufficient incentives for firms. Most of the examples regarding social responsibility in the field of intellectual property are indeed cases of the technology industry (Kretschmer et al., 2024). However, for applications of social responsibility in more traditional sectors of activities, as well as particularly significant examples regarding the leafleting of the theme of corporate social responsibility and the design of benchmarks, are coming from the non-profit sector. Social responsibility concerning intellectual property can indeed be more easily observed in the technology industry because of the exceptional ratios of financial profit on productive capital for the leading firms. These impressive financial performances are indeed the result of successful strategies of innovation, which are, in our view, constitutive of the concept of social innovation as it has developed over the past 15 years (Bedzow, 2021).

## 7.1. Classical IP Frameworks Under Digital Pressure

To strengthen the chapter, it is critical to anchor abstract intellectual property (IP) frameworks within real-world cases that demonstrate their contemporary stress points in the digital environment. For instance, the fair use and fair dealing doctrines, long cornerstones of knowledge access, are now central to litigation against generative AI companies that use vast datasets of copyrighted texts and images without explicit consent—such as The New York Times v. OpenAI and visual artists' lawsuits over AI-generated images. Similarly, the concept of derivative works is tested when diffusion models generate new artistic outputs that blur the line between inspiration and infringement. The exhaustion or first-sale doctrine, once straightforward in the physical marketplace, is complicated by NFTs and digital resale markets, where on-chain royalty provisions are often bypassed, undermining artists' claims. Even anti-circumvention rules under laws like the U.S. DMCA have provoked controversy, as they increasingly clash with right-to-repair movements in sectors like agriculture, where companies such as John Deere restrict access to software embedded in tractors, stifling both innovation and sustainability (Malik, 2024). These cases show that while the principles of IP law remain, their application in the digital realm is contested and evolving.

## 7.2. AI, Blockchain, and Global Inequalities in IP

Emerging technologies such as artificial intelligence and blockchain further intensify these dynamics, creating opportunities but also profound governance challenges. In AI, the lack of clear standards for training data disclosure and provenance exacerbates disputes: should AI models be required to catalog the datasets they rely on, and if so, how should ownership, privacy, and consent be addressed? Recent European proposals for AI regulation point toward transparency registries, while countries like Japan and Singapore lean toward flexible text-and-data-mining exceptions to stimulate innovation. Blockchain, often presented as a corrective to opacity, has enabled tamper-proof registries of creative works and programmable smart contracts that automate royalty distribution, as seen in platforms like Audius and Async Art. Yet blockchain also introduces risks of fragmentation—forked chains can undermine record authenticity, while lost private keys can erase claims of ownership altogether (Nhemi, 2023). Globally, disparities remain acute: whereas the European Union pushes harmonized frameworks (such as the Digital Services Act), many Global South countries face enforcement gaps, uneven TRIPS implementation, and a lack of mechanisms to protect Indigenous knowledge from digital misappropriation, such as cases where traditional designs from Maasai or Andean communities have been commercialized without compensation. This divergence underscores the inequity embedded within global IP governance.

## 7.3. From Theory to Policy: Toward Actionable Proposals

To move from diagnosis to solution, theoretical discussions must be recast into actionable policy proposals. One possibility is the establishment of data trusts or collective licensing mechanisms that allow creators to opt into structured agreements for the use of their works in AI training, with revenue-sharing models akin to collective rights management in music. Provenance-by-default systems, such as the Coalition for Content Provenance and Authenticity (C2PA) standard, can attach cryptographic credentials to digital works at creation, enabling verifiable chains of attribution. Governments could also legislate targeted exceptions, allowing DRM circumvention for socially valuable purposes such as cybersecurity research, accessibility for persons with disabilities, or repair of critical devices. To curb monopolistic tendencies, interoperability and portability mandates can ensure users retain control over their digital assets when moving across platforms, an issue at the center of recent antitrust actions against Big Tech. Finally, public-interest IP pools—like the WHO's COVID-19 Technology Access Pool—could be expanded to cover digital infrastructure, ensuring equitable access during crises (Kretschmer et al., 2024). Each of these proposals requires clearly designated responsibilities: regulators to establish baselines, platforms to operationalize compliance, creators to participate in licensing schemes, and civil society to provide oversight.

## 7.4. Enhancing Readability Through Transitions and Summaries

Improving the readability and coherence of the chapter can further elevate its scholarly impact. Sectional transitions can highlight not only conceptual shifts but also normative stakes—for example: "Having examined how blockchain disrupts ownership claims, the next section turns to AI, where opacity over training data poses challenges of transparency and accountability." Short end-of-section summaries could distill insights into four focal points (Bogdanov, 2024):

(1) How analog doctrines transform in digital contexts,
(2) Which actors accrue costs and benefits,
(3) Where consensus exists versus ongoing disputes, and
(4) What immediate policy levers could be piloted?

This scaffolding ensures readers—whether policymakers, academics, or practitioners—leave each section with actionable takeaways.

## 7.5. Interdisciplinary Literature and Digital Justice Perspectives

Finally, the chapter would benefit from deeper integration of interdisciplinary and contemporary literature on digital justice and technology ethics. Scholars such as Ruha Benjamin (Race After Technology) and Safiya Noble (Algorithms of Oppression) demonstrate how structural inequities manifest in digital systems, with direct relevance to IP debates. Abeba Birhane's critiques of "algorithmic colonization" shed light on the ways AI practices extract value from the Global South, while legal scholars such as Julie Cohen and Madhavi Sunder explore the intersection of IP with power, identity, and equity (Nhemi, 2023). Equally, contributions from practitioners and organizations like IT for Change, Derechos Digitales in Latin America, and the African Union's AI frameworks offer grounded perspectives on Global South realities. Including these works not only modernizes the bibliography but also reinforces the chapter's central claim: that intellectual property in the digital era cannot be disentangled from broader struggles for fairness, inclusivity, and social responsibility (Savirimuthu, 2017).

## 7.6. Successful Corporate Practices

In the following case studies, we illustrate some successful corporate practices aimed at contributing to social development by addressing real social needs and doing so in partnership with stakeholders. In all our case studies, investment in research and development by companies is what drives innovation and facilitates the development and delivery of new or enhanced goods and services to society. We also hope to demonstrate the role of intellectual property in the innovation-development-delivery process. The development and introduction of new and improved goods and services into a market economy is generally associated with patenting and trademarking (Blaskovic et al., 2023). Likewise, the preservation and enforcement of the exclusive right attached to inventions and trademarks provides a favoured avenue that facilitates an appropriate return on investment. This, in turn, contributes to sustainable development. Indeed, as a fundamental rule, capitalist development, propelled by private economic agents who, faced with the impulse of maximising the rate of return on investment, simultaneously deploy the resources to the most efficient allocation possible, contributes to the common good and the realisation of social responsibilities, as long as the rules of the game which affect private choices are symbiotic with the requirements to preserve society's endowment of resources (Kretschmer et al., 2024). We start by describing some illustrative cases of positive corporate involvement in society. Our stand, in this report, is that the positive contribution of the corporation to society is not only possible, but it is also profitable for the corporation itself, and can be sponsored by an informed set of institutional rules. We start by describing a few prominent examples, and then we draw some tentative conclusions. When questioned about the long-term future and the essence of business, the legendary founder of IBM famously said: “The business of business is more business” (Malik, 2024).

## 7.7. Failures and Lessons Learned

Much to the earners' chagrin, however, there are many other such examples. Because these practices are so common, we'd like to elaborate a little further on some unsuccessful attempts at social responsibility in business, in the hopes that businesses can learn from their mistakes. This list is not exhaustive, and not every corporation mentioned fails to include philosophy & action in their practices. But the following rundown illustrates the waffling and questionable behaviour of these companies and how they tarnish the ideals of social responsibility. The Kodak Company, founded in 1888 as Eastman Kodak, launched the concept of actually taking pictures on film (Nhemi, 2023). For a century after, Kodak was synonymous with photography, with its colour film products used in cameras worldwide. It introduced a host of innovations, including pocket cameras, instant photography, and digital cameras with integrated memory chips and colour LCD screens. It operated some of the world's biggest and best-known movie production studios. The term Kodak moment was meant to symbolise a fleeting instant that gives people pleasure so that they can cherish it forever. It was targeted at philosophers, thinkers, and the like. The corporation's failure was that they decided to focus entirely on business at the expense of these actions. This prompted the company's failure to offer digital prints in the very infancy of digital technology, and excessive reliance on slide and rare black-and-white print film (Savirimuthu, 2017). In 2012, Kodak filed for bankruptcy protection, facing more than $6 billion in debt and unable to pay bills, and was delisted from the stock market.

## 7.8. Non-Profit Initiatives

Social accountability principles motivate civil society actors to lobby for voluntary corporate engagement that takes social, environmental, and human rights impacts into account. Promotion of accountability and setting international standards is a core function of intergovernmental organisations. This is also true for the World Intellectual Property Organisation, which has made major advancements in the inclusion of non-profit organisations in its work and a few other intergovernmental organisations active in intellectual property in recent years. The World Health Organisation played a notable role in this regard in relation to health issues (Shafik, 2024b). The Trade-related Aspects of Intellectual Property Rights Agreement and Public Health Committee, combined with pandemic impulses to mobilise the public around intellectual property exceptions for health technology and to probe the measures of the Global North after the emergence of new trademarks, has been successful in moving the World Health Organization and other intergovernmental organisations to look at the intellectual property issues with a social responsibility lens. One of the most prominent civil society initiatives is Creative Commons, which enables owners of intellectual property to choose the exposure of their creation according to their wishes (Shafik, 2024g). The Digital Public Library of America connects people to the riches of our shared scholarly, cultural, and historical heritage through an innovative and open model of collaboration. Artstor is a non-profit organisation that shares communal art and visual imagery. The Social Web Working Group published a recommendation for decentralised Identifiers. The teaching and academic worlds are waking up to the opportunities of a creative commons approach. The American Association of University Professors has granted permission for universities to post academic work that the author has previously published in a journal, essentially allowing their work to go open-access without tripping over copyright or academic publisher restrictions (Shafik, 2024e).

## 8. FUTURE DIRECTIONS

The only thing we know about the future is that it is going to be different from today. Therefore, we hope that future research, policies, and actions encourage and enable a different today. The digital technology world of tomorrow will probably be more accessible, more equitable, and more productive than that of today. IP law will also likely be different one day. More balanced. More in sync with technological, social, and cultural developments. The balance has always changed over time. In different historical eras. In different countries, regions, and cultures. And the balance bounces back and forth continuously (Shafik, 2024c). To address new needs. To respond to new uses and uses. To account for new cultural realities.

Somewhere in between, the different stakeholders need to continue to engage with each other. To ensure that the voices of everyone are indeed taken into account in the different discussions, negotiations, and dealings. Inventors and brands included. Creators themselves at the core of any creative ecosystem included. Authors and performers included. Intermediaries included. Societies at large included. From this engagement, we will hopefully will not only ensure a balance in the contemporary world of identity and creativity (Nhemi, 2023). This positive collaboration can also strengthen the basic ideas behind IP law. Identity. Creativity. In order to nourish respect. To inspire future generations of creators to pursue their work. The plan. The resolve. The dream. The heavenly moonshot. To be able to write about, design, and create tomorrow should be the same for all of us. To feel empowered and inspired. In a world with fair distribution of revenue from works. And know that no matter what, the world we create together will, in turn, inspire tomorrow's generations (Kretschmer et al., 2024). The generations above us. But also at the same time the impending generations to come.

## 8.1. Trends in Social Responsibility

Numerous indicators confirm that there has been a transformation in the firm's role in society. This shift is manifested in a variety of ways, beginning with a greater interest in ethics by companies following scandals from the 1990s, and continuing with a galloping development of CSR strategies that, in just a few decades, have gone from something voluntarily adopted and declared by a small group of companies, to something which more than 90% of businesses now report on, and which is indispensable for accessing half of the invested capital in the United States and Europe (Savirimuthu, 2017). Furthermore, the current regulatory landscape, with laws that incorporate responsibility considerations into a company's strategy and the firm´s welfare obligations towards its workers, clients, the environment, and broader society, especially during the recent pandemic, is solidifying these positions. As a result of the evolution of the concept, CSR's main shortcomings are being directly tackled:

(i) CSR 2.0 is focused on solving "the grand challenges for humanity", emphasizing the pursuit of positive impacts for the majority, with the aim of mapping the universe of possible actions -and reporting them-, making it possible to choose the paths that would have the greatest value for society, and providing tools to measure them;
(ii) CSR 2.0 incorporates the firm's influence on democracy, its fight against inequality and corruption, and the oversight of the social system of market capitalism, referring to the creature—the company—who has become so powerful that it can "run away" from the government that allowed it to exist.

CSR 2.0 aims to align the interests of shareholders, stakeholders, and the broader society around the idea of creating an inspiring vision - co-created with stakeholders through a bottom-up approach - that makes the company the primary driver of social change, while generating wealth and prosperity for shareholders and investing in the talent of its workers.

## 8.2. Evolving IP Laws

As the development of digital technology redefines society and culture, social responsibility moves into a new domain of meaning. One of the most explicit expressions of evolving conceptions of social responsibility is through the development of legal norms. From labour and environmental law to antitrust legislation, the law enforcers recognised standards of corporate behaviour. Because of the importance of intellectual property to the growth of digital technology and its use and influence on users, societies, and cultures, intellectual property law must communicate an understanding of social responsibility consistent with other laws that impose costs and obligations (Malik, 2024). At the same time, the continued growth and innovation in the digital technology field depend on the continued efficacy of intellectual property laws to provide sufficient protection and economic stimulus. This means that lawmakers and politicians should constantly monitor how users and companies are using digital technology and balance their laws accordingly. In some instances, lawmakers have reflected a responsiveness to the concerns of other areas of law (Bogdanov, 2024). For example, earlier difficulties in obtaining patent protection for business methods and software led to Congress passing the American Inventor's Protection Act. A provision of the Act calls for a report from the Patent and Trademark Office describing efforts to improve the patent system and ways to improve the quality and timeliness of patent examination and the quality of patent examinations relied upon in the development of products and services based on patents. In the wake of criticism of patent examinations, the Patent Office now requires the use of mandatory electronic filing, which helps to identify issues early in the patent prosecution process by bringing important components of applications to the front (Bedzow, 2021).

## 8.3. Role of Stakeholders

Achieving the ideal balance between social responsibility and intellectual property will require the participation of multiple stakeholders. Developers need to realise that, while the laws of IP can be very clear, they can also be interpreted differently by different jurisdictions. For e-commerce companies, the issue of which jurisdiction to reside in can translate to huge legal risks. Clearer arbitration guidelines for different regions should therefore become the norm to allow for better legal clarity. Governments can help by establishing clearer IP laws to regulate the digital economy and in particular, the many private entities operating in this sector. They should examine the extent to which these entities should be held accountable for enforcing IP laws, as opposed to having the responsibility solely on the IPR owners (Malik, 2024). Further, while e-commerce is driving economic growth for many countries with boons such as job creation and access to cheap consumer goods, it can also contribute to the economic decline of others besieged by piracy. Countries with great macroeconomic imbalances can rely on global cooperation to resolve these issues. Rights holders, in turn, should take steps to properly follow the law regarding their products to avoid losing their legal protection against infringement. By working together with governments, businesses, and non-governmental stakeholders, they should educate the public about the value that IP adds to a product and the adverse effects that piracy, especially counterfeiting, can have on their lives. For e-commerce businesses, it is tempting to dismiss the issue of IP infringement as merely a question of taking down listings. However, many companies are finding themselves in the unenviable position of having a product taken down too many times, despite having ensured that it is completely legal (Bedzow, 2021; Malik, 2024). Such companies should engage with governments and rights holders, and create the right processes to work together to clear any confusion that may arise collaboratively.

## 9. CONCLUSION

We examined how the modern regime of intellectual property protection is inadequate for addressing the challenges of digital technology. The pre-digital system is not only outmoded and inadequate but actively harmful. As applied, intellectual property law has the perverse effect of distancing the products, including information and knowledge, from the commons, that is, the common intellectual capital in which all of humanity has a vested interest and which sustains further growth both in the repertoire available for individual creativity and economic development in general. However, rather than pushing back against this distortion by returning to the spirit of social responsibility underlying the original philosophy of intellectual property law, policymakers and the courts have doubled down on a creed of protectionism and ever more expansive monopolisation. The results have been all too visible and disheartening. Information and knowledge, central ingredients in any economy, are withheld from use by government and all manner of nonprofit and social enterprises, even while the invisible hand creates the demand for these products. Each new day in the 21st century is worse than the last. Economic pressure drives millions to the streets, when all that is needed to turn the tide is to open the floodgates to the commons and let access and creativity work their magic. Digital technologies hold the promise of a miracle, and with them, the intellectual technology on which they rest. What is lacking is the social infrastructure that would encourage creativity, invention, and enterprise without burdening them with the albatross of self-imposed constriction and exclusion. As we look toward the future, it is evident that social responsibility and intellectual property will continue to evolve in ways that defy linear prediction, shaped by rapid technological disruptions, shifting legal frameworks, and emerging ethical dilemmas. While the trajectory remains uncertain, one personal conviction is clear: societies must strive for a balance between protecting creators' rights and fostering open, equitable access to knowledge and innovation. This balance will not be achieved through regulation alone but through a collective ethical commitment from governments, corporations, and individuals alike to safeguard human dignity, inclusivity, and fairness in digital ecosystems. If we remain attentive to these values, even amid uncertainty, the digital age can become not merely a space of commodification but one of shared responsibility and sustainable intellectual growth.

## REFERENCES


Ahmad, J. (2019). Branding corporate social responsibility: A case study on public-listed telecommunication companies in malaysia. *Media Watch, 10*(2). Advance online publication. DOI: 10.15655/mw/2019/v10i2/49638

Akpan, J. U., & Oluwagbade, O. I. (2024). Social and Environmental Responsibility in Accounting: Beyond Financial Metrics. *INTERNATIONAL JOURNAL OF SOCIAL SCIENCES AND MANAGEMENT RESEARCH, 9*(9). Advance online publication. DOI: 10.56201/ijssmr.v9.no9.2023.pg163.188

Anwar, G. A., Hussain, M., Akber, M. Z., Khan, M. A., & Khan, A. A. (2023). Sustainability-Oriented Optimization and Decision Making of Community Buildings under Seismic Hazard. *Sustainability (Switzerland), 15*(5). Advance online publication. DOI: 10.3390/su15054385

Bedzow, I. (2021). Patents on Life: Religious, Moral, and Social Justice Aspects of Biotechnology and Intellectual Property. Edited by Thomas C. Berg, Roman Cholij, and Simon Ravenscroft. Cambridge: Cambridge University Press, 2019. Pp. 313. $110.00 (cloth); $88.00 (digital). ISBN: 9781108659802. *Journal of Law and Religion, 36*(2). https://doi.org/DOI: 10.1017/jlr.2021.25

Blaskovic, A. K., Rusk, J. D., Parker, V. C., & Payne, B. R. (2023). Cybercrime and Intellectual Property Theft: An Analysis of Modern Digital Forensics. *Lecture Notes in Networks and Systems, 560 LNNS*. https://doi.org/DOI: 10.1007/978-3-031-18458-1_36

Bogdanov, D. E. (2024). The Legal Regime of the AI Generated Results: Anthropocentrism vs. Transhumanism in the Field of Intellectual Property Law. *Lex Russica, 77*(1). Advance online publication. DOI: 10.17803/1729-5920.2024.206.1.032-053

Carvalho, L., Mota, C., & Ramos, P. (2024). Socially Responsible Investment Funds—An Analysis Applied to Funds Domiciled in the Portuguese and Spanish Markets. *Risks, 12*(1). Advance online publication. DOI: 10.3390/risks12010009

Chang, Y. L., & Ke, J. (2024). Socially Responsible Artificial Intelligence Empowered People Analytics: A Novel Framework Towards Sustainability. *Human Resource Development Review, 23*(1). Advance online publication. DOI: 10.1177/15344843231200930

Jia, T., Iqbal, S., Ayub, A., Fatima, T., & Rasool, Z. (2023). Promoting Responsible Sustainable Consumer Behavior through Sustainability Marketing: The Boundary Effects of Corporate Social Responsibility and Brand Image. *Sustainability (Switzerland), 15*(7). Advance online publication. DOI: 10.3390/su15076092

KOROL, S., & ROMASHKO, O. (2022). Corporate social responsibility in transfer pricing strategies. *Foreign Trade: Economics, Finance. Law, 122*(3). Advance online publication. DOI: 10.31617/zt.knute.2022(122)01

Kretschmer, M., Margoni, T., & Oruç, P. (2024). Copyright Law and the Lifecycle of Machine Learning Models. *IIC International Review of Intellectual Property and Competition Law, 55*(1). Advance online publication. DOI: 10.1007/s40319-023-01419-3

Long, T. B., & Blok, V. (2023). Managing the Responsibilities of Doing Good and Avoiding Harm in Sustainability-Orientated Innovations: Example from Agri-Tech Start-Ups in the Netherlands. In *Library of Ethics and Applied Philosophy* (Vol. 40). https://doi.org/DOI: 10.1007/978-3-031-14710-4_13

Malik, S. A. (2024). SDG 2: Zero hunger, food and plant-related intellectual property, and access to plant genetic resources. In *The Elgar Companion to Intellectual Property and the Sustainable Development Goals*. https://doi.org/DOI: 10.4337/9781803925233.00009

Merolla, A. J., Neubauer, A. B., & Otmar, C. D. (2024). Responsiveness, Social Connection, Hope, and Life Satisfaction in Everyday Social Interaction: An Experience Sampling Study. *Journal of Happiness Studies, 25*(1–2). Advance online publication. DOI: 10.1007/s10902-024-00710-5

Musa, S., Abubakari, M. S., & Abdulwahab, L. O. (2025). Evaluating the potential of adapting Artificial Intelligence (AI) in small and medium enterprises for competitive advantage. In *Multi-Industry Digitalization and Technological Governance in the AI Era* (pp. 233–266). IGI Global., DOI: 10.4018/979-8-3373-1681-9.ch012

Narayanan, S., & Pradhan, S. K. (2024). Exploring the research landscape of socially responsible investment through bibliometrics. In *Multidisciplinary Reviews* (Vol. 7, Issue 1). https://doi.org/DOI: 10.31893/multirev.2024022

Ndou, A. T., Madonsela, N. S., & Twala, B. (2020). The era of digital technology: Analysis of factors contributing to economic growth and sustainability. *Proceedings of the International Conference on Industrial Engineering and Operations Management,* 59.

Nhemi, S. (2023). Law Without Lawyers: Examining the Limitations of Consumer-Centric Legal Tech Services. [JIPIT]. *Journal of Intellectual Property and Information Technology Law, 3*(1). Advance online publication. DOI: 10.52907/jipit.v3i1.223

Rashid, N., Daud, W. N. W., Zainol, F. A., Salleh, F., Yazid, A. S., Endut, W. A., Yaakub, N., Ghazali, P. L., Afthanorhan, A., & Abdullah, B. (2018). The Stakeholders Perceptions towards the Corporate Social Responsibility Reporting. *International Journal of Academic Research in Business & Social Sciences*, *8*(11). Advance online publication. DOI: 10.6007/ijarbss/v8-i11/5171

Savirimuthu, J. (2017). Trademarks in the age of social media. *Journal of Intellectual Property Law & Practice*, *12*(1). Advance online publication. DOI: 10.1093/jiplp/jpw199

Shafik, W. (2023). *A Comprehensive Cybersecurity Framework for Present and Future Global Information Technology Organizations*. https://doi.org/DOI: 10.4018/978-1-6684-9018-1.ch002

Shafik, W. (2024a). Artificial Intelligence and Machine Learning with Cyber Ethics for the Future World. In *Future Communication Systems Using Artificial Intelligence, Internet of Things and Data Science* (pp. 110–130). CRC Press., DOI: 10.1201/9781032648309-9

Shafik, W. (2024b). Connected healthcare—the impact of Internet of Things on medical services. In *Artificial Intelligence and Internet of Things based Augmented Trends for Data Driven Systems* (pp. 181–217). CRC Press., DOI: 10.1201/9781003497318-10

Shafik, W. (2024c). Digital healthcare systems in a federated learning perspective. In *Federated Learning for Digital Healthcare Systems* (pp. 1–35). Elsevier.

Shafik, W. (2024d). Generative AI for Social Good and Sustainable Development. In *Generative AI: Current Trends and Applications* (pp. 185–217). Springer.

Shafik, W. (2024e). IoT-Enabled Secure and Intelligent Smart Healthcare: Beyond 5G in Enabling Smart Cities. In *Secure and Intelligent IoT-Enabled Smart Cities* (pp. 308–333). IGI Global.

Shafik, W. (2024f). Sustainable Development. In Viana Hassan, A. S. S. B. (Ed.), *Building Community Resiliency and Sustainability With Tourism Development* (1st ed., Vol. 1, pp. 1–30). IGI Global., DOI: 10.4018/979-8-3693-5405-6.ch001

Shafik, W. (2024g). The Future of Healthcare: AIoMT—Redefining Healthcare with Advanced Artificial Intelligence and Machine Learning Techniques. In *Artificial Intelligence and Machine Learning in Drug Design and Development* (pp. 605–634). Wiley., DOI: 10.1002/9781394234196.ch19

Shafik, W. (2024h). Toward a More Ethical Future of Artificial Intelligence and Data Science. In *The Ethical Frontier of AI and Data Analysis* (pp. 362–388). IGI Global., DOI: 10.4018/979-8-3693-2964-1.ch022

Shafik, W. (2025a). Data Loss Software Reason and Hardware Reason. In *Data Recovery Techniques for Computer Forensics* (pp. 27–61). Bentham Science Publishers.

Shafik, W. (2025b). Digital twins tools and technologies. In *Digital Twins for Smart Cities and Villages* (pp. 55–80). Elsevier., https://doi.org/https://doi.org/10.1016/B978-0-443-28884-5.00003-8

Shafik, W. (2025c). Ethical and legal considerations in artificial intelligence. *AI-Enabled Threat Intelligence and Cyber Risk Assessment*, 90.

Shafik, W. (2025d). Generative Adversarial Networks: Security, Privacy, and Ethical Considerations. In *Generative Artificial Intelligence (AI) Approaches for Industrial Applications* (pp. 93–117). Springer.

Shafik, W. (2025e). Human-Computer Interaction (HCI) Technologies in Socially-Enabled Artificial Intelligence. In *Future of Digital Technology and AI in Social Sectors* (pp. 121–150). IGI Global.

Shafik, W. (2025f). Machine Learning Techniques for Multicriteria Decision-Making. In *Multi-Criteria Decision-Making and Optimum Design with Machine Learning* (pp. 165–194). CRC Press.

Shafik, W. (2025g). Security, 15 Privacy, and Trust in Fintech. *FinTech and Financial Inclusion: Leveraging Digital Finance for Economic Empowerment and Sustainable Growth*, 216.

Shafik, W. (2025h). The Next Generation of Health Monitoring: Digital Twins and Medical Wearables. In *AI-Powered Digital Twins for Predictive Healthcare: Creating Virtual Replicas of Humans* (pp. 69–106). IGI Global Scientific Publishing.

Shafik, W., Singh, R., & Kumar, V. (2025). Artificial Intelligence Transparency and Explainability in Sustainable Healthcare. In *Transforming Healthcare Sector Through Artificial Intelligence and Environmental Sustainability* (pp. 165–191). Springer.

Tran, N. H. (2023). IMPACT FACTORS ON THE ADOPTION OF CORPORATE SOCIAL RESPONSIBILITY: EMPIRICAL EVIDENCE FROM AN EMERGING MARKET. *Corporate Governance and Organizational Behavior Review, 7*(2 Special Issue). https://doi.org/DOI: 10.22495/cgobrv7i2sip13

Vinueza Villagran, D. B., Amparito Cecilia, L. S., Guamán Guevara, M. D., & Luis Fabricio, G. G. (2024). Motivations for environmental social responsibility in ecuadorian banana companies. *Universidad, Ciencia y Tecnología, 28*(122). Advance online publication. DOI: 10.47460/uct.v28i122.764

Vo, N. N. Y., He, X., Liu, S., & Xu, G. (2019). Deep learning for decision making and the optimization of socially responsible investments and portfolio. *Decision Support Systems, 124*. Advance online publication. DOI: 10.1016/j.dss.2019.113097

Vulturius, G., Maltais, A., & Forsbacka, K. (2024). Sustainability-linked bonds–their potential to promote issuers' transition to net-zero emissions and future research directions. *Journal of Sustainable Finance & Investment, 14*(1). Advance online publication. DOI: 10.1080/20430795.2022.2040943

Wu, Q., Liu, X., Qin, J., Zhou, L., Mardani, A., & Deveci, M. (2022). An integrated multi-criteria decision-making and multi-objective optimization model for socially responsible portfolio selection. *Technological Forecasting and Social Change, 184*. Advance online publication. DOI: 10.1016/j.techfore.2022.121977

## KEY TERMS AND DEFININITIONS

**Algorithmic Governance:** The use of algorithms and automated decision-making systems to regulate, guide, or influence social, economic, or political processes.

**Blockchain-Based IP Protection:** The use of blockchain technology to securely register, track, and verify ownership and usage rights of intellectual property.

**Copyright Infringement Detection:** The process of identifying unauthorized use, reproduction, or distribution of copyrighted works through automated or manual systems.

**Data Sovereignty:** The principle that digital data is subject to the laws, governance, and regulatory frameworks of the nation where it is collected or stored.

**Digital Governance Frameworks:** Structured policies, norms, and mechanisms that guide the ethical, legal, and technological management of digital ecosystems.

**Digital Rights Management (DRM):** A set of technologies and policies used to control access to, distribution of, and usage rights for digital content.

**Ethical Data Stewardship:** The responsible management, use, and protection of data in ways that respect privacy, fairness, and societal values.

**Intellectual Property (IP) Ethics:** The study and practice of ensuring fairness, justice, and societal balance in the creation, ownership, and distribution of intellectual property.

**Open Access Licensing:** A publishing model that makes research outputs freely available online, usually under permissive licenses that allow reuse with proper attribution.

**Socio-Legal Accountability:** The obligation of individuals, organizations, or governments to answer for their actions within both legal frameworks and broader social norms.

# Chapter 6
# Critical Digital Competencies and Pedagogical Frameworks Within Human Rights Jurisprudence:
## Democratic Accountability and Policy Implications

**Ashraf Alam**
https://orcid.org/0000-0001-6178-1187
*Alliance University, Bengaluru, India*

## ABSTRACT

*This chapter reframes digital literacy as a justiciable facet of the right to education. Blending learning science and ethics, it defines competencies that unite critical judgment, data literacy, multimodal authorship, computational reasoning, safety, and civic responsibility. Using the A4A lens of availability, accessibility, acceptability, and adaptability, it links pedagogy to enablers such as teacher capacity, universal design, trustworthy analytics, and multilingual content. Comparative examples from Finland, Singapore, India, and sub-Saharan Africa show divergent governance and equity gaps. The analysis examines datafication, algorithmic bias, and surveillance risk while assessing the affordances of AI and immersive media. A pragmatic framework specifies design levers, learning evidence, and policy tools that align finance and accountability. Digital literacy is advanced as public infrastructure for democratic participation and dignified work across the life course.*

DOI: 10.4018/979-8-3373-8510-5.ch006

## 1. INTRODUCTION

Contemporary education is undergoing a structural inflection as digital architectures infiltrate cognition, communication, and institutional practice (Nada & Sari, 2020; Palacios-Hidalgo & Huertas-Abril, 2025). Microcomputers, broadband networks, and mobile platforms have migrated from peripheral tools to constitutive substrates of knowledge work (Mokhtari, 2023; Portillo et al., 2020). The pandemic shock of 2020 exposed this dependency when school closures displaced learning for nearly 1.6 billion students worldwide and compelled abrupt transitions to remote modalities. Within a human rights frame, this turbulence reasserts the right to education as an enforceable entitlement rather than a discretionary good (Adler et al., 2023; Kim et al., 2018). The four A principles of availability, accessibility, acceptability, and adaptability acquire concrete digital correlates that include resilient connectivity, device sufficiency, culturally and linguistically responsive content, and pedagogies that flex across modalities (Cubukcu & Bazyan, 2018; Phuapan et al., 2016). Digital literacy therefore functions as enabling capability and due process safeguard (Ahmad et al., 2023; Zadražilová & Vizváry, 2021). It secures meaningful access to instructional resources, protects learners from exclusionary design and opaque data practices, and supports participation in academic governance (Porat et al., 2018; Saliu & Bicaj, 2022). When states legislate curriculum standards, fund infrastructure, and capacitate teachers, they discharge obligations of immediate effect and progressive realization (Casillas Martín et al., 2020; Krumsvik, 2011). When they neglect these duties, connectivity deserts and device scarcity devolve into rights deficits that entrench inequality across gender, caste, disability, and geography.

Digital literacy has evolved from mechanistic routines to a composite of procedural, epistemic, and ethical competencies (García-Vandewalle García et al., 2023; Reddy et al., 2020). Taxonomies distinguish discrete skills such as search syntax, file management, or spreadsheet fluency from higher order literacies that integrate critical appraisal, multimodal authorship, and collaborative problem solving (Carretero et al., 2017; Pegalajar Palomino & Rodríguez Torres, 2023). Competence denotes a stable configuration of knowledge, skills, and dispositions that permits autonomous and accountable action in complex digital ecologies (Abrosimova, 2020; Sefton-Green et al., 2009). Contemporary frameworks enumerate domains that include information and data literacy, communication and collaboration, digital content creation, safety, and problem solving, thereby binding media studies, information science, and computational reasoning into a single architecture (Ei & Soon, 2021; Maher, 2020). A rights compatible approach extends this architecture with privacy stewardship, algorithmic transparency, accessibility by design, and linguistic inclusion so that participation is substantive rather than nominal (Cartelli, 2013; Morellato, 2014). Epistemic vigilance against misinformation protects democratic deliberation and guards the integrity of learning (Tømte et al., 2015; Koch & Fehlmann, 2025). Agency is cultivated when learners interrogate provenance, surface bias, and contest automated decisions (Martínez-Alcalá et al., 2018; Nelson et al., 2011). In this idiom, digital literacy operationalizes the right to seek, receive, and impart information while respecting the dignity and security of others.

Workforce transformation intensifies the stakes since automation and data driven systems reconfigure occupational demand while opening new roles that privilege hybrid human machine collaboration (Romero-García et al., 2020; Tomaszewicz, 2015). Recent global analyses suggest tens of millions of jobs will be displaced while a similar magnitude of new roles will emerge, with employers signaling near universal demand for digital competencies (Choudhary, 2024; Reddy et al., 2022). The right to education responds by mandating equitable pathways for reskilling across the life course, including adults and older learners who were schooled before the digital turn (Maderick et al., 2016; Tejedor et al., 2020). Policy instruments that subsidize learning credits, standardize microcredentials, and recognize prior learning translate rights discourse into portable opportunities (Brevik et al., 2019; Vuorikari et al., 2022). Institutions must invest in teacher preparation, assistive technologies, and secure learning platforms, and must enact accountable data governance that minimizes collection, limits purpose creep, and ensures effective remedies (Peters, 2024; Zhao et al., 2021). Curriculum must cultivate critical AI literacy, ethical reasoning, and civic media fluency alongside technical dexterity so that graduates can navigate algorithmic workplaces and democratic publics (He & Zhu, 2017; Li & Ranieri, 2010). When states, providers, and communities co produce these conditions, digital literacy becomes a democratizing force that advances equal educational opportunity and strengthens human capabilities (Christine, 2017; Tinmaz et al., 2023). When they fail, technocratic modernization curdles into exclusion, surveillance, and stratification that violate the spirit and letter of the right to education.

## 2. THEORETICAL FOUNDATIONS OF DIGITAL LITERACY

Digital literacy rests on convergent theories that treat learning as active, social, and distributed while grounding practice in the right to education (Darcy, 2019; Garzón-Artacho et al., 2021). Constructivism explains how learners build schemas through problem solving with technological artefacts, and constructionism shows how code and media externalize thought so that reasoning becomes inspectable and improvable (Gisbert Cervera & Lázaro Cantabrana, 2015; Reichert et al., 2020). Vygotskian mediation adds dialogic scaffolding through peers, educators, and intelligent tutors that calibrate support within the zone of proximal development (Koltay, 2011; Kuzminska et al., 2019). Connectivism and distributed cognition extend agency across networks of people, tools, and repositories, where knowledge flows along relational and technical nodes (Chan et al., 2017; Gutierrez-Angel et al., 2022). A rights-based lens converts these insights into duties for availability, accessibility, acceptability, and adaptability in digital contexts, which require resilient connectivity, device sufficiency, inclusive content, and flexible pedagogy (Table 1) (Buskqvist & Johansson, 2024; Legvart et al., 2021). When these conditions hold, learners inhabit personal learning ecologies that foster transfer, metacognition, and collaborative authorship, and digital literacy becomes not only skill acquisition but the institutional guarantee of meaningful participation in knowledge production.

*Table 1. Foundational Lenses for Digital Literacy Learning Design and Evaluation*

| Foundational Lens | Core Premise and Constructs | Mechanism of Learning in Digital Contexts | Curriculum and Pedagogic Design Levers | Assessment and Evidence Signals |
|---|---|---|---|---|
| **Constructivism and Constructionism** | Enactive cognition, artifact mediated knowledge building, equilibration, reflective abstraction, metacognitive monitoring, externalization through making | Rapid prototyping and debugging, immediate feedback loops, explanation while building, cognitive offloading with manipulatives and notebooks | Studio projects, maker tasks from blocks to text, authentic data problems, reflective design logs, scaffold fading and transfer | Analytic rubrics, version control telemetry, error taxonomy profiles, think aloud traces, confidence calibration versus accuracy |
| **Socio cultural Mediation and ZPD** | Tool mediated cognition, guided participation, internalization via dialogic scaffolding, appropriation of cultural tools, co regulation to self-regulation | Peer instruction, adaptive prompting, social annotation, collaborative documents, reciprocal teaching protocols | Role structured teams, mentoring ladders, normed peer review, talk moves, metacognitive prompts for self-explanation | Discourse move analysis, helpfulness weighted contribution analytics, time to scaffold independence, transfer growth indices, rater reliability |
| **Distributed Cognition** | Human artifact system as cognitive unit, external representations extend working memory, coordination fluency reduces cognitive load and error | Task decomposition, shared dashboards, boundary objects, workflow automation, checklist governed handoffs | Instrumented notebooks, representational fluency training, collaboration contracts, pipeline and handoff design | Coordination quality from trace logs, latency and rework rates, representation coverage, tool switch efficiency, slip and lapse reduction |

continued on following page

*Table 1. Continued*

| Foundational Lens | Core Premise and Constructs | Mechanism of Learning in Digital Contexts | Curriculum and Pedagogic Design Levers | Assessment and Evidence Signals |
|---|---|---|---|---|
| **Connectivism** | Knowledge in network topologies, competence as node discovery filtering and update, diversity confers resilience and adaptability | Personal learning environments, lateral exploration, selective subscription and pruning, balance of weak and strong ties | Network mapping of sources, community curation, federated note gardens, API based mashups across repositories | Network diversity and centrality indices, time to credible source, novelty intake without coherence loss, portfolio breadth, documented node revision |
| **Critical Digital Literacy** | Interrogation of power bias and surveillance, platform political economy, algorithmic accountability, ethics as practice | Interface deconstruction, provenance tracing, adversarial search, privacy and threat modeling, rights-based deliberation | Verification labs, model and data cards, privacy by default routines, data justice dialogues, contextual consent practices | Epistemic vigilance scores, robustness to deception, documented value tradeoffs, privacy configuration appropriateness, ethical reasoning quality |
| **Information and Media Literacy** | Strategic search, triangulation, bias mitigation, multimodal comprehension, provenance chains, calibrated confidence | Upstream source checks, credential vetting, cross language querying, structured comparisons, retrieval as augmentation | Claim evidence reasoning routines, timed fact checks, dataset lineage exercises, multimodal synthesis with uncertainty statements | Source classification precision and recall, time to justified judgment, calibration curves, sustained provenance use, post task error correction |
| **Computational Thinking and Code Literacies** | Decomposition, abstraction, algorithm design, debugging, representation choice, complexity management, testability and instrumentation | Progression visual to text paradigms, pair programming, test driven development, telemetry and profiling, code review dialogues | Unplugged to robotics, domain specific languages for rapid prototyping, sandboxed experimentation, explicit pattern libraries | Test coverage versus specification, cyclomatic complexity fit, defect taxonomy decline, rationale in review notes, pattern transfer to novel tasks |

continued on following page

*Table 1. Continued*

| Foundational Lens | Core Premise and Constructs | Mechanism of Learning in Digital Contexts | Curriculum and Pedagogic Design Levers | Assessment and Evidence Signals |
|---|---|---|---|---|
| **Competency Frameworks and Standards** | Structured progression, citizen framework with five areas twenty-one competencies eight proficiency levels, teacher framework with six dimensions three stages | Descriptors mapped to tasks, feedback aligned to levels, integration of pedagogy assessment and organization for growth | Competence mapping, stackable micro credentials, capstones aligned to upper descriptors, professional learning communities by strands | Standards aligned rubrics, e portfolios evidencing progression, inter rater moderation, periodic benchmarking, cross institution portability |
| **Synthesis and Integrated Praxis** | Multidimensional assemblage uniting cognitive social technical ethical strands, accessibility inclusion and governance by design | Multi criteria optimization, risk and impact registers, universal design for learning, offline first resilience for low resource contexts | Spiral curricula, authentic community projects, algorithmic impact assessments embedded in coursework, multilingual and low bandwidth pathways | Accessibility conformance, energy per learning hour and CO2e, equity parity metrics, reduction of avoidable harms, longitudinal transfer to civic and workplace settings |

A critical jurisprudence completes the foundation by binding epistemic practice to dignity, privacy, and non-discrimination (Milenkova & Lendzhova, 2021; Nascimbeni, 2018). Freirean consciousness invites scrutiny of platform incentives, algorithmic classifications, and data extraction that can reproduce structural inequities unless contestable by design (Mannila et al., 2018; Neagu, 2022). Evidence of weak civic online reasoning among adolescents signals a need for curricular architectures that privilege verification, provenance tracing, and bias detection alongside multimodal creation (Çebi & Reisoğlu, 2020; Indriyani, 2019). Competence frameworks operationalize this agenda by integrating information and data literacy, collaboration, content production, safety, and problem solving, while teacher standards align professional growth to ethical and technical fluency (Yang et al., 2020; Napal Fraile et al., 2018). A rights consistent implementation requires accessibility by design, transparent analytics, minimal and proportionate data collection, and remedies for automated error (Anurogo et al., 2023; Tomczyk & Fedeli, 2022b). The outcome is a multidimensional construct that prepares learners to navigate, interrogate, and co create digital systems, thereby realizing the right to education as both individual capability and collective public good within contemporary knowledge democracies.

## 3. THE EVOLVING NATURE OF DIGITAL COMPETENCIES

Digital competence has migrated from instrumental button pressing to a polycentric constellation of cognitive, ethical, and socio emotional capacities that govern participation in data saturated publics (Terry et al., 2019; Tornero et al., 2010). Information literacy now entails lateral reading, provenance tracing, and probabilistic judgment under uncertainty so that learners can discriminate signal from noise in volatile feeds (Table 2) (Fantin, 2010; Moreno-Guerrero et al., 2022). Data literacy layers numeracy with modeling sensemaking and visualization grammar while requiring scrutiny of collection pipelines and profiling logics that affect rights to privacy and nondiscrimination (Delgado-Vázquez & López-Catalán, 2022; Tomczyk & Fedeli, 2022a). Computational reasoning supplies abstraction and decomposition for tooling, yet acquires civic meaning only when yoked to interpretive rigor and accountability (Covello & Lei, 2010; Javorský & Horváth, 2014). A human rights frame converts this evolution into duties that realize the right to education through availability, accessibility, acceptability, and adaptability (Farias-Gaytan et al., 2022; Hinojo-Lucena et al., 2019). This requires resilient connectivity, device sufficiency, multilingual and accessible content, and pedagogies that honor disability, culture, and language (Bravo et al., 2021; Tveiterås & Madsen, 2022). When systems institutionalize these guarantees, digital literacy shifts from discretionary enrichment to an enforceable capability that secures epistemic agency for every learner.

*Table 2. Digital Competency Matrix for Pedagogy and Evaluation*

| Competency Stratum | Scope and Definition | Mechanisms of Acquisition | Instructional Design Levers | Measurement and Performance Signals |
|---|---|---|---|---|
| **Techno-functional Operations** | OS–filesystem fluency, CLI–GUI interoperability, troubleshooting heuristics, network hygiene, task automation | Proceduralization, chunking, automatization, error-driven learning, cognitive-load modulation | Microlabs and emulated sandboxes, spaced retrieval, job aids, performance-support systems | Task latency and error rate, MTTR, cross-platform transfer, command-repertoire breadth, automation uptake |
| **Information Literacy** | Provenance tracking, epistemic vigilance, source criticism, synthesis, credibility appraisal | Lateral reading, triangulation, argument mapping, debiasing routines, Bayesian calibration | Claim–evidence–reasoning studios, heuristic search prompts, contrastive synthesis tasks, provenance workflows | Vetting precision–recall, time-to-decision, Brier score calibration, synthesis coherence, provenance completeness |
| **Data Literacy** | Data wrangling, statistical inference, visualization grammar, uncertainty quantification, governance | Exploratory data analysis, model-based reasoning, hypothesis testing, causal diagrams, sensitivity analysis | Notebook pipelines, reproducibility scaffolds, privacy-by-design handling, versioned datasets, code review | Reproducibility hash, effect-size accuracy, generalization error, chart–question alignment, compliance to minimization |
| **Communication and Content Creation** | Multimodal rhetoric, audience design, accessibility-by-design, collaborative authorship, platform pragmatics | Narrative framing, semiotic encoding–decoding, cognitive empathy, revision cycles, feedback incorporation | Storyboarding, style guides, A11y conformance tasks, role-based collaboration, media version control | Readability indices, engagement analytics, accessibility checks, revision-depth metrics, interrater reliability |
| **Digital Safety and Well-being** | Cyber hygiene, threat-surface reduction, privacy management, psychosocial resilience, ergonomic sustainability | Threat modeling, risk appraisal, impulse control, boundary setting, affect regulation | Phishing simulacra, password-manager adoption, privacy-settings labs, screen-time hygiene, incident playbooks | Phish-click rate, secure-configuration score, security MTTR, well-being indices, hygiene adherence over time |

continued on following page

*Table 2. Continued*

| Competency Stratum | Scope and Definition | Mechanisms of Acquisition | Instructional Design Levers | Measurement and Performance Signals |
|---|---|---|---|---|
| **Digital Ethics and Citizenship** | Normative reasoning, algorithmic accountability, civic participation, commons stewardship, transparency | Moral deliberation, systems thinking, power analysis, norm internalization, reflective equilibrium | Case deliberations, algorithmic-impact assessments, guideline co-creation, participatory civic projects, audit exercises | Argumentation quality rubrics, applied fairness criteria, prosocial contribution rate, footprint audits, policy conformance |
| **Lifelong Adaptivity and Metacompetence** | Meta-learning, transferability, self-regulation, reskilling agility, horizon scanning | Metacognitive monitoring, retrieval practice, interleaving, abstraction, deliberate practice | Individual learning plans, stackable microcredentials, curated portfolios, spaced interleaving, futures-literacy drills | Learning-velocity slope, competency-diversity index, reflective depth and actionability, zero-shot transfer, cadence persistence |

Communication and creation literacies now demand multimodal authorship, audience calibration, and collaborative etiquette that traverse text, image, audio, and code while safeguarding dignity and intellectual attribution (Juškevičienė & Dagienė, 2018; Ratano, 2018). Safety and wellbeing literacy integrates threat modeling, privacy self-management, and psychosocial regulation, with attention to cyberbullying dynamics, platform addiction, and disinhibition effects that undermine inclusive classrooms (Garzón Artacho et al., 2020; McDougall et al., 2018). Digital ethics and citizenship require interrogation of algorithmic classification, content curation, and monetization so that learners can contest bias, demand transparency, and steward the commons (Martínez-Bravo et al., 2020; Tammaro & D'Alessio, 2016). Curricula therefore braid verification routines, participatory media production, and reflective metacognition with adaptive assessment that evidences transfer across contexts (Berge, 2017; Murphy, 2018). Teacher development and institutional governance must embed accessibility by design, proportional data practices, and remedy pathways for automated error to align pedagogy with rights (Andreasen et al., 2022; Cabezas-González et al., 2021). Lifelong learning architectures then sustain continuous reskilling and civic literacies across the life course, ensuring that digital competence remains a living entitlement that advances equality, autonomy, and democratic participation.

## 4. GLOBAL LANDSCAPE OF DIGITAL LITERACY EDUCATION

Global configurations of digital literacy education vary with infrastructure, pedagogy, and political economy, yet a broad consensus now treats digital competence as foundational to agency and citizenship (Feng & Xue, 2023; Ghomi & Redecker, 2019). Finland's 2014 core curriculum embedded multiliteracy and digital competence as transversal capacities alongside teacher upskilling and platform provision, which aligns with strong European benchmarking. Singapore advanced a cradle to career model through the Personalised Digital Learning Programme that achieved personal device ownership for secondary students by 2021 and mandated cyber wellness education (Table 3). India's National Education Policy and its digital architecture envision inclusive systems, although connectivity remained uneven with about half the population online in 2022, and mobile first, radio supported, and low-tech blended designs operate as pragmatic bridges. In sub–Saharan Africa, constraints in electricity, bandwidth, and teacher supply limit scale, while Kenya's early grade tablet deployments and Rwanda's ICT infused basic curriculum illustrate targeted leapfrogging. A rights-based lens reinterprets these moves as duties of availability, accessibility, acceptability, and adaptability within the right to education.

*Table 3. Global Digital Literacy Education Matrix*

| Geopolitical Archetype | Policy Architecture and Governance Instruments | Infrastructure and Access Posture | Pedagogical and Assessment Modalities | Equity, Localization, and Risk Mitigation |
|---|---|---|---|---|
| **Nordic Integrative Model (Finland)** | Transversal digital competence in core curriculum; municipal autonomy with national steering; GDPR-by-design; teacher CPD pipelines; data governance charters | Near-universal broadband; high device density; federated IAM; secure LMS/VLE; state-backed edtech procurement | Phenomenon-based inquiry; coding/media across subjects; formative learning analytics; competency rubrics; secure CBT pilots | UDL and A11y integration; Sámi/minority language resources; assistive tech provisioning; DPIA routines; privacy-by-default practices |
| **City-State Platform Model (Singapore)** | Smart Nation masterplans; PDLP device ownership; codified cyber wellness; lifelong reskilling architecture; sector-wide vendor accreditation | Nationwide fiber; 1:1 at secondary; SLS cloud; robust IAM; managed device lifecycle and MDM | Blended mastery learning; dashboards and item banks; data/coding as core; secure e-assessment with proctoring controls | Means-tested subsidies; repair depots; cyber wellness mandates; high-stakes security audits; inclusive access schemes |
| **Federal Pluralist Scale-Up (India)** | NEP 2020; NDEAR reference architecture; DIKSHA and PM eVidya; Digital University; large-scale teacher CPD | Heterogeneous connectivity; smartphone-first access; multilingual content pipelines; shared labs; incremental school networking | Radio/TV/mobile tri-channel delivery; low-tech blended models; foundation-to-TVET pathways; stackable microcredentials | Offline-first design; community learning hubs; gender/rural inclusion programs; emergent data protection; evolving A11y standards |
| **East African Leapfrog Programs (Kenya, Rwanda)** | Early-grade DLP; competence-based curriculum with coding; ICT integration; public–private compacts | Intermittent power/bandwidth; primary tablet rollouts; community hubs; solar and mini-grid augmentation | Early digital fluency; teacher ICT skilling; TVET bridges; safety and productivity suites | Local-language content (Kiswahili/Kinyarwanda); device maintenance/recycling; electrification partnerships; basic online safety protocols |

continued on following page

*Table 3. Continued*

| Geopolitical Archetype | Policy Architecture and Governance Instruments | Infrastructure and Access Posture | Pedagogical and Assessment Modalities | Equity, Localization, and Risk Mitigation |
|---|---|---|---|---|
| **European Union Benchmarking Regime** | Union-level competence frameworks; national digital strategies; cross-border interoperability and eID; quality assurance mechanisms | High household internet coverage; resilient school networks; trusted edu-clouds; data-trust frameworks | MIL mainstreamed; digital portfolios; computer-based testing; teacher professional standards with CPD | Inclusion and cohesion funds; child online protection regimes; accessibility-mandated procurement; strict privacy enforcement |
| **Latin American Localization Approach** | Curricula augmented with OER; state platforms; community partnerships; open licensing and OEP | Mixed connectivity with urban bias; school device programs; community centers; offline-capable distribution | Multimodal storytelling; media labs; civic-tech projects; offline-first content bundles; teacher CoPs | Vernacular localization; culturally responsive assets; shared-device protocols; learning circles; community facilitators |
| **Sub-Saharan Constraint Contexts** | Phased national roadmaps; multisector skill compacts; donor-aligned targets; incremental governance build-out | Bandwidth scarcity; low device-to-learner ratios; radio/SMS channels; microgrids and solar hubs | Broadcast-plus-mobile microlearning; print–digital hybrids; cluster mentoring; peer tutoring networks | Gender-responsive access initiatives; community Wi-Fi; harm-reduction playbooks; basic digital rights literacy |
| **Multilateral Coordination Layer** | MIL frameworks; comparative assessments and indicators; financing and technical assistance; open standards and reference architectures | Connectivity/device grants; shared registries; interoperability toolkits; baseline security patterns | Educator capacity building; open content repositories; evaluation toolkits; impact frameworks | Glocalization guidance; equity and sustainability criteria; trust and safety frameworks; portability and compliance support |
| **Cross-Cutting Gaps and Futures** | Convergence on competence, divergence in state capacity and pace; emergent AI governance and assurance | Persistent multidimensional divides in access/devices/usage quality; urban–rural and gender asymmetries; affordability constraints | Need resilient blended ecosystems; teacher digital didactics; trustworthy assessment; AI-personalization with guardrails | Linguistic localization; privacy/safety-by-design; green ICT and low-TCO models; targeted investment for gender/disability gaps; continuous monitoring and course correction |

Persistent multidimensional divides still undercut aspiration. Europe records roughly nine in ten residents online while Africa remains near two in five, and intrastate gaps by income, gender, disability, language, and rurality endure (Menggo et al., 2021; Nebot et al., 2021). Human rights norms require nondiscrimination and cultural rights, which elevates linguistic localization and culturally responsive curricula as core to digital inclusion (Krumsvik, 2022; Sá & Serpa, 2020). Latin American programs that adapt open resources into Quechua and Aymara and Ghanaian digital storybooks grounded in indigenous iconography exemplify substantive equality. Gender focused initiatives such as African Girls Can Code counter entrenched barriers to participation. Multilateral actors scaffold policy through frameworks, indicators, and finance, with UNESCO advancing media and information literacy, the OECD producing comparative measures through school and adult surveys, and the World Bank underwriting infrastructure and capacity. Effective governance favors glocal alignment that couples global standards with local epistemologies (Pangrazio et al., 2020; Zabolotska et al., 2021). When states institutionalize equity metrics, classroom support, and trustworthy data governance, the right to education gains full digital realization.

## 5. PEDAGOGICAL STRATEGIES FOR INTEGRATING DIGITAL LITERACY

Integrating digital literacy within curriculum requires a shift from siloed ICT units to a transversal meta competence threaded through disciplines and assessed for mastery rather than exposure (From, 2017; Røkenes et al., 2022). Competency based education sequences digital outcomes within subject ecologies so that historical inquiry deploys source verification and multimodal argumentation while STEM studios cultivate algorithmic thinking, data visualization, and reproducible notebooks (Table 4) (Kasperski et al., 2022; Mehrvarz et al., 2021). Project based learning supplies authentic problem frames where learners prototype documentaries, podcasts, simulations, or lightweight apps and thereby externalize reasoning through iterative design and reflective commentary (Cartelli, 2010; Sánchez-Cruzado et al., 2021). Gameful mechanics calibrated to self-determination theory can amplify persistence by tuning autonomy, competence, and relatedness without trivializing cognition (Marnita et al., 2023; Svensson & Baelo, 2015). Networked collaboration platforms enable synchronous and asynchronous co authorship, version control, and task orchestration that mirror contemporary workplaces (Esteve-Mon et al., 2020; Park et al., 2021). A human rights perspective transforms these choices into obligations under the right to education, which demands availability of connectivity and devices, accessibility through universal design, acceptability via culturally responsive content, and adaptability across languages, abilities, and contexts.

*Table 4. Integrated Digital Literacy Pedagogy Matrix*

| Pedagogical Modality | Learning Mechanics & Theoretical Rationale | Design Patterns, Tools, and Tasks | Inclusion, Ethics, & Safeguards | Assessment, Analytics, & Evidence |
|---|---|---|---|---|
| **Transversal Integration via Competency-Based Education** | Situated cognition, constructive alignment, mastery gradients, spiral curricula, schema automatization, metacognitive regulation | Program maps, backward design, cross-disciplinary capstones, microcredential lattices, exemplar banks, workload modeling | Device-agnostic and offline-first delivery, privacy-by-design data flows, multilingual localization, WCAG conformance, DPIA routines | Standards rubrics, learning-progression models, e-portfolio time series, telemetry dashboards, mastery transcripts, reliability checks |
| **Project-Based and Constructionist Learning** | Cognitive apprenticeship, design-thinking cycles, reflective abstraction, iterative prototyping, feedback loops, artifact-mediated reasoning | Studio workflows, cloud repositories, version control, usability tests, MVP builds, sprint retrospectives | Role rotation, UDL checkpoints, IP and consent hygiene, safe media sourcing, alternative modality pathways | Artifact and process rubrics, commit analytics, peer-rating reliability, near–far transfer tasks, reflection depth indices |
| **Gameful Learning and Motivational Engineering** | Self-determination optimization, operant reinforcement, flow regulation, spaced retrieval, desirable difficulties, adaptive scaffolding | Points–badges–levels, leaderboards with anti-gaming rules, quest chains, adaptive item banks, live quiz platforms | Opt-in competition, equitable reward curves, anti-cheat telemetry, age-appropriate gating, anxiety-aware design | Engagement telemetry, response-time distributions, pre to post learning gains, difficulty calibration curves, retention functions |

continued on following page

*Table 4. Continued*

| Pedagogical Modality | Learning Mechanics & Theoretical Rationale | Design Patterns, Tools, and Tasks | Inclusion, Ethics, & Safeguards | Assessment, Analytics, & Evidence |
|---|---|---|---|---|
| **Collaborative Knowledge-Building Ecosystems** | Distributed cognition, social constructivism, transactive memory, dialogic scaffolding, cognitive interdependence | Shared docs and wikis, kanban boards, threaded annotation, async–sync workflows, contribution protocols and roles | Netiquette charters, psychological safety, moderated escalation, timezone fairness, translation and language support | Helpfulness-weighted metrics, revision-depth indices, SNA collaboration graphs, knowledge-base quality scores, rubricized co-authorship |
| **Authentic Assessment, UDL, and Culturally Sustaining Pedagogy** | Construct-referenced evaluation, self-regulation and calibration, accessibility-first design, identity affirmation | Digital portfolios, rubricized self and peer assessment, choice of expression, assistive tech integration, captions and alt-text | Multiple means of engagement and representation, culturally resonant narratives, accommodation tracking, ethical-use guidelines | Interrater coefficients, growth-curve modeling, validity evidence and audit trails, accommodation efficacy metrics, portfolio defensibility |

Assessment architectures must evolve with pedagogy so that complex literacies are evidenced longitudinally rather than captured by isolated quizzes (Bejaković & Mrnjavac, 2020; Schröter & Grafe, 2020). Digital portfolios aggregate artifacts across media while analytic rubrics, calibrated peer review, and reflective memos surface strategy, transfer, and growth (Eraku et al., 2021; Pötzsch, 2016). Universal Design for Learning requires multiple means of engagement, representation, and expression and legitimizes assistive technologies such as captioning, alternative input, readable typography, and adjustable pacing (Cortoni et al., 2015; Gapski, 2007). Culturally sustaining pedagogy situates tasks within local narratives and vernaculars to protect identity and dignity (Hanell, 2018; Khokhar, 2016). Datafication must be governed by proportional collection, privacy by default, open standards, and contestability of automated scoring to align analytics with nondiscrimination and due process (Amdam et al., 2022; Martzoukou et al., 2024). Teacher development and institutional governance complete the system through release time, microcredentials, open resources, and trustworthy platforms with low total cost of ownership (Müller et al., 2023; Qingyi, 2023). When states and schools institutionalize these elements, integration of digital literacy becomes a rights-based transformation that yields durable learning gains and civic agency.

## 6. TEACHER TRAINING AND CAPACITY-BUILDING

Teacher capacity building must be framed as a rights-based obligation that operationalizes the right to education through professional capital rather than episodic upskilling (Orakova et al., 2024; Vaskov et al., 2021). Teachers function as epistemic agents who orchestrate inquiry, adjudicate evidence, and model ethical practice within data saturated classrooms (Levano-Francia et al., 2019; Tømte, 2015). Effective preparation integrates PCK and TPACK with media and information literacy, data and algorithmic literacy, accessibility by design, and privacy stewardship (Kim, 2019; Marsh, 2016). Preservice curricula should combine microteaching, lesson study, coached practicum, and simulation so that orchestration skills become habitual rather than incidental (He & Li, 2019; Nascimbeni & Vosloo, 2019). In service development works when it is job embedded and cumulative through coaching cycles, inquiry communities, and microcredentials that encode transparent performance standards (Kasemsap, 2018; Oberländer et al., 2020). International surveys report sizable shares of teachers who feel underprepared for digital pedagogy, which underscores the need for structured release time and mentoring rather than one off workshops (Table 5) (Rahman et al., 2021; Reddy et al., 2023). Within a human rights frame, availability requires infrastructure for training, accessibility requires inclusive pathways, acceptability requires culturally responsive content, and adaptability requires modulation across languages, disciplines, and learner needs.

*Table 5. Systemic Teacher Capacity for Digital Literacy Implementation*

| Capacity-Building Pillar | Competency Targets & Theoretical Grounding | Program Architecture & Delivery | Equity, Ethics & Safeguards | Evaluation & Evidence Signals |
|---|---|---|---|---|
| **Pre-Service Teacher Formation** | TPACK–PCK integration, SRL and metacognition, MIL, algorithmic and data literacy, UDL and classroom orchestration, basic cyber hygiene | Sequenced modules, microteaching and lesson study, simulation labs and VR, coached practicum, e-portfolio curation, capstone design studio | WCAG-aligned A11y, privacy-by-design onboarding, culturally sustaining content, low-bandwidth variants, ethical-use and minimal-data norms | Analytic performance rubrics, calibrated observations, portfolio defense, readiness benchmarks, self-efficacy scales, pre–post growth curves |
| **In-Service PD and Micro-Credentialing** | Advanced digital didactics, formative learning analytics, AI-assisted planning, assessment moderation, change leadership, SEL and trauma-informed practice, device ecosystem fluency | Blended PD sprints, modular micro-credentials and badges, job-embedded cycles, lesson-tuning protocols, sandbox experimentation, office-hours coaching | Timetabled release, multilingual assets, offline/ low-bandwidth options, DPIA for tools, consent and IP hygiene, device-agnostic delivery | Uptake and completion rates, classroom telemetry, transfer-to-practice indices, moderation reliability, Brier/ calibration scores, cost-per-competency |
| **Communities of Practice and Peer Coaching** | Social learning, knowledge brokering, transactive memory systems, inquiry stance, practitioner research, feedback literacy | PLC/CoP cadences, peer observation with structured lenses, critique protocols, shared repos and wikis, coaching triads, cross-school networks | Psychological-safety norms, anti-bias facilitation, clear escalation paths, equitable voice rotation, asynchronous participation windows | Helpfulness-weighted contributions, revision-depth metrics, SNA collaboration graphs, practitioner-inquiry outputs, retention and diffusion rates |
| **Digital Leadership and Change Enablement** | Instructional leadership, implementation science, strategic procurement, risk and compliance, data governance, evaluation use | Roadmaps and logic models, budgeted workplans, TCO/ SLA procurement, helpdesk and MDM rollout, IAM/SSO integration, comms plans | Governance charters, RBAC, ISO-aligned controls, privacy and safety playbooks, green ICT guidelines, accessibility mandates | Milestone burn-down, service reliability and MTTR, audit pass rates, adoption curves, stakeholder sentiment indices, benefit–cost and ROI analyses |
| **Human–Technical Resourcing and Sustainability** | Adaptive expertise, lifelong learning mindset, ID and technician capacity, infrastructure stewardship, knowledge retention | Release time and stipends, substitute coverage, makerspaces and media labs, device lifecycle and repair depots, tiered support desks | Equitable device allocation, assistive-tech inventory, rural and gender inclusion programs, secure configurations, safeguarding protocols | Uptime and utilization dashboards, request-to-resolution SLAs, attrition and redeployment rates, energy per learning hour, equity parity metrics |

Systemic enablement demands organizational design that protects teacher autonomy while ensuring accountability to learners (Hatlevik & Christophersen, 2013; Stopar & Bartol, 2019). Leaders should align timetables, staffing, and budgets with long horizon capability building and should evaluate platforms using total cost of ownership, security, and interoperability rather than novelty (Hatlevik et al., 2015; Kateryna et al., 2020). Professional learning needs trustworthy analytics with proportional data collection, transparent models, and contestability of machine assisted judgments so that evaluation supports growth and due process (Alarcón et al., 2020; Engen et al., 2015). Communities of practice thrive with psychological safety, anti-bias facilitation, and equitable voice rotation and can leverage open resources and local exemplars to diffuse situated craft knowledge (Instefjord, 2015; Shariman et al., 2012). Sustainability follows when schools cultivate technician pipelines, repair ecosystems, and accessible repositories that reduce downtime and vendor dependence (Blyznyuk, 2018; Marín & Castaneda, 2022). Assessment of capacity should triangulate observation, artifact portfolios, and interrater reliability so that claims of competence are defensible (Leahy & Dolan, 2010; Olimpo, 2013). When states fund human infrastructure alongside devices and connectivity, teacher empowerment becomes the hinge that turns policy rhetoric into lived realization of the right to education.

## 7. DIGITAL ETHICS, SAFETY, AND SURVEILLANCE IN EDUCATION

Digital transformation in schools has intensified datafication that captures clickstreams, gaze proxies, and psychometric traces inside learning platforms, promising early warning insights while risking a panoptic pedagogical gaze (Ferrari et al., 2012; Søby, 2015). Informational privacy, informed consent, and data sovereignty become non-negotiable where the right to education requires safe, acceptable, and dignified conditions for learning (Cartelli, 2012; López-Meneses et al., 2020). Governance must enforce purpose limitation, proportional collection, and transparent analytics with human review, contestability, and effective remedy (Cabero-Almenara et al., 2020; Sillat et al., 2021). Age-appropriate consent and child data protections must be operational rather than rhetorical, with attention to cross border transfers and vendor lock in (Davydov et al., 2020; Khan & Vuopala, 2019). The collapse of inBloom in 2014 after parental and district backlash illustrates how opaque aggregation erodes trust even when the technical stack is sophisticated (Table 6). Algorithmic bias in automated scoring, attendance via facial recognition, and behavioral risk flagging can reproduce structural inequities unless datasets, objectives, and thresholds are auditable (Krumsvik, 2014; Lee, 2014). Rights compatible learning analytics therefore integrate privacy by default, accessibility by design, and documentation that renders inference legible to teachers, students, and guardians.

*Table 6. Ethics, Safety, Surveillance, and Citizenship in Digital Education*

| Ethical–Sociotechnical Domain | Risk Topology & Normative Commitments | Governance & Technical Controls | Pedagogical & Cultural Interventions | Monitoring, Metrics & Assurance |
|---|---|---|---|---|
| **Datafication & Learning Analytics** | Panoptic telemetry, inference creep, secondary use, autonomy erosion, disproportionality, purpose-limitation violations | Data minimization, privacy-by-design/default, DPIA, RBAC/ABAC, least privilege, AES/TLS, pseudonymization, k-anonymity, differential privacy, federated analytics | Data diaries, telemetry transparency, consent literacy, data nutrition labels, learner dashboards with user override, opt-in/opt-out pathways | RoPA registers, data-flow maps, privacy-budget ledger, access-log audits, MTTR for incidents, re-identification risk scores |
| **Privacy, Consent & Data Sovereignty** | Informational self-determination, age-assurance, cross-border transfer risk, unlawful basis, sovereignty claims | Consent management with verified guardianship, data localization, DSRM workflows, de-identification pipelines, secure APIs, KMS, SOC/ISO-aligned controls | Privacy-lab practicums, consent simulations, plain-language policy refactoring, digital footprint audits, media-capture protocols | DSR turnaround SLAs, revocation latency, breach-drill cadence, audit pass rates, policy–practice concordance indices |
| **Algorithmic Accountability & Bias Mitigation** | Disparate impact, opacity, feedback loops, allocative harm, dataset shift, lack of contestability | Model/data cards, fairness constraints, pre/post bias and calibration tests, XAI toolkits, human-in-the-loop overrides, red teaming, threshold tuning | Algorithm literacy studios, counterfactual exercises, impact assessments in coursework, appeal and review channels, platform governance debates | Fairness deltas (DP/EO), ECE/MCE calibration error, subgroup error stratification, override rates, drift alarms, documentation completeness |

continued on following page

*Table 6. Continued*

| Ethical–Sociotechnical Domain | Risk Topology & Normative Commitments | Governance & Technical Controls | Pedagogical & Cultural Interventions | Monitoring, Metrics & Assurance |
|---|---|---|---|---|
| **Cyber-safety, Well-being & Affective Harm** | Cyberbullying, doxxing, phishing, grooming, online disinhibition, technostress, screen-time dysregulation | Threat modeling, transparent filters, MFA, device hardening, rate limiting, incident playbooks, trusted reporting, safe-by-default settings | Cyber hygiene drills, restorative protocols, digital empathy curricula, scenario role-plays, well-being routines, counselor escalation | Phish-click rate, incident frequency/severity, time-to-containment, recurrence rate, well-being index trends, resolution satisfaction |
| **Digital Citizenship, Rights & Civic Agency** | Speech norms, moderation ethics, misinformation propagation, IP misuse, civic disengagement, provenance gaps | AUP charters, moderation SOPs, provenance and attribution tools, open-licensing guidance, archival/takedown workflows | Civic media projects, lateral reading routines, discourse etiquette, Creative Commons production, co-designed community norms | Engagement-quality rubrics, misinformation-resistance scores, contribution helpfulness, IP compliance rates, participation parity across cohorts |

Digital ethics must also address micro social harms that compromise inclusion and wellbeing (Guzmán-Simón et al., 2017; Rambousek et al., 2016). Cyberbullying, doxxing, and harassment produce affective overload and school avoidance, with international surveys indicating that roughly one in three adolescents encounter online victimization (Atmojo, Ardiansyah, & Adi, 2023). A rights-based response aligns with the duty to provide safe learning environments and includes trauma informed protocols, trusted reporting channels, restorative conferencing, and digital empathy curricula (Krumsvik et al., 2016; Svendsen & Svendsen, 2021). Pedagogy should cultivate critical platform literacy, verification routines, and provenance tracing so that students can interrogate amplification, moderation, and monetization logics (de Vries, Piotrowski, & de Vreese, 2025; Wardhani, Hesti, & Dwityas, 2019). Schools should temper intrusive proctoring and biometric controls and should favor accessible assessment design that reduces incentive for surveillance (Abella & Rosa, 2023; Cartelli, Dagiene, & Futschek, 2012). Regulatory anchors such as child privacy statutes and data protection regimes set baselines, while institutional charters add clear purpose statements, data retention ceilings, and independent audits (Ballano et al., 2022; Mishra & Sharma, 2018). When classrooms weave civic media production, algorithmic literacy, and privacy stewardship into everyday practice, the right to education acquires contemporary meaning that safeguards dignity and enlarges agency.

# 8. EMERGING TECHNOLOGIES AND DIGITAL LITERACY

Artificial intelligence, machine learning, and immersive media recalibrate the epistemic grammar of schooling by coupling adaptive inference with embodied simulation (Calvani, Fini, & Ranieri, 2010; Skantz-Åberg et al., 2022). Intelligent tutors and recommender pipelines modulate difficulty through item response signals, while natural language interfaces scaffold discourse level revision and metacognitive planning (Shopova, 2014; Zakir et al., 2025). Virtual and augmented environments stage safe trial spaces for hazardous or rare phenomena, strengthening spatial encoding, psychomotor rehearsal, and affective presence (Al Khateeb, 2017; Koppel & Langer, 2020). Assistive AI widens participation through captioning, translation, alternative input, and personalized pacing that implement universal design principles (Table 7) (Murtadho et al., 2023; Søby, 2013). A rights-based lens converts affordances into obligations under the right to education (Martin & Grudziecki, 2006; Zhao, Llorente, & Gómez, 2021). Availability entails resilient connectivity and reliable devices (Habók & Nguyen, 2024; Røkenes & Krumsvik, 2014). Accessibility requires multilingual content, compatibility with assistive technologies, and cognitive load aware interfaces (Ferrari & Punie, 2013; Peng & Yu, 2022). Acceptability demands culturally responsive narratives and transparent model behavior (Arvianto & St Y, 2023; Indah et al., 2022). Adaptability insists on modular curricula that update as systems evolve (Marin et al., 2022; Martin, 2006). Digital literacy therefore expands into meta literacies that include reading algorithmic intent, interrogating training data provenance, and decoding persuasive architecture inside immersive worlds.

*Table 7. Affordances, Risks, and Evidence in Emerging EdTech for Digital Literacy*

| Emergent Technology Vector | Learning Affordances & Cognitive Mechanisms | Design Patterns, Tools & Implementation | Equity, Ethics & Risk Mitigations | Assessment, Analytics & Validity Signals |
|---|---|---|---|---|
| **AI Tutoring, Recommenders & Predictive Adaptation** | Hyperpersonalization, mastery pacing, immediate formative feedback, Bayesian/ DKT knowledge tracing, IRT calibration, RL sequence optimization, metacognitive nudges | Knowledge graphs, adaptive item banks, multi-armed bandits, LTI/xAPI interoperability, teacher-in-the-loop overrides, policy constraints, canary A/Bs, elastic content services | Data minimization, transparency notices, federated analytics, differential privacy, RBAC/ ABAC, bias and drift audits, age assurance, human fallback | Mastery-slope and time-to-mastery, Brier/ calibration scores, uplift heterogeneity, off-policy evaluation, SHAP/ LIME auditability, intervention MTTR |
| **Generative AI, Co-writing & Integrity** | Ideation scaffolds, rhetorical modeling, structured critique, code synthesis, metacognitive prompting, citation planning, plagiarism deterrence by design | RAG pipelines, prompt templates and guardrails, style/rubric conditioning, provenance capture, human review queues, versioned drafts, disclosure workflows | Authorship provenance, integrity policies, hallucination containment, IP/licensing hygiene, toxicity filters, watermark limits, red-team rehearsal | Originality precision–recall, hallucination rate, source-coverage ratio, rater concordance (κ/ρ), citation accuracy, disclosure compliance |
| **Immersive XR: VR, AR, MR Simulations** | Embodied cognition, spatial encoding, psychomotor rehearsal, affective presence, safe-failure sandboxes, situated transfer | Virtual labs, low-poly optimization, 6DoF/hand-eye tracking, occlusion-aware AR overlays, cross-device fallbacks, locomotion modes, session timeboxing | Cost controls, cybersickness mitigation (IPD, FOV, refresh rate), age gating, safety bubbles, hygiene protocols, inclusive interaction, offline bundles | Near/far transfer, procedural error rates, presence and workload indices (PQ, NASA-TLX), retention curves, SUS/ UEQ scores, comfort metrics |

continued on following page

*Table 7. Continued*

| Emergent Technology Vector | Learning Affordances & Cognitive Mechanisms | Design Patterns, Tools & Implementation | Equity, Ethics & Risk Mitigations | Assessment, Analytics & Validity Signals |
|---|---|---|---|---|
| **Assistive AI & Language Technologies** | Accessibility amplification, ASR/STT, TTS, live captioning, real-time translation, alt-text generation, executive-function supports | UDL-aligned integrations, accessibility APIs, on-device inference, multilingual pipelines, personalization profiles, privacy-footprint minimization | Sensitive-speech privacy, informed consent, localization fidelity, stereotype/bias checks, stigma safeguards, least-intrusive retention | Word-error rate and latency, translation quality (human judgments), WCAG conformance, SUS/A11y scores, accommodation efficacy, abandonment rate |
| **Teacher Role Reconfiguration & AI Meta-Literacies** | Orchestration over automation, ethical adjudication, algorithmic literacy, learner agency cultivation, feedback triage, risk sensing | Analytics dashboards and alerts, co-planning with AI, promptcraft PD, scenario planning and playbooks, escalation pathways, governance checklists | Professional autonomy protections, workload balancing, anti-deskilling controls, accountability delineation, change-management supports | Adoption and sustained-use curves, time-saving versus quality deltas, feedback timeliness/usefulness, climate/agency indices, incident resolution SLAs |

Governance and pedagogy must co evolve so that innovation advances dignity, privacy, and nondiscrimination (Kim et al., 2021; Lund et al., 2014). Human oversight, contestability, and proportional data practices counter predictive determinism in learning analytics (Ala-Mutka, 2011; Salganova & Osipova, 2023). Fairness auditing, robustness testing, and documentation make model behavior legible to teachers and families (Erstad, Kjällander, & Järvelä, 2021; Iordache, Mariën, & Baelden, 2017). Generative systems require provenance capture, disclosure norms, and assessment designs that privilege process evidence over mere output (Martin, 2008; Martínez-Bravo, Sádaba Chalezquer, & Serrano-Puche, 2022). Educators shift from delivery to orchestration through prompt engineering, critical source triangulation, and classroom dialogue that situates machine suggestions within disciplinary canons (Ferrari, 2012; Mbandje, Loureiro, & Lucas, 2023). Procurement should privilege openness, interoperability, repairability, and energy efficiency to align learning rights with climate stewardship (Janssen et al., 2013; Yang, 2024). Risk management must address cybersickness, biometric leakage, and equity gaps created by high capital immersive hardware through shared hubs and offline bundles (Johannesen, Øgrim, & Giæver, 2014; Ottestad, Kelentrić, & Guðmundsdóttir, 2014). When regulatory safeguards, professional capacity, and sustainable infrastructure intertwine, students gain effective remedies for harm and authentic agency in hybrid knowledge ecologies (Ala-Mutka, Punie, & Redecker, 2008; Godhe, 2019). The right to education then includes the capability to shape intelligent systems rather than merely endure them.

## 9. LIFELONG LEARNING AND WORKFORCE READINESS

Digital modernity dissolves age and institutional boundaries, recasting digital literacy as a life course capability that underwrites the right to education (Calvani et al., 2008; Sánchez-Caballé et al., 2020). A rights-based lens translates availability into resilient connectivity and public access points, accessibility into affordable devices, assistive technologies, and multilingual interfaces, acceptability into culturally responsive content and safe learning conditions, and adaptability into modular pathways that fit diverse schedules and abilities (Table 8) (Pettersson, 2018; Zakharov et al., 2021). Public libraries, community centers, and mobile laboratories operate as civic infrastructures for intergenerational transmission where geragogy, privacy stewardship, and cybersecurity hygiene are taught alongside communication platforms and telehealth navigation (Atmojo, Ardiansyah, & Wulandari, 2022; Pérez-Escoda & Rodríguez-Conde, 2015). Microlearning sequences and peer mentoring reduce cognitive load and stigma for late adopters while portfolio curation and recognition of prior learning validate tacit expertise (Bayrakcı & Narmanlıoğlu, 2021; Ilomäki et al., 2016). Equity also carries a temporal dimension since those schooled before the digital turn require second chance enfranchisement (Cartelli, 2009; Krumsvik, 2008). When states finance human support such as trainers, release time, and repair services in addition to hardware, lifelong participation becomes a realizable entitlement rather than an aspirational slogan.

*Table 8. Lifelong Digital Skills and Workforce Readiness*

| Strategic Domain | Competency Stack & Outcomes | Program Architectures & Delivery Channels | Equity, Incentives & Supports | Measurement & Labor-Market Signals |
|---|---|---|---|---|
| **Life-course Digital Inclusion & Geragogy** | Device–OS fluency; cyber hygiene; eID/eGov and telehealth navigation; privacy self-management; netiquette; digital self-efficacy | Public libraries; community hubs; mobile labs; geragogy-optimised UX; intergenerational peer mentoring; concierge helpdesks; microclinics | Subsidised devices/data; A11y toolchains; multilingual low-bandwidth modes; pacing accommodations; technostress mitigation | Task success rate; re-engagement cadence; inclusion index; support MTTR; autonomy gain; digital confidence scale |
| **Industry 4.0 Reskilling & Hybrid Skillsets** | Data/algorithmic literacy; cloud and DevOps basics; cybersecurity awareness; product analytics; collaborative problem solving; meta-learning | Bootcamps; apprenticeships; employer academies; simulated workbenches; project clinics; JIT microlearning; behavioural nudges | Stipends and paid release; training tax credits; portable learning accounts; AT for workplace inclusion; ERG mentorship | Placement and wage deltas; skill-gap closure curves; credential-to-role conversion; productivity uplift; post-reskilling retention |
| **Micro-credentials, Badges & Recognition of Prior Learning** | Modular competency atoms; stackability; evidence curation; e-portfolio literacy; assessment readiness; credit articulation | Proctored micro-assessments; digital badges/nanodegrees; role-aligned skills taxonomies; RPL mapping to degrees; issuer registries; LER wallets | Low-cost open entry; employer recognition compacts; HRIS/ LMS/LXP interoperability; transparent rubrics; anti-gaming controls | Credential acceptance rate; signal reliability; time-to-credit; portfolio defensibility; cross-provider portability; hiring conversion |
| **MOOCs & Participatory Knowledge Commons** | Self-directed learning; open-source praxis; lateral search; peer review; community moderation; knowledge co-production | MOOCs with mastery paths; open repositories; code forges and forums; cohort sprints; mobile-first offline bundles; social Q&A | Free audit tracks; scholarships; localisation and captioning; A11y conformance; safe-community norms | Completion–mastery split; persistence curves; peer-grading reliability; contribution helpfulness; employer uptake of artefacts |
| **National Skills Ecosystems & PPP Infrastructures** | Policy literacy; ecosystem navigation; lifelong-learner identity; career adaptability; civic digital agency | Learning-credit schemes; adult-education networks; broadbanded libraries/ digital labs; mobile training units; PPP regional skills hubs | Coverage guarantees; rural/gender inclusion targets; procurement with A11y/privacy clauses; stipend vouchers; outreach campaigns | Participation and parity indices; ROI/ BCR; regional skills heatmaps; re-employment velocity; longitudinal career progression |

Workforce readiness in automated economies depends on hybrid repertoires that fuse algorithmic literacy, data reasoning, platform collaboration, and ethical judgment (Gallardo-Echenique et al., 2015; Hammoda & Foli, 2024). Global labor analyses forecast large scale task reconfiguration by the mid-decade, with tens of millions of roles displaced and a comparable number created, which reframes continuing education as a social protection. Stackable microcredentials, skills wallets, and interoperable records allow competencies to travel across firms and sectors, while open course ecosystems and practice communities democratize advanced content (Makhafola et al., 2025; Tinmaz et al., 2022). Employer academies, apprenticeships, and public learning credits expand access for workers in precarious conditions and align with duties to respect, protect, and fulfill educational rights. Policy compacts should require portability, transparent assessment, accessibility by design, and privacy preserving analytics so that opportunity does not depend on surveillance. When recognition frameworks, financing mechanisms, and trustworthy platforms converge, reskilling becomes a public good that advances equal opportunity, dignified work, and democratic capability across the lifespan.

## 10. POLICY FRAMEWORKS AND GOVERNANCE MODELS

Digital literacy governance unfolds within layered jurisdictions that carry distinct histories and institutional logics, yet the right to education supplies a common normative compass (Ilomäki, Kantosalo, & Lakkala, 2011; Yazon et al., 2019). States owe duties to respect, protect, and fulfill through policies that render digital learning available, accessible, acceptable, and adaptable. India's NEP 2020 situates digital competence as transversal and is supported by the National Digital Education Architecture and a technology forum that coordinate platforms, registries, and teacher development (Table 9). The European Union's DigComp provides a portable competence lattice that informs national blueprints across member states. The United Kingdom's post 2014 computing reforms embed coding and digital literacy from primary years, while the United States relies on soft governance where the National Education Technology Plan frames direction and the ISTE Standards diffuse through state and district adoption. Centralized systems offer uniform rollouts and rapid resourcing, decentralized systems optimize local fit, and hybrid models seek coherence with subsidiarity. Rights compatible design requires each path to mitigate territorial inequities and safeguard learner dignity.

*Table 9. Policy and Governance Architectures for Digital Literacy*

| Governance Archetype & Exemplars | Normative Frameworks & Policy Levers | Implementation Infrastructure & Delivery | Risk, Compliance & Ethical Guardrails | Monitoring, KPIs & Adaptive Feedback |
|---|---|---|---|---|
| **National Integrated Strategy — India (NEP 2020, NDEAR, NETF)** | Transversal digital competence; reference architectures; curriculum and teacher standards; public financing; TCO/SLA procurement | Federated registries; DIKSHA-style content stack; device–connectivity drives; multilingual pipelines; mass CPD; Digital University pathways | Data minimization and localization; RBAC/ ABAC; DPIA; accessibility-by-design; vendor due diligence; grievance and appeal channels | Usage telemetry; learning outcome dashboards; CPD completion-to-classroom transfer; equity parity gaps; external audits; periodic policy refresh |
| **Supranational Alignment — European Union (DigComp, EDU frameworks)** | Competence taxonomies and levels; cross-border recognition; interoperability profiles; open standards; conditional funding | National blueprints aligned to union targets; secure edu-clouds; eID interoperability; portable micro-credentials | GDPR conformity; child online protections; accessibility mandates in procurement; algorithmic transparency expectations | Union–national scorecards; institutional diagnostics; longitudinal comparators; inclusion–cohesion metrics; evidence-to-policy loops |
| **Decentralized Soft-Governance — United States (NETP, ISTE adoption)** | Vision frameworks; voluntary standards with quasi-regulatory uptake; state–district autonomy; innovation grants | District LMS ecosystems; 1:1 initiatives; local PD marketplaces; library–community hub extensions | COPPA/FERPA-aligned student data protections; privacy addenda in contracts; security baselines; transparency and opt-out | State report cards; efficacy studies; engagement analytics; digital divide indices; independent evaluations informing iterative policy |
| **Hybrid Standards with Localized Delivery — Australia, UK, Canada** | National capability statements; provincial adaptation; common assessment anchors; shared resource hubs | Central standards with local timetables; blended delivery; teacher networks; regional digital leads; shared services | Privacy/safety codes; accessibility conformance; safeguarding protocols; risk registers; incident response playbooks | Standards attainment sampling; moderation reliability; participation and coverage metrics; regional benchmarking; continuous improvement cycles |

continued on following page

*Table 9. Continued*

| Governance Archetype & Exemplars | Normative Frameworks & Policy Levers | Implementation Infrastructure & Delivery | Risk, Compliance & Ethical Guardrails | Monitoring, KPIs & Adaptive Feedback |
|---|---|---|---|---|
| **Centralized Command-and-Control — France, China (unitary rollouts)** | Top-down curricular decrees; uniform credentialing; centralized funding and procurement | Rapid nationwide deployments; unified platforms; scaled teacher induction; centralized content vetting; broadcast–online hybrids | Strong compliance oversight; national data governance; approved vendor lists; security accreditation; content moderation norms | National KPI dashboards; adherence audits; completion/ readiness indices; time-to-implementation; corrective action programs |
| **Market–State–Civil Interface & Open Knowledge Governance (PPP, OER)** | PPP frameworks; open licensing mandates; public OER platforms; employer recognition of micro-credentials; role-aligned skills taxonomies | Device donations and connectivity subsidies; co-created courses; issuer registries and LER wallets; libraries as digital commons; mobile training units | Anti–vendor-lock-in clauses; IP and attribution norms; privacy-by-contract; transparency reporting; green ICT criteria | Credential acceptance and portability; signal reliability; cost-per-learner and ROI; community uptake and retention; outcomes linked to employment and civic participation |

Market actors and civil society shape implementation through public private collaboration that must be tethered to the public interest. Procurement should specify interoperability, accessibility, security, service levels, and total cost of ownership, while data governance must enforce minimization, purpose limitation, transparency, and effective remedy (Falloon, 2020; Spante et al., 2018). New York Education Law 2 D and the European Union's GDPR set enforceable constraints on vendor practices. Open educational resources counter enclosure, with Poland's national open text-books and South Africa's open learning policy signaling institutional commitment to knowledge as a commons. Monitoring and evaluation close the loop through national assessments, institutional diagnostics such as the European SELFIE tool, and global indicators linked to SDG target 4.4 that measure digital skills acquisition. A polycentric model that combines legislative guardrails, participatory oversight, and rapid feedback enables agile yet accountable policy. When such arrangements hold, digital literacy advances as a public good that realizes educational rights while future proofing learning ecosystems.

## 11. HUMAN RIGHTS JURISPRUDENCE FOR DIGITAL LITERACY

Digital literacy attains juridical gravitas when grounded in the universal grammar of rights that govern education, expression, privacy, equality, and participation. The right to education articulated in the Universal Declaration and the Covenant on Economic, Social and Cultural Rights obliges states to guarantee availability, accessibility, acceptability, and adaptability across analog and digital modalities. Contemporary jurisprudence increasingly treats meaningful internet access, safe platforms, and skills acquisition as integral to these entitlements. Indian doctrine recognized informational privacy as a fundamental right and later held that indefinite shutdowns offend constitutional guarantees and impair education and livelihoods. A Kerala High Court judgment linked student access to the internet with autonomy and scholastic opportunity. Regional tribunals have condemned disproportionate network disruptions that impair expression and information. European case law acknowledged that controlled online access can fall within protected communication where necessary for legal or educational purposes and censured bulk interception lacking strict safeguards. Across these fora, the yardsticks of legality, necessity, and proportionality now discipline digital interventions in schools and universities, converting connectivity, safety, and pedagogical usability into enforceable correlates of the right to learn.

Freedom of expression jurisprudence positions digital literacy as both capability and shield. The Human Rights Committee affirmed that Article 19 protections apply online and United Nations resolutions insist that rights offline must be protected online. The United States Supreme Court described social media as a modern public square, a rationale that informs student speech norms and platform access in education. Privacy and data protection refine the lawful perimeter for learning analytics, proctoring, and platform ecosystems. The European Charter recognizes a distinct right to data protection and the General Data Protection Regulation operationalizes purpose limitation, minimization, child sensitive safeguards, impact assessment, and rights to information and human review for automated decisions. Courts invalidated indiscriminate data retention and constrained cross border transfers lacking equivalent protections. Children's rights guidance demands safety by design, high privacy defaults, and meaningful participation by young people in decisions about their data. For learners with disabilities, the disability convention requires accessible technologies and inclusive pedagogy, which translates into captioning, alternative input methods, interoperable tools, and non-discriminatory algorithmic systems within educational settings.

Equality and non-discrimination norms supply the doctrinal lever against algorithmic bias in admissions, grading, proctoring, and resource allocation. International instruments prohibit discrimination on grounds of sex, disability, ethnicity, language, and socio-economic status, and courts increasingly treat embedded algorithms in public functions as subject to due process, transparency, and contestability. Landmark rulings have invalidated automated welfare risk scoring and scrutinized facial recognition deployments that produced discriminatory effects or lacked a clear legal basis. The emerging European Artificial Intelligence Act places heightened obligations on educational systems where foreseeable risk to fundamental rights exists, reinforcing duties of risk management, documentation, and human oversight. Socio economic rights intersect through affordability, quality, and linguistic inclusion, which requires universal service mechanisms, public access points, and localization that respects cultural and linguistic diversity. Academic freedom and institutional autonomy demand procurement that embeds audit rights, portability, accessibility, privacy, and equality safeguards to prevent vendor lock in and preserve scholarly pluralism. A rights centered governance blueprint follows, with rigorous impact assessment, independent oversight, rights by design, and effective remedies tied to financing and accreditation. Read together, these doctrines render critical digital competencies a justiciable entitlement and align educational ecosystems with dignity, equality, and democratic self-rule.

## 12. FRAMEWORK FOR ACTION

An actionable framework must treat digital literacy as a justiciable extension of the right to education and must therefore operationalize equity by design rather than retrofit it later. The four A principles that govern educational rights translate into concrete digital corollaries that include resilient last mile connectivity, device sufficiency for every learner, accessible and culturally responsive content, and pedagogies that adapt to disability, language, and context. Program charters should encode universal service obligations, zero rating for core learning portals, and assistive technologies aligned to international accessibility guidelines such as WCAG 2.1. Proportional data collection, clear consent practices, and algorithmic transparency protect dignity and autonomy while enabling responsible analytics. Curricula should embed multilingual pathways and locally resonant narratives so that epistemic inclusion precedes assessment. Equity indicators must be specified ex ante and measured ex post, including gender and rural parity in access, time to first meaningful use, rate of assistive technology uptake, and reduction in avoidable learning loss. When these safeguards are designed into infrastructure, content, and pedagogy from inception, digital modernization ceases to be a technocratic add on and becomes a rights compatible transformation that expands substantive educational opportunity.

Participatory governance forms the second axis because rights realization depends on voice, accountability, and shared stewardship. States hold primary duties to respect, protect, and fulfill, yet effectiveness rises when policymaking is co designed with teachers, learners, parents, technologists, and community knowledge holders. Deliberative councils can align standards for competency, privacy, and safety with classroom realities, while teacher unions and youth advisory panels surface frontline constraints and innovations. Public private collaboration is legitimate only when conditioned by public interest covenants that mandate data minimization, portability, interoperability, and fair licensing, with grievance redress and independent audit as non-negotiables. Philanthropic and corporate contributions should be braided into transparent compacts that privilege open standards, open educational resources, and local capacity transfer rather than vendor lock in. Civil society can monitor compliance and convene peer learning networks that diffuse effective practices across districts. This ecosystemic stance reframes digital literacy programs as social contracts whose legitimacy rests on inclusiveness, remedy, and continuous oversight, thereby giving concrete effect to the equality and accountability guarantees within the right to education.

A durable backbone requires sustainable infrastructure and scale mechanisms that convert pilots into systems. Procurement should privilege total cost of ownership, repairability, and energy efficiency, with lifecycle financing for maintenance, battery recycling, and secure decommissioning. Community ICT hubs can extend access after school hours, host intergenerational learning, and generate micro revenues for upkeep. Train the trainer architectures, microcredentialed facilitator pipelines, and local technician tracks reduce downtime and prevent dependency on external vendors. Platform choices should favor modular open-source stacks and standards-based interoperability so that content and data remain portable across providers and devices. Monitoring and evaluation must function as a learning health system that couples telemetry with qualitative inquiry, tests equity sensitive targets, and triggers course correction when gaps widen. Replicability grows through implementation toolkits, reference designs, and communities of practice that codify tacit knowledge for transfer across regions. When infrastructure stewardship, human capacity, and feedback loops co evolve, digital literacy ecosystems become adaptive public goods that honor educational rights, withstand fiscal and technological shocks, and continually regenerate equitable learning gains.

## 13. CONCLUSION

Digital literacy stands revealed as a constitutional dimension of the right to education, not an ancillary skill but a precondition for epistemic agency, civic participation, and dignified work. Across the chapter, theory, pedagogy, and governance converge on a single proposition that learners must command procedural fluency, critical judgment, and ethical discernment within algorithmically mediated environments. Constructivist, sociocultural, and critical traditions justify project-based inquiry, collaborative authorship, and reflective assessment that make students producers of knowledge rather than passive recipients. Policy architectures such as national curricular mandates and continental competence frameworks supply scaffolds only when coherently aligned with institutional capacity and classroom enactment. A rights-based analysis translates availability, accessibility, acceptability, and adaptability into tangible digital correlates that include resilient connectivity, device sufficiency, inclusive and multilingual content, and accessible platforms compliant with universal design. Duties to respect, protect, and fulfill extend to privacy stewardship, transparent analytics, and contestability of automated decisions. Systems thinking clarifies interdependence across infrastructure, teacher preparation, and governance ethics, since a sophisticated tool without pedagogy or safeguards yields little learning and many risks. The outcome is a normative and operational claim that digital literacy is integral to equal educational opportunity and must be financed, measured, and safeguarded as such.

Equity remains the decisive test of legitimacy. Persistent stratifications by income, gender, disability, language, and geography will otherwise be recoded inside new digital regimes. A human rights response joins redistributive investment with participatory governance, open standards, and linguistic localization so that inclusion is designed upstream rather than retrofitted downstream. Transnational cooperation and digital solidarity enlarge the frontier through interoperable micro-credentials, cross border teacher communities, and open curricula that lower cost and raise quality while preserving cultural specificity. Sustainable infrastructure and green information technology link educational rights to climate stewardship, while lifelong reskilling agendas operationalize a just transition in volatile labor markets. Algorithmic accountability, privacy by default, and remedy pathways protect learners from extractive surveillance and biased classification. The strategic horizon includes emergent modalities such as synthetic media, ambient artificial intelligence, and quantum scale computation, which increase capability yet amplify governance demands. The compass remains constant, public financing that treats digital literacy as a common good, institutional learning that iterates on evidence, and shared accountability that centers dignity. Societies that enact these commitments realize the right to education in its contemporary form and equip learners to shape digital systems with competence, integrity, and care.

## REFERENCES


Abella, J., & Rosa, E. D. (2023). Digital Literacy and Digital Competence of Selected Filipino Teachers: Basis for a Post-Pandemic Pedagogy.

Adler, J., Lenski, M., Tolios, A., Taie, S. F., Sopic, M., Rajdl, D., & Biemann, R. (2023). Digital competence in laboratory medicine. *Journal of Laboratory Medicine*, *47*(4), 143–148.

Ahmad, R., Mehmood, S. T., & Ijaz, S. (2023). Digital Literacy Competencies: A Study of Distance Learners of Higher Education Regulatory Authority Khyber Pakhtunkhwa. *Pakistan Journal of Distance and Online Learning*, *9*(1), 82–96.

Al Khateeb, A. A. M. (2017). Measuring Digital Competence and ICT Literacy: An Exploratory Study of In-Service English Language Teachers in the Context of Saudi Arabia. *International Education Studies*, *10*(12), 38–51.

Ala-Mutka, K. (2011). *Mapping digital competence: Towards a conceptual understanding*. Institute for Prospective Technological Studies.

Ala-Mutka, K., Punie, Y., & Redecker, C. (2008). Digital competence for lifelong learning. *Institute for Prospective Technological Studies (IPTS), European Commission, Joint Research Centre. Technical Note: JRC*, *48708*, 271–282.

Alarcón, R., Del Pilar Jiménez, E., & de Vicente-Yagüe, M. I. (2020). Development and validation of the DIGIGLO, a tool for assessing the digital competence of educators. *British Journal of Educational Technology*, *51*(6), 2407–2421.

Amdam, S., Kobberstad, L. R., & Tikkanen, T. I. (2022). Professional digital competence in strategy and management: A case study of three teacher education programs in Norway. *Nordic Journal of Digital Literacy*, (1), 16–30.

Andreasen, J. K., Tømte, C. E., Bergan, I., & Kovac, V. B. (2022). Professional digital competence in initial teacher education: An examination of differences in two cohorts of pre-service teachers. *Nordic Journal of Digital Literacy*, (1), 61–74.

Anurogo, D., La Ramba, H., Putri, N. D., & Putri, U. M. P. (2023). Digital Literacy 5.0 to enhance multicultural education. *Multicultural Islamic Education Review*, *1*(2), 109–179.

Arvianto, F., & St, Y, S. (2023). Designing an Instrument to Measure Digital Literacy Competence Using the 4D Model. *International Journal of Instruction*, *16*(4), 845–860.

Atmojo, I. R. W., Ardiansyah, R., & Adi, F. P. (2023). The Level of Classroom Teacher Digital Literacy in the Technology Dimension of the Instant Digital Competence Assessment (IDCA). In *Elementary School Forum (Mimbar Sekolah Dasar)* (Vol. 10, No. 1, pp. 165-180).

Atmojo, I. R. W., Ardiansyah, R., & Wulandari, W. (2022). Classroom Teacher's Digital Literacy Level Based on Instant Digital Competence Assessment (IDCA) Perspective. In *Elementary School Forum (Mimbar Sekolah Dasar)* (Vol. 9, No. 3, pp. 431-445). Indonesia University of Education.

Ballano, V. O., Mallari, N. T., & Sebastian, R. R. R. (2022). Understanding digital literacy, digital competence, and pedagogical digital competence: implementing online teaching for Filipino tertiary educators during COVID-19. In *Digital Literacy for Teachers* (pp. 391–409). Springer Nature Singapore.

Bayrakcı, S., & Narmanlıoğlu, H. (2021). Digital literacy as whole of digital competences: Scale development study. *Düşünce ve Toplum Sosyal Bilimler Dergisi*, (4), 1–30.

Bejaković, P., & Mrnjavac, Ž. (2020). The importance of digital literacy on the labour market. *Employee Relations: The International Journal*, *42*(4), 921–932.

Berge, O. (2017). Rethinking digital literacy in Nordic school curricula. *Nordic Journal of digital literacy, 12*(1-2), 5-7.

Blyznyuk, T. (2018). Formation of teachers' digital competence: Domestic challenges and foreign experience. *Journal of Vasyl Stefanyk Precarpathian National University*, *5*(1), 40–46.

Bravo, M. C. M., Chalezquer, C. S., & Serrano-Puche, J. (2021). Meta-framework of digital literacy: A comparative analysis of 21st-century skills frameworks. *Revista Latina de Comunicacion Social*, (79), 76–109.

Brevik, L. M., Gudmundsdottir, G. B., Lund, A., & Strømme, T. A. (2019). Transformative agency in teacher education: Fostering professional digital competence. *Teaching and Teacher Education*, *86*, 102875.

Buskqvist, U., & Johansson, E. (2024). From digital competence to digital capacity: A socio-material perspective on digitalization in preschool. *Nordic Journal of Digital Literacy*, (1), 39–51.

Cabero-Almenara, J., Romero-Tena, R., & Palacios-Rodríguez, A. (2020). Evaluation of teacher digital competence frameworks through expert judgement: The use of the expert competence coefficient. *Journal of new approaches in educational research, 9*(2), 275-293.

Cabezas-González, M., Casillas-Martín, S., & García-Peñalvo, F. J. (2021). The digital competence of pre-service educators: The influence of personal variables. *Sustainability, 13*(4), 2318.

Calvani, A., Cartelli, A., Fini, A., & Ranieri, M. (2008). Models and instruments for assessing digital competence at school. *Journal of E-learning and Knowledge Society, 4*(3), 183–193.

Calvani, A., Fini, A., & Ranieri, M. (2010). Digital Competence in K-12: theoretical models, assessment tools and empirical research. *Anàlisi: quaderns de comunicació i cultura*, (40), 157-171.

Carretero, S., Vuorikari, R., & Punie, Y. (2017). The digital competence framework for citizens. *Publications Office of the European Union, 21*(5), 222–235.

Cartelli, A. (2009). Frameworks for digital literacy and digital competence assessment. In *Proceedings of the 8th European Conference on e-Learning* (pp. 116-123).

Cartelli, A. (2010, January). Frameworks for digital competence assessment: Proposals, instruments, and evaluation. In Proceedings of informing science & it education conference (InSITE) (pp. 561-573).

Cartelli, A. (Ed.). (2012). *Current trends and future practices for digital literacy and competence*. IGI Global.

Cartelli, A. (2013). Theory and practice in digital competence assessment. In *Digital Literacy: Concepts, Methodologies, Tools, and Applications* (pp. 1367-1383). IGI Global Scientific Publishing.

Cartelli, A., Dagiene, V., & Futschek, G. (2012). Bebras contest and digital competence assessment: Analysis of frameworks. In *Current trends and future practices for digital literacy and competence* (pp. 35–46). IGI Global.

Casillas Martín, S., Cabezas González, M., & García Peñalvo, F. J. (2020). Digital competence of early childhood education teachers: Attitude, knowledge and use of ICT. *European Journal of Teacher Education, 43*(2), 210–223.

Çebi, A., & Reisoğlu, İ. (2020). Digital competence: A study from the perspective of pre-service teachers in Turkey. *Journal of New Approaches in Educational Research, 9*(2), 294–308.

Chan, B. S., Churchill, D., & Chiu, K. F. (2017). Digital literacy learning in higher education through digital storytelling approach. *Journal of International Education Research.*

Choudhary, H. (2024). Building bridges to digital inclusion: Implications for curriculum development of digital literacy training programs. *International Journal of Technology Enhanced Learning*, *16*(3), 282–296.

Christine, R. (2017). *European framework for the digital competence of educators.* Joint Research Centre.

Cortoni, I., & Cervelli, P., & LO PRESTI, V. (2015). Digital competence assessment. A proposal of operationalization of the critical analysis. *The Journal of Media Literacy Education*, *7*(1), 46–57.

Covello, S., & Lei, J. (2010). A review of digital literacy assessment instruments. *Syracuse University*, *1*, 31.

Cubukcu, A., & Bazyan, S. (2018). A study regarding the perception of digital citizenship among adults and the assessment of this perception: A digital literacy model. In *Information and Technology Literacy: Concepts, Methodologies, Tools, and Applications* (pp. 47-61). IGI Global Scientific Publishing.

Darcy, R. (2019). Infographics, assessment and digital literacy: innovating learning and teaching through developing ethically responsible digital competencies in public health. In *Annual Conference of the Australasian Society for Computers in Learning in Tertiary Education 2019* (pp. 112-120). Australasian Society for Computers in Learning in Tertiary Education.

Davydov, S., Logunova, O., Maltseva, D., Sharikov, A., & Zadorin, I. (2020). Digital literacy concepts and measurement. *Internet in Russia: A study of the Runet and its impact on social life*, 103-120.

de Vries, D. A., Piotrowski, J. T., & de Vreese, C. (2025). Developing the DigIQ: A measure of digital competence. *PLoS One*, *20*(5), e0322995.

Delgado-Vázquez, Á. M., & López-Catalán, B. (2022). From information literacy to digital competence. In *Innovation and ICT in Education* (pp. 65–75). River Publishers.

Ei, C. H., & Soon, C. (2021). Towards a unified framework for digital literacy in Singapore. *IPS Work. Pap, 39.*

Engen, B. K., Giæver, T. H., & Mifsud, L. (2015). Guidelines and regulations for teaching digital competence in schools and teacher education: A weak link?. *Nordic Journal of Digital Literacy, 10*(Jubileumsnummer), 172-186.

Eraku, S. S., Baruadi, M. K., Anantadjaya, S. P., Fadjarajani, S., Supriatna, U., & Arifin, A. (2021). Digital literacy and educators of Islamic education. *Edukasi Islami: Jurnal Pendidikan Islam, 10*(01), 569–576.

Erstad, O., Kjällander, S., & Järvelä, S. (2021). Facing the challenges of 'digital competence' a Nordic agenda for curriculum development for the 21st century. *Nordic Journal of Digital Literacy, 16*(2), 77–87.

Esteve-Mon, F., Llopis, M., & Adell-Segura, J. (2020). Digital competence and computational thinking of student teachers. [iJET]. *International Journal of Emerging Technologies in Learning, 15*(2), 29–41.

Falloon, G. (2020). From digital literacy to digital competence: The teacher digital competency (TDC) framework. *Educational Technology Research and Development, 68*(5), 2449–2472.

Fantin, M. (2010). Perspectives on media literacy, digital literacy and information literacy. [IJDLDC]. *International Journal of Digital Literacy and Digital Competence, 1*(4), 10–15.

Farias-Gaytan, S., Aguaded, I., & Ramirez-Montoya, M. S. (2022). Transformation and digital literacy: Systematic literature mapping. *Education and Information Technologies, 27*(2), 1417–1437.

Feng, L., & Xue, S. (2023). Using the DigCompEdu framework to conceptualize teachers' digital literacy. *Education Journal, 12*(3), 103–108.

Ferrari, A. (2012). *Digital competence in practice: An analysis of frameworks* (Vol. 10). Publications Office of the European Union.

Ferrari, A., & Punie, Y. (2013, April). *DIGCOMP: A framework for developing and understanding digital competence in Europe.*

Ferrari, A., Punie, Y., & Redecker, C. (2012). Understanding digital competence in the 21st century: An analysis of current frameworks. In *21st Century Learning for 21st Century Skills: 7th European Conference of Technology Enhanced Learning, EC-TEL 2012, Saarbrücken, Germany, September 18-21, 2012.* [Springer Berlin Heidelberg.]. *Proceedings, 7*, 79–92.

From, J. (2017). Pedagogical Digital Competence—Between Values, Knowledge and Skills. *Higher Education Studies, 7*(2), 43–50.

Gallardo-Echenique, E. E., de Oliveira, J. M., Marqués-Molias, L., Esteve-Mon, F., Wang, Y., & Baker, R. (2015). Digital competence in the knowledge society. *Journal of Online Learning and Teaching, 11*(1).

Gapski, H. (2007, September). Some reflections on digital literacy. In *Proceedings of the 3rd international workshop on digital literacy* (Vol. 310, pp. 49-55). Crete: CEUR-WS. org.

García-Vandewalle García, J. M., García-Carmona, M., Trujillo Torres, J. M., & Moya Fernández, P. (2023). Analysis of digital competence of educators (DigCompEdu) in teacher trainees: The context of Melilla, Spain. *Technology. Knowledge and Learning*, *28*(2), 585–612.

Garzón Artacho, E., Martínez, T. S., Ortega Martin, J. L., Marin Marin, J. A., & Gómez García, G. (2020). Teacher training in lifelong learning—The importance of digital competence in the encouragement of teaching innovation. *Sustainability*, *12*(7), 2852.

Garzón-Artacho, E., Sola-Martínez, T., Romero-Rodríguez, J. M., & Gómez-García, G. (2021). Teachers' perceptions of digital competence at the lifelong learning stage. *Heliyon*, *7*(7).

Ghomi, M., & Redecker, C. (2019, May). Digital Competence of Educators (DigCompEdu): Development and Evaluation of a Self-assessment Instrument for Teachers' Digital Competence. In *CSEDU (1)* (pp. 541-548).

Gisbert Cervera, M., & Lázaro Cantabrana, J. L. (2015). Professional development in teacher digital competence and improving school quality from the teachers' perspective: A case study. *Journal of New Approaches in Educational Research*, *4*(2), 115–122.

Godhe, A. L. (2019). Digital literacies or digital competence: Conceptualizations in Nordic curricula. *Media and Communication*, *7*(2), 25–35.

Gutierrez-Angel, N., Sanchez-Garcia, J. N., Mercader-Rubio, I., Garcia-Martin, J., & Brito-Costa, S. (2022). Digital literacy in the university setting: A literature review of empirical studies between 2010 and 2021. *Frontiers in Psychology*, *13*, 896800.

Guzmán-Simón, F., García-Jiménez, E., & López-Cobo, I. (2017). Undergraduate students' perspectives on digital competence and academic literacy in a Spanish University. *Computers in Human Behavior*, *74*, 196–204.

Hammoda, B., & Foli, S. (2024). A Digital Competence Framework for Learners (DCFL): A Conceptual Framework for Digital Literacy. *Knowledge Management & E-Learning*, *16*(3), 477–500.

Hanell, F. (2018). What is the 'problem'that digital competence in Swedish teacher education is meant to solve?. *Nordic Journal of digital literacy, 13*(3), 137-151.

Hatlevik, O. E., & Christophersen, K. A. (2013). Digital competence at the beginning of upper secondary school: Identifying factors explaining digital inclusion. *Computers & Education*, *63*, 240–247.

Hatlevik, O. E., Ottestad, G., & Throndsen, I. (2015). Predictors of digital competence in 7th grade: A multilevel analysis. *Journal of Computer Assisted Learning, 31*(3), 220–231.

He, T., & Li, S. (2019). A comparative study of digital informal learning: The effects of digital competence and technology expectancy. *British Journal of Educational Technology, 50*(4), 1744–1758.

He, T., & Zhu, C. (2017). Digital informal learning among Chinese university students: The effects of digital competence and personal factors. *International Journal of Educational Technology in Higher Education, 14*, 1–19.

Hinojo-Lucena, F. J., Aznar-Diaz, I., Caceres-Reche, M. P., Trujillo-Torres, J. M., & Romero-Rodriguez, J. M. (2019). Factors influencing the development of digital competence in teachers: Analysis of the teaching staff of permanent education centres. *IEEE Access : Practical Innovations, Open Solutions, 7*, 178744–178752.

Ilomäki, L., Kantosalo, A., & Lakkala, M. (2011). What is digital competence? In *Linked portal* (pp. 1-12). European Schoolnet (EUN).

Ilomäki, L., Paavola, S., Lakkala, M., & Kantosalo, A. (2016). Digital competence–an emergent boundary concept for policy and educational research. *Education and Information Technologies, 21*, 655–679.

Indah, R. N., Toyyibah, T., Budhiningrum, A. S., & Afifi, N. (2022). The research competence, critical thinking skills and digital literacy of Indonesian EFL students. *Journal of Language Teaching and Research, 13*(2), 315–324.

Indriyani, V. (2019, August). Digital literacy competencies for teacher education students. In *1st International Conference on Education Social Sciences and Humanities (ICESSHum 2019)* (pp. 1010-1018). Atlantis Press.

Instefjord, E. (2015). Appropriation of digital competence in teacher education. *Nordic Journal of Digital Literacy, 10*(Jubileumsnummer), 155-171.

Iordache, C., Mariën, I., & Baelden, D. (2017). Developing digital skills and competences: A quick-scan analysis of 13 digital literacy models. *Italian Journal of Sociology of Education, 9*(Italian Journal of Sociology of Education 9/1), 6-30.

Janssen, J., Stoyanov, S., Ferrari, A., Punie, Y., Pannekeet, K., & Sloep, P. (2013). Experts' views on digital competence: Commonalities and differences. *Computers & Education, 68*, 473–481.

Javorský, S., & Horváth, R. (2014). Phenomenon of digital literacy in scope of european cross-curricular comparison. *Procedia: Social and Behavioral Sciences, 143*, 769–777.

Johannesen, M., Øgrim, L., & Giæver, T. H. (2014). Notion in motion: Teachers' digital competence. *Nordic Journal of Digital Literacy*, *9*(4), 300–312.

Juškevičienė, A., & Dagien, Ė, V. (2018). Computational thinking relationship with digital competence. *Informatics in Education*, *17*(2), 265–284.

Kasemsap, K. (2018). Encouraging digital literacy and ICT competency in the information age. In *Encyclopedia of Information Science and Technology* (4th ed., pp. 2253–2263). IGI Global.

Kasperski, R., Blau, I., & Ben-Yehudah, G. (2022). Teaching digital literacy: Are teachers' perspectives consistent with actual pedagogy? *Technology, Pedagogy and Education*, *31*(5), 615–635.

Kateryna, A., Oleksandr, R., Mariia, T., Iryna, S., Evgen, K., & Anastasiia, L. (2020). Digital literacy development trends in the professional environment. *International Journal of Learning. Teaching and Educational Research*, *19*(7), 55–79.

Khan, F., & Vuopala, E. (2019). Digital competence assessment across generations: A Finnish sample using the digcomp framework. [IJDLDC]. *International Journal of Digital Literacy and Digital Competence*, *10*(2), 15–28.

Khokhar, A. S. (2016). Digital literacy: How prepared is India to embrace it? [IJ-DLDC]. *International Journal of Digital Literacy and Digital Competence*, *7*(3), 1–12.

Kim, H. J., Hong, A. J., & Song, H. D. (2018). The relationships of family, perceived digital competence and attitude, and learning agility in sustainable student engagement in higher education. *Sustainability*, *10*(12), 4635.

Kim, K. T. (2019). The structural relationship among digital literacy, learning strategies, and core competencies among south korean college students. *Educational Sciences: Theory & Practice*, *19*(2), 3–21.

Koch, C., & Fehlmann, F. (2025). Beyond digital literacy: Exploring factors affecting digital performance of university staff. *Media and Communication*, **•••**, 13.

Koltay, T. (2011). The media and the literacies: Media literacy, information literacy, digital literacy. *Media Culture & Society*, *33*(2), 211–221.

Koppel, I., & Langer, S. (2020). Basic digital literacy-Requirements and elements. *Revista Práxis Educacional*, *16*(42), 326–347.

Krumsvik, R. J. (2008). Situated learning and teachers' digital competence. *Education and Information Technologies, 13*(4), 279–290.

Krumsvik, R. J. (2011). Digital competence in the Norwegian teacher education and schools. *Högre Utbildning, 1*(1), 39–51.

Krumsvik, R. J. (2014). Teacher educators' digital competence. *Scandinavian Journal of Educational Research, 58*(3), 269–280.

Krumsvik, R. J. (2022). Digital competence across the education and health sector. *Nordic Journal of Digital Literacy*, (3), 149–154.

Krumsvik, R. J., Jones, L. Ø., Øfstegaard, M., & Eikeland, O. J. (2016). Upper secondary school teachers' digital competence: Analysed by demographic, personal and professional characteristics. *Nordic journal of digital literacy, 11*(3), 143-164.

Kuzminska, O., Mazorchuk, M., Morze, N., Pavlenko, V., & Prokhorov, A. (2019). Study of digital competence of the students and teachers in Ukraine. In *Information and Communication Technologies in Education, Research, and Industrial Applications: 14th International Conference, ICTERI 2018, Kyiv, Ukraine, May 14-17, 2018, Revised Selected Papers 14* (pp. 148-169). Springer International Publishing.

Leahy, D., & Dolan, D. (2010, September). Digital literacy: A vital competence for 2010? In *IFIP international conference on key competencies in the knowledge society* (pp. 210–221). Springer Berlin Heidelberg.

Lee, S. H. (2014). Digital literacy education for the development of digital literacy. [IJDLDC]. *International Journal of Digital Literacy and Digital Competence, 5*(3), 29–43.

Legvart, P., Kordigel Aberšek, M., & Kerneža, M. (2021). Primary School Students' Natural Science Digital Literacy Competence in Digital Learning Environments. In *International Baltic Symposium on Science and Technology Education.* Scientia Socialis Ltd. 29 K. Donelaicio Street, LT-78115 Siauliai, Republic of Lithuania.

Levano-Francia, L., Sanchez Diaz, S., Guillén-Aparicio, P., Tello-Cabello, S., Herrera-Paico, N., & Collantes-Inga, Z. (2019). Digital Competences and Education. *Journal of Educational Psychology-Propositos y Representaciones, 7*(2), 579–588.

Li, Y., & Ranieri, M. (2010). Are 'digital natives' really digitally competent?—A study on Chinese teenagers. *British Journal of Educational Technology, 41*(6), 1029–1042.

López-Meneses, E., Sirignano, F. M., Vázquez-Cano, E., & Ramírez-Hurtado, J. M. (2020). University students' digital competence in three areas of the DigCom 2.1 model: A comparative study at three European universities. *Australasian Journal of Educational Technology*, *36*(3), 69–88.

Lund, A., Furberg, A., Bakken, J., & Engelien, K. L. (2014). What does professional digital competence mean in teacher education?. *Nordic journal of digital literacy, 9*(4), 280-298.

Maderick, J. A., Zhang, S., Hartley, K., & Marchand, G. (2016). Preservice teachers and self-assessing digital competence. *Journal of Educational Computing Research, 54*(3), 326–351.

Maher, D. (2020). Pre-service teachers' digital competencies to support school students' digital literacies. In *Handbook of research on literacy and digital technology integration in teacher education* (pp. 29–46). IGI Global Scientific Publishing.

Makhafola, L., van Deventer, M. J., Holmner, M. A., & Van Wyk, B. (2025). A scoping review of digital literacy, digital competence, digital fluency and digital dexterity in academic libraries' context. *Journal of Academic Librarianship*, *51*(3), 103053.

Mannila, L., Nordén, L. Å., & Pears, A. (2018, August). Digital competence, teacher self-efficacy and training needs. In *Proceedings of the 2018 ACM Conference on International Computing Education Research* (pp. 78-85).

Marín, V. I., & Castaneda, L. (2022). Developing digital literacy for teaching and learning. In *Handbook of open, distance and digital education* (pp. 1–20). Springer Nature Singapore.

Marnita, M., Nurdin, D., & Prihatin, E. (2023). The effectiveness of elementary teacher digital literacy competence on teacher learning management. *Journal of Innovation in Educational and Cultural Research*, *4*(1), 35–43.

Marsh, J. (2016). The digital literacy skills and competences of children of pre-school age. *Medical Education*, (2), 178–195.

Martin, A. (2006). A European framework for digital literacy. *Nordic Journal of Digital Literacy*, *1*(2), 151–161.

Martin, A. (2008). Digital literacy and the "digital society". *Digital literacies: Concepts, policies and practices, 30*(151), 1029-1055.

Martin, A., & Grudziecki, J. (2006). DigEuLit: Concepts and tools for digital literacy development. *Innovation in teaching and learning in information and computer sciences, 5*(4), 249-267.

Martínez-Alcalá, C. I., Rosales-Lagarde, A., Alonso-Lavernia, M. D. L. Á., Ramírez-Salvador, J. Á., Jiménez-Rodríguez, B., Cepeda-Rebollar, R. M., & Agis-Juárez, R. A. (2018). Digital inclusion in older adults: A comparison between face-to-face and blended digital literacy workshops. *Frontiers in ICT (Lausanne, Switzerland)*, *5*, 21.

Martínez-Bravo, M. C., Sádaba-Chalezquer, C., & Serrano-Puche, J. (2020). Fifty years of digital literacy studies: A meta-research for interdisciplinary and conceptual convergence. *El Profesional de la Información*, *29*(4).

Martínez-Bravo, M. C., Sádaba Chalezquer, C., & Serrano-Puche, J. (2022). Dimensions of digital literacy in the 21st century competency frameworks. *Sustainability*, *14*(3), 1867.

Martzoukou, K., Luders, E. S., Mair, J., Kostagiolas, P., Johnson, N., Work, F., & Fulton, C. (2024). A cross-sectional study of discipline-based self-perceived digital literacy competencies of nursing students. *Journal of Advanced Nursing*, *80*(2), 656–672.

Mbandje, D. C., Loureiro, M. J., & Lucas, M. (2023). Digital competence and information literacy: Clarifying concepts based on a literature review. *Educational Media International*, *60*(3-4), 306–316.

McDougall, J., Readman, M., & Wilkinson, P. (2018). The uses of (digital) literacy. *Learning, Media and Technology*, *43*(3), 263–279.

Mehrvarz, M., Heidari, E., Farrokhnia, M., & Noroozi, O. (2021). The mediating role of digital informal learning in the relationship between students' digital competence and their academic performance. *Computers & Education*, *167*, 104184.

Menggo, S., Midun, H., & Pandor, P. (2021). Students' digital literacy competence and English study habits. In *The 1st International Conference on Education, Humanities, Health, and Agriculture.* (pp. 3-6).DOI: <ALIGNMENT.qj></ALIGNMENT>10.4108/eai

Milenkova, V., & Lendzhova, V. (2021). Digital citizenship and digital literacy in the conditions of social crisis. *Computers*, *10*(4), 40.

Mishra, P., & Sharma, P. K. (2018). Digital literacy competencies in the 21st century. *Globus Journal of Progressive Education*, *8*(2), 1–3.

MOKHTARI, F. (2023). Fostering Digital Literacy in Higher Education: Benefits, Challenges and Implications. *International Journal of Linguistics, Literature & Translation, 6*(10).

Morellato, M. (2014). Digital competence in tourism education: Cooperative-experiential learning. *Journal of Teaching in Travel & Tourism, 14*(2), 184–209.

Moreno-Guerrero, A. J., Marín-Marin, J. A., López-Belmonte, J., & Churi, P. (2022). Systematic review on digital competence in the Spanish context. *Digital Literacy for Teachers*, 495-517.

Müller, M. L., Frenz, M., & Nitsch, V. (2023). Digitale Kompetenz, Digital Literacy, Digital Competence–Eine vergleichende, strukturierte Literaturanalyse deutsch-und englischsprachiger Beiträge. *Jahrbuch der berufs-und wirtschaftspädagogischen. Forschung, 2023*, 9.

Murphy, O. (2018). Digital competences: A foundational digital literacy for all. In *Design Thinking for Digital Well-being* (pp. 16–26). Routledge.

Murtadho, M. I., Rohmah, R. Y., Jamilah, Z., & Furqon, M. (2023). The role of digital literacy in improving students' competence in digital era. *AL-WIJDÃN Journal of Islamic Education Studies*, *8*(2), 253–260.

Nada, E. I., & Sari, W. K. (2020). Digital literacy analysis of chemistry education students in using the ChemDraw application. [Jurnal Kimia Dan Pendidikan Kimia]. *JKPK*, *5*(3), 293–299.

Napal Fraile, M., Peñalva-Vélez, A., & Mendióroz Lacambra, A. M. (2018). Development of digital competence in secondary education teachers' training. *Education Sciences*, *8*(3), 104.

Nascimbeni, F. (2018). Rethinking digital literacy for teachers in open and participatory societies. [IJDLDC]. *International Journal of Digital Literacy and Digital Competence*, *9*(3), 1–11.

Nascimbeni, F., & Vosloo, S. (2019). Digital literacy for children: Exploring definitions and frameworks. *Scoping Paper*, *1*, 1.

Neagu, G. (2022). Understanding the implications of digital competence for the education process in Romania. A literature review. *Digital Literacy for Teachers*, 441-462.

Nebot, M. Á. L., Cosentino, V. V., Esteve-Mon, F. M., & Segura, J. A. (2021). Diagnostic and educational self-assessment of the digital competence of university teachers. *Nordic Journal of Digital Literacy*, (3-4), 115–131.

Nelson, K., Courier, M., & Joseph, G. W. (2011). An investigation of digital literacy needs of students. *Journal of Information Systems Education*, *22*(2), 95–110.

Nguyen, L. A. T., & Habók, A. (2024). Tools for assessing teacher digital literacy: A review. *Journal of Computers in Education, 11*(1), 305–346.

Oberländer, M., Beinicke, A., & Bipp, T. (2020). Digital competencies: A review of the literature and applications in the workplace. *Computers & Education, 146*, 103752.

Olimpo, G. (2013). Rifessioni brevi su digital literacy e digital competence. *Italian Journal of Educational Technology, 21*(1), 14–18.

Orakova, A., Nametkulova, F., Issayeva, G., Mukhambetzhanova, S., Galimzhanova, M., & Rezuanova, G. (2024). The relationships between pedagogical and technological competence and digital literacy level of teachers. *Journal of Curriculum Studies Research, 6*(1), 1–21.

Ottestad, G., Kelentrić, M., & Guðmundsdóttir, G. B. (2014). Professional digital competence in teacher education. *Nordic journal of digital literacy, 9*(4), 243-249.

Palacios-Hidalgo, F. J., & Huertas-Abril, C. A. (2025). Developing digital literacy in initial EFL teacher education: A study in a Spanish distance university. *Open Learning, 40*(1), 50–66.

Pangrazio, L., Godhe, A. L., & Ledesma, A. G. L. (2020). What is digital literacy? A comparative review of publications across three language contexts. *E-Learning and Digital Media, 17*(6), 442–459.

Park, H., Kim, H. S., & Park, H. W. (2021). A scientometric study of digital literacy, ICT literacy, information literacy, and media literacy. *Journal of Data and Information Science, 6*(2), 116–138.

Pegalajar Palomino, M. D. C., & Rodríguez Torres, Á. F. (2023, November). Digital literacy in university students of education degrees in Ecuador. [). Frontiers Media SA.]. *Frontiers in Education, 8*, 1299059.

Peng, D., & Yu, Z. (2022). A literature review of digital literacy over two decades. *Education Research International, 2022*(1), 2533413.

Pérez-Escoda, A., & Rodríguez-Conde, M. J. (2015, October). Digital literacy and digital competences in the educational evaluation: USA and IEA contexts. In *Proceedings of the 3rd international conference on technological ecosystems for enhancing multiculturality* (pp. 355-360).

Peters, S. (2024). *Digital Literacy and Competence*. Digital Foundations for Art and Design Studies.

Pettersson, F. (2018). On the issues of digital competence in educational contexts–a review of literature. *Education and Information Technologies*, *23*(3), 1005–1021.

Phuapan, P., Viriyavejakul, C., & Pimdee, P. (2016). An analysis of digital literacy skills among Thai university seniors. *International Journal of Emerging Technologies in Learning (Online)*, *11*(3), 24.

Porat, E., Blau, I., & Barak, A. (2018). Measuring digital literacies: Junior high-school students' perceived competencies versus actual performance. *Computers & Education*, *126*, 23–36.

Portillo, J., Garay, U., Tejada, E., & Bilbao, N. (2020). Self-perception of the digital competence of educators during the COVID-19 pandemic: A cross-analysis of different educational stages. *Sustainability*, *12*(23), 10128.

Pötzsch, H. (2016). Materialist perspectives on digital technologies: Informing debates on digital literacy and competence.

Qingyi, W. (2023). A Study of the Improvement of Digital Literacy from the Perspective of DigComp 2.2: The Digital Competence Framework for Citizens. *Library Journal*, *42*(383), 97.

Rahman, T., Amalia, A., & Aziz, Z. (2021, January). From digital literacy to digital intelligence. In *4th International Conference on Sustainable Innovation 2020–Social, Humanity, and Education (ICoSIHESS 2020)* (pp. 154-159). Atlantis Press.

Rambousek, V., Štípek, J., & Vaňková, P. (2016). Contents of digital literacy from the perspective of teachers and pupils. *Procedia: Social and Behavioral Sciences*, *217*, 354–362.

Ratano, P. (2018). Digital competence and digital literacy in social media usage for the visually impaired youths in Thailand.

Reddy, P., Chaudhary, K., & Hussein, S. (2023). A digital literacy model to narrow the digital literacy skills gap. *Heliyon*, *9*(4).

Reddy, P., Chaudhary, K., Sharma, B., & Chand, R. (2020, December). Digital Literacy: A Catalyst for the 21 st Century Education. In *2020 IEEE Asia-Pacific Conference on Computer Science and Data Engineering (CSDE)* (pp. 1-6). IEEE.

Reddy, P., Chaudhary, K. C., Sharma, B. N., & Chand, R. (2022). Talismans of digital literacy: A statistical overview. *Electronic Journal of e-Learning*, *20*(5), 570–587.

Reichert, F., Zhang, D., Law, N. W., Wong, G. K., & de la Torre, J. (2020). Exploring the structure of digital literacy competence assessed using authentic software applications. *Educational Technology Research and Development*, *68*, 2991–3013.

Røkenes, F. M., Grüters, R., Skaalvik, C., Lie, T. G., Østerlie, O., Järnerot, A., & Letnes, M. A. (2022). Teacher educators' professional digital competence in primary and lower secondary school teacher education. *Nordic Journal of Digital Literacy*, (1), 46–60.

Røkenes, F. M., & Krumsvik, R. J. (2014). Development of student teachers' digital competence in teacher education-A literature review. *Nordic Journal of Digital Literacy*, *9*(4), 250–280.

Romero-García, C., Buzón-García, O., & de Paz-Lugo, P. (2020). Improving future teachers' digital competence using active methodologies. *Sustainability*, *12*(18), 7798.

Sá, M. J., & Serpa, S. (2020). COVID-19 and the promotion of digital competences in education. *Universal Journal of Educational Research*, *8*(10), 4520–4528.

Salganova, E. I., & Osipova, L. B. (2023). Students' digital literacy: Competence-based approach. *Economic and Social Changes: Facts, Trends. Forecast*, *16*(1), 227–240.

Saliu, H., & Bicaj, A. (2022). The digital competence of future teachers in Kosovo. In *Digital Literacy for Teachers* (pp. 275–290). Springer Nature Singapore.

Sánchez-Caballé, A., Gisbert-Cervera, M., & Esteve-Mon, F. (2020). The digital competence of university students: a systematic literature review. *Aloma: revista de psicologia, ciències de l'educació i de l'esport Blanquerna, 38*(1), 63-74.

Sánchez-Cruzado, C., Santiago Campión, R., & Sánchez-Compaña, M. T. (2021). Teacher digital literacy: The indisputable challenge after COVID-19. *Sustainability*, *13*(4), 1858.

Schröter, T., & Grafe, S. (2020, November). Digital literacy and digital competency of university teachers. A systematic analysis of frameworks. In *Innovate Learning Summit* (pp. 144-157). Association for the Advancement of Computing in Education (AACE).

Sefton-Green, J., Nixon, H., & Erstad, O. (2009). Reviewing approaches and perspectives on "digital literacy". *Pedagogies*, *4*(2), 107–125.

Shariman, T. P. N. T., Razak, N. A., & Noor, N. F. M. (2012). Digital literacy competence for academic needs: An analysis of Malaysian students in three universities. *Procedia: Social and Behavioral Sciences*, *69*, 1489–1496.

Shopova, T. (2014). Digital literacy of students and its improvement at the university. *Journal on Efficiency and Responsibility in Education and Science*, *7*(2), 26–32.

Sillat, L. H., Tammets, K., & Laanpere, M. (2021). Digital competence assessment methods in higher education: A systematic literature review. *Education Sciences, 11*(8), 402.

Skantz-Åberg, E., Lantz-Andersson, A., Lundin, M., & Williams, P. (2022). Teachers' professional digital competence: An overview of conceptualisations in the literature. *Cogent Education, 9*(1), 2063224.

Søby, M. (2013). Learning to be: Developing and understanding digital competence. *Nordic Journal of Digital Literacy, 8*(3), 134–138.

Søby, M. (2015). Digital competence-a password to a new interdisciplinary field. *Nordic Journal of Digital Literacy, 10*(Jubileumsnummer), 4-7.

Spante, M., Hashemi, S. S., Lundin, M., & Algers, A. (2018). Digital competence and digital literacy in higher education research: Systematic review of concept use. *Cogent Education, 5*(1), 1519143.

Stopar, K., & Bartol, T. (2019). Digital competences, computer skills and information literacy in secondary education: Mapping and visualization of trends and concepts. *Scientometrics, 118*(2), 479–498.

Svendsen, A. M., & Svendsen, J. T. (2021). Digital directions: Curricular goals relating to digital literacy and digital competences in the Gymnasium (stx) in Denmark. *Nordic Journal of Digital Literacy, 16*(1), 6–20.

Svensson, M., & Baelo, R. (2015). Teacher students' perceptions of their digital competence. *Procedia: Social and Behavioral Sciences, 180*, 1527–1534.

Tammaro, R., & D'Alessio, A. (2016). Teacher training and digital competence: A pedagogical recommendation. [IJDLDC]. *International Journal of Digital Literacy and Digital Competence, 7*(2), 1–10.

Tejedor, S., Cervi, L., Pérez-Escoda, A., & Jumbo, F. T. (2020). Digital literacy and higher education during COVID-19 lockdown: Spain, Italy, and Ecuador. *Publications, 8*(4), 48.

Terry, J., Davies, A., Williams, C., Tait, S., & Condon, L. (2019). Improving the digital literacy competence of nursing and midwifery students: A qualitative study of the experiences of NICE student champions. *Nurse Education in Practice, 34*, 192–198.

Tinmaz, H., Fanea-Ivanovici, M., & Baber, H. (2023). A snapshot of digital literacy. *Library Hi Tech News, 40*(1), 20–23.

Tinmaz, H., Lee, Y. T., Fanea-Ivanovici, M., & Baber, H. (2022). A systematic review on digital literacy. *Smart Learning Environments*, *9*(1), 21.

Tomaszewicz, A. A. (2015). The impact of digital literacy on e-government development. *Online Journal of Applied Knowledge Management, 3*(2).

Tomczyk, Ł., & Fedeli, L. (2022). Introduction—On the Need for Research on the Digital Literacy of Current and Future Teachers. In *Digital Literacy for Teachers* (pp. 1–6). Springer Nature Singapore.

Tomczyk, Ł., & Fedeli, L. (2022). *Digital literacy for teachers*. Springer.

Tømte, C., Enochsson, A. B., Buskqvist, U., & Kårstein, A. (2015). Educating online student teachers to master professional digital competence: The TPACK-framework goes online. *Computers & Education, 84*, 26–35.

Tømte, C. E. (2015). Educating Teachers for the New Millennium?-Teacher training, ICT and digital competence. *Nordic journal of digital literacy, 10*(Jubileumsnummer), 138-154.

Tornero, J. M. P., Sánchez, M. O. P., Baena, G., Luque, S. G., Tejedor, S., & Fernández, N. (2010). Trends and models of Media literacy in Europe: Between digital competence and critical understanding. *Anàlisi: Quaderns de comunicació i cultura*, (40), 85-100.

Tveiterås, N. C., & Madsen, S. S. (2022). From tools to complexity?—A systematic literature analysis of digital competence among pre-service teachers in Norway. *Digital literacy for teachers*, 345-389.

Vaskov, M., Isakov, A., Bilovus, V., Bulavkin, A., & Mikhaylenko, N. (2021). Digital literacy of modern higher education teachers. In *E3S web of conferences* (Vol. 273, p. 12035). EDP Sciences.

Vuorikari, R., Kluzer, S., & Punie, Y. (2022). *DigComp 2.2: The Digital Competence Framework for Citizens-With new examples of knowledge, skills and attitudes*.

Wardhani, D., Hesti, S., & Dwityas, N. A. (2019). Digital literacy: A survey level digital literacy competence among university students in Jakarta. *International Journal of English Literature and Social Sciences*, *4*(4), 1131–1138.

Yang, H. (2024). From digital literacy to digital competence: The structure of Teacher Digital Competence (TDC). *Innovations in Education and Teaching International*, •••, 1–13.

Yang, K., Seo, S., & Ok, H. (2020). Development of self assessment tool for digital literacy competence. *Journal of Digital Convergence*, *18*(7), 1–8.

Yazon, A. D., Ang-Manaig, K., Buama, C. A. C., & Tesoro, J. F. B. (2019). Digital literacy, digital competence and research productivity of educators. *Universal Journal of Educational Research*, *7*(8), 1734–1743.

Zabolotska, O., Zhyliak, N., Hevchuk, N., Petrenko, N., & Alieko, O. (2021). Digital competencies of teachers in the transformation of the educational environment.

Zadražilová, I., & Vizváry, P. (2021, September). Digital literacy competencies and interests of elderly people. In *European conference on information literacy* (pp. 137-146). Cham: Springer International Publishing.

Zakharov, K., Komarova, A., Baranova, T., & Gulk, E. (2021, November). Information literacy and digital competence of teachers in the age of digital transformation. In *XIV International Scientific Conference "INTERAGROMASH 2021" Precision Agriculture and Agricultural Machinery Industry, Volume 2* (pp. 857-868). Cham: Springer International Publishing.

Zakir, S., Hoque, M. E., Susanto, P., Nisaa, V., Alam, M. K., Khatimah, H., & Mulyani, E. (2025, June). Digital literacy and academic performance: The mediating roles of digital informal learning, self-efficacy, and students' digital competence. [Frontiers Media SA.]. *Frontiers in Education*, *10*, 1590274.

Zhao, Y., Llorente, A. M. P., & Gómez, M. C. S. (2021). Digital competence in higher education research: A systematic literature review. *Computers & Education*, *168*, 104212.

Zhao, Y., Sánchez Gómez, M. C., Pinto Llorente, A. M., & Zhao, L. (2021). Digital competence in higher education: Students' perception and personal factors. *Sustainability*, *13*(21), 12184.

# Chapter 7
# A Victimological and Legal Analysis of Gendered Cybervictimization and Protection of Women's Rights in Digital Space

**Arpan Verma**
https://orcid.org/0009-0001-2870-3432
*Manipal University Jaipur, India*

**Parul Asthana**
https://orcid.org/0009-0003-1696-0380
*Jagran Lakecity University, Bhopal, India*

## ABSTRACT

*This chapter provides an account of Online Gender-Based Violence (OGBV) and Technology-Facilitated Gender-Based Violence (TFGBV) as overlapping phenomena that indicate the changing patterns of gender-based violence in cyberspaces. It posits a human-rights framework by investigating structures of global legal formations and victim-centered barriers presented at a territorial level. Moreover, it also points out the comorbidities that typically affect marginalized groups and criticises the drawbacks of the existing punitive-based interventions. Under the feminist and technofeminist approach, it attempts to suggest trauma-informed care, inclusive*

DOI: 10.4018/979-8-3373-8510-5.ch007

*digital governance, and structural changes. The text concludes by emphasising that addressing these two forms of violence requires the implementation of integrated, inclusive, and gender-sensitive legal, policy, and platform reforms.*

# 1. INTRODUCTION

## 1.1 Background and Rationale

Digitalization in contemporary society has furthered mediation of interactions, identities, and expressions through online platforms. Consequently, this has led to an abject transformation of the notion of justice as well (Yeasmin, 2024). The realities of gendered violence in cyberspace have started to transform what counts as harm, who qualifies as victims, and the ambit of the responsibility of states. In order to understand such metamorphosis, it is imperative to revisit rudimentary jurisprudential theories often present at the core of legal frameworks of the said subject matter. The notion of justice has an implied aim of safeguarding the vulnerable, the marginalized, and the silenced. In "A Theory of Justice," John Rawls viewed justice as fairness while contending that the legitimacy of a social institution can be assessed based on how it is benefiting the least advantaged. By laying down the "Difference Principle," Rawls has obligated socio-legal setups to mitigate inequalities in a way that is beneficial for those who are adversely placed in the societal matrix (Rawls, 1971). Even though Rawls' theory dates to the pre-digital era, its applicability is pivotal in analyzing how legal systems should deal with evolving and emerging vulnerabilities in the digital domain. Cybervictimization is a seminal issue in this regard that tends to target the vulnerabilities of the victims, posing a major threat to human rights in digital space. Ergo, based on the Rawlsian approach, it can be stated that the idea of justice in the digital era should not only further due process and proscribe questionable acts but also safeguard the dignity and security of those prone to cyber harm. Hence, domestic and legal frameworks need to recalibrate themselves by creating a conducive and safe environment that promotes equitable participation in the digital domain. Moreover, furthering the Aristotelian notion and excogitating Rawls' theory, Martha Nussbaum propounded the capability approach. From the perspective of social justice, she conceptualizes that there are certain capabilities like life, bodily health, integrity, emotions, affiliation, etc. According to her, for society to be just, these capabilities should be duly ensured and secured by the state, as these form the core of human dignity (Nussbaum, 2011). In the context of digital space, contraventions of these capabilities are frequent. Women experience tangible degradation of both physical integrity and emotional state when personal details are accessed and shared unauthorizedly, consequent to which they are subjected to online harassment. This poses an impediment to their presence in digital space. Ergo, from the perspective of the capability approach, domestic as well as international legal frameworks need to "empower" by providing accessible remedies as well as safe digital participation, thereby furthering victim-oriented justice. A victimological approach is imperative because it brings forward invisible and unseen harms of the victims that are often left unaccounted for by traditional justice frameworks (Sharma, Alam, Vatsa, 2024).

The surge in instances of Online Gender Based Violence (*hereinafter* OGBV) in the digital domain attracted international legal and policy attention. The UNHRC, vide its Resolution 20/8, affirmed that the rights of the individual existing online must be safeguarded in the same manner as the rights existing offline (UNHRC, 2012). Similarly, the Budapest Convention established the first international treaty that focused on internet and computer crime through harmonization of domestic and international laws and enhancing investigative capabilities and international collaboration. The convention does not mention gender-based violence explicitly, but experts analyze its conceptual structure to determine its relevance for cyberattacks against women (Elpaccto, 2022). General Recommendation No. 35 (2017) of the CEDAW expands the definition of gender-based violence through its acknowledgment that technology helps perpetrators commit and escalate crimes against women. The document specifies that digital violence constitutes discrimination according to Article 1 of the CEDAW Convention. It also asserts that state parties should deploy full-scale strategies for digital violence management according to the recommendation by creating laws and policies and prevention systems and compensation systems that contain digital platform regulation along with law enforcement training and victim-centric protocols. The plan requires adopting survivor-centered methods that unite structural and digital harm prevention strategies to defend women's rights for safety, dignity, and participation (CEDAW Committee, 2017). Different countries around the world have formulated specialized domestic legal frameworks. Online Safety Act, 2023, implemented in the United Kingdom, shields the users from online gendered violence in the digital domain (Barker & Jurasz, 2022). Under the Online Safety Act 2021, Australia granted its eSafety Commissioner potent authority to stop cyberbullying and handle image-based abuse and significant online threats (Nolan & Gaffey, 2024). The United States has two major federal legislations, including the Violence Against Women Act (VAWA), together with extensive state-level cyberstalking and revenge pornography legislation. The Protecting Canadians from Online Crime Act (2015) of Canada includes non-consensual image sharing as a criminal offense, and New Zealand's Harmful Digital Communications Act (2015) created digital abuse penalties through civil and criminal laws. However, despite the existence of domestic as well as international legal frameworks, OGBV exists as a persistent threat in the digital domain, augmenting instances of cybervictimization (Jeni Klugman, 2017).

The prominence of digital devices and the emergence of digital spaces have evolved public interaction and the ways in which information is accessed. However, it has also evolved ways of committing cybercrimes. Globally there is an astonishing augmentation in gender-based violence in digital spaces. As per the UN Women Report on Technologically Facilitated Gender-Based Violence, gender-based violence in the digital space is an inexorable reflection of the offline patriarchal setup that leads to algorithmic biases in platform designs and the legal status quo. This report highlights the absence of laws that are survivor-centric, inadequacy in enforcement, and inappreciable accountability of the platforms. It also reveals that intersectional harms are inconspicuous because of scarce data and research on marginalized stakeholders. The findings point towards a shift in jurisprudential focus of legal frameworks to interests and rights of the victims for combating cyber victimization (UN Women, 2024). Furthermore, a survey conducted by Plan International in 22 countries stated that 58 percent of girls between 15-22 years of age are prominently impacted by online harassment, out of which 47 percent were subjected to threats of physical or sexual violence. The study also shows that 64 percent of respondents conveyed that they suffered from emotional and psychological trauma due to these inflictions (Plan International, 2020). As per the World Bank's Digital Development Note on Gender Equality, internationally 48.4 percent of women access the internet as compared to 58.3 percent of men. From this data pool, it was found that women are 15 percent less inclined towards using mobile internet. The note also pointed out emerging online threats such as cyberstalking, online harassment, online voyeurism, etc. It states that these activities have an inordinate impact on women, causing psychological distress and preventing active participation, leading to a systemic digital exclusion (World Bank, 2021). The report of the Institute of Development Studies, UK, suggests that gender-based violence in the digital domain impacts 16 percent to 58 percent of the users internationally. Facebook comes out to be the most used platform for such aggressions. It also states that intersectional identities of the victims linking race, sexuality, or disability make them more prone to online violence. Most of the perpetrators are connected to the victims, and what motivates them to commit such acts is often rooted in displays of dominance and gender norms. The spectrum of abuse in OGBV starts with harassment before leading to physical threats. The report identifies OGBV as an attack on media freedom and democratic operations while leading to economic losses, which create an environment of constant digital danger (Hicks, 2021). Additionally, results from a 2024 study involving 2,870 women business owners from 96 low- and middle-income countries (LMICs) stated that approximately 57 percent of female business owners experienced at least one case of gender-based violence on social media networks, while 23 percent faced verbal abuse and 22 percent received unwanted sexually explicit photos. One out of five female respondents expressed fears about male customers harassing them during business interactions since negative experiences occur when men use negotiations as a means to make unprofessional advances. Also, 14% of women remain anxious about possible violent or aggressive behavior from male customers during commercial exchanges. Safety and security issues prevent 16% of women from using mobile internet, and 62% of these women have experienced personal harassment online, and this illustrates that online harassment can force women to eliminate their internet usage entirely (Alhorr et et.al., 2024). There are ample reports available, which will be analyzed further in this chapter. These reports demonstrate that OGBV exists in a broad and interconnected manner and on a global scale. These data points also show both legal structural weaknesses and platform operational issues, which cause unethical consequences for vulnerable female populations.

Considering this, the chapter will aim to examine gendered cybervictimization from the lens of OGBV. It will put forth a two-pronged analysis, one from the legal lens and another from the perspective of victimology. As digital spaces thrive because of their indispensability for communication, commerce, identity, etc., they also become a hub for gendered aggression. The central aim of this chapter will be to transcend legal positivism and deterrence schemes and instead explore the root causes of OGBV and focus on a victim-centric approach. This chapter will, firstly, establish a theoretical framework to understand online harassment as a gender-based cyber victimization phenomenon within the context of justice principles as well as a digital ethics framework. Secondly, it will critically examine international legal frameworks, as well as domestic legislation of prominent countries, and will evaluate their effectiveness as an instrument for female victims in their quest for protection from digital abuse. Thirdly, it will put forth the results and findings, and on the basis of the same, it will attempt to reach plausible conclusions and suggestions.

This chapter will be divided into 5 interlinked parts. The *first* part serves as the Introduction that provides an underpinning background by situating the emergence of online gender-based violence (OGBV) in the digital age and highlighting its relevance as a current issue in human rights. The *second* part sets the conceptual and theoretical context, introducing definitions of key terminologies and overview of underlying theories-radical feminism, techno feminism, and intersectionality—as well as visualizing their applicability to cybervictimization. The *third* part deals with a global examination of legal and policy frameworks with respect to gendered aggressions in the digital domain. Online violence against women keeps growing on digital platforms; as a result, various legal systems worldwide have started developing solutions against harassment and stalking through cyberspace and image-based abuse, including technology-enabled crimes. This part seeks to evaluate different ways countries and regions establish their laws, victim assistance systems, and institutional structures to fight cybercrimes targeting women. The analysis investigates legislative responses and policy innovations from the United States, the United Kingdom, and Australia, along with the European Union, among others, in a comparative setup. The *fourth* part posits a victimological analysis gauging the implications of technology-facilitated gender-based violence by basing the analysis strictly on reports. The *fifth* part concludes the chapter by focusing on results and findings through analysis of the entire study. This part will also incorporate suggestions intertwined with the observations and findings.

## 2. CONCEPTUAL AND THEORETICAL UNDERPINNINGS

A complete grasp of gendered cybervictimization calls for a view that unites the concepts of power, technology, and identity. Throughout this chapter, feminist victimology, social justice theory, technofeminism, digital ethics, and intersectionality are blended. When considered together, these views show how the Internet can support gender discrimination, change the experience of victims, and shape the expectations for legal and political intervention.

### 2.1 Defining Gendered Cybervictimization

Gendered online abuse aimed at women is an example of gendered cybervictimization, as it follows from traditional, unequal gendered power dynamics and is a form of subjugation that has evolved from the onset of digitization. This type of harm is not only about sexual or threatening action, but rather, it is guided through a combination of tactics that multiply its effects and lead to deep structural and emotional consequences. It is the result of how different behaviors, technology, social status, and cultural influences work together to form a chain of violence that is often directed at women. Leveraging the multifaceted features of online platforms, like anonymity, virality, and algorithmic amplification, gendered cybervictimization involves causing harm that goes beyond cyberspace to the physical world, having lasting effects on the psychology, social behavior, and physical well-being of the victim (Henry & Powell, 2023). The core act that constitutes cybervictimization is online harassment, which might involve unsolicited sexual propositions, sexist remarks, or open threats of violence. Contrary to the common terminological reference of 'trolling,' such behaviors have real psychological effects, causing anxiety and depression and making people want to avoid these online spaces (Lazarus et al., 2021). Usually, this problem coexists with other forms of digital abuse, such as cyberstalking, in which case one regularly watches a person's online activity. Apart from intimidating their victims, cyberstalkers link online crimes with real-life threats since there is always a possibility they could act dangerously offline (Patel & Verma, 2024).

Doxxing is another issue where private and often intimate personal information is shared without authorization. It became known in the 1990s, when hackers revealed the identities of individuals using fake names on the internet. The effect of doxxing transcends psychological implications, often catalyzing the perils of offline violence and social isolation. Women, in particular, are prone to this resort to self-censorship or withdrawing themselves from the digital space. Such retreats do not only happen to individuals; they are also proof that many systems fail to keep digital infrastructures free from gendered violence (Anderson & Wood, 2022). Another manifestation of gendered cybervictimization is voyeuristic virtual abuse. This incorporates image-based sexual abuse, where specific personal and intimate pictures are used and circulated in the digital space without the consent of the victim. Due to evolution and advancements in AI technology, this is done through the fabrication of images and creation of deepfake pornography. As a result, these violations attack privacy and personal sovereignty, exposing the victim to possible reputational damage, emotional trauma, and prolonged social stigma. Moreover, the permanence of data in digital space intensifies the subjugation to cybervictimization, resulting in the arduous process of getting it obliterated. This influence isn't limited to what happens in private lives; more and more, public figures and activists, as well as professionals, are made the targets to keep them silent or undermine their reputation (Huber, 2022).

## 2.2 Intersectionality and the Continuum of Digital Harm

In order to develop a keen understanding of gendered cybervictimization, it is important to recognize the intersectional nature of online harm. A woman's experience in the digital space is not only based on her gender but also a miscellany of other factors such as race, class, disability, and sexual orientation. The constant intersection of these factors with online harm constructs unique vulnerabilities and compounds the effect of online victimization (Stevens 2022). For example, a woman of color might experience abuse that includes both sexism and racism, whereas ladies who identify as LGBTQ+ can face threats that target their gender and sexuality together. Because of these mixed identities, both the nature of the abuse and the resources to respond to it may vary for each individual. According to the Continuum of Harm Theory, online gender-based violence is not an isolated incident but within a wider range of violence against women that they are subjected to throughout their lives. Digital violence tends to be coincidental with offline forms of violence; this includes domestic violence, sexual abuse, workplace harassment, etc., forming a web of oppression followed by psychological and social aftereffects.

The continuum is concretized by weaponizing technology to further image-based online abuse involving nonconsensual circulation of private and intimate pictures of the victim and deepfake pornography, suggesting that liberty and privacy can be controlled and curtailed without any due considerations. Longevity and searchability of online content multiply the severe effect of such abuse, and victims are forced to deal with the years-long reputational damage and emotional distress (Breslin, Klahr & Neria, 2020). Algorithmic amplification on various online platforms further reinforces the continuum by sensationalizing and circulating inflammatory content to augment user engagement. This inexorably amplifies adverse gendered narratives and often results in silencing users' voices and participation in digital spaces. This cycle does not only increase harm at an individual level but also codifies gender-based disparity in the system, where victimization is normalized and survivors are left with little opportunity for recourse. This suggests that the continuum of harm is a multidimensional scale that requires a multidimensional legal and policy response as the key to effective responses to gendered cybervictimization.

## 2.3 Integrating Feminist Theory, Social Justice, and Platform Accountability

It is only through a critical blend of feminist victimology, social justice theories, and techno feminism that one could develop a complete theoretical understanding of gendered cybervictimization by exploring both personal and social forces at work. Feminist victimology criticizes the gender-neutralism of the traditional legal model as it allegedly does not recognize the gendered power relations that constitute online abuse. By prioritizing the voices and choices of the victims, the feminist theory demands the creation of survivor-centered responses that would consider the short-term psychological effects of digital harm in addition to the long-term socio-political circumstances in which it occurs. This framework is further complemented by the capability approach developed by Martha Nussbaum, which underlines the necessity to provide every person with the possibility to develop and exercise their unique and foundational capabilities in the sphere of bodily integrity, emotional well-being, and engagement in public life without the risk of violence or marginalization (Nussbaum, 2011). In a digital context it implies that platforms and laws should develop conditions that allow women to feel safe and comfortable online. On the same note, the philosophy of justice promoted by Rawls accounts for the needs of the least well-off in the society, which highlights the ethical obligation towards building digital environments that safeguard and benefit females, who are the most vulnerable to online abuse (Rawls, 1971).

Moreover, techno-feminism links these normative models with critical approaches to the platform governance system and digital ethics. It is an important theoretical theory, which investigates the co-construction of gender and technology and focuses on how the digital environments are not neutral but have been cognizant of biases and exclusions of the societies in which the systems were manufactured. It has developed out of both feminist standpoint theory and cyberfeminism, which aim to investigate how technological systems (algorithms, interface design, and moderation mechanisms) frequently assume patriarchal forms and perpetuate gendered inequalities in online social environments (Gill, 2005). Techno feminists contend that women are by far the most vulnerable stakeholders to detriments posed by online platforms because such platforms are not built with consultations with the victims who suffer the most by the flaws of such platforms. As a result, reporting tools and content moderating algorithms frequently emphasize mainstream views that do not represent or acknowledge the realities of victims of cyberviolence. These regulatory structures are entirely dependent on the use of automated decision-making procedures that are opaque and usually aligned with non-intersectional sensibilities, creating a situation of under-enforcement of hate speech, as well as over-censorship of feminist counterpoint. This continues to feed the issues of so-called 'governable space' that has been termed to refer to the fact that it is the platforms themselves who control what can be discussed within the sphere of acceptability based on technocratic and profit logic as opposed to human rights or a framework of gender justice considerations (Wajcman, 2006). It points out the way platforms design algorithmic systems and content moderation policies that tend to reproduce and support gendered inequalities.

These revelations suggest that governance of platforms necessitates the transition beyond nebulous oversight of content to the incorporation of systemic governance and transparency. Digital ethics frameworks stress the importance of engaging participatory models of governance in which survivors contribute to developing safety. Ergo, an interfeminist approach to gendered cybervictimization, involving the combination of feminist and techno-feminist victimology, intersectional analyses, social justice theory, and other perspectives, is able to offer a multidimensional prism through which definitions, conceptualizations, and explanations of gendered cybervictimization can be approached. This combination, in theory, summarizes how individual experiences interact with structural conditions and require not only a punitive but also a transformative approach to be adopted by legal and policy-based solutions. In terms of approaches and moderation policies, making these solutions more inclusive and effective.

# 3. GLOBAL LEGAL AND POLICY FRAMEWORKS

## 3.1 CEDAW General Recommendation No. 35

Under International Human Rights Law, the 2017 UN Committee on the Elimination of Discrimination Against Women (CEDAW) General Recommendation No. 35 is a groundbreaking development as it specifically acknowledges online gender-based violence as a modern tool for perpetuating discrimination against women. The continuum between digital and offline violence stands out as an important highlight of this recommendation urging member states to embrace integrated legal systems that criminalize certain modes of digital violence; however, the recommendation does not impose criminalization of sexual or violent crime, posing an upstream challenge (Vijeyarasa, 2020). It specifies the need for profound national responses, which include training judicial and law enforcement members, implementing proper victim support systems, regularized data gathering procedures, and potent detection systems. Moreover, General Recommendation No. 35 introduces an intersectional approach considering the exacerbated vulnerability of women due to the various points of intersectionality, including race, ethnicity, disability, sexuality, and socioeconomic status, thus pressuring the member states to design more comprehensive policies and preventive measures that consider the multiple facets of harm (Reddock, 2022).

Despite these substantial normative additions, implementation of CEDAW General Recommendation No. 35 is patchy and shows that there are definite gaps in domestic codification, enforcement capabilities, and international cooperation globally. Although some countries like Australia, Italy, and Mexico have implemented specific legislative responses against technology-facilitated gender-based violence, most jurisdictions are not completely implementing these recommendations without a clear legal definition and, more often than not, specific reporting and enforcement mechanisms. Moreover, global collaboration required to combat transnational digital offenses is limited, which impedes the success of the Recommendation, particularly when it comes to multinational sites and attackers who might have jurisdiction. Inclusive policy analysis conducted by organizations such as EIGE and UN Women encourages digital platforms to be legally required to disclose information about online abuse and content moderation with specific details, also recommending government regulation in the form of disclosures. Lastly, the realization of the transformative nature of General Recommendation No. 35 will depend on enhanced legal specifications, capacity development of the applicators of the law, enhanced international cooperation, and sustained engagement of digital providers in the establishment of responsible and survivor-responsive digital environments (Wells & Wells, 2025).

## 3.2 UN Human Rights Council Resolution 20/8, 2012

UN Human Rights Council Resolution 20/8, adopted on July 16, 2012, is the turning point in the human rights discourse, affirming that a human right enjoyed offline must also be safeguarded online. The resolution highlights the use of universal rights in digital spaces and, particularly, the right to freedom of expression, as states have a responsibility to uphold the specified rights irrespective of the channel it is being exercised (UNHRC, 2021). The resolution highlights the internet as a central tool in the enforcement of human rights and demands the safeguard of certain rights like the right to free expression, privacy, and information rights, which are frequently violated on the internet by the knowing use of such mechanisms as surveillance, censorship, and online violence, especially against women and minorities. The international legal framework concerning gendered cybervictimization also has a key reference point in Resolution 20/8, which creates a necessary international legal premise regarding the continuous relationship between online and offline rights, which creates the normative ground to pressurize the state and digital platforms to be held accountable. It has been noted the gendered approach to digital rights is a recommended practice as it complies with Resolution 20/8 that requires states to address online violence against women (eVAW), digital surveillance, and privacy violations explicitly. Through these direct recognitions, there have been great challenges in enforcing the practicality of the resolution throughout the world, as evidenced by a lack of coherent legislation and enforcement against the cyber-based harassment of genders, a lack of adequate data needed to support the resolution, and general cultural and institutional impediments in the implementation of a comprehensive approach towards curbing gender-based harassment, especially in cyberspace. Critically, as crucial as the precedent provided by UNHRC Resolution 20/8 at an international level, further conversion of its tenets into functional and gender-sensitive legislation in national jurisdictions will continue to be a pressing step (Deane, 2024).

## 3.3 Budapest Convention on Cybercrime

One of the most detailed international instruments intended to combat crimes committed through digital technology is the Budapest Convention on Cybercrime, adopted by the Council of Europe in 2001. Its main aim is to promote international collaboration amongst nations in the normative standardization of the national laws of all countries dealing with cybercrimes such as those crimes like hacking, cyber fraud, and child exploitation material. Although it is one of the most established frameworks and procedural systems to secure electronic evidence and address cyber offenses, the Convention has traditionally been fairly gender-neutral in terms of its orientation to the topic, with its primary aspects of implementation being technical and procedural without some direct connection with a gendered approach (Tropina, 2024). Nevertheless, recent events have shown that cybercrime and gender-based violence can have substantial intersections, thus highlighting the inherent possibility of the Convention to deal with online violence, as well as the use of technology, against women. As an example, the provisions regarding computer-related crimes and content-related offenses, including the unauthorized access to computer data and systems or computer-related fraud and forgery, can be applied to prosecute some specific examples of online gender-based violence, such as doxxing, cyberstalking, or non-consensual image distribution. When assessed in a gender-sensitive context, these provisions have the potential to largely contribute to the moderation of protection mechanisms accessible to women and girls whose lives are threatened by digital forms of violence (Nguyen & Golman, 2020).

However, this potential also contains a significant weakness in the context of the Budapest Convention framework, which is the lack of explicit acknowledgement of the gendered aspect of cybercrimes alongside missing specifications that address technology-facilitated violence against women per se. In such a way, the offenses committed against women online, including gendered harassment, misogynistic trolling, and image-based sexual abuse, are frequently underreported or otherwise not addressed properly under the current cybercrime policies. Besides, the gender-neutral formulation of the Convention also restricts its effectiveness because it does not recognize the fact that women frequently have different experiences with cybercrime as compared to men in terms of both prevalence and nature due to the actuation of pernicious effects by digital technologies. In response to these shortcomings, researchers and international organizations have recommended a clearer incorporation of gender issues under the cybercrime laws. The synergies between the Budapest Convention and the Istanbul Convention have also been made more prominent: the former supplies the procedural and evidentiary tools that are needed to make prosecution effective, whereas the latter adds the necessary gender-sensitive framework, where violence against women is understood to be gender-specific and systemic. With the advantages of the two treaties, there is a powerful avenue towards further preserving women against technology-facilitated violence and providing a relevant collective legal procedural response in one jurisdiction to another (Van Der Wilk, 2021).

## 3.4 The Istanbul Convention

The Istanbul Convention, formally known as the Convention on Preventing and Combating Violence Against Women and Domestic Violence, is an important international agreement specifically defined to combat all cases of violence against women that include technology-facilitated violence. Among these provisions, the Istanbul Convention is the first to pay particular attention to the nature and manifestations of violence against women that take place online and through technological platforms and is therefore directly related to gender-based violence in other contexts and has brought together elements of a continuum consisting of abuses and harms (Grans, 2023). Such a realization is essential as it recasts cyberviolence as not just individualized cases of technology abuse but rather as symptoms of an even greater and more systemic problem of patriarchies and gender inequities, which must then be addressed by states with more seamless policy approaches (Kanbur, 2021).

Article 3 of the Convention establishes an exhaustive definition of violence against women, including the whole range of gender-based violence that involves physical, sexual, psychological, or economic violence and injuries. Importantly, this definition includes the threat, coercion, and arbitrary deprivation of liberty, which explicitly covers women who are facing cyberstalking, doxxing, and other digital threats or coercion towards women and instilling fear or feelings of psychological distress. Particularly, Article 34 requires the states to make criminal measures of stalking behaviors or other acts that involve making repeated threats to a person online that create a state of fear in their mind. In addition, Article 40 is applicable to all forms of online harassment and image-based sexual abuse, since it treats sexual harassment in general, regardless of whether it is done verbally, non-verbally, or physically, as stated in Article 40. Article 33 also mandates that psychological violence should be criminalized because psychological integrity is highly damaged in a victim under coercion and threats and because psychological harms are often perpetrated in the digital environment (Nelles, 2020).

In addition to criminalization, the Istanbul Convention focuses on a multi-sectoral and comprehensive approach that is summarized in its 4 Ps framework: prevention, protection, prosecution, and comprehensive policies. Those include gender stereotype debunking educational programs and digital safety awareness; special support services for the victims of online violence; effective prosecution procedures, including investigations and restraining orders; and policy measures to address systematic factors that drive gender-based online violence and its consequences (Rodo, 2020). The Convention strongly supports the involvement of the private sector and Internet-based technologies such as the ICT industries in order to engage them and request them to implement self-regulatory guidelines and ensure that there is digital literacy to fight off degrading online materials that are harmful to women and girls. Article 17 emphasizes the important role that needs to be played by the actors in the private sector, which requests them to establish ethical standards that can promote respect of dignity and good online spaces. And yet, along with all these measures, which are both wide-ranging and advanced in character, there are still practical difficulties. The application at the state-member level has been uneven, and various types of technology-facilitated violence are poorly covered by law or not covered at all as a result of unethical knowledgeability by enforcement organs. Furthermore, online violence has, more often than not, been normalized culturally, thus jeopardizing progress towards actualization of all of the mandates of the Convention (Faloppa, 2023). However, the Istanbul Convention is an invaluable normative framework that can serve as a robust guide and impose requirements on states to include effective gender-sensitive strategies into the national paradigm of legal regulations as well as policy priorities in their efforts to mitigate digital violence against women.

## 3.5 United Kingdom: The Online Safety Act (OSA) 2023

The Online Safety Act (*hereinafter* OSA) 2023 is the ambitious legislative initiative in the name of online safety of the United Kingdom that actively seeks to establish a safer digital environment by introducing a widespread regulatory framework. The key aim of the act is to address not only illegal content but also harmful material on the Internet and cast specific obligations and responsibilities on social media providers and search engines. At the core of the OSA is the engagement of a regulatory duty of care on these online platforms to perform comprehensive risk assessments and engage in taking proactive steps in preventing any possible harm, and particularly those affecting vulnerable segments of society, including children (Schmidt, 2024). The Act is a significant shift from the previous approach because it requires companies to locate and mitigate online harm rather than just do it out of their own volition. Interestingly, the OSA ensures more strict content moderation procedures, as well as demands transparency of online corporations towards the operation of such processes. It also provides age verification mechanisms that are immediate solutions to the issue of subjecting minors to harmful material. The legislative body of OSA is broad and multi-layered, containing 241 sections and 17 schedules that specify diverse types of harmful and unlawful content, including misinformation, sexual imagery, exploitation, and hate speech. Another very important innovation of the Act is that it enables users to challenge and report harmful content, thus strengthening the user accountability mechanisms of internet companies. Nevertheless, the Act has given platforms some form of immunity against being responsible for content that is illegal and created by other patrons, and it displays some of the uncertainty in striking the correct balance between rules and the reality of the services of online providers. Additionally, the OSA introduced a set of criminal offenses against individual online offenders, the provisions of which operationalized in January 2024, which means that the OSA also strives to manifest personal responsibilities as well as corporate ones (McGlynn et al., 2024).

Within the context of international comparisons, the OSA is modeled to conceptually and operationally interact with other legislation in this sector, like the European

Union's Digital Services Act (*hereinafter* DSA). The OSA and DSA serve to regulate big digital platforms with the focus on accountability and their own transparency as well as proactive content moderation. Nevertheless, they follow different philosophies of regulations. The DSA is a layered system with enhanced responsibilities depending on the size and effect of platforms as opposed to the more even implementation of the OSA. Moreover, DSA covers a broader scope of social issues in its regulations, whereas OSA is more individual-centric, displaying a divergent perception of the process of content management and digital platform regulation. Crucially, the OSA has also been a subject of controversy with respect to the possible implications for freedom of speech due to its current moderation guidelines, which are quite broad in nature and thus can allow the removal of excessively large amounts of content that can hurt others, though it may not be illegal (Ofcom, 2024). This has been the point of contention amidst the parliamentary process of passing the Act in light of core conflicts between public interest, online safety, and democracy, including free expression. Conversely, in other regions such as the United States, where freedom of speech is constitutionally guaranteed, it is possible to see varying degrees to which similar legislation can be applied to curtail excessive moderation, which indicates stark contrasts in online harm policies. Finally, the OSA will heavily depend on the enforcement and implementation perspective of Ofcom, which is the designated regulatory body in the UK to supervise compliance, create guidelines, and deal with collisions. This design reinforces the need for a significant amount of inter-agency and cross-border collaboration, especially in the context of the fundamentally trans-national character of digital platforms and the spread of their contents. As the OSA enters a practical implementational stage, more thorough care should be taken to avoid possible jurisdictional issues and unify regulatory regimes across borders to facilitate harmonization and ensure that the international community responds to the problem of digital safety comprehensively and collectively. To summarize, the Online Safety Act, 2023, in the UK is a historic attempt to empower digital platforms with extra responsibility towards making the internet a safer place, especially with regard to vulnerable groups. Nevertheless, no matter how impressive the intentions and all mechanisms are, the Act suffers critical issues regarding balancing between freedom of expression, effective enforcement, and international alignment. Its long-term success will rely heavily upon addressing these complexities and keeping it undergoing changes in order to provide the necessary provisions to combat emerging digital threats (Coe, 2023).

## 3.6 Australia's eSafety Commissioner

The Online Safety Act 2021 is one of the most notable policies implemented in Australia to serve as a legal framework to address online safety and confront cyber violence, online harassment, and harmful online content. This regulatory structure stands out specifically because of its proactive and far-reaching authority towards online content removal. Specifically, section 109 of the Act grants the Commissioner the power to issue so-called removal notices, which require online service providers and major global platforms to delete harmful content that can be accessed by end users residing in Australia. These orders are applicable even in a case where there are extremities of violence, i.e., recorded violent actions, and such material is considered to be objectionable according to the national classification standards in Australia. Under this framework, special attention is paid to ensuring that users, especially the vulnerable group of the population, are not exposed to severe and negative digital content. Another high-profile and contentious example of the powers of the eSafety Commissioner occurred in the aftermath of an event in Sydney in April 2024, when a stabbing attack was live-streamed on social networks and was later shared online. With most companies in the tech sector voluntarily complying with the demand, X Corp. (previously Twitter) drew particular attention as it fought back the notice to cancel the reviews by employing geo-blocking to prevent access only to the Australian users. This strategy was disputed by the eSafety Commissioner, who indicated that geo-blocking was not enough since these technological blocks could be easily hacked and the persons intending to access the banned content in Australia could do it through virtual private networks (VPNs). This has been a contentious debate that highlights some of the basic legal and operational contradictions involved with the concept of imposing national laws and regulations on internet content in the realm of the global and borderless digital world.

The legal conflict between X Corp. and the eSafety Commissioner of Australia is centered around the complex legal case of jurisdiction or territorial reach of regulatory and court decrees concerning online content. The underlying issue of conversation was whether the Australian authorities could force platforms to deactivate content worldwide, not just block it nationally. The problem bears immense impacts on global internet governance, where staking global jurisdiction interferes with the rights of other global internet users, probably overstepping jurisdiction in the process (Smith et al., 2024). According to Svantesson (2024), courts or regulatory bodies assessing the removal of content need to pay attention to both domestic and international law and strike the correct balance between the need to limit the circulation of harmful content and the need to respect international sovereignty or the right to freedom of expression. More importantly, the Australian legal system and court precedent reveal inconsistent approaches to the international universe of jurisdiction. Although as seen in earlier cases where defamation injunctions were limited locally and the courts were circumspect to grant those injunctions by the national boundaries, more recent Australian court cases, and especially the case of X v. Twitter (2017), have established worrying precedents in enforcing worldwide bans on online content without much consideration to the international consequences of that type. Although such broad swings at jurisdiction have the merit of domestic enforcement, they are fraught with foreign law issues and may lead to the establishment of unfavorable precedents that would stimulate counterclaims of extraterritorial jurisdiction by foreign nations (Svantesson & Centre for Space, Cyberspace & Data Law, 2024).

Therefore, the Australian eSafety Commissioner model, which was still robust and well-intentioned, highlights major issues associated with international content regulation. In order to overcome such complexities, the framework should pursue the adoption of clear standards with regard to global takedown orders by introducing principles of proportionality, necessity, and international cooperation. Scholars promote values that direct law courts and administrative bodies to act with a refined mind on the jurisdictional boundaries and international obligations. The integration of such principles would improve the framework of the eSafety Commissioner in Australia to guarantee a sound defense against the threats of malicious online materials without hindering international legal standards and the development of international agreement in digital policy (Dragiewicz, 2020).

Comparatively, Australia's approach to regulation with the eSafety Commissioner stands out divergently with the possibilities of any law like the Online Safety Act 2023 in the UK or the Digital Services Act (DSA) in the EU. Whereas the model used in Australia focuses on active government intervention and the right to remove through a special commissioner, the UK framework is formed on the duties of the platform and the ability of the regulator, Ofcom, to implement periodic threats on a massive scale. On the same note, the EU DSA focuses on transparency and accountability in the system, gradually introducing requirements depending on the size of the platform and the level of risk. Therefore, the eSafety Commissioner model in Australia substantially embraces a top-down centralized approach, which is distinctive both in its modus operandi and its scope, demonstrating both its advantages and its shortcomings on an international level and control over digital concerns. In summary, the eSafety Commissioner system of Australia offers a resilient, albeit contentious, framework for dealing with harmful online content, raising major concerns in internet governance and territorial global control. Whether the Australian approach will be effective and internationally acceptable in the future will greatly depend on whether it can balance its aggressive ambitions to regulate the domestic regulatory environment with deference to international law, digital rights, and cross-border digital sovereignty (ANROWS, 2022).

## 3.7 USA Violence Against Women Act

The Violence Against Women Act (*hereinafter* VAWA) was first passed by the United States in 1994 and reinstated several times; it is one of the most comprehensive legal and policy discourses created specifically to focus on violence against women, including intimate partner violence, sexual assault, and stalking. This Act signified a major policy change, highlighting violence against women as a social policy and not a personal problem that should receive a whole-scale response by law, criminal justice, and community social services. The improved responsiveness of law enforcement departments is at the core of VAWA, which was initiated through increased funding and legislative updates that were aimed to reinforce investigation procedures, services provided to victims, and offender accountability. One of the integral objectives of VAWA is to promote reporting and effective responses to the cases of domestic and sexual violence (Modi et al., 2013). In the pre-VAWA era, domestic violence was often viewed as a family matter, with few arrests and little government action. VAWA changed this strategy by providing incentives to law enforcement to move towards a pro-arrest policy, special training, and stronger victim support services. It is important to note that within the framework of the Act, the Office on Violence Against Women (OVW) was created, which distributes large amounts of federal funding in the form of grants and incentives, including the Services, Training, Officers, and Prosecutors (STOP) grants and the Arrest Program grants. These grants have been used to train law enforcement and prosecutors, create special divisions to deal with domestic/sexual violence, create policy better aimed at protecting victims and punishing perpetrators (Gover & Moore, 2020).

The use of VAWA has significantly changed the philosophy of law enforcement in the sense that officers are no longer allowed to simply sit down and watch people violate the laws against domestic violence; they are required to intervene or even arrest them at the discretion of the officer on duty. These policy alterations have brought forth both positive and negative effects. On the one hand, they have boosted the arresting and prosecuting rates, which might prevent further crimes. Conversely, there are also a few unintended, but unfortunate, side effects of mandatory arrest, including increased dual arrests and unintended punishment of the victim. These concerns exemplify the current depth and sophistication of policies that reflect the importance of making decisions on the one hand to protect the victims and on the other hand to evaluate cases to prevent collateral damage. In addition, the act has made a greater contribution to the victim support mechanisms (Aday, 2015). It authorizes the law enforcement agencies to assimilate victim advocates directly into their workforce to catalyze victim support mechanisms, facilitate reporting, and further effective coordination with the agencies of the victim service providers. It has also promoted multiagency coordination wherein there is improved cooperation between law enforcement, community organizations, health agencies, and victim advocacy groups. These synergistic platforms have played an instrumental role in treating the multidimensional and intricate character of violence perpetrated against women. Moreover, it proscribed collection of fees from the victims for collection of forensic evidence and restitution obligations on victims and promoted cross-state border enforcement of protective orders (Holbrook, 2023).

Despite these great strides, the Act has come under criticism, particularly in its uneven application and misallocation of funds on domestic violence in comparison to sexual assault. Assessments show that most of such finances have been focused on domestic violence, with sexual assault being relatively less funded. Moreover, criticism continues to surround the scope of mandatory arrest policies, as studies have reported potential negative effects on minority groups and the unforeseen effects on the victims themselves, including failure to report other incidents in the future because they fear getting punished. Comparatively, VAWA presents a revealing case in comparison to the existing frameworks around the world, such as the Online Safety Act in the UK and the eSafety Commissioner framework in Australia. In contrast to the UK, where platform accountability is the main agenda, and Australia, where the explicit regulation of digital content is defined, VAWA proposes a thorough, victim-centered approach to law enforcement response and community support. It is this combination of reforming criminal justice and victim advocacy with specialized training that sets VAWA apart in international comparative terms and makes it an innovative piece of framework (Rai et al., 2024).

## 3.8 Canada: The Online Harms Act

The Online Harms Act (Bill C-63, 2024) presented in Canada forms an effective legal and regulatory framework aiming to reduce online harm caused by harmful content on large-scale social platforms. At the core of the bill is the establishment of the Digital Safety Commission and Digital Safety Ombudsperson facilitated by the Digital Safety Office, established to monitor conformity of regulations and to act as facilitators to the users (Lau, 2024). This triad brings in a more subtle model of accountability where platforms not only regulate themselves but are overseen and directed by independent authorities. The Act outlines four key responsibilities of the service providers, such as protection of the children, the maintenance of records, responsibility, and blocking of harmful content. The type of content that raises a mandatory response involves intimate revenge content, child sexual exploitation, bullying, self-harm content, hatred, violent extremism, and genocide advocacy, and these issues have detailed definitions in legislation (Benmoussa et al., 2024). Importantly, the bill requires expedited removal of clear-cut harms (e.g., sexual violence and child sexual content) within narrow deadlines, and such obligations can be enforced through significant fines of up to 6 percent of global revenue and may even attract criminal sanctions in exceptional circumstances (Reuters, 2024).

In spite of these progressive provisions, critics and analysts highlight significant limitations of the draft legislation. Although the act creates authorities in order to safeguard children and sexual violence survivors, new technological developments, such as the use of deepfakes to commit acts of sexual abuse, are underdeveloped with vague restrictions (Lalonde, 2024). Also, the Act suggests binder obligations without specifying detailed mechanisms to control the amplification of harmful content through algorithms, which, according to many, should be inspired by European experience introducing the mechanism of algorithmic transparency and consent (Diab, 2024). Another criticism is the one between privacy and civil liberties: even though balancing free expression is key, the prospect of overstepping is high, especially in the case of the proposed formulation of Section 13 having been remodeled on a civil standard, which may be used in the case of genocide advocacy being criminalized. However, the donor aspect of the data provisions proposed in the bill is indicative of a positive trend toward providing the sustained allocation of resources toward academic research into the study of online harms, which is important as a corollary to an evidence-based policy, even despite the existing drawbacks (WSJ, 2024). Compared with the Online Safety Act in the UK and the eSafety approach in Australia, Canada has presented a well-structured and governance-based approach in its Online Harms Act, which replicates the responsibilities of care outlined in the former and recalls the structure of the latter, albeit with a lack of distinctive algorithmic action and gender-related protection, which can be noted as potential improvement points in the future (Dehlon, 2024).

## 3.9 New Zealand: Harmful Communication Act

The Harmful Digital Communications Act 2015 (*hereinafter* HDCA) of New Zealand is one of the early legislative solutions in the international context aimed at reducing cyber abuse and digital harassment. The Act came into existence to curb the damage posed by digital communications, especially in cases where the content might have a severe impact on the minds or emotional state of people. The HDCA develops an extensive set of laws, criminalizing any effort to circulate a message or publish content online with the aim of causing harm (Williamson, 2018). Notably, Section 22 makes it an offense to send digital communication with an intent to cause harm when such communication causes such harm and such harm is objectively assessed as being sufficiently serious. The statute highlights 10 principles of communication, forming the bedrock for ascertaining the harmful nature of any communication. Among them are strict restrictions on posting inciting suicide, disseminating false information, or revealing sensitive personal details. Moreover, the Act establishes a dual process, both criminal and civil, which gives victims the choice to pursue remedies either through the courts or through the civil complaint agency like Netsafe, which is the designated government body to receive, determine, and mediate complaints (Vine – Violence Information Aotearoa, 2022).

The recent events and case law have specified the strengths and limitations of the HDCA. The extent of "serious emotional distress" was clarified by the courts, which pinpointed that damage should be beyond annoyance or offense and lead to verifiable distress or psychological damage. The court in the case of Police v. B highlighted that being offended or angered by online content failed to satisfy the statutory offense under Section 22 (Harvey, 2019). At the same time, more frequent reliance on interim takedown orders and the use of civil remedies, including those used in G v. Facebook Ltd., demonstrate the expanding influence of the Act in online dispute resolution. However, critics contend that the platform does not adequately address gendered online abuse such as image-based sexual violence and deepfake pornography. They argue that the framework lacks a propensity towards recognizing gender-sensitive aggression, given the fact that a disproportionate number of women are subjected to online-based abuse (Hammond et al., 2012). In reaction to this, legal commentators and civil society groups call for a review of HDCA in order to conceptualize and incorporate evolved aspects of cyber abuse and technological progressions such as algorithmic targeting and instances of masked trolling. In comparison to other jurisdictions, HDCA is more accommodating and victim-oriented. Where the UK Online Safety Act 2023 and the eSafety Commissioner in Australia predominantly focus on regulatory control and liability of the platforms, HDCA is based more on the individual complaint processes and restorative channels. Netsafe as a mediation-based organization is contrasted to punitive or legislative enforcement models where the focus is on resolution and education rather than prosecution. However, this model has drawn criticism due to its restricted capacity to force international tech companies into compliance or combat endemic forms of online malicious acts in large amounts. The reform advocates recommend that a hybrid approach might be needed, namely, a system that incorporates civil remedies, criminal prosecutions, and platform responsibility (Pacheco & Melhuish, 2018). However, HDCA is still a significant legislative benchmark that allows achieving the balance between free expression and individual protection that may be defined by the ability to respond to more advanced, gendered aspects of harm as the digital ecosystem develops.

## 3.10 Combined Analysis and Observations

Inasmuch as legal policies, including those in the UK (Online Safety Act 2023), Australia (eSafety Commission), the USA (Violence Against Women Act, VAWA), and New Zealand (Harmful Digital Communications Act, HDCA), are likely to be expected in areas where digital harms are regulated, one of the crucial shortcomings, however, remains the lack of implementation of a survivor-centric approach. Though made with noble intentions, many legal frameworks that re-contextualize the effects of online harm are built around the systems that either rely on the state agencies or platform practices instead of focusing on the adverse experiences and the informal requirements of survivors. An example is that in New Zealand, Netsafe promotes a restorative and peacemaking pathway, but its critics suggest it does not provide cost-effective mechanisms for dealing with content removal or achieving emotional and psychological security for victims. On a similar note, in the United States, although VAWA increased the institutional backing of survivors, its framework does not appease the comprehensive handling of the rapidly changing world of digital harms, including deepfakes or gendered cyberstalking. Such cases show a bigger picture, and it is in the sense that survivors are usually seen as mere complainants but not as key stakeholders in the development of redressal systems of these legislative frameworks.

The problem of cross-border enforcement is also a matter of concern. This is one of the problems observed in the application of global content orders in Australia and the draft Online Harms Bill in Canada. Besides, the international nature of the internet makes national jurisdictions excessive and inadequate. When the Australian government faced off against X Corp in 2024 over deletion orders issued by the eSafety Commissioner, the issue of sovereignty and the right to free speech in other jurisdictions was brought into question. The issue of the enforceability of those standards outside of national boundaries became a point of contention. Canada's Digital Safety Commission was confronted by the same issue as well. The commission was confronted by the question of how it would become compliant in removing orders against platforms that have foreign headquarters. Such enforcement gaps do not only threaten to cause jurisdictional stalemates but also create a patchwork of digital protection, leaving perpetrators free to continue harming through geographical loopholes. Moreover, lacking multilateral mechanisms or agreements, particularly on cross-border online violence against marginalized populations and women, their enforcement has been uneven, and the victims have not received a comprehensive redress.

There is another structural constraint in most regimes, which is the absence of mechanisms of platform accountability that do not depend on notice-and-takedown models. Although the Online Safety Act in the UK requires risk assessment proactivity and the concept of the duty of care is offered in Bill C-63 in Canada, the enforcement is mostly reactive and based on a rather high level of harm. This issue is further compounded in legislations such as New Zealand, where voluntary obedience by platforms to the civil orders has become a barrier to compliance, as in most instances, compliance is partial and delayed. Even in places where obligations have been put in place, such as in Australia or Canada, the regulatory frameworks have not yet infiltrated the algorithmic structures that permit and scale up gender-based violence online. According to the scholars, in most cases, digital misogyny and harassment are inspired by platform design, such as recommender systems, anonymity architecture, and monetization models. Accordingly, current frameworks should shift the paradigm of harms on a user level and implement structural audits, algorithmic transparency, and systems that transfer the responsibility onto digital intermediaries that benefit monetarily, even when it is detrimental. Finally, there is a visible lack of incorporation of gender-sensitive digital frameworks within all the jurisdictions. Although both the Istanbul Convention and the CEDAW Recommendations provide an international normative base, the national legislation is not enough to make gendered analysis a part of policy development (design, implementation, and evaluation phases) on digital policy. For instance, Bill C-63 in Canada has been criticized as inadequately targeting online harms in an intersectional and gendered manner, even though women, and especially racialized and queer women, are overrepresented as the victims. Similarly, strong practices in the UK and Australia in the areas of compliance and regulatory clarity have not yet operationalized feminist principles such as participatory governance, consent-based digital citizenship, or platform co-design with the affected communities in full. In this regard, it is important to see that any future reform should not only focus on legal deterrence and systemic protection but should also be based on feminist ideas of agency, dignity, and structural fairness in order to have any chance of countering the full range of gendered cyber harms.

## 4. VICTIM-CENTRIC ANALYSIS OF TECHNOLOGY-FACILITATED GENDER-BASED VIOLENCE (TFGBV)

### 4.1 Psychological Impact

The psychological implications of TFGBV are multidimensional, far-reaching, and prolonged. Acts like cyberstalking, image-based abuse, threats of sexual violence, doxxing, and impersonation take place beyond the digital sphere and bring about dramatic emotional suffering in the real-world scenario. Trauma caused by TFGBV can be in the form of anxiety, depression, insomnia, and panic attacks, as well as symptoms related to post-traumatic stress disorder (PTSD), which can impair proper functioning of the victim in academic, employment, and social areas. A holistic report by UN Women shows that TFGBV against women prevents the realization of access to education, employment, and online elements by the victims and hence further empowers exclusion and disempowerment. The report Free to be Online?, released by Plan International, highlights the emotional toll that cyberviolence may take on young women. Out of 14,000 girls interviewed in 17 countries, over 50 percent of the girls revealed that they were anxious, scared, or threatened upon the occurrence of online abuse. Many subjects reported the feeling of shame, guilt, and powerlessness, especially in the case of non-consensual sharing of images. This mental burden usually results in abandoning digital platforms, self-restriction, and deterioration of relationships with others. Others went further to narrate their contemplation of hurting themselves or even ending their own lives due to prolonged abuse (Plan International, 2020). The studies on gender-based cyber violence also reported that women were often being forced into online sexual relations at the threat of their personal information being revealed in digital spaces. Those behind such acts were likely to have been in current or previous relationships with the victim, often resorting to social media platforms and other tools on digital devices as a medium of physical and emotional abuse. This results in lasting damage to psychology and instills symptoms of post-traumatic disorder, including depersonalization, self-accusation, and dread of revenge (Mas'udah et al., 2024).

A thematic synthesis of these reports reveals that the psychological effects of technology-facilitated gender-based violence (TFGBV) include "internalization of fear" as one of the main psychological responses to online gendered aggressions. This fear does not only involve an anticipation of further victimization but also fear of disbelief or ridicule when the incidents are reported. According to a study reporting Technology-Facilitated Gender-Based Violence: A Shared Research Agenda, due to intersectional vulnerability, the effects of gender-based violence on the well-being of women are compounded in the experiences of women of marginalized backgrounds, e.g., women of color or LGBTQ+ individuals. The report contains repeated psychological manifestations such as chronic stress, paranoia, low self-esteem, and the feeling of being followed all the time (UN Women, 2023). Moreover, the Digital Development note on Gender Equality released by the World Bank reveals that women who experience digital violence have more chances to withdraw themselves from digital economic opportunities, thus worsening their sense of helplessness and reducing self-esteem, which also impairs achievement of economic independence and social agency (World Bank, 2021).

## 4.2 Socioeconomic Impact

Technology-facilitated gender-based violence (TFGBV) triggers associated psychosocial damage and substantiates socio-economic impact on women and girls across the globe. One of the notable consequences is the digital exclusion of victims who become direct targets of online stalking, trolling, and intimidation and are forced to leave the digital realm. This kind of expulsion limits education, work, and civic engagement. According to a global survey conducted by Plan International, 57.8% of girls have explained operating out of digital platforms or expressing themselves differently after facing online abuse, leading to subversion of their digital identity and voice. Such inability suggests that women may not have the opportunity to practice anywhere in the digital world safely, directly limiting their access to life opportunities, driving the gender digital divide, and increasing socio-economic disparities (Plan International, 2020).

Moreover, in most cases, TFGBV has a direct impact on the professional and economic mobility of women. The 2024 audit conducted by the Cherie Blair Foundation for Women gives valuable information about the nexus between online abuse and economic loss. The audit discovered that one out of four women entrepreneurs was subjected to online harassment, which had directly impacted their capacity to conduct or develop their businesses. It further stated that 19 percent of the women entrepreneurs were exposed to systemic pressures to diminish their online presence, out of which 7 percent went completely offline. This resulted in quantifiable income loss and economic damage. The audit notes that digital harassment is a modern form of discrimination against the full economic engagement of women, especially those living in emerging countries whose economies rely heavily on the use of online resources to access financial systems and international clients (Alhorr et al., 2024). Statistics portray that only 33 percent of the women in developing nations use the internet as opposed to 45 percent of men. This incongruity can be ascribed mainly to online gender-based violence, which is a gendered gatekeeping tool that reproduces digital illiteracy, fosters digital fear, and compounds structural ecosystem disparities. Online gendered violence plays an economically immobilizing role on women who are contracted in informal working conditions or in a rural gig economy, and these women are unable to enjoy the digital empowerment that is normally used as a springboard to achieve sustainable livelihoods (World Bank, 2021). The UN Women OGBV Report emphasizes that women in professions with a high profile in society, e.g., journalists, activists, politicians, and entrepreneurs, are targeted by personal attacks that seek to discredit their credibility, compromise their image, and appall them into silence. Such malicious attacks not only impair their performance but also pose a detriment to their reputation, future career opportunities, and growth. Livelihood is the factor that makes many women, especially those in the Global South, wish to be visible on the web: they sell products online, they work as freelancers, and become leaders in the community. In this way, harassment effects outside of the trauma to the individual can be identified as an economic disenfranchisement (UN Women, 2023). The Digital Development Note of Gender Equality by the World Bank emphasizes that systematic online abuse leads to a restricted participation of females in the digital economy, consequently stifling economic growth and inclusivity on national grounds. Furthermore, inadequate institutional backing compounds economic hardships, as most compensation frameworks and employment protection schemes fall short of recognizing the implications of online harassment. In most cases victims are required to prove 'tangible' damage, sidelining the detrimental impacts of latent harm such as economic losses due to career alterations, reduced online engagement, or emotional burnout. Inadequate state-based rehabilitation initiatives and funding support systems create a status quo of digital vulnerability: women are under the pressure of abandoning technology to protect their mental health, which continuously leads to gendered power disparity. Thus, the socio-economic impact of TFGBV needs something much more holistic than penal responses; it needs to encompass all-inclusive digital policy, victim-centric economic aid systems, and platform responsibility that acknowledges the economic dignity of women as the key focus of digital justice (World Bank, 2021).

## 4.3 Intersectional Victimization

Technology-Facilitated Gender-Based Violence (TFGBV) can never be seen as a homogeneous experience but as an amalgamation of oppressions caused by interpositionary forces of gender, race, caste, sexuality, age, class, and ability. Digital intersectional victimization refers to how people simultaneously marginalized by many types of social identities are more exposed to targeted, recurrent, and more extreme instances of online abuse than their non-marginalized counterparts (Flynn et al., 2023). The report "Technology-Facilitated Gender-Based Violence: A Shared Research Agenda" by UN Women notes how marginalized women experience more violent, more publicly visible, and identity-based forms of violence, including but not limited to racialized and casteist slurs, targeted doxing campaigns, outing sexual orientation, and image-based abuse to shame or coerce economically. As an example, Dalit women journalists in India have also claimed to have received concomitant casteist and gendered abuse when attempting to leave a political remark on the internet, portraying the intricacies of the alliance of caste and gender in increasing the level and form of violence experienced. Furthermore, it also pointed out that disabled women are 34 percent more prone to online aggression, and the impact becomes sizable due to their structural exclusion by digital platforms failing to support their accessibility requirements. Social invisibility and administrative neglect are an additional psychological burden to these communities (UN Women, 2023).

The Left-Out Project Report (2023) vividly notes the manner in which queer women, especially trans individuals and gender non-conforming ones, are shown not only greater rates of online abuse but also more dehumanizing materials. The report revealed that 60 percent of the sampled LGBTQ individuals have encountered targeted doxxing and image-based abuse, also frequently accompanied by casteist and racist slurs. On the intersectional level, the harm is further compounded due to the silencing of the victims on more than one axis of oppression. Such aggressions are underreported as legal systems and platform moderation mechanisms fail to acknowledge the perils of the realities that victims face. Besides, the social stigma surrounding such identities is generally used in digital attacks. The special vulnerabilities of the LGBTQ+ victims mentioned by them include the risk of being forced to disclose or disclosure without consent (outed). Such types of TFGBV are not only assaults against the person; they are violations of their access to protection, family support, and legal aid. A Plan International report indicated that girls who belong to the minority ethnic and religious groups stood a greater risk of sexual threats and offensive remarks, compelling them to hide in online learning environments and civic platforms. Online violence in conflict-based societies, or in its most patriarchal form, serves as a means of censorship and control with a long-term educational and socio-political implication (The Left Out Project, 2023).

Unequal access to redress mechanisms and support services is equally produced by intersectional TFGBV. According to the Digital Development Note on Gender Equality, socio-economic disadvantages can frequently be accompanied by a low volume of digital literacy, and victims who belong to rural, low-income, or marginalized populations find it increasingly difficult to identify, report, or even recover their situation as the victims of cyber abuse. Moreover, such victims are more prone to secondary victimization within law enforcement agencies, which might perceive digital harassment as a trifle or estrange it according to the identity of the victim. This applies especially to women with disabilities, where the infrastructure to report is not accessible and many digital and legal avenues prevent them from getting protection (World Bank, 2021). The Violence Against Women Victim Support Report (2023) derails the situation even further, as it shows that marginalized women who require support when they report abuse are systematically not believed, and institutional indifference permeates the consequences of abuse. In most cases, survivors have not been able to access culturally viable, linguistically accommodating legal support, and most of the cases have been terminated as being based on the issue of community dynamics and minor offenses. It is a combination of such institutional underreaction that leaves a toxic digital environment in which the intersectionally marginalized women are left with paranoia and self-censorship, thereby solidifying such digital marginalization (Violence Against Women Victim Support: Report, 2012).

Finally, based on the reports, it can be argued that TFGBV is not just about rare instances of harassment but a systematic problem with social stratification as the main contributor to placing certain groups of people at a higher risk of being exposed and less likely to receive justice. Intersectional TFGBV makes it clear how digital disadvantages are structural, with those in the least advantaged position being the most victimized, lacking a voice, and lacking protection (Weinstein et al.,

2021). Therefore, any framework for tackling cyberviolence needs to be based on an intersectional approach that recognizes conjoined harm. Laws, site policies, and victim care networks must be acclimatized to the level of vulnerability that evolves owing to identity, geography, language, and technology access. In the absence of this, interventions are in danger of being exclusionary or ineffective, and digital spaces will remain to reinforce the same hierarchies they were supposed to eliminate. Interpretation of TFGBV through an intersectional lens is not a question of inclusion but a prerequisite of digital justice (Watson, 2023).

## 5. FINAL REFLECTION: KEY FINDINGS & SUGGESTIONS, FINAL THOUGHTS

### 5.1 Key Findings & Suggestions

An in-depth examination points towards substantial revelations about Online Gender-Based Violence (OGBV) with drastic implications for human rights. Integration of these results highlights major points that should be addressed with urgent measures and changes based on legal, victimological, and socio-economic knowledge.

Firstly, lack of harmony between the existing international mechanisms of human rights and actual practice on the national level stands out as one of the principal conclusions of the analysis. The CEDAW General Recommendation No. 35, UNHRC Resolution 20/8, the Budapest Convention on Cybercrime, and the Istanbul Convention provide sufficient, if not complete, guidelines and mandates clarifying the duty of states in the prevention and combating of OGBV. However, their implementation at the national level is disjointed and erratic. As an example, CEDAW General Recommendation No. 35 refers directly to technology-driven violence and appreciates its seriousness, including the duty of states to criminalize and act across the board with regard to such aggressions. Nevertheless, an analysis of the legal framework of several countries demonstrates that these international recommendations are poorly implemented into national legislation, resulting in a lack of protection and poor enforcement procedures. Furthermore, there is a consistent gap between technology and the law that can allow perpetrators to circumvent punishment by targeting the point of vulnerability. This mismatch highlights a very fundamental human rights challenge where victims are still not sufficiently empowered in their access to safety/dignity and justice because of a lack of protection therein on a systemic and institutional level. To fill this gap, it is important to strengthen international cooperation, align national laws with international standards, and have effective enforcement mechanisms.

Secondly, findings concern the inefficiency of survivor-based response under existing modalities. The manner in which legal frameworks like the Online Safety Act 2023 in the UK, the eSafety Commissioner in Australia, or the Harmful Digital Communications Act in New Zealand are addressing the problem is punitive: they tend to punish wrongdoers and fail to cover the full range of victim support options. The reports indicate traumatic psychological effects on the victims that include anxiety, depression, post-traumatic stress disorder (PTSD), and protracted emotional distress. As an example, the feeling of powerlessness, lack of control, and constant anxiety has been reported by victims of OGBV, as well as an overall sense of insecurity in online environments. Studies have suggested that survivors seldom have proper psychological help and counseling; this makes their condition worse, and it is harder to reintegrate them into digital worlds. This means that victims are usually isolated and stigmatized, even experiencing long-term emotional and psychological damage, without support in institutions. In order to fill these gaps, legal frameworks should include all comprehensive survivor-centered solutions that focus on emotional rehabilitation, mental health care support services, trauma-informed care needs, and long-term programs to support recovery.

Thirdly, the social and economic consequences of OGBV are multifaceted and have long-lasting implications on the economic stability of victims, their social and vocational careers, and well-being in general. Female users who are vulnerable to online harassment often suffer extreme professional consequences, such as losing their job or opportunity to develop a career, resulting in damage to a professional image and successful entrepreneurial businesses. An audit of the Cherie Blair Foundation in 2024 showed that a significant percentage of female entrepreneurs had limited their online activities or left the digital landscape completely due to online harassment, which directly affected both their economic efficiency and their viability as a business. Analogously, the World Bank note on gender equality in digital development shows the role of OGBV in deepening economic disparities, particularly among women who have to access resources on digital platforms as a source of livelihood and improved education opportunities. These results stress the need to invest in economic empowerment schemes and effective digital literacy plans in the strategies of combatting OGBV. Policymakers should understand OGBV is not only a women-specific form of violence but also an impeding economic factor, so they have to incorporate various methods that will help them to be resilient and economically empowered and engage in digital life for a prolonged length of time.

Fourthly, intersectionality plays a critical role in compounding vulnerabilities among the marginalized demographics in online gender-based violence (OGBV). According to Kimberle Crenshaw, intersectionality describes the way the multiple social identities, including gender, race, sexual orientation, disability, and socio-economic status, intersect with each other and produce deteriorating conditions of oppression (Rajani, 2022). This viewpoint is especially relevant when studying OGBV because the digital environment can increase the already existing systemic biases in society, making people who hold overlapping marginalized identities particularly vulnerable to the extreme types of digital violence. The nature of this intersectional violence is not only restricted to anonymous harassment; this violence is also in the form of targeted aggression by peers, co-workers, and even alleged like-minded people. The multidimensional risks associated with activism therefore not only compromise the cause of the racialized women activists but also subject them to punishing psychological burdens, which have the long-term effect of silencing them on the internet platform. More importantly, the policies that are informed by intersectionality are not only important in the recognition of various experiences but also in the designing of effective interventions. There is a dire need to implement policies that clearly address the issue of intersectional identities to establish safe digital spaces that could protect vulnerable activists. Failing to apply the lens of intersectionality in policies may result in an inability to deal with the harm that various groups face and continue to foster inequality. Intersectional and inclusive policy systems, therefore, become an important part of the protection of basic human rights, including the right to equality, dignity, freedom of expression, and the guarantee of access to justice.

Fifthly, the governance of digital platforms is not sufficient to curb and contain online gender-based violence (OGBV) at the moment. Regardless of laws such as the Online Safety Act of the UK or the eSafety measures in Australia, digital spaces are often ineffective in curbing potentially harmful content and guaranteeing the safety of users. Algorithmic biases and substandard moderation tend to exacerbate the potential magnitude and impact of online harm by catalyzing the circulation of abusive content. There are strong calls for the introduction of clear and accountable regulations to operate digital platforms emphasizing human rights that would demand these platforms address the content proficiently and adhere to the mechanisms of their algorithms, besides obligating accountability of such platforms. To curb gender-based violence in digital spaces, law enforcement should be enhanced, and positive cooperation between the state and the business sector should be nurtured to increase accountability. An array of important analyses highlights that digital platform regulation has not been strong enough yet to safeguard users sufficiently against OGBV, especially in relation to the censorship of damaging content and the algorithmic openness (Bansal et al., 2023). The Online Safety Act passed in the UK and the eSafety Commissioner system of Australia are major legislative efforts to protect against such issues, but in practice there is frequently a problematic reality. These frameworks obligate platforms to filter out the harmful content early, take measures to safeguard children, and put mechanisms in place to hold them accountable, yet the platforms fail because of the constraints in the technical ability, allocative resources, and enforcement of the policies. The peculiarities of managing online spaces, especially taking into account the transnational and multilingual characteristics of the material, increase the challenge of successful moderation (Aranda et al., 2022). The aims of algorithmic moderation to complement manual moderation are to increase efficiency and limit the biases and errors of manual moderation, but this is often unsuccessful, leading to overly or insufficiently moderated outcomes: at times causing the deletion of acceptable content or leaving potentially dangerous material unchecked. In addition, platform governance should have strong transparency measures that make it accountable and effective in combating OGBV (Henry & Powell, 2016). It is pointed out that moderation choices and algorithmic specifics are unclear to a greater extent, which complicates the observation of platforms and policing them by external parties. Information about content choices is often not provided to users and civil society organizations, hindering necessities to hold platforms accountable when something goes wrong in moderation. Rights of the users can be secured by responsible governance of the platform: open reporting on moderation results, a clear reason behind decisions, and intervention procedures easily accessible to users so that trust can be built around digital spaces (Manche et al., 2025).

Sixthly, public-private partnerships become an essential approach to reinforcing the platforms of governance. The platforms, the government, civil society organizations, and academic institutions are required to work in collaboration to formulate detailed, human-rights-sensitive moderation policies and norms. Mechanisms of public oversight, comprising independent digital ombudspersons or oversight agencies, would play crucial roles in furthering accountability and responsiveness. The eSafety Commissioner of Australia offers an example of government regulation in combination with the self-regulation of the industry, yet the problem of extending these practices to the use of multiple cultural environments around the world is still a major challenge. Awareness and education measures are also fundamental to any successful digital platform governance. Based on the evidence provided by Aranda et al. (2022), the awareness of online violence among people plays a significant role in the possibility to report the case and intervene. Platforms should fund thorough education programs for users, explain their moderation policies, increase digital literacy, and cultivate an active bystander intervention culture. Regular education and user guidelines enable the user to identify, report, and fight the detrimental content on their own, making the online world safer (Aranda et al., 2022).

## 5.2 Final Thoughts

To sum up, Online Gender-Based Violence (OGBV) and Technology-Facilitated Gender-Based Violence (TFGBV) are not two distinct constructs but instead connected aspects of one dynamic phenomenon, two sides of one coin that cannot be separated. Cumulatively they demonstrate how historical forms of oppression based upon gender have simply seeped into online spaces, manifesting themselves in such form as algorithms, in the designs of platforms, in the inability to moderate content, in lack of control over surveillance. Where OGBV reflects the more general gendered relations of abuse based in online interactions, TFGBV describes how it is that emerging technologies contribute to the formation, reproduction, and in many instances escalation of such harms. The consequences of such violence, which can be seen throughout this chapter, do not reside in the digital sphere only but yield severe psychological, economic, social, and political outcomes on the victims, especially when they belong to marginalized and intersectionally disadvantaged communities. The insufficiency of the legal, institutional, and technological reactions is the evidence of the necessity of a globally coordinated yet locally situated, comprehensive and rights-based approach to digital governance.

Legal reform cannot go far enough in itself. Instead, it needs an integrative approach, which will prioritize lived experiences of survivors and integrate intersectional justice, build stronger platform accountability, and promote sporting educational interventions in the field of digital citizenship and ethics. Most importantly, this chapter re-establishes the significance of acknowledging OGBV and TFGBV not as moral problems, but as a human rights issue that highly needs us to re-conceptualize notions of safety, dignity and agency as they apply to the digital world. The stories and statistics conveyed in this chapter highlight one clear trend: technological advancement will persist in reflecting and reinforcing current gender inequalities unless specific attention to the needs and voices of victims is adopted. The term victim-centricity in this context is not an idealistic goal but rather a primary necessity. As a result, we must create a digital ecosystem in which the rights of a human being, women, and gendered minorities, are not sacrificed on the throne of innovation or expediency. Digital world should not turn out to be one more battleground of oppression; instead, it should develop into a platform of power, equality, and fairness. The symbiosis of policy, technology and human rights is the only way to achieve the transformative potential of digital spaces as spaces that is inclusive and safe.

## REFERENCES

Aday, T. (2015). *The Effectiveness of the Violence against Women Act (VAWA) in Creating System-Level Change*. ScholarWorks@GVSU. https://scholarworks.gvsu.edu/spnhareview/vol11/iss1/3/

Alhorr, L., Malik, A., Javed, A., Naz, N., & Nisa, N. 2024. Empowered or Undermined? Women Entrepreneurs & the Digital Economy. *Cherie Blair Foundation*. https://cherieblairfoundation.org/wp-content/uploads/2025/03/Empowered-or-Undermined-Women-Entrepreneurs-Digital-Economy.pdf

Anderson, B., & Wood, M. A. (2022). Harm Imbrication and Virtualised Violence: Reconceptualising the Harms of Doxxing. *International Journal for Crime. Justice and Social Democracy, 11*(1), 196–209. DOI: 10.5204/ijcjsd.2140

ANROWS - Australia's National Research Organisation for Women's Safety. (2022, August 7). *Technology-facilitated abuse: Extent, nature and responses in the Australian community - ANROWS - Australia's National Research Organisation for Women's Safety*. https://www.anrows.org.au/project/technology-facilitated-abuse-extent-nature-and-responses-in-the-australian-community/

Aranda, M., García-Domingo, M., Montes-Berges, B., & Fuentes, V. (2022). Variables contributing to the awareness of online gendered violence: Focus on observers. *Social Media + Society, 8*(4). Advance online publication. DOI: 10.1177/20563051221141857

Aranda, M., García-Domingo, M., Montes-Berges, B., & Fuentes, V. (2022). Variables contributing to the awareness of online gendered violence: Focus on observers. *Social Media + Society, 8*(4). Advance online publication. DOI: 10.1177/20563051221141857

Bansal, V., Rezwan, M., Iyer, M., Leasure, E., Roth, C., Pal, P., & Hinson, L. (2023). A scoping review of Technology-Facilitated Gender-Based violence in Low- and Middle-Income countries across Asia. *Trauma, Violence & Abuse, 25*(1), 463–475. DOI: 10.1177/15248380231154614

Barker, K., & Jurasz, O. (2022). Gender-Based Abuse Online: An Assessment of Law, Policy and Reform in England and Wales. In Powell, A., Flynn, A., & Sugiura, L. (Eds.), *The Palgrave Handbook of Gendered Violence and Technology* (pp. 529–544). Palgrave Macmillan., DOI: 10.1007/978-3-030-83734-1_26

Benmoussa, M., Chénier, I., Keenan-Pelletier, M., Mason, R., Robichaud, M., Tanguay, L., Valiquet, D., Walker, J., & Research and Education. (2024). *BILL C-63: AN ACT TO ENACT THE ONLINE HARMS ACT, TO AMEND THE CRIMINAL CODE, THE CANADIAN HUMAN RIGHTS ACT AND AN ACT RESPECTING THE MANDATORY REPORTING OF INTERNET CHILD PORNOGRAPHY BY PERSONS WHO PROVIDE AN INTERNET SERVICE AND TO MAKE CONSEQUENTIAL AND RELATED AMENDMENTS TO OTHER ACTS.* https://lop.parl.ca/staticfiles/PublicWebsite/Home/ResearchPublications/LegislativeSummaries/PDF/44-1/PV_44-1-C63-E.pdf

Breslin, R. A. United States Department of Defense, Klahr, A. M., United States Department of Defense, & Neria, A. (2020). The Continuum of Harm: Examining the correlates of sexual assault victimization. In Technical Report. DOI: 10.13140/RG.2.2.33546.90565

Coe, P. (2023). Tackling online false information in the United Kingdom: The Online Safety Act 2023 and its disconnection from free speech law and theory*. *Journal of Medicine and Law*, *15*(2), 213–242. DOI: 10.1080/17577632.2024.2316360

Committee on the Elimination of Discrimination against Women. (2017). General recommendation No. 35 on gender-based violence against women, updating general recommendation No. 19 (CEDAW/C/GC/35). *United Nations*. https://docs.un.org/en/CEDAW/C/GC/35

Deane, T. (2024). Gender-Based Violence in International Human Rights Law – The efficacy of the United Nations Human Rights Legal Framework and CEDAW in addressing the issue. *The Age of Human Rights Journal*, *23*, e8662. DOI: 10.17561/tahrj.v23.8662

Diab, R. (2024, June 3). *Online Harms Act should target algorithms*. Policy Options. https://policyoptions.irpp.org/magazines/may-2024/online-harms-act-algorithms/

Dragiewicz, Molly. (2020). eSafety. (2020). Children and technology-facilitated abuse in domestic and family violence situations: Infographic. eSafety Commissioner & Australian Government.

Elpaccto. (2022). Cybercrime through a gender lens: what does it mean, how do we deal with it? https://elpaccto.eu/en/news/espanol-cibercrimen-en-clave-de-genero-que-significa-como-lo-abordamos/#:~:text=Cyberspace%20facilitates%20various%20forms%20of,out%20taking%20advantage%20of%20ICT

Faloppa, F. (2023). Participation of the private sector and the media. In *Edward Elgar Publishing eBooks* (pp. 268–283). DOI: 10.4337/9781839107757.ch23

Flynn, A., Powell, A., & Hindes, S. (2023). An Intersectional Analysis of Technology-Facilitated Abuse: Prevalence, experiences and Impacts of Victimization. *British Journal of Criminology, 64*(3), 600–619. DOI: 10.1093/bjc/azad044

Gill, R. (2005). Technofeminism. *Science as Culture, 14*(1), 97–101. DOI: 10.1080/09505430500042130

Gover, A. R., & Moore, A. M. (2020). The 1994 Violence Against Women Act: A Historic Response to Gender Violence. *Violence Against Women, 27*(1), 8–29. DOI: 10.1177/1077801220949705

Grans, L. (2023). The impact of vulnerability on state obligations in criminal proceedings on domestic violence: Interpreting the Istanbul Convention and the European Convention on Human Rights. *Women & Criminal Justice*, 1–16. DOI: 10.1080/08974454.2023.2296624

Hammond, G., & McLay, M. Mapp, Ph. D., Law Commission, Hammond, G., Burrows, J., Honoré, C., Hayward, R., & Hayward, J. (2012). *Harmful digital communications: the adequacy of the current sanctions and remedies.* https://www.lawcom.govt.nz/assets/Publications/MiscellaneousPapers/NZLC-MB3.pdf

Harvey, D. (2019). *"Case note: Police v B [2017] NZCrimLawRw 36; [2017] NZHC 526, [2017] 3 NZLR 203" [2017] NZCrimLawRw 13;[2016] NZCLR 213.* https://www.austlii.edu.au/nz/journals/NZCrimLawRw/2017/36.html

Henry, N., & Powell, A. (2016). Technology-Facilitated Sexual Violence: A Literature Review of Empirical research. *Trauma, Violence & Abuse, 19*(2), 195–208. DOI: 10.1177/1524838016650189

Hicks, J. (2021). *Global evidence on the prevalence and impact of online gender-based violence. K4D Helpdesk Report.* Institute of Development Studies., DOI: 10.19088/K4D.2021.140

Holbrook, D. (2023). Violence Against Women Act: Re-authorization and impact for forensic health professionals. *Journal of the Academy of Forensic Nursing, 1*(2), 64–68. DOI: 10.29173/jafn736

Huber, A. (2022). 'A shadow of me old self': The impact of image-based sexual abuse in a digital society. *International Review of Victimology, 29*(2), 199–216. DOI: 10.1177/02697580211063659

Kanbur, N. (2021). Istanbul Convention: Commitment to Preventing Gender-Based Violence. *The Journal of Adolescent Health, 69*(2), 354–355. DOI: 10.1016/j.jadohealth.2021.05.009

Klugman, J. (2017). Gender based violence and the law. *Background paper for World Development Report 2017*. https://srhr.dspace-express.com/server/api/core/bitstreams/87a1eef7-a563-4986-b3a9-03969a61e5af/content

Lalonde, D. (2024, June 12). *Online harms need a gender-based analysis*. Policy Options. https://policyoptions.irpp.org/magazines/june-2024/deepfake-sexual-abuse/

Lau, M. (2024, March 12). *An overview of Canada's Online Harms Act*. Tech Policy Press. https://www.techpolicy.press/an-overview-of-canadas-online-harms-act/

Manche, R., Samaah, F., Tejaswini, T., & Myakala, P. K. (2025). Empowering Safe Online Spaces: AI in Gender Violence Detection and Prevention. SSRN *Electronic Journal*. DOI: 10.2139/ssrn.5176463

Mas'udah, S., Razali, A., Sholicha, S. M. A., Febrianto, P. T., Susanti, E., & Budirahayu, T. (2024). *Gender-Based Cyber Violence: Forms, impacts, and strategies to protect women victims*. Virtual Commons - Bridgewater State University. https://vc.bridgew.edu/jiws/vol26/iss4/5

McGlynn, C., Woods, L., & Antoniou, A. (2024). Pornography, the Online Safety Act 2023 and the need for further reform. *Journal of Media Law*, 1–29. DOI: 10.1080/17577632.2024.2357421

Modi, M. N., Palmer, S., & Armstrong, A. (2013). The Role of Violence Against Women Act in Addressing Intimate Partner Violence: A public health issue. *Journal of Women's Health*, *23*(3), 253–259. DOI: 10.1089/jwh.2013.4387

Nelles, J. (2020). *Online and technology-facilitated violence against women and girls: Standards of the Istanbul Convention* [Presentation]. https://rm.coe.int/1-presentation-nelles-cyberviolence-against-women-and-ic-nov-2020/1680a0561c

Nguyen, C. L., & Golman, W. (2020). Diffusion of the Budapest Convention on cybercrime and the development of cybercrime legislation in Pacific Island countries: 'Law on the books' vs 'law in action.'. *Computer Law & Security Review*, *40*, 105521. DOI: 10.1016/j.clsr.2020.105521

Nolan, M., & Gaffey, J. (2024). Online safety and social media regulation in Australia: eSafety Commissioner v X Corp. *Griffith Law Review*, *33*(1), 2–18. DOI: 10.1080/10383441.2024.2405760

Nussbaum, M. C. (2011). Creating Capabilities: The Human Development Approach. *The Belknap Press of Harvard University Press, Cambridge, Massachusetts, and London, England 2011*. https://dokumen.pub/creating-capabilities-the-human-development-approach-0674050541-9780674050549-0674061209-9780674061200.html

Ofcom. (2024, December). *Protecting people from illegal harms online: Volume 2 – Service design and user choice*. Ofcom. https://www.ofcom.org.uk/siteassets/resources/documents/online-safety/information-for-industry/illegal-harms/volume-2-service-design-and-user-choice.pdf?v=390978

Pacheco, E., & Melhuish, N. (2018). Harmful Digital Communications in New Zealand: Annual Population Survey 2017. SSRN *Electronic Journal*. DOI: 10.2139/ssrn.3128121

Plan International. 2020. Free to be Online? A report on online abuse and harassment experienced by girls. https://www.plan.de/fileadmin/website/05._Ueber_uns/Maedchenberichte/Maedchenbericht_2020/Free_to_be_online_report_englisch_FINAL.pdf

Plan International. 2020. Free to be Online? A report on online abuse and harassment experienced by girls. https://www.plan.de/fileadmin/website/05._Ueber_uns/Maedchenberichte/Maedchenbericht_2020/Free_to_be_online_report_englisch_FINAL.pdf

Plan International. 2020. Free to be Online? A report on online abuse and harassment experienced by girls. https://www.plan.de/fileadmin/website/05._Ueber_uns/Maedchenberichte/Maedchenbericht_2020/Free_to_be_online_report_englisch_FINAL.pdf

Rai, A., Ravi, K. E., Singh, S., & Vandermolen, R. (2024). Brief review of the 2022 reauthorization of the Violence Against Women Act: Gaps and way forward. *Journal of Social Work : JSW*, *25*(1), 125–133. DOI: 10.1177/14680173241278955

Rajani, N. (2022). "I bet you don't get what we get": An intersectional analysis of technology-facilitated violence experienced by racialized women anti-violence online activists in Canada. *Canadian Journal of Law and Technology*, *20*(2), 211–250.

Rawls, J. (1971). *A Theory of Justice: Original Edition*. Harvard University Press., DOI: 10.2307/j.ctvjf9z6v

Reddock, R. (2022). CEDAW and Violence against Women: Reflections after 40 years. *Violence Against Women*, *28*(8), 1723–1727. DOI: 10.1177/10778012221086003

Reuters. (2024, February 26). Draft Canada law would force social media companies to quickly remove harmful content. Reuters. https://www.reuters.com/world/americas/draft-canada-law-would-force-social-media-companies-quickly-remove-harmful-2024-02-26/

Schmidt, H. (2024). The online safety act 2023. *Journal of Medicine and Law*, *16*(2), 202–210. DOI: 10.1080/17577632.2025.2459440

Sharma, S., Alam, T., & Vatsa, A. (2024). Justice In Digital Era: Analysing Legal and Systemic Challenges in Online Gender-Based Violence. *BPAS Journal, 44*(3), 27527-27535. https://bpasjournals.com/library-science/index.php/journal/article/view/3526/3269

Smith, M., Nolan, M., & Gaffey, J. (2024). Online safety and social media regulation in Australia: eSafety Commissioner v X Corp. *Griffith Law Review*, •••, 1–17. DOI: 10.1080/10383441.2024.2405760

Stevens, Y. (2022). Dignity, Intersectional Gendered Harm, and a Flexible Approach: Analysis of the Right to One's Image in Quebec. *Canadian Journal of Law and Technology*, *19*(2), 307–331. https://digitalcommons.schulichlaw.dal.ca/cgi/viewcontent.cgi?article=1277&context=cjlt

Svantesson, D. J. B. & Centre for Space, Cyberspace & Data Law. (2024). *Global content orders: A legal analysis of eSafety Commissioner.* https://bond.edu.au/sites/default/files/2024-06/LAW_Centre%20paper_Global%20content%20orders%20A%20legal%20analysis%20of%20eSafety%20Commissioner.pdf

*The Left-Out Project Report: The case for an online gender-based violence framework inclusive of transgender, non-binary and gender-diverse experiences.* (2023, July 22). Association for Progressive Communications. https://www.apc.org/en/pubs/left-out-project-report-case-online-gender-based-violence-framework-inclusive-transgender-non

Tropina, T. (2024). 'This is not a human rights convention!': the perils of overlooking human rights in the UN cybercrime treaty. *Journal of Cyber Policy*, 1–21. DOI: 10.1080/23738871.2024.2419517

UN Human Rights Council. (2012). *The promotion, protection and enjoyment of human rights on the Internet: Resolution 20/8.* https://documents.un.org/doc/resolution/gen/g12/153/25/pdf/g1215325.pdf?OpenElement

United Nations Human Rights Council. (2012). The promotion, protection and enjoyment of human rights on the Internet (A/HRC/RES/20/8). https://undocs.org/A/HRC/RES/20/8

Van Der Wilk, A. (2021). Protecting women and girls from violence in the digital age. *Council of Europe*, 5-64. https://rm.coe.int/protecting-women-and-girls-from-violence-in-the-digital-age-final-eng-/1680ae3a31

Vijeyarasa, R. (2020). CEDAW's General Recommendation No. 35: A quarter of a century of evolutionary approaches to violence against women. *Journal of Human Rights*, *19*(2), 153–167. DOI: 10.1080/14754835.2019.1686347

Vine – Violence Information Aotearoa. (2022). *Harmful Digital Communications Act: recent cases, changes and calls for review.* https://www.vine.org.nz/news/harmful-digital-communications-act-recent-cases-changes-and-calls-for-review

*Violence against Women Victim Support: Report.* (2012, December 7). European Institute for Gender Equality. https://eige.europa.eu/publications-resources/publications/violence-against-women-victim-support-report?language_content_entity=en

Wajcman, J. (2006). TechnoCapitalism meets TechnoFeminism: Women and technology in a wireless world. *Labour & Industry a Journal of the Social and Economic Relations of Work, 16*(3), 7–20. DOI: 10.1080/10301763.2006.10669327

Wall Street Journal. (2024, March 12). *Online Harms Act: Crime and punishment, not in that order. The Wall Street Journal.* https://www.wsj.com/opinion/crime-and-punishment-not-in-that-order-canada-hate-speech-f618e339

Watson, S. (2023). Online abuse of women: An interdisciplinary scoping review of the literature. *Feminist Media Studies, 24*(1), 51–69. DOI: 10.1080/14680777.2023.2181136

Weinstein, M., Jensen, M. R., & Tynes, B. M. (2021). Victimized in many ways: Online and offline bullying/harassment and perceived racial discrimination in diverse racial–ethnic minority adolescents. *Cultural Diversity & Ethnic Minority Psychology, 27*(3), 397–407. DOI: 10.1037/cdp0000436

Wells, M., & Wells, M. (2025, January 15). *International Solutions to Technology-Facilitated Gender-Based Violence | The Regulatory Review.* The Regulatory Review. https://www.theregreview.org/2025/01/18/seminar-international-solutions-to-technology-facilitated-gender-based-violence/

Williamson, M. E. J. B. (2018). Harmful Online Speech: An analysis of New Zealand's Harmful Digital Communications Act 2015 to combat Cyberbullying. *Kuwait International Law School Journal. Special Supplement, 3*(1), 65–140. DOI: 10.54032/2203-006-991-016

Women, U. N. 2023. Technology Facilitated Gender- Based Violence. https://www.unwomen.org/sites/default/files/2024-09/technology-facilitated-gender-based-violence-shared-research-agenda-en.pdf

Women, U. N. 2023. Technology Facilitated Gender- Based Violence. https://www.unwomen.org/sites/default/files/2024-09/technology-facilitated-gender-based-violence-shared-research-agenda-en.pdf

Women, U. N. 2023. Technology Facilitated Gender- Based Violence. https://www.unwomen.org/sites/default/files/2024-09/technology-facilitated-gender-based-violence-shared-research-agenda-en.pdf

Women, U. N. 2023. Technology Facilitated Gender- Based Violence. https://www.unwomen.org/sites/default/files/2024-09/technology-facilitated-gender-based-violence-shared-research-agenda-en.pdf

Women, U. N. 2023. Technology Facilitated Gender- Based Violence. https://www.unwomen.org/sites/default/files/2024-09/technology-facilitated-gender-based-violence-shared-research-agenda-en.pdf

World Bank. 2021. Accelerating Gender Equality in Digital Development. *World Bank Group*. 16-22. https://thedocs.worldbank.org/en/doc/61714f214ed04bcd6e9623ad0e215897-0400012021/related/Digital-Development-Note-on-Gender-Equality-November2021-final.pdf

World Bank. 2021. Accelerating Gender Equality in Digital Development. *World Bank Group*. 16-22. https://thedocs.worldbank.org/en/doc/61714f214ed04bcd6e9623ad0e215897-0400012021/related/Digital-Development-Note-on-Gender-Equality-November2021-final.pdf

World Bank. 2021. Accelerating Gender Equality in Digital Development. *World Bank Group*. 16-22. https://thedocs.worldbank.org/en/doc/61714f214ed04bcd6e9623ad0e215897-0400012021/related/Digital-Development-Note-on-Gender-Equality-November2021-final.pdf

World Bank. 2021. Accelerating Gender Equality in Digital Development. *World Bank Group*. 16-22. https://thedocs.worldbank.org/en/doc/61714f214ed04bcd6e9623ad0e215897-0400012021/related/Digital-Development-Note-on-Gender-Equality-November2021-final.pdf

World Bank. 2021. Accelerating Gender Equality in Digital Development. *World Bank Group*. 16-22. https://thedocs.worldbank.org/en/doc/61714f214ed04bcd6e9623ad0e215897-0400012021/related/Digital-Development-Note-on-Gender-Equality-November2021-final.pdf

World Bank. 2021. Accelerating Gender Equality in Digital Development. *World Bank Group*. 16-22. https://thedocs.worldbank.org/en/doc/61714f214ed04bcd6e9623ad0e215897-0400012021/related/Digital-Development-Note-on-Gender-Equality-November2021-final.pdf

Yeasmine, F. (2024). The Impact of Digital Transformation on Society: Unraveling Trends, Challenges, and Opportunities. *Eunomia, 2*(108), 53-67. https://bibliotekanauki.pl/articles/57552184.pdf

Chapter 8

# Global Governance, Digital Politics, and Human Rights Protection

**Šárka Cabadová Waisová**
https://orcid.org/0000-0001-7197-9269
*University of West Bohemia in Pilsen, Czech Republic*

**Ladislav Cabada**
https://orcid.org/0000-0001-9604-0987
*University of West Bohemia in Pilsen, Czech Republic*

## ABSTRACT

*This chapter discusses the development of global governance mechanisms in the area of digital politics, the internet, and artificial intelligence. The first part introduces key concepts and milestones in the development of governance, particularly digital politics. The next section presents a framework for protecting human rights online against the backdrop of two metanarratives. The first one is the tension between the Global North and Global South in establishing global governance and digital politics. The second metanarrative presents the tension between universal and state-centric conceptions of protecting and regulating human rights online. The final section introduces the institutional framework and soft law principles associated with the United Nations' work through the UN Hub for Human Rights and Digital Technology to develop a universal model of digital politics during the Digital Decade (2020s) and to achieve the Sustainable Development Goals by 2030.*

DOI: 10.4018/979-8-3373-8510-5.ch008

## INTRODUCTION

Digitization presents one of the most important challenges in contemporary politics. It is a paradigm that is not automatically associated with post-modernization and the transition to the information society. This means that in different types of societies or political regimes, digitalization can take very different forms, promote or suppress certain aspects or dimensions of digital transformation with different intensity, etc. This diversity poses a major challenge for both theoretical reflection on digital politics and political practice at all levels of governance.

In our analysis, we concentrate on the global level of analysis by focusing primarily on the transformations of the concept and organization of global governance in relation to the challenges of digital politics. We reflect on the mechanisms by which the UN system has integrated various aspects of digital transformation and the threats or challenges they pose. In particular, we focus on digital divide, human-centered digitization and human rights protection issues, including the new digital rights catalogue, and security challenges associated with the use of artificial intelligence.

At the same time, we focus on the geopolitical dimension of digital politics on a global scale. In other words, we examine the conflict between universal and state-centric approaches to digitization. We pay particular attention to analyzing the development of the digital politics regulatory ecosystem within the UN Hub for Human Rights and Digital Technology and the implementation of the UN General Assembly resolution on the promotion and protection of human rights in the context of digital technologies.

Finally, we reflect on the tension between global/multilateral and state-centric approaches to digital policy regulation. We discuss the frequent criticism of the global North's dominance in this area and the fact that the region's key actors — the United States and the European Union — are the biggest proponents of multilateralism and opponents of authoritarian digital policies. At the same time, however, we also consider the fact that the traditional division between the West (the Global North) and the 'post-colonial' world has recently been disrupted by two factors: the emergence of China (or rather, Sinocentric international groups) as a rival to the West; and the unilateral approach of the current US administration, which is primarily state-centric and disregards the multilateral dimension.

This transformation is also linked to the growing assertiveness and emancipation of regional powers and governance models in different parts of the Global South. These have developed under different conditions, for different reasons, and also with distinct motivations (Söderbaum, 2004, p. 4). This emancipation and plurality of regional governance models is also linked to the emergence of different models and activities of grassroots digital rights movements and, more generally, civil society resistance against various forms of digital authoritarianism, including data colonialism.

## GOVERNANCE, GLOBAL GOVERNANCE AND E-GOVERNANCE

The term "governance" is currently one of the most frequently used terms in Western social science. This is primarily due to the transformation from modern societies and states, which are characterized by strong central governments, to new forms of statehood and international systems that are usually characterized as postmodern and globalized, respectively. Hedley Bull (1995) primarily associates postmodern statehood with the European integration process. However, other actors in the international system such as Canada, Japan, or Human Security Network members (Waisová, 2025, p. 244; Waisová & Cabada, 2011) have also exhibited some of the distinctive features associated with this concept since the 1970s. These characteristics include shared sovereignty based on acceptance of multiple decision-making levels, soft borders that facilitate movement of people and goods, normative internationalism, respect for international institutions and norms that govern states, and an emphasis on human rights and acceptance of diversity and multiculturalism.

The transition to postmodern statehood is characterized by the weakening of the top-down government approach, the democratization of politics including foreign and security policy, civilian control of public policies, the involvement of various stakeholders in decision-making process, and a shift to multi-level decision-making and regionalization at subnational and supranational levels (Cooper, 2003; Sørensen, 2001).

When we try to transfer the governance mechanism from the postmodern liberal-democratic state to the globalizing international system, we naturally encounter conceptual obstacles related to the existence of other types of states. However, it is true that the cooperation of states and the international community in protecting human beings was made possible after the end of the Cold War, in particular thanks to the existence and activities of a global organization that brings states together and promotes the values declared in the Universal Declaration of Human Rights and related principles of international law (Waisová, 2025, p. 243). The tension between universalism and state-centrism remains a key challenge for the international community as it attempts to develop a functional model of global governance. At the same time, the phenomenon of multiple regionalisms (cf. Börzel & Risse, 2016) challenges the traditionally dominant Eurocentric notions of the value framework of global governance.

There is no single definition of governance, and researchers generally focus on the distinction between government and governance (see, for example, Bannister & Connolly, 2012, pp. 5-7). There is agreement that government is primarily characterized by formal institutions responsible for creating and exercising law and power within a specific territory — currently, almost exclusively the state or quasi-state. As Rhodes (1997, p. 15) states: "Government is the formal and institutional processes which operate at the national level to maintain public order and facilitate collective action."

In contrast, governance is characterized by the involvement of various institutions, tools, processes, and mechanisms. Its structure is based on networks, partnerships, and interactions between different types of stakeholders at various organizational levels within society. Unlike government, it is not possible to precisely distinguish the institutional framework for standard-setting or decision-making. This is why governance encompasses not only formalized rules and structures, but also informal practices and soft law. It is organized around the concept of multi-stakeholder committees and global governance forums. As Kooiman (2003, p. 4) states: "Governance is a broader term than government. It encompasses not only the institutions and processes of government but also the relationships between government, civil society, and the private sector."

One of the significant impulses for supporting the development of governance mechanisms beyond the scope of the normal government of a modern centralized state is the effort to strengthen accountability and transparency, as both imply the need for scrutiny and scrutiny is only necessary where there are desired forms of behavior that need to be policed" (Bannister & Connolly, 2012, p. 7). The involvement of a wide range of stakeholders should also ensure more competent decision-making and evidence-based policies.

If the difference between government and governance involves a significant normative framework, then the difference between their 'e-' versions appears, at first glance, to be primarily technical. However, Bannister and Connolly (2012, pp. 4–11) point out that the relationship between governance and e-governance is much more complicated ("e-governance cannot simply be governance with an electronic patina", p. 4) and that a specific distinction must be made between e-governance and e-democracy, as these are sometimes discussed as if they were the same. Regarding the former, the authors note that e-governance alters group dynamics, interaction possibilities, and communication tools. Notably, it shifts "the balance of power between and possibly the number of stakeholders" (p. 8). The authors then define e-governance as "the use of information and communication technologies (ICTs) in government in ways that either: (1) alter governance structures or processes in ways that are not feasible without ICT, and/or (2) create new governance structures or processes that were heretofore not possible without ICT, and/or (3) reify heretofore theoretical ideas or issues in normative governance" (p. 11).

## GLOBAL GOVERNANCE AND THE TENSIONS BETWEEN THE GLOBAL NORTH AND GLOBAL SOUTH

The conflation of e-governance and e-democracy on a global scale highlights a deeper issue regarding the conflict between universal and particularistic views of moral principles and standards. Many authors from the Global South have noted the dominance of Western, primarily American, actors in designing the theoretical frameworks of digital politics and its practical applications. As Sabhanaz Rashid Diya (2025), originally from Bangladesh, points out in the discussion on the meta-level design of contemporary AI systems: "Human beings hold a variety of contrasting but reasonable beliefs about moral values, so designing governance systems for AI with a single moral doctrine would involve imposing a set of values and judgments on other people who may not agree with them ... Second, can localized and contextualized rules be embedded in transnational technology architectures? Societies operate on varied public conceptions of justice .... Third, and most critically, which set of normative values should be encoded in AI systems or in their governance? The largest AI systems in the world are predominantly designed under sociopolitical and commercial conditions in economically advanced Western democracies" (p. 2).

Mexican author Paola Ricaurte Quijano shares a similar view. She perceives the controversy surrounding universal normative frameworks for globalization and digitalization as a geopolitical phenomenon in which the Global North, represented by the North Atlantic region, clashes with the Global South, dominated by China. "Geopolitically, two models represent the landscape of digitization: the U.S.-Eurocentric market-based model and the sinocentric state-based model. Within the Western model's sphere of influence, digitalization is viewed as a universal, indispensable, and pressing imperative" (Ricaurte, 2025, p. 12).

We will return to the tension between multiple conceptions of global digital politics several times in our text. Nevertheless, first let us return to global governance and its development after World War II. As we have demonstrated, global governance is a complex set of institutions, rules, processes, and standards that manage global affairs in the absence of a central world government. Due to the nature of international politics, in which states are the primary actors while facing challenges that transcend borders, there has been a growing need for coordination at the supranational level since World War II. The establishment of a basic framework for global governance is specifically linked to the definition and pursuit of global public goods. The management of these goods requires the adoption of global regulatory rules that all actors will respect, leading to the establishment of mechanisms that ensure fair distribution. Global public goods represent "an internally heterogeneous group ranging from international multilateral trade regimes and global financial stability ensured by international financial institutions to natural resources" (Naxera & Piknerová, 2011a, p. 13).

Unlike the traditional concept of government as a specific institution with a Weberian monopoly on legitimate violence, the global environment lacks a single authority. At the same time, the global governance environment is characterized by significant fragmentation in terms of institutions and decision-making mechanisms. Thus, in addition to states, the system of global governance is forming at both the supranational (e.g., the United Nations) and regional levels. As Naxera and Piknerová (2011b, p. 22) state: "In recent decades, global governance has also been associated with the rise of global regionalism or regionalization." Additionally, the global governance environment is characterized by the involvement of other actors, including transnational corporations and non-governmental organizations, which are organized at different spatial levels. This pluricentric and multistakeholder character is a typical feature of global governance (Weiss & Wilkinson, 2014).

The end of the Cold War and the subsequent disappearance of the bipolar confrontation provided significant impetus to strengthen and expand the concept of global governance. This opened up space to revitalize the United Nations' fundamental objectives related to promoting universal principles of human rights protection and equal access to global public goods. In the mid-1990s, the UN formed the Commission on Global Governance. The result of its work was the report Our Global Neighborhood, which presented several key areas. These included the core values of a global neighborhood (respect for life and freedom, mutual respect, equality and justice, fighting corruption, etc.), global security, managing mutual economic dependence, UN reform, and strengthening the rule of law and statehood on a global scale (Naxera & Piknerová, 2011b, p. 26).

Originally used mainly in an economic context, the concept has gradually expanded to include security, environmental, and technological issues. In particular, the goal of global governance has become to improve the coordination, efficiency, and legitimacy of global decision-making processes. These objectives are typically linked to the ideals of lasting peace, sustainable development, human rights, and economic equality. However, critics point to a democratic deficit, power inequality between the Global North and Global South, and the weak enforceability of agreements (Held & McGrew, 2007; Josukutty, 2020).

## GLOBAL GOVERNANCE, DIGITAL POLITICS AND HUMAN RIGHTS

From the outset, one of the topics predestined for transnational reflection and global regulation has been digital technology and the associated digital politics. This is primarily because the technological framework of digitalization significantly deviates from typical national regulation. As Zuboff (2019) points out, the digital space, for example, defies traditional geopolitical categories. Information spreads across borders, rendering national regulation often insufficient. This gap leads to the emergence of digital sovereignties where technological giants, rather than states, play the dominant role. Digital platforms can define the rules of communication and information distribution, giving them a quasi-sovereign character. In a world where digital technologies shape everyday life, political communication, and international security, global governance is taking on new dimensions. The internet and digital environment challenge traditional notions of state sovereignty and present new challenges regarding human rights and democratic governance (Floridi, 2014).

In its early days, the internet was overlooked or perceived as an "arcane and marginal topic of interest primarily to 'geeks' and government officials. However, in recent years, the topic has received greater attention, particularly following Edward Snowden's disclosure of classified US National Security Agency documents. This event revealed how "interconnected and vulnerable to surveillance we all are" (Verhulst et al., 2017, p. 96). Originally defined primarily by economic and technological aspects, digital politics has incorporated a key security framework that has rapidly expanded into several other areas. Therefore, it is not surprising that, alongside environmental policy, it currently represents the second cross-cutting theme of all European Union policies. The EU has declared the period from 2021 to 2030 the Digital Decade. Digital politics broadly encompasses a wide range of interrelated topics, including data collection and protection, cybersecurity, digital skills and education, the digital economy, semiconductor manufacturing, smart cities and transportation, digital identity, and the protection of personal data in the online environment (European Commission, 2020; European Commission, 2021).

The EU is undoubtedly a pioneer in the protection of digital rights and the prevention of digital authoritarianism. At the same time, however, it is important to recognize that several other key players, such as states or regional groups, engage in activities that prioritize the use of digital technologies and artificial intelligence for surveillance and the infringement of individual rights. These issues will also be further addressed in our analysis.

## DIFFERENT PERCEPTIONS OF DIGITAL GOVERNANCE AMONG STAKEHOLDERS

As shown above, global governance can be understood as a network of mechanisms, institutions, and norms governing the behavior of actors in the international system. Digital politics is becoming an integral part of this framework because it affects economic and technological processes as well as the sphere of civil rights and freedoms. The sources of global governance include international law; soft law, which contributes to the creation of rules of conduct; formal and informal structures, such as international and non-governmental organizations and agreements; and international regimes. Additionally, rules and principles adopted by private entities are developing in a new and dynamic way. However, they encroach on areas that originally fell within the competence of individual national legal frameworks. Thus, we are talking about private (global) governance. "The dramatic growth of private governance is primarily due to the development of the Internet" (Naxera & Piknerová, 2011b, pp. 22-25).

Drezner (2004) views the internet as both the greatest challenge to states as dominant actors in the international system and a test of the feasibility of building a strong global civil society. Despite all efforts, he concludes that global governance in the field of digital politics has failed to undermine the primacy of the state. This is partly because different types of states have dramatically different demands and priorities in this field. As he emphasized: "The regulation of Internet content – that is, censorship – neatly fits the outcome of sham standards. Governments have wildly divergent preferences regarding the extent to which Internet content should be regulated. Totalitarian governments such as Cuba or Saudi Arabia want absolute control over citizen access to the Internet. Authoritarian governments such as Singapore or China want to exploit the Internet's commercial opportunities while restricting the use of the Internet for political criticism. Liberal democracies also wish to place restrictions on offensive forms of content. These countries' definitions of objectionable content range from child pornography (the United States) to Nazi memorabilia (France). For this issue, there is no bargaining core among nation-states" (p. 488).

Although digital media provides a space for free speech, it is also a platform for spreading hate speech, misinformation, and extremist content. Content regulation often raises questions about censorship and freedom of speech. In authoritarian regimes, digital tools are used to silence opposition and monitor the population, a practice referred to by some researchers as digital authoritarianism (cf. Feldstein, 2019; Kaye, 2019).

Of course, the relationship between digital politics and human rights cannot be reduced to internet regulation. However, highlighting the different approaches that states take with regard to their internal political regimes and key characteristics of their security dilemmas is a useful introduction to this issue. Without geographical restrictions, the digital environment provides opportunities to circumvent or overcome national regulations. At the same time, digital politics is characterized by the increased presence and influence of transnational corporations. Companies like Amazon, Google, and Meta have become global players that impact political processes and human rights. Their economic power often exceeds that of many states. While some companies adopt codes of ethics and principles of responsibility, others are accused of failing to comply with legal and human rights standards (Douek, 2021).

## FRAGMENTED REGULATION

The tension between the global nature of the internet and fragmented regulation is evident in the different approaches to personal data protection in the EU, US, and China (Bradshaw, Millard, & Walden, 2011). The development of credit systems in China (Creemers, 2017; Dai, 2018; Qiang, 2019) and the use of facial recognition systems to persecute citizens, as in the case of the authoritarian government of Hungary cracking down on citizen gatherings, demonstrate that even Western liberal democracies are not immune to the misuse of personal data.

However, the problematic use of digital technologies and AI cannot be attributed solely to undemocratic regimes and digital authoritarianism. This was clearly demonstrated by the case of the British-American company Cambridge Analytica's use of Facebook user data to manipulate voting behavior is another example (Isaak & Hanna, 2018). An interesting example is the development and use of the Indian Aadhaar system, the world's largest biometric identification system. Since 2009, it has collected data — primarily fingerprints and iris scans — from approximately one billion people in India. However, its original purpose of establishing a robust and reliable social benefits distribution system has gradually expanded into other areas of the public and private spheres. This process of "function creep" has been accompanied by a number of problems, including extensive data leaks and malfunctions that have prevented access to public goods. In 2018, the Supreme Court restricted the mandatory use of the system in the private sector, emphasizing the need for robust personal data protection and proportionate interference with privacy (Nambiar, 2025; Supreme Court Observer, 2018).

Rashid Diya (2025, p. 6) draws attention to the possibility of "algorithmic discrimination and surveillance, as seen in facial recognition systems that produce culturally ingrained biases against people of colour." The risk of algorithmic bias, which can lead to discrimination in areas such as criminal justice, employment, and healthcare, is a common consequence of the advent of artificial intelligence. The lack of transparency in these processes makes them difficult to review and protect individuals legally (Eubanks, 2018).

The behavior of the actors also contributes to the lack of transparency. On the one hand, there are private companies whose primary goal is to maximize profit. On the other hand, there are states with very different ideas about how data should be acquired, used, and protected. However, we cannot ignore individual actors who often fail to recognize the transformation of the internet environment. As Verhulst et al. (2017, p. 96) demonstrate: "the initial *Internet of links* made computers and the information on them searchable, then the growing *Internet of data* emerged … expanding the variety, velocity and volume of data on the network ... The *Internet of people*, enabled by social and collaborative software … has similarly changed the Internet and the way it is used. We are now entering the era of the *Internet of things*, where every device from watches to refrigerators to heart monitors is getting connected, generating enormous quantities of rich and revealing data that promise further innovations and challenges in coming years". Among other things, this change brings risks of unknowingly providing personal data and its possible misuse for commercial or political purposes.

## UNITED NATIONS AND DIGITAL POLITICS

As we demonstrated above, the digital space is inherently transnational. Therefore, it is logical that the regulation and organization of this phenomenon requires supranational, ideally global, instruments. After an initial phase of humble, bottom-up internet governance, a significant change took place in the late 1990s. Announced at the World Economic Forum in Davos in January 1999, the UN Global Compact reflected the specific role of transnational corporations and sought to stimulate coordination mechanisms to create global social responsibility. This was based on the assumption that transnational corporations' activities should be ethical, moral, and responsible (Naxera & Piknerová, 2011b, p. 33-34). A few years later, at the World Summit on the Information Society (WSIS) in Geneva and Tunis (2003-2005), the foundations for multi-stakeholderism as the preferred approach to global internet governance were established. The Working Group on Internet Governance (WGIG), the Internet Governance Forum (IGF), and other forums for follow-up debates and discussions were established (Josukutty, 2020, p. 65).

The UN is striving to become a leading global authority in digital transformation. In 2020, the organization launched the Roadmap for Digital Cooperation based on the High-Level Panel on Digital Cooperation's recommendations. The panel's co-chairs were Melinda French Gates, a former Microsoft executive, and Jack Ma, the founder of the Chinese internet conglomerate Alibaba Group. The roadmap focuses on four basic principles: 1) connectivity — the goal is to achieve universal digital access by 2030; 2) digital public goods — promoting open-source software, data, and AI models for sustainable development; 3) digital inclusion — ensuring marginalized groups benefit from technology; and 4) human rights online — protecting freedom of speech, privacy, and digital rights (UN Roadmap, 2020).

The High-Level Panel on Digital Cooperation's activities resulted in the establishment of the UN Hub for Human Rights and Digital Technology, which officially launched in 2020 as part of the Secretary-General's Call to Action for Human Rights. The Hub was created to consolidate UN human rights guidance, standards, policy analysis, and recommendations related to digital rights and technologies. His remit was to cover the topics from civic space and AI to surveillance, equality, data, business, and governance. In 2023, the Hub's work was supported and refined by Resolution 78/213 on Human Rights in the Context of Digital Technologies, which was spearheaded by the Czech Republic. In May 2024, the Secretary-General's Executive Committee approved the Guidance on Human Rights Due Diligence for Digital Technology Use, which enables all UN entities to incorporate human rights safeguards into the development and deployment of digital tools. Also in June 2024, the Office of the High Commissioner for Human Rights established the Innovation and Analytics Hub to promote technology-enabled solutions for sustainable development goals and integrate data-driven strategies into its human rights initiatives (OHCHR, n.d.).

The advent of artificial intelligence has provided significant impetus for the United Nations to strengthen its activities in the field of digital policy. In November 2021, UNESCO adopted the Recommendations on the Ethics of Artificial Intelligence, which aim to provide a global framework for the ethical use of AI and promote its use for positive purposes, such as in education, climate prediction, food security, and healthcare. The recommendations also advocate for AI regulation that aligns with human rights and sustainable development goals. The ten general principles agreed upon by UNESCO are: 1) proportionality and safety; 2) safety and security; 3) equity and non-discrimination; 4) sustainability; 5) right to privacy and data protection; 6) human supervision and decision; 7) transparency and explainability; 8) responsibility and accountability; 9) awareness and education; and 10) adaptive governance and collaboration (Morandín-Ahuerma, 2023).

## DIGITAL SOVEREIGNTY, DATA COLONIALISM AND DIGITAL DIVIDE

When we look more closely at the ten general principles, we can observe that they significantly reflect security issues, platform accountability linked to the fight against misinformation, disinformation and fake news, hate speech, and online harms, but also a general effort to overcome the digital divide. It is certainly no coincidence that the initiatives presented came at a time of global pandemic, which clearly demonstrated the need for the equitable and intensive distribution of public goods associated with digital politics. “The COVID-19 crisis has made clear the central role digitalization plays in the current world, and its role in responding to a global crisis” (Burwell & Propp, 2020, p. 3). In the last decade, the internet and, subsequently, AI have undergone a profound transformation “into something like a global common, or a ‘global public resource’ that benefits and potentially empowers the entire planet” (Verhulst et al., 2017, p. 98).

However, critical studies emphasize that the internet and digital politics have become just one of many mechanisms that deepen differences between regions and groups. For instance, Josukutty (2020, pp. 64–66) discusses the evolution of the discourse on balanced information flow between the Global North and Global South since the 1970s. “The consensus is that fundamental polarization between these regions has persisted. Before the end of the Cold War, the Non-Aligned Movement and UNESCO initiated efforts to establish a New World Information and Communication Order, but these initiatives did not lead to greater balance. „In the new millennium, in the context of the breathtaking changes in the field of ICTs, the debate on information order resurfaced through the World Summit on Information Society (WSIS) and the North and South polarization over global internet governance.” In the second half of 2000s, “the differences resulted in a polarization between the North and the South at two levels. The South stood for a maximum role for sovereign state-centric arrangements and a minimum role for private players and non-state actors in the control of global internet governance. The North stood for a maximum role for the U.S., private and civil society entities and a minimum role for other sovereign states.”

This criticism suggests that digitization has become a topic around which polarization is occurring in the global environment. Information and data have thus become commodities that are fought over and can be used as tools to promote the ideas of individuals or groups. As Waisová (2011, p. 41) states: “Ownership and control of knowledge and information have become an important dimension of power. The ability to disseminate new ideas and information significantly influences behavioral frameworks and can become an important stimulus and defining feature for international political cooperation.”

Thus, data has become another public good that is the object or instrument of the digital divide. “Internet governance is increasingly becoming a conflicting issue in international relations. Consensus on a mechanism for global internet governance has been elusive on account of the differing perceptions posited by the developed and the developing countries. The domination of internet, both in its technical resources and wider public policies, by the developed countries has rendered a new dimension to North-South divide ... Digital divide, within and between nation states, has emerged as the most visible component of development divide in contemporary times" (Josukutty, 2020, p. 63).

Differences in access to the benefits of digital politics, particularly data and its use, present a challenge that the United Nations and other multilateral organizations are well-suited to address. As Allen Dafoe (2018/2019, p. 122) has pointed out in his reflections on current developments in AI: "Multilateral organizations could play a pivotal role in AI governance by providing a joint forum for the formulation, coordination, and dissemination of the cooperative norms between actors, enabling participating parties to signal sincere commitment to beneficial and shared AI development. At present, there is no single multilateral organization that has taken up this mantle, although the UN has developed a vision of pursuing "AI for Global Good," and to use it as a driver in achieving its Sustainable Development Goals by 2030."

It is the United Nations that appears to be the appropriate actor to contribute to overcoming the challenges of the digital divide in the contemporary international system. Here, on the one hand, the tensions between the Global North and Global South outlined above apply. At the same time, it should be noted that important differences also exist at lower levels of governance, such as between world regions and within states. Older structural differences between centers and (semi-)peripheries often manifest themselves within states. Furthermore, these centers tend to associate digital policy with governance concepts such as oversight and centralized authoritative decision-making rather than with a more inclusive concept of governance. As Ricaurte (2025, p. 13) points out: "In practice, digitalization processes imposed top-down from these centers of power to the peripheries, while allowing people to be integrated into the digital economy, do not contribute to global justice, as they are mainly anchored to corporate solutions based on extractive business models that have increased the concentration of capital, knowledge, and infrastructure in a handful of global players."

In addition to global activities in the field of digital politics, we should mention specific regional and national models of internet governance. Although the EU is often considered a pioneer in this area, this accolade more rightly belongs to Brazil. Brazil's approach to internet governance is frequently held up as a prime example of a multistakeholder model, combining legal, institutional and political mechanisms that emphasize public participation, the protection of user rights and transparency. This model is managed by an Internet Governance Committee established in 2003, comprising representatives from government, the private sector, academia, and civil society. The committee's activities, along with the entire ecosystem, are governed by a special 2014 law (*Marco Civil da Internet*), which codifies the basic principles, rights, and obligations of internet users, connection providers, and online applications. It also defines the responsibilities of intermediaries, privacy protection, net neutrality, and other aspects. The Brazilian model is based on ten key principles, including freedom of expression, privacy protection, net neutrality, plurality, diversity, openness, participation of civil society, accountability of stakeholders, the social purpose of the internet, and the stability, security, and functionality of the network (Igarapé Institute, 2025).

However, this system is also subject to pressures that undermine its original inclusive framework, which emerged from civil society. Since Jair Bolsonaro took office as president in 2019, there have been efforts to centralise internet governance under the authority of political institutions and limit the influence of civil society. A significant blow to the stability of the ecosystem was the 2025 Supreme Court decision that repealed two provisions of the Marco Civil da Internet: specifically, that application providers are not responsible for content, and that any intervention in content must be authorized by a court (Covington, 2025). Conversely, this decision strengthens the possibility of enforcing common principles of protecting human dignity in the digital environment by requiring the removal of unacceptable content (e.g. hate speech).

## DIGITAL AUTHORITARIANISM

At the same time, however, we cannot overlook the fundamental challenge and danger posed by the use of digital politics and artificial intelligence for subversive activities such as cyberterrorism and other forms of cyber-attacks, espionage, etc., and the authoritarian control of one's own or even foreign populations (China). Here, we must critically reflect on the fact that many authors pointing to the dominance of (some) states in the field of global governance and digital politics, in their criticism of the Global North and primarily the United States, neglect the crucial role played by China, Russia, but also North Korea and Iran in building a state-centric concept of digital politics in international relations.

The subversive activities of these states and their proxy actors often target both international and domestic audiences. Various forms of digital authoritarianism, including mass surveillance, content control, internet censorship, disinformation and propaganda activities, and repressive legislation targeting those demanding respect for digital rights from the authorities, are continuously being strengthened and supplemented in line with technological progress. Authoritarian actors are exploiting technological asymmetry and digital inequality (Feldstein, 2021).

The digital environment has also become a battleground for asymmetric conflict at various levels. One positive aspect of the fight against digital authoritarianism is that resistance is global. Non-hierarchical organisations such as Access Now,

Reporters Without Borders or Electronic Frontier Foundation offer advice and education on digital dangers, as do many quasi-governmental structures focused on combating disinformation and strategic communication. Activities that promote an open internet and decentralisation (Web 3.0, including blockchains and open networks such as Mastodon) are also important in strengthening resilience against digital authoritarianism, as is the open science mechanism.

Thus, we can hardly identify with the one-sided critique as perceived by e.g. Josukutty (2020, pp. 69-70) when he states the following: "A major argument of the North is that in matters of internet governance the role of states should be the minimum. This is necessitated by the borderless nature of the ICTs and the efficiency and flexibility of the market driven self-regulatory private governance mechanisms. But contrary to these arguments and expectations of a borderless world, internet today is controlled by states … All the forums of internet governance … and negotiations and discussion at various other institutions linked to internet governance are under new pressures as governments assert themselves more forcefully in cyberspace. The only difference is that it is controlled by the powerful states of the North led by the U.S. The powerful states continue to be the most important actors in international politics." This one-sided criticism ignores the Chinese Communist Party's specific activities toward its own population, such as the social credit system, extensive censorship, and the creation of state-controlled social networks. It also ignores the Saudi Arabian government's drastic policies against critical social network users. It fails to acknowledge that in some countries, such as North Korea and Afghanistan, non-privileged individuals are prohibited from using digital tools. In terms of protecting human rights, these activities seem to us to be a much bigger problem than state rivalries in global governance and digital policy.

In this respect, we believe a more balanced view is one that seeks to improve global governance through the involvement of different stakeholders, their mutual cooperation, and their mutual control. As Dafoe (2018/2019, p. 122) pointed out: "The market capture by a few ultra-profitable AI companies might create new forms of dependency, as many states will be forced to negotiate with whichever country – China or the United States – supplies most of their AI services." However, he does not view this as a polarizing or conflicting factor but rather as an "incentive to establish a global framework that balances private and public interests and aligns firm incentives with the common good of humanity".

## CONCLUSION

Digital policy is one of the key challenges of the current international system and internal politics of individual states. Approaches to its implementation and organization vary dramatically. In liberal-democratic states, we see numerous bottom-up activities, especially within the European Union, to set an example for building digital politics alongside the protection of human rights. In contrast, authoritarian regimes tend to misuse the technical tools of digitalization against individuals and their fundamental rights. Therefore, it is difficult to formulate generalizations in this context. This is particularly true given that some private or quasi-private corporations have emerged alongside states in the field of digital politics, particularly the internet and AI. These corporations have built an oligopoly and have become intertwined with the political sphere. One example is the current relationship between the administration of US President Donald Trump and large internet companies, as well as the surveillance of domestic internet companies and producers by the Chinese political leadership.

As we have tried to show, as in the case of other public goods, in the field of digital policy several principles and different interests of specific actors collide in the global governance environment. In this respect, the global governance of digital politics is a complex system that involves states with different power and ability to enforce or impose their own approaches, private corporations, but also global civil society based mainly on a network of NGOs. It is in the area of protecting universal human rights that we see the role of the United Nations as indispensable, albeit limited in the same way as it is for other public goods.

Without a doubt, we can still agree with the conclusions presented by Verhulst et al., when they stated that "global collective action and coordination on Internet-related issues have to date been considered by many as ineffective, too slow and often illegitimate for a global public good such as the Internet, whose value stems from interoperability. Concerns about governance fragmentation undermining the global nature of the medium arise as a result of often divergent and hard to reconcile national approaches to privacy, security, freedom of expression and access … new paradigms of governance are needed that embrace the global, distributed and open nature of the Internet. Such paradigms must integrate and embrace new tools and methods that help to realize twenty-first-century principles such as openness, collaboration and inclusiveness, along with a respect for human rights and freedom of expression (Verhulst et al., 2017, p. 96).

Clearly, the internet and the rise of AI present dramatic challenges to human rights protection. One of the most debated rights in the digital age is the right to privacy. The EU's General Data Protection Regulation (GDPR), for example, gives individuals more control over their data. "With strict requirements for consent and limits on the permissible use of personal data, the GDPR is a vindication of Europeans' fundamental right to privacy protection. But the GDPR goes even further – by controlling the movement of personal data from Europe to other jurisdictions, the GDPR provides an ambitious example of the EU's exercise of sovereignty in the digital space" (Burwell & Propp, 2020, p. 14). However, the EU is still the exception globally. "The European Union and the United States adopted different stances on the issue. The U.S. attitude toward privacy rights is based on freedom from state intervention; in Europe, privacy is considered a fundamental right to be protected by the state" (Drezner, 2004, p. 486).

The lack of a single global framework contributes to legal uncertainty and an increased risk of violations of individual rights. This also applies to freedom of speech and censorship, as well as protection against misinformation and discrimination by algorithmic decisions, as well as ensuring the primacy of human-centered AI. These challenges, along with others, complement the general and fundamental demand for universal internet access and inclusive participation in digital politics.

## REFERENCES


Bannister, F., & Connolly, R. (2012). Defining E-Governance. *e-Service Journal, 8*(2), 3–25.

Börzel, T. A., & Risse, T. (2016). Three Cheers for Comparative Regionalism. In Börzel, T. A., & Risse, T. (Eds.), *The Oxford Handbook of Comparative Regionalism* (pp. 1–25). Oxford University Press.

Bradshaw, S., Millard, C., & Walden, I. (2011). Contracts for clouds: Comparison and analysis of the terms and conditions of cloud computing services. *International Journal of Law and Information Technology, 19*(3), 187–223.

Bull, H. (1995). *The Anarchical Society: A Study of Order in World Politics*. Macmillan.

Burwell, F., & Propp, K. (2020). *The European Union and the search for digital sovereignty: building "Fortress Europe" or preparing for a new world.* Atlantic Council.

Cooper, R. (2003). *The Breaking of Nations: Order and Chaos in the Twenty-First Century*. Atlantic Monthly Press.

Covington (2025). *Brazilian Supreme Court strikes down safe harbor provision of the Marco Civil da Internet*. https://www.cov.com/en/news-and-insights/insights/2025/06/brazils-supreme-court-to-strike-down-internet-governance-safe-harbor-clause

Creemers, R. (2017). China's Social Credit System: An Evolving Practice of Control. *SSRN*. https://doi.org/DOI: 10.2139/ssrn.3175792

Dafoe, A., & Journal of International Affairs (2018/2019). Global politics and the governance of artificial intelligence. An Interview with Allan Dafoe. *Journal of International Affairs*, (Fall 2018/Winter 2019), 121-126.

Dai, X. (2018). Toward a Reputation State: The Social Credit System Project of China. *SSRN*. https://doi.org/DOI: 10.2139/ssrn.3193577

Douek, E. (2021). Governing Online Speech: From "Posts-As-Trumps" to Proportionality and Probability. *Columbia Law Review, 121*(3), 759–832.

Drezner, D. W. (2004). The global governance of internet: Bringing the state back in. *Political Science Quarterly, 119*(3), 477–498.

Eubanks, V. (2018). *Automating Inequality: How High-Tech Tools Profile, Police, and Punish the Poor*. St. Martin's Press.

European Commission. (2020). *A Europe fit for the digital age*. https://commission.europa.eu/publications/factsheets-europe-fit-digital-age_en

European Commission. (2021). *2030 Digital Compass: The European Way for the Digital Decade*. https://digital-strategy.ec.europa.eu

Feldstein, S. (2019). *The Global Expansion of AI Surveillance*. Carnegie Endowment for International Peace.

Feldstein, S. (2021). *The rise of digital repression. How technology is reshaping power, politics, and resistance*. Oxford University Press.

Floridi, L. (2014). *The Onlife Manifesto: Being Human in a Hyperconnected Era*. Springer.

Held, D., & McGrew, A. (2007). *Globalization/Anti-Globalization: Beyond the Great Divide* (2nd ed.). Polity Press.

Igarapé Institute. (2025). *The Marco Civil da Internet and data protection in Brazil*. https://igarape.org.br

Isaak, J., & Hanna, M. J. (2018). User Data Privacy: Facebook, Cambridge Analytica, and Privacy Protection. *Computer*, *51*(8), 56–59.

Josukutty, C. A. (2020). Global internet governance. *Indian Journal of Asian Affairs*, *33*(1/2), 63–78.

Kaye, D. (2019). *Speech Police: The Global Struggle to Govern the Internet*. Columbia Global Reports.

Kooiman, J. (2003). *Governing as governance*. SAGE Publications.

Morandín-Ahuerma, F. (2023). Diez recomendaciones de la Unesco sobre ética de la inteligencia artificial. In Morandín, F. (Ed.), *Principios normativos para una ética de la inteligencia artificial* (pp. 86–94). Concytep.

Nambiar, N. (2025). UIDAI deactivates 1.4 crore Aadhaar numbers of deceased across India. *The Times of India*. https://timesofindia.indiatimes.com/city/pune/uidai-deactivates-1-4-crore-aadhaar-numbers-of-deceased-sets-2-crore-target-for-year-end/articleshow/124033065.cms

Naxera, V., & Piknerová, L. (2011a). Úvodem. In Naxera, V., & Piknerová, L. (Eds.), *Globální vládnutí. Vybrané problémy* (pp. 11–15). Aleš Čeněk.

Naxera, V., & Piknerová, L. (2011b). Charakter aktérů v současném mezinárodním systému a posun od vlády k vládnutí. In Naxera, V., & Piknerová, L. (Eds.), *Globální vládnutí. Vybrané problémy* (pp. 19–39). Aleš Čeněk.

OHCHR. (n.d.). UN Hub for Human Rights and Digital Technology. https://www.ohchr.org/en/hub-human-rights-and-digital-technology

Qiang, X. (2019). The road to digital unfreedom: President Xi's surveillance state. *Journal of Democracy*, *30*(1), 53–67.

Rashid Diya, S. (2025). *Applying international human rights principles for AI governance. Policy Brieg No. 196 – February 2025. Centre for International Governance Innovation*. CIGI.

Rhodes, R. A. W. (1997). *Understanding governance: Policy networks, governance, reflexivity and accountability*. Open University Press.

Ricaurte, P. (2025). The digitalization imperative. *Dialogues on Digital Society*, *1*(1), 12–17.

Roadmap, U. N. (2020). The Secretary-General's Roadmap for Digital Cooperation (A/74/821). URL: https://www.un.org/techenvoy/sites/www.un.org.techenvoy/files/general/Roadmap_for_Digital_Cooperation_9June.pdf

Söderbaum, F. (2004). *The Political Economy of Regionalism. The Case of Southern Africa*. Palgrave Macmillan.

Sørensen, G. (2001). *Changes in Statehood. The Transformation of International Relations*. Palgrave Macmillan.

Supreme Court Observer. (2018). Constitutionality of Aadhaar Act: Judgment summary. https://www.scobserver.in/reports/constitutionality-of-aadhaar-justice-k-s-puttaswamy-union-of-india-judgment-in-plain-english/

Verhulst, S. G., Noveck, B. S., Raines, J., & Declercq, A. (2017). *Innovations in global governance: toward a distributed internet governance ecosystem. Who Runs the Internet?: The Global Multi-Stakeholder Model of Internet Governance, Centre for International Governance Innovation*. MIT Political Science.

Waisová, Š. (2011). Nevládní organizace jako aktéři mezinárodní politiky a řízení mezinárodního systému. In Naxera, V., & Piknerová, L. (Eds.), *Globální vládnutí. Vybrané problémy* (pp. 40–52). Aleš Čeněk.

Waisová, Š. (2025). Deep Co-Production of Human Security at the Science–Politics Nexus. In B. Bliesemann de Guevara et al. *Knowledge and Expertise in International Politics* (pp. 236-251). Oxford University Press.

Waisová, Š., & Cabada, L. (2011). *Ethics in Foreign Policy: Postmodern States as the Entrepreneurs of Kantian Ethics*. Peter Lang.

Weiss, T. G., & Wilkinson, R. (2014). *International Organization and Global Governance*. Routledge.

Zuboff, S. (2019). *The Age of Surveillance Capitalism*. Public Affairs.

## KEY TERMS AND DEFINITIONS

**Algorithmic Decisions:** Outcomes or choices made by computer systems using programmed rules or machine learning models, often based on analyzing large sets of data without direct human intervention.

**Cyber-Attacks:** Deliberate and malicious attempts to disrupt, damage, or gain unauthorized access to computer systems, networks, or data.

**Cyberterrorism:** The use of digital attacks or disruptions against critical computer systems or networks with the intent to cause fear, harm, or coercion for political, ideological, or religious purposes.

**Digitalization:** A process of using digital technologies to change business models, operations, or services, transforming them to create new value and improve efficiency.

**Digital Inclusion:** The effort to ensure that all individuals and communities have access to and the ability to use information and communication technologies effectively.

**Digital Privacy:** The right of individuals to control the collection, use, and sharing of their personal information in digital environments.

**E-Governance:** The use of information and communication technologies by government institutions to improve the delivery of public services, enhance transparency, and promote citizen participation in governance.

**Governance:** A system of rules, practices, and processes that aim to manage and control policy processes involving different types of stakeholders and administrative-geographical levels.

**Human-Centered AI:** An approach to artificial intelligence design and development that prioritizes human values, needs, and well-being, ensuring that AI systems are ethical, transparent, and aligned with human intentions.

**Human Rights Online:** The fundamental rights and freedoms that human beings are entitled to when using digital technologies and the internet.

**Social Credit System:** A framework that monitors, evaluates, and scores individuals' or entities' behavior to incentivize compliance and punish misconduct.

Chapter 9

# Data Science in Service of Community Anomaly Detection:

## Shaping Strategy Based on Discovered Patterns of Deviant Phenomena

**Goran Klepac**
https://orcid.org/0009-0000-6298-6790
*Algebra Bernays University, Croatia*

## ABSTRACT

*This study explores the strategic implications of identifying and analyzing patterns in deviant phenomena across various domains. By leveraging advanced data science techniques, including Benford's Law analysis, Bayesian networks, and extreme value theory, we uncover hidden regularities in seemingly random or anomalous events. Our research demonstrates how these patterns can be utilized to inform decision-making processes and shape effective strategies in fields such as fraud detection, risk management, and human rights monitoring. The study presents a novel framework for integrating statistical anomaly detection with strategic planning, allowing organizations to proactively address potential threats and opportunities. Our findings suggest that a deeper understanding of deviant patterns can lead to more robust and adaptive strategies, particularly in complex and uncertain environments. This work contributes to the growing body of literature on data-driven strategy formulation and offers practical insights for policymakers and business leaders.*

DOI: 10.4018/979-8-3373-8510-5.ch009

## INTRODUCTION

The integration of data science into the field of human rights represents a transformative approach to addressing some of the most pressing global challenges. By leveraging advanced analytical tools, machine learning, and big data, practitioners and researchers can uncover patterns of abuse, predict risks, and develop proactive interventions to safeguard human dignity.

Data science offers numerous applications for the protection and promotion of human rights.

Big data analytics can identify patterns of human rights violations, such as trafficking or forced labor, by analyzing call records, satellite imagery, or social media activity. For example, movement patterns in mobile phone data can reveal trafficking routes or exploitation hubs.

Predictive models can forecast risks of human rights abuses, such as ethnic violence or mass displacement, by analyzing historical data and real-time indicators like social unrest or economic instability.

Data science aids in disaster response by mapping affected populations and optimizing resource allocation during crises like natural disasters or armed conflicts. It also helps track displaced populations and ensure equitable distribution of aid.

Machine learning algorithms can detect anomalies in financial transactions or public procurement processes, uncovering corruption or misuse of funds that undermine human rights protections.

Advanced analytics can process large volumes of evidence (e.g., videos, images, and documents) to support investigations into war crimes, genocide, or other human rights violations.

Data science tools are used to detect and prevent surveillance abuses while promoting privacy-enhancing technologies to protect individuals from unlawful data collection and misuse.

Analyzing socioeconomic data helps identify inequality trends, monitor poverty levels, and inform policies aimed at improving access to healthcare, education, and housing.

Visualization tools and statistical analysis enhance storytelling for advocacy campaigns by presenting compelling evidence of human rights abuses to the public and policymakers.

Data science supports the development of ethical AI frameworks to prevent discrimination or bias in machine learning systems that could harm marginalized communities.

Community-driven data science initiatives empower individuals to contribute to monitoring local human rights issues while fostering transparency and accountability in governance.

Data science promotes inclusivity by identifying systemic inequalities and biases in areas such as education, healthcare, and law enforcement. Tools like algorithmic fairness frameworks ensure that AI systems used in governance or law enforcement do not perpetuate discrimination against vulnerable populations.

## BACKGROUND

As data science has great application potential in any areas where different patterns can be recognized from huge amount of data, human rights area is no exception.

There are many of scientific works which explore and give solution in area of human rights with usage of data science principles Alvarado (2017), Ball (2000), Mantelero (2021).

In data science there are different approaches in solving variety of problems Klepac (2014), Klepac (2017), and same methodology can be used in area of human rights protection.

Difference is mostly on application area and approaches due to problem type. There are some illustrative examples how data science and AI can help in human rights anomaly deviation, protection, and understanding root cause analysis Taylor (2017), Morgenroth (2021), Shah (2021), Richardson (2019), Reirer(2020).

Designing efficient technological environment which can support pattern recognition, and anomaly detection in societies for human rights protection is always the challenge Aizenberg (2020), Barocas (2017).

Different problem types, determine different approaches in data collections, methodology usage and technological solutions Brabham (2014), Sawyer (2005).

One of the most useful approaches in seeking of unusual patterns is anomaly detection Cheng (2015), Foorthuis (2021), Safdari (2024), which is not reserved only in area of human rights but can be inspiration for anomaly detection which refers to some type of deviation in area of human rights.

Anomaly detection within socio-demographic datasets is a growing area of research that leverages data science techniques to identify unusual patterns or outliers in population-related data. These anomalies can provide critical insights into societal dynamics, uncover hidden issues, and inform policy interventions. The application of data science methods to such datasets is particularly valuable in contexts like urban planning, disaster management, fraud detection, public health monitoring, corruption, class inequality.

Finding facts / patterns leads to shaping solutions and way of decreasing inequalities, corruption, public health problems and trends which generates source od human rights violations.

The advent of data science has revolutionized the way human rights are monitored, protected, and promoted. By leveraging advanced analytical tools, machine learning algorithms, and big data methodologies, data science enables the identification of patterns, prediction of risks, and formulation of proactive strategies to address human rights violations.

## ANOMALY DETECTION IN COMMUNITY DATA O R HOW DATA SCIENCE CONTRIBUTE TO HUMAN RIGHTS

### Issues, Controversies, Problems

Anomaly detection using data science is a critical tool for protecting human rights as it enables the identification of irregularities or deviations in data that may signify violations or risks. By leveraging machine learning (ML) and artificial intelligence (AI) techniques, anomaly detection can uncover hidden patterns in socio-political, economic, or behavioral datasets, providing actionable insights to address human rights challenges.

Data science plays a pivotal role in detecting patterns of irregularity in community datasets, which can reveal human rights violations that might otherwise go unnoticed. Data science enables the analysis of vast and complex datasets to identify deviations from expected norms. These anomalies often serve as indicators of potential abuses, systemic discrimination, or emerging crises.

Machine learning algorithms can process large volumes of structured and unstructured data, such as social media posts, satellite imagery, and official records, to identify unusual trends or correlations. For instance, ML tools can detect anomalies in population structures, concentration of feature characteristics for violent trends.

Temporal analysis identifies deviations over time, such as sudden spikes in hate speech on social platforms before outbreaks of violence. Spatial anomaly detection highlights geographic irregularities, such as areas with disproportionately high levels of surveillance or restricted access, which may indicate repression or discrimination.

Predictive models analyze historical data alongside real-time inputs to forecast potential human rights violations. For example, existence of some rare events which caused irregular activities in relation to ruins human rights.

Irregularities in financial records or public procurement processes can expose corruption that undermines human rights protections. These irregularities can be detected by usage of data science techniques in domain of fraud detection models.

By identifying patterns of irregularity in community datasets, data science enhances the ability to detect human rights violations early and accurately. These insights empower policymakers, advocates, and humanitarian organizations to take timely action while promoting accountability and justice.

## Data Science and Anomaly Detection Techniques and Methods

### Z-Score

The Z-score, a statistical measure, is widely used in anomaly detection due to its simplicity, computational efficiency, and ability to quantify deviations from the mean. The Z-score measures how many standard deviations (σ) a data point (X) is away from the mean (μ) of the dataset. It is calculated as:

$$z = \frac{(X - \mu)}{\sigma}$$

Z: The Z-score of the feature
X: The value of the feature.
μ: The mean of the dataset.
σ: The standard deviation of the dataset.

A high absolute Z-score (e.g., > 2,9 or < -2,9) indicates that a data point deviates significantly from the mean and may be considered an anomaly.

Mean, standard deviation, quartiles, percentiles applied on continuous variables gave an insight on existing attribute characteristics. Standard deviation is useful in finding outliers and extremes within attributes. Extreme values in variables are often milestones for further investigation regarding fraud and suspicious trends.

### Weight of Evidence (WoE) and Information Value (IV)

The Weight of Evidence (WoE) measures the strength of a predictor variable in separating two binary classes. It is based on the ratio of the proportion of non-events to events within each category or bin of the predictor variable. WoE is expressed as the natural logarithm of this ratio.

For a given bin i, the WoE is calculated as:

$$WoE = \ln\left(\frac{\text{Dnb}}{\text{Db}}\right)$$

Where Dnb represents Distribution of Non Events and Db represents Distribution of Events

A positive WoE indicates that the bin contains a higher proportion of non-events than events, negative WoE indicates that the bin contains a higher proportion of events than non-events.

The Information Value (IV) quantifies predictive power of the attribute and can be calculated as:

$$IV=\sum_{i=1}^{n}\left(Dnb_i - Db_i\right)* \ln\left(\frac{\mathrm{Dnb_i}}{\mathrm{Db_i}}\right)$$

IV value determine predictive strength of variable.

Even IV and WoE has been used as part of predictive model development, when we are talking about anomaly detection, it can be useful for investigation of deviant events or bad events concentration.

For example, we can se is there any concentration of bad water quality or criminal activities, bad health insurance in some areas or among specific situation and is observed attributes important for prediction according to human rights violation/ discrepancy.

## Benford Law

Benford's law is phenomenon discovered by Simon Newcomb and rediscovered by Benford, Klepac (2018), which describes probability of the occurrence of the first digits of the number within some data sample. This law says that the probability that the first digit D equals d (which is probability of occurrence) is given by:

$$Pr(D = d) = log\left(1+\frac{1}{d}\right)$$

This empirically proved phenomenon is much more evident in non-artificial systems where we are dealing with random events. It was proved in Benford's experiment. In recent period, especially after beginning of 90's Benford's law was renewed mostly as useful tool in area of fraud detection.

In case of illegal, immoral activities, corruptions in some society those random distribution of first digits can be ruined. Let assume principle of equality for distribution of financial help or scholarships. In case of biasing and interventions which are not in line with expected way of distribution, it can be potentially visible via Benford's law.

Benford's law give one aspect of intuition, but it is not enough for complete system. Also, we cannot claim that it is universally applicable in all situations. It depends on many factors, and Benford's law could not be universal factor for judgement about fraud. It should be critically observed, taking in consider other factors to have clear picture and serious reasons for claiming that we are dealing with suspicious cases.

## Social Networks Analysis

Social metrics are highly effective tools for uncovering hidden relationships between nodes.

Each network metric serves a distinct purpose in identifying connections and recognizing influential nodes. During the social network analysis phase, analysts can leverage a combination of different metrics to unveil concealed insights.

However, combining social metrics is not always straightforward, particularly when attempting to create filters for network structures based on these metrics. Interpreting such combinations of social network metrics can also be challenging, as can ensuring consistent periodic analysis using the same filters.

When social network data is available, it serves as a valuable resource for cognitive computing, particularly in the context of fraud detection. Identifying concentrations of influence within nodes, along with detected anomalies, can significantly aid automated fraud investigations.

For instance, suspicious activities within a multimodal network at the node level—where such activities are identified as frequent events aligning with Benford's law—can provide critical insights for uncovering potential fraud.

## Fuzzy Logic

One of the key objectives of expert fraud models is to identify suspicious activities at the individual client level. However, traditional approaches that rely on predictive models as the foundation for fraud detection may prove insufficient.

This limitation arises from the fact that predictive models typically focus on a small set of highly predictive attributes, selected based on their significant impact on the target variable. This impact is traditionally measured using attribute relevance analysis, with statistical significance serving as the primary criterion.

While statistically significant attributes are useful for identifying clear trends, they present a challenge when used as early warning indicators. If a trend becomes statistically significant, it often means it has been occurring over an extended period and has already become a recognizable pattern. As a result, traditional predictive models struggle to detect fraudulent activities that occur at an individual level or those that are subtle and infrequent.

While these models are effective for identifying broad trends and mass-scale fraudulent patterns, they fall short when it comes to providing a comprehensive early fraud detection solution.

This does not imply that predictive models should be excluded from fraud detection systems; rather, they should not serve as the sole foundation.

Fuzzy expert systems enhance fraud detection by incorporating human expert knowledge into automated solutions, enabling the identification of potential suspicious activities.

To further improve these systems, integrating elements such as Benford's law with statistical measurements can help uncover illogical patterns indicative of fraud.

This approach allows for the detection of rare and unexpected patterns without requiring explicit rules for every potential fraudulent scenario. By combining these methods, it becomes possible to identify non-obvious fraud patterns and strengthen the overall effectiveness of fraud detection systems.

A fuzzy set is an extension of a classical set. If X is the set of values and its elements are denoted by x, then a fuzzy set A in X is defined as a set of ordered pairs by flowing formula .

$$A = \{x, \mu A(x) | x \in X\}$$

Upgrade to fuzzy logic are fuzzy expert systems.

Fuzzy expert systems offer a robust framework for detecting anomalies in human rights contexts, where the data is often characterized by uncertainty, imprecision, and ambiguity. These systems leverage fuzzy logic to handle such uncertainties effectively, making them particularly suitable for identifying subtle and complex patterns of anomalies that may indicate human rights violations.

Fuzzy rule blocks allow the combination of multiple anomaly indicators—such as deviations in social network metrics or statistical irregularities—into a unified decision-making framework. This integration improves the system's ability to detect complex and interrelated anomalies

## Bayesian Networks

Bayesian networks utilize probabilistic dependencies between variables, enabling the detection of anomalies based on deviations from expected patterns. This is particularly useful in human rights contexts, where data is often incomplete or uncertain, such as reports of abuse or irregularities in social behavior

Bayesian network model for finding risk profiles should be constructed in way that target variable contains probabilities for j number of products. Parental nodes contain behavioral characteristics recognized as crucial for risk evaluation in process of attribute relevance analysis.

Formally, we can express it as:

$Pr[P_j] = Pr[\text{node parents}]$

Or more precisely as:

$$Pr\left[P_j\right] = \prod_{i=1}^{n} Pr\left[P_j \middle| Y_i, \dots, Y_n\right]$$

Where:

$Pr[P_j]$ – represents risk probability for j event, socio-demographic characteristics.

$Y_i$ – represents behavioral characteristics within Bayesian network expressed as a state value of Bayesian network node.

For discovering deviant event/ profile which has the highest risk for event j, it is necessary to find such combination of $Y_1$ to $Y_n$ values which gives maximum value of $P_j$. From the perspective of Bayesian networks, task is to find combination of evidences in nodes which will maximize value of $P_j$.

Bayesian networks support both supervised and unsupervised approaches to anomaly detection. In unsupervised settings, they can identify deviations from normal patterns without requiring labeled data, which is advantageous when dealing with low-frequency human rights violations

Unlike many machine learning models, Bayesian networks provide interpretable outputs by explicitly modeling causal relationships. This makes it easier for human rights analysts to understand and explain detected anomalies, a critical aspect when presenting findings to stakeholders or in legal contexts

## Putting It All Together

The integration of extreme value analysis, Benford's Law, fuzzy logic, and Bayesian networks creates a comprehensive framework for detecting deviations in human societies and identifying potential human rights violations. Each method contributes unique strengths to this multidimensional approach.

Extreme value analysis focuses on identifying outliers or anomalies at the tails of data distributions, which may signify rare but critical events such as sudden spikes in violence or resource deprivation in specific regions. Benford's Law, a statistical tool that identifies deviations from expected digit distributions in numerical datasets, can detect irregularities in socioeconomic or demographic data, such as fabricated reports or manipulated election results. These deviations often serve as early indicators of systemic issues or fraudulent activity. Fuzzy logic enhances this framework by introducing the ability to handle imprecise or ambiguous data common in human rights contexts. It translates complex variables—such as social network metrics or behavioral patterns—into linguistic terms (e.g., "high risk" or "moderate deviation") and applies rule-based reasoning to identify subtle anomalies. This flexibility allows for the detection of nuanced patterns that traditional binary systems might overlook. Bayesian networks complement these methods by modeling probabilistic relationships between variables, enabling the system to infer hidden dependencies and update anomaly probabilities dynamically as new data becomes available. For instance, they can combine multiple indicators—such as economic instability, social unrest, and irregular migration patterns—to predict the likelihood of human rights violations with greater accuracy. When combined, these methods form a robust anomaly detection system. Extreme value analysis and Benford's Law provide statistical baselines for identifying deviations, while fuzzy logic interprets ambiguous patterns, and Bayesian networks integrate diverse data sources into a cohesive probabilistic model. This synergy enables the detection of both explicit and subtle deviations, offering a powerful tool for monitoring societal dynamics and safeguarding human rights in complex and uncertain environments.

As with Benford's law, relying solely on statistical measures is insufficient for detecting potential fraud. By intersecting anomalies—such as extreme values or other statistical measures relevant to a specific fraud problem—with digits that significantly deviate from Benford's law, we can begin to uncover potentially suspicious patterns. This example represents a simplified concept for intuitively identifying potential fraud cases within data samples. However, this approach also requires a decision engine capable of processing and managing the identified anomalies, which will be discussed later. Traditional methods that rely on machine learning techniques, such as Bayesian networks, neural networks, decision trees, and similar models, are not fully aligned with a cognitive approach. These methods typically require the presence of a target variable, which poses a challenge when dealing with low-frequency events like fraud or corruption. In such cases, machine learning algorithms are often inefficient. Nevertheless, these algorithms can still play a role as part of the proposed solution. A more cognitive-oriented system would focus on intangible events and patterns, making it better suited for detecting subtle and infrequent fraudulent activities.

A fuzzy membership function can be defined to represent anomalies in digits identified using Benford's numbers, as well as anomalies in statistical measures and social network metrics. Each of these variables can be expressed as a linguistic variable.

The definition of a linguistic variable can include anomalies identified using Benford's numbers, statistical measures, and social network metrics. These linguistic variables can be integrated and combined through fuzzy rule blocks. In this context, social network metrics can also be incorporated seamlessly.

# CASE STUDY FROM PUBLIC DATA

## About Used Data and Data Source

The Chicago Health Atlas (https://chicagohealthatlas.orgn) is a free, interactive online platform designed to provide comprehensive health-related data for all 77 community areas in Chicago.

Developed in partnership with the Chicago Department of Public Health (CDPH), the UIC School of Public Health, Metopio, and the Otho S.A. Sprague Memorial Institute, the Atlas allows users to explore, analyze, and download data on over 160 public health indicators. These include metrics related to demographics, health outcomes, behaviors, social determinants of health, and access to healthcare resources.

The Atlas serves as a vital tool for residents, community organizations, researchers, and policymakers by enabling them to identify health challenges, monitor progress toward health equity goals, and develop data-driven solutions. It also supports initiatives like Healthy Chicago 2025 by tracking progress in reducing health disparities and closing racial life expectancy gaps.

The platform has been recognized globally for its innovation, earning a Smart Cities award in 2023 for its role in advancing community health through data accessibility. By integrating data from more than 30 partners—including local hospitals, government agencies, and research institutions—the Chicago Health Atlas empowers stakeholders to address pressing health issues and advocate for equitable resource distribution across the city.

## Use Case Description

To analyse the causes of major crimes, a systematic approach has been adopted where major crimes are defined as those exceeding one standard deviation above the mean of the entire population.

This threshold ensures that only significant deviations are considered, focusing on outliers that may indicate systemic or critical issues.

The analysis employs Information Value (IV) and Weight of Evidence (WOE) to identify and quantify the main factors contributing to these crimes.

These statistical techniques are particularly effective in determining the predictive power of independent variables relative to the dependent variable, thereby prioritizing factors with the highest influence on major crime occurrence.

The application of IV and WOE is complemented by other methodologies.

For instance, extreme value analysis is used to detect anomalies at the tails of data distributions, which often correspond to rare but impactful events. Benford's Law is applied to identify irregularities in numerical datasets, such as financial records or demographic statistics, which may signal fraudulent or manipulated data linked to criminal activities. Fuzzy logic further enhances this framework by handling imprecise or ambiguous data, translating complex variables into linguistic terms (e.g., "high risk" or "low deviation") and enabling rule-based reasoning to uncover subtle patterns. Additionally, Bayesian networks provide a probabilistic framework for modeling relationships between variables and updating anomaly probabilities dynamically as new data becomes available.

This capability is particularly valuable in integrating diverse factors such as socioeconomic conditions, peer influences, and geographic patterns, all of which are known correlates of criminal behavior. By combining these methods, the analysis achieves a multidimensional perspective, capable of identifying both explicit and implicit drivers of major crimes.

This integrated approach not only identifies key contributing factors but also provides a robust foundation for developing targeted interventions and policies aimed at mitigating major crimes and addressing their root causes effectively.

Data was used from the Chicago Health Atlas as of December 31, 2023. After construction of target variable, it was integrated with socio-demographic community data with the goal of identifying anomalies that contribute to major crimes. Major crimes were defined as incidents exceeding one standard deviation above the mean across the entire population, ensuring a focus on significant deviations. The analysis leveraged socio-demographic factors such as unemployment rates, lack of education, and other visible indicators. However, it also aimed to uncover hidden or latent factors that may underlie or drive these observable causes. By combining advanced statistical techniques, including Information Value (IV) and Weight of Evidence (WOE), the study quantified the influence of these variables on major crimes. This approach was further supported by complementary methodologies, such as extreme value analysis and probabilistic modeling, to capture both overt and subtle patterns of deviation within communities. This comprehensive framework provides a robust basis for understanding the root causes of major crimes and offers insights into potential interventions to address both explicit and implicit drivers of criminal behavior in Chicago's neighborhoods.

## Data Preparation

A comprehensive data quality analysis was conducted to ensure the reliability and validity of the dataset used for studying major crimes.

This process included the identification and correction of inconsistencies, as well as the application of data transformations where necessary to standardize variables and enhance interpretability.

Specific attention was given to handling missing values, employing appropriate imputation techniques to minimize bias while preserving the integrity of the dataset.

Extreme value analysis was also applied to identify outliers and anomalies within the data.

These extremes provided preliminary insights, revealing that crime rates are significantly more pronounced in certain areas or under specific socio-demographic conditions.

The recognition of these extremes not only highlighted critical patterns but also informed subsequent analytical steps, enabling a more targeted investigation into the factors contributing to major crimes.

By addressing data quality issues, transforming variables where required, and leveraging extreme value analysis, the study established a robust foundation for uncovering meaningful relationships between socio-demographic factors and crime rates, ultimately enhancing the accuracy and depth of the findings.

## Weight of Evidence, Information Value Results

The analysis of major crimes, based on the Weight of Evidence (WOE) and Information Value (IV) methodologies, identified key socio-demographic attributes as significant predictors. These attributes include **poverty rate**, **single-parent households**, **unemployment rate**, **food stamp usage**, **median household income**, **proportion of White population**, **9th-grade education level**, **hardship index**, and **income per capita**.

*Table 1. Information value results*

| Attribute | IV |
|---|---|
| black | 2.33 |
| eviction | 1.56 |
| latino | 1.41 |
| poverty rate | 1.26 |
| single-parent households | 1.26 |
| unemployment rate (%) | 1.26 |
| food stamp | 1.26 |
| median household income | 1.13 |
| white | 1.13 |
| 9th grade education | 0.79 |
| hardship index | 0.60 |
| income per capita | 0.51 |

WOE and IV were utilized to quantify the predictive strength of these variables in relation to the target variable for major crimes.

Poverty rate, unemployment rate, and food stamp usage emerged as critical factors, reflecting economic deprivation as a primary driver of criminal behavior.

Similarly, the hardship index and low educational attainment (e.g., 9th-grade education) highlight structural disadvantages within communities that contribute to crime.

The inclusion of median household income and income per capita underscores the relationship between economic inequality and crime rates.

Additionally, single-parent households were identified as a significant factor, emphasizing the role of family structure in shaping social stability.

These findings align with established criminological theories, such as strain theory and social disorganization theory, which link socioeconomic disadvantages to increased crime rates.

By identifying these attributes, this approach provides a data-driven foundation for targeted interventions aimed at mitigating major crimes through policies addressing unemployment, poverty, education, and community support systems.

## Findings From Benford's Law

An analysis based on Benford's Law has revealed an anomaly in the leading digit distribution of income per capita data, specifically for digit "1" in the lowest income category associated with major crimes.

This deviation suggests potential irregularities or non-conformity to expected patterns, warranting further investigation.

Furthermore, a correlation was identified between this anomaly and socio-economic factors, particularly the prevalence of single-parent households and lower levels of educational attainment.

These findings align with existing literature that highlights the interplay between family structure, income disparities, and education in influencing societal outcomes.

The significance of the digit "1" in crime data, particularly when analyzed under Benford's Law, lies in its expected frequency as the leading digit in naturally occurring datasets.

According to Benford's Law, the digit "1" should appear as the leading digit approximately 30% of the time in datasets that span multiple orders of magnitude, such as income levels or crime statistics. Deviations from this expected distribution may indicate anomalies or irregularities, such as data manipulation, reporting errors, or underlying systemic patterns.

In crime data analysis, an unusually high or low occurrence of the digit "1" as the leading digit could signal inconsistencies in reported figures or reveal socio-economic correlations.

For example, if income per capita data for areas with high crime rates shows an unexpected anomaly in the frequency of the digit "1," it might suggest deeper connections to socio-economic factors like education levels or family structures (e.g., single-parent households), which are often linked to crime trends.

## Role of Fuzzy Expert Systems

Fuzzy logic and fuzzy expert systems offer a robust framework for anomaly detection in community service applications by integrating data-driven findings with expert knowledge.

These systems are particularly effective in consolidating diverse results and identifying patterns, enabling the detection of "islands of anomaly"—localized deviations that may not conform to expected norms.

By leveraging fuzzy inference mechanisms, these systems can process uncertainty and ambiguity inherent in real-world data, offering a nuanced perspective for detecting deviations that may have implications for human rights.

For instance, fuzzy logic's ability to handle imprecise data allows it to identify subtle anomalies that traditional methods might overlook.

This is achieved through the construction of fuzzy rule bases and membership functions, which model complex relationships between variables, such as socio-economic factors or surveillance data.

The integration of expert knowledge further enhances the system's interpretability and decision-making capabilities, ensuring that detected anomalies align with human rights considerations. This approach supports the identification of systemic deviations—such as inequities or discriminatory patterns—by correlating anomalies with broader socio-economic or ethical contexts, thereby promoting transparency and accountability in community governance.

Fuzzy logic allows for the modeling of imprecise or ambiguous data, which is common in community service contexts, such as socio-economic indicators or behavioral patterns. By assigning degrees of membership to different categories, fuzzy systems can better capture subtle anomalies that traditional binary logic might miss.

Fuzzy expert systems can incorporate human expertise into the decision-making process through rule-based systems. This enables anomaly detection to align more closely with real-world complexities and expert insights, improving the interpretability and reliability of results.

By detecting "islands of anomaly" localized deviations in data fuzzy systems can highlight potential violations of human rights or inequities in service delivery.

This enables proactive interventions to address disparities and ensure equitable access to resources.

## Solution Based on Bayesian Network Model

To develop a Bayesian network with major crime as the target attribute and incorporating the specified socioeconomic factors, based on attribute relevance analysis results.

Bayesian network models for predicting major crime rates can benefit from incorporating a diverse set of socioeconomic and demographic variables to enhance their reliability and predictive power.

The inclusion of factors such as poverty rate, single-parent households, unemployment rate, food stamp usage, median household income, proportion of White population, 9th-grade education level, hardship index, and income per capita can contribute significantly to the model's accuracy for several reasons. Firstly, these variables capture various dimensions of economic hardship and social disorganization, which have been theoretically and empirically linked to crime rates in numerous studies.

Economic factors like poverty rate, unemployment, and median household income provide insights into the financial stress experienced by communities, which may influence criminal behavior.

The inclusion of food stamp usage and hardship index further refines the model's ability to capture nuanced aspects of economic distress that may not be fully reflected in income measures alone.

Demographic variables such as the proportion of single-parent households and the White population can account for family structure and racial composition, which have been associated with variations in crime rates across different communities.

Educational attainment, represented by the 9th-grade education level, serves as a proxy for human capital and potential future earnings, factors that can influence an individual's propensity to engage in criminal activities. By incorporating this diverse set of variables, the Bayesian network model can capture complex interactions and dependencies between socioeconomic factors and crime rates, leading to more robust and reliable predictions.

Furthermore, the use of county-level data for these variables allows for spatial analysis, enabling the model to account for geographic variations in crime patterns and their underlying socioeconomic determinants.

This comprehensive approach to crime prediction aligns with social disorganization theory and provides a more nuanced understanding of the multifaceted factors contributing to criminal behavior in different communities

The chance nodes in model nodes would include poverty rate, single-parent households, unemployment rate, food stamp usage, median household income, proportion of White population, 9th-grade education level, hardship index, income per capita, and major crime as the target variable.

Causal relationships would be inferred based on statistical dependencies and prior knowledge. For example, low median household income and high unemployment rates might directly influence poverty rates, which in turn could affect major crime rates.

The proportion of single-parent households and low education levels might also contribute to higher crime rates, both directly and indirectly through their impact on unemployment and income.

The hardship index, being a composite measure, would likely have incoming edges from multiple socioeconomic factors and potentially a direct link to major crime.

Food stamp usage could be an indicator of economic distress, potentially influenced by poverty rates and unemployment, and might have a relationship with crime rates.

The proportion of White population and income per capita would be included as potential factors influencing other socioeconomic variables and possibly crime rates, though care must be taken to avoid biased interpretations.

Parameter estimation would involve calculating conditional probability distributions for each node, particularly focusing on how changes in parent nodes affect the probability of major crimes.

The final network would allow for probabilistic inference, enabling policymakers to assess how interventions in various socioeconomic factors might impact crime rates, while also providing insights into the complex interplay between these societal indicators.

*Figure 1. Created Bayesian Network*

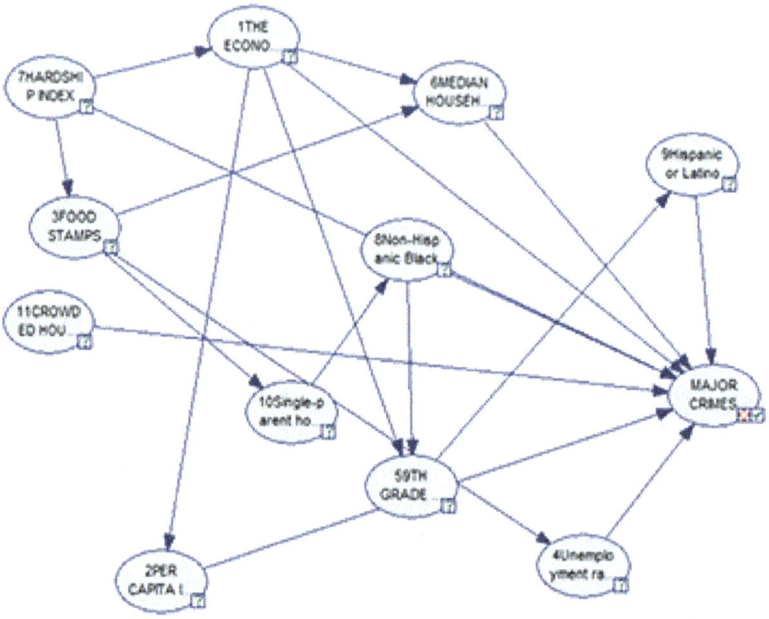


Created Bayesian networks provide a robust framework for decision-making and analysis through their capacity to facilitate both sensitivity analysis and scenario analysis, which form the foundation for informed decision-making and solution exploration.

Sensitivity analysis in Bayesian networks allows for the evaluation of how changes in input variables or parameters affect the model's outputs, enabling decision-makers to assess the robustness of their conclusions and identify the most influential factors.

This analysis can be conducted at various levels, including parameter sensitivity, evidence sensitivity, and structure sensitivity, providing a comprehensive understanding of the model's behaviour under different conditions.

Scenario analysis, on the other hand, involves exploring different possible futures or situations by manipulating the network's variables and observing the resulting outcomes.

This approach enables decision-makers to test "what-if" scenarios, evaluate the effectiveness of different interventions, and anticipate potential risks and opportunities in various situations.

The combination of sensitivity and scenario analysis in Bayesian networks creates a powerful tool for decision-making and solution finding. Decision-makers can identify optimal strategies by comparing outcomes across different scenarios, assess trade-offs between various decision options, and quantify uncertainties and risks associated with different choices.

Created Bayesian network is a tool which gives element for decision making and best possible effects for changing thing in communities in positive way.

It is long term process, which demands patience, but having clear strategy produced by data driven models can help in that direction.

## FUTURE RESEARCH DIRECTIONS

The integration of Extreme Value Analysis, Benford's Law, Fuzzy Logic, and Bayesian Networks creates a powerful framework for detecting deviations in human societies and identifying potential human rights violations.

These methods complement one another by combining statistical anomaly detection, uncertainty modelling, and probabilistic reasoning.

To further enhance this framework, additional methodologies can be integrated.

For instance, machine learning and AI-based anomaly detection can process vast datasets from diverse sources, such as social media or satellite imagery, to identify complex patterns and anomalies in real time.

Remote sensing and satellite imagery analysis provide macroscopic views of regions at risk, enabling the detection of physical evidence like burned villages or displaced populations in conflict zones.

Natural Language Processing (NLP) can analyse textual data from news reports, social media, or legal documents to identify linguistic patterns indicative of discrimination or abuse.

Social network analysis can uncover relationships between actors involved in systemic violations or identify clusters where abuses are more likely to occur.

Statistical hypothesis testing, such as chi-square tests or goodness-of-fit tests, can validate deviations detected by Benford's Law or other statistical methods to ensure that anomalies are not due to random chance.

Gap analysis can evaluate discrepancies between international human rights standards and observed conditions to prioritize areas for intervention.

By combining these methods with the EVA-Benford-Fuzzy-Bayesian framework, a multi-dimensional system emerges that leverages statistical rigor, probabilistic reasoning, qualitative uncertainty handling, and real-time capabilities.

This synergy enhances the accuracy of detecting human rights violations while enabling timely interventions across diverse contexts.

Artificial intelligence offers transformative potential in analyzing vast datasets from social media, satellite imagery, and historical records.

AI-driven tools can automate the detection of human rights abuses, categorize incidents, and visualize trends for stakeholders.

For instance, real-time monitoring systems have been developed to identify potential abuses through social media activity, empowering governments and advocacy groups to respond promptly

Future research should investigate the potential of qualitative impact evaluations to bridge gaps in understanding the social and institutional dynamics that contribute to rights violations.

These approaches can complement quantitative methods by offering context-specific insights into underlying attitudes, cultural norms, and systemic factors that drive abuses.

Additionally, incorporating network analysis could reveal connections between actors involved in systemic violations, further strengthening predictive capabilities.

## CONCLUSION

Data science has proven to be a powerful tool in identifying anomalies within communities, ultimately driving positive change.

By leveraging advanced analytical techniques, data scientists can uncover hidden patterns and outliers that may otherwise go unnoticed. These insights can lead to targeted interventions, policy adjustments, and improved decision-making processes that benefit the community as a whole.

While traditional methods such as statistical analysis and machine learning algorithms are commonly used, it's important to note that the field of data science is constantly evolving.

The approaches mentioned in existing literature represent only a fraction of the potential methodologies available to researchers and practitioners.

As technology advances and new techniques emerge, there remains ample opportunity for further research and innovation in this domain. Future studies could explore novel approaches, combining interdisciplinary knowledge and cutting-edge technologies to enhance our ability to detect and address anomalies in community settings, ultimately fostering positive societal transformations.

## REFERENCES


Aizenberg, E., & van den Hoven, J. (2020). Designing for human rights in AI. *Big Data & Society*, *7*(2). Advance online publication. DOI: 10.1177/2053951720949566

Alvarado García, A., Young, A. L., & Dombrowski, L. (2017). On making data actionable: How activists use imperfect data to foster social change for human rights violations in Mexico. *Proceedings of the ACM on Human-Computer Interaction, 1*(CSCW), 1-19.

Ball, P., Spirer, H. F., Spirer, L., & American Association for the Advancement of Science (AAAS) Science and Human. (2000). Making the Case: Investigating Large Scale Human Rights Violations Using Information Systems and. In *American Association for the Advancement of Science*.

Barocas, S., Bradley, E., Honavar, V., & Provost, F. (2017). Big data, data science, and civil rights. *arXiv preprint arXiv:1706.03102*.

Brabham, D. C., Ribisl, K. M., Kirchner, T. R., & Bernhardt, J. M. (2014). Crowd-sourcing applications for public health. *American Journal of Preventive Medicine*, *46*(2), 179–187. PMID: 24439353

Cheng, Q., Lu, X., & Liu, Z.. (2015). Mining research trends with anomaly detection models: The case of social computing research. *Scientometrics*, *103*, 453–469. DOI: 10.1007/s11192-015-1559-9

Foorthuis, R. (2021). On the nature and types of anomalies: A review of deviations in data. *International Journal of Data Science and Analytics*, *12*, 297–331. DOI: 10.1007/s41060-021-00265-1 PMID: 34368422

Klepac, G. at all. (2014). *Developing churn models using data mining techniques and social network analysis*. IGI Global.

Klepac, G. (2017). The Schrödinger equation as inspiration for a client portfolio simulation hybrid system based on dynamic Bayesian networks and the REFII model. In *Quantum Inspired Computational Intelligence* (pp. 391–416). Morgan Kaufmann.

Klepac, G. (2018). Cognitive Data Science Automatic Fraud Detection Solution, Based on Benford'S Law, Fuzzy Logic with Elements of Machine Learning // Cognitive Computing for Big Data Systems Over IoT. Cham: Springer, 2018. str. 79-95. doi: DOI: 10.1007/978-3-319-70688-7_4

Richardson, R., Schultz, J. M., & Crawford, K. (2019). Dirty data, bad predictions: How civil rights violations impact police data, predictive policing systems, and justice. *NYUL Rev. Online*, *94*, 15.

Safdari, H. (2024). De Bacco, (2024), C. Community detection and anomaly prediction in dynamic networks. *Communications on Physics*, *7*, 397. DOI: 10.1038/s42005-024-01889-y

Sawyer, S., & Tapia, A. (2005). The sociotechnical nature of mobile computing work: Evidence from a study of policing in the United States. *International Journal of Technology and Human Interaction*, *1*(3), 1–14.

Shah, N., Bhagat, N., & Shah, M. (2021). Crime forecasting: A machine learning and computer vision approach to crime prediction and prevention. *Visual Computing for Industry, Biomedicine, and Art*, *4*(1), 9. PMID: 33913057

Taylor, L. (2017). What is data justice? The case for connecting digital rights and freedoms globally. *Big Data & Society*, *4*(2). Advance online publication. DOI: 10.1177/2053951717736335

## KEY TERMS AND DEFINITIONS

**Benford's Law:** A statistical principle stating that in many naturally occurring datasets, the leading digit is more likely to be small (1, 2, 3) than large (7, 8, 9), following a specific logarithmic distribution.

**Bayesian Networks:** Probabilistic graphical models representing a set of variables and their conditional dependencies, used for reasoning under uncertainty and decision-making in complex systems.

**Data Anomaly Detection:** The process of identifying patterns or observations in datasets that deviate significantly from the expected behavior, often used to uncover fraud or errors in data collection.

**Extreme Value Theory:** A branch of statistics dealing with the behavior of extreme deviations from the median of probability distributions, particularly useful in modeling rare events.

**Forensic Data Analysis:** The application of scientific methods to digital data to detect fraud, assess data quality, or investigate anomalies, often used in legal and human rights contexts.

**Human Rights Monitoring:** The process of collecting, verifying, and analyzing information about human rights situations, often utilizing data science techniques to identify patterns and trends.

**Power Law Distribution:** A probability distribution where the frequency of an event varies as a power of some attribute of that event, often observed in natural and social phenomena.

**Statistical Inference:** The process of drawing conclusions about populations or scientific truths from data, crucial in evidence-based approaches to human rights issues.

# Chapter 10
# Convergence of Indigenous Knowledge Systems and Artificial Intelligence:
## Forging Pathways Between Indigenous Wisdom and Technological Innovation

**Cry Kuranga**
https://orcid.org/0000-0002-2801-6974
*Durban University of Technology, South Africa*

**Tlou Maggie Masenya**
https://orcid.org/0000-0001-5400-0549
*Durban University of Technology, South Africa*

## ABSTRACT

*This chapter examined the potential integration of Indigenous Knowledge Systems (IKS) and Artificial Intelligence (AI) in preserving and revitalizing indigenous wisdom. Literature review concerning harnessing the capabilities of AI in digitizing IKS, translate it into several formats to improve accessibility and visibility, and support language revitalization efforts, was analyzed. The study was guided by Self-Determination Theory and Social Contract Theory which provide crucial lenses for understanding the ethical considerations involved. The findings revealed several factors hindering effective integration of IKS and AI including ethics and social implications. This study further proposed a framework that outlines princi-*

DOI: 10.4018/979-8-3373-8510-5.ch010

*ples and guidelines that provide researchers, policymakers, community leaders and other relevant stakeholders, a platform to develop responsive solutions to culture and equitable. It is recommended that all these parties consider exploring collaborative partnerships and adopt AI technologies for preserving IKS and for long-term sustainability and inclusivity.*

## INTRODUCTION

Indigenous Knowledge Systems (IKS) present favorable options for cultural preservation, sustainable resource management, and adaptation to climate change, among others (Parlee et al., 2022; Whyte, 2017). Moreover, IKS operate in specificity, where there is no one-size-fits-all, which implies that each indigenous community defines its particular IKS (Todd, 2016; Simpson, 2017) and as such, IKS offer solutions that are adaptable and favorable to many complex problems. It only calls for the recognition, valuing and incorporating IKS as a potential source of infinite solutions to our pressing global issues. However, the existence of IKS is being contested by several factors, which include globalization and marginalization. Marginalization of IKS is not an act that began in this century, where we are witnessing IKS being sidelined in mainstream of technological and scientific discourse, rather, it is just a continuation of what started long ago in history, when colonial practices devalued and suppressed Indigenous knowledge and ways of life (Fryberg et al., 2024). Western knowledge systems were imposed on Indigenous communities, thereby suppressing their languages and cultural practices to favor Western ways of thinking (Smith, 2012). As a result, systemic bias became evident (Reyes-García et al., 2024). Globalization and rapid technological evolution also threaten IKS survival, raising concerns about cultural erosion, data sovereignty, and heritage commodification (Mazzocchi, 2022). It thus, sidelines any opportunity that points towards promoting innovation and fair development (Bremer & Meisch, 2017). Expected norms such as cultural practices and indigenous languages, are also on the decline. Typically, these factors tend to overshadow the rich and diverse knowledge that was developed over generations, thereby blocking the perspectives and practices of indigenous communities. As such, it calls for a re-assessment of knowledge hierarchies along with a commitment to epistemic justice (Shapin, 2018). It is thus vital to recognize the inherent value of IKS, and respect indigenous rights to self-determination (Anderson, 2015).

With the Fourth Industrial Revolution (4IR) bringing together digital, biological, and physical systems, technologies such as Intelligence (AI) and the Internet of Things (IoT) are instrumental in enhancing efficiency, productivity, and interconnectivity (Schwab, 2018; Xu, David, & Kim, 2018). Riding on the potential of AI, it is possible to digitize IKS, translate it into several options to improve accessibility and visibility, among others. (Berkes, 2012; Kimmerer, 2013; Tsosie, et al., 2021). Nevertheless, there are several concerns that AI is most likely to bring to Indigenous communities and IKS. The chances are very high that AI will erode indigenous data sovereignty which poses multiple risks including misappropriation of knowledge from which outsiders are most likely to benefit from commercializing indigenous knowledge without the consent of indigenous communities (Riley & Carpenter, 2015; Stevenson, 2016). Such actions are a clear act of violation of Indigenous communities' rights and cultural heritage. Again, there is a great risk of indigenous communities losing control over their own stories and histories, and such a loss can impact negatively cultural integrity and self-determination (Moreton-Robinson, 2015; Walter & Suina, 2019).

An in-depth understanding of digital colonialism and the political economy of AI infrastructure is imperative so as to critically examine the fusion of AI with IKS. A form of digital colonialism is evident when digital platforms and infrastructure that are meant to host AI-IKS are manned or controlled by multinational corporations, Indigenous data is being extracted, and Western technological standards are imposed on IKS initiatives (Couldry & Mejias, 2019). In addition, if indigenous communities are not in control of their data, algorithms that process the data and knowledge, computing resources, and regulations of AI technologies, then the political economy of AI infrastructure is evident. The political economy of AI infrastructure tends to concentrate power and wealth in the hands of a few at the expense of indigenous communities (Crawford, 2021). As such, issues to do with digital colonialism and political economy of AI infrastructure call for attention whenever considering the fusion of AI with IKS. Therefore, it becomes imperative to emphasize the importance of assessing potential risks surrounding the adoption of AI in IKS and to ensure that the technology is grounded in epistemic justice, Indigenous self-determination, and a commitment to decolonization. The following objectives are put forward:

- Determine how AI can support the preservation, revitalization and practical application of IKS.
- Determine the ethical issues and potential risks that come along with integrating AI and IKS.
- Propose a framework that guides the development of AI-IKS responsive solutions to culture and equitable.

## Artificial Intelligence: Capabilities and Limitations

Artificial Intelligence is a technology designed to perform tasks that requiring human-like intelligence (Russell & Norvig, 2016) including problem solving, learning, and natural language processing. This technology is driving digital transformation in all aspects of life, being business, social or governance and several disciplines emanate from the main tasks of AI, such as Machine Learning, Natural Language Processing, Expert systems, Robotics, and Deep Learning. Despite its advantages, AI presents several drawbacks that require attention such as privacy concerns, bias, misuse and cultural misrepresentation. Typically, AI algorithms are trained before being deployed in new instances, and this may result in unfair outcomes that reinforce existing social inequalities if the datasets used the training phase are biased (Noble, 2018). As a result, these outcomes tend to misrepresent or distort Indigenous cultures, thereby reinforcing racial hierarchies that create new forms of discrimination (Benjamin, 2023). Therefore, in the context of fusing AI with IKS, it becomes imperative to examine the following: who controls AI-IKS ecosystems; who is intended to benefit from these initiatives and how digital technologies can be controlled to avoid further marginalizing indigenous knowledge and voices. The chances are very high that if AI is not adopted thoughtfully, it may undermine indigenous self-determination and data sovereignty (Birhane, 2021).

## Synergistic Potential of Artificial Intelligence and Indigenous Knowledge Systems

Artificial intelligence can harness generational wisdom in IKS to come up with effective and sustainable solutions. The derived solution can be both environmental friendly and culturally appropriate (Bremer & Meisch, 2017; Berkes, 2017). If cutting-edge AI tools are fused with IKS, then powerful systems can be developed that are suitable to solve several challenges (Whyte, 2017; Parlee, et al., 2022). However, the potential fusion should be backed by strong ethical principles, indigenous leadership and control. As such, AI should present solutions to serve the needs and priorities of indigenous communities. Comprehensive predictive models can be developed when IKS are integrated with scientific data, thereby improving prediction accuracy. For example, traditional weather forecasting methods can be combined with satellite imagery to predict floods and droughts. This integration provide timely information to communities, which is vital for effective preparation (Kimmerer, 2013). Thus, the fusion of advanced technology and time–tested knowledge can enhance resilience and support indigenous communities. Traditional medicines have sustained indigenous communities over centuries, and therefore integrating such a powerful system that is refined over generations with cutting-edge AI technologies produces an explosion of possibilities. For instance, machine learning (ML) technology can be used to uncover intrinsic features hidden in traditional medicines which can be harnessed to create new treatments for a variety of diseases (Heinrich, 2013; Laird,

2010). Thus, fusing ancient wisdom into healthcare can create robust and effective health solutions for Indigenous communities.

There is a great risk of losing oral traditions knowledge, stories and songs developed over centuries (Crystal, 2000). Providentially, AI possess the capabilities to preserve IKS for future generations. Several IKS such as oral histories, songs, traditional ecological knowledge, stories, cultural artefacts and indigenous languages can be digitized and archived using AI technologies. Artificial Intelligence can be used to transcribe and analyze spoken words using Natural Language Processing (NLP), thereby turning conversations into text (Jha, 2023). Image recognition is ideal to identify and catalogue cultural artefacts, thereby preserving visual heritage (Smith & Wilson, 2024). Cleaning up and enhancing old audio recording can be realized using *Audio Analysis*, thereby improving quality for future listening (Gupta et al., 2021). In addition, analysis of traditional ceremonies can be done using *Video Analysis*, thereby allowing deeper understanding of cultural practices (Browne, et al., 2023). The aforementioned AI processes extract metadata which is used to create searchable databases, easing the process of finding specific information, thereby ensuring that valuable knowledge is preserved and accessible. Moreover, translating and transcribing indigenous languages using NLP aids accessibility, thus promoting linguistic diversity (Bender et al., 2020; Harlow, 2011). AI-powered language translation tools can be used to revitalize endangered languages, and in so doing, accessibility is enhanced. Consider a language-learning AI-powered application that offers personalized feedback to help learners to grasps the nuances of their native tongue or a translation tool that can provide IKS materials in native languages (Bickel, et al., 2017; Scannell, 2017). In this way, linguistic heritage is preserved while indigenous communities are empowered. Gamification makes learning more enjoyable and motivating by incorporating game-like elements which play a pivotal role in IKS revitalization. Cultural narratives also become more engaging and personal when users or the audience are involved and this tends to influence the direction of the story. Thus, a deep understanding can be established if AI-powered games and interactive storytelling are designed to teach users about indigenous culture and knowledge (Robertson & Kelley, 2021; Wang et al., 2023). Virtual Reality (VR) creates digital environments that can replicate various aspects of IKS, such as traditional ceremonies and landscapes (Jones, 2022; Kim, 2024). Augmented Reality (AR), for example, can document and showcase traditional ceremonies (Arsenault & Beaulieu, 2023; Lewis, 2024). Thus, both AR and VR foster a deeper understanding of IKS.

However, the digitization and archiving should be done in accordance with indigenous cultural protocols, intellectual property rights and data sovereignty. Several key aspects should be considered such as metadata that reflects cultural values and context to be developed to ensure that accurate representation of knowledge is upheld (Christen, 2012; Anderson, 2015). Having ethical review boards to provide guidance and accountability is crucial to ensure that all practices are respectful and responsible (Smith, et al., 2021; Carroll, et al., 2020). It is crucial to preserve, honor cultural heritage and safeguarding indigenous intellectual property rights (Riley & Carpenter, 2015). It is essential to avoid stereotypes and misunderstandings that result from misrepresenting indigenous culture (Huhndorf, 2015) and also to respect cultural protocols by safeguarding the significance and sanctity of cultural practices (O'Brien, et al., 2020). It is vital to safeguard indigenous intellectual property rights while preventing misuse (Thornberry, 2013). Moreover, to use indigenous knowledge in a manner that is respectful rather than exploiting it for commercial gain or similar purposes (Ezeanya-Esiobu, 2019). Although there is a real concern that we might lose oral traditions, as noted by Crystal (2000), much of the literature focusing on using AI for IKS usually portrays an optimistic and overly deterministic view of this technology. While several authors including Jha (2023), Smith & Wilson (2024), Gupta et al. (2021) and Browne et al. (2023) present the potential of AI technologies for digitizing and archiving IKS, their discussions tend to omit practical ways to address the inherent biases and limitations of these technologies.

Additionally, there is a significant possibility that AI-powered translation tools might misrepresent or distort cultural nuances; yet, several authors, including Bender (2020) and Harlow (2011), advocate for the use of NLP for language revitalization, often overlooking these potential pitfalls. A critical examination of who controls the technology is often lacking in the literature in which it clearly outlines who benefits from its application, and how to prevent the further marginalization of indigenous voices and knowledge. Therefore, this is a call to delve deeper into these matters rather than simply celebrating AI's potential. Robertson and Kelley (2021) and Wang et al. (2023) discussed how gamification and interactive storytelling can revitalize IKS, but the literature review often overlooks an important point such as the risk of trivializing rich cultural knowledge through basic game mechanics. Virtual reality can be used to recreate traditional ceremonies as highlighted by Jones (2022) and Kim (2024), but there is a risk of detaching these virtual experiences from their original cultural context and meaning. The literature review provides a detailed discussion of the need for community collaboration to achieve a successful implementation of IKS and technology, however, there is a gap in practical strategies to empower indigenous communities to have control over the revitalization process. There is much work in the literature review that focuses on a techno-centric view of revitalization, yet the aspects of passing down knowledge between generations and acknowledging the ongoing struggle for indigenous self-determination are being overlooked. Artificial Intelligence projects can be developed responsibly when human values, ethical principles, a strong commitment to fairness and transparency is incorporated into the development cycle so as to avoid the pitfall whereby technology is used as a weapon to colonize (Floridi, 2023). Furthermore, involving communities in the development cycle ensures that the solutions developed reflect their values and needs. Successful AI solutions are the result of fusing AI and human capabilities; thus, harnessing the strengths of both can create a better future together (Duarte, 2017).

## Data Sovereignty, Indigenous Self-determination and Cultural Appropriation

Data sovereignty is observable through self-determination, human rights, and cultural integrity. Self-determination ensures indigenous communities to freely define their own political status and freely determine their culture, social, and economic developments (UNDRIP, 2007). It is also entitled to human rights including privacy, self-expression and cultural identity (UN Declaration of Human Rights, 1948). Furthermore, it remains the exclusive responsibility of indigenous communities to preserve and safeguard their knowledge, traditions and cultural heritage (UNESCO, 2003). A community attains indigenous self-determination if it can freely define its political and economic status which supposed to align with their goals and intents (Coulthard, 2014). As such, indigenous communities can freely pursue their social and cultural interests, making impactful decisions about their future and consequently, establishing pathways that favours their well-being and promote cultural continuity (Allard-Tremblay & Coburn, 2023). Indigenous communities have rights to their land and resources and those rights empower them to manage and protect their resources in ways deemed appropriate and aligned to their customary laws and traditions (UNDRIPA Article 26, Thornberry, 2013). These marginalized communities have the right to practice their spiritual belief and cultural traditions as well as exercising their rights to pass their cultural heritage to future generations, without interference (UNDRIPA Article 11). In addition, they should control their knowledge and exercise their rights to protect it from misappropriation, determine its use and how it is shared and decide who benefits from its commercialization (UNDRIPA Article 31). Integral to self-determination is the right to establish their own systems of governance, exercising their rights to make decisions about their own affairs and be involved in decision-making processes that affect them (UNDRIPA Article 4, UNPFII, 2008).

Cultural appropriation manifests in various informed ways such as using cultural symbols, design or songs in commercial products without permission or Free Prior and Consent (FPIC) from the originating community (Ezeanya-Esiobu, 2019). For example, using a cultural song in an advertisement for profit without community consent constitutes appropriation. Indigenous cultures may also be misrepresented through stereotypical or inaccurate portrayals in media such as advertisements or movies where indigenous people are depicted in a historically inaccurate or demeaning manner (Prats, 2018). Disrespectful imitation also contributes to cultural appropriation, especially when cultural practices are adopted without observing protocols or considering their context (Huhndorf, 2001). Cultural appropriation can be deeply harmful for several reasons and it often reduces sacred or meaningful cultural elements to mere items or commodities in which their significance is stripped away (Bell, 2017). It can perpetuate or create erroneous stereotypes about indigenous cultures which may cause misinterpretation and bias (Asakawa, 2017), and infringes upon indigenous communities' rights to control cultural stories and expressions (Lomawaima & McCarty, 2025). Furthermore, cultural appropriation often involves profiting from exploitation in which dominant cultures often benefit financially from the exploitation of indigenous knowledge, thereby thereby failing to acknowledge fair compensation (Halewood, 1999, Riley & Carpenter, 2015). Knowledge exploitation occurs when a profit is generated at the expense of the indigenous knowledge without any equitable benefit-sharing or recognition for the community involved (Shiva, 2016).

## Intellectual Property Rights

Issues to do with safeguarding indigenous knowledge and culture are addressed by Intellectual Property Rights (IPR). Standard IPR tends to commodify indigenous knowledge, thereby leading to the misappropriation of cultural heritage and indigenous knowledge (Riley & Carpenter, 2015) Therefore, traditional IPR are often deemed inadequate to cover IKS because the concepts of ownership defined therein such as patents and copyrights are not well-aligned with Indigenous cultural traditions and values (Dutfield, 2000). In many indigenous cultural traditions, knowledge is considered a communal effort, therefore collectively owned by the community, rather than an individual (Fourmile, 2020). Furthermore, IKS is often transmitted orally or through practice, unlike through the expected written forms which contrasts with the requirements of copyright law. Indigenous Knowledge Systems are also dynamic in nature, thereby constantly evolving and thus contradicts the static and fixed requirements in traditional intellectual property law (Berkes, 2012).

## Analysis of Structural Inequalities, Surveillance and Global Power Asymmetries

Factors such as structural inequalities, pervasive surveillance, and global power symmetries impact the intersection of human rights and digitization. By delving deeper into the analysis of these factors we can provide a true reflection on how human rights can be violated in this digital age. If there is unequal access to technologies, limited digital literacy, and underrepresentation in the digital technology, then structural inequalities exist (Van Deursen & Van Dijk, 2019). These inequalities tend to exclude Indigenous communities to benefit from digitalization, and make them susceptible to technological harms. Surveillance is currently on the rise in the digital sphere whereby both government agencies and private organizations are busy collecting data on individuals and communities which may result in disproportionate targeting of Indigenous communities due to their political activism or cultural practices, among others (Marx, 2019). In addition, global power asymmetries drive dominant powers, usually from the West, to have control over infrastructure, standards, and governance of the internet which is likely to marginalize the voices and interests of Indigenous communities (Haggart et al., 2021). As such, Western values and norms are imposed on Indigenous cultures.

### Indigenous-Led AI Projects and Initiatives

Several AI-IKS initiatives were implemented successfully and stand as a testament to the feasibility of fusing AI with IKS to achieve equitable and responsive digital solutions. For example, the Māori media organization in New Zealand developed Te Hiku Media, an AI-IKS project that harnessed AI to revitalize the Māori language (Jones et al., 2025). This AI-IKS solution creates accurate and accessible language resources that are culturally aligned and community-driven and it tends to empower Māori speakers and learners, and enhance linguistic diversity. Another example is the Māori data sovereignty, which consists of initiatives working to empower the Māori community to have control over their data and knowledge, guided by the principles of *rangatiratanga* (self-determination) and *kaitiakitanga* (guardianship) to ensure that the use of knowledge and data benefits the community (Queniahan, 2024, Reeves et al., 2022). Moreover, indigenous community members are involved from the outset of these initiatives as part of the development teams rather than simply as end-users, which is the norm in many AI solutions. This development supports what the literature advocates by developing digital solutions that ensure indigenous communities retain their sole ownership of the IKS resources in digital formats (Kukutai & Taylor, 2016; Walter et al., 2020).

## METHODOLOGY

This research is based on a qualitative document analysis. Decolonial research principles are used as a guide to unravel the literature review focusing on epistemic justice, indigenous self-determination, equitable benefit-sharing and ethical responsibility in the development of AI initiatives for IKS (Smith, 2012). This methodology employs a critical literature review to identify and analyze the potential benefits and risks associated with the integration of AI with IKS (Smith, 2021). This critical literature review approach is most appropriate for providing an in-depth analysis of factors such as the ethical, cultural and social implications that the fusion of AI and IKS may bring to indigenous communities. It also extends to look into issues that related to data sovereignty, intellectual property rights and cultural appropriation in AI-IKS initiatives. Several policies and frameworks were put to support an equitable and responsible integration of AI and IKS which need to be revisited and assessed for their effectiveness in this regard. Peer-reviewed journal articles and book chapters, policy documents such as guidelines, legal frameworks and reports from international organizations like the UN and WIPO were reviewed. The search was performed on the following databases: ScienceDirect, Wiley, Springer, Sage, Scopus, EBSCOhost, and Google Scholar, of which only English publications were considered. The following search terms were used: "Indigenous Knowledge Systems," "Artificial Intelligence," "Data Sovereignty," "Intellectual Property Rights," "Cultural Appropriation," "AI Ethics," "Decolonization of Knowledge," "Indigenous Data Governance," "Traditional Ecological Knowledge." The data collected using the aforementioned process is then systematically analyzed using a thematic analysis approach (Braun & Clarke, 2006). This approach is a multi-step process that includes the following steps: data familiarization to gain an in-depth understanding of the content, a coding process to identify key themes, concepts and arguments in the literature review. Regrouping of themes is performed to gain broader insights which are then used to identify key findings, challenges and opportunities that relate to the integration of IKS and AI. The findings thus provide the basis on which the proposed framework to foster the integration of AI with IKS is built on. The main limitation of this study is its dependence on the existing literature review of which it may not fully capture the diverse experiences and perspectives of indigenous communities. Moreover, only English publications were considered which tend to exclude valuable insights from other languages. Despite these limitations, the proposed framework is expected to contribute a solid foundation and practical recommendations for building ethical and sustainable partnerships in AI-IKS initiatives.

## CONCEPTUAL FRAMEWORK

This chapter adopted the conceptual framework which draws on Self-Determination Theory and Social Contract Theory, and provide crucial lenses for understanding the ethical and practical considerations involved. It highlights the significance of honoring Indigenous self-determination and data sovereignty when researchers, policymakers, technologists and Indigenous communities work together. Figure 1 illustrates the conceptual framework.

*Figure 1. Conceptual Framework*

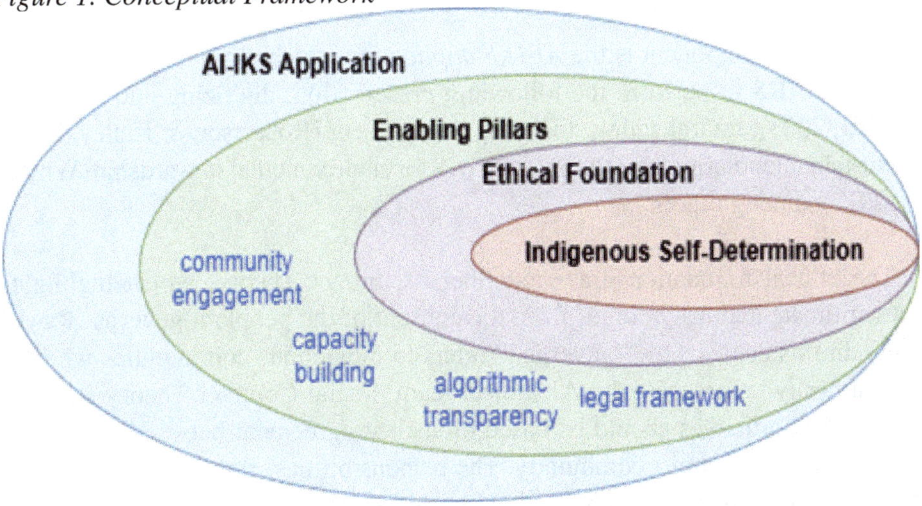


The conceptual framework is defined by four interconnected components:

a) At the core of the framework is *Indigenous self-determination*, as illustrated in Figure 1, which signifies the importance of indigenous communities' right to control their knowledge and resources (Coulthard, 2014). This aligns directly with the principles of Self-Determination Theory, which emphasizes the importance of autonomy, competence and relatedness for individual and collective well-being (Deci & Ryan, 2000). In the context of AI and IKS integration, SDT suggests that indigenous communities must have the autonomy to decide how their knowledge is used, the competence to engage meaningfully with AI technologies, and a sense of relatedness to the project's goals and outcomes. Without these three elements, this integration of AI with IKS risks undermining their inherent rights and cultural integrity.
b) The key principles for responsible AI-IKS rest on *Ethical foundation* which is based on the following concepts: Free, Prior and Informed Consent (FPIC) that ensures the Indigenous communities have the right to consent (UNPFII, 2005). Additionally, data sovereignty enforces that indigenous communities have right to their data (Kukutai & Taylor, 2016) whereas equitable benefit-sharing that guarantee fair compensation (UNDRIP, 2007). Moreover, cultural responsiveness that ensures that we develop culturally sensitive AI (Gay, 2018).
c) *Enabling Pillars* comprise essential elements that support the effective implementation of the following: community engagement which is tailored to foster collaboration (Smith, 2012); capacity building to upskill indigenous communities and provide resources; algorithmic transparency to promote understandable

AI (O'Neil, 2017) and the protection of indigenous knowledge through legal frameworks.

d) The outer component is the *AI-IKS application* which provides integration of AI and IKS to perform the following: preservation, digitizing and archiving (Jha, 2023); revitalization, fostering engagement (Robertson & Kelley, 2021) sustainable solutions, and harnessing IKS for environmental stewardship (Whyte, 2017), among others.

The ethical foundation draws on Social Contract Theory, which highlights that legitimate authority comes from the consent of the people it governs (Rawls, 1971). In this context, the "governed" refers to indigenous communities whereas the "authority" represents the AI project team. Social Contract Theory suggests that AI-IKS initiatives should be based on a clear agreement between the project team and the indigenous community. The responsibilities, rights, and obligations of each party should be clearly outlined in this agreement and negotiated openly, with a full understanding of the potential benefits and risks involved. Principles like FPIC, data sovereignty, equitable benefit-sharing and cultural responsiveness are key components of this "social contract". These principles help to ensure that the fusion of AI and Indigenous Knowledge is fair and beneficial for everyone involved.

## FINDINGS AND DISCUSSION

The findings are arranged in accordance with the objectives that informed the study.

### Potential of AI in Preservation and Revitalization of IKS

Several AI techniques possess immense possibilities either to revitalize or preserve IKS, which include natural language processing, computer vision, and machine learning. These possibilities can be leveraged to provide sustainable long-term preservation of oral traditions and cultural heritage, among others (Jha, 2023; Smith & Wilson, 2024). In addition, IKS can be revitalized using cutting edge technologies like AI gamification, virtual realities and augmented realities to create immersive and interactive experiences, making learning about Indigenous culture and knowledge much more enjoyable (Jones, 2022; Robertson & Kelley, 2021). Therefore, the capabilities of AI stand uncontested in bringing back to life the fading IKS, and also, in providing practical options for the global pressing environmental and social challenges.

## Ethical Issues and Risks Related to the Integration of AI with IKS

Several ethical issues were enumerated in the literature that focus on the integration of AI and IKS, of which the following were central to most discussions: Indigenous data sovereignty, intellectual property rights, and cultural appropriation (O'Brien et al., 2020; Tsosie et al., 2021). Indigenous data sovereignty is pivotal in AI-IKS because it ensures that indigenous communities remain sole proprietors of their resources that are expressed in digital formats, and that they have control over the collection and use of their knowledge and data in these AI initiatives. Additionally, it was discovered that traditional Intellectual Property (IP) laws are not adequate to cover all aspects of IKS and therefore, new IP laws need to be developed that are adaptable to community ownership of IKS resources (WIPO, 2024). In addition, it becomes vital to safeguard indigenous cultures from misuse and exploitation by ensuring that cultural symbols, designs, and songs are not used without obtaining Free, Prior and Informed Consent (FPIC) from the indigenous communities (Ezeanya-Esiobu, 2019). The following ethical issues are thus identified:

- *Cultural Appropriation and Commodification:* There is a significant likelihood that AI-powered tools will be used to exploit IKS for commercial gain without giving proper credit or sharing the benefits with the indigenous communities involved.
- *Algorithmic Bias and Misrepresentation:* If AI algorithms are trained on biased data, the chances of these algorithms perpetuating existing power imbalances and misrepresent Indigenous cultures are very high (Noble, 2018). These biases can lead to misrepresentations or distortions of cultural nuances in AI-powered translation processes.
- *Loss of Control and Autonomy:* The complex technicalities of AI in which external experts manage and control the systems can put indigenous communities at risk of losing complete control over their IKS. This situation can undermine their self-determination and data sovereignty.

## Framework for Equitable Partnerships and Responsible Artificial Intelligence Integration

The fusion of AI and IKS promises infinite possibilities, however, those possibilities comes along with profound ethical considerations to safeguard rights and knowledge of the indigenous communities (O'Brien et al., 2020). These ethical considerations have real-world impact on indigenous communities, and they are not just theoretical concerns (UNDRIP, 2007). This section provides a discussion on the integration of AI and IKS through the lenses of FPIC, data sovereignty, indigenous self-determination, intellectual property rights, equitable benefit-sharing, capacity building and cultural responsiveness. Technology is expected to empower indigenous communities but not to undermine them.

## Ensuring Community Agreement

First things first, a clear and accessible *AI-based IKS* project proposal is expected to be presented to indigenous communities. These communities then reach terms of agreement with such a proposal using FPIC framework as a guide and should clearly outlines essential principles that are instrumental in corning a community agreement such as the right to give or revoke their consent at any stage of the project. The project proposal should clearly state the expected benefits, potential risks and impacts (both positive and negative) the project may bring to the community (Christen, 2011). Ultimately, it should be stated clearly that the decisions made by indigenous communities whether they are positive or negative must be respected and honored to ensure that their autonomy and self-determination are upheld (Moreton-Robinson et al., 2015). It is essential to use FPIC to act as campus to point on areas that requires attention on the outset and during the project development. First point of attention is on data collection which may raise several issues such as indigenous data privacy and ownership (Christen, 2011). Indigenous communities can either state their position in terms of privacy and ownership of data, or provide guidance when enacting such rights. Secondly, there are great risks of culture misrepresentation and appropriation in AI-IKS projects. To curb these risks, FPIC can be used as a guide on the use and control of indigenous knowledge and cultural heritage in AI projects (Riley & Carpenter, 2015; Lombardi, 2019). Lastly, economic development can impact indigenous communities either positively or negatively, however, if it is negatively then it may foster inequalities (Quail et al., 2025). As such, Indigenous communities should be made aware of all possible outcomes of the project before commencement of the project.

Typically, a solution developed through the lens of FPIC is aligned to cultural values and avoids unintended harms, thereby fostering cultural preservation and revitalization (Lombardi, 2019; O'Faircheallaigh, 2021). On the other hand, technologists and researchers can build trust and long-lasting partnership with the communities (Ensminger & Henrich, 2014). In addition, such projects promote sustainable development both economically and socially which is beneficial to indigenous communities, thereby promoting cultural well-being and self-determination (Berkes, 2012). The FPIC must clearly outline the following:

- **Aim and objectives** - a discussion of the project goals and an outline of its intended outcomes to aid understanding of the project.
- **Potential impacts** - a thorough assessment of potential risks and consequences is expected, highlighting their benefits.
- **Data collection procedures** - this includes type of data that is needed and how the data is to be used to ensure transparency and proper data management practices.
- **Ownership and control of knowledge** - intellectual property rights should be well articulated to serve the interest of Indigenous community.
- **Consent** - an outline of the process of obtaining a consent where all steps involved are clearly stated in which the rights of Indigenous community are presented.

Consultations must be conducted in a culturally appropriate manner, in which indigenous protocols and customs are observed in the process to ensure that whatever is to be done is sensitive to their cultural values and traditions (Christen, 2012). This may involve holding meetings in local settings to ensure that the consultation is done in a convenient and accessible manner for community members (Moreton-Robinson et al., 2015) and also to communicate in Indigenous language that the community understands, thereby fostering trust and mutual understanding (Gilio-Whitaker, 2019). Engagement with indigenous communities should be an ongoing process from the outset to the end of the project to facilitate a check-and-balance process where updates are regularly given, and feedback is received (Berkes, 2012). This ensures that the project progresses in sync with their needs and priorities (Ojha et al., 2016). A data governance framework is supposed to be co-developed, thereby shunning all possibilities of indigenous cultural exploitations and misrepresentation in AI projects (Walter & Suina, 2019; Carroll et al., 2020). This data governance framework defines ownership, usage, protection measures (i.e data encryption and secure storage) and data access. The framework should clearly outline the procedure for dispute resolution, such as mediation or arbitration. Furthermore, indigenous communities must develop their own data management guidelines which are instrumental in defining data usage and making informed decision (Rainie et al., 2017; Kukutai & Taylor, 2016). When indigenous communities are actively involved in the project, the success rate of such a project increases because the issues to do with cultural appropriateness and values which are detrimental to the project success, are taken care of along the development cycle (Lombardi, 2019). In addition, aligning the project goals with the needs and priorities of indigenous communities promotes long-term sustainability of the project which tend to foster a sense of shared benefit along with ownership (Guttmann, 2021).

## Recognizing and Protecting Indigenous Knowledge

Since IPR is considered not to fully cover all the aspects in indigenous/traditional knowledge, therefore, it may not be adequate to protection this knowledge. However, this issue is complex and being contested. On the other hand IPR is considered to preserve indigenous culture and safeguard it from misrepresentation and distortion (WIPO, 2024) and it is considered not to adequately address all the communal and inter-generational nature of indigenous knowledge (Ogwezzy, 2012). Therefore, it is ideal to have intellectual property laws that cover issues to do with equitable benefit-sharing and protection of knowledge and resources. Indigenous communities should thus receive a fair share on all economic activities that used their knowledge and data and it remains the sole responsibility of indigenous communities to control their knowledge and resources (Gibson, 2016; Thornberry, 2013). There is therefore an urgent need to craft new legal frameworks that specifically safeguard indigenous knowledge systems to address the unique characteristics of indigenous knowledge (WIPO, 2024). These new legal frameworks should be rooted in the beliefs and values of cultural integrity, economic justice and self-determination (Thornberry, 2013). Customized legal frameworks such as *Sui generis* (of its own kind) systems are increasingly recognized as an ideal approach to safeguard the uniqueness of indigenous knowledge systems intellectual property (Marie-Vivien, 2016). In *Sui generis* systems, indigenous knowledge is considered a collective effort refined over generations, therefore, owned and protected by the community with appropriate acknowledgment and attribution (WIPO, 2024). *Sui generis* frameworks often incorporate customary laws and protocols into legal structure so as to respect indigenous practices and decision-making processes. Ideally, these systems empower indigenous communities to control and use their knowledge freely without coercion or misappropriation, while also promoting its preservation and transmission to future generations (WIPO, 2024).

## Avoiding Misuse and Exploitation of Culture

Forging partnerships at the outset of any technological initiative is imperative where the leadership of the community outlines the cultural values, ethics and priorities that should be maintained throughout the project lifecycle. Decision-making is a very sensitive area that requires mutual understanding to build trust between technologists and Indigenous communities (Smith, 2012; Kovach, 2021). Additionally, it should be clearly stated how benefit-sharing should be handled so as to ensure that indigenous communities receive appropriate compensation and recognition for the use of their resources (WIPO, 2024). It is also important to educate all team members involved in the project on issues about cultural sensitivity and potential effects of cultural appropriation (Tucks & Yang, 2012). In addition, indigenous communities should be entitled to ownership and management of the AI solutions that directly relate to the creation and use of their knowledge and resources (Duarte, 2017). Consequently, this triggers active participation which in turn fosters collaboration and innovation (Ensminger & Henrich, 2014).

## Respecting Indigenous Values and Beliefs

When AI projects are designed, developed and implemented in a culturally appropriate manner that respects indigenous values and beliefs, then cultural responsiveness goes beyond simply avoiding harm (Barnhardt, 2014). It extends to ensuring that AI solutions are sensitive to and supportive of indigenous cultures (Gay, 2018). This can be achieved by acknowledging the way indigenous cultures consider the world and its knowledge (Vickers, 2013) and that is respecting cultural protocols and customs in all project activities by involving elders and cultural experts for guidance, thus recognizing their wisdom and authority is crucial (Kirkness & Barnhardt, 2016). Using a local language when conversing with indigenous communities does not only promote inclusivity, but also participation and discourage stereotypes. This also goes along with the use of imagery that are respectful to communities' cultures which avoids misrepresentations (Ramirez, 2022). This create a conducive environment where indigenous communities feel welcomed and safe to participate, thereby building trust and confidence in the AI project development (Wepa, 2015).

Moreover, it is crucial to adapt AI technologies to reflect IKS and cultural values. In this way, the solutions which are developed will be culturally aligned with indigenous communities' ways of thinking which tend to ensure effective cultural preservation (Noble, 2018). Upholding cultural responsiveness in AI projects increase the chances of having full support of indigenous communities and earning their trust. Usually, a slight oversight on cultural responsiveness may lead to unintended harms on indigenous cultures and values (Ezeanya-Esiobu, 2019). Cultural responsiveness instils a sense of pride to indigenous communities while promoting cultural preservation (Pine & Turin, 2017). In other words, cultural responsiveness fosters equity and inclusion which promotes full participation of indigenous communities in AI initiatives (Zuboff, 2023).

## Empowering Indigenous Participation

One of effective ways to empower indigenous communities is to equip them with tools and skills that enable them to become self-sufficient that entails long-term impact (Mazany & Perry, 2013). There are several AI tools that are ideal to drive indigenous communities towards self-sufficiency and fostering their full participation in AI projects. Among the top sought skills is the ability to effectively use and manage data and this skill enables communities to make informed decisions on the use of their data and knowledge (Walter & Suina, 2019). As such, data management training should cover data collection techniques, how best to store data for longevity, perform basis data analysis and best data management practices (Meyer & Schroeder, 2023). If indigenous communities are to play leading roles in the development of AI projects, they need project management skills (Crawford, 2024). Project management training goes all its way to equip indigenous communities with skills that are essential to shape their future and nurture self-determination (Grint & Jones, 2022). More so, the moment the issue of ownership is raised, then it becomes vital to bring to our attention the protection that supposed to be attached to it such as intellectual property laws. Indigenous communities should thus be trained on how to safeguard their knowledge and cultural heritage (Rajani et al., 2018).

The existing digital divide that indigenous communities are experiencing can be narrowed down by training communities on the use of technologies and offering access to internet and computer. These technical training that focus on hands-on practices are essential to provide indigenous communities with a competitive advantage in the digital economy (Wang, 2025). Moreover, it is essential to provide training on software development and AI programming to foster visibility of indigenous communities on digital economy (Merritt, 2016). Since it has already mentioned that AI comes along with some ethical issues, therefore training in AI ethics is of paramount importance to ensure responsible AI. This training should cover methods to promote ethical development and implementation of AI projects, emphasizing the significance of fairness, transparency and accountability in the project development cycle (O'Neil, 2017). Thus, capacity building provides indigenous communities the capability to excel in AI projects by creating local expertise which is vital in the long-term sustainability of AI projects (Smith, 2021; Walter & Suina, 2019). This promotes engagement and active participation of indigenous communities in the project development (Guttmann, 2021; Berkes, 2012). The availability of local expertise also promotes innovation by unlocking novel ideas and knowledge from Indigenous communities, thereby providing more effective AI solutions (Kim et al., 2022).

## FUTURE RESEARCH DIRECTIONS

Future research should focus on the practical implementation of the proposed framework, including a thorough evaluation of its impact on indigenous communities, guided by indigenous-led evaluation methodologies. In addition, it should explore the framework's potential to address global pressing challenges, i.e social, environmental and economic. Some possible avenues to achieve these tasks include conducting pilot projects that engages indigenous communities and developing culturally rooted evaluation metrics. This can exploit the knowledge and information obtainable from lesson learned from the past endeavours. It is essential to consider cross-cultural collaboration for digital initiatives and research projects to promote ethical and cultural appropriate digital solutions that benefit all stakeholders, particularly Indigenous communities. These cross-cultural collaborations will focus on relationship building and trust, shared decision-making, cultural humility, and long-term commitment, among other things.

## CONCLUSION AND RECOMMENDATIONS

The fusion of IKS and AI holds transformative power of our current settings and beyond, and promising technological innovations that foster an equitable and sustainable future. This fusion presents limitless opportunities to tackle pressing global challenges such as climate change by tapping into refined, tried and tested indigenous wisdom and knowledge while riding on impactful technological innovations. Solutions that honor both the past and future are being developed. Artificial Intelligence can be integrated with IKS in areas such as preservation, revitalization and problem solving. However, the potential fusion should be backed by strong ethical principles, indigenous leadership and control. AI should as such, present solutions to serve the needs and priorities of indigenous communities. However, the realization of these promising solutions can be achieved when indigenous communities are engaged from the outset to the end of the project. The significance of the presence of indigenous communities is to provide a check-and-balance to promote the interests of the community, thereby decolonizing the process of knowledge production. Consequently, the existing power imbalances that retard progress must be actively challenged and addressed. Critical discussion on the integration of AI and IKS through the lenses of data sovereignty, intellectual property rights and cultural appropriation was also provided. A discussion of responsible AI was given to govern the development and implementation of AI-IKS solutions. Additionally, the presented framework aims to provide a guide for developing and implementing AI-based initiatives that align with indigenous communities' rights and culture.

Building on the findings of this work, we offer the following recommendations for researchers, policymakers, technologists and indigenous communities: AI-IKS initiatives should be grounded in the principles of indigenous self-determination to ensure that communities remains in control of their data, knowledge, and resources. This is easily achieved when FPIC is obtained from indigenous communities for all project activities and when they are involved in all decision-making matters throughout the project's lifecycle. Secondly, the proposed framework should serve as a guide for creating and implementing AI-IKS projects, which emphasis equitable benefit-sharing, cultural sensitivity and building capacity within communities. Thirdly, indigenous researchers, technologies and relevant stakeholders should strengthen capacity building within indigenous communities by providing training and resources that encourage full engagement in AI-IKS initiatives. Therefore, training indigenous communities' skills in data management and digital literacy is essential, as it is providing support for research led by indigenous communities. Finally, it is essential to establish collaboration among researchers, technologists, policymakers and indigenous communities to ensure successful integration of AI with IKS. This partnership creates a platform where knowledge is shared, foster open dialogue and nurture mutual respect. Ultimately, fostering trust between technologists, researchers and indigenous communities, leading to long-lasting relationships that benefit all parties involved and makes long-term sustainability more achievable (Auer et al., 2020; Berkes, 2012).

## REFERENCES


Allard-Tremblay, Y., & Coburn, E. (2023). The flying heads of settler colonialism; or the ideological erasures of indigenous peoples in political theorizing. *Political Studies, 71*(2), 359–378.

Anderson, J. E. (2015). Indigenous knowledge and intellectual property rights. In *International Encyclopaedia of the Social & Behavioral Sciences* (2nd ed., pp. 769–778). Elsevier Inc.

Arsenault, D., & Beaulieu, C. (2023). Augmented Reality for Documenting and Showcasing Indigenous Cultural Heritage. *Journal on Computing and Cultural Heritage, 16*(3), 45–60.

Asakawa, K. (2017). Family socialization practices and their effects on the internalization of educational values for Asian and White American adolescents. In *Conditions for Optimal Development in Adolescence* (pp. 184–194). Psychology Press.

Auer, A., Von Below, J., Nahuelhual, L., Mastrangelo, M., Gonzalez, A., Gluch, M., & Paruelo, J. (2020). The role of social capital and collective actions in natural capital conservation and management. *Environmental Science & Policy, 107*, 168–178.

Barnhardt, N. R. (2014). Creating a place for indigenous knowledge in education: The Alaska native knowledge network. In *Place-based education in the global age* (pp. 137–158). Routledge.

Bell, A. (2017). *Appropriating culture: Values, risks, and the law*. Edward Elgar Publishing.

Bender, E. M., Hovy, D., & Schofield, A. (2020). Integrating ethics into the NLP curriculum. In *Proceedings of the 58th Annual Meeting of the Association for Computational Linguistics: Tutorial Abstracts* (pp. 6-9).

Benjamin, R. (2023). Race after technology. In *Social Theory Re-Wired* (pp. 405–415). Routledge.

Berkes, F. (2012). *Sacred Ecology*. Routledge.

Bickel, B., Nichols, J., & Woodbury, A. C. (2017). *The Cambridge handbook of linguistic fieldwork*. Cambridge University Press.

Birhane, A. (2021). Algorithmic injustice: A relational ethics approach. *Patterns (New York, N.Y.), 2*(2).

Bremer, S., & Meisch, S. (2017). Co-production in climate change research: Reviewing different perspectives. *Wiley Interdisciplinary Reviews: Climate Change*, *8*(6), e482.

Browne, A.. (2023). Analyzing Traditional Ceremonies with Video AI: Insights into Cultural Practices. *Visual Anthropology Review*, *39*(3), 220–235.

Carroll, S. R., Hudson, M., Holbrook, J., Materechera, S., & Anderson, J. (2020). Working with the CARE principles: operationalizing Indigenous data governance. *Ada Lovelace Institute, 9*.

Christen, K. (2011). Opening archives: Respectful repatriation. *The American Archivist*, *74*(1), 185–210.

Couldry, N., & Mejias, U. A. (2019). The costs of connection: How data is colonizing human life and appropriating it for capitalism. In *The costs of connection*. Stanford University Press.

Coulthard, G. S. (2014). Red skin, white masks: Rejecting the colonial politics of recognition. *Minneapolis: Minnesota*.

Crawford, K. (2021). *The atlas of AI: Power, politics, and the planetary costs of artificial intelligence*. Yale University Press.

Crawford, L. (2024). The project manager. In *The Handbook of Project Management* (pp. 336–348). Routledge.

Crystal, D. (2000). *Language Death*. Cambridge University Press.

Deci, E. L., & Ryan, R. M. (2000). The "what" and "why" of goal pursuits: Human needs and the self- determination of behavior. *Psychological Inquiry*, *11*(4), 227–268.

Duarte, M. E. (2017). Network sovereignty: Building the Internet across Indian country. *Yale Journal of Law & Technology*, *19*(1), 149–200.

Dutfield, G. (2000). *Intellectual property rights trade and biodiversity*. Routledge.

Ensminger, J., & Henrich, J. (Eds.). (2014). *Experimenting with social norms: Fairness and punishment in cross-cultural perspective*. Russell Sage Foundation.

Ezeanya-Esiobu, C. (2019). *Indigenous knowledge and education in Africa*. Springer Nature.

Floridi, L. (2023). The ethics of artificial intelligence: Principles, challenges, and opportunities.

Fourmile, H. (2020). Who owns the past? Aborigines as captives of the archives. In *Terrible Hard Biscuits* (pp. 16–27). Routledge.

Fryberg, S. A., Dai, J. D., & Eason, A. E. (2024). Omission as a modern form of bias against Native Peoples: Implications for policies and practices. *Social Issues and Policy Review*, *18*(1), 148–170.

Gay, G. (2018). *Culturally responsive teaching: Theory, research, and practice*. Teachers college press.

Gibson, J. (2016). *Community resources: intellectual property, international trade and protection of traditional knowledge*. Routledge.

Gilio-Whitaker, D. (2019). *As long as grass grows: The Indigenous fight for environmental justice, from colonization to Standing Rock*. Beacon Press.

Grint, K., & Jones, O. S. (2022). *Leadership: Limits and possibilities*. Bloomsbury Publishing.

Gupta, A., Rahman, A., & Yasmin, G. (2021). Audio fingerprinting using high-level feature extraction. In *Computational Intelligence in Pattern Recognition* [Singapore: Springer Singapore.]. *Proceedings of CIPR*, *2021*, 281–291.

Guttmann, A. (2021). Commons and cooperatives: A new governance of collective action. *Annals of Public and Cooperative Economics*, *92*(1), 33–53.

Haggart, B., Tusikov, N., & Scholte, J. A. (2021). *Power and authority in internet governance: Return of the state?* Taylor & Francis.

Halewood, M. (1999). Indigenous and local knowledge: Is there a legal space? *International Review of Industrial Property and Copyright Law*, *30*(6), 795–827.

Harlow, R. (2011). Māori language regeneration: A review of research and practice. *Journal of Māori and Pacific Development*, *12*(1), 1–14.

Heinrich, M. (2013). Ethnopharmacology and drug discovery. *Comprehensive Natural Products II: Chemistry and Biology. Development & Modification of Bioactivity*, *3*, 351–381.

Huhndorf, S. M. (2015). *Going native: Indians in the American cultural imagination*. Cornell University Press.

Jha, A. (2023). AI-Powered Transcription and Preservation of Oral Histories in Indigenous Communities. *Journal of Digital Humanities*, *12*(1), 45–62.

Jones, M. (2022). Virtual Reality for Cultural Heritage Preservation: Recreating Indigenous Landscapes. *Presence (Cambridge, Mass.)*, *31*(1), 50–65.

Jones, P. L., Mahelona, K., Duncan, S., & Leoni, G. (2025). Kaitiaki: Closing the door on open Indigenous data. *International Journal on Digital Libraries*, *26*(1), 1.

Kim, A., Isaac, A., & Nadas, A. (2022). Indigenous knowledge and artificial intelligence: Opportunities and challenges. *AI & Society*, *37*(2), 645–657.

Kim, J. (2024). Immersive VR Experiences for Transmitting Traditional Indigenous Ceremonies. *Digital Applications in Archaeology and Cultural Heritage*, *32*, 100290.

Kimmerer, R. W. (2013). *Braiding sweetgrass: Indigenous wisdom, scientific knowledge and the teachings of plants*. Milkweed Editions.

Kirkness, V. J., & Barnhardt, R. (2016). First Nations and Higher Education: The Four R's— Respect, Relevance, Reciprocity, Responsibility. *The Journal of College and University Student Housing*, *42*(2).

Kovach, M. (2021). *Indigenous methodologies: Characteristics, conversations, and contexts*. University of Toronto Press.

Laird, S. A. (Ed.). (2010). *Biodiversity and traditional knowledge: Equitable partnerships in practice*. Earthscan.

Lewis, A. (2024). AR-Enhanced Learning of Indigenous Knowledge: An Interactive Approach. *British Journal of Educational Technology*, *55*(1), 78–95.

Lomawaima, K. T., & McCarty, T. L. (2025). *To remain an Indian": Lessons in democracy from a century of Native American education*. Teachers College Press.

Lombardi, L. (2019). *Indigenous Cultural Heritage Law: Protection, Management and Control*. Routledge.

Marie-Vivien, D. (2016). A comparative analysis of GIs for handicrafts: the link to origin in culture as well as nature? In *Research handbook on intellectual property and geographical indications* (pp. 292–326). Edward Elgar Publishing.

Marx, G. T. (2019). *Windows into the soul: Surveillance and society in an age of high technology*. University of Chicago Press.

Mazany, T., & Perry, D. C. (Eds.). (2013). *Here for good: Community foundations and the challenges of the 21st century*. ME Sharpe.

Mazzocchi, F. (2022). Diving deeper into the concept of 'cultural heritage'and its relationship with epistemic diversity. *Social Epistemology*, *36*(3), 393–406.

Merritt, B. (2016). The digital revolution. In *The Digital Revolution* (pp. 15–17). Springer International Publishing.

Meyer, E. T., & Schroeder, R. (2023). *Knowledge machines: Digital transformations of the sciences and humanities*. Mit Press.

Moreton-Robinson, A. (2015). *The white possessive: Property, power, and Indigenous sovereignty*. University of Minnesota Press.

Noble, S. U. (2018). Algorithms of oppression: How search engines reinforce racism. In *Algorithms of oppression*. New York university press.

O'Brien, D., Ruru, J., & Te Ahukaramū Charles Royal, C. (2020). *Routledge handbook of law and Indigenous peoples*. Routledge.

O'Faircheallaigh, C. (2021). Explaining outcomes from negotiated agreements in Australia and Canada. *Resources Policy*, *70*, 101922.

O'Neil, C. (2017). *Weapons of math destruction: How big data increases inequality and threatens democracy*. Crown.

Ogwezzy, M. C. (2012). Protection of Indigenous or Traditional Knowledge Under Intellectual Property Laws: An Examination of the Efficacy of Copyright Law, Trade Secret. *International and Comparative Law Review*, *12*(1), 5–34.

Ojha, H. R., Ford, R., Keenan, R. J., Race, D., Vega, D. C., Baral, H., & Sapkota, P. (2016). Delocalizing communities: Changing forms of community engagement in natural resources governance. *World Development*, *87*, 274–290.

Parlee, B.. (2022). Indigenous Knowledge for Climate Change Assessment and Adaptation. *Nature Climate Change*, *12*(8), 731–737.

Pine, A., & Turin, M. (2017). Language revitalization. *Oxford research encyclopaedia of linguistics*.

Prats, A. J. (2018). *Invisible Natives: Myth and Identity in the American Western*. Cornell University Press.

Quail, K., Green, D., & O'Faircheallaigh, C. (2025). Large-scale renewable energy developments on the indigenous estate: How can participation benefit Australia's FirstNation s peoples? *Energy Research & Social Science*, *123*, 104044.

Queniahan, M. (2024). Guidelines to ensure Māori Data Sovereignty in the ICT sector of Aotearoa New Zealand.

Rainie, S. C., Rodriguez-Lonebear, D., & Martinez, A. (2017). *Policy brief: Data governance strategies for federal agencies working with American Indian and Alaska Native nations*. Native Nations Institute, University of Arizona.

Rajani, K., Ranjan, T., Kumar, R. R., Patil, G., Kumar, M., Kumar, J., & Kumar, M. (2018). Traditional knowledge and its promotion through providing legal rights. In *The role of intellectual property rights in agriculture and allied sciences* (pp. 151–180). Apple Academic Press.

Ramirez, E. (2022). De/colonisation and the un/doing of critical theory. *Knowledge Cultures*, *10*(3), 150–176.

Rawls, J. (1971). *A theory of justice*. Harvard University Press.

Reeves, J., Treharne, G. J., Theodore, R., Edwards, W., Ratima, M., & Poulton, R. (2022). Understanding the data-sharing debate in the context of Aotearoa/New Zealand: A narrative review on the perspectives of funders, publishers/journals, researchers, participants and Māori collectives. *Kotuitui*, *17*(1), 1–23.

Reyes-García, V., García-Del-Amo, D., Porcuna-Ferrer, A., Schlingmann, A., Abazeri, M., Attoh, E. M., & Torrents-Ticó, M. (2024). Local studies provide a global perspective of the impacts of climate change on Indigenous Peoples and local communities. *Sustainable Earth Reviews*, *7*(1), 1.

Riley, A. R., & Carpenter, K. A. (2015). Owning red: A theory of Indian (cultural) appropriation. *Texas Law Review*, *94*, 859.

Robertson, L., & Kelley, P. (2021). Gamified Learning for Indigenous Language Revitalization: A Case Study. *Journal of Educational Technology*, *48*(2), 123–140.

Russell, S. J., & Norvig, P. (2016). *Artificial intelligence: a modern approach*. Pearson.

Scannell, K. (2017). *Language technologies for a multilingual world*. Springer.

Schwab, K. (2018). "The Fourth Industrial Revolution" Encyclopaedia Britannica Anniversary Edition: 250 Years of Excellence (1768–2018).

Shapin, S. (2018). *The scientific revolution*. University of Chicago press.

Shiva, V. (2016). *Biopiracy: The plunder of nature and knowledge*. North Atlantic Books.

Simpson, L. B. (2017). *As we have always done: Indigenous freedom through radical resistance*. U of Minnesota Press.

Smith, B., & Wilson, C. (2024). Image Recognition for Cultural Heritage Preservation: A Case Study of Indigenous Artifacts. *International Journal of Cultural Heritage*, *25*(2), 112–130.

Smith, L. T. (2012). *Decolonizing methodologies: Research and Indigenous peoples*. Zed Books.

Smith, L. T. (2021). *Decolonizing research: Indigenous storywork as methodology*. SAGE Publications.

Stevenson, S. A. (2016). Toward a narrative ethics: Indigenous community-based research, the ethics of narrative, and the limits of conventional bioethics. *Qualitative Inquiry*, *22*(5), 365–376.

Thornberry, P. (2013). Indigenous peoples and human rights. In *Indigenous peoples and human rights*. Manchester University Press.

Todd, Z. (2016). An indigenous feminist's take on the ontological turn: 'Ontology' is just another word for colonialism. *Journal of Historical Sociology*, *29*(1), 4–22.

Tsosie, R.. (2021). Indigenous Data Sovereignty and Artificial Intelligence: Opportunities for Self-Determination. *AI & Society*, *36*(4), 1325–1337.

Tuck, E., & Yang, K. W. (2012). Decolonization is not a metaphor. *Decolonization*, *1*(1), 1–40.

*UN Declaration of Human Rights*. (1948). United Nations.

UN Permanent Forum on Indigenous Issues (UNPFII). (2005). *Guidelines for implementation of the principle of free, prior and informed consent*. United Nations.

UNDRIP. (2007). *United Nations Declaration on the Rights of Indigenous Peoples*. United Nations.

UNESCO. (2003). *Convention for the safeguarding of the intangible cultural heritage*. United Nations Educational, Scientific and Cultural Organization.

UNESCO. (2023). *Local and Indigenous Knowledge*. https://www.unesco.org/en/ik (Accessed March 27, 2025)

Van Deursen, A. J., & Van Dijk, J. A. (2019). The first-level digital divide shifts from inequalities in physical access to inequalities in material access. *New Media & Society*, *21*(2), 354–375.

Vickers, P. (2013). *Understanding inconsistent science*. OUP Oxford.

Walter, M., Kukutai, T., Carroll, S. R., & Rodriguez-Lonebear, D. (2020). *Indigenous data sovereignty and policy*. Taylor & Francis.

Walter, M., & Suina, M. (2019). Indigenous data sovereignty: What does it mean in practice? *The Australian Journal of Social Issues*, *54*(2), 203–214.

Wang, X., Li, Y., Zhang, Z., & Chen, W. (2023). AI-Powered Interactive Storytelling for Cultural Heritage Education. *International Journal of Artificial Intelligence in Education, 33*(4), 800–820.

Wang, Y. (2025). Simeon Yates and Elinor Carmi (Eds.), Digital Inclusion: International Policy and Research. *International Journal of Communication, 19*, 4.

Wepa, D. (Ed.). (2015). *Cultural safety in aotearoa New Zealand.* Cambridge University Press.

Whyte, K. (2017). Indigenous climate change studies: Indigenizing futures, decolonizing the Anthropocene. *English Language Notes, 55*(1), 153–162.

WIPO. (2024). *Traditional Knowledge: Policy and Legal Options.* World Intellectual Property Organization.

Xu, M., David, J. M., & Kim, S. H. (2018). The fourth industrial revolution: Opportunities and challenges. *International journal of financial research, 9*(2), 90-95.

Zuboff, S. (2023). The age of surveillance capitalism. In *Social theory re-wired* (pp. 203–213). Routledge.

## KEY TERMS AND DEFINITIONS

**Artificial Intelligence (AI):** is a technology designed to perform tasks that requiring human-like intelligence.

**Cultural Appropriation:** Cultural appropriation is a result of misuse and exploitation of Indigenous culture and knowledge such as commercializing products without permission or consent, misrepresentation in media, exploitation of knowledge, and disrespectful imitation.

**Data Sovereignty:** The right of Indigenous communities to freely define their own political status and freely determine their culture, social, and economic developments. It encompasses human rights and cultural integrity.

**Free, Prior, and Informed Consent (FPIC):** Is a framework that empowers Indigenous communities to give or withhold their consent before using either their cultural elements or knowledge.

**Indigenous Knowledge Systems (IKS):** Frameworks that present ideal ways of understanding the world, deeply rooted in specific locations, evolved through inter-generational transmission by interaction and careful observation of the natural environment.

**Intellectual Property Rights (IPR):** Is a tool that offers solutions to issues pertaining to traditional knowledge safeguard and respect for Indigenous communities.

**Machine Learning (ML):** Is a branch of AI that provides tools and technologies to enable AI programs or systems to learn from data without being explicitly programmed.

# Chapter 11
# Child Mortality Prediction Using Machine Learning Techniques

**B. Narendra Kumar Rao**
https://orcid.org/0000-0002-7381-4828
*Sri Ramachandra Faculty of Engineering and Technology, SRIHER, India*

## ABSTRACT

*This project explores the application of machine learning techniques to predict child mortality by analyzing a dataset of 2,126 cardiotocogram (CTG) measurements, which detail fetal heart rate and uterine contraction patterns and have been meticulously classified by expert obstetricians. The study employs and compares various machine learning models, including logistic regression, decision trees, and neural networks, to assess their efficacy in identifying high-risk pregnancies. By leveraging these advanced predictive models, the research aims to enhance the accuracy of risk assessments and uncover critical patterns in fetal health data that may not be detectable through conventional methods. The ultimate goal is to support early interventions and improve child survival rates through data-driven decision-making in healthcare. This project has significant implications for enhancing predictive modeling and risk assessment in obstetrics, contributing to more effective and personalized maternal and child health care strategies.*

## 1. INTRODUCTION

Child mortality is a critical global health issue, with preterm birth being one of the leading causes of death in children below the age of five. Less weight during birth and premature gestational age are significant risk factors that contribute to neonatal

DOI: 10.4018/979-8-3373-8510-5.ch011

mortality, as well as long-term health complications for children. Early detection of fetal health anomalies can significantly reduce the risks associated with preterm births and improve the chances of survival. In this context, predictive models that identify at-risk pregnancies can be vital for providing timely interventions, ultimately saving lives and improving health outcomes for new-borns.

Child Mortality is also called as "under-5 Mortality" refers to the child death who are under age 5. It is often reported as the no of deaths in 1,000 new births and is declining globally in recent years, but still there is lot of work to be done. Infants died who are under 5 in 2022 was 4.9 million which is very low and there is 59% reduction from 1990, when 12.8 million children who are under 5 died. and cause of death of children who are under 5 are due to preterm birth complications (Obermeyer & Emanuel, 2016), pneumonia, birth asphyxia, and malaria.

Healthcare specialists to adopt the following guidelines setup by World Health organization to improve health conditions of newly born child and increase the expectancy during the under-5 age, Improve antenatal and obstetric care, Essential newborn care, Skilled delivery and emergency obstetric care, Promote nutrition, Integrated Management of Childhood Illness, Postnatal care visits, Health education and community engagement and timely vaccination. Antenatal and obstetric care involves ensuring care during pregnancy which can prevent stillbirths and neonatal deaths, hence managing complications early. Newborn care is very essential factor like thermal protection and infection prevention. Obstetric care takes care of child through appointed attendants and emergency care for the child, thereby preventing deaths from birth asphyxia. Vaccinations and nutrition immunizes the child early and protects from several common childhood illness in the so called under-5 criteria and in some cases protection for life. Integrated Management system uses protocol based system to protect child from immediate and simple sickness like pneumonia and diarrhea. Postnatal care conducts intensive care for the first 24 hours after child is born and upto a week to secure its health and make it a stable one. Health education is very desirable for families and for communities in general about newborn care and dangers aftermath. Along side the above few more considerations are as follows, Early initiation of breastfeeding, Hygienic umbilical cord care, Vitamin A supplementation, postnatal care contacts, Special care for low-birth-weight, preterm newborns and therapeutic treatments. Breastfeeding provides sufficient nutrients and immunity protection right after birth. Umbilical cord care prevents infections to both the mother and the newborn. Vitamin A supplement reduces infections that are likely to happen for the newborn. postnatal care contacts in the form of health workers by home visits within few days of birth results in early identification of health issues. Low-birth-weight and preterm newborns monitoring supports hygiene and illness monitoring. Transmittable diseases can be avoided through therapeutic treatments.

A special case of children deaths is infant mortality, and which is also includes all the deaths of children who are prior to I year of age.it remains as critical global health challenge, particularly in developing nations. and regardless of the advanced healthcare (Miotto et al., 2018), many toddlers are succumb to rescuable causes.

Machine learning (ML) is a popular tool for predicting various health outcomes, including those related to fetal health. ML models can effectively analyze complex datasets that include clinical features and physiological data (Ayres-de-Campos, Spong, & Chandraharan, 2015) from pregnancies, helping to identify patterns and predict future health outcomes. The primary challenge lies in selecting the right models and evaluating their performance to ensure accurate and reliable predictions. This study aims to apply multiple ML classifiers to predict fetal health, leveraging a dataset with clinical features such as accelerations, uterine contractions, and fetal movements.

As of current stand in literature Demographic and Health Survey applied Machine Learning algorithms like Decision trees, Random Forest, XGBoost and Naive Bayes to identify child mortality based on factors like birth intervals, socio-economic conditions, maternal age, breast feeding and other features. Gradient Boosting, stacking approaches and AdaBoost in the form of ensemble techniques are applied and have shown required performance in child mortality prediction by considering high-risk populations. Deep Learning models are also applied on Demographic and Health Survey data from multiple datasets which outperforms traditional logistic regression techniques with attributes like breastfeeding time, maternal education, antenatal visits and wealth index as primary attributes.

Predicting the risk on childs health accurately can play a very important part in early intervention and resource allocation. In this we aim to leverage ML techniques to analyse the cardiotocogram(CTG)data, and trying to offer an innovative approach to identifying high risk pregnancies and improving maternal and toddler health outcomes so that we can predict the child health in mothers womb and invent new innovative approach to prevent the child health and this decreases the mortality of the children by enabling healthcare professional to prioritize cases and allocate resources effectively. The characteristic that can be observed through cardiotocogram data is on Detection of Fetal Distress. Computerized and Deep Learning CTG Analysis and Kolmogorov-Arnold Networks (KANs) have demonstrated accurate results. The important accuracy findings from CTG includes Specificity and Negative Predictive Value, Sensitivity of abnormal CTG and Positiveness of Predictive Value. The key predictive CTG features are as given below, Bradycardia, Prolonged Decelerations, Variable Decelerations, Baseline Variability and pattern of fetal movements. Bradycardia refers to low or high heart rates and this is a case of pathology. Prolonged Decelerations in heart rate constantly is a strong indicator of upcoming hypoxia. Baseline Variability refers to heart rate above average which is normally 110-16 beats is also an indicator for monitoring.

## 2. PREDICTION AND CLASSIFICATION OF CHILD MORTALITY

In the field of public health addressing the child mortality requires advanced tools that can provide data-driven insights. Even so, healthcare systems, especially in deprived regions, they often face the limitations in access to polished technologies and professionals in the fields like machine learning, data analysis, and computational diagnostics and these elements create a significant challenges in identifying the high risk cases as early as possible and accurately.

Traditional methods for predicting child mortality risks rely majorly on the manual analysis or basic statistical techniques. And also these approaches are often insufficient for detecting fine patterns and also connections with in the data and they are critical for opportune assistance or well timed support, the delay caused by these standard methods can remarkably impact outcomes and particularly in scenarios or cases where prompt action is important.

Child mortality is a complex problem inclined in large range of medical, social, and environmental factors (Topol, 2019). Current approaches fail to comprehensively address these complexities, highlighting the need for innovative, predictive tools that leverage modern technologies.

This research bridges the gap by utilizing machine learning techniques, These models aim to empower healthcare providers by delivering actionable insights and enabling more efficient resource allocation, ultimately improving maternal and child health conditions.

The goal of this work is to give an intuition as to how machine learning can be used to fetal health prediction, specifically focusing on reducing child mortality. By determining the most effective classification model and understanding which features are most indicative of fetal health, our research contributes to the current work in the intersection of healthcare and machine learning. Early prediction of at-risk pregnancies using these models can assist healthcare professionals in taking proactive measures, potentially saving lives and improving the health of newborns worldwide.

The global burden of preterm birth and its associated risks have been widely studied due to its significant impact on child mortality rates. Harrison and Goldenberg (Harrison & Goldenberg, 2016) highlighted pre-term birth as the major reason of death among children below the age of five. They also identified Lesser weight during birth and premature gestational age as key contributors to mortality and long-term health complications. Their work emphasizes the need for early detection and timely interventions to mitigate the risks associated with preterm birth. This aligns with the objective of our study, which aims to predict fetal health to reduce child mortality risks, using machine learning techniques to analyze clinical data.

Baer (Baer et al., 2016) provided sufficient insights into the risks of mortality based on gestational age and birth weight. Their population-based study revealed how these factors influence the survival and health outcomes of newborns. Their findings contribute to understanding the importance of clinical features in predicting neonatal outcomes, which forms the basis for our approach of using clinical data to predict fetal health and preterm birth risks (Horbar et al., 2017). The integration of birth weight and gestational age with other clinical features (Sampathirao, Ramesh, & Kumar, 2025) may increase the accuracy of fetal health predictions.

The variation in neonatal intensive care unit (NICU) performance across the United States was explored by Horbar show-cased on how different unit care standards influence neonatal outcomes. This study underlined the importance of improving clinical practices and the need for standardized monitoring of newborns in intensive care settings. In the context of our work, accurate prediction models can support better NICU outcomes by identifying at-risk pregnancies early on, enabling more personalized and targeted interventions for high-risk foetuses.

Additionally, neonatal morbidities such as bronchopulmonary dysplasia, necrotizing enterocolitis, and retinopathy of prematurity have been extensively studied due to their association with preterm births. Davidson and Berkelhamer discussed bronchopulmonary dysplasia as a chronic lung disease that affects preterm infants, while Thompson and Bizzarro focused on necrotizing enterocolitis, a severe gastrointestinal condition commonly found in premature infants. Retinopathy of prematurity, as studied by Hellström, is another major concern for preterm infants. These studies reinforce the critical need for initial proof of identity of at-risk infants, making machine learning-based predictive models, such as the one developed in this paper, crucial for improving neonatal outcomes. These references establish a clear background for our research, emphasizing the importance of early detection in reducing mortality and morbidity in preterm infants. Leveraging machine learning in current context aims to enhance early detection and improve health outcomes for newborns from the risks of neonatal complications.

The common and important factors contributing to child mortality study focusses on the following, Socio-demographic, Birth characteristics, Child factors and Environmental and geographic factors. The demographic features comprises of wealth index of family, marriage age, education of parents. The birth characteristics comprise of attributes like child weight, birth rate, interval between births, postnatal care, place of delivery and other factors. The child factors comprise of size of baby, immunization history and reactions, mother feeding attributes. The Environmental and geographic factors includes residence in urban/rural and climatic conditions prevalent during birth including water resources. In developing countries Scheduled Tribe community are unreachable from above resources and in general the tribe faces higher mortality. Rural residence is one major reason which can promote mortality in view of limited healthcare facilities.

Explainable AI (XAI) methods have come a long way to make ML algorithms more transparent, interpretable and trustworthy from the viewpoint of practitioners and policy makers. XAI helps in making the stakeholders understand about the models and how they work. The commonly used XAI methods are SHAP(SHapley Additive exPlanations), LIME (Local Interpretable Model-agnostic Explanations), Feature Importance Rankings, Rule-Based Models and Decision Trees. SHAP explains about the influence of each attributes in individual predictions between global and local predictions. SHAP uses attributes like Socio-demographic and birth rate features. LIME offers explanation based on simplifying complex model tasks and approximating them. Feature Importance Rankings operates by using tree-based models to provide feature importance scores along with important attributes like socio economic changes and immunization. Rule-Based Models and Decision Trees apply direct means of explanation based on mortality risk factors and provide decision support tools.

## 2.1 Significance

ML algorithm help healthcare activists to understand and use appropriate treatments built on the predictions made by the machine learning models. They help in a long way in the form of understanding and estimating the critical risk factors resulting in child deaths like size of the family, separation between pregnancy of a woman, soci-economic status, maternal health and dietary conditions prevalent with mother etc… Secondly, data-driven decision making makes them error free and clinical decisions are superior to anticipatory treatments. Third, non-linear relationships and diverse risk factor predictions help in reducing confusions prevalent in treatments and dietary conditions. Digitization of child health information increases the insight during healthcare monitoring. The healthcare info related to the child can be digitized by the following means like Wearable Devices and Sensors, Digital Health Systems, Telemedicine platforms and Mobile Health applications. Wearable Devices and Sensors largely are used in developed nations and detect any vital sign and alerts the caregivers. Digital Health Systems links maternal and new born data streams with birth registries. Telemedicine platforms follow-up via phone and video calls and provide access to paediatric care. Mobile Health Apps enable caregivers to monitor status of the newborn online. In case of Digital Health Systems few open source platforms are available like OpenMRS, OpenEMR, GNU Health, Bahmni, OpenEHR and Hikma Health. They support digitization of child health records and provide data accessibility to all the stakeholders. Fast Healthcare Interoperability Resources supports interoperability standards which is user friendly web based application designed and built for seamless data exchange. Health Level Seven is an internationally accepted healthcare data exchange standard. International Classification of Diseases is a standard managed by WHO for coding diagnoses and caused for death. Logical Observation Identifiers Names and Codes standard is used for lab test data. All the above form an effective data exchange standard for clinical care, research and data exchange.

The importance of child mortality prediction lies in its ability to change healthcare by giving early and accurate risk assessments. Machine learning models offer a variety of benefits in this domain:

1. Improved Accuracy:

Machine learning algorithms can find intricate design and associations within data, leading to higher accuracy in predicting high-risk cases. This allows for better-targeted interventions and treatment plans.

2. Faster Decision-Making:

Automated tools can analyse high size of healthcare data in real time, allow faster identification of at-risk cases and facilitating prompt decision-making in critical situations.

3. Reduced Subjectivity:

Machine learning models provide objective assessments, minimizing variability and bias that might arise from manual or subjective evaluations (Mehrabi et al., 2021).

4. Handling Large and Diverse Data:

The ability of ML models to execute large sets of information, including cardiotocogram (CTG) data, ensures in understanding of risk across diverse populations and scenarios. ML algorithms are suitable for handling categorical, continuous, and binary features simultaneously which makes it suit for child mortality prediction. Cross-validation and hyperparameter tuning parameters help in achieving high accuracy. Ensemble Models, Gradient Boosted Trees, Recurrent Neural Networks and Deep Learning Models with Multimodal Inputs help ML algorithms in this regard.

5. Efficient Use of Resources:

Automation allows healthcare systems to optimize their resources by focusing attention on high-risk cases, reducing unnecessary interventions and improving overall efficiency.

6. Accessibility and Scalability:

Machine learning solutions can be adapted to various healthcare environments, making them valuable tools in both advanced hospitals and resource-constrained settings.

7. Driving Technological Innovation:

Integrating machine learning into child mortality prediction aligns with broader efforts to modernize healthcare through technology, contributing to the development of advanced diagnostic tools and preventive strategies.

### 2.1.1 Challenges

Although machine learning is more applicable, other challenges must be addressed for appropriate usage:

1. Limited Quality Data:

The accessibility of well-annotated, high-quality datasets relevant to child mortality is limited, which can affect the development of reliable predictive models.

2. Imbalanced Data Distribution:

High-risk cases are often underrepresented in datasets, leading to potential bias in predictions that avour more common scenarios. The key strategies to be implemented in handling imbalanced data includes the following approaches, Random Undersampling and Oversampling, Synthetic Minority Over-sampling Technique, Threshold Adjustment and Cost-Sensitive Learning. In case of imbalanced Mortality models calibration can be done through Splitting Data, Calibration Methods and few evaluation metrics.

3. Variability Across Populations:

Models trained on data from particular regions or demographics might not execute well when put in to other populations, highlighting the requirement for diverse and representative datasets.

4. Risk of Overfitting:

When trained on limited or noisy data, then these models may overfit, reducing their ability to generalize new and unseen cases.

5. Transparency and Interpretability:

Healthcare professionals require clear explanations of predictions, but many advanced ML models, particularly neural networks, work as "black boxes," making their decisions harder to explain.

6. Integration Challenges:

Use of Machine learning tools into existing healthcare workflows may not be suitable due to concerns about dependability, usability, and the need for real-world validation.

7. Data Collection Variability:

Differences in how data is collected, such as variations in CTG devices or protocols, can impact the consistency and accuracy of predictive models of machine learning.

## 3. EXISTING METHODS

Research on predicting preterm birth and neonatal morbidity has highlighted the critical role of early identification to reduce mortality rates. Harrison and Goldenberg identified pre-term birth as the major reason of death among children under five, stressing the need for better predictive models. Studies have employed machine learning to analyze clinical data for predicting neonatal outcomes. Baer focused on mortality risks based on gestational age and birth weight, using classifiers like Random Forest, which performed well in predicting neonatal outcomes due to its robustness in handling high-dimensional data.

## 3.1 Dataset

The dataset used in this work, obtained from a fetal health monitoring system, contains clinical data relevant to predicting fetal health outcomes. This dataset includes several important attributes such as baseline values, accelerations, uterine contractions, fetal movements, decelerations (light, severe, prolonged), and various histogram-based measures (e.g., histogram width, histogram mean, etc.). These features are crucial in understanding fetal health during pregnancy. The target variable, fetal health, is categorical and has three classes: 1. Normal, 2. Suspect, and 3. Pathological. The data provides a comprehensive view of different clinical metrics that help assess fetal well-being, making it suitable for machine learning applications aimed at predicting at-risk pregnancies and reducing mortality rates. The most prominent datasets include Demographic and Health Surveys, Multiple Indicator Cluster Surveys, Global Network Maternal and Newborn Health Registry, Country-Specific Health Surveys, Child and Infant Mortality Datasets (Kaggle) and many others available online. The key attributes exhibited by these datasets includes wider coverage, rich variable sets, public availability and easy usage with ML algorithms without much efforts. The best practices for data integration for best results(Demssash, Alemu, & Zerihun, 2023) relies on Geospatial linking, data harmonization, predictor selection and also applied modelling approaches. A simple workflow would comprise of the following steps, Collect Survey & Vital Data, Extract Indicators, Merge & Harmonize, Build Models, Validation, but here we discuss only on data pre-processing as others are out of the context.

## 3.2 Data Preprocessing

Data pre-processing becomes crucial in augmenting the accuracy of machine learning models. Several pre-processing steps are important for the dataset before training the models.

1. Handling Missing Values: The dataset was tested for missing values using the isnull() function. Since the dataset did not have significant missing data, no imputation was required. This ensures the models are not affected by incomplete records and maintain data integrity.
2. Removing Duplicates: Duplicated records in the dataset were found and eliminated using the drop_duplicates() function. Duplicate data can introduce bias into the model, affecting its generalizability and performance. Removing these records confirms that each data point is unique and valuable for model training.
3. Outlier Detection and Removal: Outliers in the dataset, particularly in features like accelerations, uterine contractions, and histogram values, were detected

using the Interquartile Range (IQR) method. The IQR method evaluates the difference between the first and third quartiles (Q1 and Q3), and data points out of the range [Q1−1.5×IQR, Q3+1.5×IQR] reflected as outliers. These outliers were removed as they undesirably influence the performance of ML models. The boxplots below illustrate the presence of outliers before and after their removal.

4. Feature Scaling: While not explicitly mentioned in the code, it is prominent to note that some classifiers like SVM and Logistic Regression benefit from feature scaling. Standardization (scaling attributes to have zero mean and unit variance) can increase convergence and performance for these models, safeguarding that attributes contribute unbiase to the prediction process.
5. Data Splitting: The dataset was categorized into training and testing sets from scikit-learn functions. The data was classified such that 80% was castoff for training the models, and 20% was marked for testing. This split moderates that the model can be evaluated on new data, providing a better indication of its generalizability and performance in real-world scenarios.
    1. Logistic Regression

Logistic Regression is a high powered tool for predicting child mortality and it is one of the best statistical method used in the process of predicting child mortality. The dependent variable has two outcomes during this type of regression analysis.

- **Dataset Utilization:** In this phase we collect the data that is required for child mortality prediction such as their age, height and weight of the child. The process of data cleaning and making it for the further use is done here.
- **Model Training:** For the training data (Iqbal & Jameel, 2023) we have to set a logistic regression model. Before training data we have to check the standardization like standardize the continuous variables so they may have similar scales. Model fitting is done in the process of model training for predicting child mortality.
- **Model Evaluation:** After training, we have to test the model by using test data. Here, we decide the Accuracy, Precision and Recall in the model. After this we interpret the model and make insights and check the model optimization.

2. Decision Trees

Used in classification and regression methods. It has a tree like structure which has internal nodes, branches has decision rules and leaf nodes represents outcome or predictions.

- **Feature Selection:** it is a principal move in any machine learning model to make the features used for the outcome or prediction are appropriate and redundant. In this step the main goal is to take the features that gives a good outcome. In the process of feature selection we take expert knowledge, correlation analysis and recursive feature elimination is done in this step.
- **Model Building:** After selecting meaningful and relevant features, next we have to build a decision tree model. In this process we take the performance of the selected features. We have evaluate the data.
- **Outcome Interpretation**: In the decision tree the outcome depends on both numerical and visual outputs which helps in model decisions. In this we check the accuracy, high accuracy means we are correctly predicting child mortality.

3. Neural Networks

Neural networks plays a vital role in various fields. It have become a very important tool for predicting various health outcomes, like child mortality. It works with very large data and predict complex patterns.Neural networks used in many ways like checking health care, maternal health, environmental factors and many more.

Data Collection: Data collection is a process where we collect the meaningful data such as child's age, height, weight and gender.

Data Preprocessing: The data we collected in the first step is processed here, we clean the data by handling the data and removing the outliers.

Model Selection: In this process we have to choose particular fit neural network model for better outcomes.

Model Training: After model selection we have to test the model to get accurate outcomes.

Model Evaluation: In this step we check the accuracy, precision and we evaluate the performance.

Prediction and Decision Making: In this step we predict the outcome and this helps in predicting the child mortality.

4. Support Vector Machine (SVM):

SVM is an effective classifier to identify the hyperplane that best identifies the different classes in high-dimensional spaces. It is used in linear and non-linear classification problems, especially when the dataset has many features.

5. Random Forest:

An ensemble techniques ensures that method joins multiple decision trees to decrease overfitting and improve accuracy. This algorithm is well-known for robustness and ability to use huge datasets with high-dimensional features.

6. Gaussian Naive Bayes (GNB):

A probabilistic classifier technique assumes that features are provisionally independent for a given target class. It works well when features are independent and the dataset is relatively small.

7. Other Techniques:

XGBoost technique is highly effective in case of huge population and can deliver high accurate results. To a great extent ensemble methods also provide similar results

The most important attributes on which all these models are tested includes weight during birth, immunization, environmental conditions during birth, birth intervals for parent,

## 4. MACHINE LEARNING IN CHILD MORTALITY PREDICTION

Analyzing the use of machine learning techniques to predict child death by analyzing the dateset of 2126 cardiotocogram(CTG) measurement which detail fetal heart rate and uterine contraction patterns and have been accurately classified by export obstetricians.

The Neural Network Model:

Neural Network are powerful tools for analyzing CTG data to predict to child mortality, as they can handle composite, high-dimensional, and temporal patterns in fetal heart rate (FHR) and uterine contraction data. Feedforward Neural Network (FNNs) classify CTG readings, while Convolutional Neural Networks (CNNs) detect spatial patterns in time-series or spectrogram data. Hybrid models combine CNNs and RNNs to use both spatial and temporal insights. Neural networks require preprocessing steps like normalization and data augmentation, followed by training with optimization techniques like Adam and regularization methods like dropout. While they provide high accuracy and scalability, challenges like data requirements and interpretability can be addressed using data augmentation and Explainable AI techniques. These models enable real-time predictions, aiding timely interventions and improving outcomes in maternal and fetal care.

The Decision Tree:

Decision trees are simple and interpretable models for predicting child mortality using CTG data. They split the data into branches based on attributes like fetal heart rate (FHR) variability and uterine contractions, with each branch leading to an outcome such as normal or pathological. these are simple to recognize, fast to train, and can handle both quantitative and categorical data. However, they may overfit on noisy datasets, which is mitigated by pruning or using ensemble methods like Random Forests. Their simplicity and clarity make them valuable for clinical applications where interpretability is crucial.

The Logistic Regression:

This is a supervised learning algorithm applied for binary or multi-class classification. It predicts the probability of an outcome by secure the logistic (sigmoid) function to a linear combination of input attributes. The output is a value in the range 0 and 1, representing the possibility of a specific class. Logistic regression is not difficult to execute, interpretable, and constuctive for linearly separable facts. It uses optimization techniques like gradient descent to reduce the error in the middle of expected and real results. However, it may struggle with complex, non-linear relationships unless combined with feature transformations.

Model Evaluation

Each classifier is calculated using performance metrics like accuracy, precision, recall, and F1-score. These metrics are essential in considering how suitably the models classify fetal health. Accuracy provides the overall percentage of correct predictions, while precision and recall assess the balance between false positives and false negatives. The F1-score includes precision and recall as a single metric, which is predominantly applied with imbalanced classes.

Feature Importance:

To identify which attributes contribute most to predicting fetal health, we used the Random Forest classifier to calculate feature importance. Random Forest evaluates how each feature helps in reducing the impurity (variance) in the decision trees. During the process, we can focus on the clinical metrics that provide the most predictive value, allowing for a more efficient prediction process.

Results Visualization:

To visualize the results and compare the performance of different classifiers, a line plot was created to show the accuracy scores for each algorithm. The plot offers a clear comparison of how well each model performs in terms of classification correctness.

Ethical Considerations:

To a large extent accuracy of data, unbiasedness, better data quality and generalizable predictions are crucial in success or appropriateness of the results or outcomes. Models are to remain accessible and open to all the users to make it easily applied and results are annexed as well.

## 4.1 Objective

The primary intention of this work is to develop a ML model to predict child mortality based on various socio-economic, demographic, and health-related factors. By leveraging predictive analytics, the work aims to

1. Predictive Modeling:

Evolve a robust machine learning model proficient in accurately predicting child mortality based on a dataset containing demographic, socio-economic, and healthcare-related factors.

Test and evaluate multiple algorithms (e.g., Logistic Regression Hom Forest, XGBoost) effective approach.

2. Feature Importance Analysis:

Identify the critical factors influencing child death (e.g., maternal education, access to healthcare, nutritional status).Provide insights into which variables should be prioritized for targeted interventions.

3. Support for Policy and Decision Making:

Equip policymakers and health organizations with data-driven insights to design targeted programs aimed at reducing child mortality.

Highlight areas requiring immediate attention, such as underserved regions or population (Pandey, Singh, & Verma, 2025).

4. Automation and Scalability:

Ensure the model is interpretable and user-friendly for stakeholders with minimal technical expertise.

## 4.2 Scope

The work projects on leveraging machine learning techniques to address the critical issue of child mortality. The scope includes the following:

1. Problem Domain:

Analyze factors contributing to child mortality, including socio-economic, demographic, healthcare, and environmental variables.

Understand patterns and correlations in data that may be overlooked using traditional statistical methods.

2. Data Utilization:

Work with publicly available datasets (e.g., UNICEF, WHO, DHS Program) or healthcare-specific datasets.

Pre-process raw facts by operating noise values, normalizing features, and encoding categorical variables.

3. Machine Learning Techniques:

Explore and implement supervised learning algorithms such as Logistic Regression, Random Forest, Gradient Boosting (e.g., XGBoost), or Neural Networks.

Train, validate, and test models to ensure accurate predictions.

Use explainability tools (e.g., SHAP values) for understanding model predictions.

4. Evaluation and Validation:

Assess model performance using metrics like accuracy, precision, recall, F1-score, and ROC-AUC to undertake cross-validation to ensure model generalizability.

5. Practical Applications:

Design a predictive tool for healthcare providers and policymakers to identify high-risk children.

Assist in resource allocation by highlighting regions or groups requiring immediate attention. Policy makers involve ML models to predict child death by finding high-risk groups and key-risk factors, that enable targeted interventions and resource allocation for improved child health.

6. Ethical Considerations:

Ensure data privacy and compliance with ethical standards for addressing potential biases in the dataset to avoid discriminatory outcomes. The ethical considerations require involvement from multidisciplinary teams like clinicians, ethicists, patients, family members, legal experts to ensure that applications developed using AI are deployed responsibly. Universal guidelines by policy makers are required to handle complex scenarios in clinical practice. Few key principles in this case includes Autonomy, Non-Maleficence, Justice, Transparency, privacy and Confidentiality, professional governance and accountability.

7. Future Prospects:

The model can be extended to other regions or diseases impacting child mortality. By integrating the tool into healthcare systems for real-time monitoring and prediction. Use insights for educational campaigns and preventive healthcare measures. Wearable technology provides the key for the future prospective study in this domain to improve child health with continuous monitoring (Walter et al., 2024) mechanism. This is possible by monitoring the important attributes related to cardio & respiratory factors. This proactive approach definitely avoids sudden child deaths significantly. Parent and care-givers are alerted around the clock on the well-being including location track and sudden sickness. This also ensures appropriateness in treatments offered. Even though this concept is beyond scope of this work, it is set to provide the consistent data to meet many of the challenges arising in the course of this work. This may well be applicable to developed nations caring much about this problem, seldom this happens with such countries though. Provision of live updates, timely intervention and care, remote usage, personalized care and prevention of deaths are few common advantages. Few of the wearable devices includes, VO7 Wearable Blood Pressure Monitor, Infant Temperature Monitoring Device, Smart Mattress(Iqbal, Jameel, & Malik, 2023) ECG and Breath Monitor, Wireless Neonatal Sensor System, Wearable SIDS Monitors, RFID-based Abdominal Band Sensors and Maternal-Fetal Activity Sensors used in different developed countries (Wang et al., 2022). The following are benefits of using above wearables, ECG, respiration, heart rate, and temperature monitoring, Real-time parental and clinician alerts, Cloud-based data availability, smooth and delicate designs matching child-needs (Memon & Khan, 2020). Cloud architectures scale to the data storage needs for a case like child mortality, wherein they support data-ingestion, processing and storage features (Sandvik et al., 2020). Key cloud architectures that are employed includes the following, Serverless architecture, Distributed Data Lakes and Warehouses, Big Data Processing Frameworks, Managed ML Platforms, Microservices and Container Orchestration and Edge-Cloud Hybrid Architectures. ResNet CNN architectures applied on satellite imagery for child mortality prediction is trained on cloud GPUs and deployed via serverless APIs. Cloud compute clusters are used to handle massive feature sets and cross-validation.

## 4.3 Architecture:

*Figure 1. Machine Learning model*

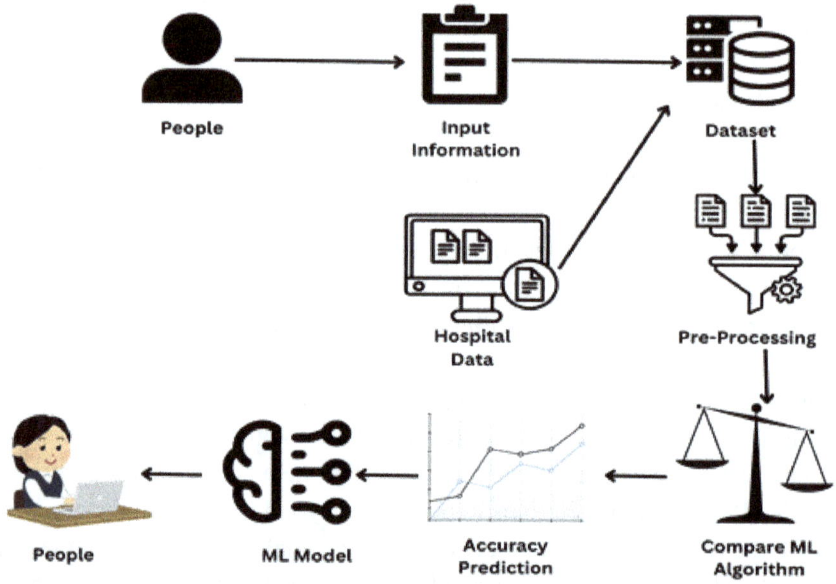


The child mortality prediction model follows a structured process. It begins with gathering datasets, which can be publicly available, collected in-house, or created from the internet. The data undergoes pre-processing, which includes feature engineering, selection, and sampling, along with data augmentation and analysis to ensure quality. Bias is detected and removed, and dimension reduction techniques are applied to optimize the data. Machine learning, decision tree, Neural Network, Logistic regression are acclimated to build the model. Once trained, and tested and fine-tuned to address overfitting and under-fitting issues (Davidson & Berkelhamer, 2017). Reinforcement learning may also be applied to improve the model. The final step involves evaluating the prototype on new, unused or new data and deploying

(Caluza, 2018) it for making predictions, ultimately contributing to child mortality prediction efforts. In deciding the appropriate algorithm to predict the child mortality

EAI platforms can be used along with the following considerations like removing imbalances, accuracy, complexity of model, interpretability, clinical relevance and data requirements. The important trade-off lies with Accuracy vs. Interpretability where complex models generally demonstrate good and accurate predictions, but they are harder to interpret and explain. This makes it unsuitable for clinical disposal. From the viewpoint of Data Availability and Quality, clinical variables increase efficiency in outcomes but burden on data collection is huge. Overfitting vs. Generalization relies on complex model overfitting and may not perform to the expectations. Cross validation techniques are generally suitable in this case. Performance Metrics take into account of multiple evaluation criteria and employs precision, F1 score to decide the trade-off. Clinical Utility uses high accuracy models to demonstrate the actual benefit through resource allocations, interventions in guidance and even identifying a simpler tool. Computational Resources and Implementation uses substantial computational resources which impact feasibility of models and data sets in use.

## 5. CONCLUSION

The application of the machine learning techniques for predicting child mortality using cardiotogram (CTG) measurements that represent a large and important change in health care analytics and risk assessment. This research has demonstrate the potential of advanced algorithms, such as logistic regression, decision trees, and neural networks, to analyse the foetal health data, offering insights that traditional diagnostic methods often overlook. The conclusions of this work underscore the ability of machine learning models to make better the accuracy of identifying high risk pregnancies, enabling timely and data-driven interventions. The leverage of these predictive techniques in healthcare can enhance maternal and child health outcomes, and they optimize the resource allocation, and reduce the risk associated with childbirth.

Machine learning can be used to accurately predict child mortality, and the results can help identify high-risk children and guide healthcare interventions. The systematic technique begin from details refinement and action, mislaid value. This implementation will ease to search for the Prediction of children's Mortality. The experimenters are motivated to use machine learning algorithms for further works related to the topic including vital ascribes that could foretell infants transience. The present results would be convenient for proceedings proactive childcare intercession. Encouraging women in education, media access, and the economic development programs are essential steps for child mortlity reduction.

The study also highlighted the importance of feature selection and data preprocessing in improving model performance. Random Forest's feature importance analysis revealed that clinical variables such as accelerations, uterine contractions, and short-term variability are key predictors of fetal health. This insight can guide healthcare professionals in focusing on the most relevant clinical indicators to predict and manage at-risk pregnancies. In conclusion, machine learning models, particularly Random Forest, hold great potential in early detection and intervention for fetal health, which can ultimately contribute to reducing neonatal mortality and improving long-term health outcomes for newborns.

Expanding the feature set to include more advanced biomarkers or integrating time-series data could lead to even more accurate predictions. Deep learning techniques, such as convolutional or recurrent neural networks, also offer even higher levels of performance, particularly in identifying complex patterns in large datasets. Additionally, exploring real-time implementation of these models in clinical settings, where they can assist healthcare professionals in making timely decisions, would be a valuable step in improving neonatal care and reducing child mortality.

## REFERENCES


Ayres-de-Campos, D., Spong, C. Y., & Chandraharan, E. (2015). FIGO consensus guidelines on intrapartum fetal monitoring: Cardiotocography. *International Journal of Gynaecology and Obstetrics: the Official Organ of the International Federation of Gynaecology and Obstetrics*, *131*(1), 13–24. DOI: 10.1016/j.ijgo.2015.06.020

Baer, R. J., Rogers, E. E., Partridge, J. C., Anderson, J. G., Morris, M., Kuppermann, M., Franck, L. S., Rand, L., & Jelliffe-Pawlowski, L. L. (2016). Population-based risks of mortality and preterm morbidity by gestational age and birth weight. *Journal of Perinatology*, *36*(11), 1008–1013.

Caluza, L. J. B. (2018). Machine learning algorithm application in predicting children mortality: Model development. *International Journal of Information System and Applications*, *10*(1), 1–6. http://www.irphouse.com

Davidson, L., & Berkelhamer, S. (2017). Bronchopulmonary dysplasia: Chronic lung disease of infancy and long-term pulmonary outcomes. *Journal of Clinical Medicine*, *6*(1).

Demssash, A. W., Alemu, T. T., & Zerihun, A. W. (2023). Using best performance machine learning algorithm to predict under-five child mortality in Ethiopia. *BMC Medical Informatics and Decision Making*, *23*, 145. DOI: 10.1186/s12911-023-01811-4

Harrison, M. S., & Goldenberg, R. L. (2016). Global burden of prematurity. *Seminars in Fetal & Neonatal Medicine*, *21*(2), 74–79.

Horbar, J. D., Edwards, E. M., Greenberg, L. T., Morrow, K. A., Soll, R. F., Buus-Frank, M. E., & Buzas, J. S. (2017). Variation in performance of neonatal intensive care units in the United States. *JAMA Pediatrics*, *171*(3).

Iqbal, F., & Jameel, F. (2023). Development and evaluation of machine learning training strategies for neonatal mortality prediction using multicountry data. *Scientific Reports*, *15*, 12345. DOI: 10.1038/s41598-023-12345-6

Iqbal, F., Jameel, F., & Malik, A. (2023). Predictive analytics in smart healthcare for child mortality prediction in Pakistan. *Frontiers in Public Health*, *11*, 1035086. DOI: 10.3389/fpubh.2023.1035086

Mehrabi, N., Morstatter, F., Saxena, N., Lerman, K., & Galstyan, A. (2021). A survey on bias and fairness in machine learning. *ACM Computing Surveys*, *54*(6), 1–35. DOI: 10.1145/3457607

Memon, S. F., & Khan, W. A. (2020). Wearable technology for infant health monitoring: A survey. *IET Cyber-Systems and Robotics*, *2*(3), 124–134. https://ietresearch.onlinelibrary.wiley.com/doi/10.1049/iet-cds.2018.5447

Miotto, R., Wang, F., Wang, S., Jiang, X., & Dudley, J. T. (2018). Deep learning for healthcare: Review, opportunities, and challenges. *Briefings in Bioinformatics*, *19*(6), 1236–1246.

Obermeyer, Z., & Emanuel, E. J. (2016). Predicting the future—Big data, machine learning, and clinical medicine. *The New England Journal of Medicine*, *375*(13), 1216–1219. DOI: 10.1056/NEJMp1606181

Pandey, P., Singh, R., & Verma, A. (2025). Predicting child mortality determinants in Uttar Pradesh using machine learning algorithms. *Children and Youth Services Review*, *150*, 105156. DOI: 10.1016/j.childyouth.2023.105156

Sampathirao, A., Ramesh, P., & Kumar, S. (2025). Feature-Based Child Mortality Prediction Using Ensemble Learning Models. *Journal of Applied Science and Technology Trends*, *2*(4), 123–132. https://jastt.org/index.php/jasttpath/article/view/264

Sandvik, K. B. (2020). Wearables for something good: Aid, dataveillance and the Khushi baby wearable digital necklace for infants initially aimed at reducing child mortality. *Information Communication and Society*, *23*(9), 1283–1299. https://www.tandfonline.com/doi/full/10.1080/1369118X.2020.1753797

Topol, E. J. (2019). High-performance medicine: The convergence of human and artificial intelligence. *Nature Medicine*, *25*, 44–56. DOI: 10.1038/s41591-018-0300-7

Walter, J. R. Querrey-Simpson Institute of Bioelectronics, Northwestern University, & Collaborators. (2024). From lab to life: how wearable devices can improve health equity by monitoring neonatal vital signs in low-resource settings. Nature Communications. https://www.nature.com/articles/s41467-023-44634-9

Wang, W., Cheng, J., Song, W., & Shen, Y. (2022). The effectiveness of wearable devices as physical activity interventions for preventing and treating obesity in children and adolescents: Systematic review and meta-analysis. *JMIR mHealth and uHealth*, *10*(4), e36943. https://pmc.ncbi.nlm.nih.gov/articles/PMC9034426/

Chapter 12

# What to Wear From Here: Analyzing the Enforceability of Dress Codes in Work From Home Jobs

**Adwait Mitra**
https://orcid.org/0009-0008-9150-1498
*O.P. Jindal Global University, India*

**Bidisha Bandyopadhyay**
https://orcid.org/0009-0009-0569-2097
*O.P. Jindal Global University, India*

## ABSTRACT

*The Covid-19 pandemic disrupted global norms, revealing both systemic flaws and new efficiencies, chief among them the shift to remote work. As businesses moved online, traditional boundaries between public and private life, and fixed working hours blurred. While employees are expected to work toward organizational goals, remote settings call for a reassessment of rights and obligations of both the employer and employee, considering the nature and location of work. Dress codes, historically tied to professionalism, safety, and branding, are now being reexamined in light of evolving freedoms of religion and expression. Clothing, as a form of personal identity, gains stronger protection within one's home. As virtual workspaces become the norm, this article traces the jurisprudence behind the enforcement of dress codes and whether that enforcement holds valid in an online workplace.*

DOI: 10.4018/979-8-3373-8510-5.ch012

## INTRODUCTION

This association of efficiency with apparel is a historic one and now faces the challenge of the 'new-normal'. The Covid-19 Pandemic radically altered the world as we knew it, and within those alterations was the critical line separating an employee's *public life* and *private life*. The first challenge in the new world order was to decisively define the new normal workplace, with 'work from home' becoming the popular narrative. Certain workplaces have a tendency to regulate the conduct of their employees, from behaving in a certain way to being dressed *'appropriately'* for the job, be it the job's ethics or its goals. Strong examples of such cases would be the front-end workers like teachers, receptionists, and doctors.

The right to dress extends beyond just a choice of mere apparel; clothes are far more deep seated and seen as a form of expression and ideology by people, fuelling the 'you are, what you wear' narrative. Restricting its application by certain workplaces has ushered dissenting uproar. Dress codes and prescribing regulations to display faith and body modifications is often perceived as complex and sensitive by the employers (Nath et al., 2016). However, Courts have still upheld that certain workplaces are within their rights to conform to certain dress codes for their employees and place reasonable restrictions upon this freedom, as long as it furthers a fair and justifiable outcome from the job itself. The Employees Appeal Tribunal upheld in the case of *Azmi v. Kirklees Metropolitan Borough Council* (Azmi v Kirklees Metropolitan Borough Council, 2007) that requiring the removal of Muslim Lady's veil, one that covers her whole face except the eyes, did not account for direct or indirect discrimination against her on the grounds of violating her religion and belief; since the requirement was targeted at maximizing the legitimate aim of providing the best quality education for students in the classroom. Employers have multiple reasons to enforce dress codes, seeking to promote healthier and safer environments for employment, whilst furthering the brand image of the organization; but they must also ensure fairness, proportionate and non-discriminatory practices, all while also considering the employee's expectation of appearance standards and their inherent need to express identity. This fair and equitable justification for dress codes must account for various expectations that different employees come with.

These codes stood justified within the conventional confines of the workplace but in the aftermath of the pandemic, do they stand to be justified when extended to the homes of these employees? Workers bound by these codes have always been free to practice and express their beliefs and ideologies outside their workplaces and dismissals on such grounds have always been tagged as unfair dismissals. However, work from home as the prevalent narrative does not just raise the question on the extension of these codes to their public lives, it also extends to their private lives. With majority of work meetings happening over Microsoft teams and majority of classes happening over Zoom, can the extension of 'formal wear' and appropriate dressing be extended to applying on workers within the premises of their homes. This extension then raises three pertinent questions:

1. Does this infringe upon the worker's freedom of expression?
2. Does it infringe upon their right to private and family life?
3. Does this infringe upon the worker's freedom of thought, conscience and religion?

Across this piece, I aim to argue in favor of enforcing dress codes against employees working from home. Part I of this essay is a developmental analysis of dress codes establishing their need; and the legitimacy behind their basic idea in the first place. Part II identifies the parameters of a modern-day worker and their work boundaries, establishing when they fall within the ambit of working conditions and hours while working from home. The lack of candid scholarship on dress codes in the online era leads me to engage with the limitations of dress codes in Parts III, IV and V of the essay dealing with the above raised questions, especially the extent of their privacy rights when working from home, and then extrapolating its link with efficiency and visual perception during work, an argument then expanded to account for online work in the conclusion.

## I. WHY DRESS CODES?

Dress codes in workplaces are increasingly becoming an imperative issue with multiple high-profile cases, and a sense of uncertainty about what today constitutes an acceptable dress code or appearance norm. The concept of dress codes is not a modern one and dates back to around 400 BC; when Hippocrates advised a physician to be *"clean in person, well dressed; and anointed with sweet smelling unguents" (Brase & Taylor, 2004)*. Leading into the modern times, today there exist certain jobs that people simply associate with certain dresses, almost to be synonymous to one another. Any primary imagination of a doctor assumes the person to be draped in a white coat, or a police officer in dark uniform with a gun; or for a lawyer to be in a black gown. Not being dressed in them often leads to questions on credibility for the employees. One argues the benefits of dress codes to be adherence by the employee's appearance to the employer's image before customers, a sense of gravitas and professionalism attached with the job, and health and safety in the workplace; all under the overarching idea of organizational unity.

Klare on the other hand argues that the primary social function of such mandated appearance is to empower employers, school officials, judges and other authority figures to enforce the dominant expectations about appearance and discipline deviance from approved social norms. He further argued that it "suppresses cultural and religious diversity and enforces conformity with a white, heterosexual and Christian image of beauty and grooming", and also exploiting and repressing female sexuality; punishing them for departing from male-created expectations about 'proper female behavior and roles', inferring the hardline stance that such rules have no place in a democratic society committed to equality and diversity. (Klare, 1992)

These dress codes have become a uniform trend with a liner spread across the world, granting them the status of convention, being referred to as the '*conventional'* dress for people pursuing those employments. Dress code norms exist both as explicit and formal, and also as informal and implicit. These jobs are most often customer-facing and front-end jobs where the employee establishes a direct point of contact with the customer: where there is direct appearance of the employee before the customer, physically or virtually. In pursuit of this, these conventions may be divided into two categories serving as reasons for the implementation and acceptance of these dress codes. There are two broad categories of dress codes for employees: 1. That is for the convenience of the customers they face; and 2. For the convenience of the employee themself. The first category entails jobs like that of police officers, doctors, teachers, flight crew, etc. The dress code assigned to this category of employees exists for the convenience of those they serve to, albeit with different purposes. For employees like police officers, doctors and flight crew; the primary purpose can be argued to be the convenience of identification; an identification that eventually leads to better social order through acceptance of situational norms instructed by them, i.e., one will always have a greater tendency to follow the instructions of a police officer in public, than that of a common man. It can be argued that for this category of people, the dress code adds a layer of legitimacy to their employment. The second category of employment is where the prescribed dress code of the employee is for their own convenience and safety. These types of employment extend to that of builders, barbers, car mechanics, etc. The dress codes prescribed to such employees help facilitate them to carry out the due course of their employment; like the barber's apron to protect their clothes from residual hair, the builder's helmet to shield them from any damage and the mechanic's protective eye-wear for protection from sparks. Thus, the second category boasts of a dress code for the protection and facilitation of the employee themselves and not the particular customer they are serving.

An independent evidence-based research conducted by Dr. Vanadana Nath, Prof. Stephen Bach and Dr. Graeme Lockwood of King's College London (Nath et al., 2016) concluded that the majority of the respondents advocated a requirement to display a 'brand-congruent physical appearance' for their customers; especially those directly facing the employees, to show a sense of being professional or appearing appropriate. This professional and appropriate presentation eventually enhanced the credibility and 'trustworthiness' of the organization's product or services. An ancillary inference was that of what the service recipient or society in general found as acceptable associated with the product or services, opposed to unaesthetic or objectionable. They further noted a trend of the comprehensiveness of dress codes being directly proportional to the size of the organization; owing to the informal nature of labor practices across the smaller firms. The researchers' direct interaction with the heads of these organizations showed that dressing trends were not discussed as a part of the recruitment process but were mostly taken for granted, i.e.,potential employees were assumed to comply with the dressing standards of the company and industry by presenting a certain look. Training in appearance management was prevalent but limited to the larger firms where employees pursued a professionalism agenda with special stress on health and wellbeing. Special reference can however be made to the enforcement of dress codes strategy in these large firms: humor and informal conversations when the transgression against the norm was minor or happened for the first time; followed by more severe and formal processes against recurrent transgressions, such as disciplinary action.

The benefits argued by the employees were that it added to their self esteem and also that it enhanced favorable perceptions of the employees in roles with repetitive interactions with their customers, adding to their legitimacy and reducing client disengagement. Even though there was minor pushback from some in the sample space noting instances of discriminatory practices based on appearance, the majority argued in favor of accepting these dress codes. Employees subject to being typecast on occasion due to faith based appearance or body modifications, had a perceived sense of adjustment towards the prejudice; highlighting the trespassers to simply overcome the said biases, like concealing the unconventional identity marker, or simply choosing more inclusive workplaces.

The reasonableness of such codes, with reference to dresses was furthered by the Employment Appeals Tribunal in the *Azmi* case (Azmi v Kirklees Metropolitan Borough Council, 2007) stating their validity so long as it was to further a legitimate aim of the work itself. The primary intent of employers in these cases could be concisely restricted to their wish for their employees to look '*conventional*'. In the case of *Samantha Elauf, Equal Employment Opportunity Commission v. Abercrombie & Fitch Stores, Inc* (EEOC v. Abercrombie & Fitch Stores, 2015). The US Supreme Court was also a strong supporter of legitimate aims as a precursor to enforcing dress codes in workplaces; as it became a binding and persuasive precedent within its local jurisdiction and internationally. Samantha Elauf was denied employment by Abercrombie due to her religious headscarf violating the company's dress code and the EEOC sued the company on her behalf. The Apex Court of USA rejected the argument that Abercrombie had not violated Title VII of the Civil Rights Act of 1964 (Title VII of the Civil Rights Act of 1964) because Elauf had not shown

Abrecrombie actual knowledge of her accommodation. Title VII of the Act advocated that an employer cannot decline employment in an attempt to avoid accommodating the prospective employee's religious belief, unless the accommodation causes undue hardship to the employer. Further, the ambit of Title VII extended to include religion as both belief and practice. The Court held that the need for accommodation need only be a motivating factor in the employer's decision, i.e., an established obligation to accommodate; and not failure to offer employment on religious grounds, over "mere neutrality with regards to religious practices". This decision was upheld by an 8-1 majority in the Apex Court.

## I.A Legal Position on Dress Codes

The one thing common to all these different forms and occasions of employment is the employment contract signed between the employer and the potential employee. These contracts range over a varied array of clauses, from standard and fundamental clauses referring to deadlines, payment and incentive structures, to more norm based structures such as annual leaves and dress codes. Even though there is no direct hierarchy within an employment contract's obligations, violating some of the clauses, such as that of dress codes is potentially inferred to be less heinous than an employee stealing from the company's resources. A survey taken by an independent Human Resources group, *XpertHR,* in 2011 revealed that the majority of dress codes were contractual, followed by written guidelines and then verbal guidelines. (Chamberlain, 2011)

Employment contracts have themselves developed over the years, transforming the initial parent (employer) - child (employee) relationship to now a more adult contractual relation between two adults. The employer is not the sole force establishing the identity and worth of the employee, the employee himself has a great role to play in it. (Kissler, 1994) These contracts have an implicit hierarchy of rights and obligations existent within them, where some are considered to be 'fundamental' parts of the contract, i.e, violating them would usually lead to a termination of the employment. The other aspects usually lead to informal or formal warnings and subsequent disciplinary action. Dress codes are usually a part of the non-fundamental aspect of such contracts, i.e., their violations are usually treated with warnings and disciplinary actions. However, the argument against this is that a fundamental aspect of any employment contract is the employee's obedience to any lawful and reasonable demand of the employer. Thus, if an employer makes it known explicitly that dress codes form a fundamental aspect of the employment contract, and a breach of them could lead to termination of employment, such a view is said to be lawful and justified.

As long as enforcing a dress code is not directly violative of protected characteristics mentioned under Section 4 of the Equality Act, 2010, such as race, religion, sex, etc.; or is not in contravention of the ECHR or Section 3(1) of the Human Rights Act of 1998, there is not much legal recourse against it. (Nath et al., 2016) Courts have generally left this area unfettered leaving the employer to exercise discretion till the point that it does not contravene with anti-discrimination laws or the freedom of expression or religion. A tribunal is *Schmidt v. Austicks Bookshops Ltd (Schmidt v Austicks Bookshops Ltd, 1977),* held that an employer is entitled to a large scope for discretion in control over the image of his establishment, including appearance of their staff. As long as this discretion does not directly transgress with the abovementioned protected characteristics, and has a genuine and legitimate business interest to further, it is lawful for employers to enforce such dress codes.

## II. WORKPLACE BOUNDARIES

Workplaces today can manifest in a variety of settings; in the outdoors, inside an office or even remotely while traveling. Employers stress on the parameters of what constitutes a workplace since it has a massive impact on the efficiency and morale of the employees. The physical area where an employee is required to carry out their respective jobs vary with the type of job at hand, and the particular company or organization they are working for. These physical spaces are usually constrained to singular locations like a manager working in a particular restaurant, a doctor working in a hospital or a techie working around their workstation on a particular floor of a building. Sometimes, these workspaces apply to the employees vicariously, say a construction worker on a building for a different entity or so on. In total, the physical extent of the workplace has a huge impact on the kind of work the employee is doing, especially with regards to his safety and wellbeing. All these argue in favor of a spatial configuration where an employer is perceived to carry out the terms of his employment contract, i.e., a space for them to engage in work related tasks.

Professional and private lives have always been separated and compartmentalized with a fine line, most often restricting the first to the confines of the four physical walls of an office. Employees have agreed upon following certain rules within those four walls, regulating their conduct, appearance and work. Such rules of conduct are often more strictly observed with front-end workers: the customer-facing ones; reflective of the employer's image. However, with the advancement of technology and more informal work structures, this compartmentalization has seen spillovers more often than not. The European Court of Human Rights recognized this as "*blurring',* i.e., 'in a time when the dividing line between work life and private life has been blurred by technology, some employers allow the use of company-owned equipment for employees' personal use, whilst others allow their employees to use their own equipment for work-related matters and still other employers permit both". (Bărbulescu v Romania, 2016)

This distinction is imperative to keep up the work-life balance of employees. The pressures of work for the employed has been intensifying. The development of an information age has introduced with it, a need for fast and speedy communication with customers, attaching a near constant availability for employees before them. Evidence from the UK (which has the longest working hours in Europe) has shown that while the average working hours have not changed dramatically, those working more than 48 hours a week have increased over the past ten years; wherein people have reported a rise in the intensity of their work. "*In the community, there is growing concern that the quality of home and community life is deteriorating." (Guest, 2002)* With growing hours and pressure, evening and weekend work are becoming more frequent, hampering the overall quality of 'family time'.

Gragnano argues through the *segmentation theory* on work-life balance that private and professional lives are inherently divided by space, function and time, right from the industrial era (Gragnano et al., 2020). His understanding is that the physical and spatial demarcation between the two helps the worker prevent overlap and spillover between these two facets of his life. It argues that employees consciously hold back thoughts, emotions and action related to work while at home, and vice versa when at work, thereby establishing a fine line in relation to family and work; skilfully sorting their lives. (Piotrkowski, 1979) Maltby and Dushman best summarize this as an employee's intuition that between 'hours 9 to 5', the employee's life is not theirs, and that the situation is tolerable because the employee accepts to be working within the timeframe stipulated as their working hours (Maltby & Dushman, 1994). Further, the structural functionalism theory argues that a person's life, which is divided into two aspects: the productive aspect and the emotional aspect; has the required necessity of a separation between work life and private life for the productive aspect to adequately fuel the aid and creation of services or goods that the worker deals with. (Bello & Tanko, 2020) There is also a sense of tension between work and private life. One of the primary reasons that returning mothers, rejoining post maternity leave, have negative work experiences is born out of this tension developed over time. Employers are expected to see work as central to their lives, with the added burden to show this centrality by working longer hours, which extends to more 'face time' with their bosses and customers, by being ever available. (Dick, 2010)

## II.A The Modern Worker

To better understand the predicaments of work-life balance, it would be pertinent to first understand what it means to be a modern day worker, and the working hours that they must dedicate. With the advent of globalization and hyper-modernization in jobs, there has been a great rise in informal work cultures, with the conventional '9 to 5' job suffering radical changes in its crux. Workers today do not have fixed hours or locations to work around and have it upon themselves to complete a certain amount of work within stipulated time frames, having the luxury to choose these time periods across their day themselves, and according to the nature, also choose to carry them out from the comfort of their homes, or other mobile locations. The Working Time Directive (Council Directive 2003/88/EC, 2003) was key in keeping up with the changing demands of this avenue. Article 1(3) of the Directive gives it a huge scope stating that it applies to 'all sectors of activity'. The European Court of Justice further expanded its scope to even include Ambulance drivers in the Pfeiffer case (Pfeiffer v Deutsches Rotes Kreuz, 2004). However, a key critique to it was its lack of a precise definition for who constituted a worker, also noted by the ECJ in *Union Syndicale Solidaires Isere v. Premier Ministre* (Union syndicale Solidaires Isère v Premier ministre, 2010). The Court decided that a worker 'must be defined in accordance with objective criteria which distinguish the employment relationship by reference to the rights and duties of the person concerned (*para.29*). The court concluded with the definition that 'the essential feature of an employment relationship, however, is that for a certain period of time, a person performs services for and under the direction of another person in return for which he receives remuneration'(*para. 32)*. Thus, the court in this judgment upholds a sense of control beyond just the terms of the work that the employer recognizes over their employees, i.e., also a sense of 'how' the work should be done.

**Article 2(1)** is a primary instrument in keeping up with the modernizing work culture, as it gives an expansive definition to working time stating it to be 'any period during which the worker is working, at the employer's disposal and carrying out his activity or duties in accordance with national laws and/or practice' (Council Directive 2003/88/EC, 2003). It would be pertinent for the course of this paper to refer to the ECJ's judgment in the SIMAP case (Sindicato de Médicos de Asistencia Pública, 2000) in detail, concerning whether the 'on-call' status of doctors constituted working hours. The court held the on-call time spent by the doctor on the premises of the employer (i.e., the medical premises) definitely constituted working hours. However, if the doctor is simply allowed to be contactable, without being on their employment premises, only the time linked to primary care service is to be constituted to be working hours. The court's observation in this case is paramount as it held while in the latter case, the doctor was still at the disposal of their employer, ‘they manage their time with fewer constraints and pursue their own interests’. The further noted that ‘stand-by at home’ however did constitute working hours in the case of firefighters due to their eight minute response time to their employer, as it ‘significantly restricted his opportunity to do other things’ (para. 50). Thus, the extent to which the employer has a right over the employee in situations of remote work is a huge factor in determining whether the employer’s actions are being constituted under working hours. Employees have different sets of interests to pursue in their private lives and it is crucial to ask that while working from home, to what extent can an employer constraint such private pursuits.

This question becomes especially relevant in the post Covid-19 phase as countries across the world have seen a massive rise in people shifting their workspaces to within the confines of their homes, and occasional cafes. Phillipa Collins (Collins, 2020) noted that in sectors such as academia, administration and IT; only 5% of people worked mainly from home according to national statistics. However, to prevent the rapid spread of covid, these numbers skyrocketed to 44% of the surveyed people(Gibbs, 2020) accepting a pattern of working from home. Lockdowns across the world created an opportunity for advancing technology to prove its merit in providing its equipment to fill in the spatial gaps between an employer and their employees, with close monitoring by employers even while the employees potentially worked from across the globe. Collins further argues that while such remote monitoring equipment has existed for many years prior to the pandemic, there was a surge of about 71% in their purchase (equipment like HubStaff and ActivTrack) during the pandemic, according to one of her sources.

Thus, with the radically changing times, the line between private and work life has indeed blurred. There is a stark change in the work culture and people now have the active, and popular choice to work from the comforts of their homes. Employers usually have a significant say in how they expect their employees to carry out their daily schedules and engage with their work and client, but does this significant say translate in the same manner when employees choose to work from within their homes, do their workplace codes of conduct extend beyond the four walls of the office, to within the four walls of their homes?

## III. RIGHT TO RESPECT FOR PRIVATE & FAMILY LIFE

Privacy has been an intrinsic human right recognized and developed over the ages now. The origins of privacy lies in prohibiting intrusive state interference with our lives. In the case of employment, employers resist hiring on the basis of a potential employee’s actions committed in their private lives, or even dismissal on the same basis. Further, technological advancements have made surveillance possible at all times, and in a secret manner. Employers can also monitor communications via email, phone calls and social media. The basis for this is consent via employment contracts but if the same is left to an employer's interpretation, workplaces would tend to be totally devoid of privacy. (Collins et al., 2019)

Privacy and a private life is advocated as a part of the Universal Declaration of Human Right (Article 12), the European Convention on Human Rights (Article 8) and the European Charter of Fundamental Rights (Article 7). However, the ambit of what falls within a person's private life is not without discourse. One conventionally symbolizes another's private life to contain any actions they commit within the boundaries of their private properties but with the lines demarcating the actions being committed within private properties beyond just private actions, the scope of private lives is made wide open for nuanced discussion. The European Court of Human Rights noted in the case of *Niemietz v. Germany (Niemietz v Germany, 1992)*, that it did not consider it possible or even necessary to attempt for an exhaustive definition of private life. Further, it would be too restrictive to limit it to the notion of 'inner circle', the space in which an individual chooses to live their own personal life according to personal choice, and completely disregard the world not encompassed within this inner circle, i.e., it must reasonably account for a person's right to develop interpersonal relations with other people. Subsequently, the Court observed that there was no principle reason for this notion of private life to exclude professional or business activities as people experience the greatest opportunity to build relationships with the outside world during work. The ECtHR observed this view to be furthered by the notion that it is not always possible to distinguish between a man's activities and put it under the heading of private or professional life very distinctly. It concluded that thus especially in the case of a person exercising a liberal profession, their work in said context may become a part and parcel of their life to such a degree it becomes impossible to know in what capacity the person is acting at a given moment of time (para 27).

However, with the increasing integration of technology and surveillance into work, the extent of this surveillance raises quite the debate. Even when working from within the office, Ewing argues that an employer can have an expectation of a reasonable amount of privacy and cannot be under the notion of being surveilled by their employer at all times. He argues that the right of workers to form relationships with each other ought to be resistant to attempt to remove private spaces at work. It could go to the extent of requiring workers to be provided with locations or time periods when they can be sure that they are free from surveillance. He further argued that this conception of reasonable expectation is however easily overridden by management decisions (Ewing, 2000). To further add to the Niemetz judgment, the ECtHR upheld that privacy is not just confined to the home, it operates in a broader space and also protects a person's 'private social life', which a person utilizes to develop social bondings with the community. It could also extend to include the notion of professional activities as a part of private life. (Fernández Martínez v Spain, 2014)

There is a great deal discussed when applying these norms to a traditional workplace, but what becomes of it when the workplace is within the confines of a person's home, i.e.,there is a greater expectation of privacy. What a person chooses to wear within the confines of their homes can be reasonably inferred to be a matter protected within the right to a private life. Article 8(1) of the European Convention of Human Rights states that '*Everyone has the right to respect for his private and family life, his home and his correspondence*'. Even a naked eye reading of this provision understands the extra insulation that the life within a person's home is provided with respect to privacy, such that '*his home*' is mentioned as an integral part of the provision. It would thus be unfair to apply the same standards of behavior to a person working from home, as are applied over them during the course of their work being done from within their office space.

Sanders argues against such standardized expectation, in relation to dismissals, as held out definitively in *Foley v. Post Office (Foley v Post Office, 2000),* and further upheld as fair in the four leading unfair dismissal cases in the UK (Sanders, 2014). Sanders argues that an employer's behavior outside of work is their own business, and that the employer should not be subject to similar scrutiny as they are during their office presence, contravening which would lead to their eventual dismissal. Even though the US has seen a rise in such dismissals based on the doctrine of vicarious liability, the UK has not followed at a similar rate (Davidson, 1998).

However, the modern problems faced during work from home face the harsh critique of not being distinguished entirely as either behavior outside of work, or within work. In terms of privacy, this creates a special set with the convergence of two spaces which have historically been distinct, with different sets of priorities and standards. In the workspace, even though the employee's interests are protected under Article 8, the employer's managerial discretion and business interests play a significant role (Collins et al., 2019). On one hand, employees are continuing in the pursuit set out by their employers, but on the other hand, can home be considered to be brought under the ambit and scope of a 'workplace', as the degree to which an employee can pursue their own interests, as laid down in the SIMAP (Collins, 2020) case is up for discourse.

Thus, reading Ewing's argument along with the SIMAP judgment, it would be a reasonable inference to demand distinction between what constitutes working hours from home and what does not. When facing customers during working hours, when there is a genuine business interest at stake, it would be justifiable to enforce dress codes: as even though the workers are within the confines of their homes, they are still under working hours, i.e., they are being paid for their time, and above all else, they are under some form of supervision or visual contact with the customer via video cameras. So, while the employee is in direct contact with their customer and there is visual contact, it would only stand to be lawful that dress codes are enforceable as the employer stands to gain a legitimate business advantage from their employee's visual appeal to their customers. With this established, it would be pertinent to now refer to certain safeguards and protected characteristics from enforcement of dress codes.

## IV. FREEDOM OF THOUGHT, CONSCIENCE AND RELIGION

**Article 9** of the ECHR advocates for everyone's right to thought, conscience and religion: to be able to practice, teach and observe it. Article 9(2) further stipulates limitations prescribed by law on a person's manifestation of their religion with respect to public order and safety in a democratic society. This provision gives the freedom to a person to practice and manifest their religion freely, especially within their private spaces. Dress codes are especially associated with freedom of religion as multiple religious ways of life prescribe certain appropriate clothing while practicing them, eg: hijabs/headscarves in Islam, turbans in Sikhism, etc.

Courts have been protective of this freedom when adjudicating over cases of dress code violations in the workplace, ordering against direct/indirect discrimination over protected attributes. In the case of *Malik v. British Home Stores*[1]*(Malik v British Home Stores, 1980),* the Employment tribunal upheld the complaint that the company's act to prohibit Malik, a Muslim woman, from wearing trousers to work constituted indirect discrimination. Similarly, in *Singh v. Great Manchester Police,* the tribunal ruled against the GMP and considered their act of telling Singh to remove his turban during riot training to amount to indirect discrimination. Murray Creevy, J. (Brase & Taylor, 2004) stated "*it is appropriate to recommend the GMP should amend its uniform and equipment policy to take into account the race and religious requirements of Sikh officers, which should come into force in due course*".

In *Noah v. Desrosiers (Noah v Desrosiers, 2008),* a Muslim woman was not hired by the respondent, for the position of a stylist at a hair salon, because of her headscarf; who had cleared that none of her employees would be allowed to cover their hair, as it was inconsistent with her business. The claimant claimed direct and indirect discrimination, of which only the claim of indirect discrimination was upheld. The tribunal held that the salon owner had a legitimate claim, which prohibited it from being a case of direct discrimination; but her practice was not a proportionate means to achieve it, amounting it to indirect discrimination. The landmark case of *Eweida v. British Airways plc. (Eweida v British Airways, 2010),* clarified that the law protects those forms of religious manifestations that are accepted as mandatory by their general practice and scriptures. The employment tribunal held that Ms.

Eweida, who had refused to conceal a crucifix in her necklace was not unjustly sent on unpaid leave as the crucifix in her apparel was by personal choice and not mandated by Christian scriptures, and thus could be made to be concealed at her employer's discretion. However, this view was overturned by a 5-2 majority of the ECtHR which held that in the balance between Eweida's religious manifestation and BA's corporate image, the tribunal had given too much weight to the latter. It further stated that a small crucifix on Eweida's apparel could not have deterred much from her corporate image and that there were no previous instances when wearing a cross had detracted BA from its corporate image (Eweida v United Kingdom, 2013).

Thus, a similar stance applies to adding legitimacy to dress codes, even when viewed from the lens of freedom of religion: as long as the employer does not violate protected characteristics of the employee (under the Equality Act or ECHR), dress codes are consistent, if backed by a lawful claim. The employee's choice of religious manifestation and the employer's corporate image need to be weighed equally, and it must then be decided if the religious manifestation indeed creates a detrimental effect over the corporate image. Sam Middlemiss argues that employers should balance between the underlying reasoning for imposition of a dress code and the eventual negative impact that is likely to be suffered by the employee. Such codes are carefully considered by employment tribunals and other legal bodies and only the ones with genuine business or safety claims are acceptable; subsequent to consideration of other alternatives. Such policies should be adequately communicated beforehand, and their negative outcomes be highlighted (Middlemiss, 2018).

## V. FREEDOM OF EXPRESSION

A person's choice on what to wear goes beyond just a mere choice of convenient apparel, it can be said to be reflective of their ideology and beliefs. People see their dresses as an extension of their personality and thought, and it forms a basis of their expression, from *blending in* to *standing out.* This expression may be impacted by a variety of things, ranging from historic ideologies, to modern trends. These have developed even further due to the creation of various cultures and subcultures like punk, goth, and more. Charles Wynn-Evanns argues that appropriate work wear is as affected by fashion trends and economic circumstances, as by legal developments, a pertinent example being the variance of what is considered to be business casual across regions and time. (Wynn-Evans, 2008)

**Article 10** of the ECHR lays down the freedom of expression subjecting it to similar limitations of law in democratic society pertaining to territorial integrity, public safety and others.

Courts have been historically protective of this freedom. Even though not directly qualifying as a case of curtailing expression in the workplace, the US Supreme Court in *Tinker v. Des Moines Community School District* (Tinker v Des Moines Independent Community School District, 1969) ruled that school students do not shed their constitutional rights to freedom of speech and expression at the school's gate and that such limitations can only be imposed if it substantially and materially interferes with the school's daily operations. This happened in the wake of students wearing black armbands to school, in protest of the US involvement in the Vietnam War.

Sklar and DeLong identify a cognitive strain known as *appearance labor* (Sklar & DeLong, 2012)- where the employee gives up a degree of expression to better fit in with the company's image, usually owing to the company's dress code policy. They establish an inverse relationship between appearance labor and quality of work, since said employees are unable to be their authentic self at work. (Powell, 2020)

A tribunal in *Boychuk v. HJ Symons Holidays*[2] *(Boychuk v H. J. Symons Holdings Ltd, 1977)* upheld it to be a fair dismissal when an employer dismissed his employee after having previously warned his employee about wearing a badge stating '*lesbians ignite'*. The decision to dismiss was considered to be a reasonable response as the employee had direct public contact and such direct interactions had the potential to create uproar with its controversial view, and also damage the company's corporate reputation and image. Thus, there is a reasonable restriction ever-present to curtail the absoluteness some might associate with their freedom to expression.

The main argument raised against freedom of expression is the enforcement of some companies to make their employees look 'conventional'. However, in *Smith v. Safeway* (Smith v Safeway plc, 1996) the Court of Appeal upheld the decision of the industrial tribunal reiterating that Mr. Smith's dismissal from Safeway, a well-known supermarket chain, for having kept a ponytail hairstyle, was not discriminatory on the grounds that Safeway's dress policy allowed women to have shoulder-length hair but forbade women from the same. Legatt, Peter Gibson and Phillips, LJJ, held that '*an appearance code that applies a standard of what is conventional applies an even-handed approach between men and women, and not one which is discriminatory'*. They further stated that a conventional standard of appearance is the appropriate criterion to be applied when considering whether a requirement operates unfavorably to any of the sexes. This was concluded with due consideration to the fact that Safeway was a competitive supermarket chain and that its enforcement of its conventional and well-groomed employees added to a legitimate business interest of better customer retention and relations.

Thus, the legal position empowers employers to enforce a conventional standard of appearance if it aims to further a legitimate business interest and does not contravene against a protected attribute. It even further establishes that such codes may not be equal for different sexes and the true test for discrimination lies in whether there is less favorable treatment to any of them.

## VI. CONCLUSION – ONLINE APPLICATION

In the new-normal world, with a huge number of jobs going online, the model of conducting said businesses have changed, but the values and nuances associated with it remain intact. The most important factor to be considered here is the primary tool of video being used during working hours – the employer is visible before the customers, and they have the luxury of developing a perception about the employer through what they look like. For instance, when a student attends a virtual class, they are still part of a virtual classroom where they are expected to behave in a certain way, even though the modes of achieving such behavior have changed. The students still see the teacher present and conducting the class, and the teacher's dress does go a long way in adding a sense of professionalism and gravity to their status, especially for younger students. Drawing from the *Azmi case*, it is the genuine purpose of best quality education that needs to be considered. Even though the place of occurrence has shifted from a physical classroom to a zoom or meets link, the purpose of the time spent attending is still education and its associated impacts. Video-consultations provided by doctors have a similar impact where being able to perceive a doctor in professional and conventional ways is likely to put the patient's mind at greater ease.

Online platforms such as Zoom, Meets and Skype have significantly tried to make their online experiences as real as possible, by extension - offline oriented, by introducing features such as 'raise hand', 'pin someone's video' and so on. The significant shift to online was brought around due to necessity but these popular companies have tried to introduce features to shift it as further back to as normal as possible via these features. Thus, even when the customer facing aspects of some of these occupations are being carried out online, the purpose behind them is the same. The customers are still having a visual and spatial perception of the employer in front of them, and this greatly contributes to their legitimacy and gravitas, that a customer develops when seeing them in real life. The employer is still a representative of the business and its interests, adding to the professionalism associated with the job, and a sense of organizational unity. Most professional meetings during the online era have been lawfully and correctly carried out in proper dress code thus, as the visual perception of employees is still vital to the meetings. Employees have gone to the extent of being dressed professionally in the top half, i.e., wearing the likes of a shirt and business jacket over pajamas. This keeps up the professional image of the employee through whatever is visible of them on screen, while also having the comfort of home clothes. This only adds to the argument that they are perceived as lawful even when working from home, since they can be seen on live video.

Thus, so long as the employer's enforcement of certain dress codes is not in contravention to the protected characteristics stipulated under the Equality Act, European Convention of Human Rights or the Human Rights Act; and exists to forward a legitimate business interest during their working hours from home, it is considered to be lawful. The same principle should apply to the employers working from home as well. If a certain employer's dress code is considered to be lawful for enforcement, it should extend to their employees who are working from home for the duration of their working hours, which play a significant role here. To the extent that the employer's work is being considered as a part of their working hours, and they are facing customers or organizational members where there is a scope to genuinely further legitimate business interests via their dress codes, i.e., there is a legitimate purpose to those dress codes: they should be considered justified and legal.

## REFERENCES


Azmi v Kirklees Metropolitan Borough Council [2007] IRLR 484 (EAT).

Bărbulescu v Romania, App. No. 61496/08, [2016] IRLR 235 (ECHR).

Bello, Z., & Tanko, G. I. (2020). Review of work-life balance theories. *GATR Global Journal of Business and Social Science Review*, *8*(4), 217–227. DOI: 10.35609/gjbssr.2020.8.4(3) PMID: 29345694

Boychuk v H. J. Symons Holdings Ltd [1977] IRLR 395 (EAT).

Brase, G. L., & Taylor, J. (2004). The white-coat effect: Physician attire and perceived authority, friendliness, and attractiveness. *Journal of Applied Social Psychology*, *34*(12), 2469–2481. DOI: 10.1111/j.1559-1816.2004.tb01987.x

Chamberlain, L. (2011, April 4). Employers ensure dress codes do not discriminate. Personnel Today. https://www.personneltoday.com/hr/employers-ensure-dress-codes-do-not-discriminate/

Collins, H., Ewing, K. D., & McColgan, A. (2019). *Labour law* (2nd ed.). Cambridge University Press.

Collins, P. (2020, September 3). The right to privacy, surveillance-by-software and the "home-workplace". UK Labour Law Blog. https://uklabourlawblog.com

Council Directive 2003/88/EC, of 4 November 2003 concerning certain aspects of the organisation of working time, 2003 O.J. (L 299) 9.

Davidson, J. E. (1998). Reconciling the tension between employer liability and employee privacy. *George Mason University Civil Rights Law Journal*, *8*(2), 145–170.

Dick, P. (2010). The transition to motherhood and part-time working: Mutuality and incongruence in the psychological contracts existing between managers and employees. *Work, Employment and Society*, *24*(3), 508–525. DOI: 10.1177/0950017010371648

Equal Employment Opportunity Commission v. Abercrombie & Fitch Stores, Inc., 575 U.S. 768 (2015).

Eweida v United Kingdom, App. No. 48420/10, [2013] ECHR 37.

Ewing, K. D. (2000). *Human rights at work.* Institute of Employment Rights.

Fernández Martínez v Spain, App. No. 56030/07, ECHR 2014.

Foley v Post Office [2000] ICR 1283 (CA).

Gibbs, C. (2020, May 7). Coronavirus, the UK economy and society, faster indicators. Office for National Statistics. https://www.ons.gov.uk/peoplepopulationandcommunity/healthandsocialcare/conditionsanddiseases/bulletins/coronavirustheukeconomyandsocietyfasterindicators/7may2020

Gragnano, A., Simbula, S., & Miglioretti, M. (2020). Work–life balance: Weighing the importance of work–family and work–health balance. *International Journal of Environmental Research and Public Health*, *17*(3), 907. Advance online publication. DOI: 10.3390/ijerph17030907 PMID: 32024155

Guest, D. E. (2002). Perspectives on the study of work-life balance. *Social Sciences Information. Information Sur les Sciences Sociales*, *41*(2), 255–279. DOI: 10.1177/0539018402041002005

Kissler, G. D. (1994). The new employment contract. *Human Resource Management*, *33*(3), 335–352. DOI: 10.1002/hrm.3930330304

Klare, K. E. (1992). Power/dressing: Regulation of employee appearance. *New England Law Review*, *26*, 1395–1436.

Malik v British Home Stores [1980] ET Case No. 2901/79.

Maltby, L. L., & Dushman, B. J. (1994). Whose life is it anyway—Employer control of off-duty behavior. *Saint Louis University Public Law Review*, *13*, 645–671.

Middlemiss, S. (2018). Not what to wear? Employers' liability for dress codes? *International Journal of Discrimination and the Law*, *18*(1), 40–58. DOI: 10.1177/1358229118757867

Nath, V., Bach, S., & Lockwood, G. (2016). Dress codes and appearance at work: Body supplements, body modification and aesthetic labour (Research Paper Ref: 07/16). Acas. https://archive.acas.org.uk/media/4566/Dress-codes-and-appearance-at-work-Body-supplements-body-modification-and-aesthetic-labour/pdf/Dress_codes_and_appearance_at_work.pdf

Niemietz v Germany, App. No. 13710/88, 16 EHRR 97 (1992).

Noah v Desrosiers t/a Wedge [2008] ET Case No. 2201867/07.

Pfeiffer v Deutsches Rotes Kreuz, Joined Cases C-397/01 to C-403/01, [2004] ECR I-8835.

Piotrkowski, C. S. (1979). *Work and the family system: A naturalistic study of working-class and lower-middle-class families*. Collier Macmillan.

Powell, C. (2020). From business suit to business beanie: Dress code, personality, and job satisfaction in the workplace [Master's thesis, Xavier University]. Xavier University Theses and Dissertations.

Sanders, A. (2014). The law of unfair dismissal and behaviour outside work. *Legal Studies*, *34*(2), 328–352. DOI: 10.1111/lest.12023

Schmidt v Austicks Bookshops Ltd [1977] IRLR 360 (EAT).

Sindicato de Médicos de Asistencia Pública (SIMAP) v Conselleria de Sanidad y Consumo de la Generalidad Valenciana, Case C-303/98, [2000] ECR I-7963.

Sklar, M., & DeLong, M. (2012). Punk dress in the workplace: Aesthetic expression and accommodation. *Clothing & Textiles Research Journal*, *30*(4), 285–301. DOI: 10.1177/0887302X12467848

Smith v Safeway plc [1996] IRLR 456 (CA).

Tinker v Des Moines Independent Community School District, 393 U.S. 503 (1969).

Title VII of the Civil Rights Act of 1964, 42 U.S.C. § 2000e et seq.

Union syndicale Solidaires Isère v Premier ministre, Case C-428/09, [2010] ECR I-9961.

Wynn-Evans, C. (2008). Discrimination what not to wear—Ongoing UK case law developments on dress codes. *Bloomberg European Business Law Review*, *2*(110), 110–116.

## ADDITIONAL READING

Azmi v Kirklees Metropolitan Borough Council [2007] IRLR 484 (EAT).

Bărbulescu v Romania, App. No. 61496/08, [2016] IRLR 235 (ECHR).

Bello, Z., & Tanko, G. I. (2020). Review of work-life balance theories. *GATR Global Journal of Business and Social Science Review*, *8*(4), 217–227. DOI: 10.35609/gjbssr.2020.8.4(3) PMID: 29345694

Boychuk v H.J. Symons Holdings Ltd [1977] IRLR 395 (EAT).

Brase, G. L., & Taylor, J. (2004). The white-coat effect: Physician attire and perceived authority, friendliness, and attractiveness. *Journal of Applied Social Psychology*, *34*(12), 2469–2481. DOI: 10.1111/j.1559-1816.2004.tb01987.x

Case C-303/98, Sindicato de Médicos de Asistencia Pública (SIMAP) v Conselleria de Sanidad y Consumo de la Generalidad Valenciana [2000] ECR I-7963.

Case C-428/09, Union syndicale Solidaires Isère v Premier ministre [2010] ECR I-9961.

Chamberlain, L. (2011, April 4). Employers ensure dress codes do not discriminate. Personnel Today. https://www.personneltoday.com/hr/employers-ensure-dress-codes-do-not-discriminate/

Charter of Fundamental Rights of the European Union. Pub. L. No. C 303/02 (2000). https://eur-lex.europa.eu/legal-content/EN/TXT/?uri=CELEX:32000X1218(01)

Collins, H., Ewing, K. D., & McColgan, A. (2019). *Labour law* (2nd ed.). Cambridge University Press.

Collins, P. (2016, September 3). The right to privacy, surveillance-by-software and the "home-workplace". UK Labour Law Blog. https://uklabourlawblog.com

Council Directive 2003/88/EC, of 4 November 2003 concerning certain aspects of the organisation of working time, 2003 O.J. (L 299) 9.

Davidson, J. E. (1998). Reconciling the tension between employer liability and employee privacy. *George Mason University Civil Rights Law Journal, 8*(2), 145–170.

Dick, P. (2010). The transition to motherhood and part-time working: Mutuality and incongruence in the psychological contracts existing between managers and employees. *Work, Employment and Society, 24*(3), 508–525. DOI: 10.1177/0950017010371648

Equal Employment Opportunity Commission v. Abercrombie & Fitch Stores, Inc., 575 U.S. 768 (2015).

Equality Act. 2010, c. 15 (UK). https://www.legislation.gov.uk/ukpga/2010/15/contents

European Convention on Human Rights, Nov. 4, 1950, E.T.S. 5.

Eweida v United Kingdom, App. No. 48420/10, [2013] ECHR 37.

Ewing, K. D. (2000). *Human rights at work.* Institute of Employment Rights.

Fernández Martínez v Spain, App. No. 56030/07, [2014] ECHR 615 (GC).

Foley v Post Office [2000] ICR 1283 (CA).

Gibbs, C. (2020, May 7). Coronavirus, the UK economy and society, faster indicators. Office for National Statistics. https://www.ons.gov.uk/peoplepopulationandcommunity/healthandsocialcare/conditionsanddiseases/bulletins/coronavirustheukeconomyandsocietyfasterindicators/7may2020

Gragnano, A., Simbula, S., & Miglioretti, M. (2020). Work–life balance: Weighing the importance of work–family and work–health balance. *International Journal of Environmental Research and Public Health*, *17*(3), 907. Advance online publication. DOI: 10.3390/ijerph17030907 PMID: 32024155

Guest, D. E. (2002). Perspectives on the study of work-life balance. *Social Sciences Information. Information Sur les Sciences Sociales*, *41*(2), 255–279. DOI: 10.1177/0539018402041002005

Human Rights Act. 1998, c. 42 (UK). https://www.legislation.gov.uk/ukpga/1998/42/contents

Joined Cases C-397/01 to C-403/01, Pfeiffer v Deutsches Rotes Kreuz, Kreisverband Waldshut eV [2004] ECR I-8835.

Kissler, G. D. (1994). The new employment contract. *Human Resource Management*, *33*(3), 335–352. DOI: 10.1002/hrm.3930330304

Klare, K. E. (1992). Power/dressing: Regulation of employee appearance. *New England Law Review*, *26*, 1395–1436.

Malik v British Home Stores [1980] ET Case No. 2901/79.

Maltby, L. L., & Dushman, B. J. (1994). Whose life is it anyway—Employer control of off-duty behavior. *Saint Louis University Public Law Review*, *13*, 645–671.

Middlemiss, S. (2018). Not what to wear? Employers' liability for dress codes? *International Journal of Discrimination and the Law*, *18*(1), 40–58. DOI: 10.1177/1358229118757867

Nath, V., Bach, S., & Lockwood, G. (2016, September). Dress codes and appearance at work: Body supplements, body modification and aesthetic labour (Research Paper Ref: 06/16). Acas. https://www.acas.org.uk/dress-codes-and-appearance-at-work-body-supplements-body-modification-and-aesthetic-labour

Niemietz v Germany, App. No. 13710/88, 16 EHRR 97 (1992).

Noah v Desrosiers t/a Wedge [2008] ET Case No. 2201867/07.

Piotrkowski, C. S. (1979). *Work and the family system: A naturalistic study of working-class and lower-middle-class families*. Collier Macmillan.

Powell, C. (2020). From business suit to business beanie: Dress code, personality, and job satisfaction in the workplace [Master's thesis, Xavier University]. Xavier University Theses and Dissertations.

Sanders, A. (2014). The law of unfair dismissal and behaviour outside work. *Legal Studies*, *34*(2), 328–352. DOI: 10.1111/lest.12023

Schmidt v Austicks Bookshops Ltd [1977] IRLR 360 (EAT).

Sklar, M., & DeLong, M. (2012). Punk dress in the workplace: Aesthetic expression and accommodation. *Clothing & Textiles Research Journal*, *30*(4), 285–301. DOI: 10.1177/0887302X12467848

Smith v Safeway plc [1996] IRLR 456 (CA).

Tinker v Des Moines Independent Community School District, 393 U.S. 503 (1969).

Title VII of the Civil Rights Act of 1964, 42 U.S.C. § 2000e et seq.

United Nations General Assembly. (1948, December 10). Universal Declaration of Human Rights (217 [III] A). https://www.un.org/en/about-us/universal-declaration-of-human-rights

Wynn-Evans, C. (2008). Discrimination what not to wear—Ongoing UK case law developments on dress codes. *Bloomberg European Business Law Review*, *2*(110), 110–116.

## ENDNOTES

1 [1980] ET/2901/79

2 [1977] IRLR 395, EAT

# Compilation of References


Abella, J., & Rosa, E. D. (2023). Digital Literacy and Digital Competence of Selected Filipino Teachers: Basis for a Post-Pandemic Pedagogy.

Acquah, E., Ganapati, S., & Choi, Y.-J. (2024). *Examining the effects of California Consumer Privacy Act (CCPA) on Organizational Data Breach Notification*. https://doi.org/DOI: 10.1145/3657054.3657082

Aday, T. (2015). *The Effectiveness of the Violence against Women Act (VAWA) in Creating System-Level Change*. ScholarWorks@GVSU. https://scholarworks.gvsu.edu/spnhareview/vol11/iss1/3/

Adler, J., Lenski, M., Tolios, A., Taie, S. F., Sopic, M., Rajdl, D., & Biemann, R. (2023). Digital competence in laboratory medicine. *Journal of Laboratory Medicine*, *47*(4), 143–148.

Ahmad, J. (2019). Branding corporate social responsibility: A case study on public-listed telecommunication companies in malaysia. *Media Watch*, *10*(2). Advance online publication. DOI: 10.15655/mw/2019/v10i2/49638

Ahmad, R., Mehmood, S. T., & Ijaz, S. (2023). Digital Literacy Competencies: A Study of Distance Learners of Higher Education Regulatory Authority Khyber Pakhtunkhwa. *Pakistan Journal of Distance and Online Learning*, *9*(1), 82–96.

Ahmed, Z. S., & Shaheen, F. (2024). The evolution of human rights in the digital age. *Al-Anfal*, *2*(1), 8–15.

Ahuja, K. (2025, March 29). *European Union Deforestation Regulation (EUDR)*. Bhatt & Joshi Associates; Bhatt & Joshi Associates. https://bhattandjoshiassociates.com/regulation-of-emerging-technologies-legal-challenges-in-the-integration-of-ai-and-blockchain-into-indian-cyber-law/

Aizenberg, E., & van den Hoven, J. (2020). Designing for human rights in AI. *Big Data & Society*, *7*(2). Advance online publication. DOI: 10.1177/2053951720949566

Akpan, J. U., & Oluwagbade, O. I. (2024). Social and Environmental Responsibility in Accounting: Beyond Financial Metrics. *INTERNATIONAL JOURNAL OF SOCIAL SCIENCES AND MANAGEMENT RESEARCH, 9*(9). Advance online publication. DOI: 10.56201/ijssmr.v9.no9.2023.pg163.188

Al Khateeb, A. A. M. (2017). Measuring Digital Competence and ICT Literacy: An Exploratory Study of In-Service English Language Teachers in the Context of Saudi Arabia. *International Education Studies, 10*(12), 38–51.

Ala-Mutka, K. (2011). *Mapping digital competence: Towards a conceptual understanding*. Institute for Prospective Technological Studies.

Ala-Mutka, K., Punie, Y., & Redecker, C. (2008). Digital competence for lifelong learning. *Institute for Prospective Technological Studies (IPTS), European Commission, Joint Research Centre. Technical Note: JRC, 48708*, 271–282.

Alarcón, R., Del Pilar Jiménez, E., & de Vicente-Yagüe, M. I. (2020). Development and validation of the DIGIGLO, a tool for assessing the digital competence of educators. *British Journal of Educational Technology, 51*(6), 2407–2421.

Aleke, N. T. (2024). The Role of Cybersecurity Legislation in Promoting Data Privacy. *Advances in Information Security, Privacy, and Ethics Book Series*, 205–244. https://doi.org/DOI: 10.4018/979-8-3373-0588-2.ch008

Alhorr, L., Malik, A., Javed, A., Naz, N., & Nisa, N. 2024. Empowered or Undermined? Women Entrepreneurs & the Digital Economy. *Cherie Blair Foundation.* https://cherieblairfoundation.org/wp-content/uploads/2025/03/Empowered-or-Undermined-Women-Entrepreneurs-Digital-Economy.pdf

Al-Kfairy, M., Alrabaee, S., Alfandi, O., Mohamed, A. T., & Khaddaj, S. (2025). Navigating ethical dimensions in the metaverse: Challenges, frameworks, and solutions. *IEEE Access : Practical Innovations, Open Solutions.*

Allard-Tremblay, Y., & Coburn, E. (2023). The flying heads of settler colonialism; or the ideological erasures of indigenous peoples in political theorizing. *Political Studies, 71*(2), 359–378.

Allen, D., Hubbard, S., Lim, W., Stanger, A., Wagman, S., Zalesne, K., & Omoakhalen, O. (2025). A roadmap for governing AI: Technology governance and power-sharing liberalism. *AI and Ethics, 5*(3), 3355–3377.

Alvarado García, A., Young, A. L., & Dombrowski, L. (2017). On making data actionable: How activists use imperfect data to foster social change for human rights violations in Mexico. *Proceedings of the ACM on Human-Computer Interaction, 1*(CSCW), 1-19.

Amdam, S., Kobberstad, L. R., & Tikkanen, T. I. (2022). Professional digital competence in strategy and management: A case study of three teacher education programs in Norway. *Nordic Journal of Digital Literacy*, (1), 16–30.

Anderson, B., & Wood, M. A. (2022). Harm Imbrication and Virtualised Violence: Reconceptualising the Harms of Doxxing. *International Journal for Crime. Justice and Social Democracy*, *11*(1), 196–209. DOI: 10.5204/ijcjsd.2140

Anderson, J. E. (2015). Indigenous knowledge and intellectual property rights. In *International Encyclopaedia of the Social & Behavioral Sciences* (2nd ed., pp. 769–778). Elsevier Inc.

Andreasen, J. K., Tømte, C. E., Bergan, I., & Kovac, V. B. (2022). Professional digital competence in initial teacher education: An examination of differences in two cohorts of pre-service teachers. *Nordic Journal of Digital Literacy*, (1), 61–74.

Angwin, J., Larson, J., Mattu, S., & Kirchner, L. (2016). *Machine bias: There's software used across the country to predict future criminals. And it's biased against blacks*. ProPublica.

ANROWS - Australia's National Research Organisation for Women's Safety. (2022, August 7). *Technology-facilitated abuse: Extent, nature and responses in the Australian community - ANROWS - Australia's National Research Organisation for Women's Safety*. https://www.anrows.org.au/project/technology-facilitated-abuse-extent-nature-and-responses-in-the-australian-community/

Anurogo, D., La Ramba, H., Putri, N. D., & Putri, U. M. P. (2023). Digital Literacy 5.0 to enhance multicultural education. *Multicultural Islamic Education Review*, *1*(2), 109–179.

Anwar, G. A., Hussain, M., Akber, M. Z., Khan, M. A., & Khan, A. A. (2023). Sustainability-Oriented Optimization and Decision Making of Community Buildings under Seismic Hazard. *Sustainability (Switzerland)*, *15*(5). Advance online publication. DOI: 10.3390/su15054385

Aranda, M., García-Domingo, M., Montes-Berges, B., & Fuentes, V. (2022). Variables contributing to the awareness of online gendered violence: Focus on observers. *Social Media + Society*, *8*(4). Advance online publication. DOI: 10.1177/20563051221141857

Arsenault, D., & Beaulieu, C. (2023). Augmented Reality for Documenting and Showcasing Indigenous Cultural Heritage. *Journal on Computing and Cultural Heritage*, *16*(3), 45–60.

Arvianto, F., & St, Y, S. (2023). Designing an Instrument to Measure Digital Literacy Competence Using the 4D Model. *International Journal of Instruction*, *16*(4), 845–860.

Asakawa, K. (2017). Family socialization practices and their effects on the internalization of educational values for Asian and White American adolescents. In *Conditions for Optimal Development in Adolescence* (pp. 184–194). Psychology Press.

Atmojo, I. R. W., Ardiansyah, R., & Adi, F. P. (2023). The Level of Classroom Teacher Digital Literacy in the Technology Dimension of the Instant Digital Competence Assessment (IDCA). In *Elementary School Forum (Mimbar Sekolah Dasar)* (Vol. 10, No. 1, pp. 165-180).

Atmojo, I. R. W., Ardiansyah, R., & Wulandari, W. (2022). Classroom Teacher's Digital Literacy Level Based on Instant Digital Competence Assessment (IDCA) Perspective. In *Elementary School Forum (Mimbar Sekolah Dasar)* (Vol. 9, No. 3, pp. 431-445). Indonesia University of Education.

Auer, A., Von Below, J., Nahuelhual, L., Mastrangelo, M., Gonzalez, A., Gluch, M., & Paruelo, J. (2020). The role of social capital and collective actions in natural capital conservation and management. *Environmental Science & Policy*, *107*, 168–178.

Ayres-de-Campos, D., Spong, C. Y., & Chandraharan, E. (2015). FIGO consensus guidelines on intrapartum fetal monitoring: Cardiotocography. *International Journal of Gynaecology and Obstetrics: the Official Organ of the International Federation of Gynaecology and Obstetrics*, *131*(1), 13–24. DOI: 10.1016/j.ijgo.2015.06.020

Azmi v Kirklees Metropolitan Borough Council [2007] IRLR 484 (EAT).

Baer, R. J., Rogers, E. E., Partridge, J. C., Anderson, J. G., Morris, M., Kuppermann, M., Franck, L. S., Rand, L., & Jelliffe-Pawlowski, L. L. (2016). Population-based risks of mortality and preterm morbidity by gestational age and birth weight. *Journal of Perinatology*, *36*(11), 1008–1013.

Ball, P., Spirer, H. F., Spirer, L., & American Association for the Advancement of Science (AAAS) Science and Human. (2000). Making the Case: Investigating Large Scale Human Rights Violations Using Information Systems and. In *American Association for the Advancement of Science*.

Ballano, V. O., Mallari, N. T., & Sebastian, R. R. R. (2022). Understanding digital literacy, digital competence, and pedagogical digital competence: implementing online teaching for Filipino tertiary educators during COVID-19. In *Digital Literacy for Teachers* (pp. 391–409). Springer Nature Singapore.

Bamberger, K. A. (2009). Technologies of Compliance: Risk and Regulation in a Digital Age. *Texas Law Review*, *88*(4), 669. https://heinonline.org/HOL/LandingPage?handle=hein.journals/tlr88&div=27&id=&page=

Banchio, P. (2022). *Reflections on a legal framework for artificial intelligence. SSRN*. https://doi.org/DOI: 10.2139/ssrn.4320870

Banchio, P. (2024). *Algorética: Una disciplina para la moderación ética de algoritmos y programas de inteligencia artificial. Zenodo*. https://doi.org/DOI: 10.5281/zenodo.12806322

Banchio, P. (2024b). *Legal framework to combat disinformation and hate speech on digital platforms. SSRN*. https://doi.org/DOI: 10.2139/ssrn.4879162

Banchio, P. (2024c). *Legal responses to disinformation and hate speech in the digital age. AI and Human Rights Law Journal,* 2(4), 26–60. *Zenodo*. https://doi.org/DOI: 10.5281/zenodo.12594869

Banchio, P. (2025). *La teoría del cibersujeto y el Reglamento Europeo de Inteligencia Artificial (IA Act): Un análisis crítico desde nuestros postulados teóricos y la regulación híbrida de la inteligencia artificial. Zenodo*. https://doi.org/DOI: 10.5281/zenodo.15127855

Banchio, P. (2025). *Reglamento de la Unión Europea sobre Inteligencia Artificial. Zenodo*. https://doi.org/DOI: 10.5281/zenodo.15127896

Bannister, F., & Connolly, R. (2012). Defining E-Governance. *e-Service Journal*, *8*(2), 3–25.

Bansal, V., Rezwan, M., Iyer, M., Leasure, E., Roth, C., Pal, P., & Hinson, L. (2023). A scoping review of Technology-Facilitated Gender-Based violence in Low- and Middle-Income countries across Asia. *Trauma, Violence & Abuse*, *25*(1), 463–475. DOI: 10.1177/15248380231154614

Bărbulescu v Romania, App. No. 61496/08, [2016] IRLR 235 (ECHR).

Barker, K., & Jurasz, O. (2022). Gender-Based Abuse Online: An Assessment of Law, Policy and Reform in England and Wales. In Powell, A., Flynn, A., & Sugiura, L. (Eds.), *The Palgrave Handbook of Gendered Violence and Technology* (pp. 529–544). Palgrave Macmillan., DOI: 10.1007/978-3-030-83734-1_26

Barnhardt, N. R. (2014). Creating a place for indigenous knowledge in education: The Alaska native knowledge network. In *Place-based education in the global age* (pp. 137–158). Routledge.

Barocas, S., Bradley, E., Honavar, V., & Provost, F. (2017). Big data, data science, and civil rights. *arXiv preprint arXiv:1706.03102*.

Bayrakcı, S., & Narmanlıoğlu, H. (2021). Digital literacy as whole of digital competences: Scale development study. *Düşünce ve Toplum Sosyal Bilimler Dergisi*, (4), 1–30.

Bedzow, I. (2021). Patents on Life: Religious, Moral, and Social Justice Aspects of Biotechnology and Intellectual Property. Edited by Thomas C. Berg, Roman Cholij, and Simon Ravenscroft. Cambridge: Cambridge University Press, 2019. Pp. 313. $110.00 (cloth); $88.00 (digital). ISBN: 9781108659802. *Journal of Law and Religion, 36*(2). https://doi.org/DOI: 10.1017/jlr.2021.25

Bejaković, P., & Mrnjavac, Ž. (2020). The importance of digital literacy on the labour market. *Employee Relations: The International Journal, 42*(4), 921–932.

Bell, A. (2017). *Appropriating culture: Values, risks, and the law*. Edward Elgar Publishing.

Bellasio, J., Slapakova, L., Quimbre, F., Stockwell, S., & Silfversten, E. (2021). *Human rights in the digital age*. RAND.

Belloso, N. M., & Petit, N. (2023). The EU Digital Markets Act (DMA): A competition hand in a regulatory glove. *European Law Review, 48*(4), 391–412.

Bello, Z., & Tanko, G. I. (2020). Review of work-life balance theories. *GATR Global Journal of Business and Social Science Review, 8*(4), 217–227. DOI: 10.35609/gjbssr.2020.8.4(3) PMID: 29345694

Bender, E. M., Hovy, D., & Schofield, A. (2020). Integrating ethics into the NLP curriculum. In *Proceedings of the 58th Annual Meeting of the Association for Computational Linguistics: Tutorial Abstracts* (pp. 6-9).

Benjamin, R. (2023). Race after technology. In *Social Theory Re-Wired* (pp. 405–415). Routledge.

Benmoussa, M., Chénier, I., Keenan-Pelletier, M., Mason, R., Robichaud, M., Tanguay, L., Valiquet, D., Walker, J., & Research and Education. (2024). *BILL C-63: AN ACT TO ENACT THE ONLINE HARMS ACT, TO AMEND THE CRIMINAL CODE, THE CANADIAN HUMAN RIGHTS ACT AND AN ACT RESPECTING THE MANDATORY REPORTING OF INTERNET CHILD PORNOGRAPHY BY PERSONS WHO PROVIDE AN INTERNET SERVICE AND TO MAKE CONSEQUENTIAL AND RELATED AMENDMENTS TO OTHER ACTS*. https://lop.parl.ca/staticfiles/PublicWebsite/Home/ResearchPublications/LegislativeSummaries/PDF/44-1/PV_44-1-C63-E.pdf

Berge, O. (2017). Rethinking digital literacy in Nordic school curricula. *Nordic Journal of digital literacy, 12*(1-2), 5-7.

Bergqvist, C. (November 12, 2023). Amazon Buy Box – Another Secret Jewel on Discrimination. *SSRN*. Retrieved from https://ssrn.com/abstract=4630315 or http://dx.doi.org/DOI: 10.2139/ssrn.4630315

Berkes, F. (2012). *Sacred Ecology*. Routledge.

Berman, S. W., & Harrington, B. (2024). *Apple App Store injunction violation*. Hagens Berman Sobol Shapiro LLP. Retrieved May 28, 2025 from https://www.hbsslaw.com/cases/apple-app-store-injunction-violation

Bickel, B., Nichols, J., & Woodbury, A. C. (2017). *The Cambridge handbook of linguistic fieldwork*. Cambridge University Press.

Binns, R. (2018). Fairness in machine learning: Lessons from political philosophy. *Proceedings of the 2018 Conference on Fairness, Accountability, and Transparency*, 1–10.

Birhane, A. (2021). Algorithmic injustice: A relational ethics approach. *Patterns (New York, N.Y.), 2*(2).

Blaskovic, A. K., Rusk, J. D., Parker, V. C., & Payne, B. R. (2023). Cybercrime and Intellectual Property Theft: An Analysis of Modern Digital Forensics. *Lecture Notes in Networks and Systems, 560 LNNS*. https://doi.org/DOI: 10.1007/978-3-031-18458-1_36

Blind, K., Niebel, C., & Rammer, C. (2023). The impact of the EU General data protection regulation on product innovation. *Industry and Innovation, 31*(3), 1–41. DOI: 10.1080/13662716.2023.2271858

Blyznyuk, T. (2018). Formation of teachers' digital competence: Domestic challenges and foreign experience. *Journal of Vasyl Stefanyk Precarpathian National University, 5*(1), 40–46.

Bogdanov, D. E. (2024). The Legal Regime of the AI Generated Results: Anthropocentrism vs. Transhumanism in the Field of Intellectual Property Law. *Lex Russica, 77*(1). Advance online publication. DOI: 10.17803/1729-5920.2024.206.1.032-053

Börzel, T. A., & Risse, T. (2016). Three Cheers for Comparative Regionalism. In Börzel, T. A., & Risse, T. (Eds.), *The Oxford Handbook of Comparative Regionalism* (pp. 1–25). Oxford University Press.

Bottoni, A. (2021). *Algoritmi, politica e diritti digitali*. FrancoAngeli.

Boychuk v H. J. Symons Holdings Ltd [1977] IRLR 395 (EAT).

Brabham, D. C., Ribisl, K. M., Kirchner, T. R., & Bernhardt, J. M. (2014). Crowdsourcing applications for public health. *American Journal of Preventive Medicine*, *46*(2), 179–187. PMID: 24439353

Bradshaw, S., Millard, C., & Walden, I. (2011). Contracts for clouds: Comparison and analysis of the terms and conditions of cloud computing services. *International Journal of Law and Information Technology*, *19*(3), 187–223.

Brase, G. L., & Taylor, J. (2004). The white-coat effect: Physician attire and perceived authority, friendliness, and attractiveness. *Journal of Applied Social Psychology*, *34*(12), 2469–2481. DOI: 10.1111/j.1559-1816.2004.tb01987.x

Bravo, M. C. M., Chalezquer, C. S., & Serrano-Puche, J. (2021). Meta-framework of digital literacy: A comparative analysis of 21st-century skills frameworks. *Revista Latina de Comunicacion Social*, (79), 76–109.

Bremer, S., & Meisch, S. (2017). Co-production in climate change research: Reviewing different perspectives. *Wiley Interdisciplinary Reviews: Climate Change*, *8*(6), e482.

Breslin, R. A. United States Department of Defense, Klahr, A. M., United States Department of Defense, & Neria, A. (2020). The Continuum of Harm: Examining the correlates of sexual assault victimization. In Technical Report. DOI: 10.13140/RG.2.2.33546.90565

Brevik, L. M., Gudmundsdottir, G. B., Lund, A., & Strømme, T. A. (2019). Transformative agency in teacher education: Fostering professional digital competence. *Teaching and Teacher Education*, *86*, 102875.

Brkan, M., Claes, M., & Rauchegger, C. (2021). European fundamental rights and digitalisation. *Maastricht Journal of European and Comparative Law*, *27*(6), 697–704. DOI: 10.1177/1023263X20983778

Browne, A.. (2023). Analyzing Traditional Ceremonies with Video AI: Insights into Cultural Practices. *Visual Anthropology Review*, *39*(3), 220–235.

Brynjolfsson, E., & McAfee, A. (2014). *The second machine age: Work, progress, and prosperity in a time of brilliant technologies*. W.W. Norton & Company.

Bull, H. (1995). *The Anarchical Society: A Study of Order in World Politics*. Macmillan.

Burwell, F., & Propp, K. (2020). *The European Union and the search for digital sovereignty: building "Fortress Europe" or preparing for a new world.* Atlantic Council.

Buskqvist, U., & Johansson, E. (2024). From digital competence to digital capacity: A socio-material perspective on digitalization in preschool. *Nordic Journal of Digital Literacy*, (1), 39–51.

Cabero-Almenara, J., Romero-Tena, R., & Palacios-Rodríguez, A. (2020). Evaluation of teacher digital competence frameworks through expert judgement: The use of the expert competence coefficient. *Journal of new approaches in educational research, 9*(2), 275-293.

Cabezas-González, M., Casillas-Martín, S., & García-Peñalvo, F. J. (2021). The digital competence of pre-service educators: The influence of personal variables. *Sustainability*, *13*(4), 2318.

Caluza, L. J. B. (2018). Machine learning algorithm application in predicting children mortality: Model development. *International Journal of Information System and Applications*, *10*(1), 1–6. http://www.irphouse.com

Calvani, A., Fini, A., & Ranieri, M. (2010). Digital Competence in K-12: theoretical models, assessment tools and empirical research. *Anàlisi: quaderns de comunicació i cultura*, (40), 157-171.

Calvani, A., Cartelli, A., Fini, A., & Ranieri, M. (2008). Models and instruments for assessing digital competence at school. *Journal of E-learning and Knowledge Society*, *4*(3), 183–193.

Calvi, A. (2024). Data Protection Impact Assessment under the EU General Data Protection Regulation: A feminist reflection. *Computer Law & Security Review*, *53*, 105950. DOI: 10.1016/j.clsr.2024.105950

Camacho, N. G. (2024). The Role of AI in Cybersecurity: Addressing Threats in the Digital Age. *Journal of Artificial Intelligence General Science (JAIGS) ISSN 3006-4023, 3*(1), 143–154. https://doi.org/DOI: 10.60087/jaigs.v3i1.75

Cameron, L. D. (2024). The Making of the "Good Bad" Job: How Algorithmic Management Manufactures Consent Through Constant and Confined Choices. *Administrative Science Quarterly*, *69*(2). Advance online publication. DOI: 10.1177/00018392241236163

Canca, C. (2022). What is Algor-ethics? In Floridi, L. (Ed.), *Ethics, Governance, and Policies in Artificial Intelligence*. Springer.

Carovano, G., & Finck, M. (2023). Regulating data intermediaries: The impact of the Data Governance Act on the EU's data economy. *Computer Law & Security Review*, *50*, 105800. DOI: 10.1016/j.clsr.2023.105800

Carretero, S., Vuorikari, R., & Punie, Y. (2017). The digital competence framework for citizens. *Publications Office of the European Union*, *21*(5), 222–235.

Carroll, S. R., Hudson, M., Holbrook, J., Materechera, S., & Anderson, J. (2020). Working with the CARE principles: operationalizing Indigenous data governance. *Ada Lovelace Institute, 9.*

Cartelli, A. (2010, January). Frameworks for digital competence assessment: Proposals, instruments, and evaluation. In Proceedings of informing science & it education conference (InSITE) (pp. 561-573).

Cartelli, A. (2013). Theory and practice in digital competence assessment. In *Digital Literacy: Concepts, Methodologies, Tools, and Applications* (pp. 1367-1383). IGI Global Scientific Publishing.

Cartelli, A. (2009). Frameworks for digital literacy and digital competence assessment. In *Proceedings of the 8th European Conference on e-Learning* (pp. 116-123).

Cartelli, A. (Ed.). (2012). *Current trends and future practices for digital literacy and competence*. IGI Global.

Carvalho, L., Mota, C., & Ramos, P. (2024). Socially Responsible Investment Funds—An Analysis Applied to Funds Domiciled in the Portuguese and Spanish Markets. *Risks*, *12*(1). Advance online publication. DOI: 10.3390/risks12010009

Casillas Martín, S., Cabezas González, M., & García Peñalvo, F. J. (2020). Digital competence of early childhood education teachers: Attitude, knowledge and use of ICT. *European Journal of Teacher Education*, *43*(2), 210–223.

Çebi, A., & Reisoğlu, İ. (2020). Digital competence: A study from the perspective of pre-service teachers in Turkey. *Journal of New Approaches in Educational Research*, *9*(2), 294–308.

Chamberlain, L. (2011, April 4). Employers ensure dress codes do not discriminate. Personnel Today. https://www.personneltoday.com/hr/employers-ensure-dress-codes-do-not-discriminate/

Chan, B. S., Churchill, D., & Chiu, K. F. (2017). Digital literacy learning in higher education through digital storytelling approach. *Journal of International Education Research*.

Chandra, R., & Sanjaya, K. (2023). Punishing the Unpunishable: A Liability Framework for Artificial Intelligence Systems. In Motahhir, S., & Bossoufi, B. (Eds.), *Digital Technologies and Applications. ICDTA 2023. Lecture Notes in Networks and Systems* (Vol. 669). Springer., DOI: 10.1007/978-3-031-29860-8_6

Chang, Y. L., & Ke, J. (2024). Socially Responsible Artificial Intelligence Empowered People Analytics: A Novel Framework Towards Sustainability. *Human Resource Development Review, 23*(1). Advance online publication. DOI: 10.1177/15344843231200930

Cheng, Q., Lu, X., & Liu, Z.. (2015). Mining research trends with anomaly detection models: The case of social computing research. *Scientometrics, 103*, 453–469. DOI: 10.1007/s11192-015-1559-9

Choudhary, H. (2024). Building bridges to digital inclusion: Implications for curriculum development of digital literacy training programs. *International Journal of Technology Enhanced Learning, 16*(3), 282–296.

Christen, K. (2011). Opening archives: Respectful repatriation. *The American Archivist, 74*(1), 185–210.

Christine, R. (2017). *European framework for the digital competence of educators.* Joint Research Centre.

Chu, N. E. (2025). The influence of surveillance capitalism on educational technology adoption. *Doi.org*. https://doi.org/DOI: 10.14288/1.0440687

Citron, D. K. (2014). *Hate crimes in cyberspace.* Harvard University Press.

Coeckelbergh, M. (2020). *AI ethics.* MIT Press.

Coe, P. (2023). Tackling online false information in the United Kingdom: The Online Safety Act 2023 and its disconnection from free speech law and theory*. *Journal of Medicine and Law, 15*(2), 213–242. DOI: 10.1080/17577632.2024.2316360

Collins, P. (2020, September 3). The right to privacy, surveillance-by-software and the “home-workplace”. UK Labour Law Blog. https://uklabourlawblog.com

Collins, H., Ewing, K. D., & McColgan, A. (2019). *Labour law* (2nd ed.). Cambridge University Press.

Committee on the Elimination of Discrimination against Women. (2017). General recommendation No. 35 on gender-based violence against women, updating general recommendation No. 19 (CEDAW/C/GC/35). *United Nations*. https://docs.un.org/en/CEDAW/C/GC/35

Cooper, R. (2003). *The Breaking of Nations: Order and Chaos in the Twenty-First Century.* Atlantic Monthly Press.

Cortoni, I., & Cervelli, P., & LO PRESTI, V. (2015). Digital competence assessment. A proposal of operationalization of the critical analysis. *The Journal of Media Literacy Education*, *7*(1), 46–57.

Couldry, N., & Mejias, U. A. (2019). The costs of connection: How data is colonizing human life and appropriating it for capitalism. In *The costs of connection*. Stanford University Press.

Coulthard, G. S. (2014). Red skin, white masks: Rejecting the colonial politics of recognition. *Minneapolis: Minnesota*.

Council Directive 2003/88/EC, of 4 November 2003 concerning certain aspects of the organisation of working time, 2003 O.J. (L 299) 9.

Council of Europe. (2018). Convention 108 +. In *European Parliament*. European Union. https://www.europarl.europa.eu/meetdocs/2014_2019/plmrep/COMMITTEES/LIBE/DV/2018/09-10/Convention_108_EN.pdf

Covello, S., & Lei, J. (2010). A review of digital literacy assessment instruments. *Syracuse University*, *1*, 31.

Covington (2025). *Brazilian Supreme Court strikes down safe harbor provision of the Marco Civil da Internet*. https://www.cov.com/en/news-and-insights/insights/2025/06/brazils-supreme-court-to-strike-down-internet-governance-safe-harbor-clause

Crawford, K. (2021). *The atlas of AI: Power, politics, and the planetary costs of artificial intelligence*. Yale University Press.

Crawford, L. (2024). The project manager. In *The Handbook of Project Management* (pp. 336–348). Routledge.

Creemers, R. (2017). China's Social Credit System: An Evolving Practice of Control. *SSRN*. https://doi.org/DOI: 10.2139/ssrn.3175792

Crystal, D. (2000). *Language Death*. Cambridge University Press.

Cubukcu, A., & Bazyan, S. (2018). A study regarding the perception of digital citizenship among adults and the assessment of this perception: A digital literacy model. In *Information and Technology Literacy: Concepts, Methodologies, Tools, and Applications* (pp. 47-61). IGI Global Scientific Publishing.

Dafoe, A., & Journal of International Affairs (2018/2019). Global politics and the governance of artificial intelligence. An Interview with Allan Dafoe. *Journal of International Affairs*, (Fall 2018/Winter 2019), 121-126.

Dai, X. (2018). Toward a Reputation State: The Social Credit System Project of China. *SSRN.* https://doi.org/DOI: 10.2139/ssrn.3193577

Darcy, R. (2019). Infographics, assessment and digital literacy: innovating learning and teaching through developing ethically responsible digital competencies in public health. In *Annual Conference of the Australasian Society for Computers in Learning in Tertiary Education 2019* (pp. 112-120). Australasian Society for Computers in Learning in Tertiary Education.

Davidson, J. E. (1998). Reconciling the tension between employer liability and employee privacy. *George Mason University Civil Rights Law Journal*, *8*(2), 145–170.

Davidson, L., & Berkelhamer, S. (2017). Bronchopulmonary dysplasia: Chronic lung disease of infancy and long-term pulmonary outcomes. *Journal of Clinical Medicine*, *6*(1).

Davydov, S., Logunova, O., Maltseva, D., Sharikov, A., & Zadorin, I. (2020). Digital literacy concepts and measurement. *Internet in Russia: A study of the Runet and its impact on social life*, 103-120.

De Hert, P., & Papakonstantinou, V. (2021, April 1). Post GDPR EU laws and their GDPR mimesis. DGA, DSA, DMA and the EU regulation of AI. European Law Blog. https://europeanlawblog.eu/2021/04/01/post-gdpr-eu-laws-and-their-gdpr-mimesis-dga-dsa-dma-and-the-eu-regulation-of-ai/

de Vries, D. A., Piotrowski, J. T., & de Vreese, C. (2025). Developing the DigIQ: A measure of digital competence. *PLoS One*, *20*(5), e0322995.

Deane, T. (2024). Gender-Based Violence in International Human Rights Law – The efficacy of the United Nations Human Rights Legal Framework and CEDAW in addressing the issue. *The Age of Human Rights Journal*, *23*, e8662. DOI: 10.17561/tahrj.v23.8662

Deci, E. L., & Ryan, R. M. (2000). The “what” and “why” of goal pursuits: Human needs and the self- determination of behavior. *Psychological Inquiry*, *11*(4), 227–268.

Delgado-Vázquez, Á. M., & López-Catalán, B. (2022). From information literacy to digital competence. In *Innovation and ICT in Education* (pp. 65–75). River Publishers.

Demssash, A. W., Alemu, T. T., & Zerihun, A. W. (2023). Using best performance machine learning algorithm to predict under-five child mortality in Ethiopia. *BMC Medical Informatics and Decision Making*, *23*, 145. DOI: 10.1186/s12911-023-01811-4

Dencik, L. (2019). Data justice and the right to protection. *International Journal of Communication, 13*, 3656–3673.

Diab, R. (2024, June 3). *Online Harms Act should target algorithms*. Policy Options. https://policyoptions.irpp.org/magazines/may-2024/online-harms-act-algorithms/

Dick, P. (2010). The transition to motherhood and part-time working: Mutuality and incongruence in the psychological contracts existing between managers and employees. *Work, Employment and Society, 24*(3), 508–525. DOI: 10.1177/0950017010371648

Douek, E. (2021). Governing Online Speech: From "Posts-As-Trumps" to Proportionality and Probability. *Columbia Law Review, 121*(3), 759–832.

Draghi, M. (2024). *The Draghi report: A competitiveness strategy for Europe*. European Commission. Retrieved April 26, 2025 from https://ec.europa.eu/commission/publications/draghi-report-competitiveness-strategy-europe_en

Dragiewicz, Molly. (2020). eSafety. (2020). Children and technology-facilitated abuse in domestic and family violence situations: Infographic. eSafety Commissioner & Australian Government.

Drezner, D. W. (2004). The global governance of internet: Bringing the state back in. *Political Science Quarterly, 119*(3), 477–498.

Duarte, M. E. (2017). Network sovereignty: Building the Internet across Indian country. *Yale Journal of Law & Technology, 19*(1), 149–200.

Dutfield, G. (2000). *Intellectual property rights trade and biodiversity*. Routledge.

Eckardt, M., & Kerber, W. (2024). Property rights theory, bundles of rights on IoT data, and the EU Data Act. *European Journal of Law and Economics, 57*(1), 113–143.

Ei, C. H., & Soon, C. (2021). Towards a unified framework for digital literacy in Singapore. *IPS Work. Pap, 39*.

Eke, D., & Stahl, B. (2024). Ethics in the governance of data and digital technology: An analysis of European data regulations and policies. *Digital Society : Ethics, Socio-Legal and Governance of Digital Technology, 3*(1), 1–15.

Elpaccto. (2022). Cybercrime through a gender lens: what does it mean, how do we deal with it? https://elpaccto.eu/en/news/espanol-cibercrimen-en-clave-de-genero-que-significa-como-lo-abordamos/#:~:text=Cyberspace%20facilitates%20various%20forms%20of,out%20taking%20advantage%20of%20ICT

Engel, C., Linhardt, L., & Schubert, M. (2024). Code is law: How COMPAS affects the way the judiciary handles the risk of recidivism. *Artificial Intelligence and Law, 33*(1). Advance online publication. DOI: 10.1007/s10506-024-09389-8

Engen, B. K., Giæver, T. H., & Mifsud, L. (2015). Guidelines and regulations for teaching digital competence in schools and teacher education: A weak link?. *Nordic Journal of Digital Literacy, 10*(Jubileumsnummer), 172-186.

Ensminger, J., & Henrich, J. (Eds.). (2014). *Experimenting with social norms: Fairness and punishment in cross-cultural perspective*. Russell Sage Foundation.

*Epic Games, Inc. v. Apple Inc.*, No. 4:20-cv-05640-YGR (N.D. Cal. 10 September, 2021). Retrieved April 27, 2025 from https://cand.uscourts.gov/wp-content/uploads/cases-of-interest/epic-games-v-apple/Epic-v.-Apple-20-cv-05640-YGR-Dkt-812-Order.pdf

Equal Employment Opportunity Commission v. Abercrombie & Fitch Stores, Inc., 575 U.S. 768 (2015).

Eraku, S. S., Baruadi, M. K., Anantadjaya, S. P., Fadjarajani, S., Supriatna, U., & Arifin, A. (2021). Digital literacy and educators of Islamic education. *Edukasi Islami: Jurnal Pendidikan Islam, 10*(01), 569–576.

Erdos, D. (2021). *Comparing Constitutional Privacy and Data Protection Rights within the EU*. University of Cambridge, Faculty of Law Research Paper No. 21/2021. Retrieved April 9, 2025 from https://ssrn.com/abstract=3843653

Erstad, O., Kjällander, S., & Järvelä, S. (2021). Facing the challenges of 'digital competence' a Nordic agenda for curriculum development for the 21st century. *Nordic Journal of Digital Literacy, 16*(2), 77–87.

Ess, C. (2009). *Digital media ethics*. Polity Press.

Esteve-Mon, F., Llopis, M., & Adell-Segura, J. (2020). Digital competence and computational thinking of student teachers. [iJET]. *International Journal of Emerging Technologies in Learning, 15*(2), 29–41.

Eubanks, V. (2018). *Automating Inequality: How High-Tech Tools Profile, Police, and Punish the Poor*. St. Martin's Press.

European Commission. (2015). *Better regulation for better results – An EU agenda* (COM(2015) 192 final). Retrieved March 31, 2025 from https://eur-lex.europa.eu/legal-content/EN/TXT/?uri=CELEX:52015DC0192

European Commission. (2019). *Ethics guidelines for trustworthy AI*. Publications Office of the EU.

European Commission. (2020). *A Europe fit for the digital age*. https://commission.europa.eu/publications/factsheets-europe-fit-digital-age_en

European Commission. (2020). *Antitrust: Commission sends Statement of Objections to Amazon for the use of non-public independent seller data and opens second investigation into its e-commerce business practices.* Retrieved May 26, 2025 from https://ec.europa.eu/commission/presscorner/api/files/document/print/en/ip_20_2077/IP_20_2077_EN.pdf

European Commission. (2021). *2030 Digital Compass: The European Way for the Digital Decade*. https://digital-strategy.ec.europa.eu

European Commission. (2022). Commission decision of 20.12.2022 relating to a proceeding under Article 102 of the Treaty on the Functioning of the European Union (TFEU) and Article 54 of the EEA Agreement Cases AT.40462 – Amazon Marketplace and AT.40703 – Amazon Buy Box. Retrieved March 4, 2025 from https://ec.europa.eu/competition/antitrust/cases1/202310/AT_40703_8990760_1533_5.pdf

European Commission. (2024). *Digital Services Act: Questions and answers*. Shaping Europe's digital future. Retrieved May 19, 2025 from https://digital-strategy.ec.europa.eu/en/faqs/digital-services-act-questions-and-answers

European Commission. (2024). *The Data Governance Act explained*. Shaping Europe's Digital Future. Retrieved March 30, 2025 from https://digital-strategy.ec.europa.eu/en/policies/data-governance-act-explained

European Commission. (2025). *Digital Markets Act: Commission designates first set of gatekeepers under the Digital Markets Act.* Retrieved April 30, 2025 from https://ec.europa.eu/commission/presscorner/detail/en/ip_25_1086

European Parliament. (2016). *General Data Protection Regulation (GDPR)*. Official Journal of the EU.

European Parliament. (2021, December 14). *EU Digital Markets Act and Digital Services Act explained | Topics | European Parliament*. Www.europarl.europa.euEuropean Parliament. https://www.europarl.europa.eu/topics/en/article/20211209STO19124/eu-digital-markets-act-and-digital-services-act-explained

European Union (2012). *Treaty on European Union*. Official Journal of the European Union, C 326/13. Retrieved March 22, 2025 from https://eur-lex.europa.eu/legal-content/EN/TXT/?uri=CELEX%3A12012M%2FTXT

European Union (2022). *Regulation (EU) 2022/1925 of the European Parliament and of the Council of 14 September 2022 on contestable and fair markets in the digital sector and amending Directives (EU) 2019/1937 and (EU) 2020/1828 (Digital Markets Act). Official Journal of the European Union, L 265*, 1–66. Retrieved March 22, 2025 from https://eur-lex.europa.eu/eli/reg/2022/1925/oj

European Union (2022). *Regulation (EU) 2022/2065 of the European Parliament and of the Council of 19 October 2022 on a Single Market for Digital Services and amending Directive 2000/31/EC (Digital Services Act). Official Journal of the European Union, L 277*, 1–102. Retrieved March 20, 2025 from https://eur-lex.europa.eu/eli/reg/2022/2065/oj

Eweida v United Kingdom, App. No. 48420/10, [2013] ECHR 37.

Ewing, K. D. (2000). *Human rights at work*. Institute of Employment Rights.

Ezeanya-Esiobu, C. (2019). *Indigenous knowledge and education in Africa*. Springer Nature.

Fahy, I. Buri, J. P. Quintais, & M. Straub (Eds.) (2023). *Putting the DSA into Practice*. Institute for Information Law (IViR), University of Amsterdam. Retrieved from https://verfassungsblog.de/wp-content/uploads/2023/02/vHoboken-et-al_Putting-the-DSA-into-Practice.pdf

Falloon, G. (2020). From digital literacy to digital competence: The teacher digital competency (TDC) framework. *Educational Technology Research and Development, 68*(5), 2449–2472.

Faloppa, F. (2023). Participation of the private sector and the media. In *Edward Elgar Publishing eBooks* (pp. 268–283). DOI: 10.4337/9781839107757.ch23

Fantin, M. (2010). Perspectives on media literacy, digital literacy and information literacy. [IJDLDC]. *International Journal of Digital Literacy and Digital Competence, 1*(4), 10–15.

Farias-Gaytan, S., Aguaded, I., & Ramirez-Montoya, M. S. (2022). Transformation and digital literacy: Systematic literature mapping. *Education and Information Technologies, 27*(2), 1417–1437.

Feenberg, A. (2010). *Between reason and experience: Essays in technology and modernity*. MIT Press.

Feldstein, S. (2019). *The Global Expansion of AI Surveillance*. Carnegie Endowment for International Peace.

Feldstein, S. (2021). *The rise of digital repression. How technology is reshaping power, politics, and resistance*. Oxford University Press.

Feng, L., & Xue, S. (2023). Using the DigCompEdu framework to conceptualize teachers' digital literacy. *Education Journal, 12*(3), 103–108.

Fernández Martínez v Spain, App. No. 56030/07, ECHR 2014.

Ferrari, A., & Punie, Y. (2013, April). *DIGCOMP: A framework for developing and understanding digital competence in Europe*.

Ferrari, A. (2012). *Digital competence in practice: An analysis of frameworks* (Vol. 10). Publications Office of the European Union.

Ferrari, A., Punie, Y., & Redecker, C. (2012). Understanding digital competence in the 21st century: An analysis of current frameworks. In *21st Century Learning for 21st Century Skills: 7th European Conference of Technology Enhanced Learning, EC-TEL 2012, Saarbrücken, Germany, September 18-21, 2012*. [Springer Berlin Heidelberg.]. *Proceedings, 7*, 79–92.

Fitsilis, F., & de Almeida, P. G. R. (2024). Artificial intelligence and its regulation in representative institutions. In *Research handbook on public management and artificial intelligence* (pp. 151–166). Edward Elgar Publishing.

Floridi, L. (2023). The ethics of artificial intelligence: Principles, challenges, and opportunities.

Floridi, L. (2013). *The ethics of information*. Oxford University Press.

Floridi, L. (2014). *The Fourth Revolution: How the Infosphere is Reshaping Human Reality*. Oxford University Press.

Floridi, L. (2014). *The Onlife Manifesto: Being Human in a Hyperconnected Era*. Springer.

Floridi, L. (2021). *The Logic of Information: A Theory of Philosophy as Conceptual Design*. Oxford University Press.

Floridi, L., & Cowls, J. (2019). A Unified Framework of Five Principles for AI in Society. *Harvard Data Science Review, 1*(1).

Flynn, A., Powell, A., & Hindes, S. (2023). An Intersectional Analysis of Technology-Facilitated Abuse: Prevalence, experiences and Impacts of Victimization. *British Journal of Criminology, 64*(3), 600–619. DOI: 10.1093/bjc/azad044

Foley v Post Office [2000] ICR 1283 (CA).

Foorthuis, R. (2021). On the nature and types of anomalies: A review of deviations in data. *International Journal of Data Science and Analytics*, *12*, 297–331. DOI: 10.1007/s41060-021-00265-1 PMID: 34368422

Foucault, M. (1977). *Discipline and punish: The birth of the prison* (Sheridan, A., Trans.). Pantheon Books.

Fourmile, H. (2020). Who owns the past? Aborigines as captives of the archives. In *Terrible Hard Biscuits* (pp. 16–27). Routledge.

Friedman, B., Kahn, P. H., & Borning, A. (2006). *Value sensitive design and information systems*. Springer.

From, J. (2017). Pedagogical Digital Competence—Between Values, Knowledge and Skills. *Higher Education Studies*, *7*(2), 43–50.

Fryberg, S. A., Dai, J. D., & Eason, A. E. (2024). Omission as a modern form of bias against Native Peoples: Implications for policies and practices. *Social Issues and Policy Review*, *18*(1), 148–170.

Gallardo-Echenique, E. E., de Oliveira, J. M., Marqués-Molias, L., Esteve-Mon, F., Wang, Y., & Baker, R. (2015). Digital competence in the knowledge society. *Journal of Online Learning and Teaching*, *11*(1).

Gapski, H. (2007, September). Some reflections on digital literacy. In *Proceedings of the 3rd international workshop on digital literacy* (Vol. 310, pp. 49-55). Crete: CEUR-WS. org.

García-Vandewalle García, J. M., García-Carmona, M., Trujillo Torres, J. M., & Moya Fernández, P. (2023). Analysis of digital competence of educators (DigCompEdu) in teacher trainees: The context of Melilla, Spain. *Technology. Knowledge and Learning*, *28*(2), 585–612.

Garzón Artacho, E., Martínez, T. S., Ortega Martin, J. L., Marin Marin, J. A., & Gómez García, G. (2020). Teacher training in lifelong learning—The importance of digital competence in the encouragement of teaching innovation. *Sustainability*, *12*(7), 2852.

Garzón-Artacho, E., Sola-Martínez, T., Romero-Rodríguez, J. M., & Gómez-García, G. (2021). Teachers' perceptions of digital competence at the lifelong learning stage. *Heliyon*, *7*(7).

Gasser, U., Ienca, M., Scheibner, J., Sleigh, J., & Vayena, E. (2020). Digital tools against COVID-19: Taxonomy, ethical challenges, and navigation aid. *The Lancet. Digital Health*, *2*(8), e425–e434. PMID: 32835200

Gay, G. (2018). *Culturally responsive teaching: Theory, research, and practice*. Teachers college press.

Geiregat, S. (2022). *Who owns 'your' (business's) digital data? New EU law in the making*. Oxford Business Law Blog. Retrieved March 19, 2025 from https://blogs.law.ox.ac.uk/oblb/blog-post/2022/12/who-owns-your-businesss-digital-data-new-eu-law-making

Genç-Gelgeç, B. (2022). Regulating digital platforms: Will the DSA correct its predecessor's deficiencies? *Croatian Yearbook of European Law and Policy, 18*, 25–60. Retrieved March 31, 2025 from https://www.cyelp.com/index.php/cyelp/article/view/485

Ghomi, M., & Redecker, C. (2019, May). Digital Competence of Educators (DigCompEdu): Development and Evaluation of a Self-assessment Instrument for Teachers' Digital Competence. In *CSEDU (1)* (pp. 541-548).

Gibbs, C. (2020, May 7). Coronavirus, the UK economy and society, faster indicators. Office for National Statistics. https://www.ons.gov.uk/peoplepopulationandcommunity/healthandsocialcare/conditionsanddiseases/bulletins/coronavirustheukeconomyandsocietyfasterindicators/7may2020

Gibson, J. (2016). *Community resources: intellectual property, international trade and protection of traditional knowledge*. Routledge.

Gilio-Whitaker, D. (2019). *As long as grass grows: The Indigenous fight for environmental justice, from colonization to Standing Rock*. Beacon Press.

Gillespie, T. (2018). *Custodians of the Internet: Platforms, Content Moderation, and the Hidden Decisions That Shape Social Media*. Yale University Press.

Gill, R. (2005). Technofeminism. *Science as Culture*, *14*(1), 97–101. DOI: 10.1080/09505430500042130

Gisbert Cervera, M., & Lázaro Cantabrana, J. L. (2015). Professional development in teacher digital competence and improving school quality from the teachers' perspective: A case study. *Journal of New Approaches in Educational Research*, *4*(2), 115–122.

Godhe, A. L. (2019). Digital literacies or digital competence: Conceptualizations in Nordic curricula. *Media and Communication*, *7*(2), 25–35.

Gover, A. R., & Moore, A. M. (2020). The 1994 Violence Against Women Act: A Historic Response to Gender Violence. *Violence Against Women*, *27*(1), 8–29. DOI: 10.1177/1077801220949705

Gragnano, A., Simbula, S., & Miglioretti, M. (2020). Work–life balance: Weighing the importance of work–family and work–health balance. *International Journal of Environmental Research and Public Health, 17*(3), 907. Advance online publication. DOI: 10.3390/ijerph17030907 PMID: 32024155

Grans, L. (2023). The impact of vulnerability on state obligations in criminal proceedings on domestic violence: Interpreting the Istanbul Convention and the European Convention on Human Rights. *Women & Criminal Justice*, 1–16. DOI: 10.1080/08974454.2023.2296624

Greenwald, G. (2014). *No place to hide: Edward Snowden, the NSA, and the U.S. surveillance state*. Metropolitan Books.

Griedlich, N., & Jerome, J. (2023). *The EU Data Act: What does it mean for you?* Deloitte. Retrieved March 28, 2025 from https://www.deloitte.com/lu/en/Industries/technology/perspectives/the-eu-data-act-what-does-it-mean-for-you.html

Grint, K., & Jones, O. S. (2022). *Leadership: Limits and possibilities*. Bloomsbury Publishing.

Gruber, J. (2025). *Judge Gonzales Rogers issues new Apple App Store ruling*. Daring Fireball. Retrieved March 24, 2025 from https://daringfireball.net/2025/04/gonzales_rogers_apple_app_store_ruling

Guest, D. E. (2002). Perspectives on the study of work-life balance. *Social Sciences Information. Information Sur les Sciences Sociales, 41*(2), 255–279. DOI: 10.1177/0539018402041002005

Gupta, A., Rahman, A., & Yasmin, G. (2021). Audio fingerprinting using high-level feature extraction. In *Computational Intelligence in Pattern Recognition* [Singapore: Springer Singapore.]. *Proceedings of CIPR, 2021*, 281–291.

Gutierrez-Angel, N., Sanchez-Garcia, J. N., Mercader-Rubio, I., Garcia-Martin, J., & Brito-Costa, S. (2022). Digital literacy in the university setting: A literature review of empirical studies between 2010 and 2021. *Frontiers in Psychology, 13*, 896800.

Guttmann, A. (2021). Commons and cooperatives: A new governance of collective action. *Annals of Public and Cooperative Economics, 92*(1), 33–53.

Guzmán-Simón, F., García-Jiménez, E., & López-Cobo, I. (2017). Undergraduate students' perspectives on digital competence and academic literacy in a Spanish University. *Computers in Human Behavior, 74*, 196–204.

Habbal, A., Ali, M. K., & Abuzaraida, M. A. (2024). Artificial Intelligence Trust, Risk and Security Management (AI TRiSM): Frameworks, applications, challenges and future research directions. *Expert Systems with Applications*, *240*(122442), 122442. DOI: 10.1016/j.eswa.2023.122442

Hacker, P. (2024). Sustainable AI regulation. *Common Market Law Review*, *61*(2).

Haggart, B., Tusikov, N., & Scholte, J. A. (2021). *Power and authority in internet governance: Return of the state?* Taylor & Francis.

Halewood, M. (1999). Indigenous and local knowledge: Is there a legal space? *International Review of Industrial Property and Copyright Law*, *30*(6), 795–827.

Hammoda, B., & Foli, S. (2024). A Digital Competence Framework for Learners (DCFL): A Conceptual Framework for Digital Literacy. *Knowledge Management & E-Learning*, *16*(3), 477–500.

Hammond, G., & McLay, M. Mapp, Ph. D., Law Commission, Hammond, G., Burrows, J., Honoré, C., Hayward, R., & Hayward, J. (2012). *Harmful digital communications: the adequacy of the current sanctions and remedies*. https://www.lawcom.govt.nz/assets/Publications/MiscellaneousPapers/NZLC-MB3.pdf

Hanell, F. (2018). What is the 'problem'that digital competence in Swedish teacher education is meant to solve?. *Nordic Journal of digital literacy, 13*(3), 137-151.

Harlow, R. (2011). Māori language regeneration: A review of research and practice. *Journal of Māori and Pacific Development*, *12*(1), 1–14.

Harrison, M. S., & Goldenberg, R. L. (2016). Global burden of prematurity. *Seminars in Fetal & Neonatal Medicine*, *21*(2), 74–79.

Harvey, D. (2019). *"Case note: Police v B [2017] NZCrimLawRw 36; [2017] NZHC 526, [2017] 3 NZLR 203" [2017] NZCrimLawRw 13;[2016] NZCLR 213*. https://www.austlii.edu.au/nz/journals/NZCrimLawRw/2017/36.html

Hatlevik, O. E., & Christophersen, K. A. (2013). Digital competence at the beginning of upper secondary school: Identifying factors explaining digital inclusion. *Computers & Education*, *63*, 240–247.

Hatlevik, O. E., Ottestad, G., & Throndsen, I. (2015). Predictors of digital competence in 7th grade: A multilevel analysis. *Journal of Computer Assisted Learning*, *31*(3), 220–231.

Heidegger, M. (1977). *The Question Concerning Technology and Other Essays*. Harper & Row.

Heinrich, M. (2013). Ethnopharmacology and drug discovery. *Comprehensive Natural Products II: Chemistry and Biology. Development & Modification of Bioactivity, 3*, 351–381.

Held, D., & McGrew, A. (2007). *Globalization/Anti-Globalization: Beyond the Great Divide* (2nd ed.). Polity Press.

Henry, N., & Powell, A. (2016). Technology-Facilitated Sexual Violence: A Literature Review of Empirical research. *Trauma, Violence & Abuse*, *19*(2), 195–208. DOI: 10.1177/1524838016650189

He, T., & Li, S. (2019). A comparative study of digital informal learning: The effects of digital competence and technology expectancy. *British Journal of Educational Technology*, *50*(4), 1744–1758.

He, T., & Zhu, C. (2017). Digital informal learning among Chinese university students: The effects of digital competence and personal factors. *International Journal of Educational Technology in Higher Education*, *14*, 1–19.

Hicks, J. (2021). *Global evidence on the prevalence and impact of online gender-based violence. K4D Helpdesk Report*. Institute of Development Studies., DOI: 10.19088/K4D.2021.140

Hinojo-Lucena, F. J., Aznar-Diaz, I., Caceres-Reche, M. P., Trujillo-Torres, J. M., & Romero-Rodriguez, J. M. (2019). Factors influencing the development of digital competence in teachers: Analysis of the teaching staff of permanent education centres. *IEEE Access : Practical Innovations, Open Solutions*, *7*, 178744–178752.

Hojnik, J. (2025). *Uvod v pravo digitalnega enotnega trga in pravni vidiki servitizacije v EU: Študijsko gradivo*. Maribor: Univerzitetna založba Univerze v Mariboru. https://doi.org/10.18690/um.pf.4.2025

Holbrook, D. (2023). Violence Against Women Act: Re-authorization and impact for forensic health professionals. *Journal of the Academy of Forensic Nursing*, *1*(2), 64–68. DOI: 10.29173/jafn736

Hopster, J. K., & Maas, M. M. (2024). The technology triad: Disruptive AI, regulatory gaps and value change. *AI and Ethics*, *4*(4), 1051–1069.

Horbar, J. D., Edwards, E. M., Greenberg, L. T., Morrow, K. A., Soll, R. F., Buus-Frank, M. E., & Buzas, J. S. (2017). Variation in performance of neonatal intensive care units in the United States. *JAMA Pediatrics*, *171*(3).

Huber, A. (2022). 'A shadow of me old self': The impact of image-based sexual abuse in a digital society. *International Review of Victimology, 29*(2), 199–216. DOI: 10.1177/02697580211063659

Huhndorf, S. M. (2015). *Going native: Indians in the American cultural imagination*. Cornell University Press.

Hyliaka, S. (2021). Human rights in the digital age: Challenges, threats and prospects. *Науковий юридичний журнал, 28*(1), 16.

Igarapé Institute. (2025). *The Marco Civil da Internet and data protection in Brazil*. https://igarape.org.br

Ilomäki, L., Kantosalo, A., & Lakkala, M. (2011). What is digital competence? In *Linked portal* (pp. 1-12). European Schoolnet (EUN).

Ilomäki, L., Paavola, S., Lakkala, M., & Kantosalo, A. (2016). Digital competence–an emergent boundary concept for policy and educational research. *Education and Information Technologies, 21*, 655–679.

Indah, R. N., Toyyibah, T., Budhiningrum, A. S., & Afifi, N. (2022). The research competence, critical thinking skills and digital literacy of Indonesian EFL students. *Journal of Language Teaching and Research, 13*(2), 315–324.

Indriyani, V. (2019, August). Digital literacy competencies for teacher education students. In *1st International Conference on Education Social Sciences and Humanities (ICESSHum 2019)* (pp. 1010-1018). Atlantis Press.

Instefjord, E. (2015). Appropriation of digital competence in teacher education. *Nordic Journal of Digital Literacy, 10*(Jubileumsnummer), 155-171.

Iordache, C., Mariën, I., & Baelden, D. (2017). Developing digital skills and competences: A quick-scan analysis of 13 digital literacy models. *Italian Journal of Sociology of Education, 9*(Italian Journal of Sociology of Education 9/1), 6-30.

Iqbal, F., & Jameel, F. (2023). Development and evaluation of machine learning training strategies for neonatal mortality prediction using multicountry data. *Scientific Reports, 15*, 12345. DOI: 10.1038/s41598-023-12345-6

Iqbal, F., Jameel, F., & Malik, A. (2023). Predictive analytics in smart healthcare for child mortality prediction in Pakistan. *Frontiers in Public Health, 11*, 1035086. DOI: 10.3389/fpubh.2023.1035086

Isaak, J., & Hanna, M. J. (2018). User Data Privacy: Facebook, Cambridge Analytica, and Privacy Protection. *Computer, 51*(8), 56–59.

Issalillah, F., & Hardyansah, R. (2024). Relevance of Privacy within the Sphere of Human Rights: A Critical Analysis of Personal Data Protection. *Bulletin of Science, Technology & Society, 3*(1), 31–39. https://inti.ejournalmeta.com/index.php/inti/article/view/39

Jangkhum, S. J., Chayutrakorn, C., Uthai, P., & Supiyanti, R. S. (2025). Risk Management in the Digital Era for SMEs. *The 15th Benjamit National and International Conference*, 211–221. https://benjamit.thonburi-u.ac.th/ojs/bmv15/article/view/99

Janssen, J., Stoyanov, S., Ferrari, A., Punie, Y., Pannekeet, K., & Sloep, P. (2013). Experts' views on digital competence: Commonalities and differences. *Computers & Education, 68*, 473–481.

Javorský, S., & Horváth, R. (2014). Phenomenon of digital literacy in scope of european cross-curricular comparison. *Procedia: Social and Behavioral Sciences, 143*, 769–777.

Jayaganesh, J., Kumar, K. S., Krishna, K. H., Tiwari, M., Vettriselvan, R., & Shelke, C. (2025). Different requirements in quality of service using an adaptive network algorithm. In *Advances in AI for cloud, edge, and mobile computing applications* (pp. 323–343). Apple Academic Press.

Jha, A. (2023). AI-Powered Transcription and Preservation of Oral Histories in Indigenous Communities. *Journal of Digital Humanities, 12*(1), 45–62.

Jia, T., Iqbal, S., Ayub, A., Fatima, T., & Rasool, Z. (2023). Promoting Responsible Sustainable Consumer Behavior through Sustainability Marketing: The Boundary Effects of Corporate Social Responsibility and Brand Image. *Sustainability (Switzerland), 15*(7). Advance online publication. DOI: 10.3390/su15076092

Johannesen, M., Øgrim, L., & Giæver, T. H. (2014). Notion in motion: Teachers' digital competence. *Nordic Journal of Digital Literacy, 9*(4), 300–312.

Jones, M. (2022). Virtual Reality for Cultural Heritage Preservation: Recreating Indigenous Landscapes. *Presence (Cambridge, Mass.), 31*(1), 50–65.

Jones, P. L., Mahelona, K., Duncan, S., & Leoni, G. (2025). Kaitiaki: Closing the door on open Indigenous data. *International Journal on Digital Libraries, 26*(1), 1.

Josukutty, C. A. (2020). Global internet governance. *Indian Journal of Asian Affairs, 33*(1/2), 63–78.

Jovanović, N. (2024). Vratarji na področju tehnologij umetne inteligence. In T. Kerešteš (Ed.), *Digitalne platforme: pravni in ekonomski izzivi* (pp. 59–79). Maribor: Univerza v Mariboru, Univerzitetna založba. https://press.um.si/index.php/ump/catalog/book/5pf24

Juškevičienė, A., & Dagien, Ė, V. (2018). Computational thinking relationship with digital competence. *Informatics in Education, 17*(2), 265–284.

Kanbur, N. (2021). Istanbul Convention: Commitment to Preventing Gender-Based Violence. *The Journal of Adolescent Health, 69*(2), 354–355. DOI: 10.1016/j.jadohealth.2021.05.009

Kan, C. H. (2024). Artificial intelligence (AI) in the age of democracy and human rights: Normative challenges and regulatory perspectives. *International Journal of Eurasian Education and Culture, 9*(25), 145–166.

Kasemsap, K. (2018). Encouraging digital literacy and ICT competency in the information age. In *Encyclopedia of Information Science and Technology* (4th ed., pp. 2253–2263). IGI Global.

Kasperski, R., Blau, I., & Ben-Yehudah, G. (2022). Teaching digital literacy: Are teachers' perspectives consistent with actual pedagogy? *Technology, Pedagogy and Education, 31*(5), 615–635.

Kateryna, A., Oleksandr, R., Mariia, T., Iryna, S., Evgen, K., & Anastasiia, L. (2020). Digital literacy development trends in the professional environment. *International Journal of Learning. Teaching and Educational Research, 19*(7), 55–79.

Kausche, K., & Weiss, M. (2024). Platform power and regulatory capture in digital governance. *Business and Politics*, •••, 1–25. DOI: 10.1017/bap.2024.33

Kaye, D. (2019). *Speech Police: The Global Struggle to Govern the Internet*. Columbia Global Reports.

Kerber, W. (2023). Governance of IoT data: Why the EU Data Act will not fulfill its objectives. *GRUR International, 72*(2), 120–135. DOI: 10.1093/grurint/ikac173

Khan, F., & Vuopala, E. (2019). Digital competence assessment across generations: A Finnish sample using the digcomp framework. [IJDLDC]. *International Journal of Digital Literacy and Digital Competence, 10*(2), 15–28.

Khokhar, A. S. (2016). Digital literacy: How prepared is India to embrace it? [IJDLDC]. *International Journal of Digital Literacy and Digital Competence, 7*(3), 1–12.

Kiilu, T. K. (2025). Challenges of democratization in the age of AI: Navigating governance, equity, and ethical dilemmas. In *Democracy and democratization in the age of AI* (pp. 203–234). IGI Global Scientific Publishing.

Kim, A., Isaac, A., & Nadas, A. (2022). Indigenous knowledge and artificial intelligence: Opportunities and challenges. *AI & Society*, *37*(2), 645–657.

Kim, H. J., Hong, A. J., & Song, H. D. (2018). The relationships of family, perceived digital competence and attitude, and learning agility in sustainable student engagement in higher education. *Sustainability*, *10*(12), 4635.

Kim, J. (2024). Immersive VR Experiences for Transmitting Traditional Indigenous Ceremonies. *Digital Applications in Archaeology and Cultural Heritage*, *32*, 100290.

Kim, K. T. (2019). The structural relationship among digital literacy, learning strategies, and core competencies among south korean college students. *Educational Sciences: Theory & Practice*, *19*(2), 3–21.

Kimmerer, R. W. (2013). *Braiding sweetgrass: Indigenous wisdom, scientific knowledge and the teachings of plants*. Milkweed Editions.

Kirkness, V. J., & Barnhardt, R. (2016). First Nations and Higher Education: The Four R's— Respect, Relevance, Reciprocity, Responsibility. *The Journal of College and University Student Housing*, *42*(2).

Kissler, G. D. (1994). The new employment contract. *Human Resource Management*, *33*(3), 335–352. DOI: 10.1002/hrm.3930330304

Klare, K. E. (1992). Power/dressing: Regulation of employee appearance. *New England Law Review*, *26*, 1395–1436.

Klepac, G. (2018). Cognitive Data Science Automatic Fraud Detection Solution, Based on Benford'S Law, Fuzzy Logic with Elements of Machine Learning // Cognitive Computing for Big Data Systems Over IoT. Cham: Springer, 2018. str. 79-95. doi: DOI: 10.1007/978-3-319-70688-7_4

Klepac, G. at all. (2014). *Developing churn models using data mining techniques and social network analysis*. IGI Global.

Klepac, G. (2017). The Schrödinger equation as inspiration for a client portfolio simulation hybrid system based on dynamic Bayesian networks and the REFII model. In *Quantum Inspired Computational Intelligence* (pp. 391–416). Morgan Kaufmann.

Klugman, J. (2017). Gender based violence and the law. *Background paper for World Development Report 2017*. https://srhr.dspace-express.com/server/api/core/bitstreams/87a1eef7-a563-4986-b3a9-03969a61e5af/content

Koch, C., & Fehlmann, F. (2025). Beyond digital literacy: Exploring factors affecting digital performance of university staff. *Media and Communication*, •••, 13.

Koltay, T. (2011). The media and the literacies: Media literacy, information literacy, digital literacy. *Media Culture & Society*, *33*(2), 211–221.

König, P. D. (2022). Fortress Europe 4.0? An analysis of EU data governance through the lens of the resource regime concept. *European Policy Analysis*, *8*(4), 409–426. DOI: 10.1002/epa2.1144

Kooiman, J. (2003). *Governing as governance*. SAGE Publications.

Koppel, I., & Langer, S. (2020). Basic digital literacy-Requirements and elements. *Revista Práxis Educacional*, *16*(42), 326–347.

KOROL, S., & ROMASHKO, O. (2022). Corporate social responsibility in transfer pricing strategies. *Foreign Trade: Economics, Finance. Law*, *122*(3). Advance online publication. DOI: 10.31617/zt.knute.2022(122)01

Kovach, M. (2021). *Indigenous methodologies: Characteristics, conversations, and contexts*. University of Toronto Press.

Kovalenko, Y. (2022). The Right to Privacy and Protection of Personal Data: Emerging Trends and Implications for Development in Jurisprudence of European Court of Human Rights. *Masaryk University Journal of Law and Technology*, *16*(1), 37–58.

Kozen, G. H. (2021). *Summary of the trial decision in Epic Games v. Apple*. Robins Kaplan LLP. Retrieved March 30, 2025 from https://www.robinskaplan.com/newsroom/insights/summary-of-the-trial-decision-in-epic-games-v-apple

Krämer, J., Colangelo, G., Richter, H., & Schnurr, D. (2023). *Data Act: Towards a balanced EU data regulation*. Centre on Regulation in Europe (CERRE). Retrieved March 19, 2025 from https://cerre.eu/wp-content/uploads/2023/04/CERRE_Data-Act_Report_April-2023.pdf

Kretschmer, M., Margoni, T., & Oruç, P. (2024). Copyright Law and the Lifecycle of Machine Learning Models. *IIC International Review of Intellectual Property and Competition Law*, *55*(1). Advance online publication. DOI: 10.1007/s40319-023-01419-3

Krumsvik, R. J., Jones, L. Ø., Øfstegaard, M., & Eikeland, O. J. (2016). Upper secondary school teachers' digital competence: Analysed by demographic, personal and professional characteristics. *Nordic journal of digital literacy*, *11*(3), 143-164.

Krumsvik, R. J. (2008). Situated learning and teachers' digital competence. *Education and Information Technologies*, *13*(4), 279–290.

Krumsvik, R. J. (2011). Digital competence in the Norwegian teacher education and schools. *Högre Utbildning*, *1*(1), 39–51.

Krumsvik, R. J. (2014). Teacher educators' digital competence. *Scandinavian Journal of Educational Research*, *58*(3), 269–280.

Krumsvik, R. J. (2022). Digital competence across the education and health sector. *Nordic Journal of Digital Literacy*, (3), 149–154.

Kumar, A. B., & Sanjaya, K. (2025a). Ethics, Algorithms, and the Rules of Evidence. *Forensic Intelligence and Deep Learning Solutions in Crime Investigation*, 103–124. https://doi.org/DOI: 10.4018/979-8-3693-9405-2.ch006

Kumar, A. B., & Sanjaya, K. (2025b). AI and Social Justice: Democratizing Technology for Inclusive Growth. In Chakraborty, S. (Ed.), *Ethical AI Solutions for Addressing Social Media Influence and Hate Speech* (pp. 163–190). IGI Global Scientific Publishing., DOI: 10.4018/979-8-3693-9904-0.ch008

Kumar, A. B., Sanjaya, K., & Saleem, M. (2025). Justice in the Age of Algorithms. *Advances in Computational Intelligence and Robotics*, •••, 191–210. DOI: 10.4018/979-8-3693-9395-6.ch009

Kuzminska, O., Mazorchuk, M., Morze, N., Pavlenko, V., & Prokhorov, A. (2019). Study of digital competence of the students and teachers in Ukraine. In *Information and Communication Technologies in Education, Research, and Industrial Applications: 14th International Conference, ICTERI 2018, Kyiv, Ukraine, May 14-17, 2018, Revised Selected Papers 14* (pp. 148-169). Springer International Publishing.

Laird, S. A. (Ed.). (2010). *Biodiversity and traditional knowledge: Equitable partnerships in practice*. Earthscan.

Lalonde, D. (2024, June 12). *Online harms need a gender-based analysis*. Policy Options. https://policyoptions.irpp.org/magazines/june-2024/deepfake-sexual-abuse/

Lau, M. (2024, March 12). *An overview of Canada's Online Harms Act*. Tech Policy Press. https://www.techpolicy.press/an-overview-of-canadas-online-harms-act/

Lawton, T. C. (2024). The New Global Electronic Economy: Consensus, Confusion, Contradictions. *Routledge EBooks*, 39–60. https://doi.org/DOI: 10.4324/9781003576990-5

Leahy, D., & Dolan, D. (2010, September). Digital literacy: A vital competence for 2010? In *IFIP international conference on key competencies in the knowledge society* (pp. 210–221). Springer Berlin Heidelberg.

Lee, S. H. (2014). Digital literacy education for the development of digital literacy. [IJDLDC]. *International Journal of Digital Literacy and Digital Competence*, *5*(3), 29–43.

Legvart, P., Kordigel Aberšek, M., & Kerneža, M. (2021). Primary School Students' Natural Science Digital Literacy Competence in Digital Learning Environments. In *International Baltic Symposium on Science and Technology Education*. Scientia Socialis Ltd. 29 K. Donelaicio Street, LT-78115 Siauliai, Republic of Lithuania.

Leiser, M. (2023). *Reimagining digital governance: The EU's Digital Services Act and the fight against disinformation. SSRN*. https://doi.org/DOI: 10.2139/ssrn.4427493

Lemieux, F. (2024). Mass Surveillance. *Emerald Publishing Limited EBooks*, 159–170. https://doi.org/DOI: 10.1108/978-1-83549-097-620242010

Levano-Francia, L., Sanchez Diaz, S., Guillén-Aparicio, P., Tello-Cabello, S., Herrera-Paico, N., & Collantes-Inga, Z. (2019). Digital Competences and Education. *Journal of Educational Psychology-Propositos y Representaciones*, *7*(2), 579–588.

Lewis, A. (2024). AR-Enhanced Learning of Indigenous Knowledge: An Interactive Approach. *British Journal of Educational Technology*, *55*(1), 78–95.

Li, Y., & Ranieri, M. (2010). Are 'digital natives' really digitally competent?—A study on Chinese teenagers. *British Journal of Educational Technology*, *41*(6), 1029–1042.

Liyanaarachchi, G., Viglia, G., & Kurtaliqi, F. (2024). Addressing challenges of digital transformation with modified blockchain. *Technological Forecasting and Social Change*, *201*, 123254–123254. DOI: 10.1016/j.techfore.2024.123254

Lomawaima, K. T., & McCarty, T. L. (2025). *To remain an Indian": Lessons in democracy from a century of Native American education*. Teachers College Press.

Lombardi, L. (2019). *Indigenous Cultural Heritage Law: Protection, Management and Control*. Routledge.

Long, T. B., & Blok, V. (2023). Managing the Responsibilities of Doing Good and Avoiding Harm in Sustainability-Orientated Innovations: Example from Agri-Tech Start-Ups in the Netherlands. In *Library of Ethics and Applied Philosophy* (Vol. 40). https://doi.org/DOI: 10.1007/978-3-031-14710-4_13

López-Meneses, E., Sirignano, F. M., Vázquez-Cano, E., & Ramírez-Hurtado, J. M. (2020). University students' digital competence in three areas of the DigCom 2.1 model: A comparative study at three European universities. *Australasian Journal of Educational Technology*, *36*(3), 69–88.

Lund, A., Furberg, A., Bakken, J., & Engelien, K. L. (2014). What does professional digital competence mean in teacher education?. *Nordic journal of digital literacy, 9*(4), 280-298.

Lundqvist, B. (2025). The objectives of regulating the digital economy indicate that there is a right to data in the Digital Markets Act with direct effect and applicability. In Engel, A., Groussot, X., & Petursson, G. T. (Eds.), *New Directions in Digitalisation. European Union and its Neighbours in a Globalized World* (pp. 29–47). Springer.

Maderick, J. A., Zhang, S., Hartley, K., & Marchand, G. (2016). Preservice teachers and self-assessing digital competence. *Journal of Educational Computing Research, 54*(3), 326–351.

Madnick, B., Huang, K., & Madnick, S. E. (2023). The evolution of global cybersecurity norms in the digital age: A longitudinal study of the cybersecurity norm development process. *Information Security Journal: A Global Perspective, 33*(3), 1–22. https://doi.org/DOI: 10.1080/19393555.2023.2201482

Maher, D. (2020). Pre-service teachers' digital competencies to support school students' digital literacies. In *Handbook of research on literacy and digital technology integration in teacher education* (pp. 29–46). IGI Global Scientific Publishing.

Makhafola, L., van Deventer, M. J., Holmner, M. A., & Van Wyk, B. (2025). A scoping review of digital literacy, digital competence, digital fluency and digital dexterity in academic libraries' context. *Journal of Academic Librarianship, 51*(3), 103053.

Malik v British Home Stores [1980] ET Case No. 2901/79.

Malik, S. A. (2024). SDG 2: Zero hunger, food and plant-related intellectual property, and access to plant genetic resources. In *The Elgar Companion to Intellectual Property and the Sustainable Development Goals*. https://doi.org/DOI: 10.4337/9781803925233.00009

Maltby, L. L., & Dushman, B. J. (1994). Whose life is it anyway—Employer control of off-duty behavior. *Saint Louis University Public Law Review, 13*, 645–671.

Manche, R., Samaah, F., Tejaswini, T., & Myakala, P. K. (2025). Empowering Safe Online Spaces: AI in Gender Violence Detection and Prevention. SSRN *Electronic Journal*. DOI: 10.2139/ssrn.5176463

Mannila, L., Nordén, L. Å., & Pears, A. (2018, August). Digital competence, teacher self-efficacy and training needs. In *Proceedings of the 2018 ACM Conference on International Computing Education Research* (pp. 78-85).

Marie-Vivien, D. (2016). A comparative analysis of GIs for handicrafts: the link to origin in culture as well as nature? In *Research handbook on intellectual property and geographical indications* (pp. 292–326). Edward Elgar Publishing.

Marín, V. I., & Castaneda, L. (2022). Developing digital literacy for teaching and learning. In *Handbook of open, distance and digital education* (pp. 1–20). Springer Nature Singapore.

Marique, E., & Marique, Y. (2020). Sanctions on digital platforms: Balancing proportionality in a modern public square. *Computer Law & Security Review, 36*(105372), 105372. DOI: 10.1016/j.clsr.2019.105372

Marnita, M., Nurdin, D., & Prihatin, E. (2023). The effectiveness of elementary teacher digital literacy competence on teacher learning management. *Journal of Innovation in Educational and Cultural Research, 4*(1), 35–43.

Marsh, J. (2016). The digital literacy skills and competences of children of pre-school age. *Medical Education*, (2), 178–195.

Martin, A. (2008). Digital literacy and the "digital society". *Digital literacies: Concepts, policies and practices, 30*(151), 1029-1055.

Martin, A., & Grudziecki, J. (2006). DigEuLit: Concepts and tools for digital literacy development. *Innovation in teaching and learning in information and computer sciences, 5*(4), 249-267.

Martin, A. (2006). A European framework for digital literacy. *Nordic Journal of Digital Literacy, 1*(2), 151–161.

Martínez-Alcalá, C. I., Rosales-Lagarde, A., Alonso-Lavernia, M. D. L. Á., Ramírez-Salvador, J. Á., Jiménez-Rodríguez, B., Cepeda-Rebollar, R. M., & Agis-Juárez, R. A. (2018). Digital inclusion in older adults: A comparison between face-to-face and blended digital literacy workshops. *Frontiers in ICT (Lausanne, Switzerland), 5*, 21.

Martínez-Bravo, M. C., Sádaba Chalezquer, C., & Serrano-Puche, J. (2022). Dimensions of digital literacy in the 21st century competency frameworks. *Sustainability, 14*(3), 1867.

Martínez-Bravo, M. C., Sádaba-Chalezquer, C., & Serrano-Puche, J. (2020). Fifty years of digital literacy studies: A meta-research for interdisciplinary and conceptual convergence. *El Profesional de la Información, 29*(4).

Martzoukou, K., Luders, E. S., Mair, J., Kostagiolas, P., Johnson, N., Work, F., & Fulton, C. (2024). A cross-sectional study of discipline-based self-perceived digital literacy competencies of nursing students. *Journal of Advanced Nursing*, *80*(2), 656–672.

Marwick, A., & Lewis, R. (2017). *Media manipulation and disinformation online*. Data & Society.

Marx, G. T. (2019). *Windows into the soul: Surveillance and society in an age of high technology*. University of Chicago Press.

Mas'udah, S., Razali, A., Sholicha, S. M. A., Febrianto, P. T., Susanti, E., & Budirahayu, T. (2024). *Gender-Based Cyber Violence: Forms, impacts, and strategies to protect women victims*. Virtual Commons - Bridgewater State University. https://vc.bridgew.edu/jiws/vol26/iss4/5

Mazany, T., & Perry, D. C. (Eds.). (2013). *Here for good: Community foundations and the challenges of the 21st century*. ME Sharpe.

Mazzocchi, F. (2022). Diving deeper into the concept of 'cultural heritage'and its relationship with epistemic diversity. *Social Epistemology*, *36*(3), 393–406.

Mbandje, D. C., Loureiro, M. J., & Lucas, M. (2023). Digital competence and information literacy: Clarifying concepts based on a literature review. *Educational Media International*, *60*(3-4), 306–316.

McDougall, J., Readman, M., & Wilkinson, P. (2018). The uses of (digital) literacy. *Learning, Media and Technology*, *43*(3), 263–279.

McGlynn, C., Woods, L., & Antoniou, A. (2024). Pornography, the Online Safety Act 2023 and the need for further reform. *Journal of Media Law*, 1–29. DOI: 10.1080/17577632.2024.2357421

Mehrabi, N., Morstatter, F., Saxena, N., Lerman, K., & Galstyan, A. (2021). A survey on bias and fairness in machine learning. *ACM Computing Surveys*, *54*(6), 1–35. DOI: 10.1145/3457607

Mehrvarz, M., Heidari, E., Farrokhnia, M., & Noroozi, O. (2021). The mediating role of digital informal learning in the relationship between students' digital competence and their academic performance. *Computers & Education*, *167*, 104184.

Memon, S. F., & Khan, W. A. (2020). Wearable technology for infant health monitoring: A survey. *IET Cyber-Systems and Robotics*, *2*(3), 124–134. https://ietresearch.onlinelibrary.wiley.com/doi/10.1049/iet-cds.2018.5447

Menggo, S., Midun, H., & Pandor, P. (2021). Students' digital literacy competence and English study habits. In *The 1st International Conference on Education, Humanities, Health, and Agriculture.* (pp. 3-6).DOI: <ALIGNMENT.qj></ALIGNMENT>10.4108/eai

Merolla, A. J., Neubauer, A. B., & Otmar, C. D. (2024). Responsiveness, Social Connection, Hope, and Life Satisfaction in Everyday Social Interaction: An Experience Sampling Study. *Journal of Happiness Studies*, *25*(1–2). Advance online publication. DOI: 10.1007/s10902-024-00710-5

Merritt, B. (2016). The digital revolution. In *The Digital Revolution* (pp. 15–17). Springer International Publishing.

Meyer, E. T., & Schroeder, R. (2023). *Knowledge machines: Digital transformations of the sciences and humanities*. Mit Press.

Middlemiss, S. (2018). Not what to wear? Employers' liability for dress codes? *International Journal of Discrimination and the Law*, *18*(1), 40–58. DOI: 10.1177/1358229118757867

Milaj-Weishaar, J. (2020). Safeguarding Privacy by Regulating the Processing of Personal Data – An EU Illusion? *European Journal of Law and Technology*, *11*(2).

Milenkova, V., & Lendzhova, V. (2021). Digital citizenship and digital literacy in the conditions of social crisis. *Computers*, *10*(4), 40.

Miotto, R., Wang, F., Wang, S., Jiang, X., & Dudley, J. T. (2018). Deep learning for healthcare: Review, opportunities, and challenges. *Briefings in Bioinformatics*, *19*(6), 1236–1246.

Mishra, P., & Sharma, P. K. (2018). Digital literacy competencies in the 21st century. *Globus Journal of Progressive Education*, *8*(2), 1–3.

Modi, M. N., Palmer, S., & Armstrong, A. (2013). The Role of Violence Against Women Act in Addressing Intimate Partner Violence: A public health issue. *Journal of Women's Health*, *23*(3), 253–259. DOI: 10.1089/jwh.2013.4387

MOKHTARI, F. (2023). Fostering Digital Literacy in Higher Education: Benefits, Challenges and Implications. *International Journal of Linguistics, Literature & Translation, 6*(10).

Monshipouri, M. (2017). Human rights in the digital age: Opportunities and constraints. *Public Integrity*, *19*(2), 123–135.

Morandín-Ahuerma, F. (2023). Diez recomendaciones de la Unesco sobre ética de la inteligencia artificial. In Morandín, F. (Ed.), *Principios normativos para una ética de la inteligencia artificial* (pp. 86–94). Concytep.

Morellato, M. (2014). Digital competence in tourism education: Cooperative-experiential learning. *Journal of Teaching in Travel & Tourism, 14*(2), 184–209.

Moreno-Guerrero, A. J., Marín-Marin, J. A., López-Belmonte, J., & Churi, P. (2022). Systematic review on digital competence in the Spanish context. *Digital Literacy for Teachers*, 495-517.

Moreton-Robinson, A. (2015). *The white possessive: Property, power, and Indigenous sovereignty*. University of Minnesota Press.

Müller, M. L., Frenz, M., & Nitsch, V. (2023). Digitale Kompetenz, Digital Literacy, Digital Competence–Eine vergleichende, strukturierte Literaturanalyse deutsch-und englischsprachiger Beiträge. *Jahrbuch der berufs-und wirtschaftspädagogischen. Forschung, 2023*, 9.

Müller, M., & Kettemann, M. C. (2024). European approaches to the regulation of digital technologies. In Werthner, H., Fleisch, E., Bauer, A., & Matthes, F. (Eds.), *Introduction to digital humanism* (pp. 655–670). Springer., DOI: 10.1007/978-3-031-45304-5_39

Murphy, O. (2018). Digital competences: A foundational digital literacy for all. In *Design Thinking for Digital Well-being* (pp. 16–26). Routledge.

Murtadho, M. I., Rohmah, R. Y., Jamilah, Z., & Furqon, M. (2023). The role of digital literacy in improving students' competence in digital era. *AL-WIJDÃN Journal of Islamic Education Studies, 8*(2), 253–260.

Musa, S., Abubakari, M. S., & Abdulwahab, L. O. (2025). Evaluating the potential of adapting Artificial Intelligence (AI) in small and medium enterprises for competitive advantage. In *Multi-Industry Digitalization and Technological Governance in the AI Era* (pp. 233–266). IGI Global., DOI: 10.4018/979-8-3373-1681-9.ch012

Nada, E. I., & Sari, W. K. (2020). Digital literacy analysis of chemistry education students in using the ChemDraw application. [Jurnal Kimia Dan Pendidikan Kimia]. *JKPK, 5*(3), 293–299.

Nambiar, N. (2025). UIDAI deactivates 1.4 crore Aadhaar numbers of deceased across India. *The Times of India*. https://timesofindia.indiatimes.com/city/pune/uidai-deactivates-1-4-crore-aadhaar-numbers-of-deceased-sets-2-crore-target-for-year-end/articleshow/124033065.cms

Napal Fraile, M., Peñalva-Vélez, A., & Mendióroz Lacambra, A. M. (2018). Development of digital competence in secondary education teachers' training. *Education Sciences*, *8*(3), 104.

Narayanan, S., & Pradhan, S. K. (2024). Exploring the research landscape of socially responsible investment through bibliometrics. In *Multidisciplinary Reviews* (Vol. 7, Issue 1). https://doi.org/DOI: 10.31893/multirev.2024022

Nascimbeni, F. (2018). Rethinking digital literacy for teachers in open and participatory societies. [IJDLDC]. *International Journal of Digital Literacy and Digital Competence*, *9*(3), 1–11.

Nascimbeni, F., & Vosloo, S. (2019). Digital literacy for children: Exploring definitions and frameworks. *Scoping Paper*, *1*, 1.

Nath, V., Bach, S., & Lockwood, G. (2016). Dress codes and appearance at work: Body supplements, body modification and aesthetic labour (Research Paper Ref: 07/16). Acas. https://archive.acas.org.uk/media/4566/Dress-codes-and-appearance-at-work-Body-supplements-body-modification-and-aesthetic-labour/pdf/Dress_codes_and_appearance_at_work.pdf

Naxera, V., & Piknerová, L. (2011a). Úvodem. In Naxera, V., & Piknerová, L. (Eds.), *Globální vládnutí. Vybrané problémy* (pp. 11–15). Aleš Čeněk.

Ndou, A. T., Madonsela, N. S., & Twala, B. (2020). The era of digital technology: Analysis of factors contributing to economic growth and sustainability. *Proceedings of the International Conference on Industrial Engineering and Operations Management,* 59.

Neagu, G. (2022). Understanding the implications of digital competence for the education process in Romania. A literature review. *Digital Literacy for Teachers*, 441-462.

Nebot, M. Á. L., Cosentino, V. V., Esteve-Mon, F. M., & Segura, J. A. (2021). Diagnostic and educational self-assessment of the digital competence of university teachers. *Nordic Journal of Digital Literacy*, (3-4), 115–131.

Nelles, J. (2020). *Online and technology-facilitated violence against women and girls: Standards of the Istanbul Convention* [Presentation]. https://rm.coe.int/1-presentation-nelles-cyberviolence-against-women-and-ic-nov-2020/1680a0561c

Nelson, K., Courier, M., & Joseph, G. W. (2011). An investigation of digital literacy needs of students. *Journal of Information Systems Education*, *22*(2), 95–110.

Neves, I. (2025). A reading of the Digital Markets Act in the light of fundamental rights. In Engel, A., Groussot, X., & Petursson, G. T. (Eds.), *New directions in digitalization: European Union and its neighbours in a globalized world* (pp. 117–164). Springer., DOI: 10.1007/978-3-031-65381-0_8

Nguyen, C. L., & Golman, W. (2020). Diffusion of the Budapest Convention on cybercrime and the development of cybercrime legislation in Pacific Island countries: 'Law on the books' vs 'law in action.'. *Computer Law & Security Review*, *40*, 105521. DOI: 10.1016/j.clsr.2020.105521

Nguyen, L. A. T., & Habók, A. (2024). Tools for assessing teacher digital literacy: A review. *Journal of Computers in Education*, *11*(1), 305–346.

Nhemi, S. (2023). Law Without Lawyers: Examining the Limitations of Consumer-Centric Legal Tech Services. [JIPIT]. *Journal of Intellectual Property and Information Technology Law*, *3*(1). Advance online publication. DOI: 10.52907/jipit.v3i1.223

Niemietz v Germany, App. No. 13710/88, 16 EHRR 97 (1992).

Noah v Desrosiers t/a Wedge [2008] ET Case No. 2201867/07.

Noble, S. U. (2018). Algorithms of oppression: How search engines reinforce racism. In *Algorithms of oppression*. New York university press.

Noble, S. U. (2018). *Algorithms of Oppression: How Search Engines Reinforce Racism*. NYU Press.

Nolan, M., & Gaffey, J. (2024). Online safety and social media regulation in Australia: eSafety Commissioner v X Corp. *Griffith Law Review*, *33*(1), 2–18. DOI: 10.1080/10383441.2024.2405760

Norman, D. A. (2013). *The design of everyday things*. Basic Books.

Novak, M. (2021). *Pravna argumentacija v teoriji in praksi*. Ljubljana: Uradni list RS.

Nussbaum, M. C. (2011). Creating Capabilities: The Human Development Approach. *The Belknap Press of Harvard University Press, Cambridge, Massachusetts, and London, England 2011*. https://dokumen.pub/creating-capabilities-the-human-development-approach-0674050541-9780674050549-0674061209-9780674061200.html

O'Brien, D., Ruru, J., & Te Ahukaramū Charles Royal, C. (2020). *Routledge handbook of law and Indigenous peoples*. Routledge.

O'Faircheallaigh, C. (2021). Explaining outcomes from negotiated agreements in Australia and Canada. *Resources Policy*, *70*, 101922.

O'Neil, C. (2017). *Weapons of math destruction: How big data increases inequality and threatens democracy*. Crown.

Oberländer, M., Beinicke, A., & Bipp, T. (2020). Digital competencies: A review of the literature and applications in the workplace. *Computers & Education, 146*, 103752.

Obermeyer, Z., & Emanuel, E. J. (2016). Predicting the future—Big data, machine learning, and clinical medicine. *The New England Journal of Medicine, 375*(13), 1216–1219. DOI: 10.1056/NEJMp1606181

Ofcom. (2024, December). *Protecting people from illegal harms online: Volume 2 – Service design and user choice*. Ofcom. https://www.ofcom.org.uk/siteassets/resources/documents/online-safety/information-for-industry/illegal-harms/volume-2-service-design-and-user-choice.pdf?v=390978

Ogwezzy, M. C. (2012). Protection of Indigenous or Traditional Knowledge Under Intellectual Property Laws: An Examination of the Efficacy of Copyright Law, Trade Secret. *International and Comparative Law Review, 12*(1), 5–34.

OHCHR. (n.d.). UN Hub for Human Rights and Digital Technology. https://www.ohchr.org/en/hub-human-rights-and-digital-technology

Ojha, H. R., Ford, R., Keenan, R. J., Race, D., Vega, D. C., Baral, H., & Sapkota, P. (2016). Delocalizing communities: Changing forms of community engagement in natural resources governance. *World Development, 87*, 274–290.

Olimpo, G. (2013). Rifessioni brevi su digital literacy e digital competence. *Italian Journal of Educational Technology, 21*(1), 14–18.

Orakova, A., Nametkulova, F., Issayeva, G., Mukhambetzhanova, S., Galimzhanova, M., & Rezuanova, G. (2024). The relationships between pedagogical and technological competence and digital literacy level of teachers. *Journal of Curriculum Studies Research, 6*(1), 1–21.

Ottestad, G., Kelentrić, M., & Guðmundsdóttir, G. B. (2014). Professional digital competence in teacher education. *Nordic journal of digital literacy, 9*(4), 243-249.

Pacheco, E., & Melhuish, N. (2018). Harmful Digital Communications in New Zealand: Annual Population Survey 2017. SSRN *Electronic Journal*. DOI: 10.2139/ssrn.3128121

Pagallo, U. (2022). The politics of data in EU law: Will it succeed? *Digital Society : Ethics, Socio-Legal and Governance of Digital Technology, 1*(1), 20. Advance online publication. DOI: 10.1007/s44206-022-00020-4

Palacios-Hidalgo, F. J., & Huertas-Abril, C. A. (2025). Developing digital literacy in initial EFL teacher education: A study in a Spanish distance university. *Open Learning*, *40*(1), 50–66.

Pandey, P., Singh, R., & Verma, A. (2025). Predicting child mortality determinants in Uttar Pradesh using machine learning algorithms. *Children and Youth Services Review*, *150*, 105156. DOI: 10.1016/j.childyouth.2023.105156

Pangrazio, L., Godhe, A. L., & Ledesma, A. G. L. (2020). What is digital literacy? A comparative review of publications across three language contexts. *E-Learning and Digital Media*, *17*(6), 442–459.

Pardo, J. L. (2020). *La educación del futuro y otros escritos*. Fondo de Cultura Económica.

Park, H., Kim, H. S., & Park, H. W. (2021). A scientometric study of digital literacy, ICT literacy, information literacy, and media literacy. *Journal of Data and Information Science*, *6*(2), 116–138.

Parlee, B.. (2022). Indigenous Knowledge for Climate Change Assessment and Adaptation. *Nature Climate Change*, *12*(8), 731–737.

Pavčnik, M. (2015). *Teorija prava: prispevek k razumevanju prava*. GV Založba.

Pegalajar Palomino, M. D. C., & Rodríguez Torres, Á. F. (2023, November). Digital literacy in university students of education degrees in Ecuador. [). Frontiers Media SA.]. *Frontiers in Education*, *8*, 1299059.

Peng, D., & Yu, Z. (2022). A literature review of digital literacy over two decades. *Education Research International*, *2022*(1), 2533413.

Perel, M., Elkin-Koren, N., & De Gregorio, G. (2021, February 10). (forthcoming). Social media as contractual networks: A bottom-up check on content moderation. *Iowa Law Review*.Paper presented at TPRC49: The 49th Research Conference on Communication, Information and Internet Policy. SSRN. https://doi.org/DOI: 10.2139/ssrn.3797554

Pérez-Escoda, A., & Rodríguez-Conde, M. J. (2015, October). Digital literacy and digital competences in the educational evaluation: USA and IEA contexts. In *Proceedings of the 3rd international conference on technological ecosystems for enhancing multiculturality* (pp. 355-360).

Peters, S. (2024). *Digital Literacy and Competence*. Digital Foundations for Art and Design Studies.

Petit, A., Wala, Z., Ciucci, M., & Martinello, B. (2024). *Evropska digitalna agenda*. In *Kratki vodnik po Evropski uniji*. Evropski parlament. Retrieved May 10, 2025 from https://www.europarl.europa.eu/factsheets/sl/sheet/64/evropska-digitalna-agenda

Pettersson, F. (2018). On the issues of digital competence in educational contexts–a review of literature. *Education and Information Technologies*, *23*(3), 1005–1021.

Peyrone, N., & Wichadakul, D. (2023). A formal model for blockchain-based consent management in data sharing. Journal of Logical and Algebraic Methods in Programming, 134, Article 100886.

Pfeiffer v Deutsches Rotes Kreuz, Joined Cases C-397/01 to C-403/01, [2004] ECR I-8835.

Phuapan, P., Viriyavejakul, C., & Pimdee, P. (2016). An analysis of digital literacy skills among Thai university seniors. *International Journal of Emerging Technologies in Learning (Online)*, *11*(3), 24.

Pine, A., & Turin, M. (2017). Language revitalization. *Oxford research encyclopaedia of linguistics*.

Piotrkowski, C. S. (1979). *Work and the family system: A naturalistic study of working-class and lower-middle-class families*. Collier Macmillan.

Plan International. 2020. Free to be Online? A report on online abuse and harassment experienced by girls. https://www.plan.de/fileadmin/website/05._Ueber_uns/Maedchenberichte/Maedchenbericht_2020/Free_to_be_online_report_englisch_FINAL.pdf

Porat, E., Blau, I., & Barak, A. (2018). Measuring digital literacies: Junior high-school students' perceived competencies versus actual performance. *Computers & Education*, *126*, 23–36.

Portillo, J., Garay, U., Tejada, E., & Bilbao, N. (2020). Self-perception of the digital competence of educators during the COVID-19 pandemic: A cross-analysis of different educational stages. *Sustainability*, *12*(23), 10128.

Pötzsch, H. (2016). Materialist perspectives on digital technologies: Informing debates on digital literacy and competence.

Powell, C. (2020). From business suit to business beanie: Dress code, personality, and job satisfaction in the workplace [Master's thesis, Xavier University]. Xavier University Theses and Dissertations.

Prats, A. J. (2018). *Invisible Natives: Myth and Identity in the American Western*. Cornell University Press.

Primec, A., Pastirk, G., & Perko, I. (2024). Sovereignty over personal data: Legal frameworks and the quest for privacy in the digital age. In Pucelj, M., & Bohinc, R. (Eds.), *Balancing human rights, social responsibility, and digital ethics*.

Putra, S., Hamsal, M., Sundjaja, A. M., & Gunadi, W. (2024). Navigating the interplay between digital innovation and ethical AI for the development of smart societies: A comprehensive literature review. In *2024 International Conference on ICT for Smart Society (ICISS)* (pp. 1–8). IEEE.

Qiang, X. (2019). The road to digital unfreedom: President Xi's surveillance state. *Journal of Democracy*, *30*(1), 53–67.

Qingyi, W. (2023). A Study of the Improvement of Digital Literacy from the Perspective of DigComp 2.2: The Digital Competence Framework for Citizens. *Library Journal*, *42*(383), 97.

Qi, Y., Sajadi, S. M., Baghaei, S., Rezaei, R., & Li, W. (2024). Digital technologies in sports: Opportunities, challenges, and strategies for safeguarding athlete wellbeing and competitive integrity in the digital era. *Technology in Society*, *77*(1), 102496. DOI: 10.1016/j.techsoc.2024.102496

Quail, K., Green, D., & O'Faircheallaigh, C. (2025). Large-scale renewable energy developments on the indigenous estate: How can participation benefit Australia's FirstNation s peoples? *Energy Research & Social Science*, *123*, 104044.

Queniahan, M. (2024). Guidelines to ensure Māori Data Sovereignty in the ICT sector of Aotearoa New Zealand.

Quintais, J. P., Appelman, N., & Ó Fathaigh, R. (2023). Using terms and conditions to apply fundamental rights to content moderation. *German Law Journal*, *24*(5), 881–911. DOI: 10.1017/glj.2023.53

Rahman, T., Amalia, A., & Aziz, Z. (2021, January). From digital literacy to digital intelligence. In *4th International Conference on Sustainable Innovation 2020–Social, Humanity, and Education (ICoSIHESS 2020)* (pp. 154-159). Atlantis Press.

Rai, A., Ravi, K. E., Singh, S., & Vandermolen, R. (2024). Brief review of the 2022 reauthorization of the Violence Against Women Act: Gaps and way forward. *Journal of Social Work : JSW*, *25*(1), 125–133. DOI: 10.1177/14680173241278955

Rainie, S. C., Rodriguez-Lonebear, D., & Martinez, A. (2017). *Policy brief: Data governance strategies for federal agencies working with American Indian and Alaska Native nations*. Native Nations Institute, University of Arizona.

Rajani, K., Ranjan, T., Kumar, R. R., Patil, G., Kumar, M., Kumar, J., & Kumar, M. (2018). Traditional knowledge and its promotion through providing legal rights. In *The role of intellectual property rights in agriculture and allied sciences* (pp. 151–180). Apple Academic Press.

Rajani, N. (2022). "I bet you don't get what we get": An intersectional analysis of technology-facilitated violence experienced by racialized women anti-violence online activists in Canada. *Canadian Journal of Law and Technology*, *20*(2), 211–250.

Rambousek, V., Štípek, J., & Vaňková, P. (2016). Contents of digital literacy from the perspective of teachers and pupils. *Procedia: Social and Behavioral Sciences*, *217*, 354–362.

Ramirez, E. (2022). De/colonisation and the un/doing of critical theory. *Knowledge Cultures*, *10*(3), 150–176.

Rashid Diya, S. (2025). *Applying international human rights principles for AI governance. Policy Brieg No. 196 – February 2025. Centre for International Governance Innovation.* CIGI.

Rashid, N., Daud, W. N. W., Zainol, F. A., Salleh, F., Yazid, A. S., Endut, W. A., Yaakub, N., Ghazali, P. L., Afthanorhan, A., & Abdullah, B. (2018). The Stakeholders Perceptions towards the Corporate Social Responsibility Reporting. *International Journal of Academic Research in Business & Social Sciences*, *8*(11). Advance online publication. DOI: 10.6007/ijarbss/v8-i11/5171

Ratano, P. (2018). Digital competence and digital literacy in social media usage for the visually impaired youths in Thailand.

Rawls, J. (1971). *A theory of justice*. Harvard University Press.

Rawls, J. (1971). *A Theory of Justice: Original Edition*. Harvard University Press., DOI: 10.2307/j.ctvjf9z6v

Reddock, R. (2022). CEDAW and Violence against Women: Reflections after 40 years. *Violence Against Women*, *28*(8), 1723–1727. DOI: 10.1177/10778012221086003

Reddy, P., Chaudhary, K. C., Sharma, B. N., & Chand, R. (2022). Talismans of digital literacy: A statistical overview. *Electronic Journal of e-Learning*, *20*(5), 570–587.

Reddy, P., Chaudhary, K., & Hussein, S. (2023). A digital literacy model to narrow the digital literacy skills gap. *Heliyon*, *9*(4).

Reddy, P., Chaudhary, K., Sharma, B., & Chand, R. (2020, December). Digital Literacy: A Catalyst for the 21 st Century Education. In *2020 IEEE Asia-Pacific Conference on Computer Science and Data Engineering (CSDE)* (pp. 1-6). IEEE.

Reeves, J., Treharne, G. J., Theodore, R., Edwards, W., Ratima, M., & Poulton, R. (2022). Understanding the data-sharing debate in the context of Aotearoa/New Zealand: A narrative review on the perspectives of funders, publishers/journals, researchers, participants and Māori collectives. *Kotuitui, 17*(1), 1–23.

Reichert, F., Zhang, D., Law, N. W., Wong, G. K., & de la Torre, J. (2020). Exploring the structure of digital literacy competence assessed using authentic software applications. *Educational Technology Research and Development, 68*, 2991–3013.

Reuters. (2024, February 26). Draft Canada law would force social media companies to quickly remove harmful content. Reuters. https://www.reuters.com/world/americas/draft-canada-law-would-force-social-media-companies-quickly-remove-harmful-2024-02-26/

Reyes-García, V., García-Del-Amo, D., Porcuna-Ferrer, A., Schlingmann, A., Abazeri, M., Attoh, E. M., & Torrents-Ticó, M. (2024). Local studies provide a global perspective of the impacts of climate change on Indigenous Peoples and local communities. *Sustainable Earth Reviews, 7*(1), 1.

Rhodes, R. A. W. (1997). *Understanding governance: Policy networks, governance, reflexivity and accountability*. Open University Press.

Ricaurte, P. (2025). The digitalization imperative. *Dialogues on Digital Society, 1*(1), 12–17.

Richardson, R., Schultz, J. M., & Crawford, K. (2019). Dirty data, bad predictions: How civil rights violations impact police data, predictive policing systems, and justice. *NYUL Rev. Online, 94*, 15.

Riley, A. R., & Carpenter, K. A. (2015). Owning red: A theory of Indian (cultural) appropriation. *Texas Law Review, 94*, 859.

Roadmap, U. N. (2020). The Secretary-General's Roadmap for Digital Cooperation (A/74/821). URL: https://www.un.org/techenvoy/sites/www.un.org.techenvoy/files/general/Roadmap_for_Digital_Cooperation_9June.pdf

Robertson, L., & Kelley, P. (2021). Gamified Learning for Indigenous Language Revitalization: A Case Study. *Journal of Educational Technology, 48*(2), 123–140.

Røkenes, F. M., Grüters, R., Skaalvik, C., Lie, T. G., Østerlie, O., Järnerot, A., & Letnes, M. A. (2022). Teacher educators' professional digital competence in primary and lower secondary school teacher education. *Nordic Journal of Digital Literacy*, (1), 46–60.

Røkenes, F. M., & Krumsvik, R. J. (2014). Development of student teachers' digital competence in teacher education-A literature review. *Nordic Journal of Digital Literacy*, *9*(4), 250–280.

Rombolà, R. (2023). *Digital Markets Act and the interoperability requirement: Is data protection in danger?* MediaLaws. Retrieved March 31, 2025 from https://www.medialaws.eu/digital-markets-act-and-the-interoperability-requirement-is-data-protection-in-danger/

Romero-García, C., Buzón-García, O., & de Paz-Lugo, P. (2020). Improving future teachers' digital competence using active methodologies. *Sustainability*, *12*(18), 7798.

Ruohonen, J., & Mickelsson, S. (2023). Reflections on the Data Governance Act. *Digital Society : Ethics, Socio-Legal and Governance of Digital Technology*, *2*(1), 10. Advance online publication. DOI: 10.1007/s44206-023-00034-9

Russell, S. J., & Norvig, P. (2016). *Artificial intelligence: a modern approach*. Pearson.

Safdari, H. (2024). De Bacco, (2024), C. Community detection and anomaly prediction in dynamic networks. *Communications on Physics*, *7*, 397. DOI: 10.1038/s42005-024-01889-y

Salganova, E. I., & Osipova, L. B. (2023). Students' digital literacy: Competence-based approach. *Economic and Social Changes: Facts, Trends. Forecast*, *16*(1), 227–240.

Sá, M. J., & Serpa, S. (2020). COVID-19 and the promotion of digital competences in education. *Universal Journal of Educational Research*, *8*(10), 4520–4528.

Sampathirao, A., Ramesh, P., & Kumar, S. (2025). Feature-Based Child Mortality Prediction Using Ensemble Learning Models. *Journal of Applied Science and Technology Trends*, *2*(4), 123–132. https://jastt.org/index.php/jasttpath/article/view/264

Sánchez-Caballé, A., Gisbert-Cervera, M., & Esteve-Mon, F. (2020). The digital competence of university students: a systematic literature review. *Aloma: revista de psicologia, ciències de l'educació i de l'esport Blanquerna, 38*(1), 63-74.

Sánchez-Cruzado, C., Santiago Campión, R., & Sánchez-Compaña, M. T. (2021). Teacher digital literacy: The indisputable challenge after COVID-19. *Sustainability*, *13*(4), 1858.

Sanders, A. (2014). The law of unfair dismissal and behaviour outside work. *Legal Studies*, *34*(2), 328–352. DOI: 10.1111/lest.12023

Sandvik, K. B. (2020). Wearables for something good: Aid, dataveillance and the Khushi baby wearable digital necklace for infants initially aimed at reducing child mortality. *Information Communication and Society*, *23*(9), 1283–1299. https://www.tandfonline.com/doi/full/10.1080/1369118X.2020.1753797

Sartor, G. (2019). The fundamental rights challenges of algorithms. *European Journal of Risk Regulation*, *10*(3), 403–416. DOI: 10.1177/0924051919861773

Savirimuthu, J. (2017). Trademarks in the age of social media. *Journal of Intellectual Property Law & Practice*, *12*(1). Advance online publication. DOI: 10.1093/jiplp/jpw199

Sawyer, S., & Tapia, A. (2005). The sociotechnical nature of mobile computing work: Evidence from a study of policing in the United States. *International Journal of Technology and Human Interaction*, *1*(3), 1–14.

Scannell, K. (2017). *Language technologies for a multilingual world*. Springer.

Schmidt v Austicks Bookshops Ltd [1977] IRLR 360 (EAT).

Schmidt, H. (2024). The online safety act 2023. *Journal of Medicine and Law*, *16*(2), 202–210. DOI: 10.1080/17577632.2025.2459440

Schröter, T., & Grafe, S. (2020, November). Digital literacy and digital competency of university teachers. A systematic analysis of frameworks. In *Innovate Learning Summit* (pp. 144-157). Association for the Advancement of Computing in Education (AACE).

Schwab, K. (2018). "The Fourth Industrial Revolution" Encyclopaedia Britannica Anniversary Edition: 250 Years of Excellence (1768–2018).

Sefton-Green, J., Nixon, H., & Erstad, O. (2009). Reviewing approaches and perspectives on "digital literacy". *Pedagogies*, *4*(2), 107–125.

Shafik, W. (2023). *A Comprehensive Cybersecurity Framework for Present and Future Global Information Technology Organizations*. https://doi.org/DOI: 10.4018/978-1-6684-9018-1.ch002

Shafik, W. (2024d). Generative AI for Social Good and Sustainable Development. In *Generative AI: Current Trends and Applications* (pp. 185–217). Springer.

Shafik, W. (2024e). IoT-Enabled Secure and Intelligent Smart Healthcare: Beyond 5G in Enabling Smart Cities. In *Secure and Intelligent IoT-Enabled Smart Cities* (pp. 308–333). IGI Global.

Shafik, W. (2025c). Ethical and legal considerations in artificial intelligence. *AI-Enabled Threat Intelligence and Cyber Risk Assessment*, 90.

Shafik, W. (2025d). Generative Adversarial Networks: Security, Privacy, and Ethical Considerations. In *Generative Artificial Intelligence (AI) Approaches for Industrial Applications* (pp. 93–117). Springer.

Shafik, W. (2025e). Human-Computer Interaction (HCI) Technologies in Socially-Enabled Artificial Intelligence. In *Future of Digital Technology and AI in Social Sectors* (pp. 121–150). IGI Global.

Shafik, W. (2025g). Security, 15 Privacy, and Trust in Fintech. *FinTech and Financial Inclusion: Leveraging Digital Finance for Economic Empowerment and Sustainable Growth*, 216.

Shafik, W. (2025h). The Next Generation of Health Monitoring: Digital Twins and Medical Wearables. In *AI-Powered Digital Twins for Predictive Healthcare: Creating Virtual Replicas of Humans* (pp. 69–106). IGI Global Scientific Publishing.

Shafik, W. (2024a). Artificial Intelligence and Machine Learning with Cyber Ethics for the Future World. In *Future Communication Systems Using Artificial Intelligence, Internet of Things and Data Science* (pp. 110–130). CRC Press., DOI: 10.1201/9781032648309-9

Shafik, W. (2024b). Connected healthcare—the impact of Internet of Things on medical services. In *Artificial Intelligence and Internet of Things based Augmented Trends for Data Driven Systems* (pp. 181–217). CRC Press., DOI: 10.1201/9781003497318-10

Shafik, W. (2024c). Digital healthcare systems in a federated learning perspective. In *Federated Learning for Digital Healthcare Systems* (pp. 1–35). Elsevier.

Shafik, W. (2024f). Sustainable Development. In Viana Hassan, A. S. S. B. (Ed.), *Building Community Resiliency and Sustainability With Tourism Development* (1st ed., Vol. 1, pp. 1–30). IGI Global., DOI: 10.4018/979-8-3693-5405-6.ch001

Shafik, W. (2024g). The Future of Healthcare: AIoMT—Redefining Healthcare with Advanced Artificial Intelligence and Machine Learning Techniques. In *Artificial Intelligence and Machine Learning in Drug Design and Development* (pp. 605–634). Wiley., DOI: 10.1002/9781394234196.ch19

Shafik, W. (2024h). Toward a More Ethical Future of Artificial Intelligence and Data Science. In *The Ethical Frontier of AI and Data Analysis* (pp. 362–388). IGI Global., DOI: 10.4018/979-8-3693-2964-1.ch022

Shafik, W. (2025a). Data Loss Software Reason and Hardware Reason. In *Data Recovery Techniques for Computer Forensics* (pp. 27–61). Bentham Science Publishers.

Shafik, W. (2025b). Digital twins tools and technologies. In *Digital Twins for Smart Cities and Villages* (pp. 55–80). Elsevier., https://doi.org/https://doi.org/10.1016/B978-0-443-28884-5.00003-8

Shafik, W. (2025f). Machine Learning Techniques for Multicriteria Decision-Making. In *Multi-Criteria Decision-Making and Optimum Design with Machine Learning* (pp. 165–194). CRC Press.

Shafik, W., Singh, R., & Kumar, V. (2025). Artificial Intelligence Transparency and Explainability in Sustainable Healthcare. In *Transforming Healthcare Sector Through Artificial Intelligence and Environmental Sustainability* (pp. 165–191). Springer.

Shah, N., Bhagat, N., & Shah, M. (2021). Crime forecasting: A machine learning and computer vision approach to crime prediction and prevention. *Visual Computing for Industry, Biomedicine, and Art, 4*(1), 9. PMID: 33913057

Shandilya, S. K., Datta, A., Kartik, Y., & Nagar, A. (2024). Navigating the Regulatory Landscape. *EAI/Springer Innovations in Communication and Computing*, 127–240. https://doi.org/DOI: 10.1007/978-3-031-53290-0_3

Shapin, S. (2018). *The scientific revolution*. University of Chicago press.

Shariman, T. P. N. T., Razak, N. A., & Noor, N. F. M. (2012). Digital literacy competence for academic needs: An analysis of Malaysian students in three universities. *Procedia: Social and Behavioral Sciences, 69*, 1489–1496.

Sharma, S., Alam, T., & Vatsa, A. (2024). Justice In Digital Era: Analysing Legal and Systemic Challenges in Online Gender-Based Violence. *BPAS Journal, 44*(3), 27527-27535. https://bpasjournals.com/library-science/index.php/journal/article/view/3526/3269

Shiva, V. (2016). *Biopiracy: The plunder of nature and knowledge*. North Atlantic Books.

Shopova, T. (2014). Digital literacy of students and its improvement at the university. *Journal on Efficiency and Responsibility in Education and Science, 7*(2), 26–32.

Sillat, L. H., Tammets, K., & Laanpere, M. (2021). Digital competence assessment methods in higher education: A systematic literature review. *Education Sciences, 11*(8), 402.

Simpson, L. B. (2017). *As we have always done: Indigenous freedom through radical resistance*. U of Minnesota Press.

Sindicato de Médicos de Asistencia Pública (SIMAP) v Conselleria de Sanidad y Consumo de la Generalidad Valenciana, Case C-303/98, [2000] ECR I-7963.

Skantz-Åberg, E., Lantz-Andersson, A., Lundin, M., & Williams, P. (2022). Teachers' professional digital competence: An overview of conceptualisations in the literature. *Cogent Education*, *9*(1), 2063224.

Sklar, M., & DeLong, M. (2012). Punk dress in the workplace: Aesthetic expression and accommodation. *Clothing & Textiles Research Journal*, *30*(4), 285–301. DOI: 10.1177/0887302X12467848

Smith v Safeway plc [1996] IRLR 456 (CA).

Smith, B., & Wilson, C. (2024). Image Recognition for Cultural Heritage Preservation: A Case Study of Indigenous Artifacts. *International Journal of Cultural Heritage*, *25*(2), 112–130.

Smith, L. T. (2012). *Decolonizing methodologies: Research and Indigenous peoples*. Zed Books.

Smith, L. T. (2021). *Decolonizing research: Indigenous storywork as methodology*. SAGE Publications.

Søby, M. (2015). Digital competence-a password to a new interdisciplinary field. *Nordic Journal of Digital Literacy, 10*(Jubileumsnummer), 4-7.

Søby, M. (2013). Learning to be: Developing and understanding digital competence. *Nordic Journal of Digital Literacy*, *8*(3), 134–138.

Söderbaum, F. (2004). *The Political Economy of Regionalism. The Case of Southern Africa*. Palgrave Macmillan.

Sørensen, G. (2001). *Changes in Statehood. The Transformation of International Relations*. Palgrave Macmillan.

Spante, M., Hashemi, S. S., Lundin, M., & Algers, A. (2018). Digital competence and digital literacy in higher education research: Systematic review of concept use. *Cogent Education*, *5*(1), 1519143.

Stevenson, S. A. (2016). Toward a narrative ethics: Indigenous community-based research, the ethics of narrative, and the limits of conventional bioethics. *Qualitative Inquiry*, *22*(5), 365–376.

Stevens, Y. (2022). Dignity, Intersectional Gendered Harm, and a Flexible Approach: Analysis of the Right to One's Image in Quebec. *Canadian Journal of Law and Technology, 19*(2), 307–331. https://digitalcommons.schulichlaw.dal.ca/cgi/viewcontent.cgi?article=1277&context=cjlt

Stopar, K., & Bartol, T. (2019). Digital competences, computer skills and information literacy in secondary education: Mapping and visualization of trends and concepts. *Scientometrics, 118*(2), 479–498.

Sunstein, C. R. (2018). *Republic: Divided democracy in the age of social media.* Princeton University Press.

Supreme Court Observer. (2018). Constitutionality of Aadhaar Act: Judgment summary. https://www.scobserver.in/reports/constitutionality-of-aadhaar-justice-k-s-puttaswamy-union-of-india-judgment-in-plain-english/

Svantesson, D. J. B. & Centre for Space, Cyberspace & Data Law. (2024). *Global content orders: A legal analysis of eSafety Commissioner.* https://bond.edu.au/sites/default/files/2024-06/LAW_Centre%20paper_Global%20content%20orders%20A%20legal%20analysis%20of%20eSafety%20Commissioner.pdf

Svendsen, A. M., & Svendsen, J. T. (2021). Digital directions: Curricular goals relating to digital literacy and digital competences in the Gymnasium (stx) in Denmark. *Nordic Journal of Digital Literacy, 16*(1), 6–20.

Svensson, M., & Baelo, R. (2015). Teacher students' perceptions of their digital competence. *Procedia: Social and Behavioral Sciences, 180*, 1527–1534.

Tammaro, R., & D'Alessio, A. (2016). Teacher training and digital competence: A pedagogical recommendation. [IJDLDC]. *International Journal of Digital Literacy and Digital Competence, 7*(2), 1–10.

Taylor, L. (2017). What is data justice? *Big Data & Society, 4*(2), 1–14.

Taylor, L. (2017). What is data justice? The case for connecting digital rights and freedoms globally. *Big Data & Society, 4*(2). Advance online publication. DOI: 10.1177/2053951717736335

Tejedor, S., Cervi, L., Pérez-Escoda, A., & Jumbo, F. T. (2020). Digital literacy and higher education during COVID-19 lockdown: Spain, Italy, and Ecuador. *Publications, 8*(4), 48.

Terry, J., Davies, A., Williams, C., Tait, S., & Condon, L. (2019). Improving the digital literacy competence of nursing and midwifery students: A qualitative study of the experiences of NICE student champions. *Nurse Education in Practice, 34*, 192–198.

The Institute of International and European Affairs. (2023). *The European digital agenda in 2023.* Retrieved April 13, 2025 from https://www.iiea.com/blog/the-european-digital-agenda-in-2023

*The Left-Out Project Report: The case for an online gender-based violence framework inclusive of transgender, non-binary and gender-diverse experiences.* (2023, July 22). Association for Progressive Communications. https://www.apc.org/en/pubs/left-out-project-report-case-online-gender-based-violence-framework-inclusive-transgender-non

Thomas, A. V. A., Kumar, A. B., & Sanjaya, K. (2025). AI-Driven Growth: Addressing Legal and Economic Complexities in the Digital Era. In *Exploring AI Implications on Law, Governance, and Industry* (pp. 1–24). IGI Global. https://doi.org/DOI: 10.4018/979-8-3373-3384-7.ch001

Thornberry, P. (2013). Indigenous peoples and human rights. In *Indigenous peoples and human rights.* Manchester University Press.

Tinker v Des Moines Independent Community School District, 393 U.S. 503 (1969).

Tinmaz, H., Fanea-Ivanovici, M., & Baber, H. (2023). A snapshot of digital literacy. *Library Hi Tech News, 40*(1), 20–23.

Tinmaz, H., Lee, Y. T., Fanea-Ivanovici, M., & Baber, H. (2022). A systematic review on digital literacy. *Smart Learning Environments, 9*(1), 21.

Title VII of the Civil Rights Act of 1964, 42 U.S.C. § 2000e et seq.

To, B. (2024). Analysis of AI-generated content and deepfakes in social media. *Urn. fi.* https://www.theseus.fi/handle/10024/857145

Todd, Z. (2016). An indigenous feminist's take on the ontological turn: 'Ontology' is just another word for colonialism. *Journal of Historical Sociology, 29*(1), 4–22.

Tomaszewicz, A. A. (2015). The impact of digital literacy on e-government development. *Online Journal of Applied Knowledge Management, 3*(2).

Tomczyk, Ł., & Fedeli, L. (2022). *Digital literacy for teachers.* Springer.

Tømte, C. E. (2015). Educating Teachers for the New Millennium?-Teacher training, ICT and digital competence. *Nordic journal of digital literacy, 10*(Jubileumsnummer), 138-154.

Tømte, C., Enochsson, A. B., Buskqvist, U., & Kårstein, A. (2015). Educating online student teachers to master professional digital competence: The TPACK-framework goes online. *Computers & Education, 84*, 26–35.

Topol, E. J. (2019). High-performance medicine: The convergence of human and artificial intelligence. *Nature Medicine, 25*, 44–56. DOI: 10.1038/s41591-018-0300-7

Tornero, J. M. P., Sánchez, M. O. P., Baena, G., Luque, S. G., Tejedor, S., & Fernández, N. (2010). Trends and models of Media literacy in Europe: Between digital competence and critical understanding. *Anàlisi: Quaderns de comunicació i cultura*, (40), 85-100.

Tran, N. H. (2023). IMPACT FACTORS ON THE ADOPTION OF CORPORATE SOCIAL RESPONSIBILITY: EMPIRICAL EVIDENCE FROM AN EMERGING MARKET. *Corporate Governance and Organizational Behavior Review, 7*(2 Special Issue). https://doi.org/DOI: 10.22495/cgobrv7i2sip13

Tropina, T. (2024). 'This is not a human rights convention!': the perils of overlooking human rights in the UN cybercrime treaty. *Journal of Cyber Policy*, 1–21. DOI: 10.1080/23738871.2024.2419517

Trstenjak, V., & Brkan, M. (2012). *Pravo EU: Ustavno, procesno in gospodarsko pravo EU*. GV Založba.

Tsosie, R.. (2021). Indigenous Data Sovereignty and Artificial Intelligence: Opportunities for Self-Determination. *AI & Society, 36*(4), 1325–1337.

Tuck, E., & Yang, K. W. (2012). Decolonization is not a metaphor. *Decolonization, 1*(1), 1–40.

Tveiterås, N. C., & Madsen, S. S. (2022). From tools to complexity?—A systematic literature analysis of digital competence among pre-service teachers in Norway. *Digital literacy for teachers*, 345-389.

*UN Declaration of Human Rights*. (1948). United Nations.

UN Human Rights Council. (2012). *The promotion, protection and enjoyment of human rights on the Internet: Resolution 20/8*. https://documents.un.org/doc/resolution/gen/g12/153/25/pdf/g1215325.pdf?OpenElement

UN Permanent Forum on Indigenous Issues (UNPFII). (2005). *Guidelines for implementation of the principle of free, prior and informed consent*. United Nations.

UNDRIP. (2007). *United Nations Declaration on the Rights of Indigenous Peoples*. United Nations.

UNESCO. (2003). *Convention for the safeguarding of the intangible cultural heritage*. United Nations Educational, Scientific and Cultural Organization.

UNESCO. (2021). *Recommendation on the Ethics of Artificial Intelligence*.

UNESCO. (2021). *Recommendation on the ethics of artificial intelligence*. Organisation for Economic Co-operation and Development. (2022, December 2). Rights in the digital age: Challenges and ways forward (OECD Papers on Risk and Regulation, No. 2).

UNESCO. (2023). *Local and Indigenous Knowledge*. https://www.unesco.org/en/ik (Accessed March 27, 2025)

Union syndicale Solidaires Isère v Premier ministre, Case C-428/09, [2010] ECR I-9961.

United Nations Human Rights Council. (2012). The promotion, protection and enjoyment of human rights on the Internet (A/HRC/RES/20/8). https://undocs.org/A/HRC/RES/20/8

United Nations. (2025). *Unsdg | Kenya's Digital Leap for a Fairer Future*. Un.org; United Nations Sustainable Development Group. https://unsdg.un.org/latest/stories/kenya%E2%80%99s-digital-leap-fairer-future

Van den Hoven, J. (2007). *ICT and value sensitive design*. Springer.

Van Der Wilk, A. (2021). Protecting women and girls from violence in the digital age. *Council of Europe*, 5-64. https://rm.coe.int/protecting-women-and-girls-from-violence-in-the-digital-age-final-eng-/1680ae3a31

Van Deursen, A. J., & Van Dijk, J. A. (2019). The first-level digital divide shifts from inequalities in physical access to inequalities in material access. *New Media & Society*, *21*(2), 354–375.

van Ooijen, I., & Uršič Vrabec, H. (2018). Does the GDPR enhance consumers' control over personal data? An analysis from a behavioural perspective. *Journal of Consumer Policy*, *42*, 91–107. DOI: 10.1007/s10603-018-9399-7

Van Wynsberghe, A. (2013). *Designing robots for care: Care centered value-sensitive design*. Springer.

Vaskov, M., Isakov, A., Bilovus, V., Bulavkin, A., & Mikhaylenko, N. (2021). Digital literacy of modern higher education teachers. In *E3S web of conferences* (Vol. 273, p. 12035). EDP Sciences.

Verhulst, S. G., Noveck, B. S., Raines, J., & Declercq, A. (2017). *Innovations in global governance: toward a distributed internet governance ecosystem. Who Runs the Internet?: The Global Multi-Stakeholder Model of Internet Governance, Centre for International Governance Innovation*. MIT Political Science.

Vettriselvan, R., & Divyaranjani, R. (2019). Human rights violations against rural women workers. *International Journal of Management Research and Social Science, 6*(1).

Vettriselvan, R., Sathya, M., & Velmurugan, T. (2018). Social inclusion at Indian small and medium mechanical engineering enterprises. *International Journal of Mechanical Engineering and Technology, 9*(8), 749–757.

Vickers, P. (2013). *Understanding inconsistent science*. OUP Oxford.

Vijeyarasa, R. (2020). CEDAW's General Recommendation No. 35: A quarter of a century of evolutionary approaches to violence against women. *Journal of Human Rights, 19*(2), 153–167. DOI: 10.1080/14754835.2019.1686347

Vine – Violence Information Aotearoa. (2022). *Harmful Digital Communications Act: recent cases, changes and calls for review*. https://www.vine.org.nz/news/harmful-digital-communications-act-recent-cases-changes-and-calls-for-review

Vinueza Villagran, D. B., Amparito Cecilia, L. S., Guamán Guevara, M. D., & Luis Fabricio, G. G. (2024). Motivations for environmental social responsibility in ecuadorian banana companies. *Universidad, Ciencia y Tecnología, 28*(122). Advance online publication. DOI: 10.47460/uct.v28i122.764

*Violence against Women Victim Support: Report*. (2012, December 7). European Institute for Gender Equality. https://eige.europa.eu/publications-resources/publications/violence-against-women-victim-support-report?language_content_entity=en

Vo, N. N. Y., He, X., Liu, S., & Xu, G. (2019). Deep learning for decision making and the optimization of socially responsible investments and portfolio. *Decision Support Systems, 124*. Advance online publication. DOI: 10.1016/j.dss.2019.113097

Vulturius, G., Maltais, A., & Forsbacka, K. (2024). Sustainability-linked bonds–their potential to promote issuers' transition to net-zero emissions and future research directions. *Journal of Sustainable Finance & Investment, 14*(1). Advance online publication. DOI: 10.1080/20430795.2022.2040943

Vuorikari, R., Kluzer, S., & Punie, Y. (2022). *DigComp 2.2: The Digital Competence Framework for Citizens-With new examples of knowledge, skills and attitudes*.

Wachter, S., Mittelstadt, B., & Floridi, L. (2017). Why a Right to Explanation of Automated Decision-Making Does Not Exist in the General DataProtection Regulation. *International Data Privacy Law, 7*(2), 76–99.

Waisová, Š. (2025). Deep Co-Production of Human Security at the Science–Politics Nexus. In B. Bliesemann de Guevara et al. *Knowledge and Expertise in International Politics* (pp. 236-251). Oxford University Press.

Waisová, Š., & Cabada, L. (2011). *Ethics in Foreign Policy: Postmodern States as the Entrepreneurs of Kantian Ethics*. Peter Lang.

Wajcman, J. (2006). TechnoCapitalism meets TechnoFeminism: Women and technology in a wireless world. *Labour & Industry a Journal of the Social and Economic Relations of Work, 16*(3), 7–20. DOI: 10.1080/10301763.2006.10669327

Wall Street Journal. (2024, March 12). *Online Harms Act: Crime and punishment, not in that order. The Wall Street Journal.* https://www.wsj.com/opinion/crime-and-punishment-not-in-that-order-canada-hate-speech-f618e339

Wallach, W., & Allen, C. (2008). *Moral Machines: Teaching Robots Right from Wrong*. Oxford University Press.

Walter, J. R. Querrey-Simpson Institute of Bioelectronics, Northwestern University, & Collaborators. (2024). From lab to life: how wearable devices can improve health equity by monitoring neonatal vital signs in low-resource settings. Nature Communications. https://www.nature.com/articles/s41467-023-44634-9

Walter, M., Kukutai, T., Carroll, S. R., & Rodriguez-Lonebear, D. (2020). *Indigenous data sovereignty and policy*. Taylor & Francis.

Walter, M., & Suina, M. (2019). Indigenous data sovereignty: What does it mean in practice? *The Australian Journal of Social Issues, 54*(2), 203–214.

Wang, Y. (2025). Simeon Yates and Elinor Carmi (Eds.), Digital Inclusion: International Policy and Research. *International Journal of Communication, 19*, 4.

Wang, W., Cheng, J., Song, W., & Shen, Y. (2022). The effectiveness of wearable devices as physical activity interventions for preventing and treating obesity in children and adolescents: Systematic review and meta-analysis. *JMIR mHealth and uHealth, 10*(4), e36943. https://pmc.ncbi.nlm.nih.gov/articles/PMC9034426/

Wang, X., Li, Y., Zhang, Z., & Chen, W. (2023). AI-Powered Interactive Storytelling for Cultural Heritage Education. *International Journal of Artificial Intelligence in Education, 33*(4), 800–820.

Wardhani, D., Hesti, S., & Dwityas, N. A. (2019). Digital literacy: A survey level digital literacy competence among university students in Jakarta. *International Journal of English Literature and Social Sciences, 4*(4), 1131–1138.

Watson, S. (2023). Online abuse of women: An interdisciplinary scoping review of the literature. *Feminist Media Studies*, *24*(1), 51–69. DOI: 10.1080/14680777.2023.2181136

Weinstein, M., Jensen, M. R., & Tynes, B. M. (2021). Victimized in many ways: Online and offline bullying/harassment and perceived racial discrimination in diverse racial–ethnic minority adolescents. *Cultural Diversity & Ethnic Minority Psychology*, *27*(3), 397–407. DOI: 10.1037/cdp0000436

Weiss, T. G., & Wilkinson, R. (2014). *International Organization and Global Governance*. Routledge.

Wells, M., & Wells, M. (2025, January 15). *International Solutions to Technology-Facilitated Gender-Based Violence | The Regulatory Review*. The Regulatory Review. https://www.theregreview.org/2025/01/18/seminar-international-solutions-to-technology-facilitated-gender-based-violence/

Wepa, D. (Ed.). (2015). *Cultural safety in aotearoa New Zealand*. Cambridge University Press.

Wesarg-Menzel, C., Ebbes, R., Hensums, M., Wagemaker, E., Zaharieva, M. S., Staaks, J. P. C., van den Akker, A. L., Visser, I., Hoeve, M., Brummelman, E., Dekkers, T. J., Schuitema, J. A., Larsen, H., Colonnesi, C., Jansen, B. R. J., Overbeek, G., Huizenga, H. M., & Wiers, R. W. (2023). Development and socialization of self-regulation from infancy to adolescence: A meta-review differentiating between self-regulatory abilities, goals, and motivation. *Developmental Review*, *69*(1), 101090. DOI: 10.1016/j.dr.2023.101090

Whyte, K. (2017). Indigenous climate change studies: Indigenizing futures, decolonizing the Anthropocene. *English Language Notes*, *55*(1), 153–162.

Williamson, M. E. J. B. (2018). Harmful Online Speech: An analysis of New Zealand's Harmful Digital Communications Act 2015 to combat Cyberbullying. *Kuwait International Law School Journal. Special Supplement*, *3*(1), 65–140. DOI: 10.54032/2203-006-991-016

Wilman, F. (2022). *The Digital Services Act (DSA) – An overview. SSRN*. https://doi.org/DOI: 10.2139/ssrn.4304586

Winner, L. (1980). *The whale and the reactor: A search for limits in an age of high technology*. University of Chicago Press.

WIPO. (2024). *Traditional Knowledge: Policy and Legal Options*. World Intellectual Property Organization.

Witt, A. (2023). The Digital Markets Act – Regulating the Wild West. *Common Market Law Review*, *60*(3), 585–612.

Wolters, P. (2024). The influence of the Data Act on the shifting balance between data protection and the free movement of data. *BILETA Special Issue*, *15*(1), 1–15.

Women, U. N. 2023. Technology Facilitated Gender- Based Violence. https://www.unwomen.org/sites/default/files/2024-09/technology-facilitated-gender-based-violence-shared-research-agenda-en.pdf

Worden, S., Svobodova, K., Côte, C., & Bolz, P. (2024). Regional post-mining land use assessment: An interdisciplinary and multi-stakeholder approach. *Resources Policy*, *89*, 104680–104680. DOI: 10.1016/j.resourpol.2024.104680

World Bank. 2021. Accelerating Gender Equality in Digital Development. *World Bank Group*. 16-22. https://thedocs.worldbank.org/en/doc/61714f214ed04bcd6e9623ad0e215897-0400012021/related/Digital-Development-Note-on-Gender-Equality-November2021-final.pdf

Wu, Q., Liu, X., Qin, J., Zhou, L., Mardani, A., & Deveci, M. (2022). An integrated multi-criteria decision-making and multi-objective optimization model for socially responsible portfolio selection. *Technological Forecasting and Social Change*, *184*. Advance online publication. DOI: 10.1016/j.techfore.2022.121977

Wynn-Evans, C. (2008). Discrimination what not to wear—Ongoing UK case law developments on dress codes. *Bloomberg European Business Law Review*, *2*(110), 110–116.

Xu, M., David, J. M., & Kim, S. H. (2018). The fourth industrial revolution: Opportunities and challenges. *International journal of financial research, 9*(2), 90-95.

Xu, X., Kostka, G., & Cao, X. (2021). Information Control and Public Support for Social Credit Systems in China. *The Journal of Politics*, *84*(4). Advance online publication. DOI: 10.1086/718358

Yang, H. (2024). From digital literacy to digital competence: The structure of Teacher Digital Competence (TDC). *Innovations in Education and Teaching International*, ●●●, 1–13.

Yang, K., Seo, S., & Ok, H. (2020). Development of self assessment tool for digital literacy competence. *Journal of Digital Convergence*, *18*(7), 1–8.

Yazon, A. D., Ang-Manaig, K., Buama, C. A. C., & Tesoro, J. F. B. (2019). Digital literacy, digital competence and research productivity of educators. *Universal Journal of Educational Research*, *7*(8), 1734–1743.

Yeasmine, F. (2024). The Impact of Digital Transformation on Society: Unraveling Trends, Challenges, and Opportunities. *Eunomia, 2*(108), 53-67. https://bibliotekanauki.pl/articles/57552184.pdf

Yeung, K. (2018). *Algorithmic regulation: A critical interrogation.* Oxford University Press.

Yıldız, C. (2023). The European Commission Accepts Amazon's Commitments. Retrieved April 8, 2025 from https://www.erdem-erdem.av.tr/en/insights/the-european-commission-accepts-amazons-commitments

Zabolotska, O., Zhyliak, N., Hevchuk, N., Petrenko, N., & Alieko, O. (2021). Digital competencies of teachers in the transformation of the educational environment.

Zadražilová, I., & Vizváry, P. (2021, September). Digital literacy competencies and interests of elderly people. In *European conference on information literacy* (pp. 137-146). Cham: Springer International Publishing.

Zakharov, K., Komarova, A., Baranova, T., & Gulk, E. (2021, November). Information literacy and digital competence of teachers in the age of digital transformation. In *XIV International Scientific Conference "INTERAGROMASH 2021" Precision Agriculture and Agricultural Machinery Industry, Volume 2* (pp. 857-868). Cham: Springer International Publishing.

Zakir, S., Hoque, M. E., Susanto, P., Nisaa, V., Alam, M. K., Khatimah, H., & Mulyani, E. (2025, June). Digital literacy and academic performance: The mediating roles of digital informal learning, self-efficacy, and students' digital competence. [Frontiers Media SA.]. *Frontiers in Education, 10*, 1590274.

Zhang, C., & Pan, L. (2024). Participatory ethical regulations: Risk challenges of artificial intelligence era and construction of governance logic. [Chinese Version]. *Bulletin of Chinese Academy of Sciences, 39*(11), 1860–1870.

Zhao, Y., Llorente, A. M. P., & Gómez, M. C. S. (2021). Digital competence in higher education research: A systematic literature review. *Computers & Education, 168*, 104212.

Zhao, Y., Sánchez Gómez, M. C., Pinto Llorente, A. M., & Zhao, L. (2021). Digital competence in higher education: Students' perception and personal factors. *Sustainability, 13*(21), 12184.

Zhou, M. M., Qu, Z., Wan, J., Wen, B., Yao, Y., & Lu, Z. (2024). Understanding Chinese Internet Users' Perceptions of, and Online Platforms' Compliance with, the Personal Information Protection Law (PIPL). *Proceedings of the ACM on Human-Computer Interaction, 8*(CSCW1), 1–26. https://doi.org/DOI: 10.1145/3637415

Zuboff, S. (2019). *The Age of Surveillance Capitalism*. Public Affairs.

Zuboff, S. (2019). *The age of surveillance capitalism: The fight for a human future at the new frontier of power*. PublicAffairs.

Zuboff, S. (2019). *The Age of Surveillance Capitalism: The Fight for a Human Future at the New Frontier of Power*. PublicAffairs.

Zuboff, S. (2023). The age of surveillance capitalism. In *Social theory re-wired* (pp. 203–213). Routledge.

# About the Contributors

**Maja Pucelj** is an assistant professor and Head of research at EMUNI. She graduated from the Faculty of Public Administration in Ljubljana and the Faculty of Management in Koper, with a master's degree from the Faculty of Government and European Studies at the New University and the European Faculty of Law. She completed her first doctorate degree at Alma Mater Europaea - ISH in the humanities and her second doctorate degree at the Faculty of Government and European Studies of the New University in the field of international studies with an emphasis on human rights. She began her career as a police officer, where she was a member of a special police unit, continuing her career path as a risk manager, head of the legal department in the field of leasing and banking, as a director of marketing in the economy and as an auditor in an audit company. Prior to joining EMUNI and FOŠ, she worked as an advisor to the Minister of Education, Science and Sport in the field of pre-school education, primary education, secondary and higher education, adult education, and the quality of education and as an undersecretary in the Service for the Implementation of Cohesion Policy at the Ministry of Education, Science and Sport. She teached or co-teached the following courses: Fundamentals of Law in Organizational Studies, Organizational Behaviour and Seminar for Doctoral Dissertation. In 2024 she received reward from Slovenian Ombudsman for the best PhD research in the field of human rights in Slovenia. In the same year she also finished International Post-doctoral programme in Globalisation and Human rights in Mediterranea International Centre for Human Rights Research. Her research interest focuses on human rights, law, social responsibility and gender equality.

***

**Ashraf Alam** currently holds the position of Research Faculty at the Centre of Excellence in Public Policy, Sustainability and ESG Research, housed within the Faculty of Law and Policy Studies at Alliance University, Bangalore. Renowned for his transdisciplinary acumen spanning education, technology, and policy studies, Dr. Ashraf has been distinguished as one of the World's Top 2% Scientists by Stanford University and Elsevier, an accolade that highlights the breadth and depth of his scholarly impact. His prolific academic output includes over fifty SCOPUS-indexed publications and more than one hundred conference presentations at esteemed national and international academic forums. His educational trajectory reflects both depth and versatility: a Ph.D. in Education from the Indian Institute of Technology (IIT) Kharagpur, an M.Ed. with a concentration in Mathematics Education, and a B.S. in Computer Science from the University of Delhi. He also holds postgraduate degrees in Public Administration (M.A.) and Mathematics (M.Sc.), supplemented by a suite of postgraduate diplomas in Higher Education, Guidance and Counselling, Educational Technology, Criminology and Police Administration, and Value Education. Dr. Ashraf is an active participant in global scholarly discourse. As Associate Editor of Frontiers in Education, he plays a pivotal role in curating and guiding intellectual contributions across the Educational, Pedagogical, and Learning Sciences. Concurrently, he serves as Founder and Director of Academic Chronicles Private Limited, where he orchestrates editorial board formation and develops strategic frameworks for peer-reviewed publishing in the Social, Behavioural, and Humanistic Sciences. His research has been disseminated through elite academic platforms, including Elsevier, Springer, Taylor & Francis, Wiley, Routledge, Sage, Emerald, and IEEE, and addresses a remarkably diverse array of topics such as pedagogical theories, educational administration, educational psychology, educational sociology, educational policy, technology-integrated learning, mathematics education, educational philosophy, educational technology, teacher education, and AI/ML in learning environments. Dr. Ashraf's scholarly rigor is further demonstrated by his success in qualifying multiple prestigious examinations including UGC-NET-JRF in both Education and Adult and Continuing Education, UGC- NET in Public Administration, and GATE in Humanities and Social Sciences. At the heart of Dr. Ashraf's intellectual ethos lies a steadfast belief in education as a catalytic and emancipatory force capable of engendering social justice, human flourishing, societal progress, and sustainable transformation. His recent explorations into 'Happiness Engineering' and holistic well- being in school ecosystems articulate a vision of education that transcends instrumentalist paradigms, prioritizing emotional intelligence, global consciousness, empathy, and psychosocial resilience among learners. His research agenda seeks to conceive educational praxis through the affordances of inclusive digital learning, gamified instructional design, and artificial intelligence (AIEd), thereby constructing robust, ethically grounded frameworks for 21st century education. At Alliance University, Dr. Ashraf remains committed to architecting pedagogical models that not only cultivate intellectual dexterity and cognitive excellence but also prepare learners for morally responsive leadership, intellectual nimbleness, and responsible global citizenship in an increasingly volatile, uncertain, complex, and ambiguous (VUCA) world.

**Ladislav Cabada** is Full Professor in Political Science and Czech History at the University of West Bohemia in PIlsen / Czech Republic.

**Goran Klepac**, Ph.D., works as a Director of Big data analytics in Croatian Telecom (T-com). Previously he worked asdirector of Stretegic development in in Raiffeisenbank Austria d.d., Croatia. In several universities in Croatia, he lectures subjects in domain of data mining, predictive analyitics, decision support system, banking risk, risk evaluation models, expert system, database marketing and business intelligence. As a team leader, he successfully finished many data mining projects in different domanins like retail, finance, insurance, hospitality, telecommunications, and productions. He is an author/coauthor of several books published in Croatian and English in domain of data mining.

**Cry Kuranga** holds a PhD in Computer Science from the University of Pretoria (UP). He is currently employed as a Postdoctoral fellow in the Department of Information Systems at the Durban University of Technology.

**Tlou Maggie Masenya** holds a PhD in Information Science from the University of South Africa (UNISA) and a Masters in Information Technology from the University of Pretoria (UP). She has 11 years of working experience as a senior lecture in the field of Information Science, Information Systems and Technology at University of South Africa, University of Zululand and Durban University of Technology. She is currently Associate Professor in the Department of Information Systems at the Durban University of Technology. She is a distinguished researcher with extensive, impressive national and international research standing and has published numerous book chapters and articles in peer-reviewed journals within the broad niche area of Digital transformation, ICT4D, Digital preservation and Data Curation, Records and Knowledge Management,Technopreneurship, Digital Entrepreneurship, Cloud Computing, Innovative Pedagogies, Disruptive Technologies and Indigenous Knowledge Systems, which had a positive impact on her scholarly growth. She recently edited four books, published by IGI- Global International Academic Publisher in 2022, 2023 and 2025. Her research publications have consistently pushed the frontiers in Information Science and Technology and related fields and have become highly cited by academics and scholars globally. she is constantly reviewing journal articles and book chapters for SAJIM, SAJLIS, Mousaion, JSASA, IFLA Journals and IGI-Global book chapters, just to name a few. She has also participated and contributed in numerous community engagement research projects throughout her academic career.

**Vinodh N** is currently pursuing his PhD as a Research Scholar at Saveetha School of Management, SIMATS, Saveetha University, Chennai. Concurrently, he serves as an Assistant Professor in the MBA Department at St. Joseph College of Engineering, Chennai, Tamil Nadu, India. He earned his Master of Philosophy (M.Phil) degree from Sri Venkateshwara University, Tirupati, and holds an MBA from Madras University, Chennai. With over Seventeen years of teaching experience across various esteemed educational institutions in Chennai, Mr. He exemplifies a strong commitment to academia and scholarly research. His contributions to the field are underscored by his publications in SCOPUS indexed journals

**Swathy P.S** serves as an Assistant Professor of Law, with academic specialization in Constitutional and Criminal Law. She is presently pursuing her Doctoral research on "The Right to Health of Tribal Women in Kerala with Special Reference to Wayanad District: A Socio-Legal Analysis." Her research interests encompass constitutional governance, human rights, gender justice, and the interface between law and public health. Ms. Swathy has contributed several scholarly papers to UGC-approved journals and actively engages in academic discourse addressing issues of social justice and legal empowerment of marginalized communities. Through her teaching and research, she seeks to promote a deeper understanding of the law as an instrument of social transformation and inclusive development

**Gal Pastirk** holds a Master of Laws (LL.M.) from the Faculty of Law, University of Maribor. He works as a research assistant at the Law Institute of ZRS Koper and EMUNI University. His areas of interest include commercial and corporate law, digital technology law, EU law, and sustainability law. He has gained practical experience through internships at courts and law firms and actively participates in academic projects and international conferences, reflecting his commitment to understanding and addressing contemporary legal and regulatory challenges in the European context.

**Andreja Primec** embarked on her career in the judiciary at the High Court in Maribor. After completing the judicial exam, she joined the Chair of Commercial Law at the Faculty of Economics and Business, University of Maribor. She holds an associate professor of law position at the same institution. Her primary focus areas in scientific research and professional endeavours encompass commercial law, European Union law, and intellectual property law. Dr Primec has authored and co-authored numerous scientific and professional publications she disseminates through national and international journals. Additionally, she presents her work at various scientific and international conferences within her home country and abroad. Her contributions reflect her expertise in interdisciplinary integration and her ability to address complex legal and societal issues.

**R. Vettriselvan**, an Associate Professor, AMET University, specialized in HRM and Marketing. He is acting as Mentor, Saraswathi Institute of Medical Sciences, Hapur. He served as Review Board member, National Council for Higher Education, Malawi, Head of the Department, School of Commerce and Management Studies, St. Eugene University, Zambia, and Director, Research and Publication, St. John the Baptist University, Malawi. He has published 31 books and 103 articles in peer reviewed journals and edited book chapters. Under his guidance two have completed and five are pursuing their PhD.

**B. Narendra Kumar Rao** is currently Working as Professor and Program Head, Department of AI&;ML in the School of Computing, Mohan Babu University, Tirupati. He is a Member of Research Advisory Committee and also Doctoral Supervisor Cluster Head in School of Computing, Mohan Babu University. His Research interests include Software Testing, Embedded Systems and Machine Learning. He has been part of several International Conferences as Convener and Conference Chair for THREE International Conferences. Has published articles in reputed Journals and Conferences. He was the convener for International Conference on Data Analytics, Intelligent Computing and Cyber Security-2021, He is editor for two Proceedings by Springer published in the year 2018 and 2022. He has been associated with IEEE, ACM, CSTA and IAENG. He has won Best Faculty Recognition, Nava Bharat Nirman Award by Information Technology Association of AP; India Servers, October, 2019 and Best Researcher Award by Integrated Research Group(IRG), Chennai for research work carried out, January, 2018. He received his Ph.D in CSE from Jawarharlal Nehru Technological University, Hyderabad.

**Karun Sanjaya** is an Assistant Professor at Symbiosis Law School, Nagpur, Symbiosis International (Deemed University), Pune, India. He is specialised in Intellectual Property Laws and is currently the Faculty-in-charge of the Centre for Intellectual Property Rights and Advocacy at SLS, Nagpur. His areas of interest include Tort Laws, Contract Laws, Cyber Laws, Intellectual Property Laws, Artificial Intelligence and allied laws. He is a recipient of the Justice Krishna Iyer Memorial Merit Award, 2019, Adv. P.F., Thomas Memorial Gold Medal, 2019, Dr. K.N. Chandrashekharan Pillai Gold Medal 2022 and Justice Krishna lyer Memorial Merit Award, 2022. He was formerly the executive editor of IILS Law Review and has authored over 70 research articles in diverse areas of law. Karun had also qualified

UGC NET with JRF (Law) and is presently pursuing his PhD from VIT School of Law, Vellore Institute of Technology, Chennai, Tamil Nadu, India.

**Wasswa Shafik** (Member, IEEE) received a Bachelor of Science degree in information technology from Ndejje University, Uganda, a Master of Engineering degree in Information Technology (Computer and Communication Networks) from Yazd University, Iran, and a PhD in Computer Science with the School of Digital Science, Universiti Brunei Darussalam, Brunei Darussalam. He is also the Founder and Research Director of the Dig Connectivity Research Laboratory (DCRLab) after serving as a Research Associate at the Network Interconnectivity Research Laboratory at Yazd University. Prior to this, he worked as a Community Data Analyst at Population Services International (PSI-Uganda), a Community Data Officer at the Programme for Accessible Health Communication (PACE-Uganda), a Research Assistant at the Socio-Economic Data Centre (SEDC-Uganda), Uganda, an Assistant Data Officer at TechnoServe, Kampala, Uganda, and Asmaah Charity Organization as Cheif Executive Officer. He has hundreds of publications with renowned publishers. His research interests include Artificial Intelligence, Neural Networks, Computer Vision, Smart Agriculture, Digital Health, and Green Computing.

**A. K. Subramani** holds a Ph.D. in Business Administration from Manonmaniam Sundaranar University, Tirunelveli, India, and has over 18 years of teaching experience. He has published 80 research articles in international journals, including two in the ABDC-A category, ten in ABDC-B, two in ABDC-C, 38 in Scopus-indexed journals, and ten in Web of Science-indexed journals. He has also presented papers at various national and international conferences. He has completed more than 35 courses through the Swayam online platform in human resource management, business analytics, and intellectual property rights. He has earned several NPTEL Star recognitions, including Evangelist, Motivated Learner, Enthusiast, and Discipline Star. He serves as a peer reviewer for reputable journals published by Inderscience and Emerald. His research interests include human resource management and organisational behaviour. He has been honoured with the Teaching and Research Excellence Award and the Distinguished Teacher Award – Management.

**Šárka Waisová** is an Associate Professor of International Relation at the University of West Bohemia in Pilsen and Senior analyst as Czech Hydrogen Technological Platform.

# Index

## A



## B



## C



## D

## E



## F



## G



## H



## I



## L



## M



## O

## P



## R



## S



## T



## W

www.ingramcontent.com/pod-product-compliance
Lightning Source LLC
LaVergne TN
LVHW080910300926
849162LV00003B/632
* 9 7 9 8 3 3 7 3 8 5 1 0 5 *